The Historical Archaeology Laboratory Handbook

Volume 1: Patterns and Analysis

Edited by John M. Chenoweth

A Society for Historical Archaeology Publication

The Historical Archaeology Laboratory Handbook Volume 1: Patterns and Analysis

13017 Wisteria Drive #395
Germantown, MD 20874, U.S.A.

Edited by John M. Chenoweth

Library of Congress Control Number: 2016944270

Cover Design by Dylan Telerski and Knic Pfost.

www.sha.org

Contents

Part II: Interpreting Dates and Meaning From Artifacts

Preface: Citations to the Original Publications

The editor and the SHA would like to extend their deepest gratitude to the authors whose work has been collected here and to the original publishers who have given permission for the works to be reprinted. Full original citations to the reprinted chapters are included below.

ADAMS, WILLIAM HAMPTON, AND SARAH JANE BOLING
1989 Status and Ceramics for Planters and Slaves on Three Georgia Coastal Plantations. Historical Archaeology 23(1):69-96.

ANDERSON, ADRIENNE
1968 The Archaeology of Mass-Produced Footwear. Historical Archaeology 2:56-65.

BALLIN, TORBEN BJARKE
2012 'State of the Art' of British Gunflint Research, with Special Focus on the Early Gunflint Workshop at Dun Eistean, Lewis. Post-Medieval Archaeology 46(1):116-142.

BEAUDRY, MARY C., JANET LONG, HENRY M. MILLER, FRASER D. NEIMAN, AND GARRY WHEELER STONE
1983 A Vessel Typology for Early Chesapeake Ceramics: the Potomac Typological System. Historical Archaeology 17(1):18-43.

BELL, EDWARD L.
1990 The Historical Archaeology of Mortuary Behavior: Coffin Hardware from Uxbridge, Massachusetts. Historical Archaeology 24:54-78.

BINFORD, LEWIS R.
1962 A New Method of Calculating Dates from Kaolin Pipe Stem Samples. Southeastern Archaeological Conference Newsletter 9(1):19-21.

BRADLEY, CHARLES S.
2000 Smoking Pipes for the Archaeologist. In Studies in Material Culture Research. K. Karklins, ed. Pp. 104-133. Rockville, MD: Society for Historical Archaeology.

BUSCH, JANE
1981 An Introduction to the Tin Can. Historical Archaeology 15(1):95-104.

—
1987 The Second Time Around: A Look at Bottle Reuse. Historical Archaeology 21(1):67-80.

CHENOWETH, JOHN M.
2006 "What'll Thou Have": Quakers and the Characterization of Tavern Sites in Colonial Philadelphia. Northeast Historical Archaeology 35:77-92.

COHEN-WILLIAMS, ANITA G.
1992 Common Majolica Types of Northern New Spain. Historical Archaeology 26(1):119-130.

DETHLEFSEN, EDWIN, AND JAMES DEETZ
1966 Death's Heads, Cherubs, and Willow Trees: Experimental Archaeology in Colonial Cemeteries. American Antiquity 31(4):502-510.

DUNNING, PHIL
2000 Composite Table Cutlery from 1700 to 1930. In Studies in Material Culture Research. K. Karklins, ed. Pp. 32-45. Rockville, MD: Society for Historical Archaeology.

GLEICHMAN, PETER J., AND DOCK M. TEEGARDEN
2005 Cartridges, Caps, and Flints: A Primer for Archaeologists. Southwestern Lore 71(3):3-27.

GRIFFITHS, DOROTHY M.
1978 Use-Marks on Historic Ceramics. Historical Archaeology 12:68-81.

GUSSET, GÉRARD
2000 A Preliminary Annotated Bibliography on Electrical Artifacts In Studies in Material Culture Research. K. Karklins, ed. Pp. 134-140. Rockville, MD: Society for Historical Archaeology.

HARRIS, JANE E.
2000 Eighteenth-Century French Blue-Green Bottles from the Fortress of Louisbourg, Nova Scotia. In Studies in Material Culture Research. K. Karklins, ed. Pp. 233-258. Rockville, MD: Society for Historical Archaeology.

HILL, ERICA
1995 Thimbles and Thimble-Rings from the Circum-Caribbean Region, 1500-1800: Chronology and Identification. Historical Archaeology 29(1):84-92.

JONES, OLIVE R.
1971 Glass Bottle Push-Ups and Pontil Marks. Historical Archaeology 5(1):62-73.

—
1993 Commercial Foods, 1740-1820. Historical Archaeology 27(2):25-41.

—
2000 A Guide to Dating Glass Tableware: 1800 to 1940. In Studies in Material Culture Research. K. Karklins, ed. Pp. 141-232. Rockville, MD: Society for Historical Archaeology.

KARKLINS, KARLIS
1982 Guide to the Description and Classification of Glass Beads History and Archaeology. Histoire et Archéologie. [Parks Canada] 59:83-117.

Kelly, Roger E., and Marsha C. S. Kelly
1977 Brick Bats for Archaeologists: Values of Pressed Brick Brands. Historical Archaeology 11:84-89.

Kenmotsu, Nancy
1990 Gunflints: A Study. Historical Archaeology 24(2):92-124.

Kidd, K. E., and M. A. Kidd
1970 A Classification System for Glass Beads for the Use of Field Archaeologists. Canadian Historic Sites, Occasional Papers in Archaeology and History 1:45-89.

Light, John D.
2000 A Field Guide to the Identification of Metal. In Studies in Material Culture Research. K. Karklins, ed. Pp. 3-19. Rockville, MD: Society for Historical Archaeology.

Lindsey, Bill
2006 Overview of BLM's Historic Glass Bottle Identification and Information Website. Technical Briefs in Historical Archaeology 1:16-20.

Lockhart, Bill
2004 An Annotated Bibliography of Bottle Manufacturer's Marks. SHA Newsletter 37(4):10-13.

—
2006 The Color Purple: Dating Solarized Amethyst Container Glass. Historical Archaeology 40(2):45-56.

Lorrain, Dessamae
1968 An Archaeologist's Guide to Nineteenth Century American Glass. Historical Archaeology 2:35-44.

Martin, Ann Smart
1989 The Role of Pewter as Missing Artifact: Consumer Attitudes Towards Tablewares in Late 18th Century Virginia. Historical Archaeology 23(2):1-27.

Maxwell, D. B. S.
1993 Beer Cans: A Guide for the Archaeologist. Historical Archaeology 27(1):95-113.

Miller, George L.
1991 A Revised Set of CC Index Values for Classification and Economic Scaling of English Ceramics from 1787 to 1880. Historical Archaeology 25(1):1-25.

—
2000 Telling Time for Archaeologists. Northeast Historical Archaeology 29:1-22.

Miller, George L., and Catherine Sullivan
1984 Machine-Made Glass Containers and the End of Production for Mouth-Blown Bottles. Historical Archaeology 18(2):83-96.

Myers, Adrian T.
2010 Telling Time for the Electrified: An Introduction to Porcelain Insulators and the Electrification of the American Home Technical Briefs in Historical Archaeology 5:31-42.

Newman, T. Stell
1970 A Dating Key for Post-Eighteenth Century Bottles. Historical Archaeology 4:70-75.

Olsen, Stanley J.
1963 Dating Early Plain Buttons by their Form. American Antiquity 28(4):551-554.

Priess, Peter J.
2000 Historic Door Hardware. In Studies in Material Culture Research. K. Karklins, ed. Pp. 46-95. Rockville, MD: Society for Historical Archaeology.

Rock, James
1984 Cans in the Countryside. Historical Archaeology 18:97-111.

Ross, Douglas E.
2009 Identification and Dating of Japanese Glass Beverage Bottles. Technical Briefs in Historical Archaeology 4:7-17.

Ross, Lester A., and John D. Light
2000 A Guide to the Description and Interpretation of Metal Files. In Studies in Material Culture Research. K. Karklins, ed. Pp. 20-31. Rockville, MD: Society for Historical Archaeology.

Samford, Patricia M.
1997 Response to a Market: Dating English Underglaze Transfer-Printed Wares. Historical Archaeology 31(2):1-30.

Scharfenberger, Gerard P.
2004 Recent Evidence for Broad Window Glass in Seventeenth-and Eighteenth-Century America. Historical Archaeology 38(4):59-72.

Singley, Katherine R.
1981 Caring for Artifacts After Excavation: Some Advice for Archaeologists. Historical Archaeology 15(1):36-48.

South, Stanley
1964 Analysis of the Buttons from Brunswick Town and Fort Fisher. Florida Anthropologist 17(2):113-133.

—
1971 Evolution and Horizon as Revealed in Ceramic Analysis in Historical Archaeology. Conference on Historic Site Archaeology Papers 6(2):71-106.

—
1978 Pattern Recognition in Historical Archaeology. American Antiquity 43(2):223-230.

SPRAGUE, RICK
2003 China or Prosser Button Identification and Dating. Historical Archaeology 36(2):111-127.

SPUDE, CATHY
n.d. Common 20th Century Artifacts - A Guide to Dating, Society for Historical Archaeology Research Resources Website, http://www.sha.org/index.php/view/page/20thCent_artifacts, accessed August 12, 2014.

STUART, IAIN
2005 The Analysis of Bricks from Archaeological Sites in Australia. Australasian Historical Archaeology 23:79-88.

SUSSMAN, LYNNE
1977 Changes in Pearlware Dinnerware, 1780-1830. Historical Archaeology 11:105-111.

—
2000 Objects vs. Sherds: A Statistical Evaluation. In Studies in Material Culture Research. K. Karklins, ed. Pp. 96-103: Society for Historical Archaeology.

TURNBAUGH, WILLIAM, AND SARAH PEABODY TURNBAUGH
1977 Alternative Applications of the Mean Ceramic Date Concept for Interpreting Human Behavior. Historical Archaeology 11(1):90-104.

VOSS, BARBARA L., AND REBECCA ALLEN
2000 Guide to Ceramic MNV Calculation Qualitative and Quantitative Analysis. Technical Briefs in Historical Archaeology 5:1-9.

WALL, DIANA DIZEREGA
1991 Sacred Dinners and Secular Teas: Constructing Domesticity in Mid-19th-Century New York. Historical Archaeology 25(4):69-81.

WEILAND, JONATHAN
2009 A Comparison and Review of Window Glass Analysis Approaches in Historical Archaeology. Technical Briefs in Historical Archaeology 4:29-40.

WELLS, TOM
1998 Nail Chronology: The Use of Technologically Derived Features. Historical Archaeology 32(2):78-99.

WHITE, CAROLYN L.
2009 Knee, Garter, Girdle, Hat, Stock, and Spur Buckles from Seven Sites in Portsmouth, New Hampshire. International Journal of Historical Archaeology 13(2):239-253.

WHITE, JOHN R.
1978 Bottle Nomenclature: A Glossary of Landmark Terminology for the Archaeologist. Historical Archaeology 12:58-67.

WILKIE, LAURIE
1996 Glass-Knapping at a Louisiana Plantation: African-American Tools? Historical Archaeology 30(4):37-49.

—
2000 Culture Bought: Evidence of Creolization in the Consumer Goods of an Enslaved Bahamian Family. Historical Archaeology 34(3):10-26.

Collecting, Updating, and Building on the Classics

John M. Chenoweth

Most American archaeologists would probably agree that artifacts, in and of themselves, are not the primary focus of our work. They are, rather, tools that we use together with context, features, strata, ecological data, and other sources of archaeological evidence to reconstruct site structure and understand past cultures (Deagan 1987: 1).

Archaeology is anthropology (Binford 1962a), and archaeology is interpretive (Hodder 1986), but all anthropological knowledge and interpretive understanding must be built on solid data, whether quantitative or qualitative. The use of artifacts as tools, as Deagan describes them in the opening quote, is a deceptively difficult matter. Only if we can answer the basic questions—what is it? how old is it?—can we then address the more important and more interpretative ones of history, process, or meaning. Archaeological field and lab work, in whatever period, is aimed at gathering this data systematically, in such a way that our data is as consistent, as comparable, and as clearly communicated as possible. The present volumes exist to provide a foundation in our knowledge of historic material culture for those new to the field and to gather in one place some of the seminal works on identifying and analyzing these "tools."

This introductory chapter serves three purposes. The first section discusses the design and structure of the three volumes that make up the Handbook and explains the overall goals of the collection. Section two, "Updating the Classics," takes note of the fact that much time has passed since some of these pieces were written. Although, on the whole, the pieces included here have stood the test of time and are important because of their foundational role in historic material culture analysis, some have been critiqued, debated, and discussed substantially in the decades since their original publication. It would seem useful, therefore, to discuss some of these debates and give a sense of the way these pieces—notably the pattern analysis and mean ceramic dating ideas of Stanley South (South 1971, I:14; South 1978, I:13)[1] and pipe stem dating ideas of Lewis Binford (Binford 1962b, I:16)—are used today. The final section points readers to the next steps in research for the topics considered in this collection. An annotated list of a handful of "must-have" books offers a place to start (though each archaeologist will differ on what books one "must" have) and a (surely incomplete) bibliography of nearly 300 works divided into sections by material gives an indication of the sheer number of works that exist to help in the process of analyzing historic artifacts.

Over the five decades or more of historical archaeology's existence as a subfield, a great store of knowledge has been amassed and more has been borrowed from historians, collectors, art historians, and others. This knowledgebase includes typologies, seriations, analyses of the physical fabric of artifacts, and histories of manufacturing techniques and the manufacturers themselves. In addition, historical archaeologists have developed techniques of analysis unique to our field. This collection is not the last word on any of these topics, but the first. The pieces included range from the earliest attempts to describe an artifact category or introduce a new form of analysis, to later refinements, to very recent comments. These works may disagree with each other and are surely incomplete. The next step for any student of historic material culture is to conduct further library research, perhaps starting with the many book-length classics of the field that could not be included here. The largest collection of such resources appears as a separate "Research Resources" section below.

Structure and Context for this Collection

The Society for Historical Archaeology has produced several very useful collections of articles used in the analysis of material culture. Though perhaps the largest such collection, this latest installment also aims to be narrower in scope than previous readers and handbooks: the focus here is on Deagan's "tools," the specifics of identification that need to be addressed before we can move on to more anthropological questions about the past. The present set aims to expand on these earlier volumes by bringing in works originally published in sources other than Historical Archaeology because some of the most used, most referenced works in the field are now somewhat difficult to find or are scattered among several journals with more limited distribution. In addition, this collection aims to start more or less at the beginning, outlining the basics of historic material culture

[1] *References to works included in* The Historical Archaeology Laboratory Handbook *will be given to their original publication followed by a Roman numeral indicating the volume within the handbook and then an Arabic numeral giving the chapter within that volume.*

analysis to readers new to the subject by presenting the seminal pieces on each of the main subjects important to the field. As such, it is comprised of more than 60 articles from over a dozen different sources. Hopefully, it will also be useful to veterans as a handbook, gathering in one place many resources to which we frequently turn.

Volume I is in two parts. There is an interpretive gap not only between artifacts and past peoples' cultures (Johnson 1999), but between the broken fragments of artifacts as they are usually found in the ground and the plates, pipes, even houses that people used in the past. Archaeologists have developed a way of looking at objects somewhat different from other scholars, in part to think about and bridge this gap. The difference between fragments and the whole pot, the lifecourse of an object as it is used and worn, how things are reused in unexpected ways, how to think about what one does not find, and a bastion of common types and terms used by archaeologists in identifying historic artifacts—all of these topics are considered in the first half of Volume I. The second half of this volume collects some of the types of analysis developed by historical archaeologists and more or less unique to our field, such as mean ceramic dating, pipe stem dating, and patterns in objects' form, cost, and other factors. These analyses are often still conducted as they were originally outlined, but, as will be discussed in the next section, many have also been the subject of expansion and critique.

Volumes II and III focus on the basics of identification of the original uses, ages, and other important properties for archaeologically recovered material: the central questions of "what is it" and "how old is it?" Many useful works on these subjects focus a great deal on the social context of the manufacture of these materials: the goals and ideas of those who created them and the way they play into broader issues such as world trade, the history of technology, changing tastes in fashion, etc. Yet when an excavator finds a ceramic sherd in the earth, in most cases, none of this is immediately apparent. Figuring out what to do with these excavated pieces is the focus of the works collected here. Once this is done, the more complex questions of their contexts of creation can (and must!) be addressed. A caveat, here, comes from an introduction to a previous SHA volume: this focus on identification is in no way meant to take issue with Brauner's (2000) statement, "An important lesson that must be woven into a materials analysis class is that determining an artifacts' function is not always as straight forward as it may seem. The physical and cultural context of an object recovered from an archaeological site must be taken into account before a meaningful functional determination can be made." Artifacts without archaeological context are just things, and there is no mechanical way to interpret artifacts. Still questions of type, date, manufacturing techniques, etc.—the focus of this collection—are starting points.

Volumes II and III are separated chronologically so that those dealing exclusively with 19th or 20th century projects, or, conversely, those whose contexts were formed before about 1800, do not have to carry the extra weight of irrelevant pieces around the lab. Due to the nature of the material considered, of course, this is not a hard-and-fast distinction: earlier material may well be found on later sites, and some articles have emphasis on one period but are applicable to the other as well. Each of these latter volumes is arranged in groups by the material of focus: first ceramic, then glass, then pieces which do not fit so neatly into large groups: metal and "small finds," the archaeologist's catch-all term for pins, buckles, marbles, buttons, gamepieces, beads, coins, nails, and just about everything else.

Updating the Classics

The processual or "New Archaeology" turn in archaeological theory occurred early in the existence of historical archaeology a subfield. This movement argued that archaeology is a science and must work by the scientific method. (For excellent introductions to archaeological theory, see Johnson (1999) or Praetzellis (2000).) By the 1970s, analysts in the new field of historical archaeology sought to deal with their data in a mathematical fashion consistent with archaeology's entry into the world of (a particular version of) formal science. Though rightly critiqued for what often became too narrow a focus on what could be said with mathematical rigor and for discounting both individuals in the past and interpretation in the present, these works were vital for increasing the interpretive ability of historical archaeology. Understandings of the past are built on top of these efforts to find patterns in the record. This said, many analysts have taken issue with aspects of this work, and this deserves some discussion, since all of these critiques and extensions cannot be included here. It is suggested that those unfamiliar with these techniques read the original articles included here (Binford 1962b, I:16; South 1971, I:14; South 1978, I:13) before proceeding.

Artifact Pattern Analysis

Many have found South's "pattern analysis" work (South 1978, I:13) to be extremely useful, and have applied it to their own sites just as he described it in the work included here. South sought patterns in the physical distribution of remains on sites and the ratios of different kinds of artifacts which could be correlated directly with different areas of past human activity. The rigidity of these patterns has been problematic to more recent researchers. Orser noted that South's work led archaeologists away from "preparing wholly descriptive reports" and towards quantification with a goal of understanding culture process (Orser 1989: 28) but overall he argued that South's ideas were essentially synchronic, collapsing many time periods into a single "signature," and that they misleadingly simplified complex social landscapes. In a similar context, Joseph suggested that such analyses were useful but could not be conducted uncritically (Joseph 1989). Critiques like these have been important for recognizing that we cannot deploy these techniques mechanically, with all archaeologists seeking, for instance, the "Carolina" or "Brunswick" artifact pattern at all sites. Indeed, South probably never intended such uncritical replication of his work. Rather, these patterns may be best used to suggest ways of looking at data that may be adapted to different contexts and different questions. A number of examples of these adaptations are presented here (I:16-20), again not as a suggestion that these are the only techniques which can or should be deployed, but as starting points to help others design analyses suited to their own work.

Mean Ceramic Dating

The practice of dating sites or deposits through the creation of an average based on the production date of the ceramics recovered there was developed by Stanley South (1971, I:14; 1978, I:13) and has been in broad use in historical archaeology ever since. To make the calculation, the number of sherds of each type is multiplied by the mean production date, a point halfway between the earliest and latest recorded (or sometimes estimated) production of that type. The results of these calculations are summed, and then the total divided by the number of sherds used in the calculation, producing a date thought to represent the approximate middle of the site's occupation or deposit's formation.

From the outset, it was clear to many that the dates produced by this formula do not necessarily correspond to the actual occupation dates of sites. In the absence of any written records, the results of these calculations can provide rough indications of occupation time periods, but for many historical sites written documentation provides a much more accurate indication of occupation. Rather, mean ceramic dates (MCDs) are useful as an expression of the average production date for many (but clearly not all) of a site's ceramic contents, and can suggest intrasite patterns and in some cases chronology. However it should be remembered that these dates need to be interpreted in concert with other lines of evidence, and may sometimes reveal trends and patterns having little to do with dating.

For instance, James Deetz's work on the Parting Ways site in Massachusetts is a well-known cautionary tale for the interpretation of mean ceramic dating (Deetz 1996: 198-199). Here, Deetz recognized that MCDs for the site tended to fall earlier than the known habitation dates, but also observed that many of the pieces recovered were of very high quality and cost for a settlement of formerly enslaved people engaged in subsistence farming. He interpreted this to be a result of "hand-me-downs" from wealthy neighbors with abolitionist tendencies intending to support the small community. Thus, the date suggests a pattern in the age of artifacts that relates more to acquisition and use practices (and through these to social interactions) than temporal occupations. In another case, my own work has compared ceramic and pipe stem dates on different parts of an eighteenth-century plantation in the Caribbean. The disjunction between the two independent lines of evidence was interpreted to show one way material culture was being consciously used to create religious identity (Chenoweth 2012). In short, mean ceramic dates cannot always be interpreted as indicating actual periods of occupation but should be compared with other lines of evidence and/or used for intrasite comparison. This point is made more generally in this collection by Turnbaugh and Turnbaugh (1977, I:15).

Beyond this interpretive question, mean ceramic dates are known to be problematic in a number of more practical ways. First, they can be distorted by types with unusually long production ranges. South recognized that tin-enameled wares or "delftwares" have a production range of more than 200 years from ca. 1600 to 1802, which could easily skew resulting MCD calculations: the listed mean production date of 1701 is problematic on a site known to be occupied only from 1750 to 1800, for instance, as it will skew the MCD earlier. South (1977: 213) suggested using 1650 as the median production date on which to base the calculations for these wares when a site is known to be of seventeenth century date and 1750 when it is known to be of eighteenth century date. Effectively, this is a circular process, as an assumption is being made about what the assemblage's MCD should look like, and then this assumption is being verified by the MCD test.

Douglas Armstrong, working on a Jamaican plantation with relatively well-established occupation dates, suggests using the approximate mid-point of occupation as the mean production date for tin-enameled wares (Armstrong 1990: 83). This suggestion avoids circularity if MCDs are not being interpreted as evidence of the actual occupation date and allows these ceramics to be considered in MCD calculations that may then be used for comparison between different parts of the site.

Other types with long production ranges have also been called into question for use in calculating MCDs. Worrying about the production ranges for stonewares, Wilkie and Farnsworth go so far as to suggest using only refined wares to calculate MCDs (Wilkie and Farnsworth 2005: 137). These wares—creamware, pearlware and whiteware, for instance—are well-known chronological indicators without the long production ranges that plague tin-enameled wares, some stonewares, and redwares. They found this technique to work well on their nineteenth century site in the Bahamas, but it introduces a different kind of bias on earlier sites. Since most of these well-dated types were not introduced until the later part of the 18th century this procedure would skew the date too late on sites with earlier occupation components, since many of the types most common in this earlier period would not be factored into the date.

Probably the best solution to this problem has only been developed in the last decade, and has received limited attention. This is the statistical method known as the best linear unbiased estimator mean ceramic date or "BLUE MCD." This method was developed in archaeological analysis by Fraser Neiman and Karen Smith (Neiman and Smith 2005) and has been used to counteract the problem of skewing due to uneven manufacturing ranges by Galle (2010; 2011) and Arendt (2013). However, there is an error in the published version of the equation in all of these sources. The correct version of the equation is given here:

$$MCD_{BLUE} = \frac{\sum_{i=1}^{t} m_i p_i \left(\frac{1}{s_i/6}\right)^2}{\sum_{i=1}^{t} p_i \left(\frac{1}{s_i/6}\right)^2}$$

It should be noted that, as far as I can determine, there are no problems with other aspects of the data or calculations in these sources, but simply that the equation was misprinted. This error may account for the limited application of this work by others in the literature, as it does address the problem of long manufacturing ranges being discussed here. The technique works by adjusting the traditional formula of South and incorporating the overall range of the dates of production into the equation so that those types with extremely long manufacturing spans play less of a factor than more tightly-dated materials. In the equation, m is the manufacturing midpoint for each type (j), p its relative frequency, and s the manufacturing span.

Bartovics dealt with the more general problem that almost all datable artifacts have ranges for production and all assemblages contain materials from distinct (though, one would expect, overlapping) ranges by calculating the partial probability of a particular piece being manufactured in a given year and incorporating frequency data for a given context. Thus a piece with a long manufacturing period is incorporated, but is less influential on the result than one with a tighter date. Rather than producing a specific date, this technique produces a chart integrating these probabilities and "the sharpest increase in decrease in probability are presumed to reflect the temporal limits of deposition" (Bartovics 1981: 167). Thus this technique produces a range of dates which represents the time span over which the assemblage was most likely formed.

Another issue concerns the calculation of MCDs based on sherd counts, as the results may be skewed by fragmentation: one vessel in many pieces will be counted more than many vessels represented by only one sherd or which are whole. The clear solution to this problem has been to calculate dates based on vessel counts (MNV) rather than sherd counts (Voss and Allen 2000, I:4). Where samples are large enough and site formation processes result in reconstructable vessels, vessel counts will better reflect the ceramics present, and using these is preferable. In some contexts, however, it can be difficult to reconstruct many vessels. This is the case on some Caribbean sites, for instance, where sandy, shallow soils and often scattered depositions can make it rare to find large portions of vessels. While MCDs must be weighed more carefully in these cases, there are other ways of accounting for fragmentation. One possibility is to calculate dates using the weights of sherds of each ware: the total number of grams of each ware can be simply used in place of counts in the original equation. This measure is somewhat rough, since different ceramic types have slightly different densities, but it can be argued that the use of weights would control for fragmentation, producing MCDs determined by how much of a particular ware was present, rather than how highly fragmented it was.

Calculating MCDs in multiple ways (by weights, sherd and vessel counts, with or without long-production ceramics, etc), and comparing them with each other and with the preceding discussion in mind might be the surest solution. The use of a simple computer spreadsheet for these calculations makes this relatively easy to do, and these comparisons themselves may produce interesting patterns as well as account for some of the vagaries of this technique. In addition, a broader application of the BLUE MCD technique will provide more information allowing us to determine how well it works to address the issues described above. Finally, as with all such techniques, the analyst needs to understand the ideas and assumptions built into any ceramic dating equation and interpret the results accordingly, rather than simply plugging numbers in and accepting the result as meaningful in a predefined way.

Pipe Stem Dating

Although other dating techniques using clay tobacco pipes have been proposed—most notably Oswald's typology (Oswald 1975) but also others based on stem length, bowl, heel and spur morphology, stem curvature and decoration (Walker 1977)—the discussion here will focus on the use of stem bore diameter, which has been the most widely used method. It should also be noted that the same comments on the use and meanings of mean ceramic dates made in the last section apply for pipe dates as well: though first perhaps intended to establish actual occupation dates, they have proven more useful as a point of comparison both within and between sites. In both cases, the context provided by other lines of evidence is vital to the interpretation of these numbers.

The technique for producing a date based on the pipe stems outlined by Binford (1962b, I:16) is itself based on an earlier observation by one of the founders of the field of historical archaeology, J.C. Harrington (1954), who showed that the diameters of the clay pipe stem bores (the holes through which smoke is drawn into the mouth) tend to reduce in size over time. Binford's article introduced a straight-line regression formula that produced a specific (though qualified) "pipe stem date" for a collection.

There has been much discussion of the reliability of this technique, and several suggestions for improvement. Walker argues that the Binford method only "appears to be accurate up to ca. 1765, after which it rapidly becomes too inaccurate to use, the dates produced being too early" (Walker 1977: 9). He also expresses doubt that the formula works well outside the US or in areas of the US where Dutch pipes were commonly imported (Walker 1977: 10), and Hanson has argued that a straight-line regression does not fit the data (Hanson 1969) although Binford responded to some of these critiques (Binford 1972). Susan White's more recent study also suggests that a straight-line regression does not produce good results (White 2004: 60). Heighton and Deagan proposed a logarithmic regression producing an exponential curve rather than a straight line (Heighton and Deagan 1972). However, the large and well-dated assemblage from Port Royal, Jamaica, proved to be much better dated by the Binford model than Heighton and Deagan's (Fox 1999: 77).

As with MCDs, sample size is an issue. Audrey Noël Hume suggested that at least 900 fragments are needed to produce "reliable" dates (Noël Hume 1963). This is an extremely stringent requirement, not met at many sites. However, this standard is suggested in order to obtain actual occupation dates, already noted to not be a strength of this kind of technique. Rather, these dates should be used primarily for comparison, and samples of far fewer artifacts seem to produce usable results for this purpose.

As in the case of ceramics discussed above, pipe dates may be skewed by fragmentation. It is also possible to use additional controls to make sure that calculations are based on how much of a particular pipe-stem bore diameter is present in each context. Dates can be calculated on counts in the usual way but also on weights (where the input is the total number of grams of each diameter recovered) or on total lengths of the pipes (where the input is the total number of centimeters of each diameter recovered). As with ceramics, the best procedure may be to calculate the dates using several of these techniques and interpret the results in the context of this discussion and the specific site being considered, and there is room for statistical improvement to this technique as well.

Other doubts about the creation of mean pipe stem dates come from questioning the assumption that bore diameters are consistent within single pipes or that the trend towards smaller diameters is universal (Alexander 1983; White 2004: 57-58). For instance, Alexander expresses doubts about some aspects of the measurement, pointing out that up to about 3% of some assemblages exhibit more than one measurement at each end. This can be caused by "finishing" wires and by pockets of air or bits of wet clay accumulating in the bore during the manufacturing process. The application of decoration via pressure can also cause the bore to constrict slightly at points. More recently, however, White conducted a study of Yorkshire pipes and concluded that "variation along the stem is not particularly pronounced" (White 2004: 60).

White's review of the debate concludes that there:

> *is no doubt that the basic theory behind stem-bore analysis is sound.... The main disadvantage of the theory, however, is that it tries to encompass a wide range of regional, chronological, production and human variables within a single mathematical formula. Pipe-makers were practical people who would have used whatever they could most easily find for the wires that would produce the stem-bores (White 2004: 58).*

White suggests that dates be given not as single numbers but as ranges (White 2004: 60), in a manner reminiscent of Harrington's original histogram (Harrington 1954).

Research Resources: Building on this Volume

As has been noted elsewhere in this introduction, the material presented here is just a starting-point for the analysis of historic material culture. This section is intended as a staging ground for research beyond these pages. It begins with a very brief selection of some of the most useful resources with a brief annotation for each. After this is an extensive (though not exhaustive) list of works not included in this collection—mainly book-length items—organized by the material(s) for which they are useful. Finding relevant resources for the identification and understanding of historic material culture requires substantial library-based research skills. One must evaluate pieces written by materials scientists and antiques collectors for their relevance, and one must sometimes make judgment calls about the reliability or applicability of these works to a particular question.

Basic Resources

Noël Hume, Ivor
1970 A Guide to Artifacts of Colonial America. New York: Knopf.

Perhaps the most widely consulted resource on historic material culture in existence, this work is divided into 44 chapters each outlining basic information on a type of artifact known from 17th and 18th-century contexts, such as pins, clocks, locks, beads, bells, and buckles. The sections titled Ceramics (British, American, and European), Stoneware, and Porcelain, in particular, offer a wealth of information on these materials and should be read in conjunction with the Ceramics Primer included here. Though much has been written about most of the topics covered in the four-plus decades since its original printing, Noël Hume's "Guide" is still the first book to which most researchers turn when learning about a new kind of artifact.

South, Stanley
1977 Method and Theory in Historical Archaeology. New York: Academic Press.

Though overlapping slightly with the pieces reprinted here (South 1971, I:14; South 1978, I:13) this work expands on these ideas with multiple examples and served as a manifesto proclaiming the entry of historical archaeology into the sciences. This book provides a set of tools historical archaeologists might use to think through their sites and artifacts. Though its language certainly represents a particular moment in the development of archaeology as a field, it still provides a way of thinking about material culture that is useful and on which researchers can build their own questions and interpretations.

Fike, Richard E.
1987 The Bottle Book: A Comprehensive Guide to Historic, Embossed Medicine Bottles. Caldwell, NJ: Blackburn Press.

While Jones (1971, II:8), Harris (2000, II:9), and Miller and Sullivan (1984, III:6) provide information on early glass manufacturing techniques and terminology, Fike is a main source on what are generically called "medicine bottles": small, rectangular, usually clear glass bottles and often with the names of pharmacists or patent medicines embossed on the sides. These were common in the nineteenth century. Fike also provides terminology and images to help in the proper description of bottles, as well as a substantial index of makers, marks, and dates, organized by the purpose of the medicine.

Majewski, Teresita, and Michael J. O'Brien
1987 The Use and Misuse of Nineteenth-Century English and American Ceramics in Archaeological Analysis. Advances in Archaeological Method and Theory 11:97-209.

This substantial, near book-length article takes on the problems archaeologists encountered when attempting to move into the analysis of nineteenth-century sites.

Due to changing technologies, there was a proliferation of ceramic types, designs, and forms which proved not only more complex but in some ways incommensurate with the techniques applied to earlier sites. The authors tackle issues of documentary sources, clarifying the different kinds of ceramic materials from this era, and providing resources for further exploring dating, decoration, and manufacturers.

Deagan, Kathleen

1987 Artifacts of the Spanish Colonies of Florida and the Caribbean, 1500-1800, vol. 1: Ceramics, Glassware, and Beads. Washington, D.C.: Smithsonian Institution.

2002 Artifacts of the Spanish Colonies of Florida and the Caribbean, 1500-1800, vol. 2: Portable Personal Possessions. Washington, D.C.: Smithsonian Institution.

This set is the place to start for any site with Spanish influence or trade, and is particularly strong with artifact types of the 16th and 17th centuries. It is intended to summarize and collect resources for Spanish materials produced over decades of work on sites in the Caribbean and Florida. Frequent images and charts help analysts identify types as well as track down relevant further research resources.

Jones, Olive R., and Catherine Sullivan

1989 The Parks Canada Glass Glossary. Quebec: Parks Canada.

This well-illustrated volume was intended to create a standardized system that could be used to catalog glass artifacts across Canadian sites. Because of the worldwide trading system in place from the early days of the North American colonies, those materials and technologies represented on Canadian sites may equally-well be found across the world in contexts dating from the seventeenth century on. This work outlines terminology and the different technologies used to make glass vessels as well as aiding the identification of form, manufacturing technique, and dating archaeological examples. This volume overlaps with but substantially expands on the information available in this collection in the Jones (1971, II:8) and Miller and Sullivan (1984, III:6) articles in particular.

Sussman, Lynne

1997 Mocha, Banded, Cat's Eye, and Other Factory-Made Slipware. Boston: Council for Northeast Historical Archaeology.

This slim volume is a special publication of the Council on Northeast Historical Archaeology (CNEHA). It is a detailed study of what are generally called "factory-turned slipwares" or "dipped" wares, the products of a suite of decorative techniques in use on creamwares, pearlwares, and other refined earthenwares. These wares are quite distinctive and are often found on late 18th and 19th century sites. Sussman's volume considers how these designs were produced, their chronology, forms, prices, and documentation.

Rickard, Jonathan

2006 Mocha and Related Dipped Wares, 1770-1939. Hanover, NH: University Press of New England.

A beautifully-illustrated volume which is more substantial than Sussman's on the same topic, this work is also more focused on the historical development of the types and the potters who made them than it is on archaeological analysis, which often must proceed from the sherd in hand rather than a knowledge of the potters themselves. However, use of Rickard's book to extend understanding of these types, their dates, development, and social functions is invaluable.

Allen, Rebecca, Julia E. Huddleson, Kimberly J. Wooten, and Glenn J. Farris, eds.

2013 Ceramic Identification in Historical Archaeology: The View from California, 1822-1940. Germantown, MD: Society for Historical Archaeology.

This recent volume gathers together extensive resources use in the analysis and identification of 19th and 20th century ceramics. Although the title suggests a geographic limitation, and each area's ceramic history will be unique, most of the types considered are found throughout the US and often far beyond, as they are the products of mass-production and were traded globally. Particularly useful is a work entitled "Ceramic Trends and Timeline from a California Perspective" (Allen et al. 2013) which is well-illustrated and provides an introduction to ceramic chronologies. The volume includes new works as well as previously published ones and is an excellent resource for up-to-date information on the complex field of nineteenth century ceramics.

Denker, Ellen, and Bert Denker

1985 The Main Street Pocket Guide to North American Pottery and Porcelain. Pittstown, NJ: Main Street Press.

Though designed as a collector's guide (as so many ceramics resources were) this book is well illustrated, including 50 color plates and many more smaller black and white images, making it useful for identification. Being focused exclusively on the products of North American potters, it fills what can often be a gap in the literature which is so focused on the products of Great Britain, the powerhouse of ceramic production in the eighteenth and nineteenth centuries. It is particularly strong in nineteenth-century wares, with examples of both utilitarian and presentation pieces.

Artifact Identification Resources Online

Of course, today many excellent resources for artifact identification exist online:

General

- SHA Research Resources Website: http://www.sha.org/index.php/view/page/research_resources
- SHA Juried Links Database: http://www.sha.org/index.php/view/juriedLinks
- Parks Canada Resources: http://www.sha.org/index.php/view/page/parks_canada_resources
- Intermountain Antiquities Computer System (IMACS) Guide, http://www.anthro.utah.edu/labs/imacs.html
- SHARD: Sonoma Historic Artifact Research Database, Anthropological Studies Center, Sonoma State University, http://www.sha.org/research/artifact_cataloging_system.cfm
- DAACS: The Digital Archaeological Archive of Comparative Slavery, http://www.daacs.org/
- Diagnostic Artifacts in Maryland, http://www.jefpat.org/diagnostic/index/htm
- Archaeological Guide to Historic Artifacts of the Upper Sangamon Basin, Central Illinois, USA: Ceramics, http://virtual.parkland.edu/lstelle1/len/archguide/documents/arcguide.htm
- Market Street Chinatown Archaeological Project, http://marketstreet.standford.edu/
- Asian American Comparative Collection: Artifact Illustrations, http://www.uiweb.uidaho.edu/aacc/illus.htm

Ceramics

- Florida Museum of Natural History Historic Ceramic Type Collection, http://www.flmnh.ufl.edu/histarch/gallery_types/
- Stoneware in the Late 1800s in San Luis Obispo's Chinatown, http://www.wolfcreekarcheology.com/Stoneware.htm
- East Liverpool Pottery District Manufacturers, Distributors, and Decorators, http://www.themuseumofceramics.org/pottery.html
- How to Interpret Diamond Marks. UK National Archives, http://www.nationalarchives.gov.uk/records/research-guides/reg-design-diamond.htm
- Official website of the White Ironstone China Association, Inc., http://www.whiteironstonechina.com/
- Historic Ceramics. User's Guide, Instructions, and Computer Codes for Use with the IMACS Site Form, http://anthro.utah.edu/_documents/imacs/473-ceramics.pdf
- The Local History of Stoke-on-Trent, England, Resources on the North Staffordshire Pottery Industry Page, containing an index of marks, background information on potters, and an illustrated guide to types, http://thepotteries.org/pottery.htm.
- Jefferson Patterson Park and Museum, Diagnostic Artifacts in Maryland, http://www.jefpat.org/diagnostic/Index.htm

Glass

- US Bureau of Land Management Historic Glass Bottle Identification and Information Website: http://www.blm.gov/historic_bottles/
- Glass Factory Marks on Bottles, http://www.myinsulators.com/glass-factories/bottlemarks.html
- Bottle Identification & Identification Website, http://bottleinfo.historicbottles.com/index.htm
- Bottles. Intermountain Antiquities Computer System (IMACS) Guide, http://www.anthro.utah.edu/labs/imacs.html

Resources for Ceramic Type Identification and Analysis

Archer, M., 1973. Engels Delfts Aardewerk, Catalogue of an Exhibition, Rijksmuseum, Amsterdam.

Archer, M., 1977. Delftware, Victoria and Albert Museum, London.

Archer, M., Morgan, B., 1977. Fair as China Dishes: English Delftware, The International Exhibitions Foundation, Washington, D.C.

1. Collecting, Updating and Building on the Classics

Atterbury, P., 1978. English Pottery and Porcelain: An Historical Survey, Peter Owen Publishers, London.

Barker, D., 1993. Slipware, Shire Publications Ltd., Princes Risborough, UK.

Blake, M.E., Freeman, M.D., 1998. Nineteenth-Century Transfer-Printed Ceramics from the Texas Coast: The Quintana Collection, Prewitt and Associates, Austin, TX.

Blaszczyk, R.L., 1994. The Aesthetic Moment: China Decorators, Consumer Demand, and Technological Change in the American Pottery Industry, 1865-1900, Winterthur Portfolio 29, 121-153.

Blaszczyk, R.L., 2000. China Mania, in: Blaszczyk, R.L. (Ed.), Imagining Consumers: Design and Innovation from Wedgwood to Corning, Johns Hopkins, Baltimore, pp. 52-88.

Brongniart, A., 1893. Coloring and Decoration of Ceramic Ware, Windsor and Kenfield Publishing, Chicago, IL.

Chipman, J., 1999. Collector's Encyclopedia of California Pottery, Collector's Books, Paducah, KY.

Claney, J.P., 2004. Rockingham Ware in American Culture, 1830-1930: Reading Historical Artifacts, University of New England, Hanover, NH.

Cluett, R., 1998. George Jones Ceramics, Schiffer Publishing, Atglen, PA.

Collard, E., 1984. Nineteenth-Century Pottery and Porcelain in Canada, McGill-Queens University Press, Montreal.

Conroy, B.J., 1998. Restaurant China: Identification & Value Guide for Restaurant, Airline, Ship & Railroad Dinnerware, Collector Books, Schroeder Publishing Co, Paducah, KY.

Cooper, R.G., 1968. English Slipware Dishes, 1650-1850, Transatlantic Arts Inc., New York.

Copeland, R., 1988. Manufacturing Processes of Tableware During the Eighteenth and Nineteenth Centuries, Northern Ceramic Society, Cumbria, England.

Copeland, R., 1999. Spode's Willow Pattern and Other Designs after the Chinese, Studio Vista, London, England.

Costello, J.G., Maniery, M.L., 1988. Rice Bowls in the Delta: Artifacts Recovered from the 1915 Asian Community of Walnut Grove, California. Occasional Publications of the Institute of Archaeology, UCLA 10., The Institute of Archaeology, UCLA, Los Angeles.

Coysh, A.W., 1970. Blue and White Transfer ware, 1780-1840, David & Charles, Newton Abbot.

Coysh, A.W., 1982. The Dictionary of Blue and White Printed Pottery, 1780-1880, Antique Collector's Club, Woodbridge.

Cunningham, J., 1982. The Collector's Encyclopedia of American Dinnerware, Collector Books, Paducah, KY.

Deagan, K., 1987. Artifacts of the Spanish Colonies of Florida and the Caribbean, 1500-1800, vol. 1: Ceramics, Glassware, and Beads, Smithsonian Institution, Washington, D.C.

Edwards, D., 1994. Black Basalt: Wedgwood and Contemporary Manufacturers, Antique's Collector's Club, Woodbridge, UK.

Ewins, N., 1997. "Supplying the Present Wants of Our Yankee Cousins…": Staffordshire Ceramics and the American Market 1775-1780, Journal of Ceramic History 15, 38-55.

Fisher, S.W., 1966. English Ceramics, Ward Lock & Co. Ltd., London.

Frelinghuysen, A.C., 1989. Fair as China Dishes: English Delftware, The International Exhibitions Foundation, Washington DC.

Furniss, D.A., Wagner, J.R., Wagner, J., 1999. Adams Ceramics: Staffordshire Potters and Pots, 1779-1998, Schiffer Publishing, Atglen, PA.

Gaimster, D., 1997. German Stoneware 1200–1900, British Museum Press, London.

Garner, F.H., Archer, M., 1972. English Delftware, Faber and Faber, London.

Gaston, M.F., 1983. The Collector's Encyclopedia of Flow Blue China, Collector Books, Paducah, KY.

Gibble, P.E., 2005. Eighteenth-Century Redware Folk Terms and Vessel Forms: A Survey of Utilitarian Wares from Southeastern Pennsylvania, Historical Archaeology 39, 33-62.

Godden, G.A., 1964. British Pottery and Porcelain 1870-1850, A. S. Barnes and Co., Cranbury, NJ.

Godden, G.A., 1964. Encyclopaedia of British Pottery and Porcelain Marks, Crown, New York.

Godden, G.A., 1966. An Illustrated Encyclopedia of British Pottery and Porcelain, Crown Publishers, New York.

Godden, G.A., 1999. Godden's Guide to Ironstone, Stone & Granite Wares, Antique Collectors' Club Ltd., Woodbridge, UK.

Godden, G.A., Jewitt, L.F.W., 1972. Jewitt's Ceramic Art of Great Britain 1800-1900, Arco, New York.

Grant, A., 1983. North Devon Pottery: The Seventeenth Century, University of Exeter, Great Britain.

Greer, G.H., 1981. American Stonewares, the Art and Craft of Utilitarian Potters, Schiffer Publishing, Exton, PA.

Griffin, J.D., 2005. The Leeds Pottery 1770-1881, The Leeds Art Collections Fund, Leeds, UK.

Grigsby, L.B., 1993. English Slip-Decorated Earthenware at Williamsburg, The Colonial Williamsburg, Williamsburg, VA.

Gurcke, K., 1987. Bricks and Brickmaking: A Handbook for Historical Archaeology, The University of Idaho Press, Moscow, ID.

Hildyard, R., 2005. English Pottery 1620-1840, V&A Publications, London.

Hunter, R.R., Jr, Miller, G.L., 1994. English Shell-Edged Earthenware, The Magazine Antiques 145, 432.

Hurst, J.G., Neal, D.S., van Beuningen, H.J.E., 1986. Pottery Produced and Traded in North-West Europe 1350-1650. Rotterdam Papers VI: A Contribution to Medieval Archaeology., Museum Boymans van Beuningen, Rotterdam.

Ketchum, W.C., 1971. The Pottery and Porcelain Collectors Handbook: A Guide to Early American Ceramics from Maine to California, Funk & Wagnalls, New York.

Ketchum, W.C., 1991. American Stoneware, Henry Holt and Company, New York.

Ketchum, W.C., 1994. American Pottery and Porcelain: Identification and Price Guide, Avon Books, New York.

Klinge, E., 1996. Duits Steengoed/German Stoneware. Rijksmuseum Aspects of the Collection Sculpture and Decorative Arts Volume 7, Rijksmuseum, Amsterdam.

Lehner, L., 1980. Complete book of American Kitchen and Dinner Wares, Wallace-Homestead, Des Moines.

Leibowistz, J., 1985. Yellow Ware: The Transitional Ceramic, Schiffer Publishing, Atglen, PA.

Lipski, L.L., 1984. Dated English Delftware: Tin-Glazed Earthenware 1600-1800, Sotheby Publications, London.

Madsen, A.D., White, C.L., 2011. Chinese Export Porcelains, Left Coast Press, Walnut Creek, CA.

Mankowitz, W., 1953. Wedgewood, B. T. Batsford Ltd., London.

Miller, G.L., 1987. Origins of Josiah Wedgwood's "Pearlware", Northeast Historical Archaeology 16, 83-95.

Miller, G.L., 1991. Thoughts Towards A User's Guide to Ceramic Assemblages, Part I: Lumping Sites into Mega-assemblages by Those That Cannot Tell Time., Council for Northeast Historical Archaeology Newsletter 18, 2-5.

Miller, G.L., 1991. Thoughts Towards a User's Guide to Ceramic Assemblages, Part II: What Does This Assemblage Represent? Council for Northeast Historical Archaeology Newsletter 20, 4-6.

Miller, G.L., 1992. Thoughts Towards a User's Guide to Ceramic Assemblages, Part III: Breaking Archaeological Assemblages into Functional Groups, Council for Northeast Historical Archaeology Newsletter 22, 2-4.

Miller, G.L., 1993. Thoughts Towards A User's Guide to Ceramic Assemblages, Part IV: Some Thoughts on Classification of White Earthenwares, Council for Northeast Historical Archaeology Newsletter 26, 4-7.

Miller, G.L., Earls, A.C., 2008. War and Pots: The Impact of Economics and Politics on Ceramic Consumption Patterns, Ceramics in America 2008, 67-108.

Miller, G.L., Hunter, R., 2001. How Creamware Got the Blues: The Origins of China Glaze and Pearlware, Ceramics in America 2001, 135-161.

Miller, G.L., Martin, A.S., Dickinson, N.S., 1993. Changing Consumption Patterns: English Ceramics and the American Market from 1780 to 1840, in: Hutchins, C.E. (Ed.), Everyday Life in the Early Republic: 1789-1828, Winterthur, Wilmington, DE, pp. 219-240.

Mountford, A.R., 1971. The Illustrated Guide to Staffordshire Salt-Glazed Stoneware, Praeger, New York.

Mudge, J.M., 1986. Chinese Export Porcelain in North America, Crown, New York.

Myers, J.E., Carredano, F.d.A., Olin, J.S., Hernandez, A.P., 1992. Compositional Identification of Seville Majolica at Overseas Sites, Historical Archaeology 26, 131-147.

Noël Hume, I., 1973. Creamware to Pearlware: A Williamsburg Perspective, in: Quimby, I.M.G. (Ed.), Ceramics in America, University Press of Virginia, Charlottesville, VA, pp. 217-254.

Noël Hume, I., 1978 [1969]. Pearlware: the Forgotten Milestone of English Ceramic History, in: Atterbury, P. (Ed.), English Pottery and Porcelain: An Historical Survey, Main Street Press, Clinton, NJ, pp. 42-49.

Noël Hume, I., 2000. If These Pots Could Talk: Collecting 2,000 Years of British Household Pottery, Chipstone Foundation, Milwaukee, WI.

Oswald, A., 1982. English Brown Stoneware 1670-1900, Faber and Faber, London.

Pollan, S.D., Gross, W.S., Earls, A.C., Pollan, J.T.J., Smith, J.L., 1996. Nineteenth-Century Transfer-Printed Ceramics from the Townsite of Old Velasco (41BO125) Brazoria County, Texas: An Illustrated Catalogue., Prewitt and Associates, Austin, TX.

Price, C.R., 1979. 19th Century Ceramics in the Eastern Ozark Border Region, Center for Archaeological Research, Southwest Missouri State University, Springfield, MO.

Rado, P., 1971. The Strange Case of Hard Porcelain, Transactions of the Journal of the British Ceramic Society 70, 131-139.

Rado, P., 1975. Hard Porcelain, Transactions of the Journal of the British Ceramic Society 74, 153-158.

Rado, P., 1988. An Introduction to the Technology of Pottery, 2nd ed., Pergamon, New York.

Ramsey, J., 1939. American Pottery & Porcelain, Hall, Cushman, & Flint, Boston.

Ray, M., 1974. Collectible Ceramics: An Encyclopedia of Pottery and Porcelain for the American Collector, Crown, New York.

Reineking-Von Bock, G., 1971. Steinzug, Katalog Des Kunstgewerbemuseum Köln, Kunstgewerbemuseum, Cologne, Germany.

Rickard, J., 1993. Mocha Ware: Slip-decorated Refined Earthenware, The Magazine Antiques 164, 182-189.

Rickard, J., 2006. Mocha and Related Dipped Wares, 1770-1939, University Press of New England, Hanover, NH.

Ross, D.E., 2012. Late-Nineteenth and Early-Twentieth-Century Japanese Domestic Wares from British Columbia, Ceramics in America 2012, 3-29.

Savage, G., Newman, H., 1976. An Illustrated Dictionary of Ceramics, Van Nostrand Reinhold, New York.

Schaefer, R.G., 1998. A Typology of Seventeenth-Century Dutch Ceramics and its Implications for American Historical Archaeology, BAR International Series 702, Oxford.

Seidel, J.L., 1990. "China Glaze" Wares on Sites from the American Revolution: Pearlware before Wedgwood? Historical Archaeology 24, 82-95.

Shlasko, E., 1989. Delftware Chronology: A New Approach to Dating English Tin-Glazed Ceramics. Unpublished MA Thesis, College of William and Mary.

Snyder, J., 1992. Flow Blue: A Collector's Guide to Pattern, History, and Values, Schiffer Publishing, West Chester, PA.

Snyder, J.B., 1997. Romantic Staffordshire Ceramics, Schiffer Publishing, Atglen, PA.

Stern, B., 2001. California Pottery: From Missions to Modernism, Chronicle Books, San Francisco, CA.

Stitt, I., 1974. Japanese Ceramics of the Last 100 Years, Crown, New York.

Stoltzfus, D., Snyder, J., 1997. White Ironstone: A Survey of its Many Forms, Schiffer Publishing, Atglen, PA.

Sussman, L., 1979. Spode/Copeland Transfer-Printed Patterns found at 20 Hudson's Bay Company Sites (Canadian Historic Sites Occasional Papers on Archaeology and History, No. 22), Parks Canada, Ottawa, ON.

Sussman, L., 1997. Mocha, Banded, Cat's Eye, and Other Factory-Made Slipware, Council for Northeast Historical Archaeology, Boston.

Switzer, R.R., 1974. The Bertrand Bottles: A Study of 19th Century Glass and Ceramic Containers, National Park Service, Washington, D.C.

Towner, D.C., 1957. English Cream-Coloured Earthenware, Faber and Faber, London.

Turnbaugh, S.P., 1985. Domestic Pottery of the Northeastern United States, 1625-1850, Academic Press, New York.

Van Rensselaer, S., 1969. Early American Bottles and Flasks, J. Edmund Edwards, Stratford, CT.

Venable, C.L., Denker, E.P., Grier, K.C., Harrison, S.G., 2000. China and Glass in America 1880-1980, from Tabletop to TV Tray, Harry N. Abrams, New York.

Voss, B.L., 2012. Status and Ceramics in Spanish Colonial Archaeology, Historical Archaeology 42, 39-54.

Wakefield, H., 1962. Victorian Pottery, Thomas Nelson & Sons, New York.

Walford, T., Massey, R., 2007. Creamware and Pearlware Re-Examined, English Ceramics Circle, Beckenham, UK.

Watkins, C.M., 1960. North Devon Pottery and its Export to America in the 17th Century, United States National Museum Bulletin 225, 17-59.

Watney, B., 1964. English Blue and White Porcelain of the 18th Century, Thomas Yoseloff, New York.

Wetherbee, J., 1980. A Look at White Ironstone, Wallace-Homestead, Des Moines.

Wetherbee, J., 1985. A Second Look at White Ironstone, Wallace-Homestead, Des Moines.

Wilcoxen, C., 1987. Dutch Trade and Ceramics in America in the Seventeenth Century, Albany Institute of History and Art, Albany, NY.

Willets, W., Lim, S.P., 1981. Nonya Ware and Kitchen Ch'ing. Ceremonial and domestic pottery of the 19th-20th centuries commonly found in Malaysia, Oxford University Press, Oxford.

Williams, P., 1981. Flow Blue China, Fountain House East, Jeffersontown, KY.

Williams, P., 1988. Flow Blue China II, Fountain House East, Jeffersontown, KY.

Resources for Clay Smoking Pipe Identification and Analysis

Alexander, L.T., 1983. More Light on the Theory of Dating Clay Pipes by Measuring Stem Hole Diameters, in: Davey, P. (Ed.), The Archaeology of the Clay Tobacco Pipe VIII, British Archaeological Reports (BAR), Oxford, pp. 235-244.

Binford, L.R., 1972. The 'Binford' Pipe Stem Formula: A Return from the Grave, Conference on Historic Site Archaeology Papers 6, 230-253.

Coney, A.P., 1980. M58: The Interpretation of Clay Pipe Scatters from Field Walking, in: Davey, P. (Ed.), The Archaeology of the Clay Tobacco Pipe III, British Archaeological Reports (BAR), Oxford, pp. 29-40.

Davey, P., 1979. The Archaeology of the Clay Tobacco Pipe I. Britain—Midlands and Eastern England. BAR British Series 63, British Archaeological Reports, Oxford.

Davey, P., 1979. The Archaeology of the Clay Tobacco Pipe II. United States of America. BAR International Series 60, British Archaeological Reports, Oxford.

Davey, P., 1980. The Archaeology of the Clay Tobacco Pipe IV. Europe I. BAR International Series 92, British Archaeological Reports, Oxford.

Davey, P., 1980. The Archaeology of the Clay Tobacco Pipe III. Britain: The North and West. BAR 78, British Archaeological Reports, Oxford.

Davey, P., 1981. The Archaeology of the Clay Tobacco Pipe V. Europe II, Parts I and II. BAR International Series 106 (i, ii), British Archaeological Reports, Oxford.

Davey, P., 1981. The Archaeology of the Clay Tobacco Pipe VI. Pipes and Kilns from the London Region. BAR British Series 97, British Archaeological Reports, Oxford.

Davey, P., 1982. The Archaeology of the Clay Tobacco Pipe VII. More Pipes and Kilns from England. BAR British Series 100, British Archaeological Reports, Oxford.

Davey, P., 1983. The Archaeology of the Clay Tobacco Pipe VIII. America. BAR International Series 175. British Archaeological Reports, Oxford.

Davey, P., 1985. The Archaeology of the Clay Tobacco Pipe IX: More Pipes from the Midlands and Southern England, Parts I and II. BAR 146 (i, ii), British Archaeological Reports, Oxford.

Davey, P., 1987. The Archaeology of the Clay Tobacco Pipe X. Scotland. BAR S175, British Archaeological Reports, Oxford.

Davey, P., Pogue, D.J., 1991. The Archaeology of the Clay Tobacco Pipe XII. Chesapeake Bay. BAR International 566, British Archaeological Reports, Oxford.

Edwards, L., 1988. The Archaeology of the Clay Tobacco Pipe XI. Seventeenth and Eighteenth Century Tyneside Tobacco Pipe Makers and Tobacconists. BAR British Series 192, British Archaeological Reports, Oxford.

Fox, G.L., 1999. The Kaolin Clay Tobacco Pipe Collection from Port Royal, Jamaica, British Archaeological Reports (BAR), Oxford.

Fox, G.L., 1999. The Archaeology of the Clay Tobacco Pipe XV. The Kaolin Clay Tobacco Pipe Collection from Port Royal, Jamaica. BAR S809, British Archaeological Reports, Oxford.

Fox, G.L., 2002. Interpreting Socioeconomic Changes in 17th-Century England and Port Royal, Jamaica, Through Analysis of the Port Royal Kaolin Clay Pipes, International Journal of Historical Archaeology 6, 61-78.

Gosse, P., 2007. The Archaeology of the Clay Tobacco Pipe XIX. Les pipes de la quarantaine: Fouilles du port antique de Pomègues (Marseille). BAR S1590, British Archaeological Reports, Oxford.

Handler, J.S., 1983. An African Pipe from a Slave Cemetery in Barbados, in: Davey, P. (Ed.), The Archaeology of the Clay Tobacco Pipe VIII, British Archaeological Reports (BAR), Oxford, pp. 245-254.

Hanson, L.H., Jr., 1969. Kaolin Pipe Stems: Boring In on a Fallacy, Conference on Historic Site Archaeology Papers 4, 2-15.

Harrington, J.C., 1954. Dating Stem Fragments of Seventeenth and Eighteenth Century Clay Tobacco Pipes, Bulletin of the Archaeological Society of Virginia 9, 1-5.

Heighton, R.F., Deagan, K., 1972. A New Formula for Dating Kaolin Clay Pipestems, Conference on Historic Site Archaeology Papers 6, 220-229.

Higgins, D., 1981. Surrey Clay Tobacco Pipes, in: Davey, P. (Ed.), The Archaeology of the Clay Tobacco Pipe VI, British Archaeological Reports (BAR), Oxford, pp. 189-293.

Jung, S.P., Jr., 2003. The Archaeology of the Clay Tobacco Pipe XVII. Pollocks of Manchester: Three Generations of Clay Tobacco Pipemakers. BAR 352, British Archaeological Reports, Oxford.

Mann, R., Rafferty, S.M., 2005. Smoking & Culture: Archaeology Tobacco Pipes Eastern North America, University of Tennessee Press, Knoxville.

Marx, R., 1968. Clay Smoking Pipes Recovered from the Sunken City of Port Royal. Jamaica National Trust Commission, Kingston.

Monroe, J.C., 2002. The Archaeology of the Clay Tobacco Pipe XVI. Negotiating African-American Ethnicity in the 17th-Century Chesapeake. BAR S1042, British Archaeological Reports, Oxford.

Noël Hume, A., 1963. Clay Tobacco Pipe Dating in the Light of Recent Excavations, Quarterly Bulletin of the Archaeological Society of Virginia 18, 22-25.

Oswald, A., 1975. Clay Pipes for the Archaeologist, British Archaeological Reports (BAR), Oxford.

Peacey, A., 1996. The Archaeology of the Clay Tobacco Pipe XIV. The Development of the Clay Tobacco Kiln in the British Isles. BAR 246, British Archaeological Reports, Oxford.

Rutter, J., Davey, P., 1980. Clay Pipes from Chester, in: Davey, P. (Ed.), The Archaeology of the Clay Tobacco Pipe III, British Archaeological Reports (BAR), Oxford, pp. 41-272.

Skre, D., 1980. Clay Pipes from the Excavation in Revierstredet 5-7, Oslo, in: Davey, P. (Ed.), The Archaeology of the Clay Tobacco Pipe IV, British Archaeological Reports (BAR), Oxford, pp. 299-318.

Tatman, C.A., 1994. The Archaeology of the Clay Tobacco Pipe XIII. The Clay Tobacco Pipe Industry in the Parish of Newington, Southwark, London. BAR 239, British Archaeological Reports, Oxford.

Walker, I.C., 1977. Clay Tobacco-Pipes, with Particular Reference to the Bristol Industry, Parks Canada, Ottawa.

White, S.D., 2004. The Archaeology of the Clay Tobacco Pipe XVIII. The Dynamics of Regionalisation and Trade: Yorkshire Clay Tobacco Pipes c1600-1800. BAR 374, British Archaeological Reports, Oxford.

Resources for Ceramic Makers' Marks Identification

Chaffers, W., 1952. The New Collector's Hand-Book of Marks and Monograms on Pottery and Porcelain, Reeves, London.

Cushion, J.P., 1980. British Ceramic Marks, Coles Publishing Co, Toronto, ON.

DeBolt, C.G., 1994. DeBolt's Dictionary of American Pottery Marks: Whiteware and Porcelain, Collector Books, Paducah, KY.

Gates, W.C.J., Ormerod, D.E., 1982. The East Liverpool, Ohio Pottery District: Identification of Manufacturers and Marks, Historical Archaeology 16.

Gibson, E.S., 2010. Ceramic Makers' Marks, Left Coast Press, Walnut Creek, CA.

Godden, G.A., 1964. Encyclopaedia of British Pottery and Porcelain Marks, Crown, New York.

Godden, G.A., 1968. Handbook of British Pottery and Porcelain Marks, Jenkins, London.

Kovel, R.M., Kovel, T.H., 1953. Dictionary of Marks: Pottery and Porcelain 1650 to 1850, Crown, New York.

Kovel, R.M., Kovel, T.H., 1986. Kovels' New Dictionary of Marks, Crown, New York.

Kowalsky, A.A., Kowalsky, D.E., 1999. Encyclopedia of Marks on American, English, and European Earthenware, Ironstone, and Stoneware (1780–1980), Schiffer Publishing, Atglen, PA.

MacDonald-Taylor, M., 1989. A Dictionary of Marks: Ceramics, Metalwork, Furniture, Tapestry, Crescent Books, New York.

Praetzellis, M., Rivers, B., Schulz, J.K., 1983. Ceramic Marks from Old Sacramento (California Archaeology Reports No. 22), Department of Parks and Recreation, Sacramento, CA.

Röntgen, R.E., 1997. Marks on German, Bohemian and Austrian Porcelains, 1710 to the Present, Schiffer Publishing, Atglen, PA.

Thorn, C.J., 1997. Handbook of Old Pottery and Porcelain Marks, Tudor Publishing Co., New York.

Resources for Glass Identification and Analysis

Blumenstein, L., 1963. Old Time Bottles Found in the Ghost Towns, Old Time Bottle Publishing Co., Salem, Oregon.

Blumenstein, L., 1966. Bottle Rush U.S.A.: The Story of Our Historic Past through Old Time Bottles, Old Time Bottle Publishing Co., Salem, Oregon.

Deagan, K., 1987. Artifacts of the Spanish Colonies of Florida and the Caribbean, 1500-1800, vol. 1: Ceramics, Glassware, and Beads, Smithsonian Institution, Washington, D.C.

Fike, R.E., 1987. The Bottle Book: A Comprehensive Guide to Historic, Embossed Medicine Bottles, Blackburn Press, Caldwell, NJ.

Giarde, J., 1980. Glass Milk Bottles: Their Makers and Marks, Time Travelers Press, Bryn Mawr, CA.

Hughes, B., 1956. English, Scottish, and Irish Table Glass, Bramhall House, New York.

Jones, O.R., 1986. Cylindrical English Wine and Beer Bottles, 1735-1850, Parks Canada, Quebec.

Jones, O.R., Smith, E.A., 1983. Glass of the British Military, 1755-1820, Parks Canada, Quebec.

Jones, O.R., Sullivan, C., 1989. The Parks Canada Glass Glossary, Parks Canada, Quebec.

Kendrick, G., 1964. The Antique Bottle Collector., Western Printing & Publishing, Sparks, NV.

Lockhart, B., 2004. An Annotated Bibliography of Bottle Manufacturer's Marks, SHA Newsletter 37, 10-13.

Lorrain, D., 1968. An Archaeologist's Guide to Nineteenth Century American Glass, Historical Archaeology 2, 35-44.

MacLeod, C., 1987. Accident or Design? George Ravenscroft's Patent and the Invention of Lead-Crystal Glass, Technology and Culture 28, 776-803.

McKearin, G.S., McKearin, H., 1948. American Glass, Crown, New York.

Miller, G.L., Pacey, A., 1985. Impact of Mechanization on the Glass Container Industry: The Dominion Glass Company of Montreal, A Case Study, Historical Archaeology 19, 38-50.

Noël Hume, I., 1968. A Collection of Glass from Port Royal Jamaica, with Some Observations on the Site, its History and Archaeology, Historical Archaeology 2, 5-34.

Parks Canada, 1985. The Parks Canada Glass Glossary for the Description of Containers, Tableware, Flat Glass, and Closures, Parks Canada, Ottawa, ON.

Switzer, R.R., 1974. The Bertrand Bottles: A Study of 19th Century Glass and Ceramic Containers, National Park Service, Washington, D.C.

Toulouse, J.H., 1969. Fruit Jars, Nelson Inc, Camden, NJ.

Toulouse, J.H., 1969. A Primer on Mold Seams, Parts 1 and 2, Western Collector 7, 578-587.

Van Rensselaer, S., 1969. Early American Bottles and Flasks, J. Edmund Edwards, Stratford, CT.

Venable, C.L., Denker, E.P., Grier, K.C., Harrison, S.G., 2000. China and Glass in America 1880-1980, from Tabletop to TV Tray, Harry N. Abrams, New York.

Wilson, B., Wilson, B., 1971. 19th Century Medicine in Glass, 19th Century Hobby & Publishing Co., Amador City, CA.

Wilson, R.L., 1981. Bottles on the Western Frontier, University of Arizona Press, Tucson.

Resources for Weapon and Weapon Accessories Identification and Analysis

Abels, R., 1967. Classic Bowie Knives, Robert Abels, Inc, New York.

Barnes, F.C., 2003. Cartridges of the World. 10th ed, Krause Publications, Iola, WI.

Bearse, R., 1966. Centerfire American Rifle Cartridges 1892–1963, A.S. Barnes & Co., South Brunswick, NJ.

Bussard, M., 1993. Cartridges of the World, DBI Books Inc., Northbrook, IL.

Chapel, C.E., 1947. The Gun Collector's Handbook of Values., Coward-McCann, New York.

Chapel, C.E., 1961. Guns of the Old West, Coward-McCann, New York.

Flayderman, N., 1994. Flayderman's Guide to Antique American Firearms and Their Values. 6th edition., DBI Books, Inc, Northbrook, IL.

Gluckman, A., 1965. Identifying Old U.S. Muskets, Rifles and Carbines, Bonanza Books, New York.

Greener, W.W., 1971. Modern Breech-Loaders: Sporting and Military, Normount Technical Publications, Forest Grove, Oregon.

Hackley, F.W., Woodin, W.H., Scranton, E.L., 1967. History of Modern U.S. Military Small Arms Ammunition. Vol. I, 1880-1939, MacMillian, New York.

Hardin, A.N., Jr., Hedden, R.W., 1973. Light But Efficient: a Study of the M1880 Hunting and M1890 Entrenching Knives and Scabbards, Taylor Publishing Company, Dallas.

Hutchins, J.S., 1970. Horse Equipments and Cavalry Accoutrements as Prescribed by G.O. 73, A.G.O., 1885. Ordnance Memoranda no. 29. 1891, Socio-Technical Publications, Pasadena, CA.

Keener, W.G., 1962. Bowie Knives from the Collections of Robert Abels and the Ohio Historical Society, Ohio Historical Society, Columbus.

Logan, H.C., 1944. Hand Cannon to Automatic: a Pictorial Parade of Hand Arms, Standard Publications, Huntington, WV.

Logan, H.C., 1959. Cartridges: A Pictorial Digest of Small Arms Ammunition, Bonanza Books, New York.

McChristian, D.C., 1995. The U.S. Army in the West, 1870–1880: Uniforms, Weapons and Equipment, University of Oklahoma Press, Norman.

McLean, D.B., 1971. Pictorial History of Firearms to 1905: the U.S. Cartridge Company Collection, Normount Technical Publications, Forest Grove, Oregon.

Peterson, H.L., 1956. Arms and Armor in Colonial America 1526–1783, Bramhall House, New York.

Peterson, H.L., 1980. American Knives, Gun Room Press, Highland Park, NJ.

Rogers, A.H., 1953. Firearms of Yesterday, Vantage Press, New York.

Russell, C.P., 1977. Firearms, Traps and Tools of the Mountain Men, University of New Mexico Press, Albuquerque, NM.

Satterlee, L.D., Gluckman, A., 1953. American Gun Makers. 2nd ed., Stackpole Books, Harrisburg, PA.

Sellers, F.M., 1983. American Gunsmiths: A Sourcebook, Gun Room Press, Highland Park, NJ.

Sharpe, P., 1987. The Rifle in America, Wolfe Publishing Co., Prescott, AZ.

Steffen, R., 1977-79. The Horse Soldier 1776–1943: The United States Cavalryman: His Uniforms, Arms, Accoutrements, and Equipments, 4 Volumes, University of Oklahoma Press, Norman.

Straube, B., 1990. Re-Examination of the English-Lock, The Bulletin of the American Society of Arms Collectors 63, 33-56.

Thalheimer, R., 1970. Percussion Revolvers of the United States, Von Hoffman Press, St. Louis, MO.

Wolff, E.G., 1968. Revolver Classification: Laboratory Textbook of Firearms Identification for Collectors and Students, Milwaukee Public Museum, Milwaukee, WI.

Resources for Other Metal and Small Finds Identification and Analysis

Albert, A.H., 1976. Record of American Uniform and Historical Buttons: Bicentennial Edition, Boyertown Publishing Company, Boyertown, PA.

Anderson, W., 1973. The Beer Book: an Illustrated Guide to American Breweriana, Pyne Press, Princeton.

Beaudry, M.C., 2006. Findings : The Material Culture of Needlework and Sewing, Yale University Press, New Haven, CT.

Brinckerhoff, S.B., 1972. Metal Uniform Insignia of the Frontier U.S. Army 1849-1902. Arizona Historical Society Museum monograph no. 3, Arizona Historical Society, Tucson.

Brinckerhoff, S.B., 1974. Early Underground Mine Lamps: Mine Lighting from Antiquity to Arizona. Arizona Historical Society Museum monograph no. 6, Arizona Historical Society, Tucson.

Brinckerhoff, S.B., 1976. Boots and Shoes of the Frontier Soldier, 1865-1893. Arizona Historical Society Museum monograph no. 7, Arizona Historical Society, Tucson.

Clifton, R.T., 1966. Clifton's Field Guide for Barbed Wire Collectors, Acobac Press, Denton, Texas.

Covill, W.E., Jr., 1971. Ink Bottles and Inkwells, William S. Sullwold Publishing, Taunton, MA.

Deagan, K., 1987. Artifacts of the Spanish Colonies of Florida and the Caribbean, 1500-1800, vol. 1: Ceramics, Glassware, and Beads, Smithsonian Institution, Washington, D.C.

Deagan, K., 2002. Artifacts of the Spanish Colonies of Florida and the Caribbean, 1500-1800, vol. 2: Portable Personal Possessions, Smithsonian Institution, Washington, D.C.

Drepperd, C., 1946. Spikes, Nails, Tacks, Brads, and Pins, The Chronicle of Early American Industries 3.

DuBois, J.H., 1972. Plastics History, Cahners Books, Boston.

Franklin, L.C., 1976. America in the Kitchen: From Hearth to Cookstove, an American Domestic History of Gadgets and Utensils Made or Used in America from 1700 to 1930, House of Collectibles/Random House, New York.

Friedel, R., 1983. Pioneer Plastic: The Making and Selling of Celluloid, University of Wisconsin Press, Madison.

Glover, J., 1969. The Bobbed Wire Bible: An Illustrated Guide to the Identification and Classification of Barbed Wire, Cow Puddle Press, Sunset, Texas.

Gurcke, K., 1987. Bricks and Brickmaking: A Handbook for Historical Archaeology, The University of Idaho Press, Moscow, ID.

Hughes, E., Lester, M., 1991. The Big Book of Buttons, New Leaf Publishers, Sedgewick, ME.

Johnson, D.F., 1948. Uniform Buttons: American Armed Forces, 1784-1948., Century House, New York.

Jordan, L., 2002. John Hull, The Mint and Economics of Massachusetts Coinage, University Press of New England, London.

Luscomb, S.C., 2006. The Collector's Encyclopedia of Buttons, 6th edition, Schiffer, Atglen, PA.

Martells, J., 1976. The Beer Can Collector's Bible, Ballantine Books, New York.

McChristian, D.C., 1995. The U.S. Army in the West, 1870–1880: Uniforms, Weapons and Equipment, University of Oklahoma Press, Norman.

Mérai, D., 2010. The True and Exact Dresses and Fashion: Archaeological Clothing Remains and their Social Contexts in Sixteenth – and Seventeenth-Century. Archaeolingua Central European Series 5, BAR S2078, British Archaeological Reports, Oxford.

Moore, S., 2005. Spoons 1650-1930, Shire Publications Ltd., Princes Risborough, UK.

Moseman, C.M., 1987. Moseman's Illustrated Catalog of Horse Furnishing Goods: An Unabridged Republication of the Fifth Edition, Dover Publications, New York.

Noël Hume, I., 1984. The Very Caterpillers of the Kingdom: or Penny Problems in the Private Sector, 1600-1660, in: Orr, D., Crozier, D.G. (Eds.), The Scope of Historical Archaeology Essays in Honor of John L. Cotter, Department of Anthropology, Temple University, Philadelphia, pp. 233-250.

Osborne, P.A., 1997. Button Button: Identification & Price Guide, Schiffer Publishing, Atglen, PA.

Petroski, H., 1992. The Evolution of Useful Things, Vintage Books, New York.

Randall, M., 1972. Early Marbles, Historical Archaeology 5, 102-105.

Russell, C.P., 1977. Firearms, Traps and Tools of the Mountain Men, University of New Mexico Press, Albuquerque, NM.

Simmons, M., Turley, F., 1980. Southwestern Colonial Ironwork: The Spanish Blacksmithing Tradition from Texas to California, Museum of New Mexico Press, Albuquerque, NM.

Snodin, M., Belden, G., 1976. Spoons, Chilton Book Company, Radnor, PA.

Steffen, R., 1977-79. The Horse Soldier 1776–1943: The United States Cavalryman: His Uniforms, Arms, Accoutrements, and Equipments, 4 Volumes, University of Oklahoma Press, Norman.

Symonds, J., 2002. The Historical Archaeology of the Sheffield Cutlery and Tableware Industry 1750-1900 (ARCUS Studies in Historical Archaeology 1, BAR 341), BAR, British Archaeological Reports, Oxford.

Thuro, C.M.V., 1976. Oil Lamps: The Kerosene Era in North America, Wallace-Homestead Book Company, Des Moines, IA.

White, C.L., 2005. American Artifacts of Personal Adornment, 1680-1820, AltaMira, Lanham, MD.

Wolfe, B., 1945. Plastics: What Everyone Should Know, Bobbs-Merrill Co., New York.

Woodhead, E.I., C., S., G., G., 1984. Lighting Devices in the National Reference Collection, Parks Canada, Parks Canada, Ottawa, ON.

Wyckoff, M.A., 1984. United States Military Buttons of the Land Services 1787-1902: A guide and classificatory System, McLean County Historical Society, Bloomington, IL.

Acknowledgements

My thanks go to all the authors of pieces that we reproduce here, as well as all the organizations who have granted permission to reprint them. Some parts of this chapter are adapted from work that appeared in my dissertation and I would like to thank my dissertation committee for their help: Laurie A. Wilkie, Rosemary A. Joyce, Kent Lightfoot, and Ethan Shagan. Thanks to Annelies Corbin and Joe Joseph for their work in shepherding this project through production, and to Robert Schuyler and Elliot Blair for discussions of the pieces included. Thanks to Sarah Roe and Norma Rahal for help with compiling the "Further Reading" section, and to Theresa Marchyok for assistance with typing and scanning.

References

Alexander, L. T.

1983 More Light on the Theory of Dating Clay Pipes by Measuring Stem Hole Diameters. In The Archaeology of the Clay Tobacco Pipe VIII. P. Davey, ed. Pp. 235-244, Vol. BAR Series 175. Oxford: British Archaeological Reports (BAR).

Allen, Rebecca, David L. Felton, and Christopher Corey

2013 Ceramic Trends and Timeline from a California Perspective. In Ceramic Identification in Historical Archaeology: The View from California, 1822-1940. R. Allen, J.E. Huddleson, K.J. Wooten, and G.J. Farris, eds. Pp. 25-52. Germantown, MD: Society for Historical Archaeology.

Arendt, Beatrix

2013 Return to Hopedale: Excavations at Anniowaktook Island, Hopedale, Labrador. Canadian Journal of Archaeology/Journal Canadien d'Archéologie 37:302-330.

Armstrong, Douglas V.

1990 The Old Village and the Great House: An Archaeological and Historical Examination of Drax Hall Plantation, St. Ann's Bay, Jamaica. Urbana: University of Illinois Press.

Bartovics, Albert F.

1981 The Archaeology of Daniels Village: An Experiment in Settlement Archaeology. Ph.D. dissertation. Department of Anthropology, Brown University, Providence, RI.

Binford, Lewis R.

1962a Archaeology as Anthropology. American Antiquity 28(2):217-225.

1962b A New Method of Calculating Dates from Kaolin Pipe Stem Samples. Southeastern Archaeological Conference Newsletter 9(1):19-21.

1972 The 'Binford' Pipe Stem Formula: A Return from the Grave. Conference on Historic Site Archaeology Papers 6:230-253.

1. Collecting, Updating and Building on the Classics

Brauner, David R.

2000 Preface. In Approaches to Material Culture Research for Historical Archaeologists. Second edition. D.R. Brauner, ed. Rockville, MD: Society for Historical Archaeology.

Chenoweth, John M.

2012 Quakerism and the Lack of 'Things' in the Early Modern. In Modern Materials: The proceedings of CHAT Oxford, 2009. B. Fortenberry and L. McAtackney, eds. Pp. 73-84. Oxford: British Archaeological Reports.

Deagan, Kathleen

1987 Artifacts of the Spanish Colonies of Florida and the Caribbean, 1500-1800, vol. 1: Ceramics, Glassware, and Beads. Washington, D.C.: Smithsonian Institution.

Deetz, James

1996 In Small Things Forgotten. New York: Doubleday.

Fox, Georgia L.

1999 The Kaolin Clay Tobacco Pipe Collection from Port Royal, Jamaica. Oxford: British Archaeological Reports (BAR).

Galle, Jillian E.

2010 Costly Signaling and Gendered Social Strategies among Slaves in the Eighteenth-Century Chesapeake: An Archaeological Perspective. American Antiquity 75(1):19-43.

2011 Assessing the Impacts of Time, Agricultural Cycles, and Demography on the Consumer Activities of Enslaved Men and Women in Eighteenth-Century Jamaica and Virginia. In Out of Many, One People: The Historical Archaeology of Colonial Jamaica. J.A. Delle, M. Hauser, and D.V. Armstrong, eds. Pp. 211-242. Tuscaloosa: The University of Alabama Press.

Hanson, Lee H., Jr.

1969 Kaolin Pipe Stems: Boring In on a Fallacy. Conference on Historic Site Archaeology Papers 4(1):2-15.

Harrington, J. C.

1954 Dating Stem Fragments of Seventeenth and Eighteenth Century Clay Tobacco Pipes. Bulletin of the Archaeological Society of Virginia 9:1-5.

Harris, Jane E.

2000 Eighteenth-Century French Blue-Green Bottles from the Fortress of Louisbourg, Nova Scotia. In Studies in Material Culture Research. K. Karklins, ed. Pp. 233-258. Rockville, MD: Society for Historical Archaeology.

Heighton, Robert F., and Kathleen Deagan

1972 A New Formula for Dating Kaolin Clay Pipestems. Conference on Historic Site Archaeology Papers 6:220-229.

Hodder, Ian

1986 Reading the past : current approaches to interpretation in archaeology. Cambridge Cambridgeshire ; New York: Cambridge University Press.

Johnson, Matthew

1999 Archaeological Theory: An Introduction. Oxford, Blackwell.

Jones, Olive R.

1971 Glass Bottle Push-Ups and Pontil Marks. Historical Archaeology 5(1):62-73.

Joseph, J. W.

1989 Pattern and Process in the Plantation Archaeology of the Lowcountry of Georgia and South Carolina. Historical Archaeology 23(1):55-68.

Miller, George L., and Catherine Sullivan

1984 Machine-Made Glass Containers and the End of Production for Mouth-Blown Bottles. Parks Canada Research Bulletin 171.

Neiman, Fraser D., and Karen Smith

2005 How Can Bayesian Smoothing and Correspondence Analysis Help Decipher the Occupational Histories of Late-eighteenth Century Slave Quarters at Monticello? Paper presented at the Society for American Archaeology conference, Salt Lake City, UT. [Available online in poster form: http://www.monticello.org/sites/default/files/media/temp/Bayesian%20Smoothing%20and%20Correspondence%20Analysis%20Poster_1.pdf].

Noël Hume, Audrey

1963 Clay Tobacco Pipe Dating in the Light of Recent Excavations. Quarterly Bulletin of the Archaeological Society of Virginia 18(2):22-25.

Orser, Charles E.

1989 On Plantations and Patterns. Historical Archaeology 23(2):28-40.

Oswald, Adrian

1975 Clay Pipes for the Archaeologist. Vol. BAR Series 14. Oxford: British Archaeological Reports (BAR).

Praetzellis, Adrian

2000 Death By Theory. Walnut Creek, CA: Altamira.

South, Stanley

1971 Evolution and Horizon as Revealed in Ceramic Analysis in Historical Archaeology. Conference on Historic Site Archaeology Papers 6(2):71-106.

1977 Method and Theory in Historical Archaeology. New York: Academic Press.

1978 Pattern Recognition in Historical Archaeology. American Antiquity 43(2):223-230.

Turnbaugh, William, and Sarah Peabody Turnbaugh
1977 Alternative Applications of the Mean Ceramic Date Concept for Interpreting Human Behavior. Historical Archaeology 11(1):90-104.

Voss, Barbara L., and Rebecca Allen
2000 Guide to Ceramic MNV Calculation Qualitative and Quantitative Analysis Technical Briefs in Historical Archaeology 5:1-9.

Walker, Iain C.
1977 Clay Tobacco-Pipes, with Particular Reference to the Bristol Industry. Ottawa: Parks Canada.

White, Susan D.
2004 The Archaeology of the Clay Tobacco Pipe XVIII. The Dynamics of Regionalisation and Trade: Yorkshire Clay Tobacco Pipes c1600-1800. BAR 374. Oxford: British Archaeological Reports.

Wilkie, Laurie, and Paul Farnsworth
2005 Sampling Many Pots: An Archaeology of Memory and Tradition at a Bahamian Plantation. Gainesville: University Press of Florida.

• • • • • • • • • • • • • • • •

John M. Chenoweth
Department of Behavioral Sciences
University of Michigan-Dearborn
4012 CASL, 4901 Evergreen Rd.
Dearborn, MI 48128

Part I: Looking At and Talking About Artifacts

Telling Time for Archaeologists

George L. Miller, with contributions by Patricia Samford, Ellen Shlasko, and Andrew Madsen

This essay presents an accumulation of data on the dates for common types of artifacts found on archaeological sites from the historical period. These dates come from a variety of sources and include a mix of types of dates. These dates are based on such things as patents, pattern registrations, dates when commercial production began, estimates of when production stopped, and the popularity ranges for various styles of wares based on makers' marks. The introductory essay discusses some of the problems in the sources of the dates presented.

Ce texte présente une accumulation de données sur les dates de types d'artefacts communs trouvés sur des sites archéologiques de la période historique. Ces dates proviennent de diverses sources et sont de plusieurs natures. Elles se basent sur divers indicateurs tels brevets, enregistrements de modèles, dates de début de production commerciale, estimations du moment où a cessé la production et périodes de popularité de divers styles d'articles d'après les marques des fabricants. Le texte évoque certains des problèmes que posent les sources des dates présentées.

Introduction

Publication of Ivor Noël Hume's *A Guide to Artifacts of Colonial America* in 1970 provided historical archaeologists with their major source for identification and dating of historical artifacts. This text became the standard reference for dating 17th- and 18th-century artifacts and to some extent artifacts from the early 19th century. As such, it is the most cited work by historical archaeologists. In this seminal work, Noël Hume presented in clear and simple terms the importance of and use of the concept of *terminus post quem* dates for dating archaeological contexts. The latest-made artifact in an archaeological context represents the earliest date that the context could have been deposited (Noël Hume 1969: 11). Unfortunately, the dating of contexts by their *terminus post quem* artifact is an under-utilized concept in historical archaeology. For some, the mean ceramic date seems to be the focus of analysis. Knowing the mid-date of a context and not knowing if it was for an assemblage that represents ten years or 100 years seems rather short sighted. It is hoped that the dates provided here will help archaeologists become more familiar with artifacts and their chronologies.

Sources for Dating Artifacts

Not all dates are created equal. Dates for artifacts used to interpret archaeological contexts come from a variety of sources that should be taken into account during the interpretation process. For example, consider the following types of sources for artifact dates.

Group 1: Dated objects

Coins, silver touch mark dates, armorial decorated wares, presentation pieces and dated ceramics and glass, manufacturers' date codes such as those used by Wedgwood, Worcester, Owens-Illinois Glass, and others (FIG. 1). One obvious question is what does the date represent? Is it the date the object was made, or does the date commemorate some event or relate to a presentation of the object?

Group 2: Known introduction dates

Patented objects, design registrations, makers' marks, model years, known date of introduction, dates of changes in technology, dates of changes in style, marks for institutionally owned wares such as used by military regiments, hospitals, hotels, schools, etc (FIGS. 2–4). Many of these dates have been estab-

Figure 1. The base to a bottle with an Owens-Illinois Glass Company mark. The bottle has an Owens suction scar to the left and top right of the parison mold line. This from the knife that cuts the glass off once it has been sucked up from the glass tank. Owens scars are very distinct, and sometimes are carried up onto the heel of the container, especially on small bottles. The Owens Automatic Bottle Blowing machine was patented in 1904. Suction scars are common on bottles made from 1903 until around 1940. Drawing by Anthony J. McNichol.

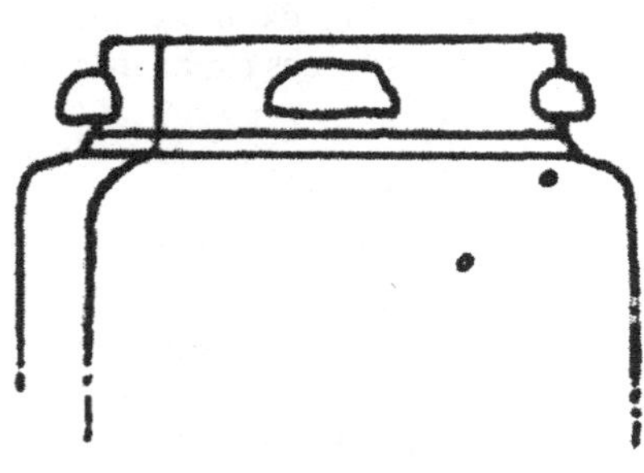

Figure 2. Lug top finish to a machine-made bottle. This type of closure was almost impossible to make on mouth-blown bottles. Lug top closures were introduced on machine-made bottles in 1906. There are many styles of lug top closures and they are still in common use today. Drawing by Anthony J. McNichol.

Figure 3. Continuous-Thread Finish. This finish on glass containers had one continuous line that overlaps itself for a quick and easy opening lid. The glass industry came together to set the first standards for the Continuous-Thread Finish in 1919 (Lief 1965: 27–29). The closure became very popular and basically replaced the cork for most containers. Drawing by Anthony J. McNichol.

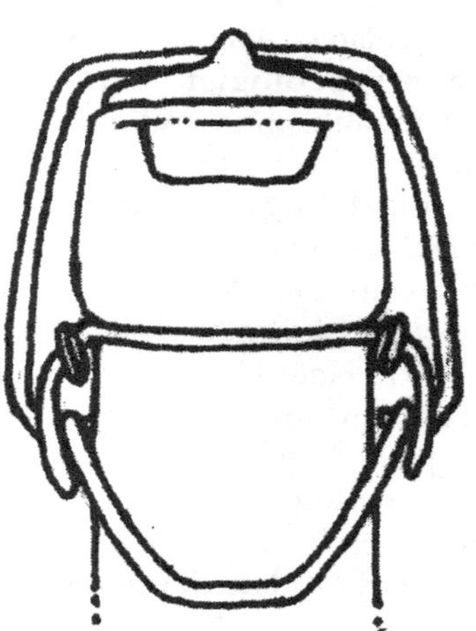

Figure 4. Bail and yoke "Lighting Stopper" stopper. Lief lists this stopper as being patented in 1882, but a patent date on the hard rubber cork on a Lighting stopper in Miller's collection has the date "Jan. 5, 1875." These closures were common on beer bottles and to a lesser extent on pop bottles until ca. 1910. They lost their market position to the crown stopper which was patented in 1892. Drawing by Anthony J. McNichol.

Table 1. Chronology for shell-edged earthenware, after Miller and Hunter 1990, keyed to Figure 5.

Figure	*Style*	*Rim*	*Mean beginning date*	*Mean end date*
5A, B	Rococo	Impressed curved lines	1784	1812
	Impressed curved lines	Even scalloped	1802	1832
5D	Impressed straight lines	Even scalloped	1809	1831
5C	Impressed bud motif	Even scalloped	1813	1834
5E, F	Embossed patterns	Patterned scalloping	1823	1835
5G, H	Impressed repetitive patterns	Unscalloped	1841	1857
	Unmolded	Unscalloped	1874	1884

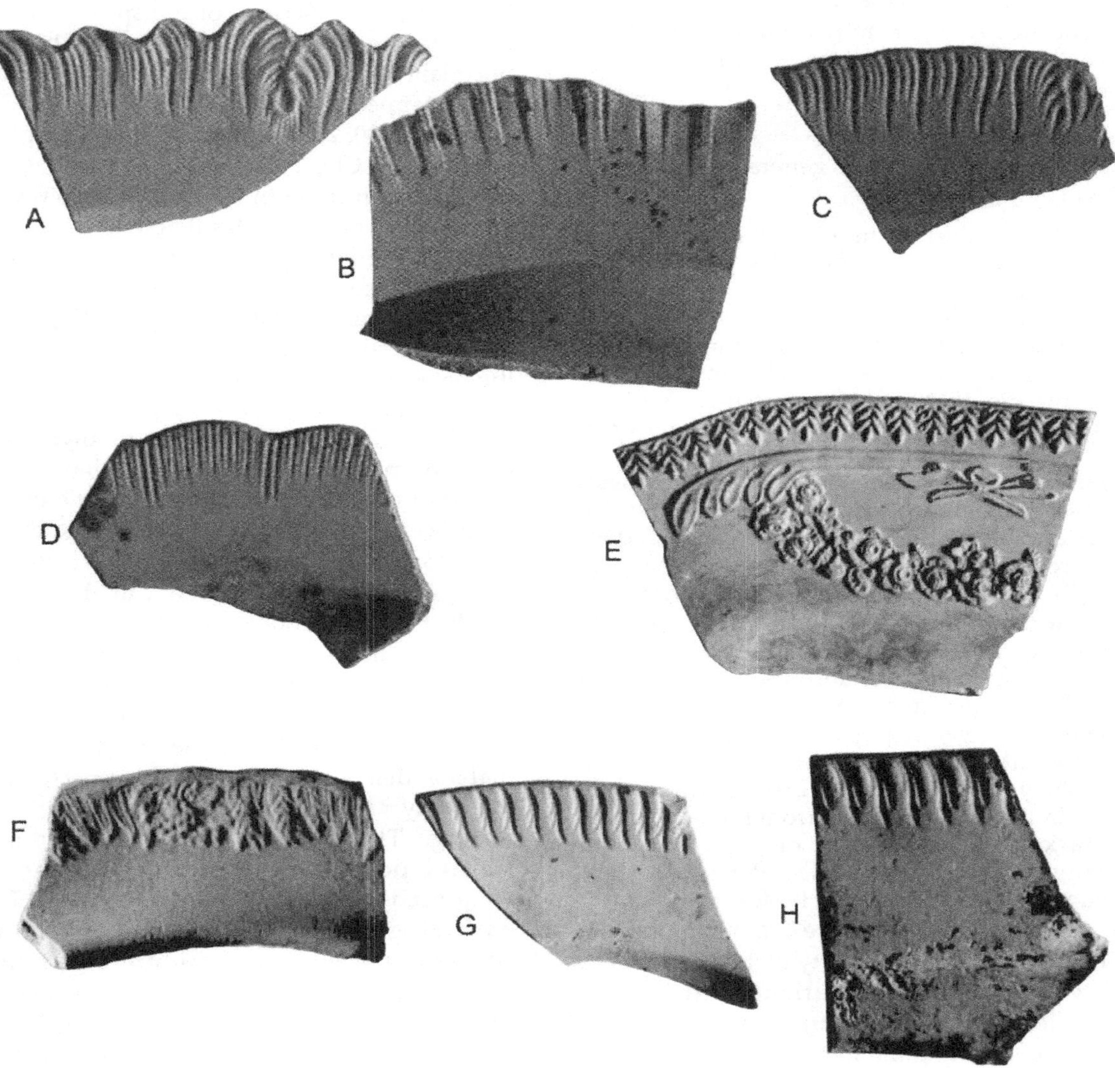

Figure 5. Bisque fired shell-edged waster sherds from Staffordshire. The chronological information on these rim types is presented in Table 1.

lished from documents such as patent office records, research in city directories, published histories, and other such sources.

Group 3: Dates by association

In most cases artifacts date the sites and contexts in which they are found. In some cases, such as shipwrecks, sites destroyed by catastrophic events, sites occupied for very short time periods, or activities such as military battles, the site often provides better dates for the objects found than our established artifact chronologies. In these cases, the dates are for a period when the artifacts were in use and deposited and generally do not represent the beginning or end date of the artifacts recovered.

Group 4: Artifact dates generated by accumulated data

The earliest example of this for historical archaeology is the Binford clay pipe stem formula dates based on the research by Pinky Harrington (Binford 1978). Later examples include Stanley South's mean ceramic date formula, based on data provided by Ivor Noël Hume (South 1978). Others have used accumulated dates from artifacts to generate ranges of popularity. Ellen Shlasko used the information from hundreds of dated delftware vessels to generate popularity curves and date ranges for the different styles of English delftwares (Shlasko 1989). Andrew D. Madsen built a similar chronology using information from dated armorial Chinese porcelain and Chinese porcelain from shipwrecks (Madsen 1995). Patricia M. Samford used the beginning and end dates from English potters' marks to generate a set of popularity date ranges for different styles in printed wares in the 19th century (Samford 1997). Likewise, I used the beginning and end dates from English potters' marks to generate a set of popularity date ranges for different styles of English shell-edged wares (Miller and Hunter 1990).

These chronologies are beginning points to further improve our ability to date the artifacts recovered from excavations. All of these studies have their limitations and raise questions concerning the meaning of the data and their reliability. For example, taking the chronology for shell edge outlined in Miller and Hunter produced the following mean beginning and end dates for the seven major decorative types (TAB. 1; FIG. 5).

Taken at face value, the above series would suggest that shell-edged wares were not being produced between 1835 and 1840 and between 1858 and 1873. Throughout the 1830s, shell edge was the most common type of plate being sold in the American market. A close look at Samford's data may reveal similar time gaps.

Andrew Madsen's data are based on Chinese porcelain decorated with English armorial designs. The British East India Company controlled the importation of Chinese porcelain to England. Because of a dispute with the London merchants who sold the Chinese porcelain imported by the Company, the Company stopped importing these wares in 1791 (Godden 1980: 28). This put an end to English armorials on Chinese porcelain at a time when the American trade in Chinese porcelain was taking off. Thus the dates that Madsen generated for the later patterns may have lasted longer in the American market (FIGS. 6–8). Anyone using the dates and chronologies in this paper should take into consideration how the dates were generated and what the limitations might be on their accuracy.

Many of the dates from the following list come from marginal sources that have been collected over the last 25 years. Some of the sources are newspaper clippings such as inventors' obituaries and company histories and promotional material about their own products. Many books and articles used were written by those involved in the antique trade. These authors commonly do not cite their sources and often come up with erroneous conclusions. While I have tried to filter out the material that is clearly wrong or suspect, there probably are cases in which the dates are wrong. The material presented here is a starting point rather than an end point for what needs to be done on chronologies. The gathering of material is a never-ending process, and what has been presented here represents a mish-mash of sources. In another five years it may be time to rework this list. I invite my colleagues to send me chronological information for a future update of this list.

One issue that has not been dealt with in this presentation is that of time lag between

Figure 6. Grape and Bamboo marly pattern on Chinese porcelain. This pattern was popular from ca. 1730 to ca. 1760 (Madsen 1995: 200). Photographed by Andrew Madsen.

Figure 7. Blue spearhead motif on Chinese porcelain. This pattern was popular from ca. 1730 to ca. 1780 (Madsen 1995: 200). Photographed by Andrew Madsen.

Figure 8. Blue trellis motif on Chinese porcelain. This pattern was popular from ca. 1720 to ca. 1795 (Madsen 1995: 200). The painting of the blue trellis pattern becomes much simpler in later examples. Photographed by Andrew Madsen.

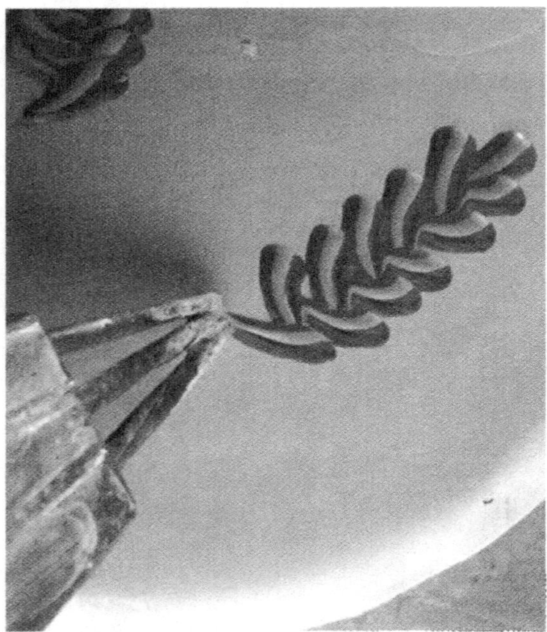

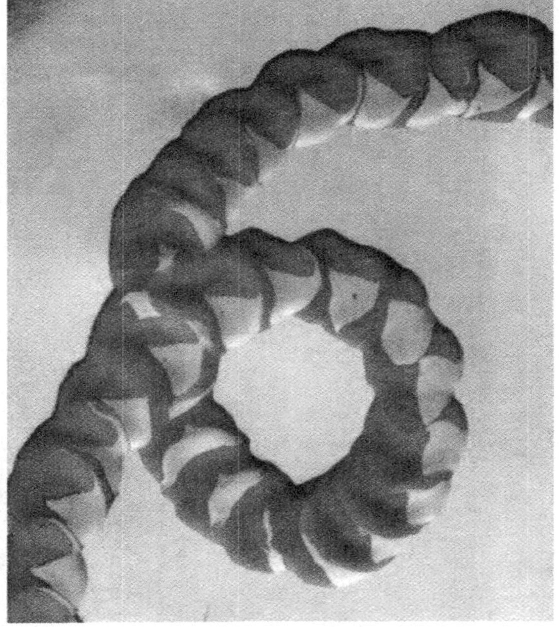

Figure 9. Don Carpentier of Eastfield Village reproducing slip decoration with a three-chambered slip trailer. The worm-like pattern on the right was called common cable by the Staffordshire potters and was created by a series of drops, each one overlapping the previous drop. This type had been called "finger trailed" in the literature. Clearly, there was not any finger trailing involved and this term should be dropped in favor of common cable. Photographs by Gavin Ashworth and are from Carpentier and Rickard 2001, courtesy of The Chipstone Foundation and *Ceramics in America*.

when an object was purchased and when it became part of the archaeological record. William H. Adams has been working on an extensive paper on this subject that will be published in the near future. In addition to the time lag based on typical length of artifact life, there is the issue of time lag from when a product is invented and when it goes into production and becomes a common item in households. Often a patent date will predate production by a number of years. Moving from an invention to funding for production can take years, and is greatly dependent on the consumers' level of acceptance of a new product. One well-documented example of this is the zipper. An early version of the zipper was patented in 1893. Zippers did not become common until 1923, however, after some of the initial bugs were worked out and the B. F. Goodrich Company began using them on their rubber boots (Panati 1987: 316–317).

It is hoped that the dates given in this paper will improve the ability of historical archaeologists to tell time when they are interpreting their contexts. Far too many archaeological reports are done after lumping whole site collections into one mega-assemblage and then applying South's mean ceramic date formula to these lumped data. Why do archaeologists excavate in a grid system and by depositional layers if they are going to lump the whole assemblage in the lab? What will a mean date tell them for a site that has been occupied for over 40 years? Historical archaeologists need to begin to work more with the dates of different contexts and the evolution of their sites. The use of the *terminus post quem* dates for excavated contexts should become more of a standard practice and archaeologists should be working toward improving their ability to describe and date the changes that took place in the sites they have excavated. The lumping of data from sites that have been occupied for more than ten years should be discouraged. Further work needs to be encouraged on the development of chronologies and typologies.

One last note: those dates that have been set in bold face are some of the most useful ones because of the frequency with which they occur in the archaeological record.

Table 2. TPQ (*terminus post quem*) List.

TABLE GLASS

Date	*Product*	*Source*
1650ca	Mold-blown table ware.	Jones 1983: 169.
1670ca	English lead crystal.	Noël Hume 1969: 186.
1690ca	Heavy baluster stem wines.	Noël Hume 1969: 189.
1725ca	Air twist stems on English wines.	Noël Hume 1969: 193.
1743	Opaque white "milk glass."	Noël Hume 1969: 196.
1750ca	Cut glass stems on English wines.	Noël Hume 1969: 193.
1750ca	Enamel twist in English stemware.	Noël Hume 1969: 193.
1825ca	Pressed glass table ware.	Jones et al. 1985.
1840	Red stained table glass.	Jones 2000: 150.
1864	Development of a colorless soda-lime glass.	McKearin & McKearin 1948: 8.
1883	Heat-sensitive glass that produces two colors, used on Hobnail, etc.	Jones 2000: 147.
1905	Pressed carnival glass.	Jones 2000: 151.
1915	Pyrex production begins.	Baker 1983: 8.
1970	Corning introduces Corelle Ware.	Panati 1987: 125.

Bottle Glass

Date	*Product*	*Source*
1730ca	Dip-mold-blown English wine bottles.	Jones 1983: 168.
1750ca	Lead glass commercial containers.	Jones 1983: 169.
1750ca	Bottles with letters blown in the glass.	Jones 1983: 169.
1750ca	Two-piece hinge molds.	Jones 1983: 169.
1821	Rickets' style three-piece mold.	Jones 1983.
1825ca	Lipping tool finish on bottles.	Jones et al. 1985.
1825ca	Post-bottom mold.	Jones et al. 1985.
1845ca	Bare iron pontil, American bottles.	Deiss 1981: 54.
1850ca	Snap-case held bottles.	Jones et al. 1985.
1858	Screw-top jar, ground lip (Mason jar).	Lief 1965: 11.
1863	Lug finish on mouth-blown canning jar.	Lief 1965: 13.
1864	Development of colorless soda-lime glass, first used on pressed glass, later on bottles.	McKearin & McKearin 1948: 8.
1867	Plate molds (other than base plates).	Toulouse 1969a: 584.
1869	Opaque white "milk glass" canning jar lid liner.	Toulouse 1969b: 350.
1870ca	Turn-paste molds.	Jones et al. 1985.
1873	Codd's Patent Ball Stopper on American bottles.	Lief 1965: 14.
1874	Patent for vented molds granted to Charles Fox.	Thomas 1977: IV.
1875	Bail and yoke "Lightning stopper."(Lief says 1882, but a Lightning stopper patent date is Jan. 5, 1875.)	Lief 1965: 13.
1876ca	Traditional ketchup bottle introduced.	*Daily Press* 1985: D1.
1876	U. S. trade-mark act prohibits refilling of bottles with registered trademarks.	Busch 1983: 193.
1879	Hutchins stopper "blob top."	Lief 1965: 14.
1880ca	Manganese decolorized glass (solarizes upon exposure to sunlight).	Miller & Pacey 1985: 44.
1886	Introduction of the milk bottle.	Lief 1965: 22.
1899	Machine-made production of narrow-mouth bottles (semi-automatic).	Miller & Sullivan 1984: 85.
1892	Crown bottle cap.	Lief 1965: 17.
1893	Machine-made production of wide-mouth containers (semi-automatic).	Miller & Sullivan 1984: 85.
1903	Owens automatic bottle-blowing machine, "suction scar," by 1917 half of bottles in U. S. made on the Owens machine.	Miller & Sullivan 1984: 85.
1906	Lug finish on machine-made bottles.	Lief 1965: 22.
1917	Cutex introduced the first commercial nail polish.	Staten 1998: 125.
1927	Introduction of plastic bottle and jar caps.	Lief 1965: 30.
1933–1964	"Federal Law Prohibits sale or reuse of this Bottle" embossed in the glass; this regulation ended in 1964.	Deiss 1981: 95; Pollard 1992.
1935	Applied color label on commercial glass containers.	Deiss 1981: 95.
1935	Non-returnable lightweight beer bottle developed, but not introduced until 1938.	Glass Container Manufacturers Inc. 1967: 32; Busch 1983: 196.
1936	Vitamin pills introduced.	Hagen 1999: A–1 & 12.
1938	Nestle's introduces instant coffee.	Hagen 1999: A–1 & 12.
1939	New non-returnable lightweight beer bottle, with stippled base.	Busch 1983: 226.
1948	Non-returnable soft drink bottle.	Busch 1983: 253.

1951	Bristol-Myers introduced roll-on deodorants.	Staten 1998: 122.
1959	Introduction of the stubby non-return beer bottle.	Glass Container Manufacturers Inc. 1967: 30.
1962	Food, Drug, and Cosmetics Act of 1962 decreed that all drugs, old or new, had to be safe and proven effective. This was the end date for many old patent and proprietary medicines.	Staten 1998: 141.
1971	32-oz. ketchup bottle introduced by H. J. Heinz Co.	*Daily Press* 1985: D1.

OTHER GLASS

Date	*Product*	*Source*
1846	Hand-made glass marbles.	Cleland 1983: 9.
1892	"Wire Glass," security window glass with imbedded wire (Schuman Patent).	*Encyc. Britannica* 1898: 1408.
1901	Machine-made glass marbles.	Cleland 1983: 9.
1906	Thermos bottles (invented in 1892) first imported to the U. S.	Panati 1987: 116–117.
1915ca	Safety glass invented in France, used for gas mask lenses. After WWI adapted to automobile windows.	Panati 1987: 158.

CHINESE PORCELAIN

Date	*Ware*	*Source*
1685	Appearance of *famille rose* Chinese porcelain.	Noël Hume 1969: 259.
1700	Armorial Chinese porcelain for English market.	Madsen 1995: 200.
1710–1730	Most popular period for Imari decoration on armorials.	Madsen 1995: 200.
1720–1790	Most popular period for *famille rose* on armorial porcelain.	Madsen 1995: 200.
1720–1795	Blue trellis border.	Madsen 1995: 200.
1730–1760	Most popular period for Grape & Bamboo border on armorials.	Madsen 1995: 200.
1730–1780	Blue spearhead border.	Madsen 1995: 200.
1740	"Batavia" ware.	Noël Hume 1969: 260.
1770–1795	Most popular period for Nanking porcelain with butterfly, scroll, & diaper border.	Madsen 1995: 165, 200.
1800–1830	Canton porcelain.	Noël Hume 1969: 262.

OTHER PORCELAIN

Date	*Ware*	*Source*
1709	German hard-paste porcelain developed in Meissen.	Savage & Newman 1976: 52.
1739	"Onion" pattern introduced on Meissen porcelain.	Röntgen 1997: 563.
1745–1795	English soft-paste porcelain.	Noël Hume 1969: 137.
1760–present	Underglaze printing on English porcelain.	Watney 1964: 52.
1768	English hard-paste porcelain.	Fisher 1966: 229.
1794–present	Bone china.	Miller 1991a: 11.
1868ca	Japanese porcelain imported to America.	Stitt 1974: 121–122.
1921	After 1921, Japanese porcelain could no longer be marked "Made in Nippon," but was to be marked "Made in Japan."	Stitt 1974: 149.

Stoneware

Date	*Ware*	*Source*
1620–1700	Poorly made bellarmines.	Noël Hume 1969: 56–57.
1650–1750	Rhenish stoneware with sprig molding, combed lines, blue and purple decoration.	Noël Hume 1969: 280–281.
1671–1775	Fulham brown salt-glazed stoneware (Dwight's patent) 1684.	Oswald, Hildyard, & Hughes 1982: 24.
1683–1810	Nottingham stoneware (lustred) production begins before 1684. Dwight sues Nottingham potters for infringement of his stoneware patent in 1684.	Oswald , Hildyard, & Hughes 1982: 102.
1690–1710	Embellished Höhr grey Rhenish stoneware.	Noël Hume 1969: 284.
1690–1715	Eler's dry-bodied red stoneware.	Noël Hume 1969: 120–121.
1700–1775	Westerwald, stamped blue floral devices, geometric designs.	Noël Hume 1969: 284–285.
1705–1930	American salt-glazed stoneware.	Ketchum 1991: 86.
1750–1780	Staffordshire refined dry-bodied red stonewares.	Barker & Halfpenny 1990: 44–46.
1750–1850	Black Basalt, also called Egyptian black.	Edwards 1994: 33–35.
1763–1775	Engine-turned red stoneware.	Noël Hume 1969: 121.
1805–1920	Albany slip.	Ramsey 1939: 21–22, 59.

White-bodied Stonewares

Date	*Ware*	*Source*
1715–1775	Slipped white salt-glazed stoneware.	Noël Hume 1969: 114–115.
1720–1730	Scratch-brown white salt-glazed stoneware, earliest dated piece is 1723. Fairly rare on American sites.	Mountford 1971: plate 58.
1720–1805	White salt-glazed stoneware, earliest dated piece, 1720. Noël Hume gives 1805 as end date, but these wares rare after 1790.	Mountford 1971: plate 53; Noël Hume 1969: 115–117.
1733–1750	Shaw brown-slipped stoneware.	Noël Hume 1969: 118–119.
1740–1765	Molded white salt-glazed stoneware.	Mountford 1971: 30, 32, 40.
1744–1775	Scratch-blue white salt-glazed stoneware.	Mountford 1971: 48–51.
1746–1775	Enameling on white salt-glazed stoneware.	Mug dated 1746, Dewitt Wallace Gallery, Colonial Williamsburg.
1750–1765	Littler's Blue.	South 1978: figure 1.
1755–1765	Transfer printed white salt-glazed stoneware.	Mountford 1971: 60–62.
1765–1795	Debased scratch-blue white salt-glazed stoneware (scratch-and-fill technique continues on pearlware).	Noël Hume 1969: 118.
1805–1840	Stone Chinas, decorated.	Miller 1991a: 8–9.
1813–1900	Mason's ironstone china; these dates should not be used for undecorated ironstone, see White Granite above.	Noël Hume 1969: 131; Miller 1991a: 9–10.
1835–present	Bristol white-glaze lined wares.	Oswald, Hildyard, & Hughes 1982: 19.
1842–1930	White granite, also know as white ironstone. (see also Miller 1991b, 1991c, 1992).	Miller 1991a: 10; 1993: 5–6.
1896	Rolled chip-resistant rim introduced on hotel wares.	Conroy 1998: 325.
1908	Underglaze decal printing on hotel wares.	Conroy 1998: 350.
1933	Narrow marley hotel ware plates introduced.	Conroy 1998: 325.

Coarse Earthenware

Date	*Ware*	*Source*
1624–1720	Dutch/North German-style redwares and slipwares.	Fayden 1993: 179–191.
1630–1660	Metropolitan slipware.	Noël Hume 1969: 103.
1635–1710	North Devon sgraffito slipware.	Watkins 1960: 53–54.
1675–1760	North Devon gravel-tempered ware.	Watkins 1960: 58–59.
1660–1745	North Midlands combed slipware.	Noël Hume 1969: 107, 134–136.
1720–1775	Buckley ware.	Noël Hume 1969: 132–135.
1745–1780	Flat-rimmed Iberian storage jars with sandy pink body & vestigial folded rim.	Noël Hume 1969: 144.
1750–1810	Coarse agate ware.	Noël Hume 1969: 132.
1835–1860	Hand-made terra cotta field-drain tiles in U. S.	Klippart 1861: 27.
1848–present	Machine-made terra cotta field-drain tiles.	Klippart 1861: 27.

Tin-glazed Earthenware

Date	*Ware*	*Source*
1628–1718	Bird-and-rock motif on English delftware.	Shlasko 1989: 39.
1628–1673	Overall powdered decoration on English delftware.	Shlasko 1989: 39.
1628–1724	Barrel-shaped mugs or drinking pots in English delftware.	Shlasko 1989: 39.
1645–1776	Armorial English delftware.	Shlasko 1989: 39.
1645–1728	Caudle cups in English delftware.	Shlasko 1989: 39.
1671–1788	Oriental landscapes on English delftware.	Shlasko 1989: 39.
1682–1709	Globular-shaped mugs or drinking pots in English delftware.	Shlasko 1989: 39.
1687–1703	Green/turquoise glaze on English delftware.	Shlasko 1989: 39.
1696–1788	Dot-&-diaper painted borders on English delftware.	Shlasko 1989: 39.
1700–1800	Everted rim, plain delftware ointment pots.	Noël Hume 1969: 204–205.
1708–1786	Sponge decoration used on English delftware.	Shlasko 1989: 39.
1709–1774	Painted marley panels on English delftware.	Shlasko 1989: 39.
1710–1740	Mimosa pattern delftware.	Noël Hume 1969: 108–111.
1725–1788	Scratched decoration used on English delftware.	Shlasko 1989: 39.
1729–1793	Rim-painted lines on English delftware.	Shlasko 1989: 39.
1730–1830	Pedestal-footed delftware ointment pots.	Noël Hume 1969: 204–205.
1738–1764	Powdered decoration used with stencils on English delftware.	Shlasko 1989: 39.
1745–1765	Ogee-shaped mugs or drinking pots in English delftware.	Shlasko 1989: 39.
1747–1768	*Bianco-sopra-bianco* decoration on English delftware.	Shlasko 1989: 39.
1748–1774	Cracked-ice pattern on English delftware.	Shlasko 1989: 39.
1750–1770	Fazackerly palette on delftware (Liverpool mug inscribed "T. F. Fazackerly 1757").	Garner & Archer 1972: 33.
1752–1771	Blue-glazed English delftware.	Shlasko 1989: 39.
1775–1780	Rouen faience on American sites, earlier and later on Canadian sites.	Noël Hume 1969: 141–142.
1783–1793	Glass-bottomed mugs and drinking pots in English delftware.	Shlasko 1989: 39.

REFINED EARTHENWARE

Date	*Ware*	*Source*
1610–1660	Marbleized North Italian red slipware.	Noël Hume 1969: 77.
1725–1750	"Astbury" ware, white sprigged and trailed.	Barker & Halfpenny 1990: 23–27; Noël Hume 1969: 123.
1740–1775	Refined agate ware.	Barker & Halfpenny 1990: 31–33.
1740–1800	"Jackfield."	Noël Hume 1969: 123; Barker & Halfpenny 1990: 34–35.
1830–1940	American yellow ware.	Ramsay 1939: 61.

REFINED WHITE-FIRING EARTHENWARE

Date	*Ware*	*Source*
1740–1770	Clouded wares & mottled glazes on molded wares.	Noël Hume 1969: 123; Barker & Halfpenny 1990: 50–57.
1759–1775	Wedgwood's green glaze, a refinement of earlier green glazes used by other Staffordshire potters.	Noël Hume 1969: 124–125; Barker & Halfpenny 1990: 63.
1762–1820	Creamware, dates dependent on the shade of the creamware. Dark colored creamware dates from ca. 1762 to ca. 1780. See light-colored creamware.	Noël Hume 1969: 125–126.
1765–1815	Enameled creamware.	Noël Hume 1969: 126–128.
1770–1825	Lined: enameled or underglaze brown or blue lines parallel to rims of creamware & pearlware tableware. Later as green lines on hotelware.	Finer & Savage 1965: 116–118; Miller 1991a: 7.
1774–1800	Shell-edged creamware.	Miller & Hunter 1990: 202–204; Hunter & Miller 1994: 433–435.
1775–1810	China glaze, Chinese motifs, blue painted.	Miller 1987: 87; Miller & Hunter 2001.
1775–1830	Underglaze floral blue painting on pearlware.	Miller 1987; Miller & Hunter 2001.
1775–1820	Light-colored creamware: gets lighter in shade through time. This in part results from refining iron out of the lead glaze. By 1790, light-colored creamware referred to as CC ware & was cheapest refined ware. Rare on tea wares after 1812, but continued on toilet ware well into the 19th century.	Noël Hume 1969: 126–128; Miller 1991a: 5; Miller 1993: 4–6; Miller, Martin, & Dickinson 1994: 222–223.
1779–1830	Pearlware, blue-painted, non-Chinese motifs.	Miller 1987: 87.
1780–1815	Rococo shell-edged blue or green under the glaze.	Miller & Hunter 1990: 115; Hunter & Miller 1994: 434-436.
1782–1810	Variegated (dipt) pearlware.	Miller 1987: 91; Miller 1991a: 6–7.
1790–1820	Dipt creamware.	Noël Hume 1969: 132; Rickard 1993: 184.
1790–1840	Lustre decoration.	South 1978: figure 1.
1795–1810	Polychrome-painted China glaze wares with Chinese patterns.	Miller & Hunter 2001.
1795–1830	Underglaze painted polychrome pearlware, floral patterns.	Miller 1991a: 8.
1795–1840	Mocha.	Miller 1991a: 7; Rickard 1993: 184.
1800–1835	Even scalloped blue or green shell-edged pearlware with impressed patterns.	Miller & Hunter 1990: 116.

1805–present	White ware production begun at Wedgwood, not common on American sites until after 1820.	des Fontaines 1990: 4.
1805–1840	Stone Chinas, decorated.	Miller 1991a: 8–9.
1810–1840	London- or Grecian-shaped teacup.	
1810–1833	Brown lines painted parallel to the rim of tableware, underglaze, usually on creamware. Blue lines usually occur on pearlware.	Miller 1991a: 7.
1811	Introduction of the three-chambered slip cup for making common cable dipt wares (FIG. 9).	Rickard 1993: 185.
1813–1900	Mason's ironstone china.	Noël Hume 1969: 131.
1820–1835	Embossed blue- and green-edge ware.	Miller & Hunter 1990.
1830ca	Appearance of chrome colors on painted white wares, underglaze red being a good indication of this. Stems of flowers for this group usually painted black vs. brown on earlier polychrome-painted wares.	Miller 1991a: 8.
1840–1860	Unscalloped blue shell-edge with simple repeating lightly impressed patterns.	Miller & Hunter 1990: 117.
1842–1930	White granite begins as a vitrified ware, but later white granite often just a high-fired earthenware.	Miller 1991a: 10.
1845–1930	Cut-sponge stamped wares.	Miller 1991a: 6.
1851	Victorian Majolica.	Wakefield 1962: 84.
1865–1895	Blue shell-edged, unscalloped & unmolded.	Miller & Hunter 1990: 117.
1870–present	"Bright gold" gilding, also known as "liquid gold" on English wares.	Miller 1991a: 10.
1875–1890ca	"Ivory" body introduced in U. K.	Samford 1997: 19.
1933	Narrow marley hotel ware plates introduced.	Conroy 1998: 325.

PRINTED WARES

Date	*Ware*	*Source*
1762	Overglaze printing on creamware first shipped to America.	Price 1948: 35.
1783–1830	Underglaze printing on pearlware.	Shaw 1829: 214.
1790–1830	Underglaze black printing. Jug dated 1790 in a Litchfield auction catalog.	Litchfield 1990.
1795–1830	Willow pattern on pearlware.	Noël Hume 1969: 130.
1800–present	Royal coat of arms as part of potters' makers' mark.	Godden 1964: 11.
1807–1830	Stippling in printed pearlwares.	Coysh & Henrywood 1982: 9.
1809–1825	Brown-printed pearlware.	Miller 1991a: 9.
1810–present	Printed pattern names as part of makers' mark.	Godden 1964: 11.
1828–present	Red, green, purple, and brown-printed white wares.	Shaw 1829: 214.
1845	Flow blue printed wares first imported to North America.	Collard 1984: 17.
1875–1900	Japanese-style patterns printed on English wares.	Miller 1991a: 9.
1890–present	Decalcomania on English wares.	Shaw 1900: XIX.
1908	Underglaze color decals introduced.	Conroy 1998: 350.

MEAN BEGINNING AND END PRODUCTION DATES FOR PATTERNS ON PRINTED WARES

Date	*Pattern or color*	*Source*
1797–1814	Chinese patterns on China glaze/pearlware (22 patterns).	Samford 1997: 6.
1813–1839	British views (401 patterns).	Samford 1997: 6.

1816–1836	Chinoiserie-style patterns (33 patterns).	Samford 1997: 6.
1819–1835	Negative dark blue patterns (122 patterns).	Samford 1997: 20.
1819–1836	Pastoral views (88 patterns).	Samford 1997: 6.
1820–1842	Exotic views (214 patterns).	Samford 1997: 6.
1826–1838	American views (192 patterns).	Samford 1997: 6.
1826–1842	American historical views (49 patterns).	Samford 1997: 6.
1827–1847	Classical views (104 patterns).	Samford 1997: 6.
1831–1846	Two-color printed wares (18 patterns).	Samford 1997: 20.
1831–1851	Romantic views (376 patterns).	Samford 1997: 6.
1833–1849	Floral central patterns (56 patterns).	Samford 1997: 6.
1841–1852	Gothic views (20 patterns).	Samford 1997: 6.
1868–1878	No central view (11 patterns).	Samford 1997: 6.
1881–1888	Brown-printed patterns on ivory body (24 patterns).	Samford 1997: 20.
1882–1888	Japanese views (44 patterns).	Samford 1997: 6.
1883–1889	Black-printed patterns on ivory body (26 patterns).	Samford 1997: 20.

METALS, NAILS, AND OTHER FASTENERS

Date	*Material or product*	*Source*
1790–1810	Machine-cut nails with hand-finished heads.	Nelson 1968: 6.
1805–present	Cut nails with machine-made heads.	Nelson 1968: 6.
1839	Machine-made railroad spikes.	Drepperd 1946: 69.
1846	Self-starting gimlet-point wood screw patented Aug. 20, 1846	Devoto 1943: 214.
1850	Small wire nails introduced in France.	Nelson 1968: 7.
1860ca	Large wire nails become common after ca. 1885.	Nelson 1968: 7.
1901	Galvanized roofing nails introduced.	Fontana et al. 1962: 50.

CONTAINERS

Date	*Material or product*	*Source*
1837	Commercial production of goods canned in metal containers began.	Keen 1982: 316.
1898	Crimped top "Sanitary can."	Keen 1982: 316.
1928	Key-opened vacuum-packed coffee can.	Keen 1982: 318.
1935	Crown cap on beer cans.	Keen 1982: 319.
1953	Marketing of canned soft drinks (attempted in 1938, but failed).	Busch 1983: 246.

ARMS RELATED

Date	*Material or product*	*Source*
1814–1816	Percussion cap patented, iron or pewter before 1816.	Logan 1959: 3.
1816	Copper percussion cap.	Logan 1959: 3.
1846	Brass or copper cartridge cases for ammunition.	Logan 1959: 5.
1850	Shotgun cartridges.	Logan 1959: 6.
1852	Minie Ball introduced in France.	Logan 1959: 6.
1866	Rim-fired cartridges.	Logan 1959: 8.
1871	Bottle-necked cartridges.	Logan 1959: 9.
1958	Introduction of plastic-bodied shotgun shell.	Bussard 1993: 384.

Electrical and Lighting

Date	*Material or product*	*Source*
1859	Drake drills first oil well; cheap kerosene caused an increase in lamp and lamp chimney production.	Thur 1976: 15.
1865	Production of glass electrical insulators with internal threads for attaching to pole begins.	Cleland 1983: 6.
1870ca	Hand-crimped lamp chimney tops.	Davis 1949: 155.
1876	First commercial application of arc lighting of streets, later department stores.	Weitz 1930: 28.
1878	Dust-pressing of electrical insulators (oil mixed with clay before insulator is mold-pressed).	Jameson 1958: 663.
1879	Machine crimped lamp chimney tops.	Davis 1949: 155.
1879	Invention of the carbon-filament light bulb.	Jarvis 1958: 214.
1888	Introduction of the ceramic part of the spark plug.	Jameson 1958: 663.
1895	Machine-made electric light bulbs.	Scoville 1948: 331.
1901	Mercury vapor lamps (fluorescent lights) introduced.	Weitz 1930: 35.
1906	Tungsten filament light bulbs introduced.	Weitz 1930: 6.
1911	Neon lighting introduced.	Weitz 1930: 46.
1926	Light bulbs with frosted interior surfaces.	Weitz 1930: 17.
1959	First commercially viable alkaline batteries introduced.	*The Times* 1999: D–10.
1999	Introduction of multicolored extension cords.	*The Times* 1999: D–10.

Other Metals and Processes

Date	*Material or product*	*Source*
1743ca	Introduction of Sheffield Plate, fusing silver to copper with heat.	Luscomb 1967: 177.
1788	Enameled cast-iron cooking pots developed in Germany.	Panati 1987: 100.
1820	Seamless lead pipes.	Chadwick 1958: 627.
1824	German silver or nickel silver.	Chadwick 1958: 608.
1835	Machine-made horseshoes.	Chappell 1973: 104.
1836	Practical process for galvanizing iron created in U. K.	Chadwick 1958: 624–625.
1840	Electroplating patent taken out in U. K.	Chadwick 1958: 633.
1840	Brass key-hole covers & sleeves on iron padlocks "do not seem to have been used on iron padlocks until the nineteenth century, most of them dating no earlier than 1840."	Noël Hume 1969: 251.
1840	Cylinder locks patented by Linus Yale.	Noël Hume 1969: 249.
1844	Galvanized corrugated iron roofing introduced in U. K.	Chadwick 1958: 625.
1858	Can opener patented.	Petroski 1992: 187.
1865	James H. Nason receives patent on December 26, 1865, for coffee percolator.	*The Times* 1998: A–10.
1867	Commercial production of enameled tin pots for cooking begins in the U. S.	Keen 1982: 296.
1884	Ball-bearing roller skates patented December 9, 1884.	*The Times* 1996a: A–12.
1886	Invention of barbed wire.	Cleland 1983: 61.
1893	Zipper patented in 1893, not in common use until improvements in 1913.	Panati 1987: 316–317.
1891	Aluminum household items appear on the market; aluminum cookware production begins in 1903.	Trench & Luty 1918: 343; Panati 1987: 101.
1896	Introduction of tooth paste in a squeeze tube.	Staten 1998: 105.

1898	Paper clip patented.	Petroski 1992: 63.
1908	Electric coffee pot introduced.	Kovel & Kovel 2000b: AA–3.
1910	Electric toaster introduced.	Kovel & Kovel 2000b: AA–3.
1911	Electric frying pan introduced.	Kovel & Kovel 2000b: AA–3.
1918	Electric waffle iron introduced.	Kovel & Kovel 2000b: AA–3.
1921	Stainless steel flatware (knives, forks, & spoons) introduced.	Bidwell & Haughton 1999: E–1.
1935	Electric blender introduced.	Kovel & Kovel 2000b: AA–3.
1937	Home model of the electric coffee grinder.	Kovel & Kovel 2000b: AA–3.
1956	Electric can opener introduced.	Kovel & Kovel 2000b: AA–3.
1981	First computer mouse came onto the market.	Stefton 2001: B–1.

RUBBER, PLASTIC, AND OTHER SYNTHETICS

Date	*Material or product*	*Source*
1851	Hard rubber buttons patented.	Luscomb 1967: 91.
1863	The term *Linoleum* coined by F. Walton for new English floor covering.	*Webster's New World Dictionary* 1982.
1868–1920	Celluloid plastic (imitation of ivory, amber, coral, tortoise shell, and mother-of-pearl).	Wolfe 1945: 15.
1870	Rubber fire and garden hose.	Panati 1987: 165.
1871	Rubber bottle corks.	Panati 1987: 165.
1871	Rubber fruit jar rings and other gaskets.	Panati 1987: 165.
1871	Asphalt paving, first used in Philadelphia.	Parrington 1983: 21.
1876	Portland Cement first produced in U. S in 1876, but output not significant until invention of rotary kiln in 1899.	Cleland 1983: 93.
1887	Wooden clothes pins with steel springs patented June 28, 1887.	Schneringer 2001: cover.
1900	Flat disk records invented in Germany in 1895, overtook cylinder records by 1900.	Thorgerson & Dean 1977: 8.
1902	"Fisheye" cut pearl buttons.	Claassen 1994: 55.
1905	First marketing of aspirin, invented in Germany in 1899.	Shartar & Shavin 1981: 6.
1907	Bakelite plastic, black electrical parts, telephone parts.	Wolfe 1945: 19.
1915	Pyralin plastic, tooth brushes, combs, pens, baby toys, kitchen gadgets.	Wolfe 1945: 22.
1917	Asphalt roofing advertised, but probably produced earlier.	Luetkemeyer Co. 1917: 2126.
1917	U. S. Rubber introduced Keds™ (first rubber-soled canvas-top gym shoe).	Panati 1987: 299.
1922	Introduction of the Popsicle™ stick.	*Daily Press* 1986b: B–15.
1924ca	Introduction of Easter Bunny as marketing device.	*Progressive Grocer* 1924: 17.
1938	Introduction of the Nylon-bristle tooth and other brushes.	Panati 1987: 209.
1938	Federal law required listing ingredients on many types of foods.	Kovel & Kovel 2000a: AA–3.
1940	Melmac™ plastic, used by the Navy during WWII, commercial production of table ware after the war.	Wolfe 1945: 29.
1943	Postal codes introduced, the precursor to ZIP codes.	Kovel & Kovel 2000a: AA–3.
1944	Invention of Styrofoam™ by Ray McIntire of Dow Chemical.	Anonymous 1996: 25.

1945	Tupperware™ introduced.	Panati 1987: 129.
1947	Introduction of aluminum foil.	Panati 1987: 113.
1951	Introduction of Diners Club, first credit card.	*The Times* 2000: D–4.
1954	Introduction of the frozen TV dinner.	Berry 1999: AA–5.
1955	Velcro™ in production by mid-1950s.	*Daily Press* 1990: B–5.
1957	Introduction of pink plastic yard flamingo.	*The Times* 1996b: A–15.
1957	Child-proof cap introduced on St. Joseph's Aspirin for Children™ (not required by law until 1972).	Staten 1998: 53.
1958	Disposable one-use ballpoint pen introduced by Bic.	Busch 1983: 334.
1959	Introduction of the Barbie™ doll.	Lord 1994.
1959	American Express introduces first plastic charge card.	*The Times* 2000: D–4.
1961	Teflon™ nonstick coating on pans.	*Daily Press* 1986a.
1961	Plastic milk bottle.	Busch 1983: 284.
1962	Styrofoam™ cups.	Busch 1983: 120.
1962	Pull-tab pop & beer can closures.	Keen 1982: 31.
1963	Postal ZIP codes introduced.	Kovel & Kovel 2000a: AA–3.
1963	Vinyl siding for buildings introduced.	Hoagland 1997: 5.
1972	Child-resistant caps required by law for aspirin containers.	Glass Packaging Institute n.d.
1973	Bar codes introduced.	Kovel & Kovel 2000a: AA–3.
1973	Federal law requires nutrition information to be listed on food packages.	Kovel & Kovel 2000a: AA–3.
1975	McDonalds™ introduces polystyrene "clamshell" package for its burgers.	Petroski 1992: 221.

Acknowledgments

I would like to thank Robert H. Hunter Jr. and The Chipstone Foundation of Milwaukee, Wisconsin for providing color photographs from their journal *Ceramics in America* to illustrate this article. The first issue of *Ceramics in America* was published during the summer of 2001. I would also like to thank Anthony J. McNichol for the glass drawings he did for this publication. I began compiling this list of dates while employed at Parks Canada and much of the information came from my former colleagues in Ottawa.

References

Anonymous
1996 Obituary of Ray McIntire, invented Styrofoam at Dow Chemical. *Time* 147(7): 25.

Baker, John C.
1983 *Pyrex: 60 Years of Design.* Tyne and Wear County Council Museum, England.

Barker, David, and Pat Halfpenny
1990 *Unearthing Staffordshire: Towards a New Understanding of 18th-century Ceramics.* City of Stoke-on-Trent Museum and Art Gallery, Stoke-on-Trent, England.

Berry, Walter
1999 Inventor Enjoying Limelight for TV Dinner Innovation. *The Times* (Burlington County, NJ) November 19: AA–5.

Bidwell, Carol, and Natalie Haughton
1999 20th Century Brought Soda, Appliances, Instant Coffee, Chocolate Bars. *The Times* (Burlington County, NJ) December 29: E–1.

Binford, Lewis R.
1978 A New Method of Calculating Dates from Kaolin Pipe Stem Samples. In *Historical Archaeology: A Guide to Substantive and Theoretical Contributions*, ed. by Robert L. Schuyler, 66–67. Baywood Publishing Company, Inc., Farmingdale, NY.

Busch, Jane Celia
1983 The Throwaway Ethic in America. Ph.D. diss., American Studies, University of Pennsylvania, Philadelphia.

Bussard, Mike, ed.
1993 *Cartridges of the World.* DBI Books Inc., Northbrook, IL.

Carpentier, Donald and Jonathan Rickard
2001 Slip Decoration in the Age of Industrialization. *Ceramics in America* 1: 115-134.

Chadwick, R.
1958 The Working of Metals. In *A History of Technology. Volume V: The Late Nineteenth Century c. 1850–1900*, ed. by Charles Singer, E. J. Holmyard, A. R. Hall, and Trevor I. Williams, 605–635. Oxford University Press, New York.

Chappell, Edward
1973 A Study of Horseshoes in the Department of Archaeology, Colonial Williamsburg. In *Five Artifact Studies*, ed. by Ivor Noël Hume, 100–116. Occasional Papers in Archaeology 1. Colonial Williamsburg Foundation, Williamsburg, VA.

Claassen, Cheryl
1994 Washboards, Pigtoes, and Muckets: Historic Musseling in the Mississippi Watershed. *Historical Archaeology* 28(2).

Cleland, Charles E.
1983 *Tombigbee Historic Townsites Project Code Book*. Michigan State University, East Lansing, MI.

Collard, Elizabeth
1984 *Nineteenth-Century Pottery and Porcelain in Canada*. McGill-Queens University Press, Montreal.

Conroy, Barbara J.
1998 *Restaurant China: Identification & Value Guide for Restaurant, Airline, Ship & Railroad Dinnerware*. Volume 1. Collector Books, Schroeder Publishing Co., Inc., Paducah, KY.

Coysh, A. W., and R. K. Henrywood
1982 *The Dictionary of Blue and White Printed Pottery 1780–1880*. Antique Collectors' Club, Woodbridge, Suffolk, England.

Daily Press
1985 Ketchup Industry Strives to Cut Mustard. *The Daily Press* (Newport News, VA) July 7: D–1.
1986 Teflon Making 25th Anniversary. *The Daily Press* (Newport News, VA) January 19.
1986 The Popsicle on a Stick. *The Daily Press* (Newport News, VA) March 13: B–13.
1990 Obituary for George de Mestral, inventor of Velcro. *The Daily Press* (Newport News, VA) February 13: B–5.

Davis, Pearce
1949 *The Development of the American Glass Industry*. 1970 reprint ed. Russell & Russell, New York.

Deiss, Ronald William
1981 *The Development and Application of a Chronology for American Glass*. Midwestern Archaeological Research Center, Illinois State University, Normal.

des Fontaines, John
1990 Wedgwood Whiteware. *Proceedings of the Wedgwood Society* 13: 1–8.

Devoto, Bernard
1943 *Year of Decision: 1846*. Little, Brown & Co., Boston.

Drepperd, Carl
1946 Spikes, Nails, Tacks, Brads and Pins. *The Chronicle of Early American Industries* 3(8), August, 1946.

Edwards, Diana
1994 *Black Basalt: Wedgwood and Contemporary Manufacturers*. Antique Collectors' Club, Woodbridge, Suffolk, England.

Encyclopedia Britannica New American Edition
1898 Glass, Wire. Volume 3: 1408. Werner Co., New York.

Fayden [Janowitz], Meta P.
1993 Indian Corn and Dutch Pots: Seventeenth-Century Foodways in New Amsterdam/New York. Ph.D. diss., City University of New York, New York.

Finer, Ann, and George Savage, eds.
1965 *The Selected Letters of Josiah Wedgwood*. Cory, Adams, and Mackay, London.

Fisher, Stanley W.
1966 *English Ceramics*. Ward Lock & Co. Ltd., London.

Fontana, Bernard L., J. Cameron Greenleaf, Charles W. Ferguson, Robert A. Wright, and Doris Frederick.
1962 Johnny Ward's Ranch: A Study in Historic Archaeology. *The Kiva* 28(1 & 2).

Garner, F. H., and Michael Archer
1972 *English Delftware*. Faber and Faber, London.

Glass Container Manufacturers Inc.
1967 *Glass Containers 1966*. Glass Container Manufacturers Inc., New York.

Glass Packaging Institute
n.d. Closures: Tops in Consumer Protection. Pamphlet, Washington, DC.

Godden, Geoffrey A.
1964 *Encyclopedia of British Pottery and Porcelain Marks*. Crown Publishers, New York.
1980 *Godden's Guide to Mason's China and the Ironstone Wares*. The Antique Collectors' Club Ltd., Woodbridge, Suffolk, England.

Hagen, Tom
1999 A Century of Memories: Depression Exerts Profound Change on Trenton Economy. *The Times* (Trenton, NJ) May 9: A–1, A–12.

Hoagland, Alison K.
1997 Industrial Housing and Vinyl Siding: Historical Significance Flexibly Applied. Paper presented at the conference, "Preservation of What, For Whom?" Goucher College, Baltimore, MD.

Hunter Robert H., Jr., and George L. Miller
1994 English Shell Edged Earthenware. *The Magazine Antiques* 165(3): 432–443.

Jameson, Irene
1958 Ceramics. In *A History of Technology. Volume V: The Late Nineteenth Century c. 1850–1900*, ed. by Charles Singer, et al., 658–670. Oxford University Press, New York.

Jarvis, C. Mackechnie
1958 The Distribution and Utilization of Electricity. In *A History of Technology. Volume V: The Late Nineteenth Century c. 1850–1900*, ed. by Charles Singer, et al., 208–234. Oxford University Press, New York.

Jones, Olive
1983 The Contribution of the Ricketts' Mould to the Manufacture of the English "Wine" Bottle, 1820–1850. *Journal of Glass Studies* 25: 167–177.
2000 A Guide to Dating Glass Tableware. In *Studies in Material Culture Research*, ed. by Karlis Karklins, 141–232. The Society for Historical Archaeology, Tucson, AZ.

Jones, Olive, and Catherine Sullivan, with contributions by George L. Miller, E. Ann Smith, Jane E. Harris, and Kevin Lunn
1985 *The Parks Canada Glass Glossary for the Description of Containers, Tableware, Flat Glass, and Closures*. National Historic Parks and Sites, Canadian Parks Service. Ottawa, Ontario.

Keen, Sharon
1982 Metal Container Artifact Class. In *Artifact Analysis Manual for Historical Archaeology*, ed. by Dana-Mae Grainger. Manuscript report. Parks Canada, Prairie Region, Winnipeg, Manitoba.

Ketchum, William C., Jr.
1991 *American Stoneware*. Henry Holt and Company, New York.

Klippart, John H.
1861 *The Principles and Practice of Land Drainage*. Robert Clarke & Co., Cincinnati, OH.

Kovel, Ralph, and Terry Kovel
2000a Antiques. *The Times* (Burlington County, NJ) February 6: AA–4.
2000b Antiques: Kitchen Gadgets are Hot Property. *The Times* (Burlington County, NJ) May 7: AA–3.

Lief, Alfred
1965 *A Close-up of Closures*. Glass Container Manufacturers Institute, New York.

Litchfield Auction Gallery
1990 Auction Catalogue for a sale to be held October 5th, 6th, and 7th, 1990.

Logan, Herschel C.
1959 *Cartridges: A Pictorial Digest of Small Arms Ammunition*. Bonanza Books, New York.

Lord, M. G.
1994 *Forever Barbie: The Unauthorized Biography of a Real Doll*. William Morrow, New York.

Luetkemeyer Company
1917 *The Luetkemeyer Company Hardware Catalog*. Cleveland, OH.

Luscomb, Sally C.
1967 *The Collector's Encyclopedia of Buttons*. Bonanza Books, New York.

McKearin, George S., and Helen McKearin
1948 *American Glass*. Crown Publishers, New York.

Madsen, Andrew David
1995 "All sorts of China ware . . . large nobel

and rich Chinese bowls:" Eighteenth-century Chinese Export Porcelain in Virginia. Master's thesis, College of William and Mary, Williamsburg, VA.

Miller, George L.
1987 Origins of Josiah Wedgwood's Pearlware. *Northeast Historical Archaeology* 16: 80–92.
1991a A Revised Set of CC Index Values for English Ceramics. *Historical Archaeology* 25(1): 1–25.
1991b Thoughts towards a Users' Guide to Ceramic Assemblages: Part One. Council for Northeast Historical Archaeology *Newsletter* 18: 2–5.
1991c Thoughts towards a Users' Guide to Ceramic Assemblages: Part Two. Council for Northeast Historical Archaeology *Newsletter* 20: 4–6.
1992 Thoughts towards a Users' Guide to Ceramic Assemblages: Part Three. Council for Northeast Historical Archaeology *Newsletter* 22: 2–4.
1993 Thoughts towards a Users' Guide to Ceramic Assemblages: Part Four. Some Thoughts on Classification of White Earthenwares. Council for Northeast Historical Archaeology *Newsletter* 26: 4–7.

Miller, George L., and Robert H. Hunter, Jr.
1990 English Shell Edged Earthenware: Alias Leeds, Alias Feather Edge. *Thirty-Fifth Wedgwood International Seminar* 201–232.
2001 How Creamware Got the Blues: The Origins of China Glaze and Pearlware. *Ceramics in America*, 1: 135-161.

Miller, George L., Ann Smart Martin, and Nancy S. Dickinson
1994 Changing Consumption Patterns: English Ceramics and the American Market from 1770 to 1840. In *Everyday Life in the Early Republic*, ed. by Catherine E. Hutchins, 219–247. Henry Francis du Pont Winterthur Museum, Winterthur, DE.

Miller, George L., and Antony Pacey
1985 Impact of Mechanization in the Glass Container Industry: The Dominion Glass Company of Montreal, a Case Study. *Historical Archaeology* 19(1): 38–50.

Miller, George L., and Catherine Sullivan
1984 Machine-Made Glass Containers and the End of Production for Mouth-blown Bottles. *Historical Archaeology* 18(2): 83–96.

Mountford, Arnold R.
1971 *The Illustrated Guide to Staffordshire Salt-glazed Stoneware*. Praeger Publications, New York.

Nelson, Lee H.
1968 Nail Chronology as an Aid to Dating Old Buildings. American Association for State and Local History Technical Leaflet 48. *History News* 24(11).

Noël Hume, Ivor
1969 *A Guide to Artifacts of Colonial America.* Alfred A. Knopf, New York.

Oswald, Adrian, in collaboration with R. J. C. Hildyard and R. G. Hughes
1982 *English Brown Stoneware 1670–1900.* Faber & Faber, London.

Panati, Charles
1987 *Panati's Extraordinary Origins of Everyday Things.* Harper & Row, New York.

Parrington, Michael
1984 The History and Archaeology of Philadelphia Roads, Streets, and Utility Lines. *Pennsylvania Archaeologist* 53(3): 19–31.

Petroski, Henry
1992 *The Evolution of Useful Things*. Vintage Books, New York.

Pollard, Gordon
1992 Glass Bottles: A Chronology of Some Major Developments. Handout, Council for Northeast Historical Archaeology annual meetings, Fort Edward, NY.

Price, E. Stanley
1948 *John Sadler: A Liverpool Pottery Printer.* Privately printed.

Progressive Grocer
1924 These Western Merchants Cash in on Easter Business. *The Progressive Grocer* 3(4): 17–18.

Ramsey, John
1939 *American Pottery & Porcelain.* Hall, Cushman & Flint, Boston.

Rickard, Jonathan
1993 Mocha Ware: Slip-decorated Refined Earthenware. *The Magazine Antiques* 164(2): 182–189.

Röntgen, Robert E.
1997 *Marks on German, Bohemian and Austrian Porcelains, 1710 to the Present.* Schiffer Publishing Ltd., Atglen, PA.

Samford, Patricia M.
1997 Response to a Market: Dating English Underglaze Transfer-printed Wares. *Historical Archaeology* 31(2): 1–30.

Savage, George, and Harold Newman
1976 *An Illustrated Dictionary of Ceramics*. Van Nostrand Reinhold, New York.

Schneringer, Kenneth
2001 *A Catalog Collection*. Catalog Number 141. Woodstock, GA.

Scoville, Warren C.
1948 *Revolution in Glass Making: Entrepreneurship and Technological Change in the American Industry 1880–1920*. Harvard University Press, Cambridge, MA.

Shartar, Martin, and Norman Shavin
1981 *The Wonderful World of Coca-Cola*. Capricorn Corporation Inc., Atlanta, GA.

Shaw, Simeon
1900 *History of the Staffordshire Potteries and the Rise and Progress of the Manufacture of Pottery and Porcelain; with Reference to Genuine Specimens and Notices of Eminent Potters*. Scott Greenwood and Company, London.
1829 *History of the Staffordshire Potteries and the Rise and Progress of the Manufacture of Pottery and Porcelain; with Reference to Genuine Specimens and Notices of Eminent Potters*. 1968 reprint ed. Beatrice C. Weinstock, Great Neck, NY.

Shlasko, Ellen
1989 Delftware Chronology: A New Approach to Dating English Tin-Glazed Ceramics. Master's thesis, College of William and Mary, Williamsburg, VA.

South, Stanley
1978 Evolution and Horizon as Revealed in Ceramic Analysis in Historical Archaeology. In *Historical Archaeology: A Guide to Substantive and Theoretical Contributions*, ed. by Robert Schuyler, 68–82. Baywood Publishing Company, Inc., Farmingdale, NY.

Staten, Vince
1998 *Did Trojans use Trojans? A Trip inside the Corner Drugstore*. Simon & Schuster, New York.

Stefton, Dru
2001 The Mouse that Roared. *The Times* (Burlington County, NJ) April 30: B–1, 2.

Stitt, Irene
1974 *Japanese Ceramics of the Last 100 Years*. Crown Publishing, Inc., New York.

Thomas, John L.
1977 *Picnics, Coffins, Shoo-Flys*. Maverick Publications, Bend, OR.

Thorgerson, Storm, and Roger Dean, eds.
1977 *Album Cover Album*. Paper Tiger, A & W Visual Library, New York.

Thuro, Catherine M. V.
1976 *Oil Lamps: The Kerosene Era in North America*. Wallace-Homestead Book Company, Des Moines, IA.

The Times (Burlington County, NJ)
1996 On This Day in History. Patent Granted for Ball-bearing Roller Skates. *The Times* (Burlington County, NJ) December 1: A–12.
1996 The Plastic Pink Flamingo Yard Ornament Now 25 Years Old. *The Times* (Burlington County, NJ) May 29: A–15.
1998 On this Date. *The Times* (Burlington County, NJ) December 26: A–10.
1999 Changes in Electrical Appliances. *The Times* (Burlington County, NJ) August 27: D–10.
2000 Key Dates in the 50-year History of the Credit Card. *The Times* (Burlington County, NJ) March 12: D–4.

Trench, C. S. J., and B. E. V. Luty, eds.
1918 *Metal Statistics 1918*. 11th annual edn. The American Metal Market Company, New York.

Toulouse, Julian Harrison
1969a A Primer on Mould Seams, Part 2. *Western Collector* 7(12): 578–587.
1969b *Fruit Jars*. Nelson Inc., NJ.

Wakefield, Hugh
1962 *Victorian Pottery*. Thomas Nelson & Sons, New York.

Watkins, C. Malcolm
1960 North Devon Pottery and its Export to America in the 17th Century. *United States National Museum Bulletin* 225: 17–59. United States Government Printing Office, Washington, DC.

Watney, Bernard
1964 *English Blue and White Porcelain of the 18th Century*. Thomas Yoseloff, New York.

Webster's New World Dictionary of the American Language
1982 Linoleum. Simon & Schuster, New York.

Weitz, C. E.
1930 *Electrical Illuminates Prepared Especially for Home Study*. International Correspondence School, Scranton, PA.

Wolfe, Bernard
1945 *Plastics: What Everyone Should Know*. Bobbs-Merrill Co., New York.

George L. Miller is the Laboratory Director at URS Corporation in Florence, New Jersey. He has his B.A. degree from Wayne State University and has been working in material culture research for over 30 years. He has held research positions at the Historic St. Mary's City Commission, Parks Canada, Colonial Williamsburg, and the University of Delaware. He has published articles on the economic history of ceramics and glass in *Historical Archaeology, Northeast Historical Archaeology*, and *Winterthur Portfolio*.

Patricia M. Samford is Archaeologist and Head of Museum Services at Tryon Palace Historic Sites and Gardens in New Bern, North Carolina. She has her B.A. and M.A. degrees from the College of William and Mary, and a Ph.D. from the University of North Carolina at Chapel Hill. She has been working in archaeology and research for over 20 years. She has held positions at the Colonial Williamsburg Foundation and is currently adjunct professor at East Carolina University. She has published articles on ceramics in *Historical Archaeology* and *Early American Life*. She co-authored a children's book on archaeology with David Ribblett and has published on African-American archaeology.

Ellen Shlasko is an Assistant Professor of Anthropology at the University of Memphis in Memphis, Tennessee. Her primary research interest is the archaeology of plantation life, but she is also involved in research in the areas of Civil War archaeology, the formation of ethnic identity, and ceramic analysis. She holds an M.A. from the College of William and Mary and a Ph.D. from Yale University.

Andrew D. Madsen is a professional archaeologists residing in Frederick, Maryland. He has a B.A. in anthropology and history from the University of California, Berkeley, and an M.A. in anthropology from the College of William and Mary in Virginia. His research interests have focused on the chronological aspects of Chinese export porcelain and artifact conservation. He has held positions at Colonial Williamsburg, the Virginia Department of Historic Resources, the James River Institute for Archaeology, and R. Christopher Goodwin & Associates, Inc. He has presented papers at the Society for Historical Archaeology and the Mid-Atlantic Archaeological Conference meetings and has taught workshops on Chinese porcelain.

George L. Miller, Laboratory Director
URS Corporation
561 Cedar Lane
Florence, NJ 08518
george_miller@urscorp.com

Patricia Samford, Archaeologist
Tryon Palace Historic Sites & Gardens
P.O. Box 1007
New Bern, NC 28563
psamford@tryonpalace.org

Ellen Shlasko
Anthropology Department
316 Manning Hall
University of Memphis
Memphis, TN 38152–0001

Andrew Madsen
364 Madison Street
Frederick, MD 21701

A Primer in Historical-Period Ceramics

John M. Chenoweth and Meta F. Janowitz

This introduction is intended to be, as the title states, a "primer" for students beginning their study of ceramics excavated from North American sites occupied from the sixteenth through the twentieth centuries, particularly those connected to English, French, and Dutch trading networks. Archaeological ceramics are usually divided first by "type." A type is a specific kind of pottery defined by a certain set of attributes, such as temper, color, hardness, porosity, etc. (Orton et al. 1993: 11-12). In historical archaeology, analysis usually begins with division by clay type into "wares" such as stonewares, earthenwares, or porcelains.

Another important aspect of analysis is the shape of a ceramic vessel, referred to by archaeologists as "form." For many eighteenth, nineteenth and twentieth century vessels, these will be familiar and most sources use recognizable terms like "plate," "bowl," "creamer," etc. Often, of course, we encounter only partial vessels whose original shape is difficult to determine. For these, a basic distinction is often made between "hollowware" (such as bowls and porringers) and "flatware" (such as plates and platters). These classifications can be useful for discussing fragments, and can sometimes be used to assess human behavior (e.g. Adams and Boling 1989, I:21)[1]. Examples of earlier, less-familiar, vessel forms can be found in Beaudry et al. 1988, II:2; Deagan 1987; Gibble 2005; Greer 2005[1981]; Hurst, Neal, and van Beuningen 1986, Ketchum 1991a, 1991b; Noël Hume 1970; Pearce et al 1992, Waselkov and Walthall 2002, and Wilcoxen 1987, among others.

Ceramic Bodies and Wares

The importance of vessel form notwithstanding, historic ceramic typologies usually start with the "body" of the ceramic—the material of which it is made, visible in breaks, as distinct from surface treatments such as glazes. The different kinds of bodies are initially separated primarily by color (a result of clay type and source and firing conditions), temper (materials like sand, grit, or ground ceramic added to adjust the properties of a clay—or by the absence of visible temper), vitrification (glassiness), and hardness (determined, for the most part, by the temperature achieved in firing). A particular combination of body attributes and surface treatments is called a "ware." The practice of focusing on wares in creating typologies of historic ceramics was borrowed from prehistorians and some have called its applicability to historic materials into question, arguing that color and design were of greater importance to those who made and sold these pieces (Majewski and O'Brien 1987; Miller 1980). These are valid points for many situations, though different questions require different data. Sometimes variables such as original cost (Miller 1991, I:17), color (Wilkie 2000, I:19), or form (Chenoweth 2006, I:20) are most important, but the use of ware-based types, recognized as etic types that may not have been recognized by potters or their customers, has proven useful for chronological and other interpretations and is still common. The basic division of ceramic bodies and descriptions of some common ware types are outlined below.

Non-Kiln Fired Earthenwares

The focus in historical archaeology is most often on wares manufactured by specialist craft potters using some form of a potter's wheel or by workers in factories using potter's wheels and molds. These wares can show considerable variation, but much less so than those created by hand by individual potters, and so it is possible to recognize world-wide types of craft shop or industrial wares. However, people are resourceful, the knowledge of pottery making was widespread, and pottery was made long before the use of closed kilns. Where resources (good clay, wood or other materials for firing, knowledge, and freedom of time and action) allowed, people often made pottery for themselves and for limited distribution to others. As a group, these materials can be referred to as "low-fired" earthenwares as they were typically open fired (simply baked in an open fire rather than in a kiln), often being heated to little more than 600°c. These pieces have a wide range of appearances, generally being red and brown in body but having substantial variation in color and form (FIGURE 1a). Such pieces are not glazed. For complete analysis of these materials, one needs the same expertise as for prehistoric ceramics—the knowledge of how to interpret evidence of firing conditions, forming methods, surface

[1] *References to works included in* The Historical Archaeology Laboratory Handbook *will be given to their original publication followed by a Roman numeral indicating the volume within the handbook and then an Arabic numeral giving the chapter within that volume.*

modifications, etc. (Orton, et al. 1993; Rye 1988; Shepard 1956). Such materials appear more often on historic sites or parts of sites associated with earlier dates and poorer occupants or in particular parts of the world where indigenous ceramic traditions persisted.

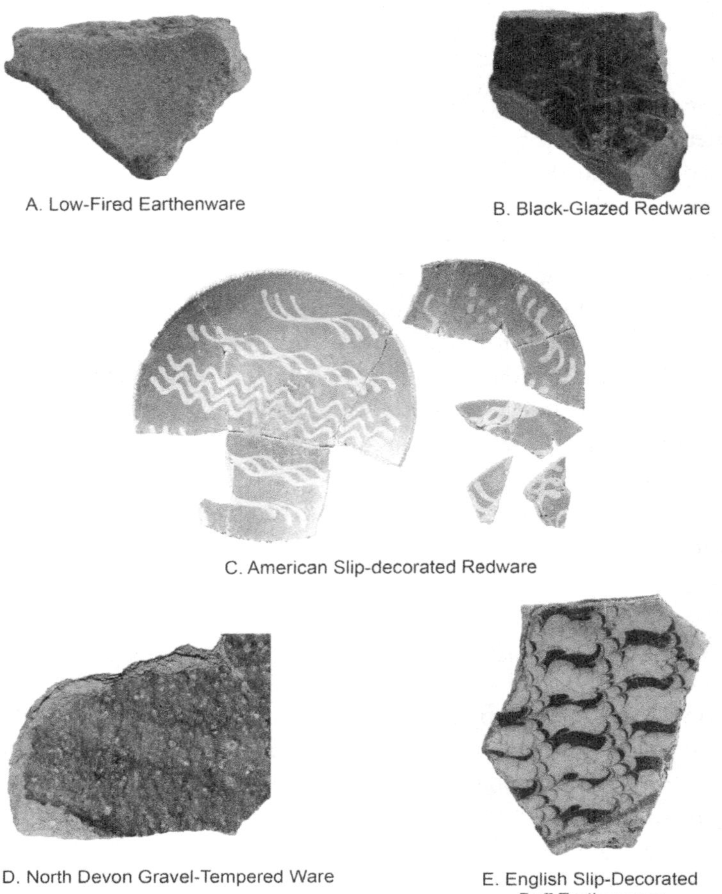

Figure 1. A. Non-kiln fired or "low-fired" earthenware (photo by John Chenoweth); B. black-glazed redware (photo by John Chenoweth); C. American slip-decorated red earthenware (photo by Rob Tucher); D. North Devon gravel-tempered ware (photo by John Chenoweth, courtesy of the Grosscup Museum of Anthropology); E. English Slip-Decorated Buff Earthenware (photo by John Chenoweth).

Kiln-Fired Coarse Earthenware

Fired to about 900-1200°c and often composed of minimally refined clays, coarse earthenware is often reddish, brownish, or tan in color. These materials are generally soft-bodied (they can occasionally be scratched with a fingernail) and porous unless glazed (a small drop of water placed on an unglazed portion of the vessel, especially a broken edge, quickly sinks into the surface). Since many coarse earthenwares were of a utilitarian nature (they were used for cooking and daily eating or storage more than for formal meals or display) these materials were often glazed only on the inside. Although requiring a kiln and thus usually the work of specialist craft potters, there is still substantial variation in coarse earthenwares. Two broad categories of coarse earthenware are often termed "red earthenware" and "buff-bodied earthenware" based on their body colors, although in practice each of these can be broken down into much more specific types based on how they were decorated or where and by whom they were made.

"Red earthenware" (in short form "redware") is the name used for a medium-to-soft, red-bodied coarse earthenware found on most sites dating from the seventeenth to the last decades of the nineteenth century (Denker and Denker 1985; Ketchum 1983,1991b), though it was most common before the second quarter of the nineteenth century. It was most often coated with lead glaze, which could be colored brown or black (FIGURE 1b), although redware is also found with an uncolored lead glaze, which makes the glazed surface appear a smooth reddish or chocolate brown, depending on the color of the body, where not otherwise decorated. More utilitarian, less costly pieces of redware were often glazed only on one side. These wares were inexpensive, and manufactured in the Americas as well as Europe (Barber 1970[1903], 1976[1893]; Turnbaugh 1985). The unglazed surfaces of redware vessels can resemble the unglazed red pottery usually used for flowerpots today. Because of the long history of red earthenware production and the many different types that have been produced, it can be difficult to identify particular makers or dates without substantial experience.

The most common type of decoration on red earthenware vessels is slip decoration. Slips will be discussed more below, but slip is clay that has been thinned with water to the consistency of heavy cream. Some archaeologists separate red-bodied slip-decorated vessels into a separate "slipware" ware type, though it is more accurate to describe them as red earthenwares with slip decoration. Slip was usually applied to the surface of vessels using a slip-cup, a hollow vessel with holes into which from one to six (rarely more) goose quills were inserted, allowing the potter to make designs or even writing (Figure 1c; Barber 1970; Ketchum 1991b). The slip was made from a clay whose color contrasted with the body of the vessel, most often white (which appears light yellow under the lead glaze). Brown or dark brown slip was used occasionally or the white slip could be dyed green or dark yellow. Some slip decorated vessels can have patches of green coloring in the glaze (Myers 1980).

One of the earliest and most coarse types of red earthenware found on New World sites in relatively small quantities is North Devon gravel-tempered ware (Figure 1d). North Devon coarse earthenwares are usually lead glazed and often have a firing core (a grey center to the body, from reduction conditions during firing) fading to orange or pink closer to the exterior, and the gravel-tempered variety is defined, as the name suggests, by the large size (sometimes 1mm or more in diameter) of the temper. Although variants of North Devon ceramics were manufactured earlier and later, gravel-tempered examples typically date from roughly 1675-1725 (Maryland Archaeological Conservation Lab Website, http://www.jefpat.org/mac_lab.html, hereafter "MAC").

The most common type of buff-bodied coarse earthenware found on non-Hispanic North American sites was imported from Great Britain and was decorated with dark brown slips (Figure 1e). This ware is often referred to simply as "lead glazed slipware" (Noël Hume 1969) but it is more precise to identify it as "English Slip-Decorated Earthenware" (Grigsby 1993) to distinguish it from American-made slip-decorated vessels, which are almost always red bodied. Slips were used in a variety of ways to decorate vessels: they could be trailed in simple or complex patterns, even portraits. Contrasting colors could also be layered on top of each other and cut to show the underlying color, or two or more slips could be placed side by side on a vessel and then combed through (as in Figure 1e) or the vessel rotated to mix the two and create a joggled or marbled effect (MAC, Cooper 1968). English slip-decorated earthenwares were imported into North America from about 1670 to 1795 (South 1971, I:14). This broad date range can sometimes be narrowed using vessel forms or decorations (Grigsby 1993; MAC 2002b, Noël Hume 1969).

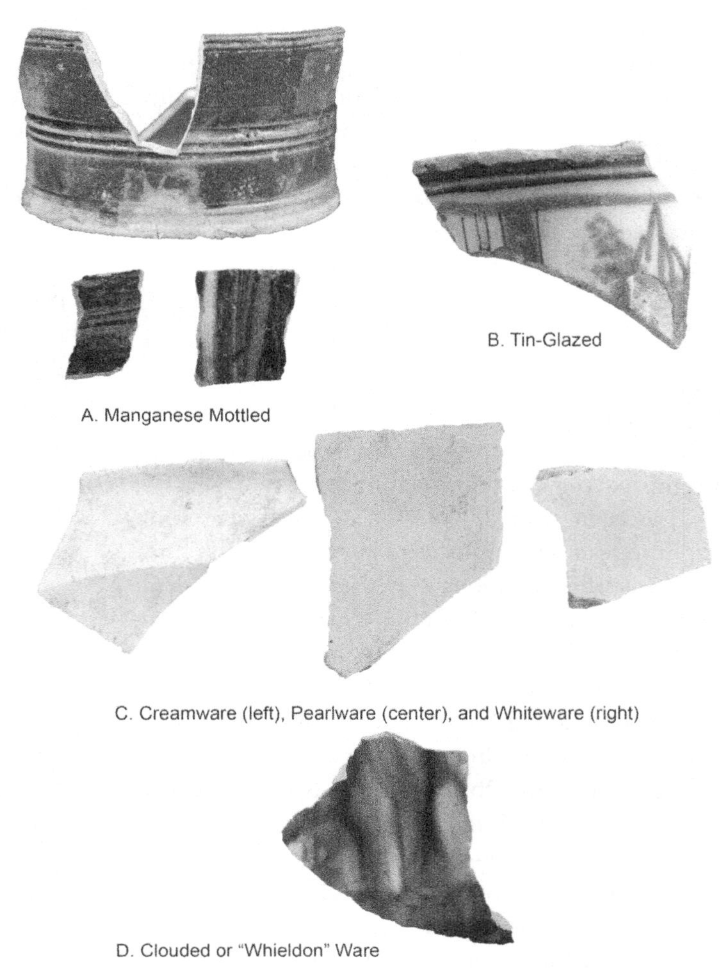

Figure 2. A. manganese mottled ware vessel on top (photo courtesy of The George Washington Foundation, by Zac Cunningham) and sherds on bottom (photo by John Chenoweth); B. tin-glazed or tin-enameled ware (photo by John Chenoweth); C. creamware (left), pearlware (center), and whiteware (right) (photo by John Chenoweth); D. clouded, tortoiseshell or "Whieldon" ware (photo by John Chenoweth, courtesy of the Grosscup Museum of Anthropology).

Another type of buff-bodied earthenware is called "manganese mottled," and sometimes "mottled ware," "Staffordshire mottled," or "Midlands mottled" (Figure 2a). It was made in England between about 1680 and 1780 and has a compact, fine body which can vary in color from light to dark buff, covered completely (except for exteriors of bases) by a yellow-to-brown lead glaze that has been mottled with streaks or spots of darker color (MAC). When streaked, this can give pieces a wood-grained look, particularly for small fragments. See discussion of "mottled ware" in Williams (2003). This type can sometimes appear similar to nineteenth-century Rockingham ware, discussed below, but can be distinguished by manganese mottled having a less-refined, softer but generally thinner body and greater unevenness or mottling in the glaze, which is not usually as shiny, thick, or brown as Rockingham. The mottling, or uneven patches of color in Rockingham vessels are also more diffuse and irregular, compared to the more spotted or wood-grained streakiness of manganese mottled. The decorations and forms are also different (MAC).

Refined Earthenwares

Tin-Glazed or Tin-Enameled Wares, Delftware, Faience, or Maiolica

Many names are applied to this type. During the seventeenth century the importation of very expensive Chinese porcelain painted in blue on a white background spurred European potters to create less costly imitations. The first successful imitations were these, which we shall refer to as tin-glazed earthenwares. Usually decorated in blue with copies of or derivations from Chinese motifs, these ceramics are a very soft-bodied earthenware coated with a glaze containing both lead and tin oxide, which creates a thick, opaque white covering, sometimes called an "enamel" (FIGURE 2b). This glaze is quite distinct from the body on which it sits, and it can be described as appearing like a "candy-coating" sitting on chocolate: it floats on top of the body and easily chips off with wear or weathering. The enamel itself is usually white (although often with a light blue tint) but can be Robin's egg or a deeper blue. It was commonly painted with various pigments to create designs in several colors, almost always free-hand, as in FIGURE 2b. Blue is by far the most common color although polychrome colors were also used: "cobalt blue, manganese purple, copper green, antimony yellow, and an orange derived from iron rust" are often seen (Noël Hume 1970: 106). Though applied on top of the opaque glaze, the motifs are not technically "overglaze" designs, as seen on some other types of ceramics discussed below, because the colors become part of the glaze during the final firing. Tin-glazed vessels were often highly decorated with either Chinese-derived or European motifs. The most common vessel forms were plates, followed by bowls, particularly punch bowls of all sizes. The bodies of tin-glazed vessels are most often white, creamy, or buff colored and are very soft, easily scratched with a fingernail and have a "chalky" feeling. Some French tin-glazed wares have red bodies.

Tin-glazed vessels were made in many European countries but most of the vessels found in North American contexts were made in Great Britain, the Netherlands, or France. Noël Hume (1970:106) discusses the misnomer "delft"—which implies production in that Dutch city—and clarifies that this ware is essentially the same as that called "maiolica" in Spanish contexts or "faience" in French ones, at least in their general descriptions. Some European ceramic historians reserve the term "maiolica" for vessels that have tin glaze on their faces and lead glaze on their backs, regardless of their country of origin (Hurst, Neal, and van Beuningen 1986). Determining the place of origin from sherds and even whole vessels is difficult without considerable experience, but see Archer and Morgan 1977; Austin 1994; Deagan 1987; Cohen-Williams 1992, II:3; Noël Hume 1977; Waselkov and Walthall 2002. Tin-glazed vessels were produced in the Netherlands and England from the late sixteenth century, but the technology was widespread in Europe and dates to much earlier periods (Tite et al. 2008). Tin-glazed tablewares were replaced by other refined earthenwares during the course of the third quarter of the eighteenth century (Martin 1989, I:11) although vessels used for drug storage and dispensing (ointment pots) were made well into the nineteenth century.

Creamware, Pearlware, and Whiteware

Refined earthenwares with light colored bodies and lead glazes were developed during the mid-eighteenth century in Staffordshire, England by full-time potters in large workshops and factories. They were almost always more expensive than coarse earthenware or even tin-glazed vessels, and were made generally in tea and tableware forms rather than in utilitarian storage or cooking forms. The three most commonly found ware types are creamware, pearlware, and whiteware, all of medium hardness (the body can be scratched with a metal implement but not with a fingernail) with a lead glaze (after about 1805 the glazes had much less lead in their compositions) which is applied as a liquid and fires to a very smooth surface (Noël Hume 1969: 19).

The principal differences between the three ware types are subtle distinctions of glaze and body color and the types of decorations (FIGURE 2c). Creamware has a cream-colored body with a clear glaze that appears yellow or yellow/green where it pools, (particularly around footrings) while pearlware's glaze appears blueish or greenish/blue in its puddling (Noël Hume 1970: 130); pearlware bodies also have a slightly blue hue. The blue in the glaze and in the body are the result of adding cobalt to whiten the original creamware body and glaze (Miller and Hunter 2001). Whiteware, bright white in both body and glaze (although some vessels also have slight blue puddling, particularly those with blue painted or painted motifs) was developed about 1805 but does not become common on North American sites until about 1820 (Miller et al 2000:13, I:2). Creamware was made between about 1762 and 1820 and pearlware between about 1775 and 1840 (ibid and Barker 2002). Recent research (Chenoweth and Farahani 2015) has investigated the nature of these color variations with mechanical color measurement and statistical analysis, showing that there is overlap between the three types as ceramic historians have long suggested. However, this study also showed that about 85% of the time, the measured sherds did fall into relatively clear groupings based on color alone. Even though these groups would not have been those recognized by contemporaries, this needs to be considered when interpreting these types.

Contemporary distinctions were centered more on decoration. Creamware can be decorated with painted or printed motifs applied over the glaze but was most often left undecorated (except for molded rim motifs on plates; see Noël Hume 1970:116); pearlware and whiteware are almost always decorated with painted or printed motifs applied under the glaze. As George L. Miller has pointed out, the changes from creamware to pearlware to whiteware were evolutionary rather than revolutionary and there were many potters making these wares who each had their own slightly different body and glaze formulas (Miller 1991b, 1991c, 1992, 1993). Thus, when considering if a sherd or vessel is creamware, pearlware, or whiteware, the decoration of the piece should be taken into account, particularly when dealing with ceramics made ca. 1805-1840, the long period of transition from classical pearlware to whiteware. Decorations provide a better dating tool than simple discussion of ware type. For example, vessels painted with muted "earth tone" polychrome colors are dated 1795 to 1830 while those with brighter "chrome" colors are dated after ca. 1830 (MAC 2002c), and a variant known as "China Glaze" (dating 1775 to about 1810) is usually distinguished by a pearlware body with chinoiserie, underglaze, blue decoration and sometimes Chinese-inspired vessel forms (Miller 1993). Other types of decoration used on refined earthenwares such as lathe-turning and engine-turning (Rickard 2006; Sussman 1997), transfer-printing, luster, and decals each have a well-known development allowing for both more precise dating and discussions about cost and fashion (see Miller 1991, I.17, and see below for descriptions of these techniques).

Creamware was developed by Josiah Wedgwood but he did not create it single handedly. Beginning about 1740, potters in Staffordshire began to make refined earthenwares with cream colored bodies that, unlike most earlier earthenwares, were fired twice: first to create a "bisque" or "biscuit" body and second after decorations and lead glaze were applied to create the finished vessel (MAC, Noël Hume 2001: 204, 209). The lead glaze used on this cream-colored body was yellowish rather than clear and potters applied splotches of various metal oxides to the biscuit-fired vessels to create a surface called "clouded" or "tortoiseshell" in shades of brown, gray, green, purple and/or yellow (Figure 2d; MAC 2002). Clouded wares were made between about 1740 and 1780 (MAC ibid, Noël Hume 1970:123-124). These wares are sometimes called "Whieldon ware," for the Staffordshire firm of Thomas Whieldon. In 1759, Whieldon and Wedgwood together developed a distinctive deep green glaze for use on the cream-colored bodies, which is sometimes called "Green Glazed" ware. This glaze, used alone or in combination with light or dark yellow glazes to create a variety of fruit and vegetable shaped teawares (particularly melon, pineapple, and cauliflower tea and coffee pots) was made until the early 1780s (MAC). Dates for these developments have been refined over the past decades, and so these may disagree slightly with earlier publications but represent current best estimates.

The terminology used by some ceramic historians and archaeologists for light bodied refined earthenwares can be confusing. The term "Queensware" was used by both potters and merchants to refer to creamware and in the nineteenth century it continued to be used, especially in merchants' newspaper advertisements, for what archaeologists now call whiteware. The potters, and some modern archaeologists, refer to wares made after about 1820 as CC, which stands for "cream colored" or "common colored," with the latter term replacing the former in the last half of the nineteenth century (Miller 1980: 27).

Other Refined Earthenwares

There are other types of twice-fired refined earthenwares as well. "Astbury," made in Britain from about 1725-1750, is a red-bodied earthenware with a lead glaze, giving it a smooth "ginger or light-chocolate-brown" finish and is often decorated with lines of white slip or white sprigged motifs ("sprigging" is decoration made by molding small shapes such as flowers and then applying them separately to a pot, so that the result stands out from its surface). British "Jackfield-type," made from about 1740 into the early nineteenth century, is "purple to gray" in body but this is hidden by a deep black, glossy glaze (Noël Hume 1970: 123). Both can be distinguished from coarse redwares by the thinness, consistency, and hardness of their bodies and the fact that Astbury and Jackfield-type are not used for utilitarian forms but for teawares and mugs. However care needs to be exercised when working in areas, such as Philadelphia and the places where Philadelphia potters sent their wares, because these potters also made thin-bodied black glazed wares from the late eighteenth throughout most of the nineteenth century (Magid and Means 2003; Myers 1980; Turnbaugh 1986). Jackfield-type can be distinguished from these domestic wares, in general but not infallibly, by the color of the body and the glossiness of the glaze: Jackfield-type bodies are usually dark red/purple with a very uniform glass-like glaze; American-made fine bodied red earthenwares can have dark red bodies (the body color depends on firing conditions) but the bodies are often redder than Jackfield-type vessels and their glazes are less glass-like. American black-glazed vessels, in particular tea pots made during the nineteenth century, were often molded rather than turned on a wheel, as can be seen in their elaborate shapes. When an attribution is in doubt, it is better to classify the vessel simply as red-bodied with black glaze.

By the middle of the nineteenth century, a more vitrified, denser, heavier, and harder ware became quite common (vitrification is to become "glass-like" from melting and rehardening). This is often called "ironstone" by archaeologists but Miller (1993) suggests that "white granite" is better as a broader term for the ware and that "ironstone" should refer to those pieces made in the first half of the nineteenth century with semi-vitrified, white bodies and Chinese-inspired decorations, including a slight bluish tint to the glaze (Godden 1999). Though harder than whiteware—hard enough that it cannot be scratched with metal—it is softer than porcelain and is not translucent, as porcelain is (Majewski and O'Brien 1987: 120). The technique for making this ware was patented in 1813 by Charles James Mason, but he had many imitators and similar ceramics were widespread by 1827 when Mason's patent expired (Dieringer and Dieringer 1997). These earlier pieces were often decorated with Chinese motifs (Miller 1993). Starting around 1845, English producers exported huge amounts of unpainted ironstone vessels decorated with molded designs to the United States; this is what Miller argues should be called "white granite." Miller also notes that this material was sometimes given a slight blueish tint in order to whiten it or make it similar to contemporary porcelains (Miller 1993). The bluing was added to the body of the ceramic in some cases, as opposed to being in the glaze alone, and this is a defining feature of white granite. Hardness and vitrification will distinguish this material from pearlware, as would any a priori knowledge of chronology of decorative techniques and forms. These unpainted, semi-vitrified, heavy bodied wares were the mainstay of English pottery exports to the US from about 1850 to 1880 and continued to be popular well into the twentieth century (Majewski and O'Brien 1987:114; Miller et al 2000, I:2).

"Yellowware" is, as the name states, a yellow- or buff-bodied refined earthenware with a light yellow or clear glaze (FIGURE 3a). Production of yellowware began in the late eighteenth century in England but it did not come into common use in the United States until domestic production began in 1827 (Goldberg 2005, Leibowitz 1985, MAC). It was used for many of the same cooking and other food preparation functions as red earthenwares and, to a great extent, replaced these earlier vessels in the kitchen. Yellowware is most common in food preparation and service forms (bowls, pans, pitchers and pie plates in particular) followed by toilet wares, especially chamber pots. American factories produced large amounts of yellowware vessels from the middle of the nineteenth into the middle of the twentieth centuries, and some is still made today (Ketchum 1987). Many yellowwares were left undecorated or were decorated only with molded motifs although many had applied slip lines or bands and some have the variety of slip decoration called "mocha" (Sussman 1997).

Sometimes considered a version of yellowware and sometimes classed entirely separately is a type known as "Rockingham ware" (FIGURE 3b). Made first in England, then later in the United States, Rockingham is defined by a very glossy, brown, often mottled glaze over a body much like yellowware: yellow or buff (occasionally white) in color and quite thick and hard. It almost always has molded decorations (MAC). Small fragments

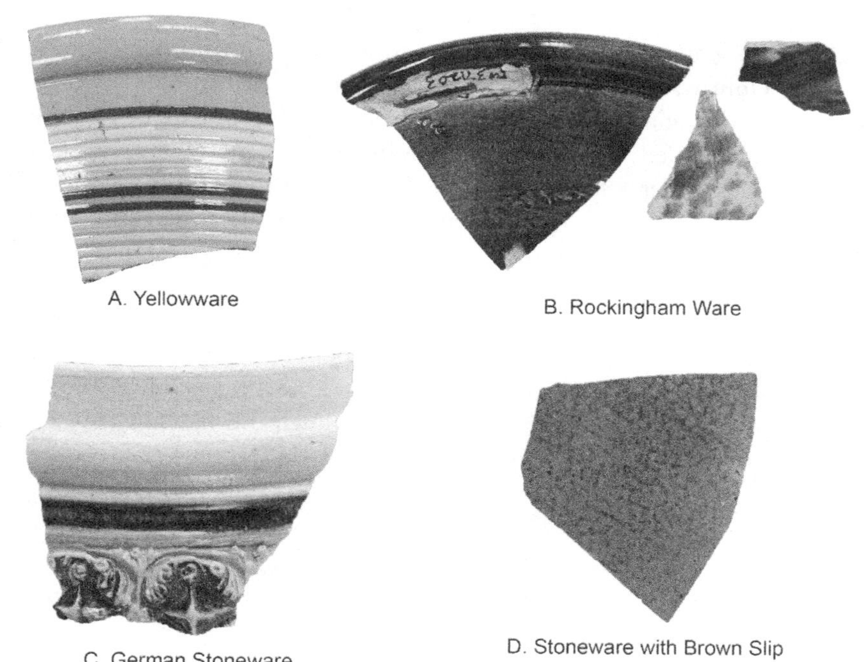

Figure 3. A. Yellowware (photo by John Chenoweth, courtesy of the Grosscup Museum of Anthropology); B. Rockingham ware (photo by John Chenoweth, courtesy of the Grosscup Museum of Anthropology); C. German-made stoneware (photo from South Ferry Site, Courtesy of the New York City Archaeological Repository, by Rob Tucher); D. stoneware with mottled brown surface (photo by John Chenoweth, courtesy of the Grosscup Museum of Anthropology).

can appear to have a wood-grain appearance as a result of the mottling, but this should not be confused with the earlier type known as "Manganese Mottled" which it can sometimes resemble. This type is known for display pieces, such as teapots or table pitchers, which are often highly decorated with molded designs. Rockingham is given various dates, but most sources agree that it was common from about 1830 to the middle of the twentieth century. For more, see Claney (2004).

A final type of refined earthenware deserves mention because it combines multiple clays in a single piece. "Agate" wares are produced by combining multiple colors of clay, folded over each other but not evenly mixed, producing a "marbled" appearance much in demand on some high-quality wares; this technique was also used to improve the quality of poor clays, and thus appears in a coarse fashion on utilitarian ware (Noël Hume 1970: 132). Agate wares can be confused with manganese mottled and with ceramics decorated to have a wood-grain or marbled appearance, but the distinction is that in agates the colored bands appear throughout the body, not just in the surface decoration.

Stonewares

Stoneware clays are not as abundant as earthenware clays; as a consequence pre-nineteenth century stoneware potteries, generally located near clay sources, were not as common as those making red earthenwares. Stonewares are identified primarily by the hardness of their bodies (they cannot be significantly scratched with metal) coupled with a lack of complete vitrification. Stonewares are non-porous, meaning that, unlike earthenwares, they do not need to be glazed to be watertight. However, they are most often salt-glazed (see below) although clay slip glazes and wood ash and lime (alkaline) glazes were also used, the latter especially in the American Southeast where alkaline became particularly common in the Edgefield District of South Carolina (Greer 2005[1981]: 202).

There is a great variety in stonewares, as they were produced from late medieval times until the mid-twentieth century (and are still in production by craft potters today). Many were coarse utilitarian wares, but others, notably the type referred to as "white salt-glazed stoneware" were in high demand for teawares and formal dinner services.

German salt-glazed stonewares have had the longest period of production and were distributed worldwide from the sixteenth through the nineteenth centuries (Figure 3c). Salt glazing was developed during the late Middle Ages in the German Rhineland (hence the common grey stonewares with blue and incised decoration are sometimes referred to as "Rhenish" stonewares), where there were abundant deposits of stoneware clays, and the technique spread to England in the late seventeenth century (Gaimster 1997, Oswald et al 1982). The most common German-made vessels found on North American sites are drinking vessels and jugs of various shapes. German stonewares were decorated in a variety of ways, most commonly with incised and painted designs, applied sprigged motifs, or painted motifs (MAC).

Cobalt blue was used as a color for the painted designs (as in Figure 3c) along with, occasionally, manganese purple. Most German stonewares have light gray or gray bodies but one early type, Siegburg or Höhr ware, which is not decorated with blue, is white or very light gray bodied. Some vessels were covered with a mottled brown slip; many brown-slipped vessels have no other decoration but the best-known brown-slipped vessels are the so-called "bartman" jugs, which have medallions of bearded men's faces near or on their necks. Some bartmans also have medallions on their bellies, often the arms of a city or a family's coat of arms.

Brown-slipped salt-glazed stoneware, made in imitation of German vessels, was produced in England beginning in the 1670s and was made throughout the eighteenth century (MAC). "English Brown" or "Fulham-type" stonewares are often light grey in body, although their color may vary through buff to light brown (Green 1999: 147; Noël Hume 1970:112), and their surfaces gain a "pebbly" appearance when an iron-brown slip is applied partially revealing the grey body beneath (FIGURE 3d). "Nottingham-type" stonewares are also grey in body and have a brown to light brown slip described as "finely textured" (Noël Hume 1970: 113) or "burnished" (MAC) which completely obscures the grey body beneath. Some vessels have a thin layer of white slip between the body and the brown slip, which can be seen on broken edges. Nottingham-type stonewares were made from about 1683-1810 (Miller et al 2000:10, I:2).

The English potters' next stoneware development was a white slipped or "dipped" ware. "Dipped" stonewares are described by Noël Hume as having a grey body which is dipped in a thick engobe (a covering slip) slip so as to appear opaque white before receiving the usual salt glaze (Noël Hume 1970: 114). The vessels often have a band of brown iron-oxide slip around their rims where the white engobe does not completely cover the body. This technique might have been developed as early as the 1690s (Noël Hume 2001:199) and continued until the last quarter of the eighteenth century (Miller et al 2000:10, I:2).

White dipped stonewares are distinct from "white salt-glazed stoneware" (FIGURE 4a) a fully white-bodied stoneware developed in England about 1720. White salt-glazed stoneware became the tableware of choice for many households during the middle decades of the eighteenth century, especially after the ca. 1740 development of plaster molds that allowed for the production of plates and other vessels with elaborate molded motifs (Noël Hume 1970: 115-116). White salt-glazed vessels were replaced in popularity by creamwares in the mid-1760s but continued to be made into the earliest nineteenth century, although they are rare in tea – and

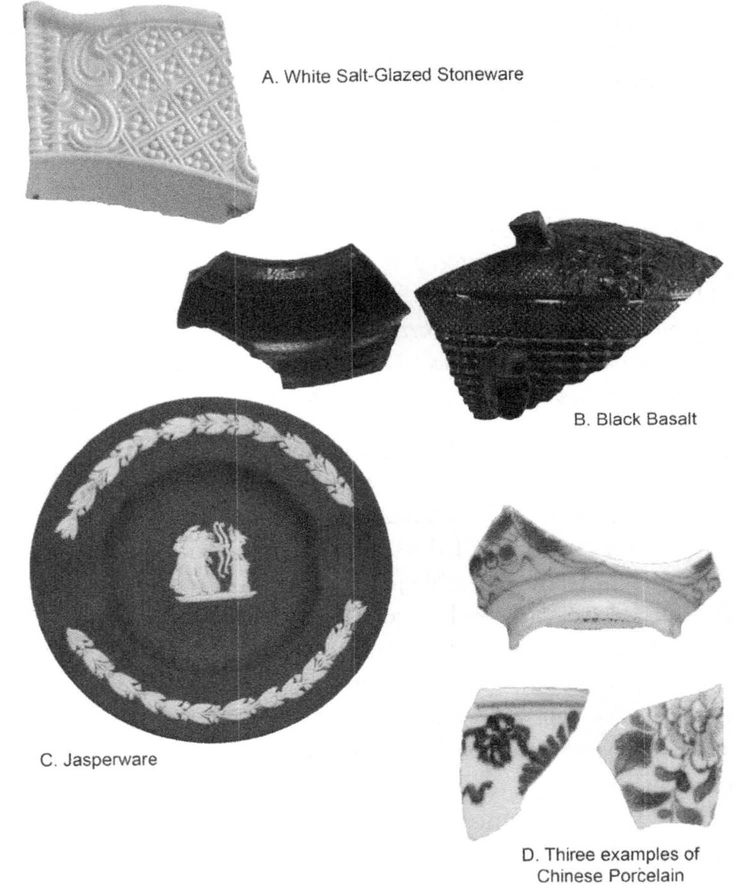

Figure 4. A. white salt-glazed stoneware (photo by John Chenoweth); B. black basalt (photo by John Chenoweth, courtesy of the Grosscup Museum of Anthropology); C. Jasperware (photo by John Chenoweth, courtesy of the Grosscup Museum of Anthropology); D. three examples of Chinese porcelain (photo from South Ferry Site, Courtesy of the New York City Archaeological Repository, by Rob Tucher).

tableware forms after about 1790 (Miller et al 2000:10, I:2). Starting possibly as early as 1735 (Noël Hume 2001:206) but certainly by ca. 1742 (MAC), white salt-glazed teawares were often decorated with simple incised motifs filled in with cobalt blue ("scratch blue"); the bodies of scratch blue vessels are usually light gray rather than white. Somewhat later, about 1760-65, vessels, often chamber pots, with blue that is not confined to the incised lines (called "debased scratch blue") began to be made; this decorative technique was used until about 1795 (Noël Hume 1970: 117-118).

English and other European potters also made dry-bodied (i.e. unglazed) stonewares; these vessels have very fine-grained, thin bodies that can be decorated with sprigged or lathe or engine-turned motifs (see below for descriptions of these decorative techniques). The first dry-bodied type made was red, in imitation of Chinese red stoneware teawares, but this ware was made only for a short period of time, ca. 1675-1700 (MAC). English potters resumed production of red stoneware in the 1740s or early 1750s and it continued into the 1780s, often with engine-turned motifs (MAC). Wedgwood's version of red stoneware, called "rosso antico," first made in 1776, was produced into the nineteenth century.

Other colors of fine-bodied stoneware were also made. "Black Basalt" (Figure 4b) is deep black and is usually dry-bodied but is occasionally glazed, generally on the interiors of vessels but also sometimes on both surfaces (Noël Hume 1970: 121-2). Cane ware is light buff-colored and dry-bodied (except for glaze occasionally applied around the rims of tankards); most popular between about 1800 and 1820 it was made in a variety of mold-decorated forms (MAC). Jasperware (Figure 4c), a dry-bodied stoneware developed by Wedgwood by 1780 and still made today, is characterized by the application of white sprig-molded designs on a matte, colored background (MAC). Although it is the most widely produced dry-bodied stoneware, it is seldom found in North American archaeological contexts. Light blue jasper is the most popular color, but it was and is also made in other colors, including lilac, sage green, dark blue, chocolate, and pink.

The stonewares made by North American potters were of the coarse, rather than fine-bodied type (Greer 2005[1981], Ketchum 1991a, Webster 1971). Salt-glazed stoneware potters became established in New York, Pennsylvania, and Virginia during the first decades of the eighteenth century (Skerry and Hood 2009). These potters were trained in Germany or in England and continued to make vessels using the techniques of their homelands. The first potters, especially those working in New York City, made some tableware forms and even teapots (Janowitz 2008) but by the beginning of the nineteenth century most stoneware potters were making a limited variety of forms: primarily jugs, jars of various shapes, bottles, chamber pots, mugs, churns, and ink wells. Salt-glazed stonewares were made in many areas of the United States and Canada, especially after the construction of canals in the early nineteenth century (the Erie Canal in particular) made transport of stoneware clays away from their areas of origin economically feasible. American stonewares can be plain or decorated with painted, painted and incised, slip trailed, or stenciled motifs (Ketchum 1991a, Webster 1981); the earliest stonewares sometimes had sprigged motifs, perhaps made in molds brought by the potters from Germany (Janowitz 2008).

Porcelain

Porcelain is a fully vitrified (glass-like) ceramic, translucent except where thick-bodied, with a glaze usually almost completely fused with the body, especially in higher quality products (Figure 4d). First produced over a millennium ago in China it became a major export commodity shipped to Europe after 1600 and is found on sites connected to European trading networks worldwide. In European and American contexts it is considered to be generally more expensive than any other type discussed. Decorated with cobalt blue painted under the glaze or overglaze enamels in several colors, most seventeenth and eighteenth century porcelains found on North American sites are probably Chinese in origin, because, even though British and European potters made different types of porcelain at this time, their products were generally of lower quality and even more expensive than the Chinese vessels (Noël Hume 1970: 257).

Almost as soon as Chinese porcelain vessels came into Europe, European potters tried to imitate them. At the same time as European earthenware potters were producing blue-painted tin-glazed wares as less-expensive substitutes for Chinese porcelain, other potters—and alchemists—were attempting to produce porcelain but they were hampered by their lack of knowledge concerning the necessary clays and potting techniques (Atterbury 1979, Cushion and Cushion 1982, Gleeson 2000, Godden 1966, Miller and Hunter 2001, Rado 1971:131). Various body and glaze formulas were created with greater or lesser success. Many of these European porcelains were "soft paste" or "artificial," meaning that they were made using assorted ingredients, for instance ground soapstone or glass, to replace the missing clays used to make genuine "hard paste" porcelain, such as Chinese porcelain (MAC). Hard paste porcelain was produced in Europe beginning in 1709 in Germany and 1768 in England but it was expensive and rare (Miller et al 2000:9, I:2). English soft-paste porcelain vessels were made between about 1745 and 1795 (Noël Hume 1970:137) and can be found in limited numbers in archaeological contexts, often—after 1760 (Miller et al 2000:9, I:2)—with blue underglaze printed motifs.

"Bone China," a type of soft paste porcelain, was and is the most successful non-Asian porcelain. It is made with a substantial amount of pulverized bone ash mixed into the clay which produces a fine, often very thin and delicate, translucent body (Majewski and O'Brien 1987: 115). Bone china has been produced successfully from 1794 onwards in England (Miller et al. 2000:9, I:2) and later in other parts of the world, including Ireland and the United States. It can be distinguished from hard-paste porcelain because it is often slightly ivory-colored (although most English-made bone china vessels are a brilliant white) and the glaze can "crackle slightly" and become discolored in archaeological contexts (Majewski and O'Brien 1987: 127). Another way to distinguish between hard-paste, soft-paste, and bone china vessels is through the use of a short-wave UV light. In a dark room under this light, most hard-paste porcelain sherds will show dark purple surfaces, most soft-paste sherds will shine light purple/mauve, and bone china surfaces will appear white. These reflected colors can be affected by decorative motifs and glaze compositions but this technique is generally reliable.

Distinguishing between types of porcelain can help in dating sherds, although porcelain varieties in general had a long production span and so are often less useful for dating purposes than refined earthenwares. Some dates can be assigned based on particular decorative motifs on Chinese porcelain (Madsen and White 2011:51-137). For example, blue painted "spearhead" motifs, although made as early as the 14th century, were most popular on teawares and plates imported into North America between ca. 1722 and 1797 (Madsen and White 2011:75). The pattern referred to by Noël Hume (1970) and others as "Nanking" and by Madsen and White as "Third Period Pavilion Landscape" was most common ca. 1780-1820; the familiar pattern called "Canton" by Noël Hume (1970) and "Fourth Period Pavilion Landscape" by Madsen and White was popular ca. 1785 to the middle of the nineteenth century (Madsen and White 2011:83-86). "Batavian" or "Batavian Brown" type vessels, which have their exteriors covered in brown slip, had a longer period of popularity, between ca. 1685 and 1793, although rare earlier examples have been found (Madsen and White 2011:123-125).

Chinese porcelain vessels came to colonial North America through European ports but, as soon as the American Revolution was over, US merchants, particularly Philadelphia merchants, sent ships to trade directly with China. During the late-eighteenth and early-nineteenth centuries many teawares painted with simple overglaze motifs arrived in eastern ports; some of the border and secondary motifs on these and earlier vessels can be dated. The "husk chain," a "simple repeating pattern of arrowhead-shaped" elements in a band, seen on plate cavettos and teacup and saucer rims, was common ca. 1765-1810 (Madsen and White 2011:117). The "half-circle and dot" motif was common on vessels made ca. 1780-1800 (Madsen and White 2011:118-119). For nineteenth and twentieth century assemblages, porcelain vessels often can be dated by comparing them to motifs and shapes made by known potteries (Atterby et al 2005, Collard 1967, Cushion and Cushion 1992, Denker and Denker 1985, Frelinghuysen 1989, Godden 1966, Mudge 1986, among others).

Surface Modifications

Ceramic Glazes

Other factors to be considered when identifying ceramics include the glaze and decoration. The glaze is a shiny, glassy coating that could be created in several ways. The most common were lead glaze and salt glaze. Lead glaze, used most frequently on earthenwares, can be applied to leather hard vessels before firing or to bisque-fired vessels before a second firing. As noted above, after about 1805 lead, because of its harmful properties, was replaced to a great extent by other components—in particular borax (MAC)—for use on refined earthenwares but it remained in coarse earthenware glazes until at least the end of the century (Janowitz 2013). Lead glaze generally is quite smooth and often has a slight yellowish or greenish tint, although iron and manganese were used frequently to give the glaze a brown or black color. Under magnification lead glaze appears crazed or cracked, often in patterns much like shattered glass, with some bubbles or inclusions (Figure 5a).

Salt glaze is identified by a characteristic "orange peel" pitting, which is usually visible without magnification, especially in strong light when one tilts the piece back and forth slowly. Sometimes, the pitting is more subtle and appears most clearly under about 60x magnification as an un-fractured more-or-less rolling surface with a great number of bubbles in the matrix of the glaze and the presence of some pits, appearing like craters at the bottom of which are burned pockets of inclusions (FIGURE 5b). Salt glaze is created during firing: when the kiln reaches a high enough temperature, common salt is shoveled into the kiln either through apertures near the top of the kiln or through portals near the firing box. The salt molecules separate into their component elements—sodium and chlorine—and the sodium combines with silica and other elements on the surfaces of vessels to create the salt glaze. Some vessels, especially jugs, have heavier salt glaze on their exteriors than on their interiors because their narrow mouths hinder the entrance of the sodium vapors.

A. Lead Glaze under 60x Magnification

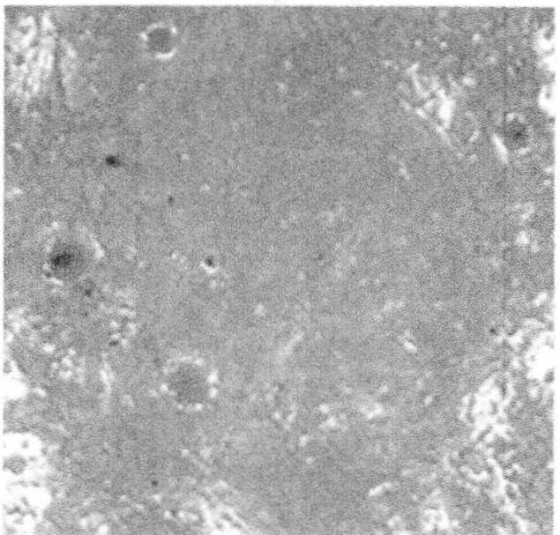

B. Salt Glaze under 60x Magnification

C. Albany Slip Glazed Wide-Mouth Jar

D. Jug with Bristol Glaze on body and and Albany Slip Glazing on top

Figure 5. A. lead glazing under 60x magnification (photo by John Chenoweth); B. salt glazing under 60x magnification (photo by John Chenoweth); C. Albany slip-glazed wide-mouthed jar (photo by Thomas Kutys); D. jug with Bristol glaze on bottom and an Albany slip glaze on the top and interior (photo by Thomas Kutys).

Several other kinds of glaze exist, and three particularly common on North American stonewares merit comment. Natural "slip" glazes are prepared using a slip (a slurry of clay and water) made with particular clays known to melt and vitrify—therefore to form a glaze—at stoneware firing temperatures. Some eighteenth century potters used a variety of slips on the interiors of their vessels, whose colors ranged from light pink/tan to brown (Janowitz 2008). Beginning in the early nineteenth century, potters located sources for slips that would give a uniform dark brown color. A particularly well-known variety is the Albany slip glaze (Figure 5c), named for the location in upstate New York where the clay that provided this slip was found (Greer 2005[1981]:194), which produces a rich chocolate color (although the color can vary from milk chocolate to very dark chocolate; compare the vessel in 5c to the Albany glaze on the top of the jug pictured in Figure 5d). Common from the 1820s until the middle of the twentieth century, this glaze is often found on the inside of vessels which have a salt glaze on the exterior. Alkaline glazes are produced by mixing sand, clay, and wood ash (hence "wood ash glaze"), all cheaply available for use on inexpensive utilitarian pots. This forms a durable surface which is very shiny and clear, but often colored with trace elements and textured from drips and runs or separations of its elements (sometimes including individual un-melted grains of sand). "Bristol" glazes (Figure 5d, lower half of vessel) were popular in the late nineteenth and into the twentieth centuries, and produce a durable, smooth, white surface, sometimes marked with tiny pin-hole defects resulting from gasses escaping during firing. They are often found on the exterior of vessels with interiors and top halves glazed with Albany slip (as in Figure 5d). After about 1920 Bristol glazes are generally found alone (Greer 2005[1981]: 212). For much more on stoneware glazes see Cheek (2016), Majewski and O'Brien (1987: 109-111), and Greer (2005[1981]: 179-214).

Decorative Techniques

Decoration can take many forms. Painted colors can come before glazing (underglaze) or after (overglaze). In the case of the latter, the design is less permanent and tends to wear off, sometimes leaving behind a "ghost" image. Lab analysts are often cautioned to examine ceramics, especially porcelain, in advance of washing them to see if they have any trace of overglaze decoration, which might be damaged by washing. The earliest underglaze decorations had a limited pallet of colors because they needed to survive the firing which hardens the glaze. Blue was most common, and was created by using cobalt, which was unaffected by the high temperatures. Other underglaze colors, including green, yellow, and orange, began to be used on pearlwares starting about 1795. Starting shortly before 1830, brighter colors, based on the use of chrome, began to be used. For more on using ceramic colors as a chronological tool see the discussion of "underglaze painted earthenwares" on the Maryland Archaeological Conservation Lab site.

Ceramic surfaces may also be treated with a "slip," a liquid form of clay that can be trailed or painted on ceramics before firing. A slip made of the same clay as the body of the ceramic (a "self-slip") is sometimes applied over the whole of a vessel in order to increase its smoothness and evenness of color, or a slip of a different color can be applied to change the appearance of a piece or to make a design or lettering. Slips can also be applied in lines of different colors and then "combed" to produce a pattern, as in FIGURE 1e. Vessels can be incised before the clay is fired, which is termed "sgraffito" ("scratched" in Italian). Sometimes this is done by itself but more often the vessel is covered evenly with a slip which is then cut away in places to make a design the same color as the piece's body, in contrast to the slipped surface.

Starting in the 1770s, colored slips were used in a variety of ways to decorate creamwares, pearlwares, and whitewares (MAC, Rickard 2006, Sussman 1997). Colored slips were applied in bands, lines, and other patterns to vessels using slip cups, containers that allowed potters to draw with slip, often while the vessel was turning on a horizontal lathe. Vessels with such decorations have been called "dipped," "dipt," or "dip't," "factory turned slipwares" or "annular" wares, although the last should be reserved for vessels decorated with annular bands (Figure 6a). These ceramics are sometimes called "mocha" by collectors, but archaeologists generally use this term only for the "dendritic" or tree-like pattern sometimes included in this group (Figure 6b). Different motifs and decorative techniques can provide fairly narrow date ranges (see the MAC website). These ceramics were also often decorated with rouletted motifs and/or "diced" or incised designs (discussed below as "engine-turning").

By the end of the eighteenth century, English potteries began using thin metallic films as part of their decoration in an effect known as "luster" or "lustre" shown in Figure 6c (Samford 2013). Luster is an overglaze decoration, which may fade or wear off in archaeological examples. If present, however, it can be a good guide to chronology (MAC). Luster could be used to cover an entire vessel, especially teapots, giving them the appearance of metal, or it could be used in painted or stenciled motifs.

Another major development in ceramic decoration was transfer printing, in which a design was cut into a copper plate. Colorants were applied to the copper plate and a thin sheet of paper was pressed onto it. The paper was then laid onto a bisqued vessel with the colors still wet, "transferring" the design onto the ceramic, a relatively cheap way to replicate detailed designs (FIGURE 6d, and for an example of the process see https://www.youtube.com/watch?v=9P7sIvxtLho). Painted motifs can be distinguished from transfer printed ones by the lack of regularity in their designs and the appearance of individual brush strokes (Figures 2b and 4d, for example). Transfer printing was introduced in the middle of the eighteenth century on porcelain but was rare and quite expensive at first, eventually becoming widespread on pearlwares by the early 1790s. Overglaze transfer printing in black or red using sticky "bats" rather than paper transfers was used earlier on creamwares (Miller et al 2000:13, I:2), usually resulting in somewhat thicker lines than paper transfers. The earliest underglaze paper transfer prints were in blue, and black was introduced by 1790 with brown by 1809; red, green, and purple transfer printing were available by 1828 and multi-colored prints began to be made about 1840 (MAC; Majewski and O'Brien 1987:142-3; Miller et al. 2000:13, I:2). The particular scenes and designs depicted are very useful for dating as many were produced for a limited time (see, for example, Coyshe and Henrywood 1982, 1989; Furniss et al 1999; Samford 1997, III:2; Sussman 1977, II:4; many websites also exist with examples and useful information, including AmericanHistoricalStaffordshire.com, PrintedBritishPotteryAndPorcelain.com, and SpodeCeramics.com.)

A variation of transfer printing called "flow blue" was introduced around 1835 (Snyder 1992) (FIGURE 6e). Chemicals were added to the kiln when a batch of ceramics with underglaze decoration was being fired

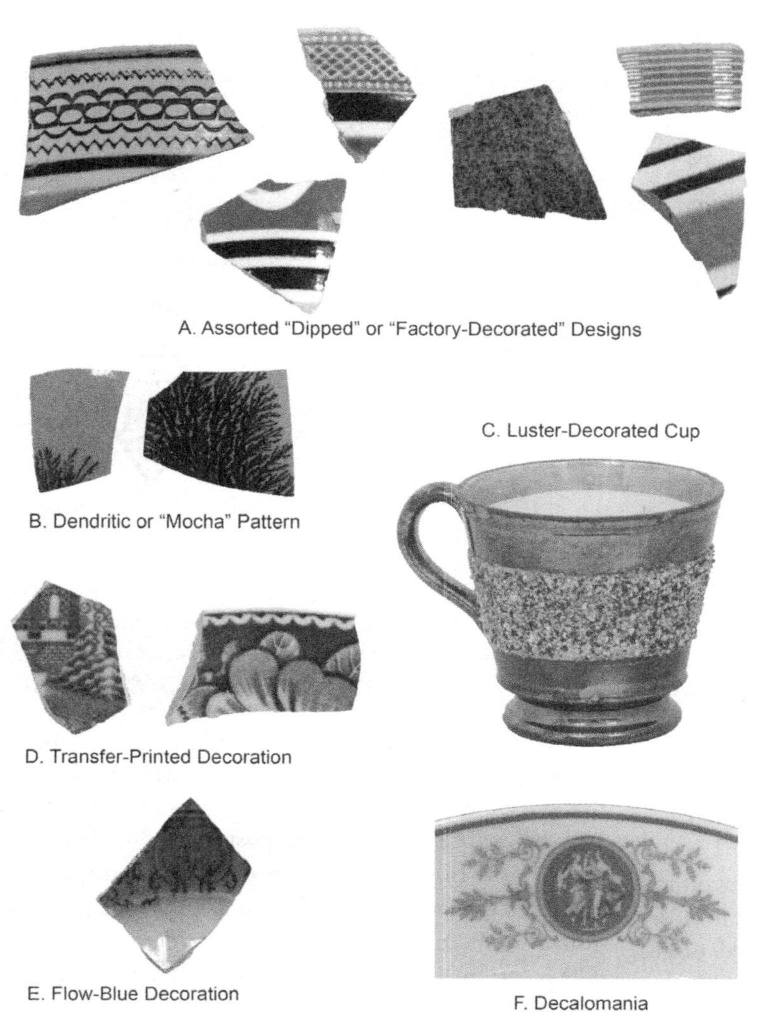

Figure 6. A. an assortment of dipped (also known as "dipt" or factory-decorated) slipwares, including engine-turned, banded, rouletted, and speckled motifs (photo by John Chenoweth); B. dendritic (tree-like) design often known as "mocha" and classed along with dipped slipwares (photo by John Chenoweth, courtesy of the Grosscup Museum of Anthropology); C. a luster-decorated cup with a gritted band around the center, the luster decoration appearing pink on the pearlware slip interior and golden elsewhere (photo by Thomas Kutys); D. examples of transfer prints, including a fragment from the "Willow" pattern (left) and a bold floral motif (right) (photo by John Chenoweth); E. flow-blue decoration (photo by John Chenoweth, courtesy of the Grosscup Museum of Anthropology); F. decalomania decoration (photo by Laurie A. Wilkie).

which caused the colorant to flow or spread into a hazy, cloudy pattern (Majewski and O'Brien 1987: 143). The original design was still visible, but behind a cloud. This was most often done with blue; hence it is best known as "flow blue," though examples exist of flow mulberry and grey along with, very rarely, yellow, black, brown, and green. Most examples are on ironstone bodies.

Decalomanias or "decals," products of a process in which a design is printed onto a thin film which is then applied overglaze to the ceramic, began to be common on refined earthenwares about 1890 and an underglaze version of this technique was introduced in 1908 (Miller et al. 2000:13, I:2). The process is similar to transfer printing, but the result can be distinguished by the use of shading and a full range of colors (Figure 6f) as well as a very slightly raised design which can often be felt when running a finger over the surface, whereas transfer-printed designs are entirely smooth (Majewski and O'Brien 1987:146-147). Decal decorations replaced transfer printed motifs by the early twentieth century and remained the most popular form of decoration on refined earthenwares well into the middle of the century (MAC).

In addition to painted and printed designs, ceramics can be molded and cut into many shapes. Designs can be cut freehand into ceramics that have dried to the leather-hard stage before firing ("sgraffito") or they can be cut through ("pierced" motifs) or stamped and molded pieces of clay can be added to create raised designs (called "sprigging"). One technique, developed about 1760 and adopted shortly thereafter by Wedgwood and other Staffordshire potters, was to use a complex lathe to cut a variety of patterns into vessels, usually called "engine-turning" (Figure 6a, top left corner; Hawkins 1999, Rickard and Carpentier 2004, Sussman 1997:26ff). The motifs could be simple repetitive lines or other geometric configurations or could be complex patterns that cut through different layers of colored slips to create elaborate designs (for a demonstration of the process of using a complex lathe, see https://www.youtube.com/watch?v=n-7twF5_chU).

Flatwares, such as plates, often had their rims molded in different patterns, called "shell edge," "feather edge," etc. (Figure 7a). Feather edge motifs were left uncolored but shell edge and other edge motifs on pearlware and whiteware vessels were almost always painted, usually in blue or green, rarely in other colors. These designs are useful for dating, as different designs were very popular at different times between about 1780 and 1860. See Miller et al. (2000, I:2) as well as Hunter and Miller 1994; MAC; Majewski and O'Brien 1987: 149; Noël Hume 1970: 116 for more images and dates. Other molded decorations, such as molded floral motifs or geometric designs, were used in the nineteenth century and began to be commonly impressed on white granite wares about 1840 (Dieringer and Dieringer 2002; Majewski and O'Brien 1987: 153; Miller et al 2000:13, I:2; Wetherbee 1996). These rim motifs were left uncolored. By the latter half of the nineteenth century, whole vessels were shaped into hexagonal, octagonal or oval pieces, decorated with panels or otherwise molded.

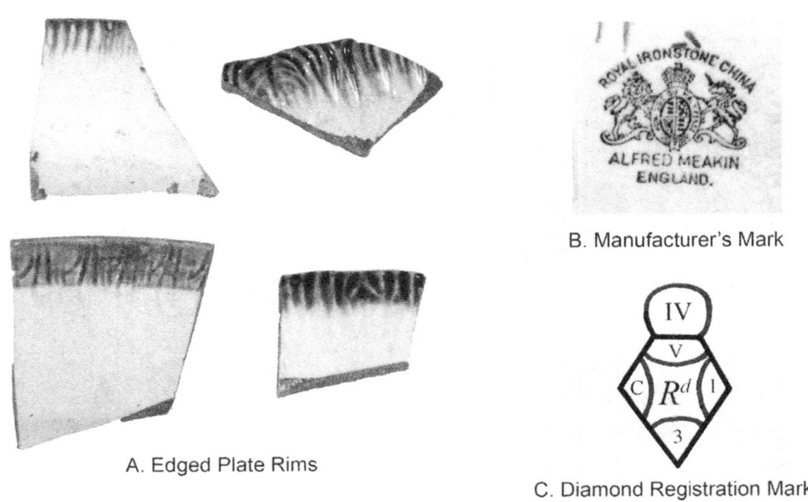

Figure 7. A. Examples of edged plate rims (photo by John Chenoweth); B. example of a manufacturer's mark (photo by John Chenoweth, courtesy of the Grosscup Museum of Anthropology); C. example of a "Diamond" pattern registration mark, giving the registration date of January 1, 1850 (drawing by John Chenoweth).

Makers' Marks and Patent Registrations

All of these divisions by ware, decoration, and glaze produce a complex number of traits for identifying ceramic vessels and sherds. One of the most fortunate strokes in archaeological work is to encounter a shortcut: many manufacturers placed marks which identify who made their pieces and where, often including pattern or dating information (Figure 7b). Though rare before 1800, after this date for English pieces (and somewhat later for American pieces) it is not uncommon to encounter sherds which identify the maker quite specifically, and this is almost always the best indicator of chronology or other factors of interest. Dozens of websites and books now exist to translate between these often cryptic marks and the information desired, and several of these are listed in the "Research Resources" section of the introduction to this volume.

Some useful general trends in marks can be summarized. Majewski and O'Brien (1987: 167), drawing largely on (Godden 1964), have collected a number of temporal markers: the use of the term "Ltd." postdates 1855, "trademark" 1862, and "Bone China" (as a marketing term, not to be confused with the ware of the same name described above) usually indicates a twentieth-century date. In 1891, the US government passed the McKinley Tariff Act, requiring all imports to identify their country of origin; this is why we have "Made in China" stickers on so much that we buy today. This requirement applied to ceramics as well, and so most marks that include a country of origin post-date this year.

From 1842 to 1883, the British Patent Office registered ceramic patterns which are often recorded on the pieces made in these patterns as a "diamond mark" (Figure 7c). It is important to note that the dating here records the registration of the pattern, not the manufacture of the piece, but these marks can give close production ranges and yield the name of the company that produced the piece when cross-referenced with patent indexes. The Roman numeral at the top represents the material for which the pattern was intended, and will be "IV" for ceramics. Three of the other figures give the month, day, and year of the registration following a code (the fourth is the number of items registered together, or "bundle"). See tables 1 and 2 for the coding. These diamond marks were replaced by simple, sequential registration numbers in 1884, and these, labeled "Rd." or "Rd. No." are equally useful; see Godden (1964:526-528) and Birks (2013) for the details.

Year	Year Code	Year Placement	Month Placement	Day Placement
1842	X	Top	Left	Right
1843	H	Top	Left	Right
1844	C	Top	Left	Right
1845	A	Top	Left	Right
1846	I	Top	Left	Right
1847	F	Top	Left	Right
1848	U	Top	Left	Right
1849	S	Top	Left	Right
1850	V	Top	Left	Right
1851	P	Top	Left	Right
1852	D	Top	Left	Right
1853	Y	Top	Left	Right
1854	J	Top	Left	Right
1855	E	Top	Left	Right
1856	L	Top	Left	Right
1857	K	Top	Left	Right
1858	B	Top	Left	Right
1859	M	Top	Left	Right
1860	Z	Top	Left	Right
1861	R	Top	Left	Right
1862	O	Top	Left	Right
1863	G	Top	Left	Right
1864	N	Top	Left	Right
1865	W	Top	Left	Right
1866	Q	Top	Left	Right
1867	T	Top	Left	Right
1868	X	Right	Bottom	Top
1869	H	Right	Bottom	Top
1870	C	Right	Bottom	Top
1871	A	Right	Bottom	Top
1872	I	Right	Bottom	Top
1873	F	Right	Bottom	Top
1874	U	Right	Bottom	Top
1875	S	Right	Bottom	Top
1876	V	Right	Bottom	Top
1877	P	Right	Bottom	Top
1878	D	Right	Bottom	Top
1879	Y	Right	Bottom	Top

1880	J	Right	Bottom	Top
1881	E	Right	Bottom	Top
1882	L	Right	Bottom	Top
1883	K	Right	Bottom	Top

TABLE 1. Coding for "Diamond" Registration Marks 1842-1883.

Month	**Month Code**
January	C
February	G
March	W
April	H
May	E
June	M
July	I
August	R
September	D
October	B
November	K
December	A

TABLE 2. Coding for Months in "Diamond" Registration Marks 1842-1883.

References

Adams, William Hampton, and Sarah Jane Boling
1989 Status and Ceramics for Planters and Slaves on Three Georgia Coastal Plantations. Historical Archaeology 23(1):69-96.

Archer, Michael, and Brian Morgan
1977 Fair as China Dishes: English Delftware. The International Exhibitions Foundation, Washington, D.C.

Atterbury, Paul J., editor
1979 European Pottery and Porcelain. Main Street Press, New York.

Atterbury, Paul, Ellen Paul Denker, and Maureen Batkin
2005 Miller's Twentieth-Century Ceramics: A Collector's Guide to British and North American Factory-Produced Ceramics. Octopus Publishing Group Ltd., London.

Austin, John C.
1994 British Delft at Williamsburg. The Colonial Williamasburg Foundation, Williamsburg, Va.

Barber, Edwin Atlee
1968[1904] Marks of American Potters. Cracker Barrel Press, Southampton, New York. Reprint of 1904 edition, Patterson and White, Philadelphia. (Available online at: http://trentonhistory.org/Made/Marks.html)

1970[1903] Tulip ware of the Pennsylvania-German Potters: An Historical Sketch of the Art of Slip-Decoration in the United States. Reprint of 1903 edition, Dover Publications Inc., New York

1976[1893] Pottery and Porcelain of the United States. Feingold and Lewis, New York.

Barker, David
1991 William Greatbatch: A Staffordshire Potter. London: Jonathan Horne Publications.

2002 Pearlware. In Encyclopedia of Historical Archaeology, edited by Charles E. Orser, Jr, pp. 415-416. Routledge, London and New York.

Beaudry, Mary C., Janet Long, Henry M. Miller, Fraser D. Neiman, and Gary Wheeler Stone
1988 A Vessel Typology for Early Chesapeake Ceramics: the Potomac Typological System. In Documentary Archaeology in the New World. M.C. Beaudry, ed. Pp. 51-67. Cambridge: Cambridge University Press.

Birks, Steve
2013 Ceramics Marks. Electronic document, http://www.thepotteries.org/mark/reg.htm, accessed September 16, 2013.

Charles D. Cheek
2016 Bristol Glazed Stoneware on Rural Indiana Farms: Effects of Technology Adoption on Consumer Choice. Historical Archaeology 50(2).

Chenoweth, John M.
2006 "What'll Thou Have": Quakers and the Characterization of Tavern Sites in Colonial Philadelphia. Northeast Historical Archaeology 35:77-92.

Chenoweth, John M., and Alan Farahani
2015 Color in historical ceramic typologies: A test case in statistical analysis of replicable measurements. Journal of Archaeological Science: Reports 4:310-319.

Claney, Jane Perkins
2004 Rockingham Ware in American Culture, 1830-1930: Reading Historical Artifacts. Hanover, NH: University of New England.

Cohen-Williams, Anita G.
1992 Common Majolica Types of Northern New Spain. Historical Archaeology 26(1):119-130.

Collard, Elizabeth
1967 Nineteenth-Century Pottery and Porcelain in Canada. McGill University Press, Montreal, Canada.

Cooper, Ronald G.
1968 English Slipware Dishes, 1650-1850. Transatlantic Arts Inc., New York.

Coysh, A.W., and R.K. Henrywood
1982 The Dictionary of Blue and White Printed Pottery, 1780-1880, vol. I. Baron Publishing, Woodbridge, Suffolk, England.

1989 The Dictionary of Blue and White Printed Pottery, 1780-1880, vol. II. Antique Collectors' Club Ltd., Woodbridge, Suffolk, England.

Cushion, John and Margaret Cushion
1992 A Collector's History of British Porcelain. Antique Collectors' Club Ltd., Woodbridge, Suffolk, England.

Deagan, Kathleen
1987 Artifacts of the Spanish Colonies of Florida and the Caribbean, 1500-1800, vol. 1: Ceramics, Glassware, and Beads. Washington, D.C.: Smithsonian Institution.

Denker, Ellen, and Bert Denker
1985 The Main Street Pocket Guide to North American Pottery and Porcelain. The Main Street Press, Pittstown, New Jersey.

Dieringer, Bev, and Ernie Dieringer
1997 White Ironstone China. In White Ironstone: A Survey of its Many Forms. D. Stoltzfus and J. Snyder, eds. Pp. 11-12. Atglen, PA: Schiffer Publishing.

Dieringer, Ernie and Bev Dieringer
2001 White Ironstone China: Plate Identification Guide, 1840-1890. Schiffer Publishing, Ltd., Atglen, Pennsylvania.

Frelinghuysen, Alice Cooney
1989 American Porcelain 1770-1920. The Metropolitan Museum, New York.

Furniss, David A., J. Richard Wagner, and Judith Wagner
1999 Adams Ceramics: Staffordshire Potters and Pots. Schiffer Publishing Ltd., Exton, Pennsylvania.

Gaimster, David
1997 German Stoneware 1200 – 1900: Archaeology and Cultural History. British Museum Press, London.

Giannini, Robert L. III
1981 Anthony Duché Sr., Potter and Merchant of Philadelphia. The Magazine Antiques CXIX (1): 198-203.

Gibble, Patricia E.
2005 Eighteenth-Century Redware Folk Terms and Vessel Forms: A Survey of Utilitarian Wares from Southeastern Pennsylvania. Historical Archaeology 39(3):33-62.

Gleeson, Janet
2000 The Arcanum: The Extraordinary True Story. Grand Central Publishing Company

Godden, Geoffrey A.
1964 Encyclopaedia of British Pottery and Porcelain Marks. New York: Crown.

1966 An Illustrated Encyclopedia of British Pottery and Porcelain. Crown Publishers Inc., New York.

1999 Godden's Guide to Ironstone, Stone and Granite Ware. Antique Collectors Club, Woodbridge, Suffolk, England.

Goldberg, Arthur F.
2003 Highlights in the Development of the Rockingham and Yellow Ware Industry in the United States—A Brief Review with Representative Examples. In Ceramics in America 2003. edited by Robert Hunter. Chipstone Foundation, Milwaukee, pp. 26-46. (http://www.chipstone.org/publications/CIA/2003/Goldberg/goldbergindex.html)

Green, Chris
1999 John Dwight's Fulham Pottery, Excavations 1971-79. London: English Heritage.

Greer, Georgeanna H.
2005 American Stonewares, the Art and Craft of Utilitarian Potters, 4th edition. Atglen, PA: Schiffer Publishing. [Originally published 1981.]

Grigsby, Leslie B.
1993 English Slip-Decorated Earthenware at Williamsburg. The Colonial Williamsburg Foundation, Williamsburg, Virginia.

Hawkins, John
1999 Staffordshire Engine-Turned Pottery ~ 1760-1780. Bulletin of the Society of Ornamental Turners Vol. 20 Num. 100. Electronic document, http://www.jbhawkinsantiques.com/uploads/articles/StaffordshireEngineTurnedPottery1.pdf

Hunter, Robert R., Jr, and George L. Miller
1994 English Shell-Edged Earthenware. The Magazine Antiques 145(3):432-443.

Hurst, John G., David S. Neal, and H.J.E. van Beuningen
1986 Pottery Produced and Traded in North-West Europe 1350-1650. Rotterdam Papers VI: A Contribution to Medieval Archaeology. Museum Boymans-van Beuningen, Rotterdam, The Netherlands.

Janowitz, Meta F.
2008 New York City Stonewares from the African Burial Ground. Ceramics in America 2008. Robert Hunter editor. The Chipstone Foundation, Milwaukee, Wisconsin. pp 41-66.

2013 Decline in the Use and Production of Red-Earthenware Cooking Vessels in the Northeast, 1780–1880. Northeast Historical Archaeology 42:92-110.

Ketchum, William C., Jr.
1983 Pottery and Porcelain. Alfred A. Knopf, New York.

1987 American Country Pottery. Alfred A. Knopf, New York.

1991a American Stoneware. Henry Holt and Co., New York.

1991b American Redware. Henry Holt and Co., New York.

Leibowitz, Joan
1985 Yellow Ware: The Transitional Ceramic. Atglen, PA: Schiffer Publishing.

Madsen, Andrew D. and Carolyn L. White
2011 Chinese Export Porcelains. Left Coast Press, Walnut Creek, CA.

Magid, Barbara A. and Bernard K. Means
2003 In the Philadelphia Style: The Pottery of Henry Piercy. In Ceramics in America 2003, Robert Hunter, editor, Pp. 47-86. Milwaukee, WI: Chipstone Foundation.

Majewski, Teresita, and Michael J. O'Brien
1987 The Use and Misuse of Nineteenth-Century English and American Ceramics in Archaeological Analysis. Advances in Archaeological Method and Theory 11:97-209.

Maryland Archaeological Conservation Lab
2002 "Diagnostic Artifacts in Maryland." Maryland Department of Planning, Jefferson Patterson Park and Museum. http://www.jefpat.org/diagnostic/Index.htm (accessed July 2016).

Miller, George L.
1980 Classification and Economic Scaling of nineteenth-Century Ceramics. Historical Archaeology 14:1-40.

1991 A Revised Set of CC Index Values for Classification and Economic Scaling of English Ceramics from 1787 to 1880. Historical Archaeology 25(1):1-25.

1991b Thoughts Towards a Users' Guide to Ceramic Assemblages: Part One. Council for Northeast Historical Archaeology Newsletter 18:2-5.

1991c Thoughts Towards a Users' Guide to Ceramic Assemblages: Part Two. Council for Northeast Historical Archaeology Newsletter 20:4-6.

1992 Thoughts Towards a Users' Guide to Ceramic Assemblages: Part Three. Council for Northeast Historical Archaeology Newsletter 22:2-4.

1993 Thoughts Towards a Users' Guide to Ceramic Assemblages: Part Four. Council for Northeast Historical Archaeology Newsletter 26:4-7.

Miller, George L., Patricia M. Samford, Ellen Shlasko, and Andrew D. Madsen
2000 Telling Time for Archaeologists. Northeast Historical Archaeology 29:1-22.

Miller, George, and Robert R. Hunter Jr.
2001 How Creamware Got the Blues: The Origins of China Glaze and Pearlware. In Ceramics in America 2001, Robert Hunter, editor, pp. 135 – 161, Chipstone Foundation, Milwaukee, WI.

Mudge, Jean McClure
1986 Chinese Export Porcelain in North America. Clarkson N. Potter Inc., New York.

Myers, Susan H.
1980 Handcraft to Industry: Philadelphia Ceramics in the First Half of the Nineteenth Century. Smithsonian Institution Press, Washington D.C.

Noël Hume, Ivor
1969 Pottery and Porcelain in Colonial Williamsburg's Archaeological Collections. Williamsburg, VA: Colonial Williamsburg Foundation.

1970 A Guide to Artifacts of Colonial America. New York: Knopf.

ORTON, CLIVE, PAUL TYERS, AND ALAN VINCE
1993 Pottery in Archaeology. Cambridge: Cambridge University Press.

OSWALD, ADRIAN, R.J.C. HILDYARD, AND R.G. HUGHES
1982 English Brown Stoneware, 1670-1900. Faber and Faber, London.

PEARCE, JACQUELINE, J.E.C. EDWARDS, D. LAKIN
1992 Border Wares: Post Medieval Pottery in London 1500-1700. Museum of London, London, England.

RADO, PAUL
1971 The Strange Case of Hard Porcelain. Transactions of the Journal of the British Ceramic Society 70:131-139.

RICKARD, JONATHAN
2006 Mocha and Related Dipped Wares, 1770-1939. Hanover, NH: University Press of New England.

RICKARD, JONATHAN AND DONALD CARPENTIER
2004 The Little Engine that Could: Adaptation of the Engine-Turning Lathe in the Pottery Industry. In Ceramics in America 2004, Robert Hunter, editor, Pp. 78-99. Milwaukee, WI: Chipstone Foundation.

RYE, OWEN S.
1988 Pottery Technology: Principles and Reconstrution. Washington, D.C.: Taraxacum.

SAMFORD, PATRICIA M.
1997 Response to a Market: Dating English Underglaze Transfer-Printed Wares. Historical Archaeology 31(2):1-30.

2013 Identifying and Dating Luster-Decorated Wares. In Ceramic Identification in Historical Archaeology: The View from California, 1822-1940. R. Allen, J.E. Huddleson, K.J. Wooten, and G.J. Farris, eds. Pp. 493-498. Germantown, MD: Society for Historical Archaeology.

SHAW, KENNETH
1962 Ceramic Colors and Pottery Decoration. Dublin: Alex. Thom & Co.

SHEPARD, ANNA O.
1956 Ceramics for the Archaeologist. Washington, DC: Carnegie Institution of Washington.

SKERRY, JANINE E. AND SUZANNE FINDLEN HOOD
2009 Salt-Glazed Stoneware in Early America. University Press of New England, and Colonial Williamsburg.

SNYDER, JEFFREY
1992 Flow Blue: A Collector's Guide to Pattern, History, and Values. West Chester, PA: Schiffer Publishing.

SOUTH, STANLEY
1971 Evolution and Horizon as Revealed in Ceramic Analysis in Historical Archaeology. Conference on Historic Site Archaeology Papers 6(2):71-106.

SUSSMAN, LYNNE
1977 Changes in pearlware dinnerware, 1780-1830. Historical Archaeology 11:105-111.

1997 Mocha, Banded, Cat's Eye, and Other Factory-Made Slipware. Boston: Council for Northeast Historical Archaeology.

TITE, M., T. PRADELL, AND A. SHORTLAND
2008 Discovery, Production and Use of Tin-Based Opacifiers in Glasses, Enamels and Glazes from the Late Iron Age Onwards: A Reassessment. Archaeometry 50(1):67-84.

TURNBAUGH, SARAH PEABODY
1985 Introduction. In Domestic Pottery of the Northeastern United States, 1625-1850. S.P. Turnbaugh, ed. Pp. 1-29. New York: Academic Press.

WASELKOV, GREGORY A. AND JOHN A. WALTHALL
2002 Faience Styles in French North America: A Revised Classification. Historical Archaeology 36(1):62-78.

WEBSTER, DONALD BLAKE
1971 Decorated Stoneware Pottery of North America. Charles E. Tuttle Co., Rutland Vermont.

WETHERBEE, JEAN
1996 White Ironstone: A Collector's Guide. Antique Trader Books. Dubuque, Iowa.

WILCOXEN, CHARLOTTE
1987 Dutch Trade and Ceramics in America in the Seventeenth Century. Albany Institute of History and Art, Albany, New York.

WILKIE, LAURIE
2000 Culture Bought: Evidence of Creolization in the Consumer Goods of an Enslaved Bahamian Family. Historical Archaeology 34(3):10-26.

WILLIAMS, PETER
2003 The Talbot Hotel Pit Group. In Ceramics in America 2003. edited by Robert Hunter. Chipstone Foundation, Milwaukee. (http://www.chipstone.org/article.php/79/Ceramics-in-America-2003/The-Talbot-Hotel-Pit-Group)

Guide to Ceramic MNV Calculation Qualitative and Quantitative Analysis

Barbara L. Voss and Rebecca Allen

ABSTRACT

Although calculating the minimum number of vessels (MNV) is common in many historical archaeological studies, the method is not consistently applied. Reasons for using MNV methodologies to describe a ceramic assemblage are deceptively simple. As others have pointed out, overall counts and ceramic weight can provide relative information on the distribution of ceramics across a particular site and the formation of the archaeological record. Most practically, MNV ceramic counts (rather than individual sherd counts) best illustrate how items were used before they entered the archaeological record.

Introduction

> "People don't use sherds, they use vessels."
> Barbara Voss,
> *The Archaeology of El Presidio de San Francisco*

Historical archaeologists commonly record ceramics in the field and in the laboratory. Minimum Number of Vessel (MNV) counting is by no means a new idea, but one that bears highlighting for future studies. In brief, MNV counts describe the minimum number of original items that can account for the fragmentary specimens present in the archaeological assemblage. MNV counts are not a substitute for specimen counts or specimen weight. Instead, MNV counts provide substantially different information that can contribute to interpretation of depositional and post-depositional processes, site chronology, and social behaviors such as purchasing patterns and the historical use of ceramic vessels.

Methods for determining MNV counts are varied, although there are essentially two methods of calculating MNV counts (Rice 1987:292–293): the quantitative and the qualitative. Quantitative MNV assessments are based on counts and measurements of rim sherds, bases, or handles. The advantage of quantitative techniques is that they are replicable and relatively expeditious. They are particularly useful for quantification of mass-produced ceramics for which vessel attributes (form, size, glaze, and decoration) are highly standardized. Quantitative MNV assessments may result in a disproportionately low vessel count for handcrafted and undecorated vessels. This is because quantitative MNV methods usually disregard body sherds and do not take paste composition, temper/inclusions, glaze, and manufacture technique into account.

Qualitative MNV counts subjectively assess and group together sherds that likely represent a single vessel. This method is not as replicable (i.e., MNV groupings vary from analyst to analyst). Its strength is that it allows the analyst to take multiple attributes into account and is less likely to undercount undecorated and handcrafted vessels disproportionately. To compensate for the subjective nature of this process, defining attributes for each MNV grouping should be clearly recorded. This permits other analysts to reevaluate the MNV groupings for future studies.

In defining MNVs, the analyst should consider all ceramic sherds within a given ware type category (e.g., majolica, blue transfer print, stoneware, etc.). For each sherd there are three possibilities: (1) a sherd could be assigned to a group of specimens representing a MNV with shared attributes; (2) a sherd may have unique attributes, not shared with other specimens, that indicate that it represents a MNV; or (3) a sherd could have attributes that would allow it to be assigned to more than one MNV grouping. Sherds falling into the third category should be set aside and excluded from MNV calculations.

As a result, only a fraction of the ceramic sherds within a given ware category can generally be assigned to an MNV grouping. Typically, the more abundant the sherds in a ware category, the lower the frequency of sherds assigned to MNV groupings. This is because the more MNV groupings are defined for a particular ware type, the more likely it is that a given sherd will share characteristics with more than one MNV. For example, a body sherd could have the same paste, glaze, and decorative attributes as an 8 cm diameter rim sherd and a 12 cm diameter rim sherd. The resulting minimum-vessel groupings consist of a sherd or group of sherds that uniquely share a constellation of specific attributes, including vessel form, rim form, vessel diameter (at rim and/or base), manufacture method, decoration, paste characteristics (including paste color and inclusions/temper), and surface treatments.

In grouping sherds into MNVs, it is best to be rigorously conservative. If there is any possibility that two sherds *could* be from the same vessel, they should be grouped together even if their attributes are somewhat different. For example, two rim sherds with slightly different rim profiles can be grouped together if intravessel variation can account for variation in rim profiles. Likewise, two sherds with different paste colors but similar inclusions/temper can be grouped if it is possible that color differences could be attributed to differential firing of the vessel. These considerations reduce the possibility that spurious or fictitious minimum vessels are created during the subjective minimum-vessel grouping process.

Regardless of the admitted imperfections embodied within both quantitative and qualitative analysis, the importance of defining minimum-vessel groupings cannot be overstated. To put it simply, people don't use sherds; they use vessels (Voss 2002:661). Identifying minimum numbers of vessels brings the archaeologist one step closer to reconstructing the functional and symbolic role of ceramic artifacts in the past.

MNV Estimation in the Field

When recording historic ceramics on a site, think in terms of MNV (Figure 1). How many plates? cups? bowls? Stating the number of sherds can be deceptive in terms of site characterization: 1 sherd can equal 1 pot, 8 sherds can represent 1 bowl, or 80 sherds can represent 1 large platter. Breakage can occur both during original use of the vessel and also long after the sherds are discarded. For example, a single ceramic sherd can be easily broken into multiple fragments by vehicles driving through a site, or by human or animal trampling. Conversely, buried sherds or surface sherds in less-accessible areas of a site are less likely to be affected by postdepositional breakage. These examples illustrate why sherd count alone can be an unreliable measure of how the site was used, and the count cannot be used to characterize the overall artifact assemblage.

Instead of counting sherds, learn to look instead at the numbers of rim sherds, bases, or other attributes to help determine how many whole artifacts were once on the site, not the number of broken pieces. Learn how to make MNV estimates. Site records are usually not intended to be the end-all of information about an archaeological site, but are meant to characterize both

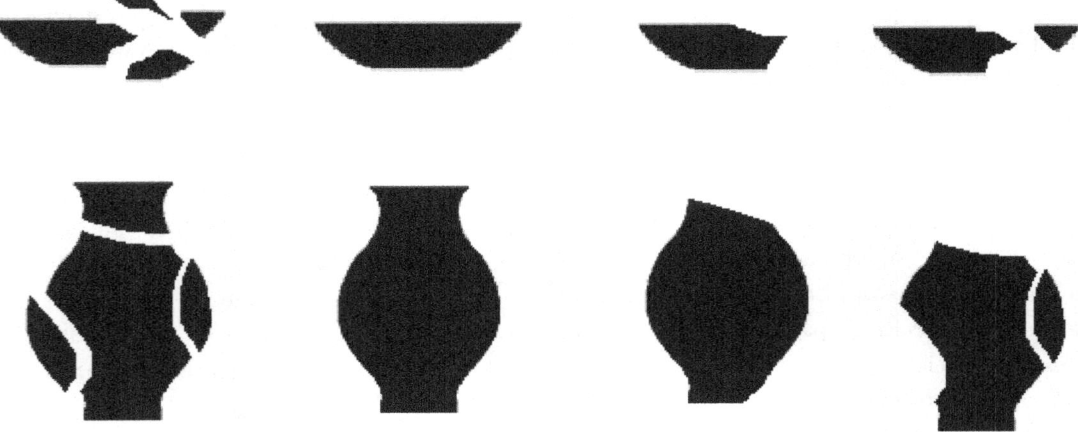

Figure 1. Each row shows the equivalent of one MNV. A single vessel can be represented by several sherds that can reconstruct the vessel in its entirety with several fragments missing, but with characteristic form such as a base or rim. (Illustration by R. Allen, 2009.)

the kind and general function of occupation or use. Knowing the ceramic MNV can help to clarify site use and characterize the overall artifact assemblage and/or its relationship to features. Is the site a trash dump? domestic assemblage? industrial waste site with byproducts? temporary camp site?

Given the limited time that is normally available for site recordation, most archaeologists use qualitative MNV calculation methods in the field. The majority of historic ceramics can be divided into three general categories that can provide a starting place for estimating MNV: (1) earthenware, (2) porcelain, and (3) stoneware.

The following categories (revisited in the laboratory discussion later in this article) can further help to estimate MNV in the field: vessel form (bowl, cup, plate, jar, etc.); manufacture style (molding, casting, pinching, etc.); surface treatment and decoration (transfer print, painting, base marks, etc.); body characteristics (color, temper); and external modifications (burning, drilling, etc.).

For example, a concentration of ceramics from a trash-dumping area could be described as 14 sherds of white improved earthenware (Figure 2). This says little about the site function or the site association. Using MNV methodologies, the assemblage could be estimated as: ≅4+ white earthenware plates, ≅2 white earthenware cups, ≅2 white earthenware saucers, and ≅6+ white earthenware flatware vessels; the MNV estimation determined by makers' marks and body shape.

The advantage to this characterization is that it suggests a domestic assemblage, and perhaps even represents one household dumping event within the larger city trash dump. Noting the presence and kinds of makers' marks is also important to dating the assemblage. Interpretations gathered from field assessments of ceramic MNV can then be evaluated in conjunction with any available documentary evidence.

Figure 3 shows a similar probable domestic assemblage, where body decoration as well as makers' marks and body

Figure 2. White improved earthenware from a trash-dump area. (Photo by R. Allen, 2002.)

Figure 3. White improved earthenware with additional body decoration from a trash-dump area. (Photo by R. Allen, 2002.)

shape can be used to determine MNV. Remember, the point of estimation in the field is not to be exact—given two minutes, five archaeologists may come up with five different estimations. The purpose is to assist in better characterizing the site's use and content rather than simply counting (or estimating) the number of sherds. If exact vessel shapes cannot be determined, the more generic terms of *flatware* (plates, saucers, etc.) or *hollowware* (cups, bowls, etc.) can also be used.

Figure 4 shows a possible domestic assemblage that is more industrial (oil cans, etc.), where it is not practical to estimate ceramic MNV. In this instance, metal cans are the more prominent artifacts, and description of these materials can better help to characterize the site and its assemblage. The presence of white improved earthenware can be noted but not necessarily counted, especially if time is limited.

MNV Recordation in the Laboratory

In the laboratory, MNV recordation becomes more sophisticated, and both quantitative and qualitative methods can be used. Figure 5 is adapted from sample minimum-vessel recordation sheet intended for one form per vessel that was developed for a ceramic-analysis project that included both hand-formed and mass-produced ware types, and used quantitative as well as qualitative methods to determine MNV groups. A recordation sheet such as this can be adapted to fit the particular attributes of a given ceramic assemblage as well as the research goals of the project.

Vessel attributes recorded for each MNV can be roughly divided into eight major categories. Seven of these are categories of primary attributes that can be interpreted directly from the specimens themselves. These are: ware type, form, method of manufacture, surface treatment

Figure 4. An assemblage from a trash area for which it is not practical to estimate ceramic MNV. (Photo by R. Allen, 2002.)

and decoration, body characteristics, burning, and completeness. Many other scholars have made suggestions for standardized procedures for recording these attributes: Colton (1953), Shepard (1956), Rye (1981), Chase (1985), Miller (1986), Rice (1987), Sinopoli (1991), and Orton et al. (2003). The sample MNV recordation sheet considers these previous examples. The eighth major category includes those attributes which provide additional information when interpreted with documentary sources, such as makers' marks or the trade names of decorative patterns.

In the laboratory, analysis generally proceeds in five steps: (1) Subdivide the ceramic specimens into ware types; (2) For each ware type, determine whether quantitative or qualitative MNV assessment is most appropriate. All other things being equal, quantitative methods are more reliable for mass-manufactured ceramics, while qualitative methods are more appropriate for hand-formed and workshop-produced ceramics; (3) Whether using qualitative or quantitative MNV methods, identify which attributes will be most meaningful in determining MNV groupings for that ware type. For example, analysis of vessel form and decoration will likely generate the strongest MNV groupings for mass-produced tableware ceramics with standardized pastes and glazes. Hand-formed vessels will require careful analysis of surface treatment and body characteristics to avoid undercounting MNVs. Highly fragmented ceramic specimens of any origin may also require greater attention to paste and glaze characteristics; (4) Once the method and attributes have been determined for a given ware type, sort the ceramic sherds into MNV groupings using the selected attributes, setting aside any sherds with attributes of more than one MNV group. Cross-mending analysis, discussed later in this article, may also be conducted during this step; and (5) Record the selected attributes for each MNV

		Vessel # *15*			
		Waretype: *unglazed earthenware*			
1. Vessel Form:	10. Decoration				
hollowware	Interior: *undecorated*				
2. Rim Form:	Exterior: *undecorated*				
unknown					
3. Rim Diameter:	11. Colors	13. Burning			
unknown	Interior: *7.5YR 5/2*	Interior: *No*			
4. Base Diameter:	Int. mar.: *N2.75 to N2.0*	Int. mar. *Yes*			
unknown	Core: *N2.75 to N2.0*	Core: *Yes*			
5. Vessel Height:					
unknown	Ext. mar.: *N2.75 to N2.0*	Ext. mar. *Yes*			
6. Thickness	Exterior: *5YR 6/8*	Exterior: *No*			
Minimum: *11 mm* Maximum: *8.2 mm*					
7. % of Vessel:	12. Inclusions/Temper	14. Cross Mended Sherds			
0-5 %	Material: *sand, plant, white rock (not shell)*	Catalog #	# of sherds	Unit	Stratum
		122	*1*	*HF*	*9*
8. Manufacture:	Volume (%): *30%*	*668*	*1*	*YH*	*13*
handbuilt	Particle size: *common nonplastic particles up to 3 mm or less*				
9. Surface Treatment:	Regularity: *good-fair*				
Interior: *brushed*					
		15. Other affiliated sherds			
		Catalog #	# of sherds	Unit	Stratum
Exterior: *brushed*	Rounding: *sub-rounded to angular*	*1624*	*1*	*MIX*	*4*
Comments: *Thick bodied, coarse temper visible to eye*					

Figure 5. Example form, with sample answers given in italics. Adapted from ceramic MNV groupings from the Funston Avenue Archaeological Research Project, Presidio of San Francisco. (Form created by B. Voss, 1999, adapted by R. Allen 2010.)

group, adjusting as needed. Repeat steps 2 through 5 for each ware type in the ceramic assemblage.

Although it is not strictly necessary, cross-mending analysis is also recommended while determining MNV groupings. In cross-mending, analysts look for sherds that directly mend together, providing incontrovertible evidence that these sherds were once part of the same vessel. Cross-mending can provide greater precision in evaluating vessel form and vessel size. The distribution of cross-mended sherds within and between excavation units, stratigraphic layers, and archaeological features can also provide valuable information about depositional and post-depositional processes.

Sections below describe recording procedures for MNV attributes. It is not necessary to record all attributes for each MNV group. Rather, the ceramic analyst should thoughtfully consider which attributes will be most meaningful in determining MNV groupings for each ware type and which attributes will be most useful in addressing research questions related to the assemblage as a whole. Similarly, while this guide uses metric measurements, the ceramic analyst could select English measurements if preferred.

Vessel Form

Vessel form is one of the more relevant attributes related to interpretations of vessel function. Overall vessel form (Field No. 1 on the MNV recordation) can be recorded at one of three nested levels: at the most basic level, open or closed (as determined by orifice shape); second, flatware or hollowware; and third, whenever possible, specific vessel shape (e.g., bowl, cup, plate, or jar).

Additional form attributes recorded include rim form (Field No. 2), rim diameter (Field No. 3), base diameter (Field No. 4), vessel height (Field No. 5), and minimum and maximum thickness (Field No. 6). Rim and base diameters can be measured using the curve-fitting method (Rice 1987:223) to the nearest even-numbered centimeter (e.g., 2 cm, 4 cm, 6 cm, etc.). Unless more than 50% of the vessel is present (recorded in Field No. 7), curve fitting readings carry some ambiguity and the 2 cm interval best represents the level of accuracy that can be obtained. In cases where the diameter cannot be determined within a 2 cm interval, a range of diameters can be recorded (e.g., 12–18 cm).

Vessel Manufacture

Rice (1987:124) defines six procedures of vessel manufacture: pinching/drawing, slab modeling, molding, casting, coiling, and throwing. Each can leave characteristic marks on the vessel body and in the cross-section view of the vessel paste provided by the broken surfaces of ceramic sherds. These are noted when visible and described in Field No. 8. Surface qualities of the vessel that are related to manufacture are also sometimes recorded in Field No. 9, "Surface Treatment."

Surface Treatment and Decoration

Surface treatments can be undertaken to change the functional characteristics of a vessel (e.g., to reduce porosity) and/or to alter its appearance. These can include smoothing, burnishing, glazing, slipping, rouletting, or any combination of these methods. Surface treatments are noted in Field No. 9 for both the interior and exterior of the vessel. Decorative treatments of ceramic vessels such as painting, transfer printing, or decals are closely related to surface treatments and are recorded in Field No. 10, again for both the interior and exterior surface of the vessels.

Body Characteristics

As noted above, body characteristics are standardized for most mass-manufactured ceramics and may not need to be analyzed in detail beyond identification of ware type. For locally produced and hand-formed ceramics, body characteristics are key variables that can differentiate sherds that may look identical at first glance but which represent multiple original vessels.

The body of each vessel consists of the mixture of clays, nonplastic chemically inert temper/inclusions, and flux, that together provide the vessel with structural integrity before, during, and after the firing process. At this stage of analysis only macroscopic attributes of the vessel body are recorded. This includes the body color (Field No. 11), which can be recorded for the vessel interior surface, interior margin, core, exterior margin, and exterior surface using the Munsell color system of hue, chroma, and value. Where applicable, color recordation also includes the colors of any surface treatments and decorative elements. If color variation is present, record multiple colors to represent the range of color present throughout the sherd and/or MNV. Because of the limitations of the Munsell color system for extremely light and extremely dark colors, the Munsell neutral value scale can also be used when appropriate.

Recording the color of the vessel body provides considerable information about the parent clay and manufacture conditions of the vessel. First, the general color of the fired body can indicate the type of clay used to prepare the vessel: primary, or residual clays possess a high iron content and when fired range in color from yellow to red, while secondary deposits of clay usually have a low ferrous content and a high organic content, yielding gray, black, white, and cream colors. The color of the body core also indicates whether the ceramic was fired in a reducing or oxidizing environment: a dark core can indicate that the vessel was fired in a reducing environment or was fired at too low a temperature, or for too short a period of time to completely oxidize the organic material present in the clay (Rice 1987).

The second vessel body attribute is the inclusions/temper present in the vessel (Field No. 12). These inclusions can occur naturally within the parent clay, can be inadvertently incorporated during vessel preparation, and/or can be intentionally added. To record the inclusions/temper of each vessel, cleaned sherd edges should be inspected under a binocular microscope at 10× to 40× magnification. The material, volume, particle size, regularity/sorting, and rounding can all be recorded. Inclusions/temper attributes are particularly useful in distinguishing between handcrafted vessels of similar outward appearance.

Burning

Evidence of burning is indicated by the presence or absence of soot residues, and can generate important information about vessel function and pre- and post-depositional transforms that may have affected the ceramic sherds. Burning (Field No. 13) is recorded for the interior, interior margin, core, exterior margin, and exterior of each vessel, and is noted as absent, partially present, or present.

Because burning occurs after vessel manufacture, burning alone should not be used to determine MNV grouping. Nonetheless, systematic recordation of burning can provide important information to interpret vessel use and post-use transformation. In general, burning on part or most of the exterior of a ceramic vessel may be a strong indication that the vessel was used in cooking. Soot on the interior of the vessel probably accumulated after discard; soot on the broken edges of ceramic sherds would indicate burning after breakage. Both interior and margin burning suggest incineration, either intentional or accidental, before or after deposition.

Vessel Completeness

Sherds composing a minimum-vessel group are enumerated in two fields: Field No. 14, "Cross-mended sherds," lists all sherds that have been physically mended together, allowing reconstruction of part of the vessel; and Field No. 15, "Other affiliated sherds," lists all unmended sherds that uniquely share the vessel's diagnostic attributes. Together the cross-mended and unmended sherds are examined with respect to the percentage of the vessel represented (Field No. 7). This is subjectively assessed to one of six ranges: 0–5%, 5–25%, 25–50%, 50–75%, 75–100%, and 100%.

It should be remembered that the percentage of the vessel present within a minimum-vessel grouping is almost certainly an underestimate of its actual completeness. While this practice ensures that only those sherds *uniquely* matched to each minimum vessel's description are included in the grouping, it undoubtedly artificially suppresses measures of vessel completeness.

Conclusions

Both in the field and in the laboratory, MNV analysis yields more accurate archaeological evidence, and better represents and interprets the actual use of the artifacts. Further, MNV analysis is particularly useful for intrasite and intersite comparative studies because MNV counts provide some correction to the biases that can be introduced through depositional and postdepositional processes. While this technical brief focuses exclusively on ceramic specimens, the field and laboratory methodologies described here can be adapted to quantify other functional items such as glass containers and tablewares, metal canisters, and clothing parts such as buttons and shoes. Many of the MNV principles and techniques presented can also be adapted for other kinds of artifacts found in the historic archaeological record. As with ceramics, defining MNVs for these categories is deceptively simple, and better suited as the subject of other technical briefs.

Archaeologists sometimes perceive ceramic MNV analysis to be time consuming and expensive. It need not be so. Critical assessment of the range of ceramic attributes to be considered allows the field archaeologist or laboratory researcher to focus analysis on those characteristics that are most likely to identify the original vessels that generated the assemblage. Most importantly, MNV analysis brings archaeologists closer to understanding what objects were actually used by the historical communities being studied through their research.

ACKNOWLEDGMENTS

This text was adapted from Barbara Voss's dissertation and from field identification guides put together by Rebecca Allen and others. Barbara Voss thanks the National Park Service and the Presidio Trust which sponsored her dissertation research at the Presidio of San Francisco National Historic Landmark District. Rebecca Allen has also benefited from discussions with R. Scott Baxter, Kimberly Wooten, and Julia Huddleson. We also both extend our thanks to Thad Van Bueren and the article reviewers.

REFERENCES

Chase, Philip G.
1985 Whole Vessels and Sherds: An Experimental Investigation of Their Quantitative Relationships. *Journal of Field Archaeology* 12(2):213–218.

Colton, Harold Sellers
1953 *Potsherds: An Introduction to the Study of Prehistoric Southwestern Ceramics and Their Use in Historic Reconstruction.* Northern Arizona Society of Science and Art, Flagstaff.

Miller, George L.
1986 Of Fish and Sherds: A Model for Estimating Vessel Populations from Minimal Vessel Counts. *Historical Archaeology* 20(2):59–85.

Orton, Clive, Paul Tyres, and A. G. Vance
2003 *Pottery in Archaeology*. Cambridge University Press, Cambridge, UK.

Rice, Prudence
1987 *Pottery Analysis: A Sourcebook*. University of Chicago Press, Chicago, IL.

Rye, Owen S.
1981 *Pottery Technology: Principles and Reconstruction*. Taraxacum, Washington, DC.

Shepard, Anna O.
1956 *Ceramics for the Archaeologist*. Carnegie Institution of Washington, Washington, DC.

Sinopoli, Carla M.
1991 *Approaches to Archaeological Ceramics*. Plenum Press, New York, NY.

Voss, Barbara L.
2002 *The Archaeology of El Presidio de San Francisco: Culture Contact, Gender, and Ethnicity in a Spanish-Colonial Military Community.* Doctoral dissertation, Department of Anthropology, University of California, Berkeley. University Microfilms International, Ann Arbor, MI.

Barbara L. Voss
Department of Anthropology
450 Serra Mall, Building 50, Main Quad
Stanford University
Stanford, CA 94305-2034

Rebecca Allen
Past Forward, Inc.
P.O. Box 969
Garden Valley, CA 95633

LYNNE SUSSMAN

Objects vs. Sherds: A Statistical Evaluation

Introduction

This project grew out of a discussion paper on the methodology of using ceramics to interpret archaeological sites. Naturally the subject of object and sherd counts arose. It happens that material culture researchers are singularly unqualified to discuss sherds. Archaeologists almost never deal with them. By this is meant that by the time the material is studied, the forensic science of sherd distribution on a site has already taken place. The archaeologist has presumably studied the material as refuse. We are usually concerned with the character of the material before it was discarded, or rather as if it had never been discarded. We treat the material as objects belonging to the occupants. The distinction between the two approaches is obvious and valuable. You cannot understand your site unless you view the artifacts as garbage (sherds); you cannot understand the occupants unless you view the artifacts as possessions (objects). In this work concern is with ceramics in their roles as possessions.

It will not come as a surprise to anyone who has read numerous archaeological reports that archaeologists are occasionally guilty of blurring the duality of archaeological material. The most irresponsible type of blurring is the failure to establish the links, or the lack thereof, between the refuse and the occupants. (The material found in the ravine all must have belonged to the occupants of the nearest house.) The second type of blurring concerns numbers–counts of sherds indicate the same thing as counts of objects. It is not quite so obvious how heinous the latter practice is. The purpose of this paper is to describe the consequences of treating sherd counts as equivalents to object counts.

The assemblages and their contents as described here are real, so are their physical and cultural attributes (Chism 1972; Sussman 1972). The research questions, however, have been made up purely to explore the object vs. sherd counts (MacLeod 1990; Sussman 1990).

Chi-Square

Archaeologists are well aware of the weaknesses of sherd counts. They know that objects do not neatly break into equal numbers of sherds. They are not blind to the fact that they sometimes recover a complete object and sometimes a tiny fragment. There is published literature on the subject of deriving reliable object counts from sherds (Burgh 1959; Egloff 1973; Chase 1985). To their credit, archaeologists are almost universally in agreement that object counts are desirable, the problem being how to arrive at them. Few are willing to say that one sherd represents one object, a statement that is obvious if sherd counts are used in chi-square statistical tests. A statistician would strongly discourage the comparison of sherd counts using chi-square tests. This test requires that the counts are of independent individuals, not related groups of individuals.

Still, it is tempting to use sherd counts as pretend object counts, especially when they have already been compiled to study deposition on the site. What would happen if the warnings of the statistician are ignored? What would be the ramifications of statistically comparing distributions of artifacts if only sherd counts are used?

First, to appreciate the effect of sherd counts on site interpretation, one must be reasonably confident that the differences found are not results of cultural or depositional effects, or excavation technique. Comparing ceramics from a 16th-century monastery and a 19th-century landfill site will produce significant differences that far outweigh sherd/object counting.

The ideal test situation would be several rich sites (or distinct components of a site) which shared the same date range, cultural affiliation, depositional character, and excavation techniques. Lower Fort Garry comes as close to this ideal as any site investigated. It was a large Hudson's Bay Company post with buildings that were occupied contemporaneously (Chism 1972). The ceramics in every structure came largely from the Fort Store, and it was almost all tableware or toilet articles made of the same material (transfer-printed white earthenware). Most of it was made by a single manufacturer (Sussman 1972). All structures selected were excavated using the same techniques and recording methods, and all structures were completely excavated. The surface collection, ravine dump, and unprovenienced artifacts were eliminated.

The structures were compared with one another, looking for statistically significant differences in counts of four item types (cups, saucers, plates, and bowls) and separately, in counts of four decorative types (plain, molded, painted, and transfer-printed). This was done once (for each pair of structures) using object counts and again using sherd counts. The chi-square values of these comparisons of item frequencies are presented in Tables 1 and 2.

Even the statistician was surprised at these results. It was expected that the chi-square values would be inflated using sherd counts. After all, there were a lot more sherds than objects. What was not expected were the enormous chi-square values for sherd count comparisons that were absolutely meaningless. Comparisons of the same material using object counts proved to have chi-square values that were much more believable. An extreme example is the comparison between the blacksmith's shop and the fur loft; this comparison has a chi-square value of 199.9 when sherds are counted and a chi-square value of 1.37 when objects are counted.

To grasp the weirdness of the sherd-count comparisons, the chi-square values were divided into four types according to their confidence level. Confidence levels of less than 95% were not considered as being significant. This is Group 1, identifiable in the tables as plain unadorned numbers. Note that only three comparisons out of 45 are not significantly different when sherd counts are used. If really interpreting the site, the researcher would now be obliged to wrestle with the reasons why the counts of the various items were so different in every building. Note also that 32 of the same 45

TABLE 1. CHI-SQUARED VALUES COMPARING FREQUENCIES OF CUPS, SAUCERS, PLATES, AND BOWLS BETWEEN PAIRS OF STRUCTURES–USING SHERD COUNTS

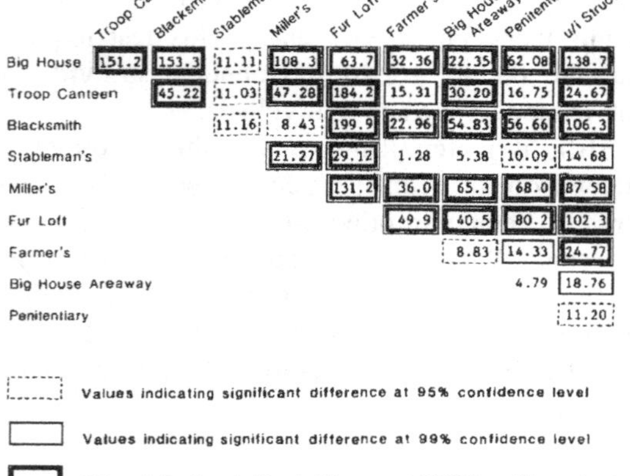

	Troop Canteen	Blacksmith	Stableman's	Miller's	Fur Loft	Farmer's	Big House Areaway	Penitentiary	u/i Structure
Big House	151.2	153.3	11.11	108.3	63.7	32.36	22.35	62.08	138.7
Troop Canteen		45.22	11.03	47.28	184.2	15.31	30.20	16.75	24.67
Blacksmith			11.16	8.43	199.9	22.96	54.83	56.66	106.3
Stableman's				21.27	29.12	1.28	5.38	10.09	14.68
Miller's					131.2	36.0	65.3	68.0	87.58
Fur Loft						49.9	40.5	80.2	102.3
Farmer's							8.83	14.33	24.77
Big House Areaway								4.79	18.76
Penitentiary									11.20

Values indicating significant difference at 95% confidence level

Values indicating significant difference at 99% confidence level

Values indicating significant difference at 99.99% confidence level

TABLE 2. CHI-SQUARED VALUES COMPARING FREQUENCIES OF CUPS, SAUCERS, PLATES, AND BOWLS BETWEEN PAIRS OF STRUCTURES–USING OBJECT COUNTS

	Troop Canteen	Blacksmith	Stableman's	Miller's	Fur Loft	Farmer's	Big House Areaway	Penitentiary	u/i Structure
Big House	6.92	3.30	1.23	19.9	10.2	3.92	1.95	4.12	4.77
Troop Canteen		4.51	1.25	5.25	12.6	3.82	7.68	3.36	1.24
Blacksmith			3.13	11.42	1.37	5.98	6.46	6.60	3.85
Stableman's				8.16	7.41	0.64	2.21	0.92	1.04
Miller's					20.5	15.5	17.6	12.5	8.86
Fur Loft						12.2	11.3	11.6	7.61
Farmer's							3.96	0.30	1.08
Big House Areaway								3.46	6.32
Penitentiary									1.30

Values indicating significant difference at 95% confidence level

Values indicating significant difference at 99% confidence level

Values indicating significant difference at 99.99% confidence level comparisons are *not* significantly different when object counts are used!

Group 2, distinguished by a broken-line box around the values (7.81 to 11.34), is made up of those comparisons that are different with confidence levels from 95% to just below 99%. Differences at these levels are considered statistically significant.

Group 3, distinguished by a solid-line box around the values (11.42 to 21.11), is made up of those comparisons that are different with confidence levels from 99% to just below 99.99%. These are high confidence levels. A conclusion that the differences are real would be considered very safe for these cases.

Group 4, distinguished by a double line box around the values (higher than 21.11), is made up of those comparisons that are different with confidence levels at 99.99% and higher. The chance of any difference this great occurring randomly is considered almost astronomically remote. Yet note that most of the sherd count differences were this great. Thirty of the comparisons were significantly different at this level when sherds were counted; not one comparison was significantly different at this level when objects were counted.

To say that the chi-square values using sherd counts are inflated is such an understatement as to miss the point. Not only are extremely significant differences found that do not exist, but the real differences are lost in all of the noise. When object counts were used, all of the thirteen significant differences found involved either the miller's house or the fur loft. The fact that something potentially interesting was happening at these structures is not at all apparent when sherd counts were used.

Comparisons of counts for decoration types produce similar results. Of 21 comparisons, 18 are significantly different at a 99.99% confidence level when sherds are counted, whereas only one comparison is significantly different at that level when objects are counted.

Correlational Statistics

Correlational statistics are the perennial favorites of the social and medical sciences. They are meant to answer questions such as "is there a positive relationship between blue eyes and musical genius?" They are often used in an exploratory way, to identify areas of promising research.

For this exercise, it was decided to look for a positive relationship between serving dishes (platters, tureens, gravy boats, etc.) and toiletware (washbasins, ewers, and chamber pots). This is not as farfetched as it may sound. These items can be considered optional household effects, compared to the basic cups, saucers, plates, and bowls.

The statistical analysis used was a Pearson's correlation of frequencies of servers with toilet articles. The frequencies are relative to the combined number of cups, saucers, plates, and bowls. The results of the object-based frequencies and the sherd-based frequencies can be seen in the two scattergrams depicted in Figures 1-2. The object-based frequencies are so different from the sherd-based frequencies, at first it was thought that the scattergrams must be wrong. Each dot represents a structure. The horizontal axis is the percentage of servers found (relative to cups, saucers, plates, and bowls). The vertical axis is the percentage of toiletware found. An ideal positive correlation would lie in a diagonal line from lower left to upper right. The correlation coefficient using objects is +.25, indicating a definite, though not strong, tendency to find servers in the same relative quantities as toilet articles and vice versa. The correlation coefficient using sherds is -.06, indicating absolutely no tendency for the two types of articles to be found together. (Note: correlation coefficients have values ranging from +1 indicating perfect positive correlation, to 0 indicating no relationship between quantities, to -1 indicating perfect negative correlation.) If the scattergrams are again studied it can be seen why there are difficulties in using sherd counts as proportions. As an example, note the dot lying along the bottom axis to the far right. This dot represents a structure wherein no toiletware, but some servers were found. When these servers were counted as objects they made up about 8% of the assemblage, but when they were counted as sherds they made up about 32% of the same assemblage. Obviously one or two servers broke into numerous pieces. It is this variation in the numbers of sherds representing articles which masks any relationship between the articles.

These Pearson's correlation coefficients are intended to provide only an approximate first look at the data. The data were not transformed (as counts or proportions normally are prior to any rigorous statistical analysis) and no statistical

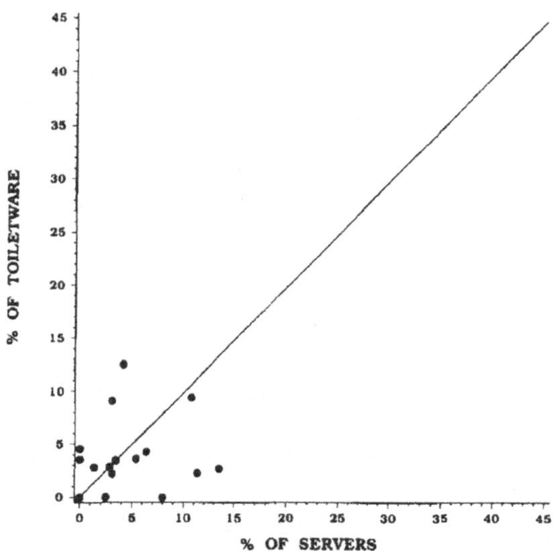

FIGURE 1. Correlation between toiletware and servers: using object counts. (Drawing by Dorothea Larsen.)

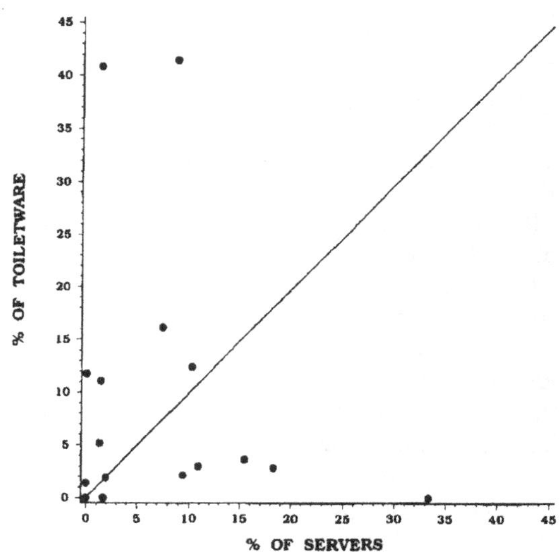

FIGURE 2. Correlation between toiletware and servers: using sherd counts. (Drawing by Dorothea Larsen.)

tests were run to determine the significance of the coefficients. In the normal course of research, relationships would be explored by just such simple analysis. At a preliminary stage, rigor is less important than indications of promising areas of research. This is what is so disturbing about the results of these correlations. If sherd counts had been used, thinking that their proportions were accurate enough for at least indications of relationships, the researcher would have immediately abandoned any exploration of server/toiletware relationship. One could hardly get less encouragement than a correlation coefficient of -.06.

Proportions

Archaeological material is often reported, not as counts, but as proportions of some total. Proportions cannot be compared statistically, unless the numbers (counts) they are based on are considered. Without them, there is no mathematical way of knowing the significance of any differences observed in proportions of two assemblages; one assemblage could consist of two examples, while the other could consist of thousands. This is a fact that, mystifyingly, is ignored in some archaeological reporting. There are reports which carefully tabulate proportions without mentioning counts–as if proportions provided more, rather than less, information.

Initially, because of this, there was no intention of comparing the proportions based on sherds with those based on objects. It was questioned, however, whether the proportions arrived at using sherds even *appeared* to be the same (or close enough to make no difference) as the proportions arrived at using objects. Figures 3-12 depict bar graphs showing proportions of items and decorative types for the five structures with the greatest amount of ceramics. With the understanding that, for comparative purposes, there is no mathematical significance to the sizes of the bars, the results of many of the comparisons were sufficiently *different looking* to be interesting to anyone concerned with a sherd-equals-object hypothesis. Any difference under 25% was considered to be insignificant. That is, if the relative difference calculated as

$$\frac{\text{Difference between object-and sherd-based proportion}}{\text{Object-based proportion}} \times 100\%$$

is *more* than 25%, it is safe to say that this difference is a deformity caused by the sherd counts. On the graphs, the sherd proportions that are unacceptably different from the object proportions are flagged with a thumbs-down hand. Those that are acceptable are flagged with a check-mark. Proportions based on counts of less than ten were not considered; these are the unflagged bars. The numerical code for the items translates as follows: 1=saucers; 2=cups; 3=plates; 4=bowl; 5=pitcher; 6=serving dish; 7=washbasin; 8=ewer; 9=chamber pot; 10=other; 11=unidentified. The numerical code for decoration types translates as follows: 1=molded;

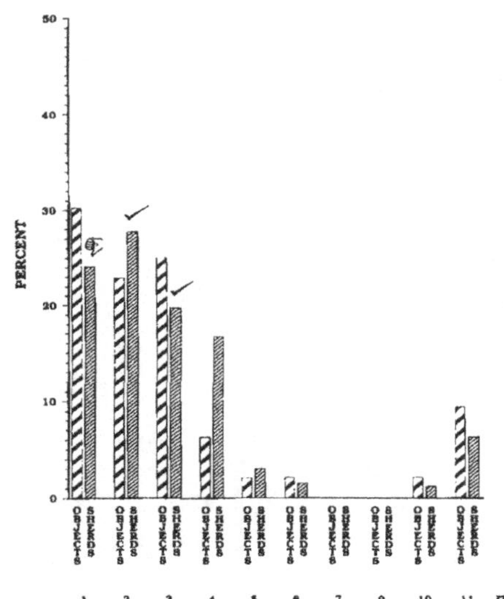

FIGURE 3. Troop canteen: comparison of object and sherd proportions by item (total objects, 96; total sherds, 336). (Drawing by Dorothea Larsen.)

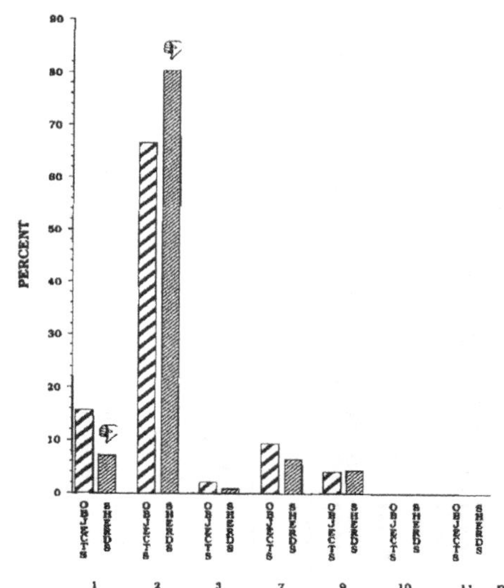

FIGURE 4. Troop canteen: comparison of object and sherd proportions by decoration (total objects, 96; total sherds, 336). (Drawing by Dorothea Larsen.)

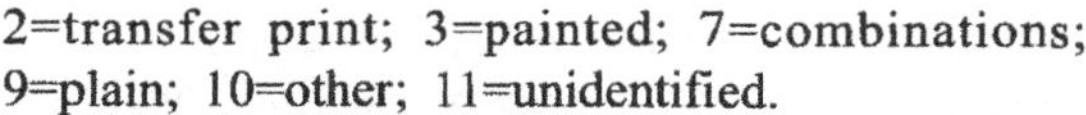

2=transfer print; 3=painted; 7=combinations; 9=plain; 10=other; 11=unidentified.

Looking at these graphs, one has to conclude that sherd proportions are unreliable reflections of object proportions. They may be very close in some cases and highly different in others. The graph of the unidentified structure is an extreme example. If trying to identify the building's function based on proportions of item types, quite different data would be used depending on whether sherd or object proportions were used. The problem with proportions of anything is that an abnormally large or small occurrence of a single type will affect all the other proportions. The proportions of sherds, not surprisingly, seem to be affected by the size of the items–the large serving dishes and toilet articles producing more sherds than their smaller counterparts in the assemblage.

The object and sherd proportions based on decoration are much closer to each other. This is due partly because decoration *on this site*

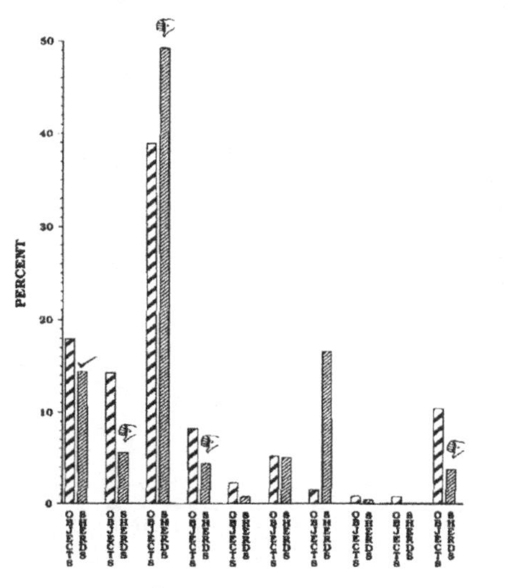

FIGURE 5. Big house: comparison of object and sherd proportions by item (total objects, 134; total sherds, 690). (Drawing by Dorothea Larsen.)

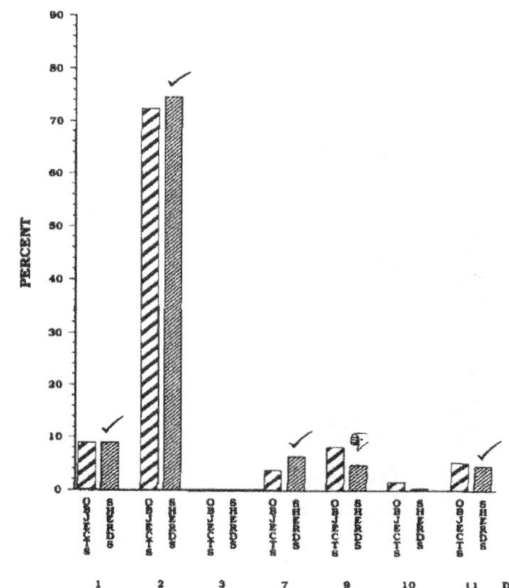

FIGURE 6. Big house: comparison of object and sherd proportions by decoration (total objects, 134; total sherds, 690). (Drawing by Dorothea Larsen.)

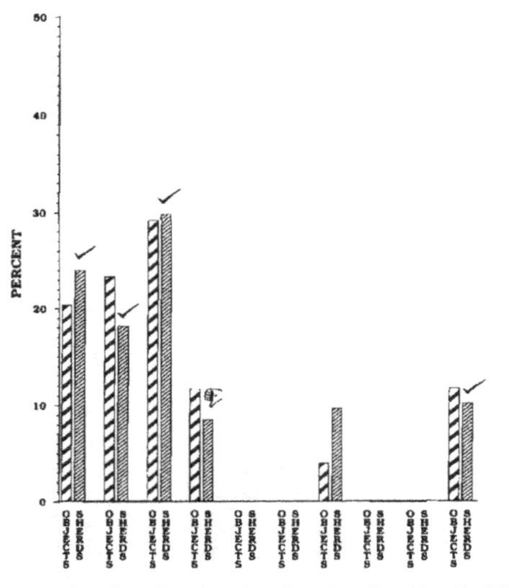

FIGURE 7. Farmer's house: comparison of object and sherd proportions by item (total objects, 103; total sherds, 188). (Drawing by Dorothea Larsen.)

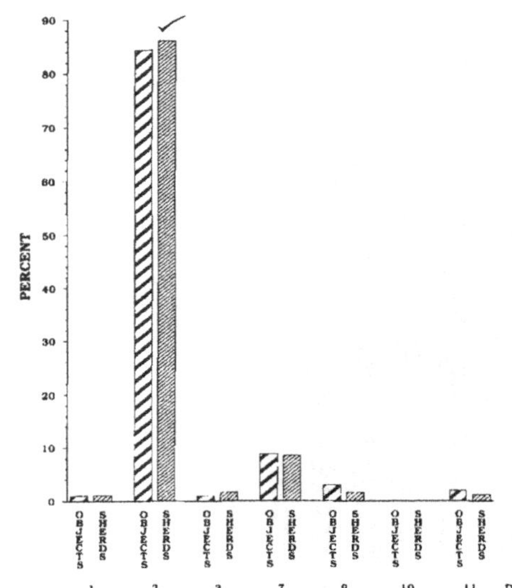

FIGURE 8. Farmer's house: comparison of object and sherd proportions by decoration (total objects, 103; total sherds, 188). (Drawing by Dorothea Larsen.)

is not related to vessel size, and partly to the extraordinary dominance of a single decorative type (60% of all ceramics on the site are transfer-printed). It is not necessary to count either sherds or objects to conclude that every structure's ceramic assemblage is made up largely of transfer-printed pieces.

When the assemblages from all of the structures are combined, the differences between proportions of items based on sherd counts and those based on object counts are smaller. The bar graphs (Figures 13-14) compare proportions of items based on sherds with those based on objects for the whole site. If questions are asked about the site generally (such as, what are the most common items from the site?), both the sherd counts and the object counts tell the same thing. If conclusions about the site are to be accomplished by comparing proportions of some of the larger items such as washbasins, chamber pots, and servers, then these conclusions are on shakier ground. The data on more than half the item types are unreliable if proportions based on sherd counts are used.

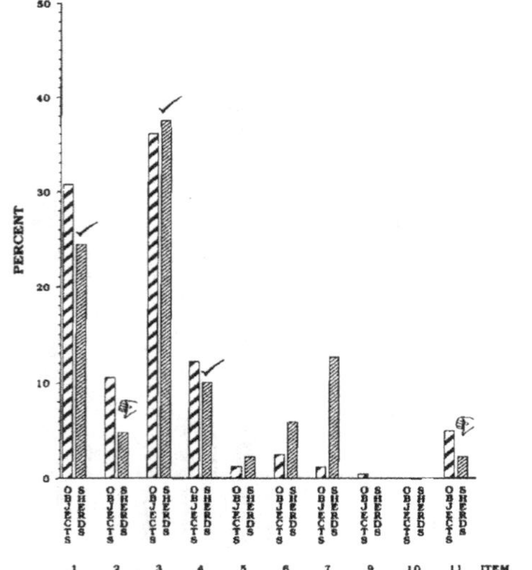

FIGURE 9. Fur loft/store: comparison of object and sherd proportions by item (total objects, 247; total sherds, 1639). (Drawing by Dorothea Larsen.)

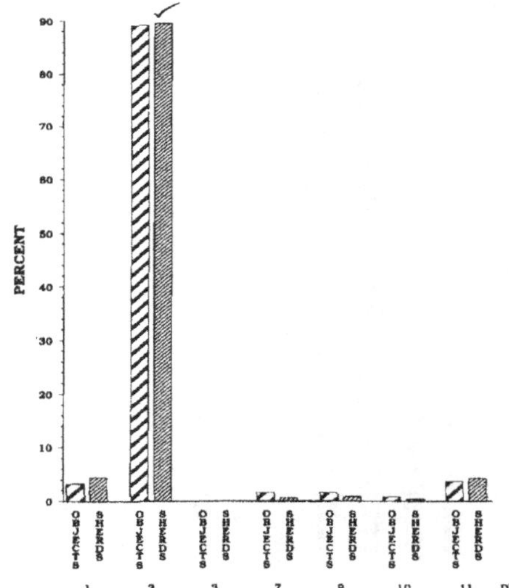

FIGURE 10. Fur loft/store: comparison of object and sherd proportions by decoration (total objects, 247; total sherds, 1639). (Drawing by Dorothea Larsen.)

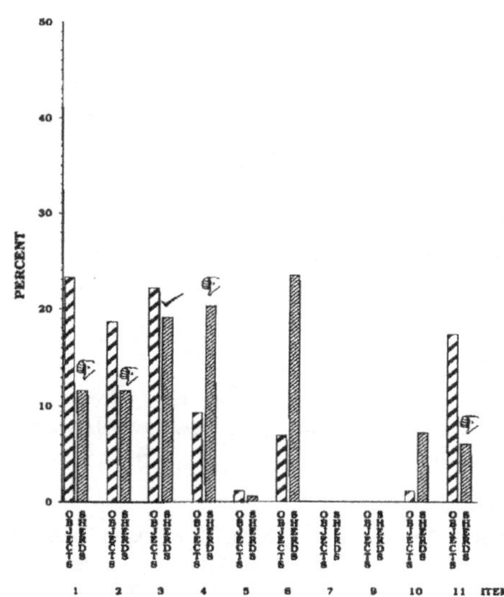

FIGURE 11. Unidentified structure: comparison of object and sherd proportions by item (total objects, 86; total sherds, 345). (Drawing by Dorothea Larsen.)

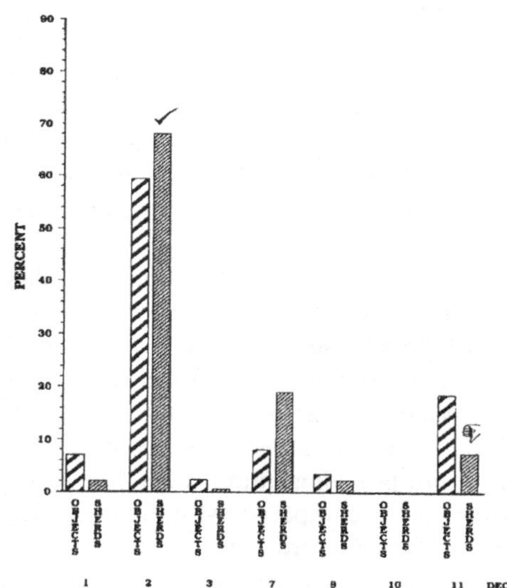

FIGURE 12. Unidentified structure: comparison of object and sherd proportions by decoration (total objects, 86; total sherds, 345). (Drawing by Dorothea Larsen.)

Conclusions

The purpose of this exercise in duplicate counting has been to see what happens when sherd counts are used as the equivalents of object counts. These are the results:

1. When sherd counts are used directly, the results can be truly nightmarish. It is now obvious why statisticians discourage chi-square tests with sherd counts.

2. When sherd proportions are used to compare occurrences of traits between structures (i.e., between samples that are much smaller than the whole site), the results are alarmingly different from those using object proportions. On the basis of our results, correlation statistics using sherd frequencies are almost as bad as chi-square tests using sherd counts.

3. When comparing proportions by themselves, one can only evaluate the *appearance* of difference or likeness between sherd counts and object counts. Based on this intuitive approach, it is my impression that if using a large sample (7790 sherds equaling 1938 objects have been

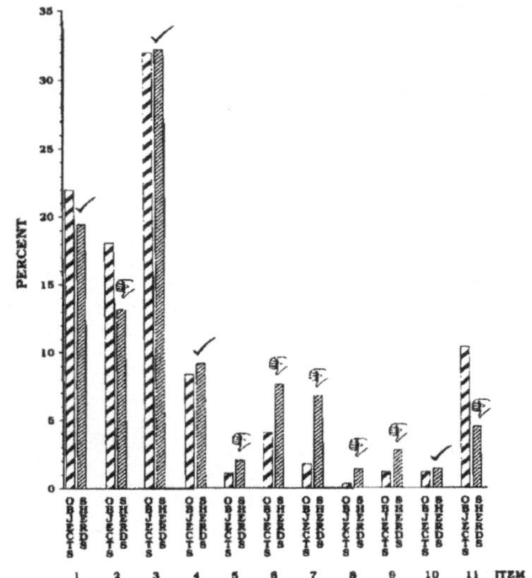

FIGURE 13. All structures: comparison of object and sherd proportions by item. (Drawing by Dorothea Larsen.)

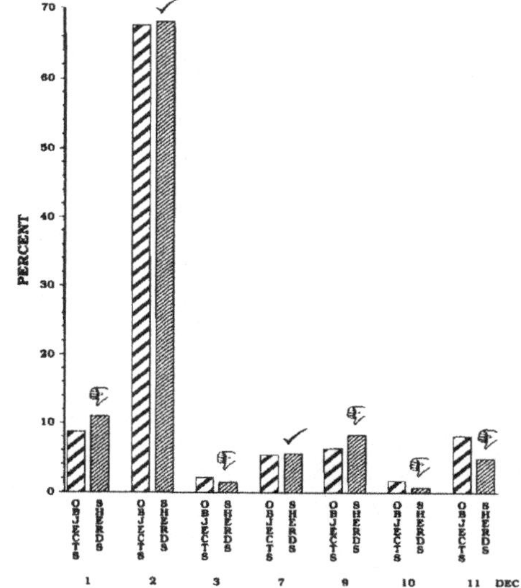

FIGURE 14. All structures: comparison of object and sherd proportions by decoration. (Drawing by Dorothea Larsen.)

recovered from Lower Fort Garry), and if counting traits that are not linked to vessel size (knowing this might be problematical), there is a reasonable hope that the proportions based on sherd counts approximate those based on object counts. On the other hand, these proportions can never be used comparatively because they have no mathematical validity.

The simple statistics and counting described in this work are standards in the repertoire of archaeological research. They are used to demonstrate differences or similarities among groups. When archaeologists report on the quantities of ceramic found at their sites, they presumably are providing information that allows these sites to be compared with others. The numbers they provide are meant to be used rigorously. That is, differences among the ceramic types themselves or among the sites will be looked for using just the techniques used in this paper. The question has been: are groups of sherds equivalent to groups of objects? Yes? No? Sort of? Sometimes? The answer did not prove to be a surprise: no. The surprise lay in the degree of the differences that resulted when the same material was counted as sherds and as objects. Based on what has been seen with the data from a respectably large site, it is concluded that for any serious research purposes, sherd counts cannot be used as substitutes for object counts.

ACKNOWLEDGEMENTS

I am grateful to Duncan MacLeod, the anonymous statistician whose presence is so evident in the text above. I relied not only on his statistical expertise but on his nose for intellectual trickery. Thanks are also due to the computer analyst, Richard Aylesworth and to Dan Pittman who entered the data into an electronically retrievable form.

REFERENCES

Burgh, Robert F.
1959 Ceramic Profiles in the Western Mound at Awatovi, Northeastern Arizona. *American Antiquity* 25(2):184-202.

Chase, Philip G.
1985 Whole Vessels and Sherds: An Experimental Investigation of their Quantitative Relationships. *Journal of Field Archaeology* 12:213-218.

Chism, James V.
1972 Excavations at Lower Fort Garry, 1965-67. *Canadian Historic Sites: Occasional Papers in Archaeology and History* 5. Ottawa, Ontario.

Egloff, B. J.
1973 A Method for Counting Ceramic Rim Sherds. *American Antiquity* 38(3):351-353.

MacLeod, Duncan
1990 Analysis of Data to Compare Accuracy of Object-Based and Sherd-Based Information. Manuscript, Parks Canada, Ottawa, Ontario.

Sussman, Lynne
1972 The Ceramics from Lower Fort Garry. Parks Canada, *Manuscript Report Series* 87. Ottawa, Ontario.
1990 Catalogue of Sherds and Objects Excavated at Lower Fort Garry. Manuscript, Parks Canada, Ottawa, Ontario.

Lynne Sussman
Low, Québec J0X 2C0
Canada

DOROTHY M. GRIFFITHS

Use-Marks on Historic Ceramics: A Preliminary Study

ABSTRACT

Researchers have traditionally relied on object shape as the basis for inferences on artifact utilization at historic sites, ignoring the problems of multiple use, consumer substitution of one functional shape for another, and intensity of utilization of different artifacts. The methodology tends to posit a greater degree of homogeneity in consumer activities than may have existed in the past. The analysis of residual marks (or use-marks) produced during the actual use of an object is one of the procedures which can deal with this problem. Ceramic artifacts in particular lend themselves to this type of analysis owing to their physical properties.

A preliminary examination of scratches on various 18th century lead-glazed earthenwares from Canadian historic sites in the Parks Canada collection, and in collections of similar material in England, has shown that use-marks provide readily observable attributes for the investigation of actual artifact utilization.

Investigations in material culture research include the correct identification of building or area function, the range of activities, and the spatial arrangement of such activities, as well as the precise dating of structural and non-structural remains. Historical documents usually lack sufficient data on normal living patterns and behavior (normal is here used to mean whatever was regarded as commonplace by the person who wrote the document). The majority of this information must be obtained from analyses of the type, quantity, distribution, and contexts of artifacts recovered from excavation. In addition, historical data may conflict concerning function and activities at a site, or they may have been recorded for only a limited segment of the occupation. Thus the artifact studies serve also to expand or cross-check the validity and adequacy of documentary data.

While the dating of artifacts is relatively simple, the identification of artifact utilization and the derivation of inferences on site/structure function, patterns of activity, site population, social stratification, or social interaction are considerably more complicated. In order to draw such inferences researchers have, in the past, relied on type-specific attributes, such as the ware type (e.g., creamware), object shape (e.g., dinner plate) and decoration (e.g., blue-painted). Heavy reliance has also been placed on catalogs, advertisements, or illustrations (compiled or commissioned by the ceramic manufacturers) as a means of developing indices of artifact utilization. These indices, in conjunction with physical attributes, are rarely conclusive or specific enough to permit more than broad generalisations to be made on artifact use.

Morphological attributes, including the shape of an essentially complete object, can be used for determination of the function for which the object was produced. However, since the consumer is equally an active agent in determining the specific use of an object, such information provides only a gross framework for beginning analysis of the utilization of objects recovered from a site. Thus problems of multiple use of an object and the substitution of one functional shape for another (usually as a result of the scarcity of certain functional shapes) are critical problems to be considered within site interpretation. To conduct valid contextual analyses, investigations must begin with the correct identification of object function at a site.

One of the procedures for increasing and clarifying information on object function and utilization is through detailed observations of the residual marks produced during the actual use of an object. Due to the intrinsic nature of the material, ceramics is one of the classes of artifacts amenable to use-mark analysis. Since use-marks occur on sherds, the function of the original object may be identified even when only fragments remain. Observations based on preliminary examinations of ceramics from Fort Beauséjour and other Canadian historic sites and collections of excavated and mu-

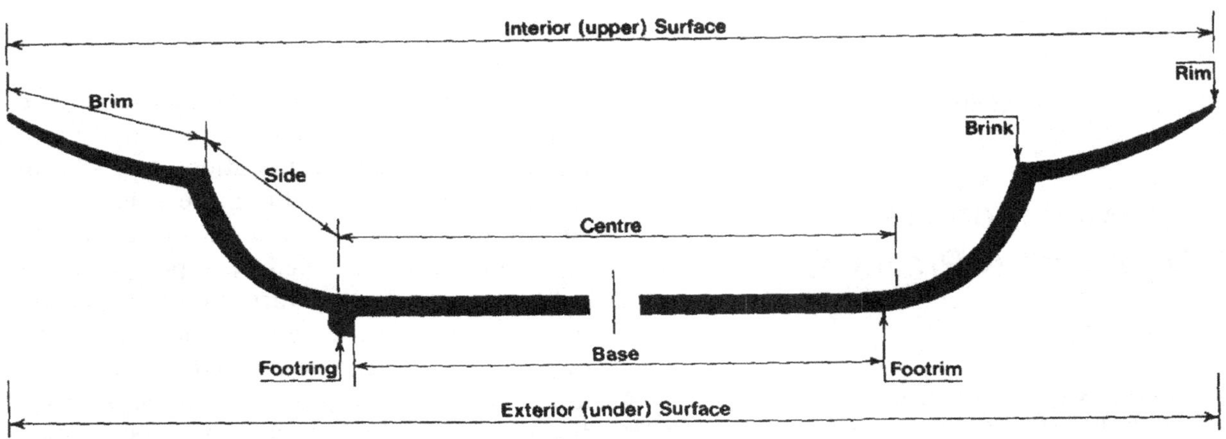

FIGURE 1. Parts of a Plate (Terminology). N.B. Half sections of two different plates are drawn. The terminology applies to platters as well as all sizes of plates.

seum specimens in England indicate that the study of use-marks is feasible with historic ceramic material.

During the initial stages of this research, it was assumed that use-mark analysis would facilitate the identification of *object shape*. That is, it would be possible to examine the use-marks on sherds from certain portions of an object and then be possible to state that they were once part of a dinner plate. This assumption was only partly correct, and the major usefulness of this research is in the identification of *object function*. Thus a researcher may examine the use-marks on sherds from certain portions of an object and be able to state that they were once part of an object used as a dinner plate.

There is a substantial difference between object shape and object function although fortunately the two are often congruent. As utilized in this paper, the former term is the shape created by the manufacturer to serve a certain function and (to promote its sale) usually named by him in such a way as to indicate the purpose for which it was intended. Thus the factory pattern books are replete with such terms as teapot, coffeepot, tea cup, coffee cup, sugar bowl, etc. Object function is the term for the function(s) actually served by the object during its useful life, from the time it was bought to that point when it was broken and finally discarded.

Since shapes of ceramic vessels are legion, it was initially necessary to limit the study to those shapes most commonly recovered from historic site excavations, viz., soup and dinner plates; tea, coffee and beverage cups, and bowls; slop and utility bowls; mixing, punch, and washbowls; and chamberpots. There is ample evidence, however, that sherds from vessels serving other functions (such as mugs, jugs, teapots, coffeepots, meat dishes, etc.) will be identifiable after more study. Further, it was decided to limit the scope of the study to one category of use-marks, i.e., scratches into the fabric and glaze of a vessel.

Finally, it was deemed necessary to select a glaze type which would be relatively easily marked during use by such implements as knives, forks, spoons, etc. Therefore 18th century lead-glazed earthenwares were chosen for the study and, in view of the very extensive series of ware types covered by this glaze (ranging from coarse earthenware through fine earthenware to soft paste porcelain), the scope of the study was further nar-

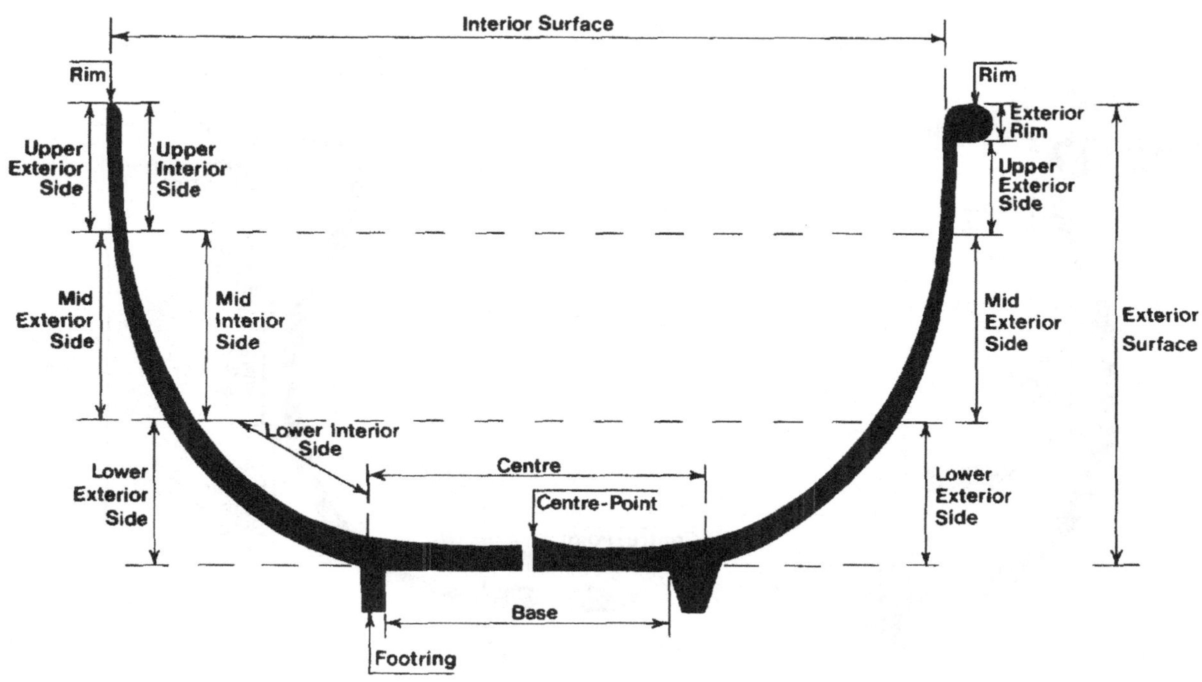

FIGURE 2. Parts of a Bowl (Terminology). N.B. Half sections of two different bowls are drawn. The terminology applies to cups as well as all sizes of bowls. Handles are excluded.

rowed to a fine earthenware group of ware types in which vessels were produced which were, generally speaking, socially accepted alternatives of each other during use. These ware types are: tin-glazed earthenware, Astbury and Jackfield type red earthenware, cream colored earthenware, creamware, and pearlware. It must be borne in mind that all these ware types were not in use simultaneously, but from about 1740-1800 some were used together (along with white stoneware which was omitted from this study because of its harder fabric and salt glaze), and as one ware type faded from popularity, another in this group took its place.

Apart from making the study more manageable, these ware types were selected because there are a number of morphological shapes, common to all the wares, which were produced in considerable quantity (e.g., beverage wares, teawares, dinnerwares, and toiletwares). Thus it was envisioned that scratches, peculiar to the shapes and functions under investigation, would become more apparent across all the ware types and, by their prevalence, would help to identify and dismiss those random scratches that might be expected to occur as a result of the sherds being jostled together during excavation, washing, and sorting.

During the course of this research it has been most useful to examine the use-marks on modern ceramics in constant, specialized use at home and in restaurants. This was of assistance in discerning the original tentative use-mark categories and varieties.

The observations indicate consistent differences in the marks left by various methods of utilization. For example, objects consistently used as dinner-plates are characterized by the

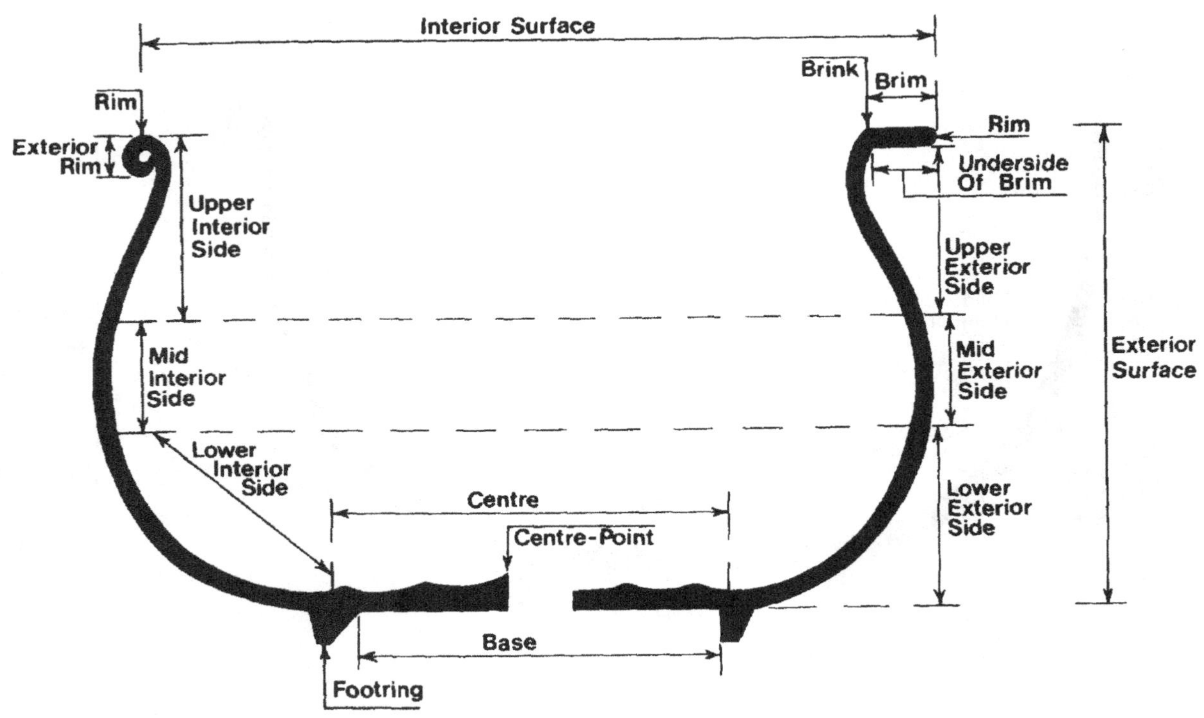

FIGURE 3. Parts of a Chamberpot (Terminology). N.B. *Half sections of two different chamberpots are drawn.* Handles are excluded.

presence of two varieties of use-marks: "knife cuts" and "fork-or-spoon scratches (Figures 14, 15, 16)." In contrast, objects consistently used as soup plates are characterized by the presence of only the latter type of use-marks. Although these are basically the same as those on dinner-plates, the incidence of the longer, curving lines is greater, "knife cuts" being almost entirely absent (Figures 5, 6, 7).

Some seven categories of use-marks have been identified on the basis of research thus far. These consist of:

1. *Fire-blackening* of the outside of the vessel resulting from its being placed upon, over, or beside a cooking fire or of the inside of a vessel being used to contain fire or hot coals.
2. *Cracking of the fabric and/or crazing of the glaze* of a vessel resulting from localized contact with heat or intense thermal shock.
3. *Spalling* of the surface of a vessel, usually the interior, possibly resulting from the crystallization of salt impurities carried into the fabric of a vessel by various liquids and left behind, to form crystals, when the liquid medium evaporates.
4. *Scratches* into the fabric and/or glaze of a vessel resulting from the use of cooking utensils or cutlery or even certain types of cleaning or storage (Figures 5-17).
5. *Staining* of the fabric and/or the glaze-crazing of a vessel.
6. *Etching* of the glaze when attacked by various acidic liquids stored in the vessel.
7. *Deposits* on the fabric and/or glaze resulting from long storage, insufficient cleaning, or high temperature cooking of contents.

These categories are divided into varieties.

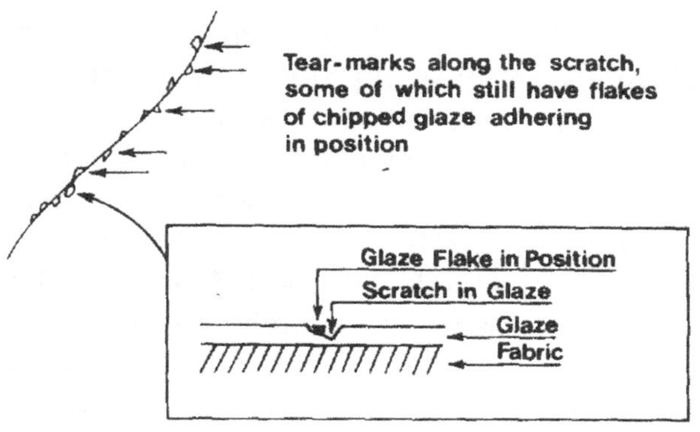

FIGURE 4. "Jostled" Scratch. Diagram in plan and in section of a non-use-related scratch which may appear similar to scratches in category #4.

For example, category four includes such distinctive use-mark varieties as:

a. knife cuts
b. fork or spoon scratches
c. stirring scratches
d. beating marks
e. abrasion (e.g., of the footring)
f. scouring scratches
g. storage marks

Among the category four use-marks, four varieties are most diagnostic of object function; the other three being primarily useful in the identification of type and degree of useage. The four most diagnostic marks are: knife cuts, fork or spoon scratches, stirring scratches, and beating marks.

Category 4 use-scratches become more easily visible if the glaze is rubbed with a soft lead pencil and then lightly wiped clean with a soft dry cloth. Where the glaze is unscratched the pencil lead will wipe free, but a deposit will be left in the scratches. This pencil lead washes off easily, but care should be taken not to allow it to enter joins between sherds, nor onto unglazed areas of the vessel since it is very difficult, if not well-nigh impossible, to eradicate it from these areas.

There is not space here to discuss the many varieties of use-marks, but as an example, it may be of interest to describe some of those mentioned above. Knife cuts, fork or spoon scratches, footring abrasion, and storage marks are found on objects consistently used as dinner plates. Knife cuts are the heaviest, cut most deeply into the glaze, and they tend to have distinct little tears along the edges of the cut where flakes of glaze have been chipped off by the knife blade. They usually form fairly straight lines of various lengths, depths, and widths, occasionally ending in a tiny hook. Generally, they are scattered all over the plate center (for vessel terminology see Figures 1, 2, 3) in haphazard directions, rarely continuing *onto* the plate sides. The heaviest of the knife cuts often seem to be in the middle of the plate center or run from side

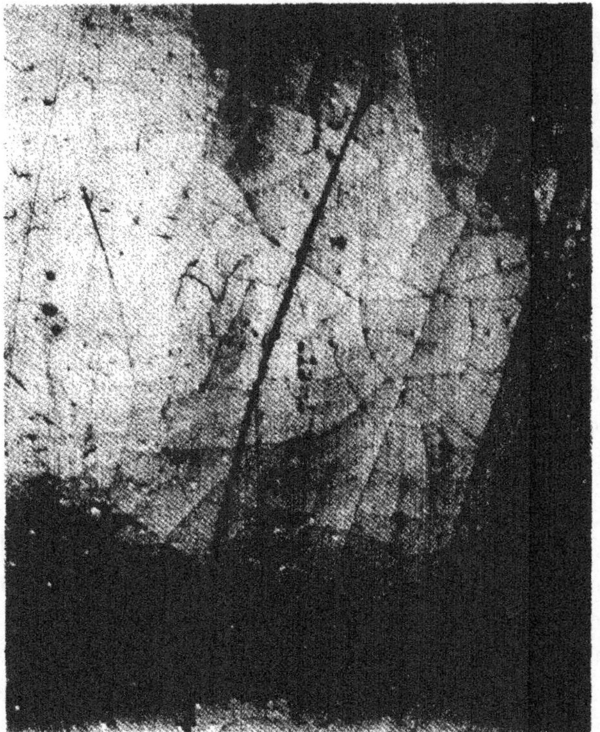

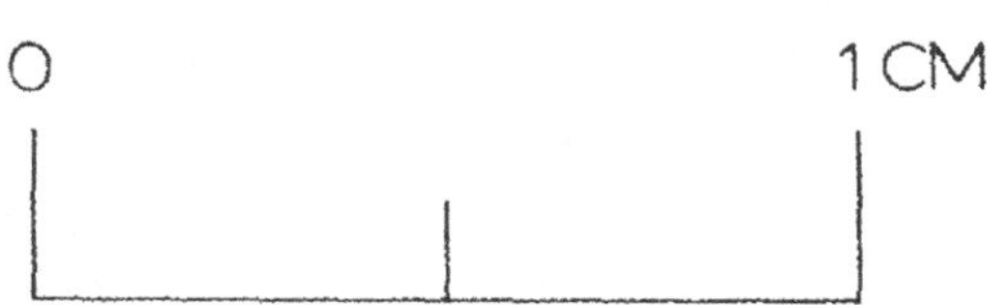

FIGURE 5. Soup plate, center (detail); light use, spoon-scratches; use history known. Late 19th century creamware, Staffordshire, England.

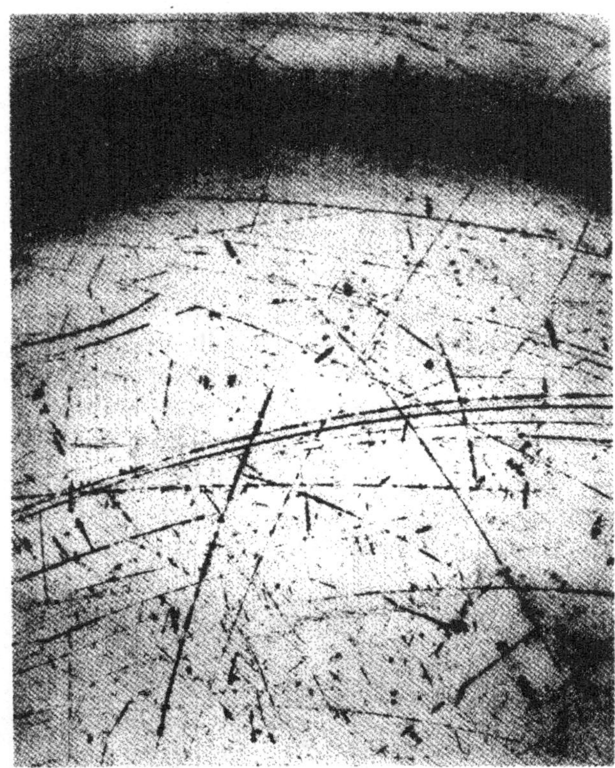

FIGURE 6. Soup plate, center (detail); heavy use, spoon-scratches; use history known. 20th century white earthenware, Staffordshire, England.

to middle. The fork or spoon scratches are much lighter than the typical knife cut and, more often than not, they cover the plate center (often extending on the plate sides) with a haze of short random lines or they curve in longer, sweeping lines over and around the plate center. Short zigzag lines are also common. Minute tears along the edges of these scratches may be discerned with the aid of a magnifying glass, but generally they appear to be smooth scratches (especially by comparison with the knife cuts), and their depth does not vary so much (see Figures 5-7, 14-17).

In contrast, objects consistently used as soup plates are characterised by the presence of the fork or spoon scratches, usually accompanied by the supporting footring abrasion and storage marks. Although the fork or spoon scratches are basically the same as those occurring on dinner plates, the incidence of the longer, curving lines is greater, knife cuts being almost entirely absent (see Figures 5-7).

Use-marks on the footrim or footring take the form of simple abrasion dulling the brilliance of the glaze or scratching it with short, haphazard, criss-cross lines. On the whole the degree of useage indicated on the footring usually agrees with that on the plate center (see Figure 17). Plates with few or no cutlery marks do not normally exhibit worn footrings; moderate cutlery marks are usually reflected by moderate to deep wear in the glaze of the footring; extensively worn plates, heavily

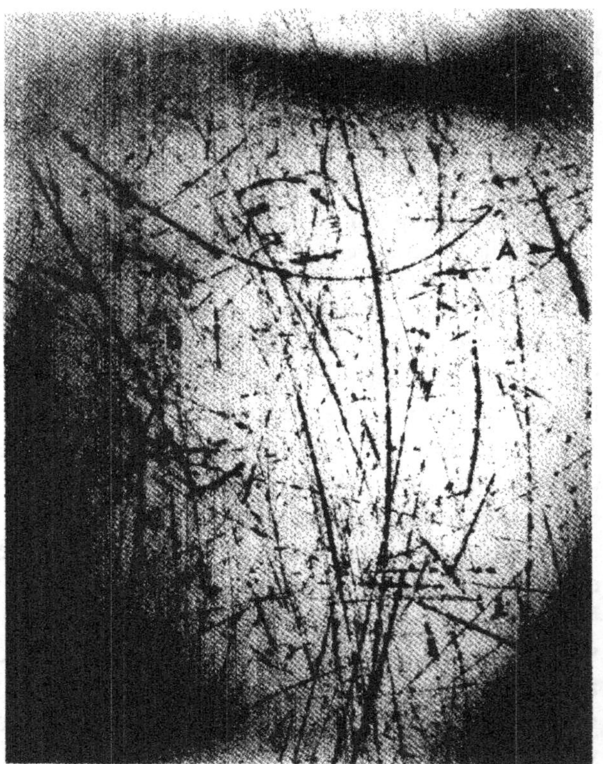

FIGURE 7. Soup plate, center (detail); heavy use, spoon-scratches, some knife-cuts (A and B). 20th century white earthenware, Staffordshire, England.

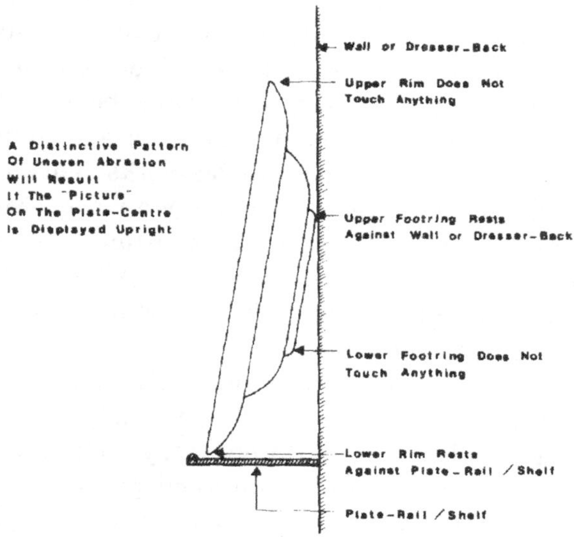

FIGURE 8. Plate display. Abrasion will result where the surfaces of the object touch those of its support. If a picture on the plate center is displayed upright, a distinctive pattern of uneven abrasion will result. See for example, figures 9 to 13.

marked by cutlery, usually have well worn footrings—even to the extent of the glaze being almost completely worn through or, in a few extreme cases, even the fabric itself being worn.

When the footring exhibits less useage than is indicated by the plate center, it may indicate that the plate was customarily used on a non-abrasive surface (perhaps that a tablecloth was habitually used by the owner of the plates, especially if several plates of the same pattern exhibit the same peculiarity) or that they were stored more carefully than normal (either on cloth covered shelves or stacked with cloth or paper inserted as a buffer between them).

When the footring exhibits more useage than is manifested by the plate center, it may indicate one or several types of use or storage:

1. The use of cutlery that was not hard enough, or sharp enough, to scratch the glaze.
2. Useage in a capacity other than as a soup plate or dinner plate, e.g., serving dish, cake plate, pie dish, etc. In such cases other categories of use-marks should support the inference, such as widespread food staining in the glaze-crazing and even in the fabric of the object, if it had been used as a pie dish.
3. Storage in stacks but without the use of a buffer material; in these case (depending upon the form of the vessel—i.e., which parts of one vessel were likely to touch which parts of another during stacking) the brink and underside of a plate or the perimeter of the plate center may exhibit faint abrasions corresponding approximately to the diameter of plate footrings. It may be that, in addition to the plate footrings of one plate abrading the glaze of the one beneath it, the gritty dust that accumulates on objects stored for any length of time was enough to add a few scratches between touching surfaces whenever they were next moved, especially among the lowermost vessels of a heavy stack.

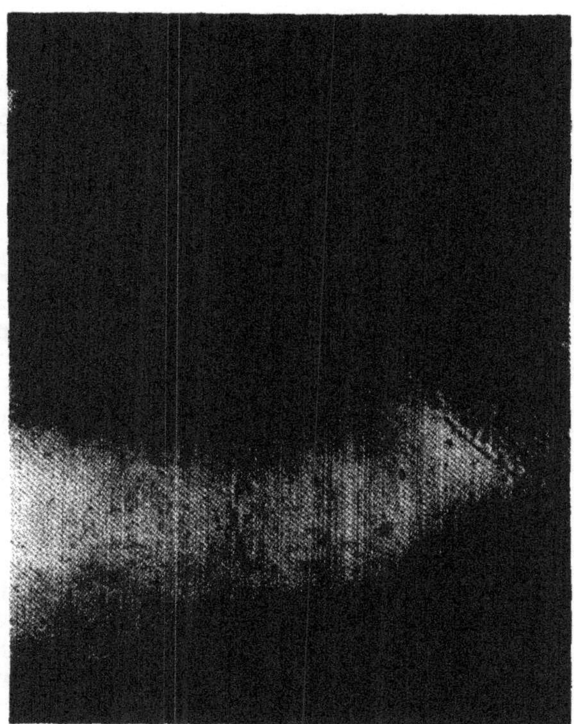

FIGURE 9. Dinner plate, center (detail); decorative use, note absence of use-marks; use history known. Third quarter of the 18th century, tin-glazed earthenware, probably Bristol, England.

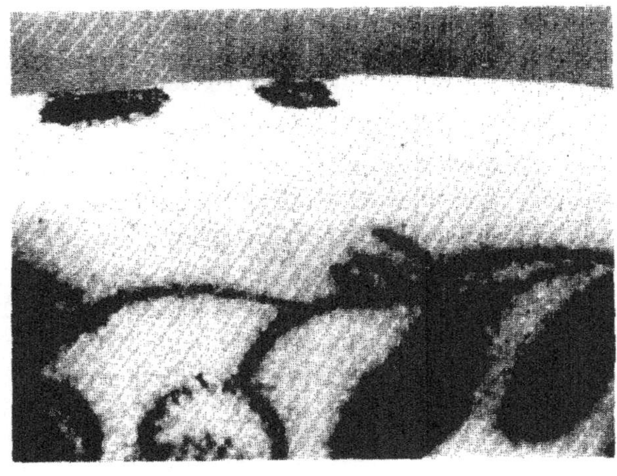

FIGURE 10. Dinner plate, upper rim (detail); decorative use, some chipping but little or no abrasion; use history known. Third quarter of the 18th century, tin-glazed earthenware, probably Bristol, England.

4. Hanging against a wall or dresser-back. In such cases if there are no holes for suspension in the rim or footring there should be some chips around the rim indicating the use of pewter or wire hangers or staining at certain points on the rim or the footring resulting from contact with the metal hanger (especially if iron wire was used).
5. Leaning against a wall or dresser-back, which should cause some abrasion of the rim by friction between the rim and the shelf on which it stood. If the plate bears a pattern (e.g., a scene) which is meant to be viewed from one angle, it is likely that it would have been placed on the shelf in an "upright" position. Therefore it would be expected that abrasion of the rim corresponding to the bottom of the picture and abrasion of the footring (caused by friction between the footring and the wall or dresser-back against which it was leaning) corresponding to the top of the picture would appear (Figures 8-13).

Teabowls, coffee cups, and beverage bowls exhibit "stirring marks" in a haze of shallow, sweeping lines in random directions around and over the center of the vessel and up onto the lower sides. Occasionally shorter, straighter lines rather resembling "beating marks" have been noted. These may, perhaps, be accounted for by individual idiosyncrasies in stirring additional substances, such as milk or sugar, into the beverage. Also some teabowls and coffee cups have been noted with worn footrings and fabric or glaze-craze staining, but with no stirring marks. This may indicate that the individual who used such vessels did not add other substances to the beverage being drunk, though whether this was through choice or force of circumstances is open to question.

The presence of a group of drinking vessels from a site, some of which exhibit stirring marks while others do not, may well indicate private instead of institutional possession of these objects. This is the case since it is highly unlikely that vessels, provided by the establishment for the use of all, would consistently fall to the user who did not, for example, take sugar in his tea.

Depending upon the shapes and functions under consideration, an object may exhibit one or more categories of use-marks. Thus a

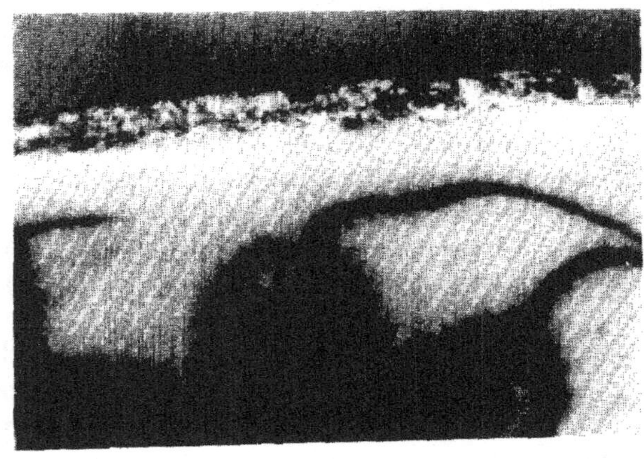

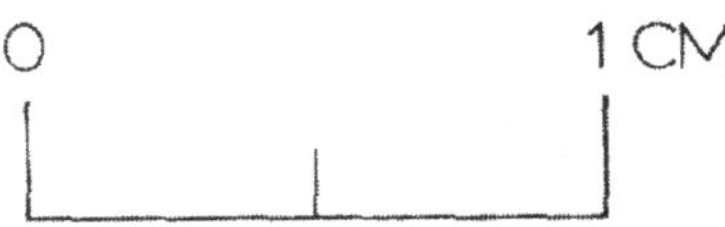

FIGURE 11. Dinner plate, lower rim (detail); decorative use, some chipping but very extensive abrasion. The glaze is completely worn away and even the fabric is abraded. Use history is known. Third quarter of the 18th century, tin-glazed earthenware, probably Bristol, England.

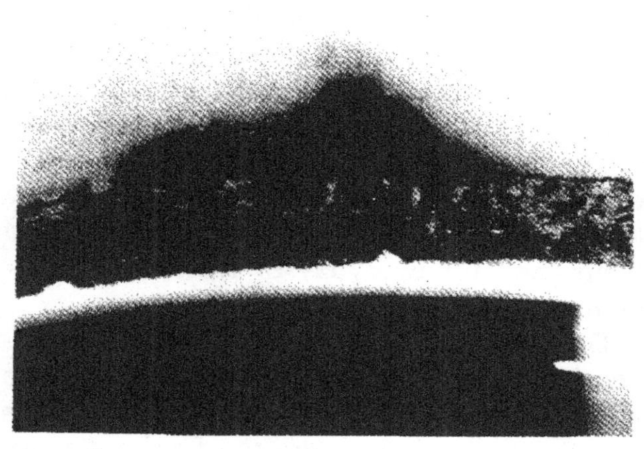

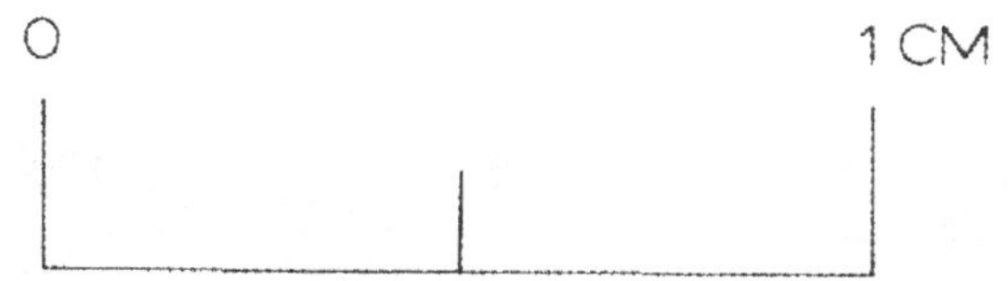

FIGURE 12. Dinner plate, upper footring (detail); decorative use, very extensive abrasion. The glaze is completely worn away and even the fabric is abraded. Use history is known. Third quarter of the 18th century, tin-glazed earthenware, probably Bristol, England.

dinner plate may be most easily identified by two varieties in the scratches category, i.e., the knife cuts and the fork or spoon scratches, but it is also likely to have heat related glaze-crazing (especially on the plate base and center) and perhaps even cracks in the fabric. In many cases, a certain amount of food staining is found in the crazing and the cracks.

Use-mark analysis provides a set of object specific attributes which relate particularly to the useful life of each object, and which may be utilized in terms of the specific use of each object from a site. Eventually, when the field of use-marks is more fully explored, artifacts excavated from historic sites may be studied in relation to each other according to the type and degree of use-marks they all received during use. This will enable archaeologists and material culture researchers to make more meaningful statements about excavated site material.

Use-mark research can be of assistance at several different stages of research. It can facilitate the sorting of sherds into functional groupings by type and, possibly, by degree of useage. In addition it can promote the assessment of object-quantities for activity pattern and site population studies by making cross-mending easier, especially among the multitude of curved side and flat base sherds. It is these types of sherds which occur so commonly in excavations and often fail to exhibit other features which can be used to sort them.

Use-mark research will assist in identifying shape function categories within the varieties of object shape. Thus comparisons can be made between the useage intended by the manufacturer and the actual treatment by the user of historic ceramic objects. This should also promote the identification of patterns of activity within and between different areas of a site. By examining similar object-shapes it will be possible to compare the type, variety,

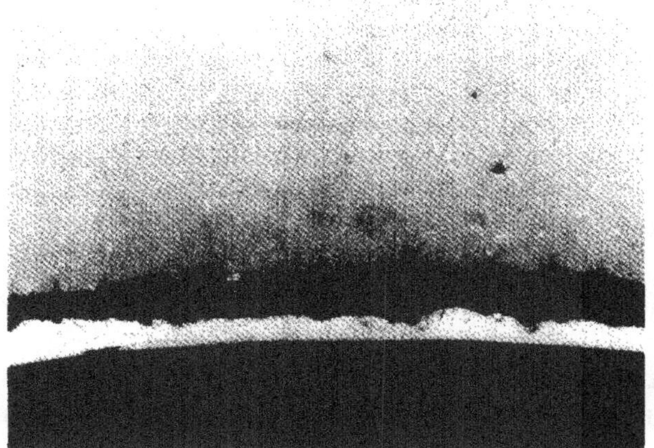

FIGURE 13. Dinner plate, lower footring (detail); decorative use, moderate abrasion. The glaze is completely worn away on the most prominent outer edge, but remains intact on the normal resting surface. Use history is known. Third quarter of the 18th century, tin-glazed earthenware, probably Bristol, England.

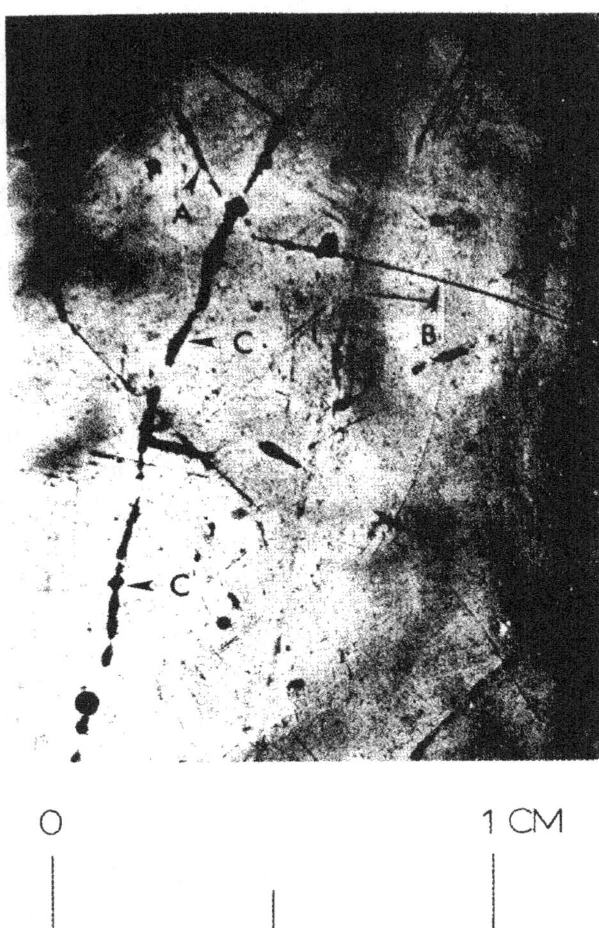

FIGURE 14. Dinner plate, center (detail); light use, knife cuts? (e.g., A), fork-spoon-scratches (e.g., B), long unusual cutting or gouged mark (C); use history not known. Late 18th century creamware, England.

and degree of use-marks. Analyses can also be undertaken to determine which objects should be omitted from an initial activity pattern study, i.e., those that arrived on the site broken in transit, were discarded, and thus were never used on that site.

Use-mark analysis further can be undertaken as an ancillary means of assessing the social status of one group of site occupants relative to another. For example, if one group constantly used a particular variety of moderately expensive ceramics whereas another group used the same variety of ceramics only occasionally, it might be possible to infer that the former group was more affluent than the latter. Of course, hopefully higher status would be indicated not only by use-wear but also by the presence of a greater quantity and variety of objects than in the lower status home. But without an indication of the degree of useage, a researcher would not necessarily know whether such a group of objects had been used for everyday or for special occasions.

Despite the optimism this writer feels concerning the utilization of use-mark analysis as a research tool in site interpretation, it is necessary at this juncture to offer cautionary notes regarding its use and to indicate some of

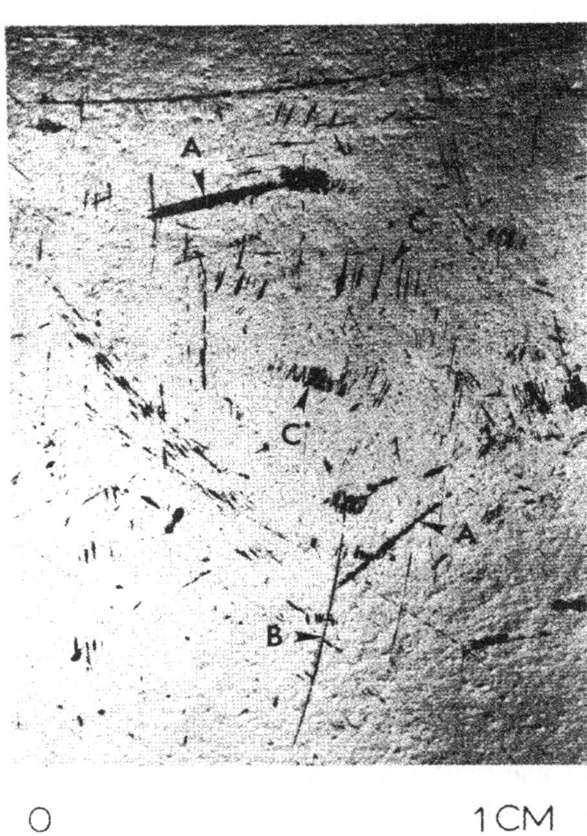

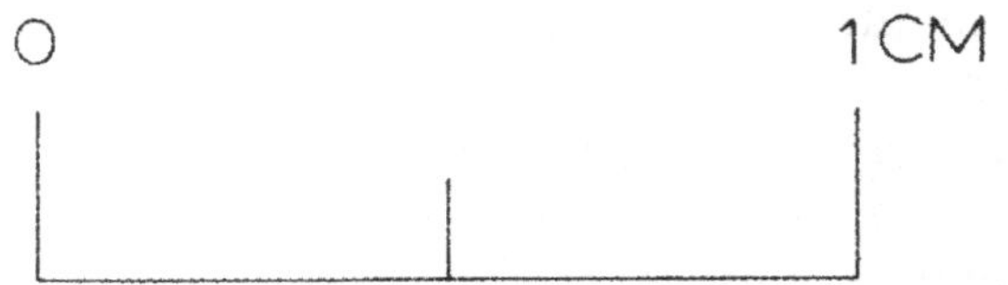

FIGURE 15. Dinner plate, center (detail); light to moderate use, knife-cuts (e.g., A), fork-mark (e.g., B), stacking/storage abrasion? (e.g., C); use history known. 20th century vitrified white earthenware, Staffordshire, England.

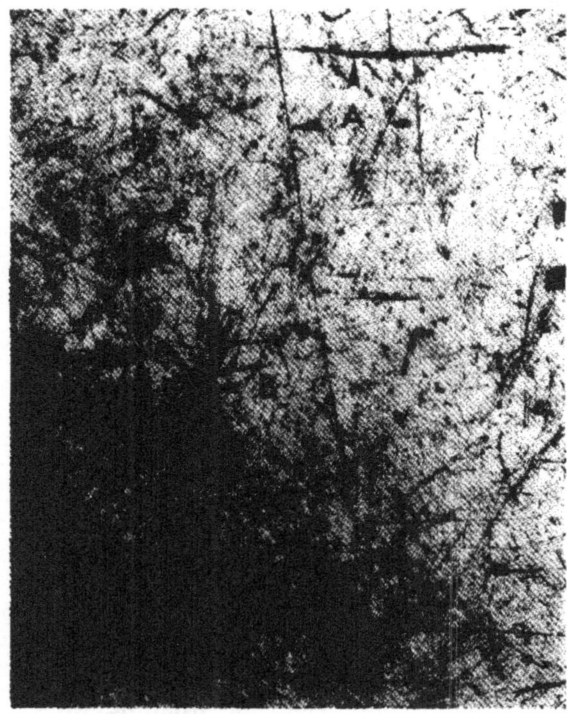

FIGURE 16. Dinner plate, center (detail); moderate to heavy use, knife-cuts (e.g., A), fork/spoon-marks (e.g., B), stacking/storage abrasion (short parallel scratches, e.g., C); use history not known. Second quarter of the 19th century white earthenware, Staffordshire, England.

the implications in terms of artifact processing and conservation and display techniques.

There are several pitfalls awaiting the unwary which, if not realized and allowed for, may skew the results of interpretive research.

1. Although a vessel may have been manufactured to serve a specific function, once it was in normal use on a historic site, it may have been used for another purpose. For example, occasionally soup plates were used as dinner plates, saucers were used as flowerpot stands, and handleless jugs were used as flower vases. When this occurs there should be some use-marks to indicate this re-use or conversion to other use. This serves to emphasize the point that *all* the use-marks on an object must be taken into account when identifying object function.
2. At the risk of seeming redundant, it is necessary to reiterate that use-mark analysis will *not* permit a researcher to examine a sherd and state that it was once part of a dinner plate. Instead it *will* be possible to examine it and state that it was once part of an object *used* as a dinner plate. This emphasizes the fact that the smaller the portion of a vessel under consideration, the less that can confidently be stated about the object of which it once formed a part. Only by gathering together sherds with similar use-marks and finding cross-mends among them until at least a portion of a vessel is assembled and a

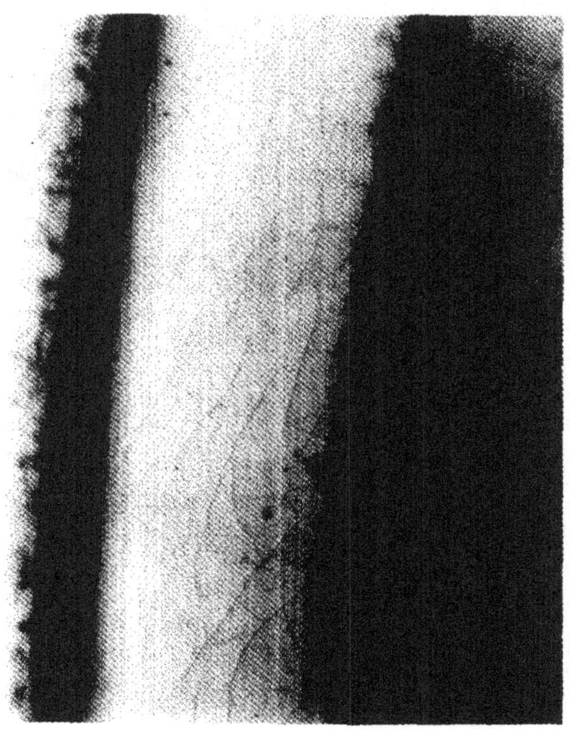

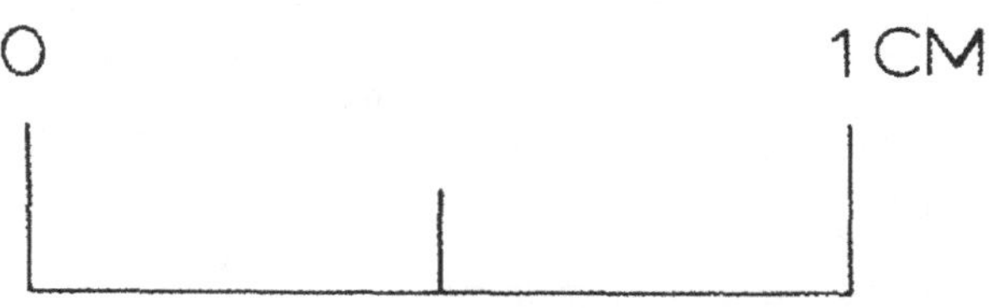

FIGURE 17. Dinner plate, center (detail); moderate to heavy use. This is a double footring and both footrings show abrasion, but on the one normally in contact with the table top, the abrasion is worn well into the glaze and staining of the abrasion and the underlying fabric has occurred. Use history not known. Second quarter of the 19th century white earthenware, Staffordshire, England.

pattern emerges, will it be possible to analyze all the use-marks (or absence thereof) to draw inferences about the type and degree of use the vessel originally received.

3. It should be noted that the definition of the degree of use-marks (that is light, moderate, extensive, etc.) varies between one object shape/function and another. A certain number of scratches per square inch on a dinner plate may be regarded as light useage, whereas the same number of scratches per square inch may be graded as moderate useage on a soup plate and as extensive on a meat dish.
4. It is important to note that different types of glaze will exhibit different degrees of use-marks, even when vessels of the same object shape and function have received the same degree of useage. For example, a creamware dinner plate with X number of scratches per square inch may be graded as showing moderate use. However, it may be that moderate useage on a white saltglazed stoneware dinner plate is represented by only half as many scratches per square inch because the harder glaze was less easily marked by cutlery. Similarly, a white earthenware dinner plate of the second half of the 19th century with the same degree of useage may be represented by even fewer scratches because its harder glaze was also less subject to abrasion.
5. It is possible that one or more objects which had been well used at one site were packed and transported to another site where, arriving broken in transit, they were immediately discarded. Such objects, especially a large quantity of them, could easily skew interpretation of the intensity and even type of activity inferred from the site material. This serves to illustrate the point that all of the excavated material must be used to draw inferences for site interpretative research.
6. Care must be taken to distinguish between category 4 scratches and those scratches which occur on sherds as a result of careless excavation and processing techniques. Jostling scratches can look like a knife cut (Figure 4) but are usually too deep and less straight or too light and aimless. A knife cut that extends to the edge of one sherd usually must continue onto the sherd adjoining that edge. It would be too much of a coincidence for the vessel to have broken just at the end of the knife cut, preventing it from continuing onto the adjoining sherd. Jostling scratches usually halt at the crossmend joints between sherds.
7. While it is difficult to distinguish between use-spalling and that caused by frost action or by soil salts during burial, there is one method to assist the analyst. Before the excavated material is sorted into ware types, it should be scanned for spalling common to groups of sherds of different ware types and different object shapes. If spalling occurs randomly among sherds of different ware types and/or different object shapes from a distinct layer or area of the site, it is likely that this is evidence of frost action or soil salt. If comparatively few sherds are spalled in any layer or area, or if the distribution of spalling is non-random, this spalling is likely to be use related, and the sherds may be grouped together.
8. The relative scratching properties of implements made from horn, wood, silver, pewter, and steel and whether they scratch only when sharp remain to be investigated. Is it possible that silver, pewter, and steel cutlery leave slightly different marks in the glaze?

There are several implications to be considered in terms of excavation, processing, conservation, and display procedures. During excavation, processing, and subsequent display, care should be taken not to add spurious use-marks (especially those resembling category 4) such as scratches from trowelling, screening, bagging, and sorting and storage marks during display. During washing, and later conservation, use-marks in categories 1 (fire blackening), 5 (staining), and 7 (deposits on the fabric and/or glaze of a vessel) should not be removed. At present many sherds with use-marks such as fire blackening of the outside of a cooking pot or dried tea from the inside of a broken tea cup reach the analyst in an almost pristine condition. Also, for illustration purposes, it is common practice to bleach out the fabric staining of category 5. Continuing these practices will skew the final results of use-mark research.

Although this study concentrated on 18th century lead glazed fine earthenwares, it is the author's impression that coarse earthenware, white saltglazed and other stonewares, and porcelain (whether soft paste, bone china or hard paste) are amenable to use-mark analysis. Those objects similar to the ones mentioned herein are likely to exhibit similar types of use-marks, while different objects, such as cooking pots, are likely to bear marks peculiar to their use and distinctly different to those outlined above. As an example, it would be wise to check the inside of a fire blackened cooking pot to see if it has stirring marks. Such marks might be left by a metal implement while stirring the contents during cooking. If no such marks are present, it could indicate that either a wooden implement was used for stirring or that the contents did not require stirring—such as water boiling. In the latter case, a ring of mineral deposit might remain as evidence of such useage.

The 18th century saltglazed, the 19th century "feldspathic" glazed fine stonewares, and the 19th century fine earthenwares have been omitted from the study. The salt and feldspathic glazes are much harder than the lead glaze of the 18th century fine earthenwares and are, therefore, less liable to be easily scratched by cutlery. However, it does seem that white stoneware vessels may be found to exhibit a certain (though probably fainter) degree of the use-marking. It may be that after more intensive research the other ware types will also be found to show some identifiable use-marks.

It was found during initial stages of this research that many of the fine earthenware vessels post dating 1850 exhibited less use-marking than was common on earlier vessels. There are probably a number of reasons for this, e.g., a growing population, flourishing economy, technologically advancing industry, an increasingly settled society, and an expanded transportation system interacted together to result in a greater quantity and variety of goods being available to more people at more moderate prices than ever before. It is also known that throughout the 19th century earthenware manufacturers were striving to produce a leadless glaze, and as a result of their experiments, the glazes made during that period contained progressively less lead. Such glazes as the boro-silicate and refined feldspathic glazes, only fluxed with lead, are harder than the pure lead variety and less subject to the same degree of abrasion. Hence, the absence of marks on this ware cannot automatically be taken as an absence of use, therefore, the hardness of these types of glazes must be borne in mind.

Use-marks on ceramics have been discussed to the exclusion of use-marks on other materials such as glass, metal, wood, leather, etc. This should not be taken as an indication that such marks do not occur on these other materials, nor that they are any less amenable to identification and function analysis. There is evidence to the contrary. It is likely that further study will reveal instances where the use-marks are similar to those occurring on ceramics, though perhaps differing in degree. In other instances where use-marks are entirely different from those on ceramics, new categories will have to be developed.

Analyses of use-marks, pioneered by Semenov (1964), has produced sophisticated results in prehistoric studies. Provisional results of this research indicate potential for application in historic period studies. In conjunction with documentary data from the factories, analysis can be undertaken on variability in consumer practices in the past, and assessments can be made on the relationship between producer and consumer. It is clear also that, without a reliable index for measuring variability in artifact utilization, social interpretations will be biased. When sufficient information has been gathered, more meaningful conclusions, in terms of type and variety of site activity, can be drawn from analyses of excavated site material.

ACKNOWLEDGEMENTS

I would like to thank my colleagues in the Material Culture Research Unit, National Historic Parks and Sites Branch, Parks Canada, and other colleagues and friends—too numerous to name—for their assistance and critical discussions. George Van Der Vlugt, now with the Conservation Division, National Historic Parks and Sites Branch, developed an ingenious method to photograph the detailed views of use marks on ceramics. DiAnn Herst, Acting Head of the Archaeology Section, National Historic Parks and Sites Branch, provided encouragement and assistance during the course of the research. Finally, James V. Sciscenti, Head, Environmental Impact Assessment Unit provided many invaluable criticisms on theoretical orientation and thrust of the research.

An earlier version of this paper was presented at the 1977 meetings of both the Society for Historical Archaeology and the Canadian Archaeology Association which met in Ottawa, Ontario.

REFERENCE

SEMENOV, S. A.
1964 *Prehistoric Technology*. Barnes and Noble, London.

DOROTHY M. GRIFFITHS
NATIONAL HISTORIC PARKS AND SITES BRANCH
PARKS CANADA
OTTAWA, ONTARIO K1A OH4

JOHN R. WHITE

Bottle Nomenclature: A Glossary of Landmark Terminology for the Archaeologist

ABSTRACT

Recognizing the lack of uniformity in the literature with regard to bottle nomenclature, an attempt is made to provide some degree of consistency. The problem does not lie entirely with the terminology currently being used but rather with a lack of a precise definition of that terminology. Although not exhaustive, the glossary should be of assistance to the average archaeologist.

Introduction

Some efforts more than others take their rise out of necessity. So it is with the following—a respectfully complete, though somewhat short of exhaustive, glossary of bottle nomenclature.

Recent work carried out at two historic archaeological sites in Northeastern Ohio, the Eaton (Hopewell) Furnace (33MH9) and the Austin Log House complex (33MH11) led to the recovery of hundreds of bottles and bottle fragments of various ages dating from the present back to the 1840's. When the time came to describe these ubiquitous artifacts, the writer found himself in a quandary of fair proportions, being totally unprepared for the abundance of terms being used to define and describe just the landmarks on glass bottles and jars. The examination of texts and treatises on bottles and bottlemaking soon led to the inevitable conclusion that: 1) authors often have their own idiosyncratic terms for some landmarks; 2) some terms are used in different ways (some slightly different, some grossly different) by different authors; 3) terms in common usage by the layman are often (if not usually) too imprecise (or even incorrect) for use in descriptive reports, and 4) somehow, some degree of uniformity had to be brought to the material. Answers to letters written to numerous experts reinforced this need.

The problem does not lie in the terminology used in describing types of containers or types of materials. There are, fortunately, a number of experts who can tell the archaeologists new to the field almost everything they need to know about shapes, uses, dates, material, styles, makers, and methods of bottle or glassmaking. Unfortunately for most archaeologists—and again this is especially true of the investigator newly arrived in the field of historic sites archaeology—the question they need most answered is that for which the answer is least available—the correct term to use in describing the bits and pieces of the artifact itself. In short, there is a need for a lexicon of bottle nomenclature.

It is true that at the back of some (but certainly not most) longer articles and texts there is a glossary of terms. But a perusal of these glossaries leaves the reader with the distinct impression that while the more unusual terms or those being applied in a unique way are defined, the more casual (and what end up being most vague) terms are the ones which most often are left undefined. Terms such as base, neck, lip, bead, collar, etc. are assumed to be part of the reader's vocabulary and are ignored. it seems that these "easy" words are by far the most difficult to grasp, the most elusive. Their elusiveness lies in their generality, their universality, their ultimate simplicity.

It is the goal of this paper to contain some of this elusiveness. Some of the definitions given herein can be found elsewhere in other forms, some stated in ways which the reader might perhaps find preferable to those here listed. However, most readers will find this lexicon more complete than most, at least in the area of bottle landmarks. As stated at the outset, this endeavor arose out of need; it is not exhaustive, especially to the bottle expert, but it should help the average archaeologist.

GLOSSARY

Applied lip: A lip applied to the neck after the bottle has been formed. It might be straight (Figure 1a), flaring (Figure 1b), or contracting (Figure 1c) or just a ring of glass trailed around the opening. Many forms exist.

Bail: That part of a toggle device which is connected to the lever wire and passes over the lid holding it in place on the bottle or jar. Also called *yoke*. (Figure 3).

Basal diameter: The diameter across the base of round or polygonal bottles.

Base: The surface of the bottle on which it rests when in an upright position; the bottom (Figure 3).

Bead: A raised ridge of glass having a convex section which encircles the neck of a bottle. The term itself can be applied to any such circle or molding; also a modifier indicating its specific location e.g. closure bead (Figure 1d), collar bead, (or beaded collar) (Figure 1e), etc.

Beaded seal: A bottle that makes its seal or point of maximum contact on a beaded ridge which encircles the bottle neck (Figure 1f).

Bernadin disc: A metal (usually tin) disc placed over wired cork stoppers to prevent them from being cut deeply by the taut wire. These discs were often made with scalloped edges to prevent slippage (Figure 1g).

Black glass: The name given to a thick, dark olive green glass. Often a container for porter or ale.

Blob top: The name given to the thick, rounded lip usually applied to the neck of bottles containing carbonated liquids (Figure 1h).

Bottle glass green: The natural aquamarine color of bottle glass resulting from the presence of iron oxides in the sand.

Bottom plate: The shallow depression in the bottom of machine-made bottles and jars designed to allow for stability and to serve as a nest for the closure of another bottle when stacking containers.

Bull's eye: The small, thick, translucent concentration of glass occurring on pieces of crown glass. It is the point at which the pontil was attached during rotation.

Bust-off and grind lip: Found on wide-mouthed bottles, it consists of a lip which was broken or sheared from the blowpipe and subsequently ground to a satin smoothness (Figure 1i).

Buttons: Small knobs or protruberances on the neck of bottles around which the lever wire of a toggle device was wrapped (Figure 1j).

Chip marks: See *whittle marks*.

Closure: A device, such as a cork, cap, stopper, etc., used to seal a bottle.

Closure Sidewall: The portion of the closure between the rolled edge and the top of the skirt (Figure 1k).

Closure skirt: The vertical part of a closure which fits to the outside of the bottle finish. It includes the *closure sidewall, curl* or *rolled edge,* and/or *flange* (Figure 1k).

Codd ball stopper: See *Codd stopper*.

Codd "face": The appearance of a "face" given to Codd stopper bottles by virtue of the addition of a pair of indentations in the bottle below the neck. These indentations served to catch the marble before it could reseal the bottle.

Codd stopper: (After Hiram Codd) A closure consisting of a glass marble held by pressure against a ring of cork or rubber which rested in a groove which encircled the inside top of the neck. The seal was broken by pressing down on the marble and sending it down into the bottles' contents (Figure 1l). Also *Codd ball stopper*.

Coil: See *continuous thread*.

Cold mold marks: See *whittle marks*.

Collar: A band, bead, or ring of glass applied to and encircling the finish of a bottle. It may sit immediately adjacent to the lip or some distance below it (Figure 2i).

Continuous thread (C.T.): A continuous spiral projecting glass ridge encircling the finish of

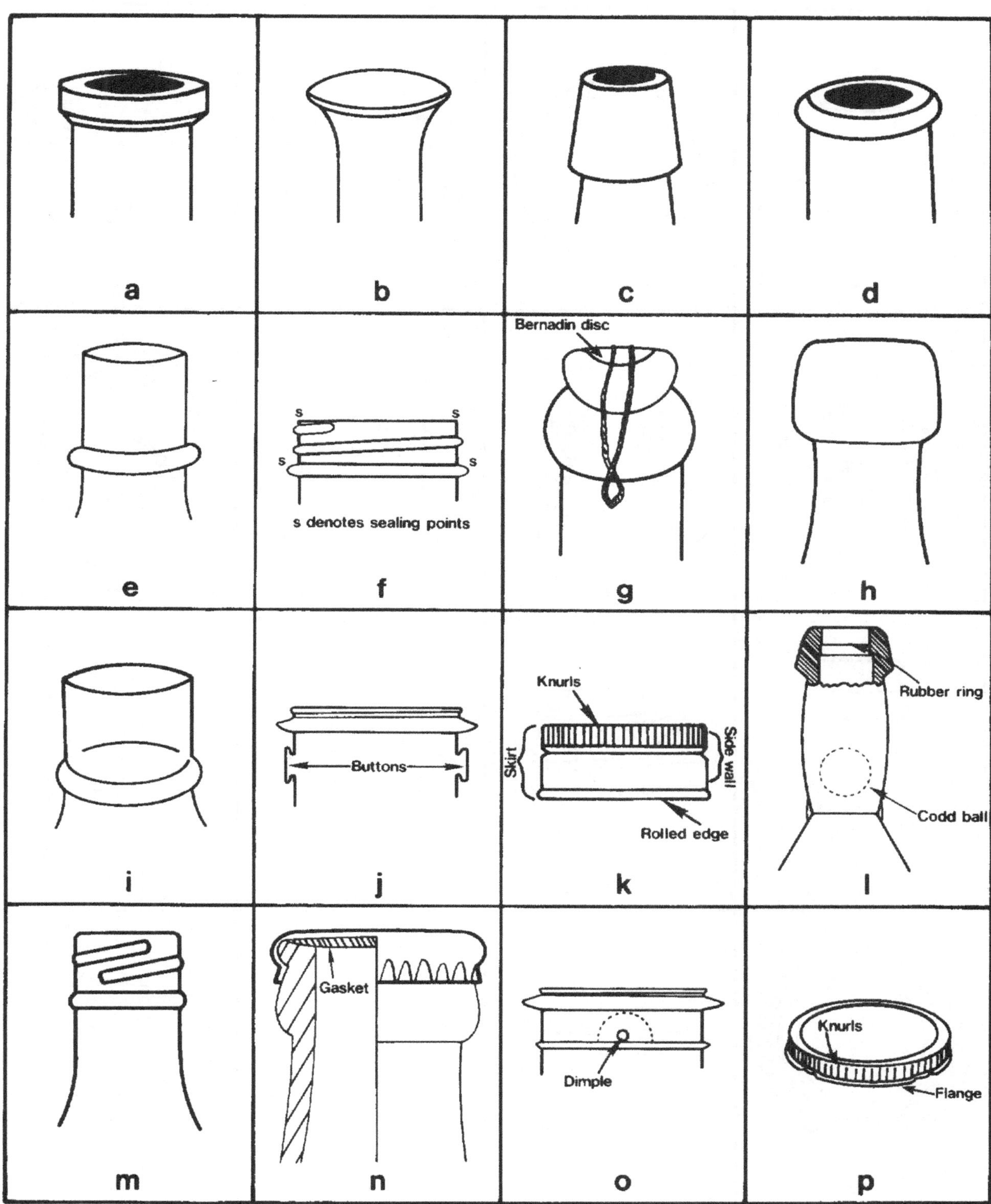

FIGURE 1. Illustrations of bottle landmarks and nomenclature.

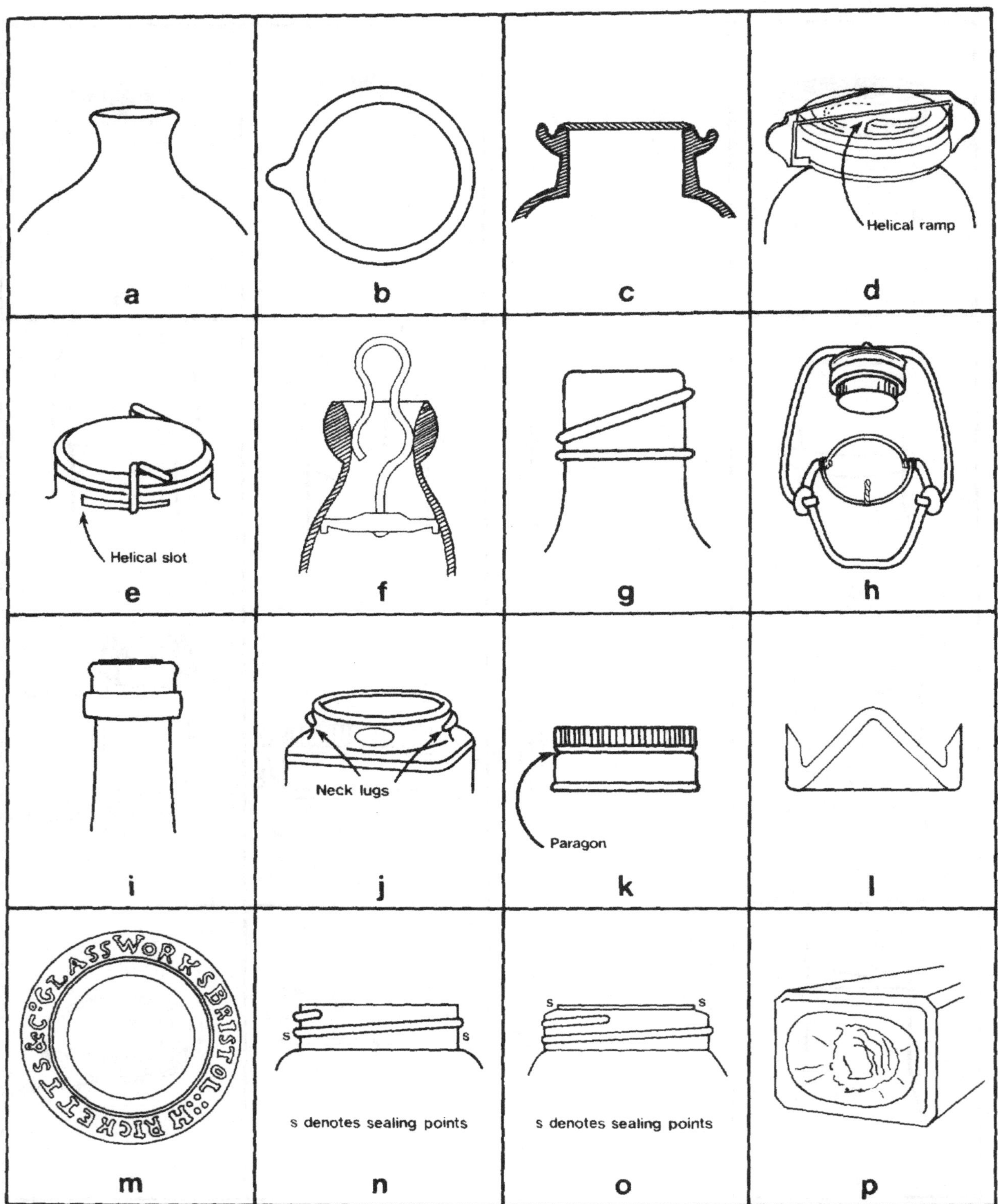

FIGURE 2. Illustrations of bottle landmarks and nonmenclature.

a bottle intended to mesh with the thread of a screw-type closure. Also called *helix* or *coil* (Figure 1m).

Cover groove: In Lightning-type closures it is a groove of varying lengths which sits atop the closure and receives the yoke or bail. It keeps the closure from slipping (Figure 3).

Crown cap: A metal closure usually faced with cork which has its edges crimped over the rounded lip of a bottle (Figure 1n).

Curl: See *rolled edge.*

Cut glass: Glass decorated by incising the surface with iron or stone wheels.

Date line: The vertical mold seam or mold line on a bottle. Called such because it can often be used to approximate the date of manufacture. Also called *seam* or *seam line* (Figure 3).

Dimple: The small depression or hole on the bottle neck into which the lever wire of a toggle device is hooked (Figure 1o).

Dish base: A concavity in the base of a bottle which is somewhat shallower than a push-up or kick.

Embossed lettering or embossing: The raised letters, figures, trademarks, etc. on a bottle.

Filamented ring: A ring on the base of early machine-made bottles formed when a gob of glass was severed after being drawn into the mold.

Finish: The neck formation i.e., that part of the bottle between the shoulder and the top. Often used to designate specifically the upper portion of the neck to which the closure is affixed (Figure 3).

Flange (closure): That part of the closure that protrudes from the bottom of the sidewall and eventually becomes the rolled edge or curl (Figure 1p).

Flared lip: A lip that spreads outward so as to create an opening whose diameter is wider at the top than at any other point on the neck (Figure 2a).

Flashing: The method where a decorative effect is achieved by dipping white or clear glass in a batch of colored glass to coat it. Also called *plating.*

Flat base: A base which is as flat as production will allow.

Flint glass: A heavy, leaded glass of high quality with high refractive power, and great luster used in the choicest cut glassware.

Frosted: The sand-blasted or satiny appearance given to glass as a result of exposure to the abrasive nature of the elements.

Gasket: A liner applied between the sealing surface of the bottle lip and the closure to provide the ultimate seal (Figure 1n).

Gilding: The method wherein glass is decorated by painting brown gold oxide on it then refiring it.

Goose pimples: See *whittle marks.*

Graphite pontil: See *bare-iron pontil mark,* under *pontil scar.*

Greatest diameter: See *maximum diameter.*

Green glass: The relatively coarse glass used chiefly for utilitarian bottles. It is a silicate of lime and soda and is greenish in tint from the iron impurities in the sand.

Griffen gasket: A rubber ring gasket used on canning jars having a thumb tab or projection which allows graspability (Figure 2b).

Ground pontil: The smooth and often slightly concave circle which remains after the rough pontil scar has been ground off. Also called *polished pontil.*

Grooved-ring: A groove encircling the mouth of some early bottles into which a closure having a male counterpart was nestled and sealed (Figure 2c).

Helical ramp: A circular ramp on the outside top of glass lids which was designed to receive a neck yoke and was employed in tightening the seal by a rotating action (Figure 2d).

Helical slot: Slots or grooves in the bottle finish which were designed to receive a closure

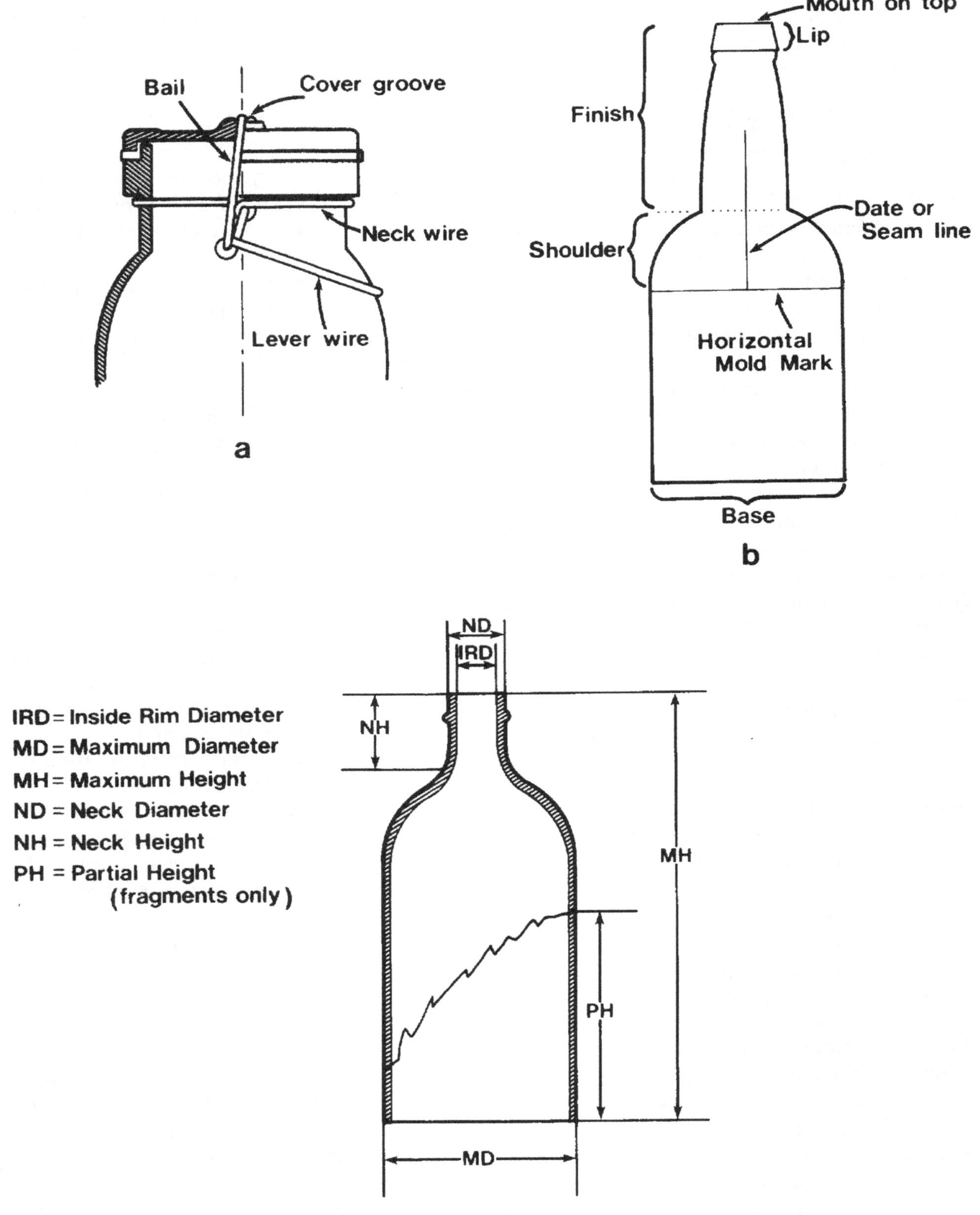

FIGURE 3. Illustrations of landmarks and nomenclature. a, lever closure; b, bottle anatomy; c, points of measurement.

with a corresponding lug or other such projection (Figure 2e).

Helix: See *continuous thread.*

Horizontal mold marks: Mold marks which encircle the bottle (Figure 3).

Hutchinson stopper: An internal stopper composed of a stiff wire with a loop at one end and a rubber disc on the other. The disc served as a seal between the liquid and the neck and was dislodged by pushing downward on the exposed wire loop (Figure 2f).

Improved pontil: See *bare-iron pontil mark* under *pontil scar.*

Infolded lip: The lip is folded into the opening creating a smooth exterior surface and a slight interior ledge. This inner ledge can be detected by rotating a finger around the inside of the neck.

Inside rim diameter: The diameter immediately inside the mouth of the bottle (Figure 3).

Interrupted thread (I.T.): Threads on the bottle that are not continuous throughout the circumference of the finish but are gapped to receive a cap with lugs (Figure 2g).

Kick or *kick-up:* See *Push-up.*

Knurl: Series of vertical indentations around the top of a closure skirt which allow for gripping during application and removal (Figure 1k, p).

Lady's leg: Collector's term for bottles with long curving necks.

Laid-on ring: Ranging from crude to refined, this consisted of a glass ring or bead trailed around and/or slightly below the opening and fused to the bottle. It was added to strengthen the opening or neck (Figure 2i)

Lever: A closure device, the movement of which, applies pressure to hold a lid against the sealing surface of the bottle (Figure 3).

Lever wire: That part of a toggle device which is raised or lowered to loosen or tighten a seal (Figure 3).

Lightning stopper: An external stopper, usually made of porcelain, with a rubber ring encircling it as a sealant and held in place on the bottle by a bent wire attached to the stopper and anchored to the outside of the neck just below the rolled lip (Figure 2h).

Lip: The edge or margin of glass immediately surrounding the bottle opening (Figure 3).

Lipping tool marks: See *swirling.*

Looping: Decoration made up of colored loopings or beads of glass of one or more colors added to a bottle body of a different color.

Maximum diameter: The maximum diameter in circular or polygonal bottles measured at any point. Also *greatest diameter.* (Figure 3).

Maximum height: The distance measured from the base of the bottle to the maximum height i.e., the top of the lip (Figure 3). Also called *total height.*

Membrane: The liner or secondary closure which adheres to the lip of a bottle or jar and is a separate unit from the lid. It usually is made from paper and must be peeled off or torn through to get to the product.

Metal: A glassmaker's term for glass either in the molten or finished state.

Mold line: Raised lines or ridges left on the body of a piece of mold-made glass. The marks are created when the hot glass is forced out the interstices between parts of the mold (Figure 3).

Mouth: See *top.*

Neck: See *finish.*

Neck diameter: The diameter measured at the point of junction of the shoulder and the neck (Figure 3).

Neck height: Distance measured from the junction of the shoulder and neck to the top of the lip (Figure 3).

Neck lugs: Projections or spurs on the bottle neck which act to engage the closure. Interrupted thread projections are often referred to as neck lugs (Figure 2j).

Neck swirls: See *swirling.*

Neck wire: In Lightning-type closures, it is the part of the wire holding device which articulates directly with the bottle neck (Figure 3).

Opalescence: Trait due to moisture on the glass surface leaçhing out or dissolving the soda within the glass and depositing it on the surface of the bottle. Opalescence may take the form of nacreous discoloration or whitish, scale-like patina.

Open pontil mark: See *blowpipe pontil* under *pontil marks.*

Overlay: A method of decorating glass by applying several layers of glass, usually of different colors, then cutting through one or more layers to provide a contrast of hues.

Panel: Square or rectangular insets on one or more sides of rectangular bottles on which are raised letters or figures giving content information, manufacturer, etc.

Paragon: The depression encircling the outside top of continuous thread bottle caps (just below the knurl) designed to give them rigidity (Figure 2k).

Partial height: The distance measured from the base to the maximum height extant short of total height. Used to denote fragment sizes only (Figure 3).

Plate glass: A refined silicate of lime and soda rolled into sheets and used in the better windows and mirrors.

Plating: See *flashing.*

Point of seal: See *sealing surface.*

Pointed base: A bottle base which rather than being round is more plummet-or torpedo-shaped. Also called *torpedo base.*

Polished pontil: See *ground pontil.*

Pontil scar or mark: The irregular scar left on the base of the finished bottle after removal of the pontil (Figure 2p). Pontil marks may be of various types, including a.) *glass-tipped pontil marks* are comparatively small (usually <30 mm) and characterized by an excess of glass left on the base or by a scar caused by the removal of small bits of glass from the base; b.) *sand pontil marks* are larger than the glass-tipped ones and consist of a thin line of glass chips encircling the push-up and enclosing a pebbled surface caused by the grains of sand, some sand may be embedded in the base; c.) *blowpipe pontil marks* are distinct ring-shaped marks with the same diameter as the neck; as with the sand pontil, scar glass may be left on or torn out of the base; as the only area of contact is the ring of glass, any markings, etc. remain as undisturbed on the inside as they do outside; also called *tubular pontil scars;* and *open pontil marks;* and d.) *bare iron pontil marks* are circular marks covered with a reddish or black ferric oxide deposit; the push-up associated with this scar is often distorted; also called *improved pontil* or *graphite pontil.*

Prunts: Blobs of glass added as decoration to bottles and glassware and molded into various shapes such as leaves, seals, etc.

Push-up: The characteristic wherein the base of the bottle is pushed up into the body of the bottle forming a more or less deep basal concavity; also called *kick, kick-up* (Figure 2l).

Quilting: Wavy lines or ribbons of glass swirled or cross-notched on the outside of a still-hot blown flask as decoration. Also called *trailing.*

Quatrefoil: The impression left in the top of the push-up by a pontil-like rod having its end divided into quadrants.

Ribbing: Protruding ridges on bottles and other glass objects produced either by the use of molds or by tooling.

Rickett's ring: A lettered ring encircling the push-up on the underside of a bottle base usually bearing such information as the address of the manufacturer or the volume of the bottle (Figure 2m).

Rigaree: Parallel lines of ribbons added as decoration to the sides of bottles and glassware.

Rolled edge: The turned in (or out) portion of

the open end of the closure skirt, usually to form a tubular structure. Also called *curl* or *wire* (Figure 1k).

Round base: A bottle base which is completely round having no flat surface at all. This bottle cannot stand on its own.

Screw band: A screw-cap, generally used with canning jars, with a cut-out center. It is used to hold down a sealing disc.

Screw thread, inside: Where the screw threads for holding the closure are on the inside of the neck.

Screw thread, outside: Where the screw threads are on the outside of the bottle neck. They receive screw-on caps rather than stoppers.

Sealing surface: The surface of the bottle or jar on which the closure makes maximum or sealing contact. Also called *point of seal.*

Seam or seam line: See *date line.*

Sheared top: A bottle top that has been cut off by shears while still in a soft state. It may be fire-polished or not.

Shoulder: The part of the bottle between the base of the neck and the point on the bottle at which the sides turn inward toward the neck (Figure 3).

Shoulder seal: A bottle that makes its seal or point of maximum contact on the apex of the shoulder (Figure 2n).

Sick glass: Glass whose surface has been corroded by long exposure to moisture.

Snap case mark: Barely noticeable and shallow indentations in the sides of a bottle caused by the snap case grasping the hot, pliable glass.

Spot crown: A cork lined crown cap having a smaller disc of aluminum or other material centrally located on the cork liner. These spots prevented the imparting of an off-taste to the bottle contents.

Stopper: A closure which fits inside the neck of a bottle rather than atop or outside e.g. a cork, bung, plug, etc.

Straps: Flat, wide ridges (or "straps") of glass running vertically up both sides of bottles which are narrower fore and aft than they are left to right. The straps usually measure between ¼ and ½ inch in width and up to ⅛" thick depending on the bottle size.

Sun coloring: Glass turned either amethyst or amber by the action of the sun on manganese oxide and selenium contained therein.

Swirling: The vague marks encircling the neck of bottles which have had lips applied by the rotation of a lipping tool. Also called *lipping tool marks.*

Tears: Bubbles of air imprisoned in the glass.

Toggle: A bottle locking and sealing device consisting of at least two elements, usually wires or bails, which present three fulcrums or centers of force. The familiar lightning closure is one type of toggle (Figure 3).

Top: The part of the bottle incorporating the lip and the opening the lip surrounds. Also called *mouth* (Figure 3).

Top seal: A bottle that makes its seal or point of maximum contact on the top (Figure 2o).

Torpedo base: See *pointed base.*

Total height: See *maximum height.*

Trailing: See *quilting.*

Tubular pontil scar: See *blowpipe pontil scar* under *pontil scar.*

Vertical mold marks: Mold marks which run in the direction of the bottle's length.

Whittle marks: Rough marks of a stippled or wavy nature on the surface of a hand blown bottle. Actually a misnomer as these marks result from blowing the bottle in a mold which has not been properly warmed. Also called *chip marks* or *cold mold marks.*

Window glass: A relatively crude silicate of lime and soda made into window panes.

Wire: See *rolled edge.*

Wired cork stopper: Cork stoppers which are wired into place on the bottle neck. Modern champagne bottles are usually corked in such a manner (Figure 1g).

Yoke: See *bail.*

REFERENCES

The following articles and books, though not specifically cited, were valuable sources of insight in the compilation of this glossary.

ADAMS, JOHN P.
1969 *Bottle Collecting in New England*. New Hampshire Publishing Co. Somersworth, New Hampshire.

BAUMAN, RICHARD
1968 "Glass and Glasswares." In *Handbook for Historical Archaeology, Part 1*, edited by John Cotter, pp. 30–36.

BROSE, DAVID
1967 "The Custer Road Dump Site: An Exercise in Victorian Archaeology." *The Michigan Archaeologist* 13(2):37–128.

COHEN, HAL L.
1975 *Official Guide to Bottles Old and New*. House of Collectibles, Florence, Alabama.

FERRARS, PAT AND BOB FERRARS
1966 *A Bottle Collector's Book*. Western Printing and Publishing Company, Sparks, Nevada.

FREEMAN, LARRY
1964 *Grand Old American Bottles*. Century House, Watkins Glen.

HUNT, CHARLES
1959 "Dating of Mining Camps with Tin Cans and Bottles." *Geotimes* 3(1):8–10, 34.

JONES, OLIVE
1971 "Glass Bottle Push-ups and Pontil Marks." *Historical Archaeology*, 5:63–73.

KENDRICK, GRACE
1971 *The Antique Bottle Collector*. Pyramid, New York.

LIEF, ALFRED
1965 *A Close-up of Closures*. Glass Container Manufacturers Institute, New York.

LORRAIN, DESSAMAE
1968 "An Archaeologist's Guide to Nineteenth Century American Glass." *Historical Archaeology* 2:35–44.

NEWMAN, T. SNELL
1970 "A Dating Key for Post-Eighteenth Century Bottles." *Historical Archaeology* 4:70–75.

NOEL HUME, IVOR
1970 *A Guide to Artifacts of Colonial America*. Alfred Knopf, New York.

TIBBITS, JOHN C.
1967 *John Doe, Bottle Collector*. Heirloom Press, Santa Cruz.

TOULOUSE, JULIAN
1969 "A Primer on Mold Seams." *Western Collector* 7, (11), Pt. 1:526-535; (12), Pt. 2:578-87.
1971 *Bottlemakers and Their Marks*. Thomas Nelson, Inc., New York.

WILSON, REX
1961 "A Classification System for 19th Century Bottles." *Arizoniana*, 11(4):2–6.

JOHN R. WHITE
PROFESSOR
DEPARTMENT OF SOCIOLOGY A
ANTHROPOLOGY
YOUNGSTOWN STATE UNIVER
YOUNGSTOWN, OHIO 44555.

LAURIE A. WILKIE

Glass-Knapping at a Louisiana Plantation: African-American Tools?

ABSTRACT

During the analysis of glass artifacts recovered from undisturbed archaeological contexts at Oakley Plantation, West Feliciana Parish, Louisiana (16WF34), a number of glass sherds were found to have retouching and edge damage consistent with wear found on utilized lithics. Of these, 35 sherds were determined to exhibit significant evidence of use as tools. These tools were recovered from four African-American assemblages dating from the 1840s through the 1930s. This paper discusses the analysis of these tools, whether variations among the tools are representative of distinct types, a review of the occurrence of similar tools at other sites, and whether the tools can be considered to be of uniquely African-American origin.

Introduction

During archaeological excavations in 1991 and 1992, 35 utilized glass sherds were recovered from assemblages dating from the 1840s to the 1930s at Oakley Plantation, West Feliciana, Louisiana (Table 1). These investigations were conducted as a follow-up to an earlier surface survey by Holland and Orser (1984), and further explored several features identified by them. In each instance of glass tool occurrence at the site, strong oral historical or documentary evidence associates the archaeological assemblages with African-American occupants.

Oakley Plantation was founded in 1796 as a cotton plantation in Feliciana Parish of Spanish West Florida. At its economic peak in the 1840s, the plantation comprised over 3,000 acres of land and over 200 slaves (Wilkie 1994). The plantation remained in the ownership of the same family and was continuously farmed by African Americans until the 1940s. In 1947, 100 acres of the plantation, including the planter's house and plantation yard area, were sold to the State of Louisiana for preservation and interpretation as the Audubon State Commemorative Area.

Three loci excavated during the 1991 and 1992 field seasons provided the archaeological materials for this study (Figure 1). These areas were defined as features in the Holland and Orser (1984) surface collection, and to maintain continuity for management purposes, feature numbers used by Holland and Orser were retained. Each of Holland and Orser's (1984) features—better thought of as loci—represented clusters of archaeological features associated with two house areas. The loci investigated included a cabin and yard area which were occupied throughout the antebellum and postbellum periods (Features 5, 29) and a house built by 1920 and occupied until 1949 by Sam Scott and his wife Nettie Scott (Feature 30). Specific details of excavations at each of these areas are given in the following discussion.

Mean Artifact Dates, a variation on South's Mean Ceramic Date method, which incorporates datable artifacts such as metals and glass in addition to ceramics, were used to date the assemblages. The author has found that manufacturing date ranges on artifacts such as glass, plastic, and rubber can provide tighter chronological control for late 19th- and early 20th-century sites than ceramics alone. For a detailed discussion of individual features and strata, see Wilkie (1994) and Wilkie and Farnsworth (1992, 1993).

TABLE 1
NUMBER OF TOOLS RECOVERED FROM EACH AFRICAN-AMERICAN ASSEMBLAGE AT OAKLEY

Assemblage	Mean Artifact Date (MAD)	Number of Tools Found
Features 5 and 29 (Antebellum)	1842–1843	5
Feature 5 (Silvia Freeman family)	1897	22
Feature 5 (Delphine and Eliza Freeman family)	1923	8
Feature 30 (Samuel and Nettie Scott)	1938.5	0

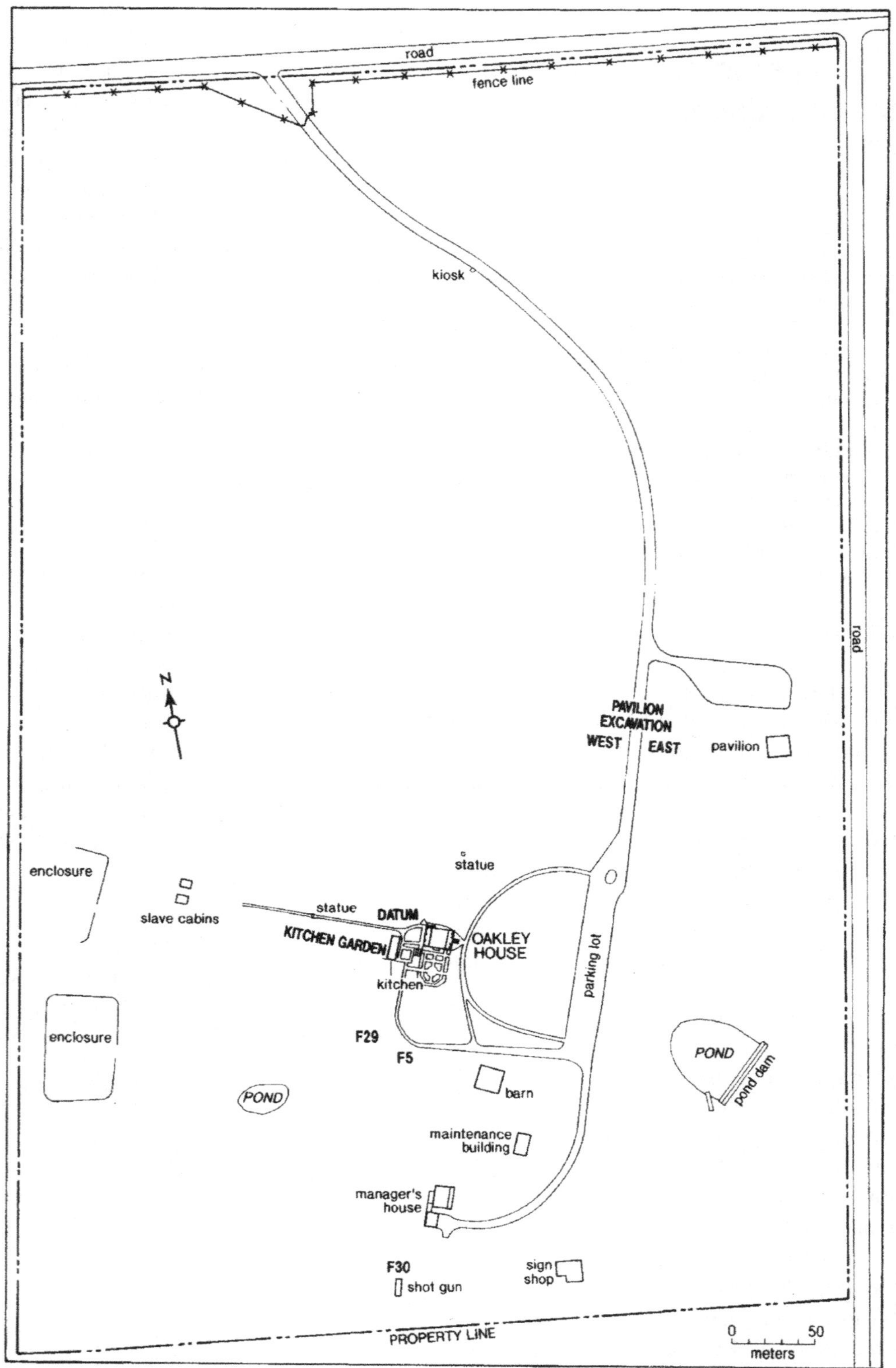

FIGURE 1. Archaeological Features at Oakley Plantation associated with African Americans.

Feature 5

The area designated Feature 5 was described by Holland and Orser (1984) as a possible house site. In 1991 the area was tested with four 1-m units and three shovel test pits. The brick foundation of a pier and beam house were identified in association with mid- to late 19th- and early 20th-century materials.

Further testing was undertaken in 1992 to determine the preservation of the structural remains and the extent of the yard area deposits. A 7-x-9-m excavation grid (Grid A) of 1-m units was laid out and oriented along the brick foundations found in 1991 to insure that as far as possible, excavation units outside versus under the structure would be distinct. Both a second 3-m square grid (Grid B) was laid out to the west of Grid A and three additional 1-m units were placed to the south of Grid A to examine further a major artifactual concentration found in 1991.

During the course of excavation, a number of archaeological features were encountered at this locus, including three shallow trash pits, 25 postholes representing the extent of the house, a brick-mining pit, and three trenches. Each of these components was excavated separately, and color, diameter, shape, and depth recorded. This information was important in establishing the chronology of, and associations between, archaeological features at this locus.

Large quantities of material cultural remains were recovered from undisturbed contexts immediately around and under the house, and in the western yard area of the house. Materials recovered from stratigraphic levels and archaeological features determined to be of the same age through their *termini post quem* have been treated as single assemblages. In this way, three assemblages representing activities related to three occupations of the house were identified archaeologically.

Antebellum materials were recovered in the southwestern area of Grid A from a dark grayish-brown mottled clay overlying the sterile clay level and from two small trash pits and provided a Mean Artifact Date (MAD) of 1842.5 (Wilkie 1994:178). Above this level was a yellowish-brown to dark yellowish-brown mottled loam which contained artifacts dating to the end of the 19th century. Additional materials from this time period were recovered from postholes and another small pit. Materials from this level provided a MAD of 1897 (Wilkie 1994:180–181). A brownish-yellow loam overlying the 19th-century strata contained early 20th-century materials which provided a MAD of 1923 (Wilkie 1994:182–183).

Historical Context for Feature 5

The construction of the cabin at Feature 5, based upon its architectural style and archaeological remains, probably took place in the 1840s (Wilkie 1994). Given the proximity of the cabin to the planter residence, the antebellum materials recovered from Feature 5 are most probably associated with an enslaved family that worked in the great house.

Henry Cummings and John Hulbert, former tenants of Oakley, both described this feature during interviews as corresponding to the location of the "cook's house" which was lived in by the African-American Freeman family (Cummings 1991; Hulbert 1992). Most clearly, they remembered a woman named Delphine Freeman working in that capacity during the 1920s and 1930s but thought that her mother had also been a cook. Delphine Freeman had inherited the position from her mother, Silvia Freeman (Wilkie 1994:199–201).

Silvia Freeman and her family worked as domestic servants for the Matthews family through the late 19th and early 20th centuries. The late 19th-century materials from Feature 5 are most likely associated with their occupation of the cabin. Silvia Freeman's employment began sometime in or prior to 1886, when William Wilson and Isabelle Matthews owned the plantation. After Isabelle Matthews's death, Silvia Freeman and her family continued to work as domestics for Lucy and Ida Matthews.

The earliest documentary evidence available for Silvia Freeman is found on her marriage license. On 5 June 1875, Lewis Freeman paid

$50.00 for a license to marry Sylvia [sic] Hill. The date of their actual marriage was not recorded by the parish (West Feliciana Parish Records 1875). Lewis Freeman's family is known to have lived in this ward and parish as early as 1870, but Silvia Hill does not appear in the 1870 West Feliciana census (U.S. Bureau of the Census [USBC] 1870). In 1880, the census shows Silvia Freeman living with Lewis Freeman and their two sons, Joseph and John, at Oakley. Lewis Freeman's occupation was listed as "planter" and Silvia Freeman's as "farming" (USBC 1880).

The earliest reference to Silvia Freeman working in the house as the cook is an 1886 ledger entry in the Oakley Collection. No mention of Lewis Freeman is made in the ledger; however, Silvia Freeman's youngest child was born in 1889 and bears the last name Freeman, suggesting that Lewis Freeman had passed away no earlier than 1888. By 1900, Silvia Freeman is listed as a widow in the manuscript census (USBC 1900).

Silvia Freeman appears to have passed away between 1900 and 1910; she does not appear in the 1910 census. By 1910, Eliza Freeman, presumably "Lizzie" in the 1900 census, and Delphine Freeman were both still living at Oakley. Eliza was working as a servant and Delphine as a cook (USBC 1910).

The Freeman daughters appear in the 1920 census as well; Eliza is listed as "Louisa" Freeman, and still employed as the Matthews house servant (USBC 1920). Henry Cummings (1991) remembers Eliza and Delphine Freeman living together at the plantation through the 1930s but had no clear recollection of their daughters. The 20th-century materials recovered from Feature 5 are most probably related to the Freeman sisters' occupation.

Feature 29

Feature 29 was not previously identified by Holland and Orser (1984). During the 1991 surface collections, a concentration of mid-19th-century artifacts was found eroding at a tree base located to the northwest of, and in close proximity to, Feature 5. A 1-m unit was subsequently excavated to a depth of 40 cm below the surface at this locus. Large quantities of household refuse dating to the 19th century were recovered (Wilkie and Farnsworth 1992). Two additional 1-m units were excavated in 1992 to define further the deposit. Both 1992 units were excavated to depths of 40 cm below the surface and contained concentrations of antebellum household materials. No evidence of architectural remains was found at this loci. Intact, antebellum deposits including pearlwares, shell-edged whitewares, and green-glazed redwares, were recovered, concentrated between 20 and 30 cm deep. These materials place the MAD of this locus at 1843 (Wilkie 1994:185), comfortably within the antebellum period and very close to the 1842.5 date for the antebellum materials recovered at Feature 5.

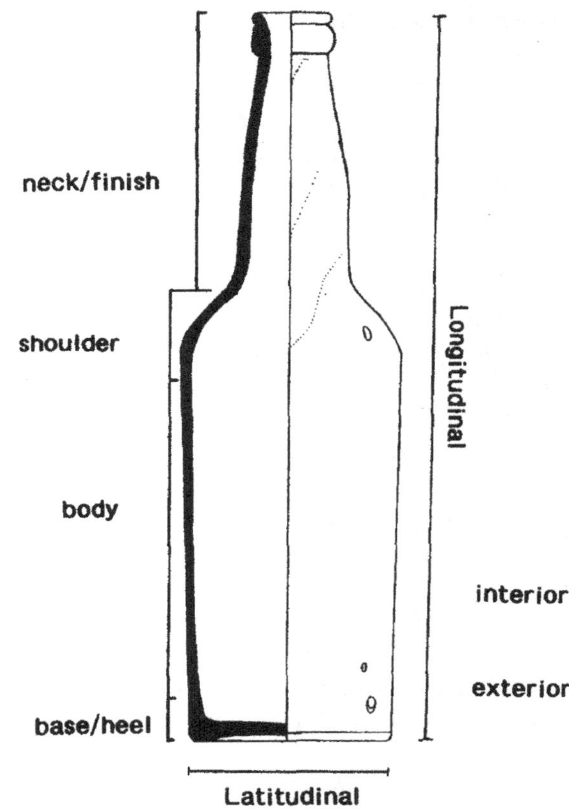

FIGURE 2. Terms used to describe bottle anatomy and sherd orientation during analysis.

TABLE 2
CONTINGENCY TABLE: RETOUCH VERSUS ANGLE EDGE

Edge Angle	Retouched	Not Retouched
Less than 35°	0	11
Greater than 35°	24	0
Total	24	11

Although it has not been possible to determine which enslaved family may have been associated with the antebellum deposits at Features 5 and 29, the spatial and chronological proximity of these deposits suggests that the two groups of artifacts may both represent the activities of the same enslaved African-American family. Accordingly, glass tools from the antebellum period deposits at Features 5 and 29 were analyzed as a single group.

Feature 30

Feature 30 is the location of the only standing tenant house remaining in the park, and excavations in this area were directed in relationship to this architectural feature. During testing in September 1991, a 5-m grid was excavated north of the house to test the extent of a midden deposit first identified in the summer of 1991. These units contained large quantities of glass, plastic, ceramic, and metal artifacts dating between the 1920s and the 1940s, all concentrated in a soft, black oily midden soil that was 15 cm thick close to the building, and thinning to only a couple of cm thick at the west and north edges of the grid. The back room of the house served as the kitchen, thus likely explaining the large concentration of artifactual materials behind it. The MAD for this feature is 1938.95 (Wilkie 1994:187).

This house is known to have been built about 1920 by African-American Sam Scott. Henry Cummings (1991) remembered Sam, also called Sammy, living in the house with his wife, and for a time, his father. Sam and his wife had no children. John Hulbert (1992), the Scotts' nephew, was also able to provide information about the family. According to Hulbert (1992) and Cummings (1991), the Scotts were the only family to live in this house; therefore, the assemblage recovered here must be associated with them. While no glass tools were recovered from this assemblage, this feature was the only one at Oakley Plantation to produce steel razor blades. The possible impact of razor blades on glass-knapping traditions will be discussed below.

Description of the Glass Tools

In analyzing the 35 glass tools—nearly all made from fragments of glass bottles or jars, it was necessary to define descriptive terms that both reflected the nature of the raw materials used to construct the tools as well as those attributes of the tools which were functionally meaningful. To achieve this end, a standardized set of descriptive terms was used during analysis to describe the portion of the original bottle being utilized, the orientation of the sherd in the original vessel, and the interior and exterior of the bottle. The description of bottle components is drawn from Jones and Sullivan (1985:77, Figure 52) and is comprised of finish, neck-finish, shoulder, body, heel, and base.

In lithic analysis, flake tools typically are described and measured relative to the bulb of percussion (Keeley 1980; Vaughan 1985). Since glass sherds lack such a percussion bulb, it is necessary to use other means to describe them. The form and use of bottle sherds as tools is in part dictated by the original shape of the vessel. To describe the orientation of the utilized edge relative to the sherd's original position in the bottle, the circumference of the bottle is called the latitudinal plane, and the vertical aspect of the bottle is called the longitudinal plane. Therefore, utilized edges that would have been parallel to the base or finish of the intact bottle are referred to as longitudinal edges, and those that would have been perpendicular to the base and finish are referred to as latitudinal edges (Figure 2).

Other variables considered as potentially important attributes include the presence/absence of retouching, the angle of the utilized edge, the shape of the utilized edge, the distribution of use wear along the utilized edge, and placement of the contact edge or leading aspect (Keeley 1980:21) relative to the interior or exterior of the original vessel. To determine whether different attributes were meaningfully linked, contingency tables were constructed to determine if there were meaningful relationships between attributes and, therefore, typological differences between the tools (Sackett 1989).

This level of analysis formed the foundation for microwear analysis and for identifying relationships between use and morphology. Through this analysis, meaningful relationships were established between retouching, edge angle, and sherd orientation. In addition, some patterns related to the portion of the bottle utilized, and the nature of the tools has been established.

Correlating Attributes

Visual observation indicated that the tools fell into two rough groups, including those that had no retouching (n = 11) and those that were unifacially retouched (n = 24). To determine whether retouching may have served a functional purpose, a contingency table was constructed comparing the presence of retouch and the angle of the utilized tool edge. A general relationship has been established by lithic researchers between angle edge and use. For instance, whittling activities are usually associated with acute angles, whereas planing is usually associated with more obtuse edge angles (Keeley 1980:16–17). These criteria were compared, since edge angles had been observed to cluster below 35 degrees and above 45 degrees. The contingency table relating these two variables demonstrated that all of the tools with retouch had edge angles of greater than 35 degrees, while all tools lacking retouch had edge angles smaller than 35 degrees (Table 2). When a second contingency table was constructed relating longitudinal/latitudinal edge utilization with presence/absence of retouching, a correlation was found. All tools with retouching, a total of 24, were utilized on the latitudinal edge of the sherd, while all of the unretouched sherds were utilized on their longitudinal edge (Table 3). A comparison of edge angle by assemblage demonstrated that 60 degrees was the most common edge angle, with Silvia Freeman's assemblage demonstrating the greatest variation (Table 4).

Glass bottles/jars served as the raw material for all but two of the tools, with wine bottles being the most commonly used. The other two tools were made from tumbler sherds. Addi-

TABLE 3
CONTINGENCY TABLE: RETOUCH VERSUS LONGITUDINAL/LATITUDINAL UTILIZATION

Utilization	Retouched	Not Retouched
Latitudinal Edge	0	11
Longitudinal Edge	24	0
Total	24	11

TABLE 4
CONTINGENCY TABLE: EDGE ANGLE AND ASSEMBLAGE OF RETOUCHED TOOLS[a]

	Assemblage		
Edge Angle	Antebellum	Silvia Freeman	Delphine and Eliza Freeman
40°	0	1	0
50°	0	3	6
60°	1	6	2
70°	0	5	2
80°	1	0	0
Total	2	15	7

[a] Retouched tools listed in Table 3 comprise these tools.

tional comparisons were made to determine whether certain components of the bottles were preferred for retouched versus unretouched tools. Components of the bottles used for tools fell into the categories heel and base, neck and finish, shoulder, and body. Both heel and base and neck and finish are combined because tools were derived from both of these elements, as compared to body and shoulder sherds, which did not contain portions of any other bottle part. This analysis demonstrated that body sherds were most often used for tools. Base and heel sherds were only used to manufacture retouched tools (Table 5), but were by no means the exclusive choice for these tools.

Given the variety of bottle parts represented, several tables were then constructed to compare the distribution of bottle parts being utilized. Within each of the assemblages, body sherds were the most common. Shoulder sherds, used for both retouched and unretouched tools, were only associated with the assemblage of Silvia Freeman (Table 6). Whether the selection of the shoulder sherds represented a personal preference or a functional decision may be clarified when microwear analysis is conducted.

Visual observation suggested that the shape of the contact edge, in addition to edge angle, may be an important attribute for the retouched tools. Retouched tools were found to have concave-or convex-shaped contact edges. Comparison of the shape of the contact edge with bottle part (Table 7) demonstrated that convex edges were almost exclusively associated with body sherds. Analysis of edge angle with the shape of the contact edge (Table 8) demonstrated that convex contact edges were associated with edge angles of 50–70 degrees, while concave contact edges were associated with a broader range of edge angles (40–80°).

TABLE 5
CONTINGENCY TABLE: RETOUCH AND BOTTLE ANATOMY

Bottle Part	Retouched	Not Retouched
Heel and Base	4	0
Neck and Finish	1	3
Shoulder	3	1
Body	16	7
Total	24	11

TABLE 6
CONTINGENCY TABLE: ASSEMBLAGE VERSUS BOTTLE ANATOMY

Bottle Part	Antebellum	Silvia Freeman	Delphine Freeman
Heel and Base	1	1	2
Neck and Finish	1	2	1
Shoulder	0	4	0
Body	3	15	5
Total	5	22	8

Other correlations failed to reveal meaningful trends. A comparison of edge angles with bottle parts found no correlations. An ambiguous correlation is related to the orientation of leading edges. The majority of the recovered tools utilized the exterior wall of the bottle as its leading or contact edge. However, five examples of interior wall contact edges were included in the assemblage of Silvia Freeman (Table 9). The use of interior versus exterior walls may represent a personal preference, as this decision affects how one grips the tools.

Exploring Potential Functions

Several conclusions can be drawn from the above analysis. First, there are clear correlations between the presence/absence of retouch, edge angle and utilized sherd edge, suggesting the presence of at least two tool types. The first type can be defined primarily as retouched, the second type as unretouched (Figure 3).

All retouched sherds are worked on a latitudinal edge and have an edge angle of greater than

35 degrees. The steep edge angle that these tools possess suggest that they functioned as scrapers. The reason for the selection of the latitudinal edge for working may be related to comfort in gripping the finished tool or may reflect differences in ease of knapping along the edges. Given that these tools are retouched, their production required a certain degree of knapping ability and investment of time. They appear, therefore, to be intentionally produced tools.

Convex and concave contact surfaces were noted among the retouched tools; however, it is unclear whether these are meaningful attributes. Concave edges had a broader range of edge angles and bottle body sherds associated with them than did the convex edges. Further exploration of these issues through microwear analysis and comparison with other assemblages is necessary further to define the significance, if any, of these differences.

Bottle bases and heels were used exclusively for retouched tools. Bottle body sherds were the most common (24 of the 35 tools). Shoulder sherds (n = 4) were only utilized by Silvia Freeman's family. Likewise, Silvia Freeman's assemblage is the only one to include contact edges on the bottle interior. Without an additional level of analysis, such as microwear, or the comparison of these tools with similar examples from other sites, it is not possible to determine which patterns reflect the preferences of the tool knappers/users or represent functional differences.

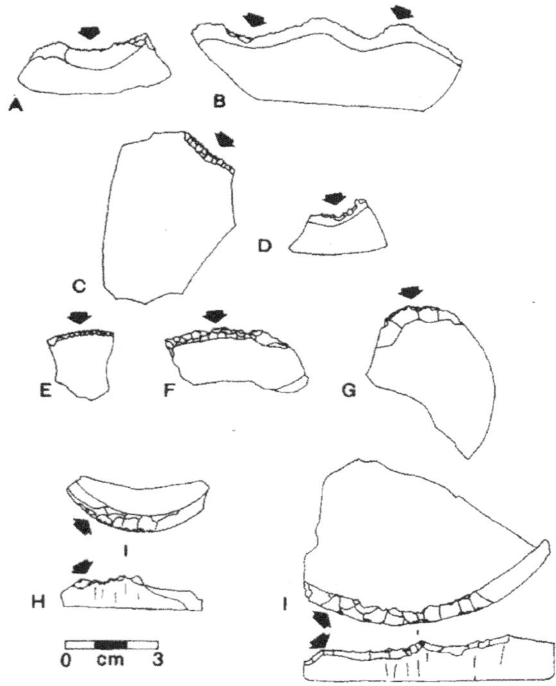

FIGURE 3. Examples of retouched and unretouched tools from Oakley Plantation: A–B, unretouched tools; C–I, retouched tools. Arrows indicate utilized edges.

All of the unretouched sherds exhibit edge wear damage—scarring, pitting, and chipping—on their longitudinal or utilized edges, and all have edge angles of less than 35 degrees. Longitudinal edges are potentially longer and straighter than are latitudinal edges, suggesting that such tools may have been used for cutting rather than scraping. Since longitudinal tools lack retouching, it is not clear whether they were intentionally produced or if glass sherds from broken bottles were selected to be used as expedient tools when necessary. They may, in fact, represent tools of convenience rather than forethought.

Examination of the unretouched tools demonstrates that the wear damage on eight of the 11 was irregularly distributed along the length of both surfaces. This form of wear is typically associated with longitudinal motions, such as sawing or cutting (Vaughan 1985:20). The remaining three examples exhibit dense scarring on both edge surfaces. The motion associated with this distribution is less clear, for such wear has been found associated with both transverse and longitudinal motions (Vaughan 1985:20–21). However, the general pattern suggests that these tools were likely to have been used for cutting rather than scraping.

Putting the Tools in Context

Oral history and an evaluation of other cutting tools recovered from the African-American assemblages at Oakley can provide some insight into tool use. Mintz and Price (1976:48) have documented the use of broken bottles by Africans during the middle passage to shave tradi-

TABLE 7
CONTINGENCY TABLE: CONTACT EDGE SHAPE VERSUS
BOTTLE PART ANATOMY, RETOUCHED TOOLS[a]

Bottle Part	Contact Edge Shape	
	Convex	Concave
Base and Heel	0	4
Shoulder	1	2
Body	10	6
Neck Finish	0	1
Total	11	13

[a]Table 3 comprises this same sample.

tional designs in their hair. The practice of using broken glass as a razor was common in the Bahamas until the 1930s (Ferguson 1995).

In Louisiana, John Hulbert (1992), a former tenant of Oakley, remembers glass tools used on the plantation to smooth axe and hoe handles in the 1930s. He indicated that making such tools was not a skill he possessed, stating that some people on the plantation knew how to break glass in a certain way to make a tool. He compared the use of these tools to the way a razor blade was used for the same purpose. His description suggests that the production of these tools was a specialized skill not shared by the entire tenant population.

John Hulbert's comment that only a few people had the skill to create these tools suggests that by the 1930s, when he was a child, this glass tool tradition may have been becoming less common. The Scott assemblage, Feature 30, contains none of these artifacts but does contain an artifact type not found in the other assemblages: razor blades. Razor blades are a versatile tool that can be used for cutting as well as scraping, depending upon the angle at which they are held. This metal tool can perform the tasks of the glass tools and maintains a functional edge for a longer period of time.

To determine whether there may be a relationship between the appearance of razor blades and the disappearance of glass tools in the Scott assemblage, a review of Oakley Plantation commissary ledgers from the 1890s to 1920 was conducted. These ledgers did not include any purchases of razor blades (Matthews 1889–1891, 1890–1901a, 1890–1901b, 1890–1901c; Matthews and Matthews 1902–1920a, 1902–1920b). The ledgers are nearly complete through the 1890s, and less complete for the remainder of this time period. However, enough of the records are available to demonstrate that razor blades, if available during this time period, were not commonly purchased. Archaeologically, the only other evidence of cutting tools recovered were two broken pairs of scissors from Silvia Freeman's assemblage.

The lack of razor blades in Oakley's commissary records may be related to the cost of purchasing these items. Razor blades, or blades for safety razors, were relatively expensive when first introduced. The 1897 Sears, Roebuck catalog ran the following advertisement for the Star Safety Razor:

> An invention which obviates all danger of cutting the face. It is especially adapted to old and young, and is indispensable to travelers, miners and persons camping out. Blades of best steel and fully concave, which can be easily removed and placed in handle for strapping (Israel 1968:112).

The Star Safety Razor sold for $1.50, and extra blades for $1.00. Similarly, straight blade prices started at $.60, and single-bladed pocket knives at $.25, although both items were most commonly available in the $1.50 price range (Israel 1968:112). In 1891, Silvia Freeman was earning $4.00 a month, and had been working at that salary for at least two years (Matthews 1889–1891). The purchase of a knife or razor would therefore represent a significant portion of her monthly income.

No safety razors are listed in the 1900 Sears, Roebuck catalog (DBI Books 1970). By 1908, 10 safety razor blade replacements could be purchased through Sears, Roebuck and Company for a price of $.50 (Schroeder 1971:775). Straight razors were still the razor most commonly available through the catalog, with the cheapest option costing $.96 (Schroeder 1971:773). Prices for pocket knives are not available in this edition of the catalog. The 1927 Sears, Roebuck Catalog advertised 10-packs of razor blades for as low as $.54 (Mirkin 1970:529). Straight razors could be purchased for no less than $1.25 (Mirkin 1970:529), while pocket knives ranged in price from $.79 to $1.89 (Mirkin 1970:510).

The cost of razor blades dropped relative to straight razors and pocket knives between the 1890s and the 1930s. It is possible that the availability of this cheap, commercially-made alternative eventually rendered glass-knapping obsolete. It is also possible that the Scotts, as an individual family, simply did not possess the knapping skills or chose not to participate in this practice. An understanding of glass tools in a broader regional and chronological context is necessary before such conclusions confidently can be drawn.

Razor blades are commonly used today by African Americans in rural Louisiana for cutting, scraping, and whittling (Bibens 1994). If kept in the proximity of the house, razor blades can be easily stored and used. Pocket knives are certainly a safer portable option. While not the focus of this paper, it is interesting to note that preliminary analysis by the author of artifacts from a late 19th- to early 20th-century trash pit at Crawford Park, 1MB99, an African-American midwife's house site in Mobile, Alabama, has also identified glass tools. All of the tools from that site are retouched and, given the outcome of the Oakley analysis, were probably used as scrapers. While no glass knives have been identified as yet, two pocket knives have been recovered. Again, razor blades may be present at the Scott house instead of glass tools because they may have represented a functional substitution of one artifact type for another.

TABLE 8
CONTINGENCY TABLE: CONTACT EDGE SHAPE AND
EDGE ANGLE, RETOUCHED TOOLS[a]

Edge Angle	Contact Edge Shape	
	Convex	Concave
40°	0	1
50°	3	3
60°	5	4
70°	3	4
80°	0	1
Total	11	13

[a] Table 3 comprises this same sample.

TABLE 9
CONTINGENCY TABLE: LEADING EDGE FACE AND ASSEMBLAGE

Assemblage	Leading Edge Face	
	Interior Edge	Exterior Edge
Antebellum	0	5
Silvia Freeman	5	17
Delphine and Eliza Freeman	0	8
Total	5	30

Glass Tools: A Distinctive African-American Trait?

Intentionally worked glass artifacts are not a new phenomenon and have been recovered from both Native American and other African-American archaeological sites. This discussion will focus upon examples recovered from plantation contexts. Two antebellum and two postbellum planter assemblages were recovered from Oakley Plantation. Neither glass tools nor razor blades were recovered from any of the planter contexts, and Native Americans have not been clearly associated with the sites where these particular tool types were recovered.

TABLE 10
ARCHAEOLOGICAL SITES WHERE WORKED GLASS HAS BEEN RECOVERED FROM NON-NATIVE AMERICAN CONTEXTS

Site	State	Site Type	Date	Ethnic Affiliation
Oakley Plantation[a]	Louisiana	Plantation	1840s–1940s	African American
Riverlake Plantation[b]	Louisiana	Plantation	1840s–1990s	African American
St. Rose Plantation[c]	Louisiana	Plantation	1790–1810	African American and Euroamerican
Bennett House[d]	Louisiana	Plantation	1840–1860	African American and Euroamerican
Crawford Park[e]	Alabama	Urban house	1890–1910	African American
Garrison Plantation[f]	Maryland	Plantation	early 19th c.	African American
Monticello[g]	Virginia	Plantation	18th–19th c.	African American
Levi-Jordan Plantation[h]	Texas	Plantation	?	African American and Euroamerican

[a]Wilkie (1994)
[b]Site currently under study by the author
[c]Wilkie and Tannert (1994)
[d]Port Hudson State Commemorative Area Archaeological Collections, Louisiana
[e]Site currently under study by the author
[f]Klingelhofer (1987)
[g]Patten (1992)
[h]Anonymous SHA manuscript reviewer (1995, pers. comm.)

In Maryland, Klingelhofer (1987:114–115) found an intentionally chipped tumbler at Garrison Plantation, and reported that similar artifacts had been recovered in Virginia. Patten (1992:6) reports the recovery of chipped glass from Monticello, as well as from other Virginia tidewater sites. The author has identified isolated examples of glass tools from the Bennett House and St. Rose Plantation, both in Louisiana. As noted earlier, significant numbers of these tools are currently under analysis by the author from Crawford Park, and from Riverlake Plantation, Pointe Coupee Parish, Louisiana. Excavations at Riverlake Plantation were focused on the African-American quarters buildings, which have been continuously occupied from the 1840s until the 1990s. Analysis of these materials is ongoing, but the glass tools from these sites will be compared with those from Oakley to determine if broader regional patterns are visible. Of the sites known to the author to contain glass tools, the vast majority come from contexts that are either clearly African American or from contexts which may have been used jointly by African Americans and Euroamericans (Table 10). Such tools have been recovered from both rural and urban settings. At this point, however, published reference to glass tools recovered from strictly Euroamerican contexts has not been found.

What is not clear, however, is whether glass tools are more likely to be recognized in African-American assemblages by archaeologists aware of their presence in other African-American sites. It is important that non-African-American contexts for such tools be explored so that it can be determined whether their production and use is tied to a distinct ethnic heritage or whether they were broadly used by many ethnic groups. The association of such tools with predominately female contexts at both Oakley Plantation and Crawford Park also suggests that glass flake tools, like prehistoric lithics (Gero 1991), deserve further attention for their potential engendered meanings.

Conclusion

Thirty-five utilized glass sherds from African-American contexts have been recovered from Oakley Plantation, West Feliciana Parish, Louisiana. Attribute analysis of these glass sherds has demonstrated that the sherds easily divide into two major groups which seem to be functionally significant, one group of unretouched sherds serving as knives, and the other group of retouched sherds serving as scrapers. Additional differentiations may be identifiable in conjunction with microwear analysis.

The tools were recovered from three different African-American assemblages at Oakley Plantation dating 1840–1930. No glass tools were recovered from the latest African-American assemblage, dating 1920–1940. It is unclear if the absence of tools from this context represents the abandonment of the tradition by this time period or simply represents the nonparticipation of this family. It is suggested that cheaper, commercially manufactured cutting tools such as razor blades may have replaced glass tools at this time.

In closing, the tools discussed in this paper were drawn from strictly African-American contexts. It is unclear at this juncture whether these tools are distinctly African American in nature or if they have only been recognized in African-American contexts. The majority of glass tools reported in the literature have been recovered from rural settings, and it may be that closer examination of glass from Euroamerican rural contexts will reveal the presence of similar practices.

ACKNOWLEDGMENTS

The author would like to thank the Louisiana State Division of Archaeology and the National Park Service for funding archaeological research at Oakley Plantation. Additional assistance was provided by the University of California, Los Angeles, Friends of Archaeology, and students from UCLA and Louisiana State University, who participated in field schools at the site. Finally, I would like to thank Paul Farnsworth, Christopher R. DeCorse, Daniel G. Roberts, and two anonymous reviewers for their comments on this manuscript.

REFERENCES

Bibens, David
1994 Interview at Riverlake Plantation. Notes on file, Department of Geography and Anthropology, Louisiana State University, Baton Rouge.

Cummings, Henry
1991 Videotaped Interview at Oakley Plantation. On file, Department of Geography and Anthropology, Louisiana State University, Baton Rouge.

DBI Books
1970 *Sears, Roebuck and Co. Consumer Guide, Fall, 1900.* DBI Books, Northfield, IL.

Ferguson, "Papa D"
1995 Oral History Interview, Crooked Island Bahamas. Notes on file, Department of Anthropology, University of California, Berkeley.

Gero, Joan M.
1991 Genderlithics: Women's Roles in Stone Tool Production. In *Engendering Archaeology: Women and Prehistory*, edited by Joan M. Gero and Margaret W. Conkey, pp.163–193. Blackwell, Cambridge.

Holland, Claudia C., and Charles E. Orser, Jr.
1984 A Preliminary Archaeological Investigation of Oakley Plantation, Audubon State Commemorative Area, West Feliciana Parish, Louisiana. Report on file, State Division of Archaeology, Baton Rouge, Louisiana.

Hulbert, John
1992 Interview in Baton Rouge. Notes on file, Department of Geography and Anthropology, Louisiana State University, Baton Rouge.

Israel, Fred L.
1968 *1897 Sears, Roebuck Catalogue.* Chelsea House, NY.

Jones, Olive, and Catherine Sullivan
1985 *The Parks Canada Glass Glossary.* Government Publishing Centre, Québec.

Keeley, Lawrence
1980 *Experimental Determination of Stone Tool Uses.* University of Chicago Press, Chicago, IL.

KLINGELHOFER, ERIC
1987 Aspects of Early Afro-American Material Culture: Artifacts from the Slave Quarters at Garrison Plantation, Maryland. *Historical Archaeology* 21(2):112–119.

MATTHEWS, ISABELLE
1889–1891 Plantation Ledger Kept by Isabelle Matthews. Oakley Collection. Audubon State Commemorative Area, St. Francisville, LA.
1890–1901a Store Receipts. Oakley Collection. Audubon State Commemorative Area, St. Francisville, LA.
1890–1901b Store Receipts, James Pirrie Bowman Papers. Louisiana and Lower Mississippi Valley Collections. Hill Memorial Library, Louisiana State University, Baton Rouge.
1890–1901c Store Receipts, Turnball-Slocum Papers. Louisiana and Lower Mississippi Valley Collections. Hill Memorial Library, Louisiana State University, Baton Rouge.

MATTHEWS, LUCY, AND IDA MATTHEWS
1902–1920a Store Receipts. Oakley Collection. Audubon State Commemorative Area, St. Francisville, LA.
1902–1920b Store Receipts, Turnball-Slocum Papers. Louisiana and Lower Mississippi Valley Collections. Hill Memorial Library, Louisiana State University, Baton Rouge.

MINTZ, SIDNEY, AND RICHARD PRICE
1976 *The Birth of African-American Culture.* Beacon Press, NY.

MIRKIN, ALAN (EDITOR)
1970 *1927 Edition of the Sears, Roebuck Catalogue.* Bounty, NY.

PATTEN, DRAKE
1992 Mankala and Minkisi: Possible Evidence of African-American Folk Beliefs and Practices. *African-American Archaeology* 6:5–7.

SACKETT, JAMES R.
1989 Statistics, Attributes, and the Dynamics of Burin Typology. In Alternative Approaches to Lithic Analysis, edited by Donald O. Henry and George H. Odell. *Archaeological Papers of the American Anthropological Association* 1:51–82.

SCHROEDER, JOSEPH J.
1971 *1908 Sears, Roebuck Catalogue.* DBI Books, Northfield, IL.

UNITED STATES BUREAU OF THE CENSUS (USBC)
1870 Population Census, West Feliciana Parish, Louisiana. U.S. Government Printing Office, Washington, DC.
1880 Population Census, West Feliciana Parish, Louisiana. U.S. Government Printing Office, Washington, DC.
1900 Population Census, West Feliciana Parish, Louisiana. U.S. Government Printing Office, Washington, DC.
1910 Population Census, West Feliciana Parish, Louisiana. U.S. Government Printing Office, Washington, DC.
1920 Population Census, West Feliciana Parish, Louisiana. U.S. Government Printing Office, Washington, DC.

VAUGHAN, PATRICK C.
1985 *Use-Wear Analysis of Flaked Stone Tools.* University of Arizona Press, Tucson.

WEST FELICIANA PARISH RECORDS
1875 Marriage License of Lewis Freeman and Silvia Hill. Marriage Book C, No. 161. Recorded 5 June 1875. West Feliciana Parish, LA.

WILKIE, LAURIE A.
1994 *"Never Leave Me Alone": An Archaeological Study of African-American Ethnicity, Race Relations and Community at Oakley Plantation.* Ph.D. dissertation, Archaeology Program, University of California, Los Angeles. University Microfilms International, Ann Arbor, MI.

WILKIE, LAURIE A., AND PAUL FARNSWORTH
1992 National Register Testing at Oakley Plantation (16WF34), West Feliciana Parish, Louisiana, 1991. Report on file, State Division of Archaeology, Baton Rouge, LA.
1993 National Register Testing at Oakley Plantation (16WF34), West Feliciana Parish, Louisiana, 1992. Report on file, State Division of Archaeology, Baton Rouge, LA.

WILKIE, LAURIE A., AND STEPHANIE TANNERT
1994 An Archaeological and Historical Investigation of Site 16SC77 Discovered During Construction of State Project No. 700-19-0001 F.A.P. No. HES-373-1(004), St. Rose-Destrehan Highway Route LA 48, St. Charles Parish. Report on file, State Division of Archaeology, Baton Rouge, LA.

LAURIE A. WILKIE
DEPARTMENT OF ANTHROPOLOGY
UNIVERSITY OF CALIFORNIA
BERKELEY, CALIFORNIA 94720–3710

JANE BUSCH

Second Time Around: A Look at Bottle Reuse

ABSTRACT

Until recently, glass bottles were generally used more than one time. This study investigates customs of bottle reuse in the United States during the 18th and 19th centuries, with particular attention to the secondhand bottle business and returnable bottle systems. Effects of bottle-manufacturing machinery and reasons for the decline of bottle reuse are discussed. The implications of reuse for the analysis of bottles from archaeological sites are considered.

Introduction

Bottles are seductive. Bottle shapes and markings often indicate function and provenience, inviting archaeologists to guess the tastes, wealth, connections, and habits of the people who used the bottles. Nevertheless, archaeologists know that empty bottles were often reused for different purposes. Consider an empty soda pop bottle, embossed with a Philadelphia address, found at a house site in rural Pennsylvania. The occupant of the house might have received the bottle filled with homemade catsup from a relative in New York city. Reuse must be considered whenever bottles are found, and it complicates analysis.

The following account traces the history of bottle reuse in the United States from the 18th century, when bottles were relatively scarce and valuable, through the development of complicated collection systems during the 19th century, to the decline of bottle reuse following World War I. It is possible to see the extent, and the limits, of bottle reuse, and some patterns for specific bottle types and different geographic areas. This information should help to interpret bottles from archaeological sites. Furthermore, the history of bottle reuse is part of the history of trash disposal, a basic concern in all archaeology.

Reuse in the Eighteenth Century

Bulk packaging in ceramic and wooden containers was the norm during the 18th century. Glass bottles were relatively expensive, and the demand was greater than the supply. Most bottles were imported, a costly process. American glassworks produced some bottles, but they were hampered by shortages of capital and skilled labor and by inadequate transportation. In 1800 only eight glassworks are known to have been operating in the United States (McKearin and Wilson 1978:7, 28–68, 229).

New and old bottles were more than containers for other goods; they had trade value and property value. Brewers, snuff manufacturers, druggists, and other entrepreneurs who needed bottles to market their products gave cash or goods for new and old bottles (McKearin and Wilson 1978:229, 260, 262, 289). Peter Barbour offered money or snuff for bottles in the *Boston Gazette* in 1756 (Dow 1927:280–81). Jonathan Nash advertised "a good price" for quart bottles for his New York brewery in 1769 (Baron 1962:61). In 1779, Harmon & Lewis of Philadelphia offered "the highest price for empty claret bottles" (McKearin and Wilson 1978:223). Merchants attempted to conserve their supply of bottles by offering lower prices when bottles were returned. In May 1774, a New York brewer offered a dozen bottles of beer for 10 shillings, or 7 shillings if the bottles were returned (Baron 1962:62). A dealer in Hartford, Connecticut, in 1797 reduced his price for a dozen bottles of porter from 16 shillings, 2 pence, to 12 shillings when the bottles were returned (McKearin and Wilson 1978:230). In another approach to the shortage, customers provided their own bottles, as seen in this 1766 advertisement from the *Virginia Gazette:* "Any person who sends bottles and corks may have them carefully fitted and corked with beer and porter at 6s. or with ale at 4 s. the dozen" (Baron 1962:62). Sam Hudson sold cider in the same manner in Philadelphia during the Revolutionary War, when bottles became even scarcer (McKearin and Wilson 1978:230).

Seals were applied to wine and liquor bottles to

identify them as private property. Wine merchants used bottles with seals bearing their initials to designate ownership and to insure return of the bottles for refilling. Among affluent gentlemen, who could afford to custom order bottles from England, sealed bottles were fashionable for private use (McKearin and Wilson 1978:204). The chattel value of bottles is also evident in household inventories, which frequently list empty bottles. The estate left by Samuel Ruggles in 1716 included a small case with eight bottles among the hall furnishings. The 1763 inventory of the estate of Robert Oliver listed a case with small bottles in the setting parlour, and a case with two bottles in the dining room. Inventories list bottles in cellars, garrets, back rooms, and out of doors, often in large quantities: one-half gross (72) in the 1737 estate of Jacob Williams, one gross (144) in the 1732 estate of William Tailor. In the 1771 inventory of the estate of James Foster, $1\frac{1}{2}$ gross (216) quart-size bottles were valued at 48 shillings. By comparison, two brass kettles were valued at 40 shillings in the same estate (Cummings 1964).

Archaeological excavations have shown that bottles could be kept for decades before they were discarded. Wine bottles excavated from the John Custis house well in Williamsburg were at least 20 years old when they were deposited (Noël Hume 1974:188). A trash pit at Rosewell mansion in Virginia was filled sometime between 1763 and 1772, but most of the bottles (from a total of more than 350) were manufactured between 1725 and 1750 (Noël Hume 1962:172). At Wormslow plantation in Georgia, wine bottles manufactured between 1735 and 1760 were found in trash pits with artifacts post-dating 1770 (Kelso 1979:95).

The Growth of Supply and Demand

After the War of 1812 the supply of bottles more closely approached the demand. Bottle imports from England resumed at the end of the war. At the same time, the domestic glass industry was encouraged by protective tariffs, a greater supply of capital and skilled labor, and new roads and canals. In 1820 there were at least 33 glasshouses operating in the United States (McKearin and Wilson 1978:68–70, 230; Scoville 1948:7, 50). By 1880 there were 169 glasshouses in operation, with an annual output of bottles approximately seventy times greater than in 1820 (Scoville 1948:7, 64). Innovations in bottle manufacturing increased productivity. Full-size piece molds, adopted in America circa 1810, facilitated unformity and speed (McKearin and Wilson 1978:216, 219, 293, 410). Refinements in the division of labor culminated in the shop system, introduced around 1860 and dominant after 1870. During the same period, workers began to be paid by the piece instead of by the day, and the limit on the day's output was abolished (Scoville 1948:22; Anonymous 1905a:6). After 1880, productivity was augmented by the adoption of gas fuel, the tank furnace, and the annealing lehr (Scoville 1948:28–29, 76–77, 176–77, 337). In 1892, semi-automatic machinery was introduced into the production of wide-mouth glass containers (Scoville 1948:155). In 1899, U.S. glass container production totalled 7,780,000 gross, compared to 1,480,000 gross just twenty years earlier (Davis 1949:221; Anonymous 1955:3).

Growth in bottle manufacturing was accompanied by a decline in bottle prices (McKearin and Wilson 1978:223–24; Scoville 1948:48, 213, 249). Lower prices combined with changes in American life to expand the bottle market. Urbanization and a rising standard of living expanded substantially the markets for products that were formerly produced at home, such as liquor and canned food, and for products that were previously consumed in small quantitites, such as patent medicines and carbonated beverages. Glass container use grew along with the increased demand for packaging of all kinds. With the development of roads, canals, steamboats, and railroads, more packaging was needed to protect and preserve goods during shipment. Sealed glass containers helped to assure consumers that the contents were pure and sanitary. Brand names on bottles reinforced consumer confidence. Packaging was also adopted to make it easier for customers to bring home and store their purchases.

Glass bottles were common by the end of the

19th century. What was the effect on their value? In 1899, beer, soda, and whiskey bottles were valued at $3.75 per gross, roughly half their cost earlier in the century, but this was still expensive compared to other products (Scoville 1948:213). The skilled labor required in glassblowing kept the cost high: in the 1870s the wages of skilled glassmen were one-third to two-thirds greater than the wages of other skilled craftsmen, and two to three times greater than the wages of ordinary laborers (Scoville 1948:32–33). Furthermore, the demand for bottles had grown so much that it was still greater than the supply. To meet this demand in 1899, a number of houses petitioned the bottle blowers' union to operate part of the summer, when glassworks traditionally closed due to the heat (Anonymous 1899a:1). More than a billion new bottles were produced that year, but old bottles retained enough value to be saved and used again.

The Secondhand Bottle Business

In the first decades of the 19th century, people continued to reuse bottles much as they had during the 18th century. In the 1830s it was still customary for consumers to bring empty bottles directly to merchants in return for cash (McKearin and Wilson 1978:232, 289). Druggists continued this custom into the 20th century, charging customers for new prescription bottles, then refunding the charge if the bottle was returned, or omitting the charge if the bottle was refilled. Customers also brought their own bottles to druggists to be filled; sometimes these were medicine bottles, sometimes they were not (Anonymous 1903a:487; Hague 1913:135; Leslie 1840:211; Anonymous 1899b:11; Anonymous 1902a:18). Merchants such as druggists who used large numbers of bottles kept many as permanent store furnishings, refilling them as needed. The "shop furniture" used by druggists was even passed on from father to son (Munsey 1970:174). Similarly, bars and saloons served whiskey from bottles but purchased it by the barrel. It was the bartender's job to fill bottles from the barrel, as described in an 1869 manual: "The most unpleasant duties of the bartender are in the morning, when the bottles and decanters, reduced by the draughts of the day and night previous have to be refilled; the tumblers, used just previous to closing, washed, and everything put in order for the day's operations (Anonymous 1869; preferatory).

These simple cycles of bottle reuse were overshadowed by the growth of large businesses devoted to the trade in used bottles. As American commerce developed, the distance between manufacturers, merchants, and consumers increased, and middlemen moved in to facilitate the transfer of goods between them. In this case, used bottle dealers transferred empty bottles from consumers back to merchants and manufacturers. Information on the origin and early development of the secondhand bottle trade is elusive. First, there had to be enough used bottles to make the business profitable. A dealer named George Bartholf claimed to have started the first used bottle business in New York City in the late 1840s (Anonymous 1928:109–10). By 1878, soda bottlers were organizing against secondhand bottle dealers who unethically sold their bottles (Anonymous 1878:36). The secondhand bottle trade in Pittsburgh was reportedly founded in 1883 (Anonymous 1899c:7). The largest bottle dealer in Detroit started out in 1885 (Anonymous 1957:6). By the 1890s the secondhand bottle business was firmly established and thriving in America's cities.

In an 1896 report, New York City's Department of Street Cleaning described a flourishing business in used bottles:

> The trade in old bottles, for example, is enormous, several large establishments being devoted to it. At one store I was told that 5,000,000 bottles were kept in stock, that carload lots were received from different large cities, and that expensive exports were made to Europe (Department of Street Cleaning 1896:70–71).

In 1908 the secondhand bottle trade in New York state handled an estimated 2,000,000 gross bottles a year, at a value of $4,500,000 to $6,500,000 (Anonymous 1908a:32). Dealers received bottles from servants and employees who recovered them from private residences, restaurants, saloons, and hotels. Hotels were an important source, regularly collecting empty bottles even from the guest rooms and sending them to dealers by the wagon load. Many bottles arrived at the secondhand bottle dealer via pushcart men and junk shops. Large numbers of bottles were recovered from the dumps (Department of Street Cleaning 1896:34, 70–71; Anonymous 1903b:74; Anonymous 1905b:1; Anonymous 1899d:18). In New York city, ''scow-trimmers'' collected bottles from the waterfront garbage dumps. They set aside registered bottles belonging to soft drink and beer bottlers, and sold the remaining ''mixed'' bottles to bottle dealers for $1.50 a barrel. In 1896, New York's scow-trimmers collected approximately 500 barrels of mixed bottles a week, or 26,000 barrels a year (Department of Street Cleaning 1896:117).

Secondhand bottle dealers paid from one-half to two cents each for bottles around the turn of the century and sold the bottles for fifty cents less per gross than new bottles (Anonymous 1903b:74; Anonymous 1905b:1). Customers for used bottles were varied and widespread. In 1899 Jacobson Brothers of Pittsburgh sent an eight carload shipment of wine and champagne bottles to Puerto Rico and Cuba (Anonymous 1899c:7). The market for wine bottles was particularly good since few were manufactured in the United States. Secondhand bottle dealers distributed used European wine and champagne bottles to American wineries and to the fruit juice and gaseous water industries in upstate New York (Anonymous 1903b:74; Anonymous 1934a:10; Anonymous 1908b:13). Distilleries, bucket shops, and saloons provided a ready market for used whiskey bottles; illegal refilling of branded bottles with cheap whiskey was widespread (Anonymous 1903b:74; Anonymous 1908c:17). The South Carolina Dispensary, a legitimate customer, used as many secondhand whiskey bottles as possible for economy (Anonymous 1905c:88). Empty liquor bottles were also traditionally used in the sale of linseed oil, turpentine, and similar products (Anonymous 1938a:7). Embossed patent medicine bottles were purchased by the original medicine manufacturers or by imitators, and were used for bluing and ammonia (Anonymous 1903b:74; Blanc 1913:39). Large ink and mucilage bottles were returned to the manufacturers; cologne and perfume bottles went to the cheap scent manufactories on New York's East Side (Anonymous 1903b:74).

The Returnable Bottle System

The returnable bottle system complemented the used bottle business in the recovery of empty bottles. Returnable soda water bottles were used in New York city as early as the 1840s but did not become common until bottled soda became popular following the invention of the Hutchinson stopper in 1879 (McKearin and Wilson 1978:242–43; Riley 1958:97–98). Similarly, returnable beer and milk bottles became common after the 1870s. Lager beer was first bottled successfully in 1873, and the first known delivery of milk in glass containers was in 1878 (Anonymous 1909a:4; Munsey 1970:191). Under the returnable system, bottles were considered the legal property of the bottler, and customers were obligated to return them to the bottler for refilling. Bottles were embossed with the bottler's name, and frequently the reminder ''This Bottle Not To Be Sold'' or ''This Bottle To Be Washed And Returned'' (Wilson and Wilson 1968:170–77; McKearin and Wilson 1978:179, 242). Returnable bottles were practical when distribution was localized, as was generally the case with soda pop, beer, and milk. Their advantage was elimination of the cost of the bottle from the price of the product. Products such as patent medicine were expensive enough to absorb the price of the bottle, but a few cents added to the price of a bottle of soda would hurt sales. In the early 1900s a bottle of soda sold for 5¢; selling the bottle with the contents would have added an additional $2\frac{1}{2}$¢ (Scoville 1948:213). The returnable bottle system seemed sensible for these inexpensive, rapidly-consumed products, but it established ''the bottle question'' as the number one bottler headache.

The *National Bottlers' Gazette* called the bottle question ''the monstrous evil which every year saps the life from this otherwise prosperous trade (Anonymous 1882:3). In 1883 bottle loss was estimated at roughly 65 percent (Anonymous 1883:25). An 1896 report on the bottling business in the United States reported a total capital investment of $41,573,469 and an annual loss in bottles of more than $3,500,000 (Department of Street Cleaning 1896:119). To fight bottle loss, bottlers banded together in trade associations. The Pennsylvania Bottlers' Association, the Maryland Bottlers' Association, the Missouri Bottlers' Association and their counterparts throughout the United States secured the passage of state laws protecting the property rights of registered trademark bottles. They organized the recovery of bottles from other bottlers, private households, and dumps, setting up central bottle exchanges and clearing houses where bottles were sorted and returned to their rightful owners. Bottle exchanges received the most bottles from member bottlers who acquired other members' bottles mixed with their own empties. With many small soda and beer bottlers operating in one area, empties were inevitably scrambled. The exchange was foremost a means of getting these bottles back to their proper owners.

Bottle exchanges also directed the recovery of bottles lost to careless and illegal users. In an 1855 advertisement in the *Savannah Daily News*, one bottler warned: "I hereby caution all persons particularly those engaged in bottling against either buying, selling, using or in any way depriving me of my bottles bearing my name John Ryan" (Schmeiser 1968:8). Seventy years later the *National Bottlers' Gazette* was still deploring the activities of the "bottle louse" who used competitors' bottles (Carr 1926:122). The bottle louse had plenty of opportunity to appropriate bottles left for collection or simply abandoned by customers. Dishonest dairymen ensured a supply of milk bottles by collecting their competitors' empties from the doorsteps when they made their morning deliveries (Hagerman 1912:68). Saloons sold a large proportion of the bottled soda in the 19th century, and the bottling trade papers bitterly criticized the "always careless and too often unscrupulous" saloon keeper who sold soda and beer bottles to used bottle dealers, who sold them in turn to the bottle louse (Anonymous 1878:36). The Trade-Mark Act of 1876 prohibited the refilling of bottles that had registered trademarks blown in the glass, and subsequent state laws prohibited the sale of these bottles (Anonymous 1878:36; Peters 1902:24). By 1906, twenty-one states had laws imposing fines for dealing in registered bottles (Anonymous 1906a:30). The laws reduced, but did not eliminate the sale and reuse of registered bottles, and bottle exchanges hired detectives to track down violators (Anonymous 1905d:66; Carr 1926:122). Under the protective laws, bottlers were able to seize their property in raids and prosecute the violators. In 1921, within four months, the Massachusetts Bottlers' Exchange took more than 60,000 bottles in raids and prosecuted 30 bottlers for illegally using registered bottles (Anonymous 1921:34). Though dramatic, raids actually brought back fewer bottles than member exchanges and dump collections.

Large numbers of beer and soda bottles were lost to housekeepers who kept them for their own use, particularly in the fall (Anonymous 1900:56). "That period of the year when the good housewife begins to bottle her ketchup and make her preserves is at hand, and it is also the season when the Pennsylvania Bottlers' Protective Association makes its greatest efforts to prevent the bottles of its members from being utilized for purposes that necessitate hiding them in cellars and closets until gentle spring comes around again" (Anonymous 1902b:84). The shapes of beer and soda bottles made them particularly popular for home preserving. In 1901 the Pennsylvania Bottlers' Association found in Philadelphia homes over one million bottles filled with ketchup, sauces, corn beer, root beer, fruit wines, and other "exhilirating drinks" (Anonymous 1902b:84). Bottlers seldom prosecuted housewives, but they did confiscate the bottles (Anonymous 1902b:84; Anonymous 1905d:66). In the 20th century, bottle loss to home preserving declined, except during Prohibition. In 1922 the *National Bottlers' Gazette* attributed a shortage of soft drink bottles almost entirely to their use for home brew (Anonymous 1922:18).

Bottles taken by housekeepers and competing bottlers were lost to their legitimate owners, but they were still in use. Many bottles, however, were simply discarded. A bottle detective observed in 1905:

> Beer bottles are treated very much the same as boxes in which fried oysters are taken home. As soon as the box is done with it is thrown to one side to find the ash heap and finally the dump. The same is true with beer bottles. Many a man will take home a bottle or two of beer with his box of oysters and when the bottle is emptied it is thrown out with the oyster box (Anonymous 1905d:66).

Whereas saloon keepers legally or illegally returned bottles for refilling, consumers were more likely to throw bottles away. Archaeologists excavating late 19th century dumps in Atlanta found only fragments of beer bottles at a tavern dump but found whole bottles at domestic dumps (Dickens and Bowen 1980:54). Bottle exchanges followed the example set by used bottle dealers in recovering bottles from city dumps. In the 1890s a contractor for the New York Bottlers' and Manufacturers Association paid the scow-trimmers 50¢ a barrel to collect soda bottles, which he washed, sorted, and delivered to the exchange (Department of Street Cleaning 1896:119–20; Anonymous 1899:18). In 1895 the New York Association recovered 1,132,018 beer, soda, and siphon bottles from New York city and Brooklyn dumps. Milk bottlers were recovering 100,000 bottles a year from the New York dumps during the same period (Department of Street Cleaning 1896:119–20). In 1905, 453,475 milk bottles and 1,915,354 beer and soda bottles were recovered from the New York dumps (Anonymous 1906b:36; Anonymous 1906c:34). The New York Association found that dump bottles accounted for a consistently higher percentage of small soda bottles than of other bottles. In 1909 dump bottles accounted for 7% of the siphon bottles recovered, 20% of the quart-size bottles, 27% of the weiss beer bottles, 41% of the lager beer bottles, and 62% of the soda bottles recovered. Customers were understandably more careless with the smaller, cheaper bottles (Anonymous 1909b: 46–48). By the early 1900s, all of the state associations were recovering bottles from the dumps.

Reuse and Disposal ca. 1900

In 1900 a bottle manufacturer wrote:

> In no other country in the world is the consumption of glass bottles so great as in the United States. The reason for this is to be found in the greater material prosperity of the people of this country as compared with those of the old world. Here it is not the custom to preserve a bottle after it has once served the purpose for which it was originally intended (Tatum 1900:8).

Bottlers and bottle dealers recovered many bottles only after they were discarded, and recovery was far from complete. Used bottle dealers operated primarily in cities, even as far west as San Francisco, but the cost of collecting and shipping bottles from sparsely populated areas was generally too high to make the business profitable. Similarly, long distance "shipping brewers" found it too expensive to retrieve bottles used to ship beer across the Rocky Mountains (Cochran 1948:177; Kurtenacker 1914:58). In western mining towns, empty beer and liquor bottles were so abundant that in some towns they were used to build houses and sidewalks (Starry 1968:20–23; Baron 1962:254). In others they were just dumped. Even within the cities, bottles did not always make it to the city dumps, where they might be recovered, but were frequently broken or deposited in backyard dumps and vacant lots. A bottle detective described this scene in 1906: "In the various empty lots, especially those adjoining flat houses, many bottles, the greater number of them broken, can be found. It is so much easier to throw bottles out of the window." He noted that few bottles bearing the dates 1903 and 1904 were still in use (Brand 1906:28).

Consumers discarded empty bottles because they accumulated more than they needed. Housewives still used large quantities of glass containers for storage, home brewing, and preserving, but the number of bottles coming into the home was increasing. In 1910, twenty glass containers were produced for every person in the United States (Anonymous 1910a:1). Some of these glass containers contained prepared foods that the housewife formerly made herself, so the need for glass containers in the home was decreasing while the supply was increasing. A thrifty homemaker observed in 1916: "There is a vast array of bottles and jars accumulated in the course of a few months in the average home, in which pickles, cream cheese, dried beef, and various other kinds of edibles are sold, and there is a vast array of uses to which they can be put instead of being thrown away." (Farmer 1916:89–90). That same year, *Scientific American* noted that a very large portion of the bottles manufactured annually in the United States were thrown away after one use (Anonymous 1916a:56). Even where bottles were redeemable for cash, many people did not bother to redeem them. As the New York City Department of Street Cleaning reported:

> Old bottles are handled in every junk-shop, besides forming the sole stock in trade of a considerable number of dealers, large and small. But although they can be used over and over again, and are always exchangeable for cash, bottles are to be found in very load of garbage that reaches the dump (Department of Street Cleaning 1896:117).

Impact of the Bottle Machine

In 1903, when Michael Owens began marketing his automatic bottle manufacturing machine, the *New York Post* estimated that half of the bottles used in a year were lost and half were used again (Anonymous 1903b:74). Machine manufacturing did not at first affect this balance, although the effects on cost and productivity were immediate. The first Owens machines produced 35.4 gross pint beer bottles in an $8\frac{1}{2}$ hour day, while a shop of glassblowers and assistants produced 15 to 20 gross in the same time. Furthermore, the Owens machine could operate around the clock to produce at least 100 gross pint beer bottles in 24 hours. Productivity increased in subsequent models of the Owens machine; a 1917 model produced about five times as many bottles per day as a 1905 model. Greater productivity and the elimination of skilled bottle blowers combined to reduce the cost of production. Machine operators were paid $.20 an hour in 1906, compared to glass blower wages of $7.00 a day. The total labor cost for one gross of pint beers produced by an Owens machine between 1903 and 1907 was approximately $.10, compared to $1.50 by manual production. In 1916, factories using glassblowers paid 51.49% of the sales value of their annual product in wages. Owens machine licensees paid 31.38% of their product sales value in wages and machine royalties (Scoville 1948:65, 155–56, 159–62, 205, 211).

By 1917, when the Owens Bottle Machine Company opened the first completely mechanized glass factory, Owens machines accounted for 50% of the glass containers produced in the United States (Meigh 1960:25; Scoville 1948:184). There were also more than 300 semi-automatic bottle machines in use. Comparatively simple and inexpensive, semi-automatic machines were more practical for small orders and helped to fill the gap in machine supply created by the Owens Bottle Machine Company's limited licensing policy. Gob feeding devices that could be attached to semi-automatic machines to make them fully automatic were available for jars in 1915 and for bottles in 1918 (Scoville 1948:162, 180–89; Meigh 1960:36–38). In the 1922–23 glassblowing season, automatic machines, either Owens or gob-feeding, produced 80% of the glass containers made in the United States. In 1924–25, automatic machines accounted for 90% of glass container production (Davis 1949:213).

When machine manufacturing began, the growing bottle market readily absorbed the additional output. Machine manufacturing actually increased the demand for bottles by producing bottles that were notably more uniform in weight and capacity than bottles hand blown into molds. Uniform size assured both retailers and consumers that they were not being cheated in the sale of bottled products and encouraged the use of glass containers in place of bulk containers. While the growing demand was thus helping to prevent overproduction, the Owens Company was limiting the number of its licensees toward the same end (Scoville 1948:212, 214). In 1909 the president of the bottle blowers union reported optimistically: "Even with all the machines in operation last season, and every bottle maker in the country employed, the stocks of ware now on hand are lighter than at any former time" (Anonymous 1909c:1). Instead of lowering prices, machine users turned lower production costs into extra profits, even charging 50¢ to $1.00 more per gross because of the superior quality of their product (Scoville 1948:212; Anonymous 1910b:1; Anonymous 1909d:10).

In 1909 this balance began to falter. The bottle blowers took wage cuts of 20% in 1909 and another 20% in 1912, hoping to preserve the market for handblown bottles by reducing the price. Owens licensees retaliated by reducing their bottle prices (Scoville 1948:212–13). In 1911 the Owens Bottle Machine Company reported average price reductions for the company and its licensees of 10 to 20% over 1908 (Anonymous 1911a:1). One licensee, the American Bottle Company, reduced its pint beer bottles from $3.75 to $2.60 per gross before Word War I ended the price war. During the war years, 1914 to 1918, prices rose throughout the glass industry, though less rapidly than prices in general (Scoville 1948:213–14).

Meanwhile, machines with ever-increasing productive capacity were steadily replacing the bottle blowers. Overproduction was inevitable. In 1911, the *National Glass Budget* reported that there would be a delay in the resumption of bottle blowing following the summer break: "The longer a general resumption is delayed, the better it will be for the market as the year advances, since there is a producing capacity in excess of consumptive requirements" (Anonymous 1911b:1). In 1919, glass container production reached 22,295,000 gross, more than three times the number of glass containers produced in 1899 (David 1949:221). The Owens Company discontinued a machine that produced three hundred four-ounce prescription bottles per minute because its output was too great for the market (Anonymous 1942:10). Nevertheless, in 1934 the automatic bottle machines in use were capable of producing 100,000 bottles a day, or 700,000 a week, and *Modern Packaging* reported: "You seldom have call for a full week's production on any single bottle, except in such exceptional instances as that caused by the legalization of beer and liquor" (Anonymous 1934b:35). In 1936, standard twelve-ounce returnable beer bottles cost $2.80 per gross, the equivalent of $1.73 in 1911 dollars (Anonymous 1936a:3; U.S. Bureau of the Census 1975: 210–11). By comparison, pint beer bottles in 1911 cost $2.75 per gross (Scoville 1948:213). Machine manufacture accelerated the steady increase in bottle supply and decrease in bottle value that began during the 19th century, bringing the industry to the critical point where the supply of bottles surpassed the demand.

Decline of the Secondhand Bottle Business

Bottle manufacturers had always viewed used bottle dealers as a nuisance, but the competition took on new meaning with the arrival of machine manufacturing and overproduction. When the bottle blowers felt threatened by machinery, they channeled much of their anger toward their old enemies the bottle dealers. In 1905 the Glass Bottle Blowers Organization of the United States and Canada resolved to send a circular to all labor organizations in the country, asking them to encourage their families and friends to break all bottles before throwing them away (Anonymous 1905b:1). In the end, neither the bottle blowers nor the bottle dealers could compete with the bottle machines. While machine manufacturing was reducing the cost of producing new bottles, rising labor costs were increasing the cost of recovering old bottles. In *Municipal Refuse Disposal*, the American Public Works Association cited the high cost of labor for collecting and sorting materials as the primary cause of the decline of all forms of waste salvage (American Public Works Association 1961:308–9).

While the price advantage of used bottles was slipping, legislation to regulate the liquor industry crippled the secondhand bottle trade. Liquor bottles and imported wine bottles were the staples of the secondhand bottle business. In 1914, 2,689,000 gross liquor bottles and flasks were manufactured in the United States. The Eighteenth Amendment was ratified on 29 January 1919, and went into effect the following year. By 1919 liquor bottle production had already dropped to 993,000 gross (Barnett 1926:89). With liquor bottles practically eliminated, many bottle dealers undoubtedly went out of business, like the Kansas junk dealer who had to quit the bottle business in 1916 after Prohibition took effect in his state (Anonymous 1916b:73). On the other hand, there was a great demand for bottles suitable for bootleg liquor. Before 1920, the consumption of bottled liquor increased where local prohibition laws forced the closing of saloons (Anonymous 1910c:3). When Atlantic City began to enforce its Sunday Closing Law in 1913, the beaches became littered with bottles: "In a search made from Young's Ocean Pier to the Million Dollar Pier by one of the employees, 232 flasks of the pint and half-pint variety were discovered. This condition prevails only on Monday, following 'dry' Sundays" (Anonymous 1913:38). During Prohibition, bottle dealers who were able to maintain supplies of suitable bottles and were willing to deal with bootleggers must have flourished.

On 5 December 1933, the Eighteenth Amendment was repealed. Liquor boards prohibited the sale of bulk liquor in casks in the effort to establish tight control and prevent the resurgence of anything resembling the old time saloon (Anonymous 1933:32). Liquor was sold only in bottles, and well-established bootleggers took up the old practice of refilling the branded bottles of legitimate dealers (Anonymous 1935a:23; Anonymous 1935b: 12). In 1934, a Federal Alcohol Control administrator estimated that one gallon of illegal liquor was sold for every legal gallon (Anonymous 1934c:13). On 1 January 1935, the federal government enacted legislation prohibiting the resale, purchase, or use of used liquor bottles, even by the original filler. All liquor bottles were embossed "Federal Law Forbids Sale or Re-Use of This Bottle." Used bottles were supposed to be destroyed. Before mid-January, one million empty liquor bottles were seized in a raid on three New York secondhand bottle dealers (Anonymous 1935a:23; Anonymous 1935d:92). By August the price of bootlegged bottles had reportedly increased 500%. Sales of legal liquor and new liquor bottles increased: 5,663,000 gross liquor and wine bottles were shipped for domestic consumption in 1935, 7,447,000 gross were shipped in 1936 (Anonymous 1935d:483; Anonymous 1936b:3; Glass Container Manufacturers Institute 1960:54). By 1938 the law was pronounced successful in largely curtailing bootlegging (Anonymous 1938b: 705). As an aside, *Business Week* noted: "So far no one has worried about the problem of final destruction. The old liquor bottle may become as bothersome an outcast as the dulled razor blade" (Anonymous 1935a:23).

After 1935 the secondhand bottle business survived on a greatly reduced scale. In 1938 New York city's used bottle dealers did a million dollar annual business, a fraction of their sales volume at the beginning of the century. They dealt primarily in wine bottles, with a large share of food and beer bottles (Anonymous 1938c:16). Used bottle dealers tried to collect and sell the nonreturnable beer bottles introduced in 1935. These special lightweight beer bottles were strong enough for one filling but not necessarily for two; some broke when returned to the fillers (Anonymous 1940a:12; Anonymous 1940b:15). Lightweighting was applied to other glass containers, and, combined with the use of faster filling machinery, may have contributed to the decline of the used bottle business.

Public health was another contributor. People had long been concerned about using bottles recovered from dumps. In the early 1900s, some customers required secondhand bottle dealers to deliver their bottles packed in boxes as if they were new bottles from the glass factories (Anonymous 1903b:74). In 1899, the Pennsylvania legislature passed a law prohibiting the collection of bottles from refuse and the sale of any goods in previously used bottles (except for milk, soft drink, beer, and prescription bottles). The stated purpose of the bill was to protect the public health, but the state's important glass manufacturing industry was reported to be behind the bill (Anonymous 1899c:7; Anonymous 1905e:54). Although this particular law was not enforced, it shows an awareness of possible health hazards from bottle reuse. In the 1930s, state pharmacy boards began issuing regulations requiring new bottles for all liquid prescriptions (Husa 1941:653).

After World War II, new methods of waste collection and disposal further discouraged the recovery of old bottles (Darnay and Franklin

1972:14, 22, 98). In 1961, *Municipal Refuse Disposal* cited only one company that salvaged bottles, and their efforts were limited to returnable deposit bottles (American Public Works Association 1961:308–9). Apart from some trade in returnables, the used bottle market no longer existed. In the late 1960s, when consumers concerned about solid waste began voluntarily bringing their used bottles to recycling centers, the bottles were crushed and used for cullet.

Deposits on Returnable Bottles

During the period when the used bottle business was declining, the returnable bottle system was actually growing stronger through the use of deposits. As early as 1877, the trade journal *Carbonated Drinks* proposed a deposit system as the solution to the bottle loss problem (Anonymous 1877:3). No one questioned the wisdom of deposits. Without them, only a sense of honesty and responsibility motivated customers to return bottles, and this had proven insufficient. Customers actually had more incentive to sell bottles to dealers than return them to bottlers. A deposit provided incentive for return and defrayed the cost of the bottle when it was not returned. But bottlers delayed adopting a deposit system for fear that they would lose business, particularly if neighboring bottlers continued to "give bottles away" (Anonymous 1931:118). When significant numbers of bottlers began to charge deposits they usually adopted the system at the state or regional level to minimize unfair competition. In 1903 Milwaukee brewers began charging deposits on all bottles leaving the city (Anonymous 1903c:70). The Bottlers Association of (Washington) D.C. began placing a 2¢ deposit on every bottle in 1906 (Anonymous 1906d:31). Nebraska bottlers adopted a deposit system in 1909, followed by Kansas bottlers in 1911, and so forth (Anonymous 1911c:51). The trade journal *American Bottler* chronicled the spread of deposits and their benefits. One example cited was a Massachusetts brewery which used an average of 16.6 bottles to bottle a barrel of beer before they began charging deposits, and only 13.8 bottles per barrel with deposits (Nicholson 1916:39).

Deposits were widespread in the soft drink industry by the 1920s. Under the 1934 National Recovery Act Code of Fair Competition for the Bottled Carbonated Beverage Industry, deposits became mandatory (Carr 1926:122; Anonymous 1934d:39). The Code required a deposit no less than one-third of the replacement value of bottles and cases (Anonymous 1934e:11). In practice, 2¢ per bottle became normal. Following repeal, the brewing industry adopted deposits as standard practice, although they posed a problem for long-distance shipping brewers (Anonymous 1934f:3). Dairies were also using deposits in the 1930s, particularly for milk purchased at retail stores (Anonymous 1938d:3, 7; Anonymous 1946:65). Combined with more organized systems of pick-up and delivery, deposits reduced bottle loss far more effectively than bottle exchanges and dump collections, which were generally discontinued. When a Virginia bottler recovered bottles from the city dumps in 1949, the *National Bottlers Gazette* reported it as a curious incident (Anonymous 1949:39). Bottle loss was 3 or 4% in 1947, not insignificant, but still a fraction of the loss typical at the turn of the century (Comptroller General of the U.S. 1980:40).

Decline of Returnable Bottles

Returnable bottles for soda pop, beer, and milk were at their strongest during the 1930s and 1940s. The value of a 2¢ deposit encouraged bottle returns during the Depression; materials shortages enforced returns during World War II. In 1947, beer bottles travelled an average of 32 round trips from brewer to market, and soda pop bottles travelled an average of 24 round trips (Comptroller General of the U.S. 1980:40; Organization for Economic Cooperation and Development 1978:39). Yet it was during this period that nonreturnable containers began to threaten the use of returnable bottles. Paper milk bottles were used as early as 1902, but it was the square paper carton, introduced in 1934, that became a serious competitor to glass (Anonymous 1902c:68; Anonymous 1934g:50; Anonymous 1935e;125; Anonymous 1936c:16). Nonreturnable bottles and cans for beer were introduced in 1935 (Beer Can Collectors of America 1976:3; Anonymous 1935f:3). After World War II, nonreturnables progressed rapidly and steadily. By 1952, nonreturnable containers accounted for 30% of packaged beer and 37% of packaged milk (Anonymous 1959:79; Anonymous 1953:14). In the soft drink market, the progress of nonreturnables was slower; nonreturnable bottles were first used for soft drinks in 1948, and soft drink cans were not used successfully until 1953 (Anonymous 1948:107; Anonymous 1961:25). In 1978, nonreturnable containers accounted for 62% of packaged soft drinks and 89% of packaged beer (Comptroller General of the U.S. 1980:31). In 1976, nonreturnables already held 98% of the packaged milk market (Serchuk 1978:37).

Conclusions

When reuse is taken into account, as it must be, site interpretation based on bottles is more difficult. At the least there is the possibility of time lag between the dates of manufacture and disposal of bottles, reducing their usefulness in dating sites. Trade networks based on names and places marked on bottles are subject to error because bottles were often reused by different people in different locations. Furthermore, bottles can no longer be seen as an easy guide to consumer behavior. The relationship of what people consume to what they discard to what the archaeologist ultimately finds is complex. When efficient bottle collection systems are present, the evidence that a person drank a lot of soda pop, for example, would be removed or reduced. Of course an archaeologist would not base conclusions only on the absence of physical evidence. However the presence of a bottle, such as a wine bottle, does not necessarily indicate that wine was consumed for the bottle might have contained something else.

Despite these difficulties, archaeologists can still use bottles in site analysis. To begin with, awareness that reuse is a possibility will help to avoid simplistic interpretation. When a bottle must be dated, archaeologists should look for wear such as scratches and abrasions to indictate how long a bottle was used, as well as the way it was used. Wear patterns on bottles could be analyzed as they are on ceramics. Bottles can help to determine trade networks when conclusions are based on a sample rather than on isolated instances, particularly when evidence from bottles is combined with evidence from other artifacts and from historical research. For example, historical research shows that in the early 20th century the South Carolina Dispensary used secondhand liquor bottles, an important clue to archaeologists at early 20th century South Carolina sites. When commercial and industrial sites are excavated, archaeologists should note the variety of packages found there; excavation of a dairy site might yield bottles from other dairies in the area, or from other areas. Although the shape or label of a bottle is not an automatic indicator of its contents, in some cases traces remain of the last product it held, traces that can be analyzed. Again, historical research provides clues: European wine bottles were used to bottle fruit juices and gaseous waters in upstate New York, liquor bottles were customarily reused for paint products, and so forth. Site-specific historical research should provide more clues.

There are some rough guidelines as to where bottles were more likely to be reused than discarded. Bottle dealers were most active within and between cities. In contrast, large numbers of beer and liquor bottles shipped full to frontier mining towns were discarded when empty. Commercial users seem to have been more inclined than consumers to return bottles, at least at urban sites. One might hypothesize that at rural domestic sites, where packaged products were less common than in cities, bottles had greater value for reuse in the home. Analysis of dump sites has shown that small bottles were discarded more readily than large bottles.

If bottles seem less useful in determining dates, trade networks, and consumption patterns, consider that the decision whether to reuse or discard a bottle is itself an aspect of consumer behavior. If an archaeologist observes that the occupants of a site were discarding whole, usable bottles, that may reveal something about those occupants. Perhaps they were too wealthy, or too careless, to care about redeeming bottles for cash. It could be a sign that scavengers and bottle exchanges were absent in that particular area. Conversely, absence of usable bottles in a trash deposit might be linked to immigrant status; there is historical evidence that European immigrants were more accustomed than Americans to reusing bottles (Department of Street Cleaning 1896:119; Tatum 1900:8). Multiple use reduces the certainty of bottle interpretation, but it adds dimension. With more careful and sophisticated analysis, the result can be a richer, more complete knowledge of an artifact and the society where it was used.

ACKNOWLEDGMENTS

I would like to thank LuAnn DeCunzo, Judith McGaw, George Miller, and Robert Schuyler for their comments on earlier versions of this paper. Thanks also to Joseph Gallagher, Olive Jones, Kevin Lunn, and Karl Roenke for sending information on bottle reuse.

REFERENCES

American Public Works Association, Committee on Refuse Disposal

1961 *Municipal Refuse Disposal.* Public Administration Service, Chicago.

Anonymous

1869 *Steward and Barkeepers' Manual.* Jesse Handy & Company, New York.

1877 The Bottle Question. *Carbonated Drinks: An Illustrated Quarterly Gazette* 1(1):2–3.

1878 Protect Your Bottles. *Carbonated Drinks: An Illustrated Quarterly Gazette* 1(4):36.

1882 A New Proposition to Bottlers. *National Bottlers' Gazette* 1(1):3–4.

1883 Recovering Lost Bottles. *Carbonated Drinks: An Illustrated Quarterly Gazette* 6(3):24–25.

1899a The Glass Market. *National Glass Budget* 15(3):1–2.

1899b Familiar Bottles. *Meyer Brothers Druggist* 20(1):11.

1899c Pittsburg's Junk Bottle Industry. *National Glass Budget* 15(11):7.

1899d The Trade in Old Bottles. *Liquor Trades' Review* 7(26):18.

1900 Recovery of Bottles in Auburn, N.Y. *American Carbonator and American Bottler* 20(235):56.

1902a Unlawful Filling of Bottles. *American Carbonator and Bottler* 22(253):18.

1902b Bottles Lost by Thousands. *American Carbonator and American Bottler* 22(261):84.

1902c Paper Bottles for the Bottling Trade. *American Carbonator and American Bottler* 22(261):68.

1903a A Grave Source of Danger. *Bulletin of Pharmacy* 17(12):487.

1903b A Bottle Establishment. *American Carbonator and American Bottler* 23(266):74.

1903c Pay for Bottles. *American Carbonator and American Bottler* 23(263):70.

1905a A Government Bottle Report. *National Glass Budget* 21(18):6.

1905b Out-Gazams the Gazabos. *National Glass Budget* 21(12):1.

1905c To Buy Bottles. *American Carbonator and American Bottler* 25(290):88.

1905d The Washington Bottle Exchange. *American Carbonator and American Bottler* 25(288):66.

1905e Pennsylvania Law Against Refilling Bottles. *American Carbonator and American Bottler* 25(295):54.

1906a The Bottle Laws of the States. *American Bottler* 26(6):30–31.

1906b Milk Bottlers' Federation. *American Bottler* 26(3):36.

1906c Bottlers' and Manufacturers' Association. *American Bottler* 26(1):32–35.

1906d Washington's New Deposit System. *American Bottler* 26(11):31.

1908a Property Rights in Plain Bottles. *American Bottler* 28(6):32–33.

1908b Second-Hand Bottles. *Bar and Buffet* 6(25):13.

1908c Whisky Bottles Too Often Refilled. *Bar and Buffet* 5(20):17.

1909a The Export Beer Bottle. *National Glass Budget* 25(7):4.

1909b Association Affairs. *American Bottler* 29(11):46–48.

1909c The March of Progress. *National Glass Budget* 25(4):1–2.

1909d Thatcher Milk Bottle Catalogue. *National Glass Budget* 25(12):10.

1910a Bottles and Their Making. *National Glass Budget* 25(36):1.

1910b Bottle Machine Statistics. *National Glass Budget* 25(50):1.

1910c A Very Short Bottle "Crop." *National Glass Budget* 26(10):3.

1911a The Owens Bottle Machine. *National Glass Budget* 27(29):1.

1911b The Glass Bottle Situation. *National Glass Budget* 27(15):1–3.

1911c Kansas Bottlers Enforce the Deposit System. *American Bottler* 31(5):51–52.

1913 Bottles Strew the Beach. *American Bottler* 33(8):38.

1916a Glass Bottles. *American Bottler* 36(12):55–56.

1916b Bottle Business Slumps in Western Kansas. *American Bottler* 36(9):73.

1921 Exchange Saves Bottles. *American Bottler* 41(3):31.

1922 Curbing Bottle Losses. *National Bottlers' Gazette* 41(489):118.

1928 Forty Years Ago. *National Bottlers' Gazette* 47(557):109–112.

1931 Forty Years Ago. *National Bottlers' Gazette* 50(590):117–19.

1933 John Barleycorn Dresses Up. *Modern Packaging* 7(4):29–43.

1934a Glass Container Officials Report on Its Activities. *National Glass Budget* 50(22):3.

1934b The Materials of Packaging, No. 2: Glass Containers. *Modern Packaging* 8(2):33–39.

1934c Change Our Control Methods and Curb the Bootlegger. *National Glass Budget* 50(1):13.

1934d Code Approved! *National Bottlers' Gazette* 53(628):39–42.

1934e Rules Governing Deposits on Soft Drink Bottles. *National Glass Budget* 50(19):11.

1934f Business Holding Despite Adverse Conditions. *National Glass Budget* 50(6):3.

1934g New Paper Milk Bottle. *Scientific American* 151(1):50.

1935a Outlaw Empties. *Business Week*, January 12:23.

1935b Non-Refillable Bottles. *Business Week*, March 16:12.

1935c Fight to Stop Illegal Liquor Business Continues on Front of Package Control. *Glass Packer* 14(2):92–93.

1935d Bulk Liquor Means Bootlegging. *Glass Packer* 14(8):483–84.

1935e Paper Containers. *Food Industries* 7(3):125–26.

1935f New No-Deposit Beer Bottle Makes Its Bow to the Trade. *National Glass Budget* 51(16):3.

1936a The "Steinie" Joins "Stubby" in Defense Against Cans. *National Glass Budget* 52(19):3.

1936b Glass Bottle Sales Active; But Beer Bottle Menaced. *National Glass Budget* 51(40):3.

1936c Container Conflict. *Business Week*, March 21:16.

1938a No Early Improvement Seen in the Container Industry. *National Glass Budget* 54(7):3.

1938b 10 Years Progress in Glass Packaging. *Glass Packer* 17(11):668–71.

1938c Glass Containers Continue to Gain in Popularity. *National Glass Budget* 54(27):16.

1938d Glass Container Industry Faces an Uncertain Year. *National Glass Budget* 53(37):3.

1940a Annual Report of Glass Container Association by Ackerman Constructive. *National Glass Budget* 56(4):3.

1940b News and Notes Relative to the No-Deposit Beer Bottle. *National Glass Budget* 56(1):14–15.

1942 Recent Developments in Glass Container Litigation. *National Glass Budget* 57(38):3.

1946 Raise the Bottle Deposit? *National Bottlers' Gazette* 64(768):64–67.

1948 One-Way for Soda. *Modern Packaging* 22(3):106–8.

1949 Bottler Combs City Dumps for Empties. *National Bottlers' Gazette* 67(804):39.

1953 Milk Packaging Trend in Glass—Paper Containers. *National Glass Budget* 69(14):3.

1955 O–I Provides Pertinent Glass Container Facts. *National Glass Budget* 71(27):3

1957 Max Jacob Prominent Cullet Dealer for Sixty Years. *National Glass Budget* 73(12):6.

1959 Bottles and Cans Make Vast Strides. *Modern Brewery Age* 59(17):79.

1961 Marketing-Packaging Trends. *National Bottlers' Gazette* 80(956):25–26.

Barnett, George F.

1926 *Chapters on Machinery and Labor.* Harvard University Press, Cambridge; reprint ed. 1969, Southern Illinois University Press, Carbondale.

Baron, Stanley

1962 *Brewed in America: A History of Beer and Ale in the United States.* Little, Brown and Company, Boston.

Blanc, Joel

1913 When Truth Telling Does Not Advertise. *The American Bottler* 33(9):39–40.

Brand, Joseph

1906 Where Do the Bottles Go? *American Bottler* 26(1):28.

Carr, Frank P.

1926 How to Operate a Bottle Exchange. *National Bottlers' Gazette* 44(528):122.

Cochran, Thomas C.

1948 *The Pabst Brewing Company.* New York University Press, New York.

Comptroller General of the United States.

1980 *States' Experience with Beverage Container Deposit Laws Shows Positive Benefits,* PAD-81-08. General Accounting Office, Washington, D.C.

Cummings, Abbott Lowell (Editor)

1964 *Rural Household Inventories.* Society for the Preservation of New England Antiquities, Boston.

Darnay, Arsen and William E. Franklin

1972 *Salvage Markets for Materials in Solid Wastes.* U.S. Environmental Protection Agency, Washington, D.C.

Davis, Pearce

1949 *The Development of the American Glass Industry.* Harvard University Press, Cambridge.

Department of Street Cleaning

1896 *A Report on the Final Disposition of the Wastes of New York.* Department of Street Cleaning, New York.

Dow, George Francis

1927 *The Arts and Crafts in New England, 1704–1775.* Wayside Press, Topsfield, Mass.

Farmer, Lizzie C.

1916 *A-B-C of Home Saving.* Harper and Brothers, New York.

GLASS CONTAINER MANUFACTURERS INSTITUTE
1960 *Glass Containers, 1960.* Glass Container Manufacturers Institute, New York.

HAGEMAN, E. F.
1912 The Bottle Question. *American Bottler* 32(11):68–69.

HAGUE, GEORGE W.
1913 Practical Suggestions. *Meyer Brothers Druggist* 34(5):135.

HUSA, WILLIAM J.
1941 *Pharmaceutical Dispensing*, 2d ed. Husa Brothers, Iowa City.

KELSO, WILLIAM M.
1979 *Captain Jones's Wormslow.* University of Georgia Press, Athens.

KURTENACKER, CARL
1914 The Desirability of the Plain Bottle. *American Bottler* 4(5):58–59.

LESLIE, ELIZA
1840 *The House Book: or, A Manual of Domestic Economy.* Carey and Hart, Philadelphia.

MCKEARIN, HELEN AND KENNETH M. WILSON
1978 *American Bottles and Flasks and Their Ancestry.* Crown Publishers, New York.

MEIGH, EDWARD
1960 The Development of the Automatic Glass Bottle Machine. *Glass Technology* 1(1):25–50.

MUNSEY, CECIL
1970 *The Illustrated Guide to Collecting Bottles.* Hawthorn Books, New York.

NICHOLSON, JAMES R.
1916 Deposit Saves Large Sums. *American Bottler* 36(5):39.

NOËL HUME, IVOR
1962 Excavations at Rosewell, Gloucester County, Virginia, 1957–59. *United States National Museum Bulletin*, no. 225. Contributions from the Museum of History and Technology, paper 18, Washington, D.C.
1974 *All the Best Rubbish.* Harper and Row, New York.

ORGANIZATION FOR ECONOMIC CO-OPERATION AND DEVELOPMENT
1978 *Beverage Containers: Re-Use or Recycling.* OECD Publications, Paris.

PETERS, W. A.
1902 Trade Marks in the Bottling Industry. *American Carbonator and American Bottler* 22(251):24.

RILEY, JOHN J.
1958 *A History of the American Soft Drink Industry: Bottled Carbonated Beverages, 1807–1957.* American Bottlers of Carbonated Beverages, Washington, D.C.

SCHMEISER, ALAN
1968 *Have Bottles Will Pop.* Michalan Press, Dixon, California.

SCOVILLE, WARREN C.
1948 *Revolution in Glassmaking: Entrepreneurship and Technological Change in the American Industry, 1880–1920.* Harvard University Press, Cambridge.

SERCHUK, ALAN
1978 Milk Packaging Still in Transition. *Modern Packaging* 51:37–40.

STARRY, ROBERTA W.
1968 Bottle Houses. *Old Bottle Magazine* 1(11):20–23.

TATUM, C. A.
1900 Druggists Glassware. *National Glass Budget* 15(47):8.

U.S. BUREAU OF THE CENSUS
1975 *Historical Statistics of the United States, Colonial Times to 1970*, Bicentennial ed., part 1. Government Printing Office, Washington, D.C.

WILSON, BILL AND BETTY WILSON
1968 *Spirits Bottles of the Old West.* Wilson and Wilson, Wolfe City, Texas.

JANE BUSCH
WESTERN RESERVE HISTORICAL SOCIETY
10825 EAST BOULEVARD
CLEVELAND, OHIO 44106

JOHN D. LIGHT

A Field Guide to the Identification of Metal

Introduction

Despite the fact that the excavation of an historical site normally yields an abundance of metal, this material is not extensively understood by archaeologists. Difficulties often begin in the field lab, and erroneous descriptions applied there can remain attached to an object for a long time. Usually problems relate to identification and description; the person in the lab is constantly asking: what is the stuff made of and what do I call it? For example, is it possible to call iron everything made from the element iron, and what is brass and how can it be differentiated from any other yellow metal? This field guide has been written to help solve these problems.

It should be emphasized that this is neither a laboratory guide to metals, nor a discourse on the artistic nuances between the metal of one era and that of another. Neither does it deal with every known metal as some, such as cobalt and platinum, are uncommon or of minimal importance or both. For these and other metals not discussed herein, consult general works like Tomlinson (1851) and Tylecote (1992). The only purpose of this guide is to suggest terminology and explain the cogent features for which one should look when attempting to provide the rudimentary, but accurate, descriptions which are required of field lab staff. Accordingly, there are only brief descriptions of alloy percentages such as may be necessary to give a minimal description of something, and the technology of manufacture is usually avoided. For example, rolled gold is mentioned, but the means used to make dissimilar metals roll together evenly is left unsaid. Antimony and bismuth are mentioned, not because they are found archaeologically, but because they are important as alloys in some common metals.

So, too, although processes of production and manufacture of metals often need to be expounded for the greatest clarity, space constraints in this article permit only rudimentary mention of production methods or manufacturing techniques. Further reading is, therefore, required for a clear understanding of the subject. Some good general works include Van Nostrand (1947), Mullins and Shaw (1968), Doyle (1969), Knauth (1974), Dick (1975), and Brady et al. (1997).

The principal metals are discussed in alphabetical order. A brief glossary of unfamiliar terms is provided at the end of the guide.

Aluminum

Aluminum is a lightweight, soft white metal, tending to blue. It is very malleable and ductile, and can be polished; indeed, one of its early uses was to serve as a replacement for silver on reflectors. This was not because it was less costly–in fact, it was a rare and expensive metal originally–but because its long-term performance was better than silver. Aluminum and most of its alloys resist corrosion very well in air because a film of protective oxide forms on the bare metal surface. If subjected to prolonged exposure, the oxide becomes a dull bluish-gray.

The fairly recent discovery of metallic aluminum (1825) and its even more recent application to the production of objects (the first aluminum item was a royal baby rattle, ca. 1855), make it useful for dating. Meager commercial production of aluminum began in England in the 1860s and 1870s, but it was World War I that provided the real growth for the aluminum industry. During the war, 90% of all the aluminum produced was consumed by the military, but after the war it became increasingly available to consumers. Between the wars, numerous alloys were developed and innovative production techniques were generated so that after the shortages of World War II, aluminum became universally available to the consumer.

During the 19th century, aluminum was used for jewelery, ornaments, reflectors, novelty items, and wire for embroidery, including military banners and epaulets. Aluminum leaf sometimes replaced silver leaf. Napoleon III saw the possibilities it offered for lightweight military equipment and stimulated research into aluminum metallurgy.

Pure and industrial research into the metallurgy of aluminum has produced a bewildering array of alloys and production techniques. Commercially viable aluminum alloys have been made with the following metallic and nonmetallic elements: silver, copper, lead, bismuth, manganese, magnesium, silicon, zinc, lithium, chromium, platinum, nickel, and tin. Although they were the first ones developed, only iron-aluminum alloys lack a commercial use. For this reason, only the designation aluminum or aluminum alloy should be given to an object in the field lab.

Aluminum is not normally difficult to identify. The best indications are weight and color. Although the oxide can resemble tin oxide in color, the lack of weight will betray aluminum.

Antimony

Antimony is a bluish-white, extremely brittle metal which is not found commercially in its pure form. Its only commercial use is as an alloy with other metals, particularly copper and tin, with which it forms Babbitt's metal for bearings, and copper, zinc, and tin with which it forms Britannia metal. Another alloy, called tutania after its English inventor William Tutin who produced it in 1770, is 32 parts antimony, 8 parts brass, and 7 parts tin. It was used for such things as buckles, buttons, and spoons. In most alloys, however, antimony is undesirable because it imparts its inherent brittleness to the alloy.

Arsenic

Arsenic was once regarded as a metal (Partington 1835:118; Ure 1848:82) because its physical properties resembled those of metals, but it is now classified as a semimetal because it does not resemble metals in its chemical properties (Brady et al. 1997:68). It is a common constituent of the ores of many metals but, although it appears as an ingredient in various alloys and compounds, arsenic is never found archaeologically in pure form. It is volatile, steel-gray in color, brittle, about as hard as copper, and extremely poisonous. It is now chiefly used industrially in pigments, bearing metal, lead shot, and glass production as well as in poisons, insecticides, and herbicides. Historically, it was used in glass production and is found in alloys, especially copper alloys such as "white tombac." It is generally undesirable as an alloy because it imparts its inherent brittleness.

Bismuth

Bismuth is a reddish-white, extremely brittle metal which is not found commercially in its pure form. Its only commercial use is as an alloy with other metals. The addition of bismuth to an alloy lowers the melting point, which makes it particularly useful for such things as solders and printers type metal.

Copper

Copper is a soft, orangey-red metal which is both very malleable and very ductile. It has been used continuously since antiquity, and is very possibly the earliest known metal. It may readily be remelted, alloyed, and cast, or reused in some other way; so, despite the fact that it is the second most common metal after iron, it is never found as scrap in the same quantities. Copper does not cast well because it flows poorly into a mold and sets badly on its surface in the mold. However, because of its ductility and malleability, it rolls and hammers easily; so most copper objects are hammered, drawn, rolled, or stamped.

Pure copper is commonly found. For example, because it is an excellent conductor, and because impurities lower its conductivity, electrical apparatus–like wire and bus bars–are ordinarily pure copper. Water tubes and pipes are also made from pure copper because of its easy solderability and general resistance to corrosion, and in the days of black powder, barrel straps, scoops, etc., were copper because it will not spark. Copper's conductivity led to its service in cookware, a usage which continues today. Copper-clad wooden hulls, sheathed as protection against borers which avoid copper, are well known as are the distinctive sheet roofs, green from a protective film of carbonate, on many famous buildings.

Despite the very common nature of these objects, the most frequent use of copper is in alloys, both as the principal metal and as an additive. There are three principal alloys of copper: bronze, brass, and nickel-silver. The subject of copper alloys is vast, and numerous books, many very current, have been written on the topic, among them Hughes and Rowe (1986); Fennimore (1996); Brady et al. (1997). Earlier sources like Ure (1848) and Tomlinson (1851) also have good articles on many metals including such copper alloys as bronze and brass. What follows here is only meant to cover the salient points.

Copper Alloy

Copper can be alloyed with many metals and, through the centuries, almost every conceivable alloy has been attempted. In this work, copper is discussed as an additive under the principal metal. As the primary metal, copper is alloyed in a wide variety of ways. Although some authorities, especially more modern ones, maintain that there are two broad categories for all copper alloys–bronzes and brasses (Van Nostrand 1947:198)–it is generally conceded that there are three common alloys: bronze, brass, and nickel-silver (Ure 1848:338 ff.; Child and Townsend 1988:11; Gentle and Feild 1994:447-448). In the simplest terms, bronzes are copper-tin alloys, brasses are copper-zinc alloys, and nickel-silvers are brass with nickel added. It is not uncommon, however, to find an alloy of copper, zinc, and tin in various ratios.

As with all alloys until around the late 19th century, the proportions of each metal in the mixture were but indistinctly known by the founder. Copper alloys were mixed by eye for particular characteristics, such as color and hardness, and they were mixed with metals which were never perfectly refined. Copper alloys, like pewter, were also often remelted and reused. Furthermore, the crucibles were small (Singer et al. 1958:609) and it was not unusual to cast a single object from two or more crucibles containing imprecisely mixed alloys. For example, a late 18th-century candlestick belonging to a colleague (P. Dunning collection), has a mottled bronze-brass appearance, although it was likely intended to be bronze. What appears to have happened is that two crucibles, each containing slightly different mixtures, have been poured together into the neck of the mold. This object is far from unique.

Despite the fact that the colors of copper, brass, bronze, and nickel-silver are different and easily differentiated, the difficulty of knowing exactly what alloy is involved it makes advisable in most field lab situations to use the term "copper alloy" rather than a specific term. Even for someone who is familiar with the problems of identification, terms such as "probable brass" or "probable bronze" are often more useful for an initial catalogue than a precise designation. Nickel-silver, on the other hand, is frequently marked as such (EPNS: electro-plated nickel-silver), and it is probably just as easy to identify it uniquely as it is to identify it as a copper alloy.

All copper alloys can be easily plated, and many varieties were. They can also be used as a plating, one example being brass over ferrous metal.

Copper alloys are also commonly joined together by a form of soldering called brazing. Brazing refers to a group of soldering processes in which the filler metal is a non-ferrous alloy with a melting temperature higher than approximately 1000ºF, but less than the melting temperature of the metal(s) to be joined. In practice this often means an alloy of copper and zinc, so the process of soldering with brass is called brazing. Sometimes tin or silver are part of the filler metal.

BRONZE

Bronze is a copper-tin alloy. It was the first deliberate alloy known in antiquity (Meier 1970:4), a development so significant that an "age" was named after the metal. The bronze statuary, weapons, and axes of classical antiquity are well known, as are the famous Chinese bronzes. Bronze, being hard and brittle, is very difficult to work, so the normal method of manufacture is by casting. In this regard, it is a superior metal. Even so, lead, which increases the fluidity of molten bronze, was frequently added, especially to artistically important pieces or pieces which had to set up finely. The color of bronze varies with the alloy, but it can be anywhere from brown through coppery-orange and red-gold to pale gold. It is always darker and redder than brass.

Unlike pewter, bronze is extremely resonant, and it is often used for bells. Bronze alloys are noted for toughness and strength, as well as the ability to wear well and resist corrosion. For this reason cannon, bushings, pressure castings, gears, and the like were frequently made of a bronze, and the metal was often named for its purpose, such as gunmetal and bell metal. One kind of bronze which has a specific name is speculum. A very brittle metal which is one-third tin and two-thirds copper, speculum was used for the mirrors of telescopes because it has a brilliant blue-white color and can take a very high polish.

BRASS

The uses to which brass were put are legion. Tableware, kitchen utensils, personal items of adornment, lighting devices, scientific implements, tools, writing implements, building hardware, locks, weapon furniture, and marine fixtures are just some of the manifold uses of brass.

Brass is a copper-zinc alloy. Though not nearly as old as bronze, it has, nevertheless, been known for many centuries, but it is a more difficult alloy to achieve because at the melting temperature of copper, zinc is volatile. The whiteness of the zinc modifies the redness of the copper when it is alloyed, so that at 95% copper, the mixture is quite coppery-red. As more zinc is added, it becomes more pale, until at about 75% copper and 25% zinc, the alloy is a very sallow yellow. Then, as more zinc is added, the mixture becomes a deeper yellow until at about 30% copper it suddenly turns white. Together with the color changes come changes in ductility, fusibility, hardness, and malleability. These traits also change with the addition of aluminum, antimony, arsenic, iron, lead, nickel, and/or tin, all of which have at one time or another been alloyed with brass in various proportions.

Most brass was cast because it is an excellent casting metal. It will take fine, detailed designs in the mold, and can be decorated and highly polished afterwards. Decoration is commonly found on brass objects because it is easy to engrave, etch, paint, plate, punch, or raise. Brass can be drawn, rolled, spun, stamped, or wrought as well, though some alloys were better suited for one or another of these processes. Brass, for example, was difficult to spin, and a practical means of using this known process was only developed for brass in 1851 (Kauffmann 1979:78-79). Special alloys were devised for one or more of these manufacturing methods, as well as for specific usages. Names were often developed, especially during the 19th century, for specific alloys, not only to denote special characteristics, but also for marketing. Some of the more common names (besides just plain brass) were bath metal, Dutch gold, gilding metal, latten, Manheim gold, Muntz metal, pinchbeck, Prince's or Prince Rupert's metal, red brass, similor, standard English brass, tombac, and yellow metal (Fennimore 1996:18).

Brass is ductile and malleable, takes plating (tin or zinc) very well, and itself serves as a plate for ferrous metal. It can be easily remelted and cast and reused in other ways, so it is not found in large quantities as scrap. Blacksmiths formerly scavenged brass objects and them into pieces small enough to serve as raw material for brazing. The corrosion products of brass are green, though it is characteristically resistant.

NICKEL-SILVER

Nickel-silver is an alloy of copper, zinc, and nickel. The Chinese produced it for centuries, and it was imported into Europe under the name paktong. Europeans had been both searching for its secret and making objects using the imported metal since the 18th century, but it did not go into production in Europe until the late 1820s (Gentle and Feild 1994:448). It is brass with nickel added, thus some authorities wish to classify it as a kind of brass, but it was not historically understood, probably because of its color, in that manner. It is a distinctive, hard, tough, very versatile metal which can be cast, drawn, hammered, rolled, spun, and stamped.

As with other copper alloys, its composition can vary considerably and, not infrequently, a different name goes with a different composition.

For example, Ure (1848:341) gives the following percentages for nickel-silver according to the purpose for which it is intended: as a silver substitute - 50% copper, 25% zinc, 25% nickel; as an alloy for rolling - 60% copper, 20% zinc, 25% nickel [sic]; as an alloy for candlesticks, bells, etc. - 60% copper, 20% zinc, 20% nickel, 3% [sic] lead ; and "genuine" German silver - 40.4% copper, 31.6% nickel, 25.4% zinc, 2.6% iron. Aside from German silver, names which have been used for nickel-silver include, among others, white copper, Argentine (argentan), electrum, Nevada silver, paktong (also pakfong, packfong, and petong), tutenag (also toothenague, and tooth and egg—an old name for zinc mistakenly applied to paktong), and Silveroid.

The alloys vary widely, thus so does the color which can range from white to several shades of pale yellow. It resists tarnishing and corrosion very well. Fortunately, nickel-silver is frequently marked. Unfortunately, despite the nickel content, it is not magnetic.

When it was first produced, nickel-silver was used as a base for fused silver plate (Sheffield plate), but when electro-plating superseded the old plating methods in the 1850s, nickel-silver became the preferred base metal because any wearing away of the silver was not immediately obvious. Cutlery was produced in both plain nickel-silver and EPNS. The former, of course, was the cheaper of the two.

Ferrous Metal

Ferrous metal is the term for any metal, whether pure or an alloy, whose principal ingredient is the element iron (Fe). Iron is the most abundant metal on the planet, but it is not found in nature (except for a few meteorites) in a usable form. To obtain iron, its ore must be processed in some manner.

Unlike most other metals, iron is magnetic, and the vast majority of ferrous metals are magnetic, so this is a good test if one is unsure about the identity of a metallic object. Unfortunately, a few modern ferrous alloys are non-magnetic, as are some of the products of the decomposition of iron. All iron made before the last quarter of the 19th century is magnetic.

Cast Iron

Cast iron, as its name implies, was once molten. In its molten state, it was poured into some form of mold or channel either to produce a finished product, like a stove or cannon, or to produce an object of manageable size for further processing, like pig iron. Cast iron is high in carbon content (approximately 3% to 4.5%), making it brittle and subject to fracture under a sufficient impact load. It cannot be forged by a smith and apart from remelting in a blast furnace, it can only be reused with great difficulty.

There are three basic types of cast iron: "gray," "mottled," and "white." Gray cast iron contains a relatively high proportion of carbon present in the form of flake graphite, whereas in white cast iron the carbon is combined chemically with other elements and is therefore not "free" as it is in graphitic carbon. Mottled cast iron is a mixture of gray and white in varying degrees and, therefore, falls between the two in any descriptive categories. Although white cast iron is finer, has a higher carbon content, is harder, more resistant to wear and compression, and is more brittle than the more-coarse gray cast iron, it is unwise to attempt the classification of iron without sufficient experience and proper expertise. All three types of cast iron are subject to brittle fracture; they break in such a way as to show little or no evidence of plastic deformation. In other words, like ceramic, cast iron does not bend. Like ceramic, too, cast iron may be mended.

If the break in the cast iron is fresh, the surface of the fracture will betray the variety of cast iron by its appearance. The surface of a fresh fracture of gray cast iron will appear gray because of the graphitic carbon, the mottled iron will appear uniformly speckled; and the white cast iron will likely show columns of crystals, like ice crystals on a window, pointing to the surface of the mold, along with sporadic black spots. Should casting defects be present, they are liable to be more obvious in white cast iron than in other irons.

Despite these distinctions, it is appropriate to stress that any attempt to classify cast irons (indeed any metals) without sufficient experience and training is fraught with difficulties. It is best in a field lab simply to class the material as "cast iron" and defer further analysis.

Wrought Iron

From the discovery of the production of iron until this century, the common ferrous material has been wrought iron, also known just as iron. Wrought iron was *the* common smith's stock until the early part of this century. Its current rarity is a major obstacle for those engaged in historic craft enactment who give more than lip service to historical accuracy because both the techniques and the processes of manufacture vary, sometimes considerably, between wrought iron and its modern equivalent, mild steel. Aston and Story (1942) present a good introduction to wrought iron.

Iron was made either by the direct process in bloomeries or by the indirect process in blast furnaces. In either case, it was forged (wrought) by hammers and, in later periods, rolled in mills before it reached market. Wrought iron contains slag which, through hammering or rolling, becomes aligned in stringers throughout the body of the piece. These stringers are called either grain (because of the obvious similarity to wood grain) or fiber by a smith. Metallurgists prefer tighter usage, referring to stringers as fiber, reserving the term grain for crystalline structures within metals. It is these stringers, however, which give iron its unique properties. Its heterogeneity makes it easy to recognize if the surface has corroded enough to make this characteristic visible. If not, it looks much like any other ferrous metal.

Steel

Before the modern steel-making processes, steel was any mixture of iron and carbon containing up to 1.7% carbon and minor amounts of other elements (such as manganese, silicon, and phosphorous) depending on the ore. Carbon steel is harder and more durable than iron. It, like most steels, has a critical transformation temperature range during which it undergoes changes in properties. This characteristic allows for heat treating (annealing and tempering) in order to achieve maximum softness or hardness or the right balance of the two.

Although steel could be made directly in a bloomery, the common method of making iron and steel from about the 16th century on was in the blast furnace where steel could not be made directly. Pig iron from the blast furnace was used to make wrought iron. All the carbon was burned off the pig and the resulting "bloom" was forged or rolled into sheets or bars of wrought iron. The carbon-free iron, however, did not wear well and carbon had to be reintroduced (the commercial process was called cementation) to give it hardness and durability. This resulted in added cost, and steel was both costlier and in shorter supply than iron. The first reintroduction of carbon into iron was called blister steel. If blister steel were run through the process a second time it was called shear steel. A third time produced double-shear steel. Each step made the steel more expensive, so blister steel tended to be used for coarse applications and shear steels for more refined purposes. The important thing to stress here, however, is that wrought iron and carbon steel made from wrought iron are visibly indistinguishable.

It should be noted, too, that iron and steel can also be, and often were, welded together to make a single object, such as an iron pick with steel points. A good weld will leave little trace on an uncorroded object, so it may appear that there is only one material present.

Although they look the same, iron and steel were used differently. They can often be differentiated by this means. For example, files were always steel, as were the business ends of tools (the faces of hammers and the bits of axes), while the central portions of tools and bolts were almost invariably iron. It is impossible (and also not the place here) to list all the potential variations. It needs to be pointed out, however, that the distinction between iron and carbon steel can be made by one who is familiar with ferrous artifacts. Without this familiarity (as in a normal field lab situation), it is best to refer to the material as ferrous metal, *not* iron or steel, and defer closer identification. Barraclough (1976) provides more information on steel.

Cast Steel

In 1740, a new steel–crucible steel, also known as cast steel–was introduced to the commercial market. The inventor of the commercial process, Benjamin Huntsman, took blister steel, melted it in a glass-furnace crucible, skimmed off the slag which rose to the top (the material which produced the wrought iron fiber) and cast the material in an ingot. The ingot could be forged like any other steel, but having been molten and cast, it was a homogeneous carbon steel which no longer had a fibrous structure. It was, therefore, sought after for fine or delicate applications in which the fiber could be considered an inconvenience, such as watch springs, table knives, and fine files. Cast steel was extremely scarce and correspondingly expensive; however, by about 1800, it became fairly common to see knife blades marked "cast steel." This became a quality mark and, like other quality marks, it was sometimes abused.

Although cast steel is a homogeneous ferrous metal which is easy to differentiate from wrought iron or steel made from wrought iron, it is impossible to distinguish cast steel visually from most modern steels; indeed, in the late 19th century, objects made of Bessemer steel (Gale 1967:95) were often marked "cast steel" (which was true in the very literal sense) in order to gain market share.

Mild Steel

Mild steel is the modern equivalent of wrought iron but without the slag stringers which give iron its fibrous structure. After the invention of the Bessemer process in 1856, mild steel gradually replaced wrought iron as the everyday stock of the blacksmith, who used it to make all of the objects normally made of iron. Today, wrought iron is unavailable commercially in the western world, having been replaced by mild steel. Without training and experience, it is not possible to identify it visually.

Mild steel is highly ductile and malleable, though less so than wrought iron, but it has greater tensile strength. Mild in this context means soft (as in mild weather), and though mild steel may contain as much as 0.25% carbon, it cannot be tempered. With no, or virtually no, carbon, it is known as very mild steel. It may be case hardened; turned into steel on its surface by being packed in carbon and "baked." Historic craft enactments by smiths are usually hampered by having to use mild steel in place of wrought iron because it changes the work patterns of traditional blacksmithing.

Alloy Steels

Alloy steels, of which there are now many, began to appear in the last quarter of the 19th century. After the Bessemer process for making steel was discovered in 1856, it was realized that other elements than carbon could be mixed with iron on a commercial basis. In 1868, R. F. Mushet produced the first of the true alloy steels by producing a tungsten alloy called self-hardening steel. This steel made machine tools more effective. Other alloys using chromium, nickel, and manganese followed quickly. Some of these alloys could not be worked by hand blacksmiths, but appeared only in machine-made forms.

Trying to distinguish most alloy steels from mild steel or cast steel is a task best left to an analytical lab, so "ferrous metal" is the best designation for field lab purposes.

STAINLESS STEEL

One easily recognizable form of alloy steel which has been commercially available only since the 1920s is stainless steel. All stainless steels, of which there are dozens, contain chromium in the alloy. There are three types of stainless alloys: austenitic, ferritic, and martensitic. They are impossible to differentiate visually.

Austenitic stainless steels are the most common. They contain nickel and small amounts of carbon, but sometimes manganese and nitrogen are used as nickel substitutes. If these steels are improperly heat treated, they can be prone to a kind of decomposition called intergranular corrosion, and if small specks of corrosion are present on a stainless steel object, it is likely austenitic stainless. Ferritic stainless steels contain high chromium and no nickel, while martensitic stainless steels contain balanced amounts of nickel, carbon, and chromium.

Austenitic stainless, which is the most expensive, is used where oxidation resistance and strength at high temperature are needed in addition to corrosion resistance. Food preparation equipment and machinery are typical applications. The cheapest, ferritic stainless steels, tend to be used where less strength, and even less corrosion resistance, can be tolerated, such as in automobile body trim. Finally, martensitic stainless is the hardest and is used for things like cutlery and razor blades where wear resistance is at a premium.

The best quick way to distinguish between the various varieties of stainless steel is magnetism. Austenitic stainless steels are non-magnetic, while the other two types are magnetic.

Plated Ferrous Metal

There are five metals commonly used to plate ferrous metal: tin, zinc, brass, nickel, and chromium. The plate is always thin enough to allow the magnetism of the ferrous metal to be evident.

BRASS PLATE

Iron objects can be plated with brass either by dipping or electroplating. It was common in the last 150 years to plate such things as bedsteads, lamps, and architectural fittings with brass. Magnetism will reveal if a "brass bed" is solid or plated.

CHROMIUM PLATE

Chrome is a blue-white, very hard metal which is extremely resistant to corrosion and can be polished to a mirror finish. It has been around for most of the 20th century, but only after World War II did it become common to use it for commercial electro-platings on such things as automobile trim. The bright color and high shine are the best keys for quick identification purposes.

Another thing to look for is the fact that when chrome is plated over base metals, it tends to flake or peel. For this reason it is usually plated over a thin coating of nickel or, occasionally, copper. All three of these metals can produce greenish corrosion products, so the color is not a reliable guide.

NICKEL PLATE

Nickel is only occasionally found in its pure state on such things as scalpel handles, but its normal use is as either a plating or an alloy. As a plating on ferrous metal, it was used on a multitude of things such as car parts, the tops of salt and pepper shakers, and bicycle fittings. Nickel is a hard metal and resists scratching and abrasion well.

Nickel plate is shiny and white. It does not corrode easily, but when it does, the oxide is a faint yellowish-green which remains very hard, though not as hard or shiny as chrome.

TIN PLATE

Tin is very seldom found in its pure form. It takes a high polish and is also non-toxic, thus it was used at one time as a foil wrap for candies and cigarettes but, after World War II, it was replaced by aluminum foil. Tin is a soft, silvery-white metal which sometimes has a yellow tinge from the oxide. When it corrodes it is dull gray. Its lack of toxicity, coupled with its stability and resistance to corrosion, led to its widespread use as a coating for a wide variety of food containers including copper cookware, early Sheffield plate, and tin cans.

The most common use for tin is in making tin-plate, or plated ferrous metal, from which tin(ned) cans are made. Although iron has been tinned since the middle ages, tin-plate has only become commonplace since the early 19th century. John and Simcox (1966) give more information on tin-plate.

ZINC PLATE

Zinc plating on ferrous metal is known as galvanizing. Originally, and still frequently, steel plate was dipped in molten zinc, but today the zinc is often deposited electrolytically. Freshly applied zinc is bright, but it becomes drab quickly. Dipped zinc is easily identified by its blue-gray color and dull, camouflage-suit-like pattern, or mottled finish.

Galvanizing is used on metal exposed to the elements, such as corrugated iron, roofing, and garbage cans. Although the first patent for "zincing" iron was granted in 1837 (Hunt 1863:559), it only became common in the 1860s.

One 19th-century process, of Morewood and Rogers, used galvanizing on tin-plate for even greater protection.

The value of zinc plating lies in the fact that zinc itself is corrosion resistant and that it is above iron and steel on the galvanic scale. This means that it will corrode preferentially to the iron substrate, thus protecting it. The ferrous metal will not begin to corrode until most of the zinc has disappeared. The difficulty is that acids and alkalis both readily attack zinc, so it cannot be used in most places where tin plate is common.

Modern electrolytic platings are more evenly applied and dried so it is harder to identify them. They also retain the original bright blue-silver color of zinc better, which can sometimes be confused with chrome. It is usually smaller exposed objects which are electrolytically galvanized, such as nuts, bolts, screws, and bicycle parts.

Gold

Pure gold is yellow, soft, malleable, and very heavy. It is known as a "noble" metal because it does not tarnish or corrode. It is seldom found pure, but is usually alloyed with some metal like silver or copper in order to harden it. An ancient silver-gold alloy was known as electrum. Alloys with a gold content below 75% (18 carat) can tarnish.

There are numerous gold alloys which are designated by the term carat, or the measure of concentration by weight based upon 24 units. Carat is used to describe the purity of an alloy; so if 22 of the 24 parts of the ounce (gram) are gold, it is called 22 carat. If 10 of the 24 parts are gold, it is 10 carat, and so on. The other parts of the alloy are not specified, but silver, copper, and platinum are common additions. The addition of copper produces "red gold," while the addition of silver or platinum produces "white gold."

Substantial pieces of gold are required by law to be hallmarked, except for coins which are produced according to a legal standard which may vary slightly from place to place. Coins, which are made from very high carat alloys known as fine gold, can vary from 19 to 22 carats according to the jurisdiction.

Although gold is legally supposed to be hallmarked, the fact is that much gold is not. This is because it is easy to remelt and cast gold, and a jeweler often cannot guarantee the gold content of the new alloy. For example, a client may request that a jeweler manufacture a new piece from several bits of "old gold." Even if the jeweler knows the number of carats in each piece of old gold, it is still difficult, if not impossible, to know exactly the number of carats in the new piece, though this may be roughly estimated. The "other metal or metals" are almost always unknown.

For this reason, jurisdictions set standards for alloys. In Britain, for example, the standard alloys are 22, 18, 15, 12, and 9 carats. Only pieces of like carats are supposed to be melted together to make new pieces, but this is impossible to control. If, as in the example above, the "old gold" were a mixture of 12 and 9 carat pieces, the new piece of jewelery cannot be stamped by the jeweler according to the legal standards. It was, accordingly, safer and easier for the jeweler to ignore the hallmark. The lack of a hallmark on what is obviously gold, therefore, should not cause concern.

Gold is usually easy to identify because of its color and nobility, despite the fact that different alloys give various tints. The alloys, on the other hand, are impossible to classify visually unless a mark is present. Marks can be obtained from a number of standard reference works such as Jackson (1964).

Gold also appears in the form of a number of coatings including the following.

Gold Leaf

Gold leaf is very thin gold foil applied with glue over some molded or carved substrate.

Gilding

Gilding is the application of a surface layer of gold over some base metal, the varieties of which are legion. Sometimes a particular gilded metal has a name, as has gilded copper or copper alloy which is known as ormolu. From the last half of the 19th century to the present, gilding has almost always been done by electroplating. The operator can produce a very thin layer, and this, coupled with the fact that the pure gold of the electroplated layer does not wear well, means that objects gilded during this period now often show little evidence of gilding.

The other sort of gilding common before electroplating was mercury gilding. Mercury and gold were heated together to form a paste which was then applied to the base metal. The mercury disappeared as vapor upon heating, and the gold was left upon the object. This could be buffed or left matte but, in either case, mercury gilding invariably produced a thicker layer.

Rolled Gold

Rolled gold is a sandwich of metals, with two outside layers of gold or gold alloy enclosing a core metal like silver or nickel-silver. This is then rolled into a sheet of the desired thickness which is subsequently used in the manufacture of jewelery. Gold wire or braid can also be made this way.

Lead

Lead, which has been known for several millennia, is a very heavy, soft, malleable, and slightly ductile metal. When the surface is freshly exposed, it is a silvery-blue color, but the oxide which forms fairly quickly is dull gray. When oxidized, it is very resistant to corrosion. It is not uncommon to find "pure" lead archaeologically because of its softness, malleability, and corrosion resistance. It was often used for channeling water in pipes, drains, and gutters or pump wells in ships, and masons used it to anchor building hardware. Its heft made it useful for weights, and sailors used it for sounding leads to gauge depth. As shot or bullets, it was sometimes pure, sometimes alloyed, and always ubiquitous. Lead is most typical encountered as an alloy.

The earliest lead alloys were with tin, which is also an ancient metal. Tin and lead are soluble in each other, so virtually any proportion of each is possible. When lead predominates in these alloys, the metal is colored a dull metallic blue, but when tin is the major element, the color is yellowish-white. In broad general terms, and roughly speaking, when the two metals are mixed in equal parts they yield solders. When the tin is high, pewter is produced, and when lead predominates, the mixture creates bearing metals, battery grids, and toy soldiers. Of course, lead need not be alloyed with tin alone. The addition of silver to lead (95%-97% lead and 3%-5% silver) produces a high-temperature solder, and antimony, bismuth, and copper are often found singularly or in combination with either lead and/or tin.

The addition of antimony and/or bismuth to lead or lead-tin alloys greatly increases their hardness, ductility, and casting abilities. For this reason, printing type is almost always made of lead-antimony-tin alloys. The addition of bismuth to lead-tin lowers the melting point and gives a fusible alloy. Copper increases the hardness, and lead-based bearing metals usually have copper in them to make them wear better.

Lead is easy to recognize from its color, weight, and malleability, but it should be borne in mind that it alloys easily and that lead alloys are extremely common. There are numerous clues, some of which have been suggested here, which can be followed. For example, if something which is very clearly lead is also hard, that is a transparent indication of an alloy. Nevertheless, no alloy can be determined with precision outside of an analytical lab, so in an archaeological field lab, the best designation is probably "lead or lead alloy."

Solder

Soldering involves the joining of two pieces of metal, either of the same or different composition, by another metal compound or alloy which melts and fuses at a lower temperature than those being joined. The joining is thus effected by surface adhesion without melting the base metals, as in welding.

While a number of metals and alloys were used as iron solders, lead-based alloys, often with the addition of zinc or tin, were common because of the low melting temperature of lead. A zinc compound called spelter was used to solder brass, but was also sometimes used on iron. Brazing, a specialized form of soldering, is described in the section on "Copper Alloy."

Magnesium

Magnesium is a light, malleable, silver-white metal which is ductile when heated. It is not likely to be found in its pure form archaeologically, but it might not be unusual to discover it in one of its alloys, almost always an aluminum alloy, as a surface find on some sites.

Although it was discovered in 1808, and isolated in 1828, the metal was not used industrially until the 1910s, when it was employed in photographic flash powder and as a deoxydant in nickel alloys. World War II gave a great impetus to its production. During the war, it was used for lightweight castings, as well as for incendiary bombs and flares because it burns with an intense white light. Today there are many commercial uses for magnesium, but it is most familiar as a lightweight alloy with aluminum and zinc in engine castings and as airframes, etc. It is still used in flares.

Mercury

Mercury, which has been known since antiquity, is the only metal which is liquid at room temperature. It will not stick to glass as do other liquids and, at room temperature, it is slightly volatile. Its liquid nature and its silver-white color give rise to its other name, quicksilver. If inhaled or ingested, it has a poisonous effect on the body.

Mercury forms alloys, always known as amalgams, with most metals, but not with iron and platinum. Almost every child who declines to brush regularly becomes acquainted with an amalgam. Mercury is or has been used in scientific apparatus, electrical switches, pigments (vermilion), the manufacture of explosives, the recovery of gold and silver by the amalgamation process, and various medical treatments.

Mercury is very easy to identify. If it is found during excavation, it should be kept in a sealed container.

Nickel

Nickel is a hard, silver-white, scratch- and abrasion-resistant, ductile, malleable, magnetic metal which is resistant to tarnishing and corrosion and is capable of taking a high polish. It has been used by the Chinese in argentic and cupric alloys for nearly two millennia, but it was not isolated until the Swede Cronstedt did so in 1751, partly because of its very high melting point (1455°C). It was subsequently occasionally used in its pure state, especially in the late 19th century, for such things as fancy livery and scalpel handles, but is now normally used almost exclusively either as a plating or as an alloy. As an electroplating on ferrous metal, it was used on such things as car parts and bicycle fittings. Nickel plate is shiny and white. When it corrodes, the oxide is a faint yellow-green which remains very hard; indeed, nickel is harder than iron.

As an alloy, nickel is used with many metals, including aluminum, chromium, copper, steel, tin, and zinc. Most goes into the production of austenitic stainless steels. Nickel is usually alloyed with another metal as the base, but high-nickel alloys such as the monels, which are essentially nickel-copper alloys used for such things as marine applications and household appliances, are usually identified by their magnetism. The identification of nickel alloys is only possible in an analytical laboratory with the proper equipment, thus hard white magnetic metals should be classified in the field lab only as nickel alloys.

Silver

Pure silver is a very bright, white noble metal capable of taking a high polish. It is soft (though not as soft as gold or lead) and, as a consequence, it is almost never found pure. Silver is most frequently alloyed with copper. Though there are numerous silver-copper alloys–like hard silver (83.33%), coin silver (90%), and Britannia silver (95.8%)–the most common and famous alloy is sterling silver which contains 92.5% silver. Unlike gold, British sterling (and

Britannia) silver are consistently hallmarked because the alloy standards do not present an insoluble problem to the jeweler. Silver of other countries may have more complex hallmarking or may not be hallmarked at all. Marks can be obtained from a number of standard reference works like Currier (1970).

Although silver is a noble metal which resists corrosion, it is highly prone to tarnishing from sulfur. Any sulfur-containing material or atmosphere such as wool, eggs, or coal smoke will thus stain silver rapidly. The initial tarnish is blue/purple, but this deepens to a brown/black color.

Silver, being a costly metal, was often applied over cheaper base metals so that it could be made available to a wider public and, indeed, silver plate is more common than sterling. The chief plating methods are reviewed below. Numerous reference works (Blair 1987) document other, more unusual, methods.

Silver Leaf

Silver leaf, like gold leaf, is thin foil applied with glue over some molded or carved substrate.

Close Plating

Before the invention of electroplating, close plating was the only effective way to plate ferrous metal. It has been used since about the 14th century, but it became widely used in the 19th century for objects which required both beauty and durability. Close plating is common on such things as fancy horse livery, clothing accessories, candle snuffers, and so on. It is not unusual to find it stamped with maker's marks.

The process was as follows: cleaned iron or steel was dipped in molten tin. The object was then wrapped with silver foil and heated with a smoothing iron until the silver was soldered to the ferrous metal beneath. This produces a hard surface which can be polished.

Close plating can be identified by magnetism and by the presence of typical iron corrosion wherever the surface layer has been breached. It is also common for the silver to flake wherever the soldering is imperfect.

French Plating

Known in England as French plating, this was a method of covering brass and copper with silver. The object to be plated was polished, heated, and then bathed in nitric acid in order to prepare the surface to accept the silver. Pure silver leaf was then burnished onto the base, pressure and heat causing the silver to adhere. Though it remained in use after the advent of electroplating in the 1840s, French plating was incapable of standing heavy use, and did not provide a really permanent plate (Hughes 1970:9-10).

Electroplating

Electroplating began to be used commercially on many different metals in the 1840s. Silver was usually electroplated over some alloy of copper like Britannia metal or nickel-silver.

Aside from the fact that these pieces were usually marked with the familiar EP (this always means "electro-plated with silver") stamps–EPBM (Electro-Plated Britannia Metal) or EPNS (Electro-Plated Nickel-Silver)–the easiest way to identify plate is to look for worn patches. Usually a yellow or red tinge beneath the silver will betray the copper alloy.

Old Sheffield Plate (Fused Silver Plate)

Sheffield plate is similar to rolled gold. Essentially, it is a sandwich with silver as the bread on either side and a copper alloy as the filling, although on rare occasions the sandwich was "open-faced." When heated, fused, and rolled into sheets, it was used to make all manner of items. The process was developed in the 1740s, and superseded by electro-plating 100 years later (Wyler 1949:5, 8).

The silver layer of old Sheffield plate is thicker than EP silver, and it was frequently stamped with a maker's mark. Despite these differences, the distinction between different kinds of plating should probably not be attempted in a field lab.

Although old Sheffield plate was developed in Sheffield and most of the production came from there, it was not the only place where it was produced. The wider and broader term, "fused silver plate," is preferred by most authorities today.

Imitation Silver

Most silver imitations were unsuccessful. Pewter, for example, served often as a silver substitute (Child 1988:12) and sometimes as an imitation (Massé, Michaelis, and Kauffman 1971:36), but it fooled few because of the dominant tin content of pewter. Occasionally, an alloy appeared which became a successful imitator of silver. One such, called melchior, which was popular in the early 20th century, was a mixture of copper (55 parts), nickel (23 parts), zinc (17 parts), iron (3 parts), and tin (2 parts) (Massé, Michaelis, and Kauffman 1971:36). It is usually copper-nickel alloys like melchior and nickel-silver which are the most effective silver imitators.

Tin

Tin is very seldom found in its pure form. It takes a high polish and is also non-toxic, thus it was used at one time as a foil wrap for candies and cigarettes, a task which aluminum foil took over after World War II. Tin is a malleable silvery-white metal with a bluish tinge, which sometimes has a yellow tint from the oxide. It corrodes dull gray. It is softer than zinc but harder than lead and is ductile at 100ºC.

The two most important uses for tin are as a protective plating for copper and, especially, for ferrous metal (see Ferrous Metal and Tin Plate), and as an alloy, often with copper and zinc, in several important metals like bronze, bell metal, and bearing metal. Most often tin is an additive, but there is one very common alloy in which it is the principal metal: pewter.

Pewter and Britannia Metal

What follows is not meant to be a treatise on pewter, but rather to show how complex the subject is. Books have been written on pewter (Michaelis 1971; Cotterell et al. 1972), and much of what has been written is contradictory. Despite this, pewter is a recognizable metal, although it reminds one of what Mr. Justice Potter of the U.S. Supreme Court once said about pornography: "I can't define it, but I know it when I see it." Cotterell says the same (Cotterell et al. 1972:39-40)!

Pewter, which has been known since antiquity, is a tin alloy. Aside from its lack of resonance (it "clunks" when tapped), the fact that it is an alloy with a high tin content is about the only universally true statement which can be made about pewter. The various other metal additions have usually been added to the tin merely for the purpose of strengthening it, although sometimes economics (usually greed or lack of capital) have made strange alloys. Though there are standards regarding pewter's formulation today, these either did not always exist or were not followed, and there have been an astonishing variety of compositions through the years (Cotterell et al. 1972:39, 50-51). This has been exacerbated by the fact that it is very easy to remelt and recast pewter, and this was frequently done (Peal 1971:15). Pewter objects may occasionally have different parts of them (such as the handle and the body of a tankard) cast from different crucibles or spoons containing different alloys, or even have the same body cast from two different spoons of slightly different alloys, the one spoon not holding enough for the complete object. This appears to have been the case with a 16th-century pewter object from the Basque shipwreck site at Red Bay, Labrador (Dunning 1990).

The variety of deliberate formations has been further complicated by the fact that accidental and conscious additions, sometimes in considerable quantities, as well as trace elements, often show up in pewter alloys. Antimony, lead, copper, bismuth, zinc, silver, mercury, iron, nickel, and arsenic, either as deliberate or accidental additions, have all appeared in pewter (Unglik 1984:22). Romano-British pewter, a tin-lead alloy, varied from 47% to 99.2% tin, although the norm was between 62% and 80% tin. This carried through the Middle Ages (Peal 1971:79). Though most knew the dangers of lead and tried to regulate it, the regulations were seldom, if ever, effective. In the late Middle Ages, a tin-copper alloy began to appear (Peal 1971:26, 87). This alloy, in about a 4:1 ratio, is what is often referred to as "fine pewter" (Massé, Michaelis, and Kauffman 1971:51). Antimony was then added to the mix in varying proportions from 100:17 to 9:1 (Pemberton's alloy) (Massé, Michaelis, and Kauffman 1971:51). The systematic, deliberate addition of antimony appears to have begun in the 18th century, and as the use of antimony increased, the use of lead declined. Modern pewter, by definition, contains no lead, though, in fact, trace amounts are often found.

Late in the 18th century, James Vickers developed a new, improved pewter called Britannia metal which is more durable and has better molding qualities than pewter. Britannia metal is an alloy of tin, antimony, and copper. There are several varieties of Britannia metal, a typical one being Queen's Metal: 88.5% tin, 7.1% antimony, 3.5% copper, and 0.9% zinc (Child and Townsend 1988:12). Some collectors will refuse to accept Britannia metal as a type of pewter, not for scientific reasons, but because it is both "late" and defined. Nevertheless, it is accepted by most as a variety of pewter simply because it is a tin alloy (Peal 1971:171), and this should be the classification used by archaeologists. Britannia metal is often stamped "BM" and frequently plated (see Silver).

Pewter objects can be cast in molds, hammered from plate or both, lathe turned after molding, stamped, or formed by spinning. Stamping and spinning are invariably confined to Britannia metal among the pewters (Massé, Michaelis, and Kauffman 1971:54; Cotterell et al. 1972:40) because these are industrial processes which require not only a consistent alloy but also the harder, more ductile, nature of Britannia metal. A case may be made that Britannia metal largely displaced pewter because of industrial exigencies (Montgomery 1973:17-19), especially as the ability of Britannia metal to take electroplating became known (Massé, Michaelis, and Kauffman 1971:54).

Britannia metal is the hardest, thinnest, and lightest of the pewters, but all have the unmistakable look and feel of tin. The colors vary depending on the alloy, and everything from a shiny silvery-blue to a dark dull gray may be found.

Lead pewters suffer from "pewter disease," an affliction mentioned by most commentators on pewter (Massé, Michaelis, and Kauffman 1971:69; Peal 1971:26-27). It is characterized by pock marks or boils which appear on the surface of the metal, and is due to an imperfect alloy–a separation of one of the constituent elements from the others. Cotterell even suggests that pewter disease is a way by which one can tell fake from real pewter (Cotterell et al. 1972:41)

Zinc

Zinc is a bluish-white metal which was not isolated as a metal until the 18th century, although it was known for centuries before. It is not found commercially in its pure form. Acids and alkalis attack zinc rapidly. Like tin, its two most important uses are for plating, especially for ferrous metal where the process is called galvanizing (see Ferrous Metal and Zinc Plate), and as an alloy, often with copper, nickel, and tin, in several important metals like brass, Britannia metal, and nickel-silver. Today it is sometimes used as a base in some die-casting alloys, but mostly as an additive in aluminum, copper, and magnesium casting alloys. It is harder than both tin and lead.

Collectors sometimes refer to any zinc-alloy castings of whatever composition as spelter (Perry 1974:186). Spelter is a commercial name for molten zinc which comes from the name (*spailter* or *speauter*) given by 17th-century Dutch traders to the zinc brought from China. The name was also applied to a yellowish zinc compound used to solder brass. Its color was imparted by the small amount of copper it contained.

Glossary

Alloy: The combination of metals by fusion. When mercury is one of the metals, the alloy is termed an amalgam. Alloys acquire new properties which are different than the original metals. They are usually designated by the chief or base ingredient; for instance, a copper alloy will be mostly copper.

Annealing: Annealing is a process which makes use of the ability of steel to "soften" when it is heated above its critical transformation temperature and then slowly cooled. The process was crucial in the days when only carbon steel existed because, to work a carbon-steel object with a carbon-steel file, the one had to be soft and the other hard. Although a smith almost always used the term to refer to the softening of steel, it has a wider meaning and can refer to the softening of other metals or to the slow, controlled cooling of materials like glass.

Block tin: Pure tin, cast into blocks.

Brazing: The process of soldering with brass is called brazing. It involves joining two pieces of metal by fusion using an alloy of copper and zinc (brass), and sometimes tin or silver, which melts and fuses at a lower temperature than the pieces being joined.

Brittle: Subject to disintegration under pressure, especially under impact loads.

Ductile: Often confused with malleability (q.v.), ductility is the ability of a metal to remain together without cracking or breaking when drawn. Metal for wire must be ductile.

Fusibility: Before metals are rendered liquid by heating, they become pasty. It is at this temperature that they will fuse. All metals are fusible, but the temperature at which this occurs varies greatly among metals: from a few hundred degrees Celsius for tin, bismuth, and lead, to thousands of degrees for nickel, manganese, and tungsten.

Malleability: A malleable metal can be beaten into thin sheets without cracking or breaking. It is often confused with ductility (q.v.). Brittle metals are not malleable; thus, wrought iron is malleable, cast iron is not.

Pig iron: The tapping of a blast furnace involved removing a ceramic dam in order to allow the molten contents of the furnace to flow out into a channel dug into the sand floor in front of the blast furnace. The fancied appearance to a suckling animal together with the weight of the metal caused the main channel to be called the sow and the side channels, pigs. This is pig iron. The only use of pig iron (besides ballast for ships) was to make wrought iron.

Soldering: Soldering involves joining two pieces of the same or different metals by another metal or alloy which melts and fuses at a lower temperature than those being joined. While a number of alloys were used as iron solders, lead-based alloys, often with the addition of zinc or tin, were common. Brazing (q.v.) is a specialized form of soldering.

Spinning: An industrial process whereby sheet metal is made into a hollow vessel by the pressure of a roller against the sheet which is being held by a spinning lathe tailstock. The sheet is pressed into a form block on a revolving headstock spindle. Many vessels made of copper alloy and Britannia metal were spun.

Welding: Welding is the process of uniting two or more heated pieces of fusible metal by compression (usually hammering). There were other means of joining metal, namely riveting, brazing, or soldering, but welding, when it could be used successfully, was the most effective of these. Forge welding was eventually replaced by gas and electric welding both of which were faster and required less skill. These processes were developed in the late 19th century, but they were not practicable until the 20th century.

Conclusion

The task of rectifying a very large blind spot in historical archaeological research begins with the ability to identify correctly metals; but it only begins here. On historical sites, objects made of metal are simultaneously both the most profuse and the least understood of artifacts. Archaeologists who are able accurately to identify unmarked Staffordshire pearlware teaware and date it to the half decade are often unable even roughly to describe how an axe was manufactured, or even from what material it was made.

There are a number of reasons for this situation, not the least of which is the enormous complexity of the subject. Metal objects are made from a great number of substances and come in a bewildering number of forms. Furthermore, most metals corrode, obscuring surface details and often reducing an object to a handful of rusty fragments. This is further complicated by the fact that relatively little has been written about archaeological metal. Add to all this the difficulty, if not impossibility, of dating most metal (which renders it archaeologically "unhelpful"), as well as the all too frustratingly real-time constraints under which archaeology operates in today's hyper society, and there is every incentive for the researcher to defer or ignore the hard task of learning about and mastering metals and metal artifacts.

Still, these are not acceptable excuses. Metal is generally part of every archaeological assemblage and it demands interpretation. It is in our collections, but not in our site reports. We are thus losing information, sometimes a great deal of crucial information. Assuming a desire to correct the deficiency, the long slow process of reversing the existing apathy towards archaeological metal must begin by each of us being able to answer the question: what is the stuff made of and what do I call it?

REFERENCES

ASTON, JAMES, AND EDWARD B. STORY
1942 *Wrought Iron: Its Manufacture, Characteristics and Applications.* A. M. Byers, Pittsburgh, PA.

BARRACLOUGH, K. C.
1976 *Sheffield Steel.* Mooreland, Buxton, Derbyshire, England.

BLAIR, CLAUDE (EDITOR)
1987 *The History of Silver.* Macdonald, London, England.

BRADY, GEORGE S., HENRY R. CLAUSER, AND JOHN A. VACCARI
1997 *Materials Handbook,* 14th edition. McGraw-Hill, New York, NY.

CHILD, ROBERT E., AND JOYCE M. TOWNSEND (EDITORS)
1988 *Modern Metals in Museums.* Institute of Archaeology, London, England.

COTTERELL, H. H., ADOLPHE RIFF, AND ROBERT M. VETTER
1972 *National Types of Old Pewter.* The Pyne Press, Princeton, NJ.

CURRIER, ERNEST M.
1970 *Marks of Early American Silversmiths.* Robert Allan Green, Harrison, NY.

DICK, WILLIAM B.
1975 *Dick's Encyclopedia of Practical Receipts and Processes, or How They Did it in the 1870's.* Funk and Wagnalls, New York, NY.

DOYLE, LAWRENCE E.
1969 *Manufacturing Processes and Materials for Engineers.* Prentice-Hall, Englewood Cliffs, NJ.

DUNNING, PHIL
1990 Sixteenth-Century Domestic Metals Recovered from Red Bay, Labrador (Sites 24M and 29M). Manuscript, Parks Canada, Ottawa, Ontario.

FENNIMORE, DONALD L.
1996 *Metalwork in Early America: Copper and Its Alloys.* Henry Francis du Pont Winterthur Museum, Winterthur, DE.

GALE, W. K. V.
1967 *The British Iron and Steel Industry: A Technical History.* David and Charles, Newton Abbot, Devon, England.

GENTLE, RUPERT, AND RACHAEL FEILD
1994 *Domestic Metalwork: 1640-1820,* revised and enlarged by Belinda Gentle. Antique Collectors Club, Woodbridge, Suffolk, England.

HUGHES, G. BERNARD
1970 *Sheffield Silver Plate.* Praeger, New York, NY.

HUGHES, RICHARD, AND MICHAEL ROWE
1986 *The Colouring. Bronzing and Patination of Metals.* Crafts Council, London, England.

HUNT, ROBERT (EDITOR)
1863 *A Supplement to Ure's Dictionary of Arts, Manufactures and Mines.* D. Appleton, New York, NY.

JACKSON, CHARLES JAMES
1964 *English Goldsmiths and Their Marks.* Dover, New York, NY.

JOHN, W. D., AND ANNE SIMCOX
1966 *Pontypool and Usk Japanned Wares with the Early History of the Iron and Tinplate Industries at Pontypool.* The Ceramic Book Company, Newport, England.

KAUFFMAN, HENRY J.
1979 *American Copper & Brass.* Bonanza, New York, NY.

KNAUTH, PERCY
1974 *The Metalsmiths.* Time-Life, New York, NY.

MASSÉ, H. J. L. J., RONALD F. MICHAELIS, AND HENRY J. KAUFFMAN
1971 *Chats on Old Pewter.* Dover, New York, NY.

MEIER, JERZY W.
1970 *Non-Ferrous Metals Casting, History and Forecast.* Department of Energy, Mines and Resources, Ottawa, Ontario.

MICHAELIS, RONALD F.
1971 *Antique Pewter of the British Isles.* Dover, New York, NY.

MONTGOMERY, CHARLES F.
1973 *A History of American Pewter.* Henry Francis du Pont Winterthur Museum, New York, NY.

MULLINS, WILLIAM W., AND MILTON C. SHAW (EDITORS)
1968 *Metal Transformation.* Gordon and Breach, New York, NY.

PARTINGTON, CHARLES F.
1835 *The British Cyclopædia of the Arts and Sciences.* Orr & Smith, London, England.

PEAL, CHRISTOPHER A.
1971 *British Pewter and Britannia Metal.* Peebles Press, London, England.

PERRY, EVAN
1974 *Collecting Antique Metalware.* Doubleday, New York, NY.

SINGER, CHARLES, E. J. HOLMYARD, A. R. HALL, AND TREVOR I. WILLIAMS (EDITORS)
1958 *A History of Technology*, Volume 5. Clarendon Press, Oxford, England.

TOMLINSON, CHARLES (EDITOR)
1851 *Cyclopædia of Useful Arts.* James S. Virtue, London, England.

TYLECOTE, R. F.
1992 *A History of Metallurgy.* The Institute of Metals, London, England.

UNGLIK, HENRY
1984 A Case of a Broken Pewter Flagon from Red Bay, Labrador: Nondestructive Analysis by X-Ray Fluorescence Spectroscopy. Manuscript, Parks Canada, Ottawa, Ontario.

URE, ANDREW
1848 *A Dictionary of Arts, Manufactures and Mines.* D. Appleton, New York, NY.

VAN NOSTRAND
1947 *Van Nostrand's Scientific Encyclopedia.* Van Nostrand, New York, NY.

WYLER, SEYMOUR B.
1949 *The Book of Sheffield Plate.* Crown, New York, NY.

JOHN D. LIGHT
MATERIAL CULTURE RESEARCH
ONTARIO SERVICE CENTRE
PARKS CANADA
1600 LIVERPOOL COURT
OTTAWA, ONTARIO K1A 0M5
CANADA

ANN SMART MARTIN

The Role of Pewter as Missing Artifact: Consumer Attitudes Toward Tablewares in Late 18th Century Virginia

ABSTRACT

Ceramic assemblages have long been scrutinized by archaeologists. Yet, remarkably little attention has been given to food-related objects not found in the archaeological record. This study assesses the role of pewter—one such "missing artifact"—as an alternative and companion to ceramics, and thus provides a documentary framework of consumer choice amidst social and marketing pressures. Probate inventories of Albemarle County, Virginia, from 1770 to 1799 reveal a nearly standard presence of pewter in households of varying economic levels even after the introduction of the "fashionable" creamware, and the slow addition of ceramics to—not substitution for—pewter in more wealthy households. Comparing pewter and creamware purchases at contemporary retail stores estimates the time between an object's purchase and its recording in the probate process, and demonstrates real regional variability and rural conservatism. Finally, a consumer's view of pewter is attempted through an understanding of its economic and symbolic value and its uses within a household.

Introduction

Archaeologists have long used ceramics as primary evidence for the study of historic cultures. The technical and decorative variation of ceramic artifacts, their widespread use, and their availability in a large continuum of cost provides important evidence about choices of acquisition and use. Recent excellent publications in historical archaeology have also focused upon ceramics as sensitive barometers of social and economic status and ethnicity (Miller 1980; Felton and Shultz 1983; Herman 1984). Certainly well-suited to examine the role of ceramics, these studies are nonetheless restricted by a reliance on archaeologically retrievable goods and fall short in the study of the full range of behavioral patterning. Of course, while the limitations of the archaeological record cannot be changed, what can be altered is the analytical focus. By considering the social and economic value of using certain kinds of ceramics within a framework of the full range of available choices, perhaps some more sophisticated statements can be made about the materials and behavior that are recovered.

In a sense, ceramics have become a proxy for all tablewares, a fatally simplistic assumption. For example, pewter, a major component of tableware items for two centuries, is seldom recovered in archaeological excavations. Three simple reasons explain its absence. First, pewter's durability prevented significant breakage and discarding and, second, its resale value for recasting provided a major outlet for its disposal. Finally, if discarded, as a metal alloy it suffered varying degrees of decomposition in the ground.

The absence of pewter tablewares, and to a far lesser extent, those of wooden and silver, skews our archaeological data in important ways. A brief example will suffice. John Otto's now-famous study of planter, overseer and slave sites in Cannon's Point, Georgia, revealed some compelling differences in "social status and access to material resources" through ceramic distribution. Because the evidence of the slave population indicated a greater reliance on hollow table wares, one inference was that they had a greater reliance on stews than roasts (Otto 1975:120,360).

While not directly reflective of Otto's sample population, a study of Albemarle County probate inventories from 1770 to 1799 raises some important questions about "missing artifacts." For example, when both pewter and ceramic items were combined, there was no correlation between wealth and the number of hollow wares, such as bowls and basins. One could not predict the other. More important, 88 per cent of those particular hollow ware forms were pewter, leaving few bowls and basins likely to even become part of an archaeological assemblage. Hence a change in the patterning of ceramic forms did not necessarily represent a change in all forms.

Analysis of these probate inventories demonstrates that until the opening decades of the 19th century, pewter was the common, if not predominant, material of serving items in Albemarle County, Virginia. This study will examine patterns of pewter ownership within different economic groups and look for changes after the introduction of the certainly less expensive and allegedly more fashionable creamware—tablewares so appropriate for the high-style dining behaviors documented among the elite in long-settled and urban regions. Comparing pewter sales at local retail stores will help assess the lapse in time between the purchase of an object and its recording in probate inventories, as well as estimate regional preferences in purchasing patterns. Finally, an attempt will be made to re-create the consumer's view of pewter through its market and symbolic value and its uses within the household.

Tablewares in Probate Inventories

Historical archaeologists have begun to stress the need for studying evidence discrete from the archaeological record (for example, see Beaudry et al. 1983). Probate documents from county courts are particularly popular data as they enumerate and evaluate slaves and household goods upon the death of an encumbered county resident. A 1774 guide for procedures of probate in Maryland listed the items to be inventoried:

> All the singular goods, chattels, wares, and merchandise such as ready money, household furniture, clothing, negroes, stock of cattle, corn, the crop on hand begun in the lifetime of the deceased and every sort of property in and about the house what kind soever, not being a freehold or parcel of it or fixed to it (the convenient apparel of the widow according to her degree excepted) (Vallete 1774:3).

Custom seemed to allow a widow her clothing, and at least protected a bed and a pot from eager creditors. Virginia law also provided that all food and liquor set aside for family use should not be sold or accounted for. Other exclusions included gifts and legacies made before death even though bequests made through wills remained a part of the estate until settlement (Hening 1823:150). Even though quite inexpensive items were listed, others were lumped or excluded.

The major problem with the study of probate records is not the quality and quantity of information available in the extant inventories. The overall possibility of retrieving accurate information from existing records is excellent. But because Virginia law provided several ways to bypass the probate process, the nagging problem remains of the actual representation of those whose estates reached probate. Under-representation of the very poor skews probate evidence towards the wealthy. Yet even if every estate was appraised, inventories would be further biased towards the wealthier population merely due to the recording of goods owned at death, an event which usually occurred at a later stage in the goods accumulation cycle (Carr and Walsh 1980). Thus the probate population is not a perfect reflection of the living population.

Overriding these considerations of bias, however, is the rich detail of their evidence of past household consumption. The data chosen for this study represented a 30 year period, 1770–1799, in Albemarle County, lying in the central piedmont of Virginia (Figure 1). One hundred and seventy households reached probate in those years, and their estates contained 2872 items relating to food preparation and serving (see Table 1 and Appendix).

Lying west of the fall line and at the eastern base of the Blue Ridge Mountains, present-day Albemarle County contains some 735 square miles, widely varying from east to west in topography, soils, drainage, and climate. Most of the area is within the Piedmont Physiographic Province characterized by rolling hills dissected by many small streams. The western portion, however, contains higher elevations and steeper slopes where many small, rapidly flowing streams cut narrow valleys. Most of these streams drain into the Hardware or the Rivanna Rivers, both tributaries of the James, which forms the southern border of the county (Hantman 1985:9–11). These waterways served as crucial linkages eastward, especially before the improvement of roads leading to the fall line. One late 18th century traveller reported that the area's temperate climate created what some called "the garden of the United States" (Weld 1799:206).

TABLE 1
FOODWAYS OBJECTS IN PROBATE INVENTORIES: ALBEMARLE COUNTY, VIRGINIA, 1770–1799

CERAMIC ITEMS:
Baking pan
Basin
Bottle
Bowl
Breakfast plate
Butter boat
Butter pot
Can
Chamber pot
Coffee cup
Coffee pot
Cream pot
Creamer
Crock
Cruet
Cup
Custard Cup
Desert plate
Dish
Ewer
Fruit basket
Jar
Jug
Lid
Milk pot
Muffin plate
Mug
Mustard pot
Ointment pot
Oval dish
Oval plate
Pan
Pap boat
Patty pan
Pickle bottle
Pickle leaf
Pickle pot
Pitcher
Plate
Platter
Pot
Punch bowl
Salad dish
Sauce boat
Saucer
Slop bowl
Spoon boat
Stand
Sugar bowl
Sugar pot
Sweet meat dish
Tea Canister
Tea pot
Tureen
Twiffler
Water jug
Water vessel

OTHER FOOD—
WAYS
ITEMS;

Baking pan
Basin
Basket
Beer glass
Bird roast
Bottle
Bowl
Bread baker
Bread toaster
Bread tray
Butter tub
Cannister
Canteen
Case knife
Cask
Castor
Chafijkn dish
Chamber pot
Cheese toaster
Coffee Mill
Coffee pot
Collander
Cork screw
Cover
Crute
Cup
Decanter
Dish
Divided spoon
Dough chest
Dripping pan
Dutch oven
Ewer
Fat Jafr
Fat pot
Flask
Flesh fork
Fork
Frying pan
Funnel
Glass
Grater
Gravy Spoon
Grid iron
Hand dish
Hook
Jack
Kettle
Kitchen furniture
Knife
Ladle
Measure
mortar and pestle
Mug
Mustard pot
Nutmeg grater
oven
Pan
Pan Handle
Patty pan
Pepper box
Phial
Plate
Plate holder
Plate warmer
Porringer
Pot
Pottle Pot
Punch bowl
Punch lakde
Rack
salt cedllar
Salt glass
Salver
Sauce pan
Shaving basin
Sieve
Sifter
Skillet
Skimmer
Soup spoon
Spice mortar
Spinder
Spoon
Spit
Square bottles
Stand
Stew pan
Stilliards
Sugar box
Sugar dish
Sugar tongs
Tankard
Tea board
Tea cannister
Tea kettle
Tea kitchen
Teapot
Teaspoon
tin
Tongs
Tray
Trivet
Tumbler
Vessel
waiter
Warming pan
Wash basin
Wash bowl
Wash noggin
Water polate
Wine glass

The piedmont region of Virginia was one of the first great frontiers of the Chesapeake. Previously held back by fears of Indians and frontier policy, the colony began to expand in the early 18th century past the fall line up the James River Valley. Beginning in the 1720s, large land grants were made to wealthy eastern planters in what was then the western portion of Goochland County, but another decade would pass before owners regularly settled their families there. By the time the sepa-

TABLE 2
LAND AND SLAVEOWNING: VIRGINIA AND MARYLAND, 1782–1783

Region	Piedmont Va	Shenandoah Valley, Va	Southside Va	Northern Neck Va	Western Shore, Md
County	Albemarle[a]	Frederick	Charlotte	Richmond	Calvert
Land					
% owning land	87.0	60.0	67.0[b]	70.0	49.0
% of all landowners:					
100 acres or less	8.5	8.0	8.0	23.5	29.2
1000 +	8.0	4.0	7.0	5.5	2.8
Slaves					
% owning slaves	54.0	20.0	63.5	62.5	56.0
% of slaveowners:					
12 or more slaves	9.0	3.5	10.5	16.5	10.0

Sources: [a]Data from Ayres, 1966. All other from Risjord, 1978.
[b]Land ownership in 1790.

rate county of Albemarle was established in 1744, much of the prime land in its present boundaries, especially along the rivers, had already been patented and a quarter of the landowners owned nearly three-quarters of the land (Watts 1947:15). Devereux Jarrett, a tutor moving from New Kent County to Albemarle in the 1750s, found an employer who owned "great possessions in lands, slaves, etc. etc." that he feared as "gentlefolk," one who moved in a different world from simple men of poor beginnings like himself. Yet despite the early establishment of a landed aristocracy, Jarrett found Albemarle County in those early years to be "nearly a frontier county," and the "manners of the people were generally more rough and uncivilized than in the more interior parts of the country (Matthews 1957: 23,20). As "nearly a frontier county," Albemarle remained a land of some opportunity for those of limited means. Many gained land and moderate prosperity, and by 1765 moderate sized farms (under 400 acres) were the homes of over 70 per cent of the landowners (Ayres 1966:47). Tobacco was the prime crop, although by no means the only one, and many farmers dragged their weighty hogsheads to the nearest creek or river where it was floated down the James. Others, enticed by high prices at the fall line at Fredericksburg, carried their produce overland. But the rapidly expanding population soon encouraged local marketing facilities, a process eased in 1789 when two tobacco inspection stations were established in the county (Moore 1976).

By this time, however, many Albemarle County residents had begun moving in earnest toward the cultivation of wheat and other crops especially suited to the deep upland clays. Economic diversification and entrepreneurial activities added to the wealth of long-established families, as well as that of the sons of the tidewater that were increasingly pushed westward. The population in Albemarle County swelled so rapidly that the county was divided twice before the Revolution. By 1790, 12,000 residents made their home within the present day boundaries, blacks forming just under half of that number. The population would increase by nearly a quarter before the century's end.

Rapid population growth suggests that many who came were able to prosper. Table 2 demonstrates that the wealth of Albemarle County at the end of the Revolution was remarkably well distributed compared to many regions of Virginia and Maryland. Nearly 90 per cent of the households owned some form of land, and over half had slaves. There were few small farms, although planters owning more than 1000 acres were perhaps more prominent than in the other sample counties. A comparison of the size of landholdings between Albemarle and the coastal counties of Middlesex, Gloucester, Elizabeth City, Princess Anne, Accomac, and Northampton further high-

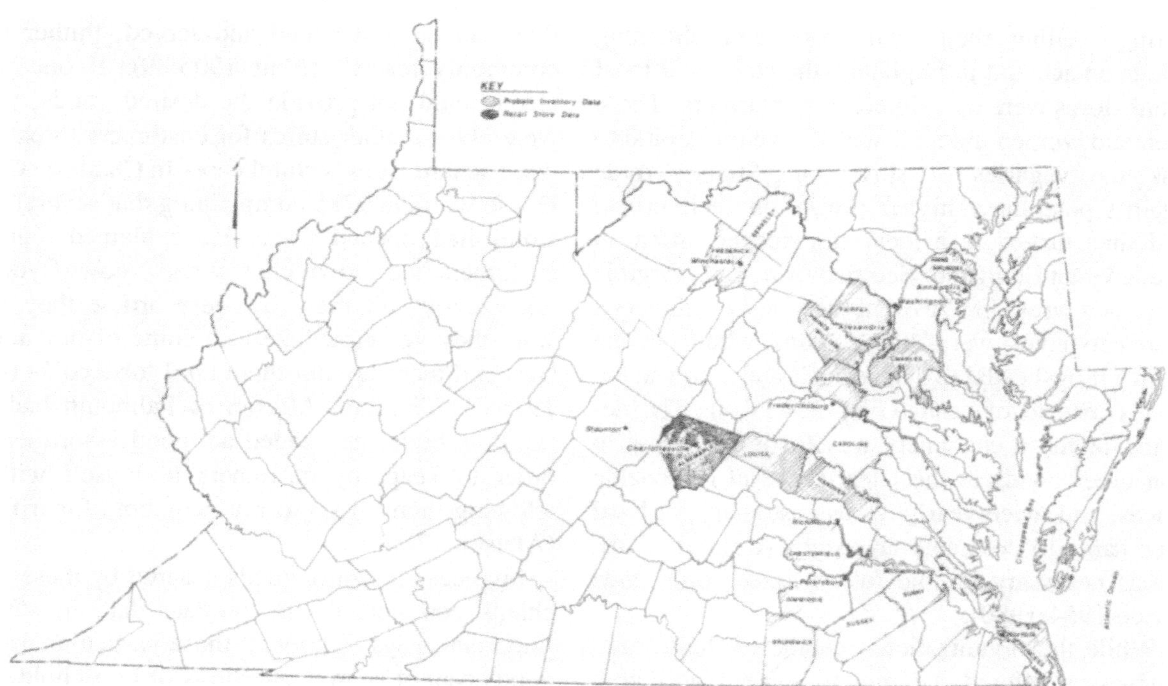

FIGURE 1. County locations of probate inventory and retail store data base.

lights the relatively equal prosperity of the Piedmont region. While two-thirds of the farms in Albemarle County were between 100 and 400 acres, less than half of those in those tidewater counties were of a similar size. The number of upper middling landowners—those owning 400 to 1000 acres—was doubled in Albemarle. Finally, there were four times the number of small farms (under 100 acres) in the long-established region than in Albemarle (Main 1954; Ayres 1966).

Thus, many residents of Albemarle County had access to capital in the form of farms and enslaved labor at least by the 1780s. Yet the expansion and opportunity for poorer men in a "frontier" society was to a large extent over. As population pressures and improvement pushed land prices higher, mobility in the piedmont became more restricted, just as it had in the tidewater. So too, a small group of elite consolidated their wealth and political power into a network linked by kinship and friendship. Joining that small group was increasingly limited to those men born to wealth (Kulikoff 1986: 160–161).

Tablewares in Retail Stores

Additional data for this study was gathered from the records of 19 Virginia and Maryland merchants in business between 1740 and 1800 (see Appendix and Figure 1). Like the village shops of England, these stores supplied the colonists with "every individual article necessary in life such as linens, woollens, silks, paper, books, iron, cutlery, hats, stockings, shoes, wine, spirits, sugars, etc. and even jewelry" (Smyth 1784:II,99). Such objects were usually purchased on credit, with payment made in crops, cash, or services. Thus, someone like Devereux Jarrett, the Albemarle County tutor, could begin to "get some credit in a store" and venture into debt for a new suit of clothes (Mathews 1957:32).

These kinds of year-round facilities mushroomed across the two colonies after the Tobacco Inspection Acts of Virginia in 1730 and Maryland in 1747, keenly jostling for customers and their crops. While even some of the wealthier planters were abandoning the consignment system of marketing—selling their own crops and obtaining goods on account in England—the patrons of local retail stores were most likely lesser farmers. These men and women did not usually have the capital to risk the vagaries of slow trans-Atlantic trade against potentially higher profits on their crops, and thus turned to a local storekeeper, often an agent for an English or Scottish firm. One Virginia merchant wrote in 1767 that the "best customers a store can have" were "those people who have one or two h[ogsheads] to dispose of" and who wanted goods instead of cash (Gill 1984:IV,4). The demand of these customers was for local access to consumer goods in the latest styles at reasonable prices, and twice-yearly it was customary for local merchants to complete an extensive order of the goods necessary for the following season's trade (Price 1954,1980).

While the organizational details of these retail businesses differed, a common problem faced both Scottish factor and local entrepreneur. By the eve of the Revolution, nearly one-quarter of all titheables may have been merchants (Bergstrom 1980: 219). So many merchants made competition fierce to obtain business at all. As early as 1743, Francis Jerdone reported 25 stores within 18 miles of his own in piedmont Louisa County, and four or more were expected in the next year (Jerdone 1743). Yet, in the west, Cumberland was deemed "a very proper place for a Merchant" in 1752 because it was on navigable water and there was no store within 10 miles (O'Mara 1983:233). Soon, however, competition for crops and customers would be felt even in backcountry places where stores moved in "to supply the real and imaginary necessities" of settlers and their wives. Thus, as "wealth and population increased, wants were created, and many considerable demands, in consequence, took place for the various elegancies as well as necessaries of life" (Eddis 1969:51–52).

As markets became more competitive, the selection of goods for sale became even more important for attracting and keeping business. John Mair's popular *Book-keeping Modernized* recommended varied stock for an 18th century retail store in Virginia or Maryland, and "the greater variety . . . the better; for wherever planters find they can be best suited and served, thither they commonly resort" (Mair 1905:89). If one merchant could not provide the desired goods, there were always other stores for customers to patronize. Richard Blow's storekeeper in Charlotte Court House wrote in 1785 complaining that several new stores had opened there. He explained that his customers had grown choosy and "now if you do not exactly suit them in every article they may want they go immediately to some of our neighbors and there lay out there [*sic*] tobacco" (Teute 1976:81). William Allason of Falmouth had the same problem: he needed a "good assortment in order to keep my customers to myself without allowing them to go to my neighbors for trifles" (Allason 1760).

Invoices recording goods ordered by these merchants complement the probate data in several important ways. Although these particular lists of goods cannot answer questions of household consumption (i.e. *who* bought what), they can help override a major problem of probate evidence: the accumulation of goods over a lifetime or even several generations. Merchants' records thus provide much better dating control. Secondly, if stores in a number of communities have similar patterns in the goods they stocked, a horizon in material culture is suggested and the representativeness of the Albemarle County data may be confirmed.

Changes in Anglo-American Society and Tableware Production

The temporal limits of this study were chosen for several reasons. The most important was the testing of the impact of a specific historical process on 18th century Virginians. An alleged radical transformation of English consumer attitudes towards objects resulted in a spending boom that reached "revolutionary proportions" by the third quarter of the century. Large and small, inexpensive and dear, consumer goods representing the pursuit of fashion and conspicuous consumption were becoming a part of life for all but the indigent, each group participating to their own ability. The propellants of this tidal wave of mass consumption were rumbles of social and economic change, beginning in England and spreading to the colonies. Seemingly disjointed in their genesis, widespread economic, cultural and structural changes would come together by the end of the century to produce new abilities, desires, and methods of obtaining goods. One signal of this new consumer society was the demand for fashionable new ceramic items, a desire created by intense and innovative marketing of Josiah Wedgwood and other Staffordshire potters (McKendrick et al. 1982).

How did these changes in the cosmopolitan center affect consumers across the Atlantic? The American colonies had emerged as a significant foreign market for British manufactured goods, the destination, in fact, for almost half of the glass and earthenware exported in 1770 (McCusker and Menard 1985:284). Even after England lost the monopoly on her colonial market, the Staffordshire industry maintained a dominant position as supplier of ceramics. One Englishman observed just after the American Revolution that there would be little competition with British production of "Porcelain and Earthen ware of all Qualities, except the most Gross and Common . . . The importation has been and must be made from Great Britain, on account both of the quality and price" (Sheffield 1783:7). By no means were all of these items utilitarian; Benjamin Franklin claimed in 1766 that the greatest part of all British exports were "mere articles of fashion, purchased and consumed, because the fashion in a respected country" (Larabee 1969:143). Ceramics clearly matched his description, at least as seen in orders from some Virginia merchants. For instance, John Wilkins was insistent in his 1773 London order: he wanted "one dozen fashionable sugar dishes, newest fashion ware" (Wilkins c. 1773). Current ceramic vogue was the paramount concern, for whatever the coming fashion would soon be demanded by his Northampton County customers.

Archaeological and documentary sources should reflect these supposed profound changes. Archaeological evidence seems to show that the rise of the Staffordshire pottery industries made ceramics so inexpensive, plentiful, and desired that they filled virtually every white home in the British Empire. Ivor Noël Hume points out, for instance, that creamware is present on "most American sites of the late 18th and early 19th centuries" (Noël Hume 1969:125). Evidence from 18th century retail stores demonstrates that consumers flocked to purchase the new creamwares in a variety of dining and tea forms, leaving older styles languishing on store shelves (Martin 1988). One would believe that ceramics, and especially creamware, had become the predominant tableware item.

"Quite new in its appearance, covered with a rich and brilliant glaze, bearing sudden alternations of heat and cold, manufactured with ease and expedition and consequently cheap," creamware could naturally outpace its rivals like the oldfashioned and expensive pewter (Coombe 1790: VI, 934). As a matter of fact, Neil McKendrick claims that by the third quarter of the 18th century "one no longer spoke of common pewter but of common Wedgwood" (McKendrick et al. 1982:103). The creamware of Wedgwood and others was arriving in this country "in such quantities and so cheaply that it was supplanting all other tablewares and crowding the pewter plate right off the table" (Sprackling 1958:7).

To best evaluate how—if—and when this hypothetical pewter plate came to fall of the household table requires a bit of background. Other scholars have shown that a majority of households in 17th century Virginia and Maryland used pewter plates (Beaudry et al. 1983:25). Indeed, Gloria Main discovered that pewter ware was the third "priority" in Maryland households of young fathers between 1650 and 1720, falling in frequency only behind beds and iron cooking utensils. This choice cross-cut class lines, forming a continuum with over 90 per cent of those in the top two-thirds of wealth owning pewter, and even half in the bottom five per cent of the population. Overall, 88 per cent of these households contained at least one item of pewter (Main 1982:242).

The dominance of pewter in Virginia and Maryland households before 1700 seemed to be representative of much of the British empire. The unfortunate result was a virtual saturation of the

British and American markets by the mid 18th century (Hatcher and Barker 1974:280). The pewterers had a compound dilemma: the durability of their product limited replacement demand by those who already owned it, and the nature of their medium limited the ways designs could be used to make it fashionable. Even if the forms were slightly modified, a more important problem was the restriction of surface decoration, for it was just this surface ornament that differentiated ceramic prices and popularity. While there were two basic grades of pewter, common and hard, there were many levels of price—and hence social status—in ceramic items (Miller 1980) (see Figures 2 and 3).

Another change lay far beyond the pewter industry itself. A transformation in the drinking habits of British and American society did not favor pewter. Between 1722 and 1833 British beer consumption decreased an estimated 50 per cent per capita, with pewter vessels preferred by many for its drinking. In the same period, per capita tea consumption rocketed from one ounce to two to three pounds. Hot beverages were the potter's domain. While the British liked their beer warm, they did not want their tea cold. Pewter conducted heat, especially to human lips, and cooled tea. Despite production of pewter tea and coffee pots, the influx of tea drinking was highly detrimental to the pewterer; he could never emulate delicate china teacups, and with changing tastes his own wares looked increasingly bulky (Hatcher and Barker 1974:281).

The final cause contributing to pewter's downfall was the aforementioned wooing of public taste by Staffordshire entrepreneurs. The tensions felt in the pewter industry as its popularity waned and that of its competitors rose can be seen through the reaction of the Cornwall tin miners, the first and major link in the chain of pewter production. As tin prices plummeted, an Exeter paper of 1776 reported a mob of tinners which rose "in consequence of the introduction into that country of large quantities of Staffordshire and other earthenwares." The crowd went to a neighboring town and broke all the wares for sale. From there they went to the next town where "because they could not force their way into the Town Hall where large

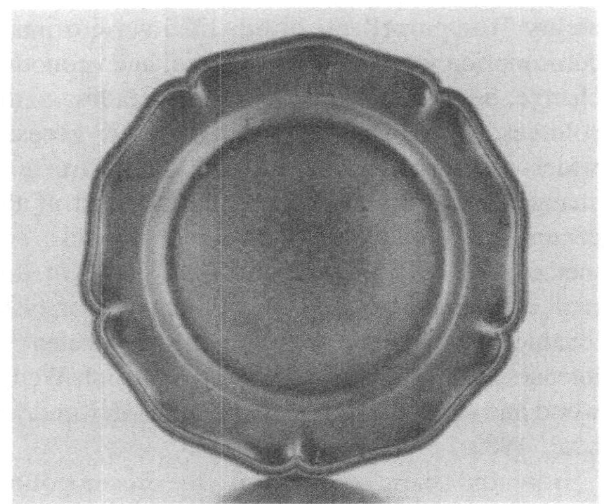

FIGURE 2. Pewter plate, London, Thomas Chamberlain, 1750–1770 (Photograph courtesy of the Colonial Williamsburg Foundation).

amounts of Staffordshire and other wares were lodged," set about to burn it down, a job only averted by the town alderman going with them to a pewterer's and ordering a quantity of pewter dishes and plates. Josiah Wedgwood himself noted in his journal of June 5, 1775 that he had been advised "not to trust myself among the miners of Cornwall, the tin trade being then low, and they being persuaded that the use of Queen's ware was the cause of it" (Hatcher and Barker 1974:286).

A rough scenario is set. A transformation occurred in the production of ceramics just as the British pewter industry was struggling, perhaps even providing the catalyst for pewter's demise. According to historical accounts of British tableware production, a simple change had occurred: innovatively marketed and technologically improved ceramics replaced pewter as the common tableware.

Part of the appeal of these new ceramics was their social value. Josiah Wedgwood's acquisition of royal patronage for his new creamware was brilliant marketing that sent consumers scrambling. By 1767 Wedgwood's experience with such patronage had taught him that "if a Royal, or Noble introduction be as necessary to the sale of an

FIGURE 3. Creamware plate, overglaze transfer print of the seal of Virginia, 1770–1785 (Photograph courtesy of the Colonial Williamsburg Foundation).

Article of Luxury as real Elegance & beauty, then the Manufacturer . . . will bestow as much pains, and expence too, in gaining the former of these advantages, as he wd. on bestowing the latter'' (McKendrick et al. 1982:108). First royalty was impressed, then nobility flattered, then the wishes of the common people to be like their betters were finally realized—each group's purchases separated by the appropriate quality, decorations, forms, and hence price. The powerful engine of social emulation was in high gear in mid 18th century society. As Henry Fielding complained, ''the nobleman will emulate the Grandeur of the Prince and the Gentleman will aspire to the proper state of a Nobleman; the tradesman steps from behind his Counter into the recent place of the Gentleman. Nor doth the confusion end there: It reaches the very Dregs of the People, who aspire still to a degree beyond that which belongs to them'' (McKendrick 1985:21–22). Soon such complaints would be echoed across the Atlantic where one post-war traveller blustered that ''this mania for luxury has reached such an extent that the wife of the laboring man wishes to vie in dress with the wife of the merchants, and the latter does not wish to be inferior to the wealthy women of Europe'' (Bayard 1950:130–131). From the wish for ease and comfort sprang emulative spending—the common man's ''petty vanity for tricking out himself and his family in the flimsy manufactures of Britain'' (Lemay 1987: 847).

These complaints illustrate the material effects of the challenge to traditional ideas about class structure and relations in 18th century Anglo-American society (Corfield 1987). Focusing on the Chesapeake colonies, the evidence has also mounted exponentially for sweeping changes in the economy, social structure, architecture, and material culture of the region (Kulikoff 1986; Isaac 1982; Neiman 1978; Carr and Walsh 1985, 1988). Social stratification and the importance of social rituals as class delineators are a major tenet of these recent studies. Specialized spaces in manorial brick houses provided an appropriate environment for such social rituals as the fashionable, elaborate serving of labor-intensive and exotic foods on fine ceramic tablewares; an elegant atmosphere and a genteel activity to demonstrate one's enhanced position to the lesser classes and reinforce one's membership in a colony-wide political and economic elite (Bushman 1984:345–383; Douglas and Isherwood 1979:66). All of these behaviors—and their props— became demarcators of class membership, visible indicators of the way people lived at the top of the social hierarchy. Not institutionally disbarred, the lesser classes at least perceived the chance to be received in the circles above, further spurring social emulation to close the gap to those above and increase the distance from those below.

In this process, fine ceramics, like the socially-correct creamware, gained heightened importance as social symbols. If a new concern for fashionable and elaborate dining had emerged among the middling ranks, the demand for the appropriate supporting artifacts—such as fine ceramic tablewares—should be seen in their household inventories. Thus, both from society and the market, historical evidence suggests change, not continuity, in the use of pewter or ceramics in 18th century Virginia.

Albemarle County Probate Records

But are those changes reflected in the household possessions of those that lived and died in late

18th century Albemarle County, Virginia? The answer from the probate evidence of 170 households is clear: despite large-scale changes in British tableware production and the heightened importance of fine ceramics in dining, pewter was not immediately replaced by ceramics in Albemarle County homes.

The number of households containing some type of ceramic remained static from 1770 to the end of the century; there was no large influx as would be produced by the revolutionary and universal introduction of creamware by 1762 and later refined earthenwares. Similarly, pewter remained a standard presence in households of all economic levels. Eighty per cent of all the households represented in Albemarle County probate inventories in those three decades contained pewter, 80 per cent contained ceramics, and about 70 per cent contained both pewter and ceramic.

The ubiquitous ownership of pewter reported between 1650 and 1720 seems to have remained surprisingly constant for households of the next several generations. Does this mean that dining behaviors remained unchanged? One way to test this proposition is to examine the presence of pewter and ceramic serving items in those households of varying economic ranks and through time. Plates were the most basic and numerous item, and those inventories listing at least one plate—either pewter or ceramic—were selected as test cases. Of that group of plates found in Albemarle County probate inventories, about two-thirds were pewter. Each household contained a median of about a dozen plates, and only a quarter of these were ceramic. However, the large number of ceramic plates in *some* households pulled the mean to 21, of which almost half were ceramic. The continued predominance of pewter in Albemarle County is again suggested.

Did the frequency of pewter change in households of differing wealth? Cautioning that the very poorest were probably not represented in the probate process, the percentage of households in each wealth category that owned at least one pewter plate did not change greatly as one progressed up the economic scale. At no economic tier did fewer than 70 per cent of the households own pewter,

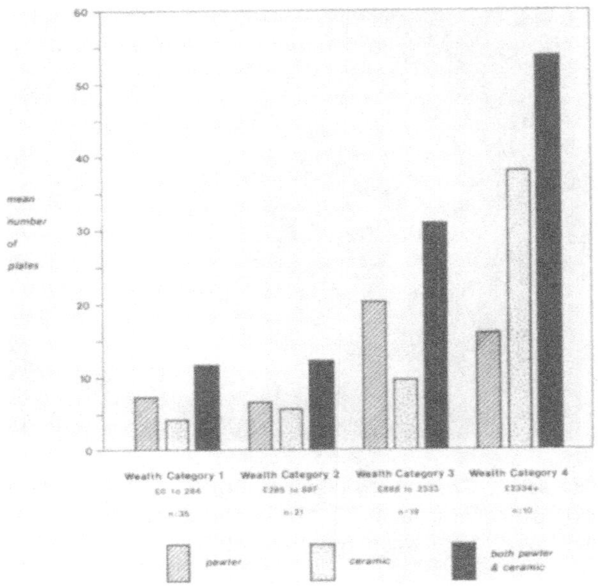

FIGURE 4. Mean number of plates by wealth category, Albemarle County, 1770–1799.

and the percentages were nearly identical at the top and bottom end of society.

Nevertheless, the frequency of ceramics does suggest some differences among economic groups: the presence of ceramics markedly increased as one's wealth increased. While little more than a third of the bottom tier owned ceramic plates, that number steadily increased to two-thirds in the top echelon. Thus, even though pewter was standard in all groups, the frequency of ceramics increased up the economic scale. The poorest households were most likely to have pewter, but the richest chose both pewter and ceramic.

Turning from presence/absence of pewter plates to the mean number of plates, these patterns are again confirmed. Figure 4 presents the mean numbers of plates in these probate records, while Table 3 presents the basic statistical data to evaluate those averages. The most obvious trend is expected: the wealthier a household, the more plates of all categories owned. Within each group there was also significant variation in the quantities owned, a characteristic which increased significantly with wealth. For example, the marked

TABLE 3
DESCRIPTIVE STATISTICS FOR PLATES IN HOUSEHOLDS OF VARYING WEALTH: 1770–1799

	WEALTH GROUP 1	WEALTH GROUP 2	WEALTH GROUP 3	WEALTH GROUP 4
ALL PLATES				
MEAN	11.5	12.2	30.7	53.8
MEDIAN	7.0	7.0	19.0	38.0
STD DEV	12.1	9.5	25.6	57.3
MAXIMUM	66.0	36.0	97.0	156.0
PEWTER PLATES				
MEAN	7.3	6.6	21.0	15.7
MEDIAN	6.0	6.0	14.0	12.0
STD DEV	5.2	6.5	22.6	13.0
MAXIMUM	21.0	23.0	97.0	45.0
PRESENCE[a]	85.7	71.4	100.0	90.0
CERAMIC PLATES				
MEAN	4.2	5.6	9.7	38.1
MEDIAN	0.0	3.0	5.0	18.5
STD DEV	9.4	8.4	11.1	54.2
MAXIMUM	48.0	36.0	30.0	144.0
PRESENCE[a]	37.1	52.4	63.1	70.0
N[b]	35	21	19	10

[a]Percentage of households
[b]Number of inventories listing at least one plate

difference between the mean and median figures in the richer households suggests a tendency to own either large numbers of ceramic plates or perhaps none at all. The number of ceramic plates rose rapidly with one's wealth level, increasing ninefold from top to bottom. In contrast, the number of pewter plates, although naturally increasing in wealthier households, did not increase in such large numbers. The mean number of pewter plates showed a much smaller increase from top to bottom, and it was the third wealthiest group that owned the largest number.

The bottom 70 per cent of the population, Wealth Groups 1 and 2, were remarkably similar in their ownership of pewter plates. An average of about a dozen plates graced their tables. These plates were most often pewter. Yet if an Albemarle County resident's rank moved just above the bottom half of the population to Wealth Group 2, one in two added a half dozen ceramic plates to the pewter ones in his home. However, it was in the top third of the population that dining behavior may have become quite different. The inventories of those households just below the economic elite, Wealth Category 3, contained at least twice the number of plates as those less wealthy below them. While every householder in this group had pewter plates, two-thirds also had ceramic.

Yet, the wealthiest households in Albemarle County, the top nine per cent of the decedent population, still managed to separate themselves from those below through their material goods. The number of plates jumped so dramatically that ownership of several sets of ceramics is suggested. Men and women in this group could choose between three dozen ceramic plates or more than a dozen pewter ones. While the group below had more pewter plates on average, more of Wealth Group 4 chose ceramics—and in large numbers. It is only at the top of the economic scale that ceramic plates outnumbered pewter ones.

Were there changes in pewter ownership as a generation matured and died in the late 18th century? While the retention of pewter from an earlier era might be expected for those dying in the beginning years of the sample, part of the group setting up a household in 1770 may have just been entering the probate population by the end of the century. This cohort would not necessarily have already made the initial investment into pewter as ceramics had become more popular. Yet while there were differences between the consumer choices in the estates of *some* of these men or women and those of the previous generation, no clear picture of change emerges. Mean numbers of all plates decrease, as well as the mean number of ceramic and pewter plates. But large differences between mean and median numbers and large standard deviations, particularly in ownership of ceramics, imply quite different choices within these households in each time period. There may have been a transitional period, or variability among economic groups may have masked changes across time.

Attempting to divide the population into economic groups by decade produces a sample size too small to be statistically significant, but one quite tentative generalization might be offered. While the number of pewter plates remains steady in households at each tier of the economic hierarchy in each time period, the mean number of ceramic plates among the elite tripled after 1780. Yet the median number of ceramic plates remained constant in this group in the same periods. It seems again that some households, particularly at the top of the economic scale, were acquiring large numbers of ceramic plates, but by no means were all making such purchases. This addition of ceramic to—not substitution for—pewter after the Revolution helps explain another trend over time. While fewer than half of the plates between 1770 and 1779 were ceramic, two-thirds were ceramic in the final decade of the century.

But, again, what of the seeming lack of change over time in the vast majority of the population—the middling and lower ranks that continued to choose pewter over ceramic? Perhaps this later generation were investing in differing ceramic *forms* than their fathers, evidence that would be hidden in considering plates alone. If so, ownership of *any* ceramics should increase by the end of the century. Combining all forms into a simple presence/absence test also enables the inclusion of ''parcels'' of pewter and ceramic in the probate lists, lumped groupings of goods where no form was designated.

Even so, the ownership of pewter, ceramic or both pewter and ceramic is relatively static in these 30 years, although there was some slight decrease in the number of households owning tablewares at all (Figure 5). Perhaps there was a change in the population itself: for example, more probate inventories in this time period did not include a full range of household goods and thus fewer decedents may have succeeded in setting up their own household after the Revolution.

Two sample years, 1815 and 1825, were arbitrarily chosen to test if a significant decline in pewter ownership took place in households in Albemarle County in the early 19th century. About half of those 26 households that entered probate in 1815 had some form of pewter. A decade later, however, fewer than a quarter of the dozen inventories listed pewter. The slight decreases occurring in the 18th century quickly accelerated by the first quarter of the 19th century. Pewter was then no longer common in Albemarle County households.

Two salient patterns are seen in this data. First, there are no significant changes in pewter ownership in probate inventories through the end of the 18th century, although a slight decrease may be indicated. Pewter remained standard for most families, while some households were slowly adding ceramic plates. Changes in production and marketing in the late 18th century were not immediately reflected in the consumer behavior of the Albemarle County probate population. According to the probate data, there were fewer ceramic plates than pewter ones in the last three decades of the 18th century in Albemarle County, but this would markedly change in the coming generation.

The second important evidence is that there were distinct differences in the patterning of ceramic and pewter usage by varying economic groups. If those in the wealthier groups owned ceramic plates, they owned large numbers. But only in the uppermost echelon of society did ceramic plates outnumber pewter ones. Many in

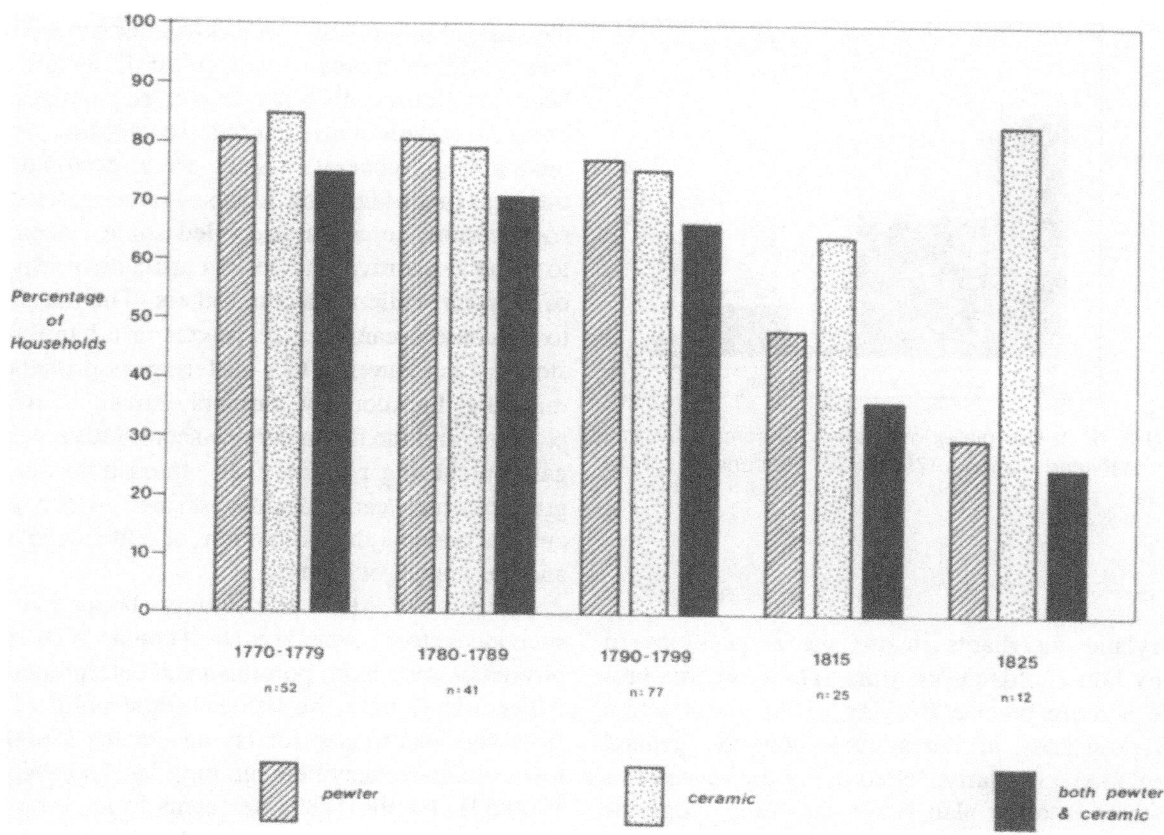

FIGURE 5. Presence of pewter and ceramics in Albemarle County households, 1770–1825.

this elite group acquired a large number of the more fashionable new ceramic wares so appropriate for large-scale entertaining, and here ceramic plates outnumbered pewter ones. Looking to those just below the elite, the upper middling ranks that may also have had disposable income to invest in items of social display, some did certainly choose to separate themselves from those below through the investment in more ceramic tablewares. But most still selected pewter, albeit in far larger numbers that their less wealthy neighbors. If the proposition is valid that the purchase of ceramic tablewares suggests a participation in the consumer frenzy promoted by Wedgwood, then the middling ranks of Albemarle County do not seem to have been fooled by such fashion manipulation. Similarly, if the ownership of fine ceramic tablewares suggests an attempt to emulate elite fashionable high-style dining behaviors, then those households do not seem to have been participating in the anxious social drama of the 18th century Chesapeake colonies.

Virginia and Maryland Retail Stores

Such answers only open a Pandora's box of questions. Is the inventory evidence so blurred with the lifetime accumulation of objects that changes in consumer behavior are masked? Were Albemarle County residents representative of Virginia society as a whole? One way to answer both of these questions is through the use of independent historical documents. While probate inventories represent the acquisitions of one household for many years, invoices of goods sent to Virginia and

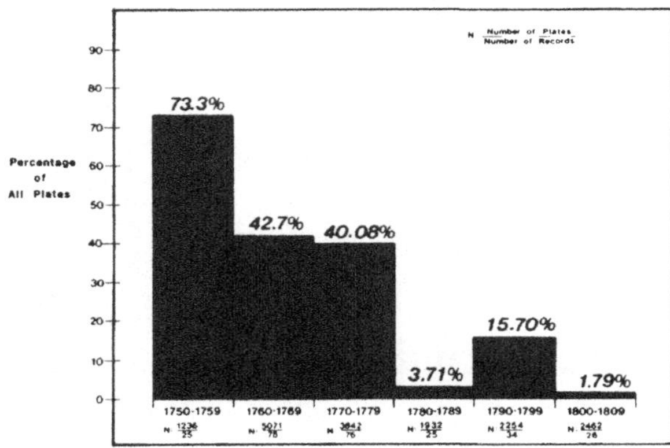

FIGURE 6. Pewter plates ordered in 19 sample Virginia and Maryland stores, 1750–1810: Percentage of all plates.

Maryland merchants record the acquisitions of many households at one time. These records provide a more precise tracking of the introduction and popularity of items throughout the general population. Similarly, by studying the inventories of stores in other places, we can better judge the consumer behavior of Albemarle County.

The decline in the importance of pewter plates in 19 sample stores is dramatic (Figure 6). Between 1750 and 1759, three-fourths of the plates were pewter. Fifty years later that number was less than two per cent. With each decade, fewer of the plates imported were pewter, their number particularly plummeting during the chaos of the Revolution and its immediate aftermath. A partial explanations for this abrupt plunge may lie in the materials of pewter, tin and lead. Both were necessary to the war effort. In any event, total exports of pewter from Britain dropped 75 per cent between 1772 and 1780 (Schumpeter 1960).

Even as the sale of pewter declined, that of creamware skyrocketed. The trickle of creamware that began in the late 1760s would become a flood in the Chesapeake in only a few years, pushing aside not only pewter but white salt glazed stonewares and tin-enameled earthenwares as well (Martin 1988). The purchase of creamware by so many people in so short a time could not have merely been for functional reasons. Even if all had the same ability to buy, each consumer carried into these different stores certain cultural, social, and behavioral norms that may have led one to purchase a certain item, another to abstain. Some modes were general, others were personal. A different mix of cultural values—some matching a social norm, some varying—led some customers to respond positively to certain artifacts or aspects of artifacts while neglecting others. The decisions to purchase creamware or pewter in a handful of stores, each catering to a differing assortment of middling backcountry farmers, small tidewater planters, and the urban service sector create aggregate purchasing patterns that demonstrate the degree to which each locality ascribed to one such cultural value—the emulation of elite behaviors and the appeal of fashion.

Residents of Albemarle County shopped at one such local store, owned by Dr. Thomas Walker. A physician, merchant, politician and entrepreneur in Albemarle County, he held multiple political offices and was trustee for laying out the fledgling town of Charlottesville beginning in 1763 (Woods 1900:53). By the 1780s he seems to have ranked among the wealthiest men in the county (Moore 1976:84). Walker's store was in operation in the new county seat at least by 1768 and his family papers from 1764 to 1769 included invoices for his retail business. During this time he imported 30 dozen plates—two-thirds pewter and the remainder of white salt glazed stoneware. His customers were probably the middling ranks of Albemarle County society, and he would have extended credit for their purchases throughout the year, answering requests like "please send by the Bearer a quart stone or earthen Bowl and one of your largest Tumblers" (Maury 1768).

Even though later data is not available for this store, we can assume from other merchants' records that the percentage of ceramic plates in his stock should have increased over time. The customers that came in the 1770s to purchase sugar or salt or coarse osnaburg would undoubtedly see the gleaming creamware plates, so delicate and refined and new. Did they buy them, carefully tucking them in straw or carrying them in their laps across the jolting back country roads?

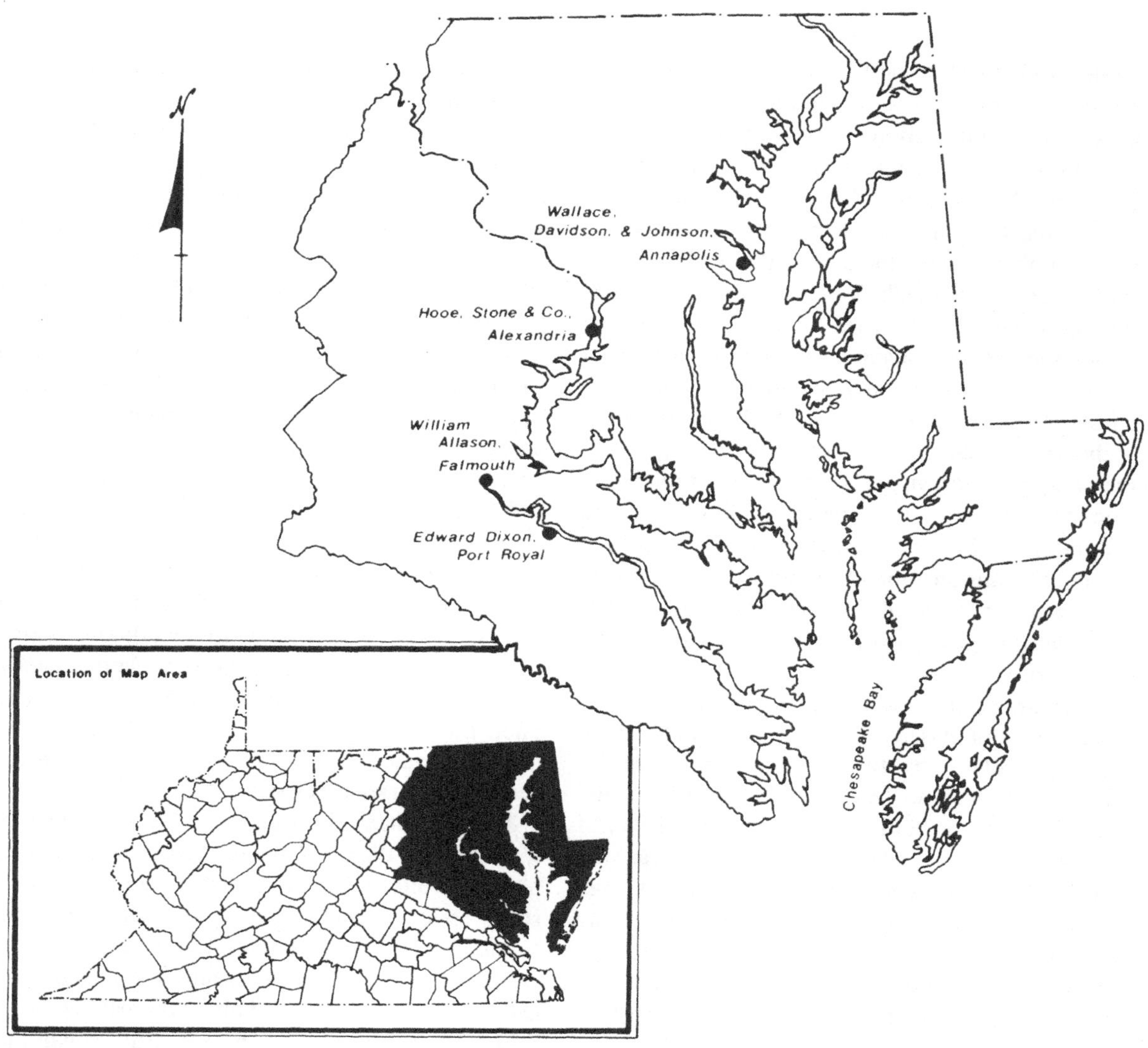

FIGURE 7. Locations of four sample merchants, c. 1760–1784.

While some were won by the new fashions, as a group they were not. The number of pewter tablewares in households of the lower 70 per cent of the Albemarle County probate population, those most likely to have been local store customers, remained almost static from 1770-1799—ranging from 55 to 65 per cent of all tablewares, matching the stock of Walker's store as much as 30 years earlier. If the middling sorts purchased creamware in large amounts instead of pewter in the 1770s, perhaps it was by the young setting up household, for such behavior was not seen in the middle-aged ranks that died by the end of the century. But the wealthy Dr. Walker was not so immune to a sense of status display, purchasing queen's ware serving items in quantities in 1772 and 1773 for his own use. Walker's seven queen's ware dishes, however, were not to become probate evidence for some 24 years.

Did the consumer behavior of Albemarle County represent Virginia society at the end of the 18th century? The stock of retail stores demonstrates some local, or perhaps regional, variation in consumer demand. Four contemporary stores with excellent documentation can serve as quick examples (Figure 7). William Allason was a merchant in Falmouth, Virginia from 1760 to 1774. On the fall line of the Rappahanock River, his store drew a large number of customers from the piedmont and the upper Shenandoah Valley, nearly a quarter travelling the 80 miles from Frederick County. The importance of the consumers of that western market led Allason to open a satellite store in Winchester before a feared Indian attack forced him to withdraw (Spoede 1973). Between 1760 and 1774 the majority—about two-thirds—of the plates stocked in his store were pewter. Allason ordered tin-glazed earthenware (delft) in the 1760s, sold in small but constant quantities until he introduced creamware in 1770. After that time, the leftover delft plates lingered on his shelves until the closing of his store.

In contrast, creamware plates sold quickly; his customers purchased 172 plates in only three years. Porcelain, by far the most expensive ceramic plate, had no buyers for three years, and even then Allason could only rid himself of half of his original order of twelve. Pewter was the workhorse of his tablewares—demand was high and he re-ordered it consistently even after adding creamware to his stock. While 270 creamware plates were ordered in 1770 and none after, he added twice that number of pewter in the next four years.

Just down the Rappahanock River was the store of Edward Dixon. A retired sea captain, gaining land and slaves through a well-placed marriage, Dixon had settled in Port Royal in Caroline County as an agent for an English mercantile firm. A merchant with an extensive commission trade in tobacco and grain exports, he also managed the inspection warehouse, as well as keeping a blacksmith shop. (Bergstrom 1980:211). An invoice and inventory book records store transactions there from 1767 to 1774. In that first year he ordered 96 delft and 144 pewter plates, of which about half of each remained in stock a year later. After another year a little more than a third of the original delftware plates remained, and he would only sell seven in the next two years. But his pewter sold out and he replenished his stock of it in March.

So far the transactions at his store are not so different from those at William Allason's. But after the introduction of creamware, Dixon ordered no more pewter plates. His customers instead chose 28 dozen creamware plates in the next four years. The patrons of Dixon's store were demanding expensive and fashionable ceramics, and in his store is the earliest creamware documented in Virginia: enameled cream colored teas in 1768. Enameled porcelains and copper plated (overglaze transfer printed) coffee pots were all available to his customers.

A third example is the firm of Hooe, Stone and Company, running a commission house and store in prosperous Alexandria, with satellite stores on both sides of the Potomac at Dumfries, Virginia, and Portobacco, Maryland. Invoice books, extant from 1771 to 1784, record large-scale dealings in grains to Europe, Britain, and the West Indies. Their transactions were only slowed by the Revolution; shipments of ceramics continued through neutral countries (Preisser 1977).

The first plates Hooe and Stone received in 1771 were three dozen "white stone barley corn plates," followed by two dozen more of "white stone" two years later. During this same time their suppliers also shipped four dozen pewter plates. By 1774, 80 per cent of the white salt-glazed plates had been sold, as well as half of the pewter. As in Edward Dixon's store, there was little demand for other types of plates after the introduction of creamware. The first creamware was top-of-the-line: over four dozen "gold-bordered" queen's ware table and desert plates, costing two to three times undecorated creamware and more than blue-and-white porcelain. While these luxuries were slow-sellers, Hooe, Stone and Company ordered more than 500 plain creamware plates in the next 11 years, as well as six dozen porcelain ones. They also stocked two "compleat dining setts Queens Ware," each containing 240 pieces. Such matched sets included all the props for the serving of abundant and elaborate foods in the highly-schematic diagrams illustrated in contemporary cookbooks. With the inclusion of items such as barrel-shaped mugs "painted and gilded with the four parts of the world," an impressionistic picture arises of truly urban difference in lifestyle, a "level of conspicuous consumption almost never matched in the countryside" (Walsh 1983:112).

This impression is only reinforced by the items for sale in other urban places. The partnership of Wallace, Davidson, and Johnson formed in Annapolis in March 1771. With £1000 capital contributed by each partner, Joshua Johnson was dispatched to London to purchase goods for a new store. Despite increasing competition in the Annapolis trade, Johnson felt their business would have the advantage, "our goods being better in quality, more fashionable and better chosen . . . for my having time and seeing them myself." He instructed his partners to "enumerate the articles and describe them but leave the fashion and quality to me" (Papenfuse 1975; Price 1979:21,11).

His first shipment of goods was equal to the firm's whole capital, forming at once an inventory about three times the value of William Allason's. That initial order included 11 dozen creamware table, dessert, and soup plates, and six dozen more table plates were re-ordered a few months later. Yet no pewter plates were included in the two schemes of goods requested or shipped that year. Annapolis residents wanted not only creamware plates, but a wide assortment of the proper matching serving pieces: three different varieties of salad dishes (oblong, octagonal, and pierced), cruets for condiments, egg cups and pickle stands and salts. Marketed separately, their price would be in reach of a far greater part of the population than the complete sets sold by Hooe, Stone, and Company. Perhaps they are evidence that those of lesser economic abilities were also concerned with the kinds of high-style dining dictated in contemporary cookbooks. Aptly enough, one such recipe book, Hannah Glasse's *The Art of Cookery Made Plain and Easy,* was included in the first shipment, containing instructions for preparation of the kind of "side or corner dishes" those forms would contain (Glasse 1797:134). Creamware was the overwhelming tableware of choice for the residents of Annapolis.

The customers of these stores differed in their demands for expensive and fashionable goods. Although Allason successfully added creamware to his stock, it was in addition to pewter. In contrast, creamware replaced pewter to a large extent in Edward Dixon's store. Pewter was insignificant in the stock of Hooe, Stone, and Company in Alexandria, while two grades of creamware were available there; a small number of gold-bordered plates were sold as well as a huge volume of common creamware plates. But Wallace, Davidson and Johnson did not even stock pewter plates in their new store in Annapolis. They sold several sizes of creamware plates for a soup, main, and dessert course, as well as a large complement of matching serving pieces.

The bulk of customers at stores in places like Annapolis and Alexandria were not the wealthiest urban elite, many of whom continued to make direct requests to an agent in England, but those that catered to the elite themselves; artisans, ordinary keepers, and the broad range of a growing service sector (Papenfuse 1975:28). It was in these more urban places that sociability, both private and public, was an important part of daily life (Clark 1988). Even the 800 residents of declining Yorktown, Virginia spent their time "dining together, drinking punch and playing billiards" at the end of the 18th century. One function of this conviviality was social display, an opportunity for the rich man "to shew the stranger his splendid furniture, his fine English glass, and exquisite china" (La Rochefoucauld 1799:II,21,38). Nor was this limited to the wealthy: one early 19th century critic lampooned urban society as a citadel of bandboxes where "fashion intermeddled with everything and descended to all ranks to seek for votaries" (*Norfolk Gazette and Publick Ledger,* January 26, 1814). For example, in early 19th century Williamsburg, Virginia, over one-third of the lower-middling ranks of society owned some portion of a group of luxury goods related to entertaining at dinner or tea parties, such as table or tea wares of silver, plate or cut glass, or mahogany dining tables, sideboards or chairs. Yet only three per cent of the same economic group in surrounding rural York County had such items in their households (Smart 1986:84). These urban/rural contrasts are clearly documented in the types of goods purchased at local urban stores.

A second distinction may be found even between rural areas. While many of William Allason's customers were drawn from the western piedmont and "backcountry," Edward Dixon's patrons were mostly drawn from established tidewater families. Creamware was becoming increasingly common and popular for those of the "middling and lower sorts" in the east. Lorena Walsh and Lois Carr found that even one-third of the poorest Talbot County households on Maryland's Eastern Shore had some creamware by the 1790s, and among the richest, sets of 100 or more pieces of ceramic were common. Pewter continued at all levels of wealth, but with far less frequency than in Albemarle County (Lorena Walsh 1984, pers. comm.).

The predominant tableware items in late 18th century Virginia and Maryland were pewter and ceramics. Most ceramics were less expensive and perhaps more fashionable than pewter. But if the unbreakable pewter was already owned, the purchase of a dozen creamware plates—no matter what the cost—was unnecessary, even frivolous. If none other than functional meanings were attached, new products would only slowly move into a community, mainly as new households made their purchasing decisions based on long- or short-term economic value. But if *social* value was attached to their real value; if prestige could be consolidated by their purchase; then innovation would take place more quickly. Thus the acquired social value of queen's ware plates—the successful status marketing by Wedgwood and others and the desire for social emulation—was recognized most markedly in Annapolis, Alexandria, and the tidewater region. In the more recently settled piedmont and backcountry, however, such fashion trends and social desires were more muted. Thus, the data from Albemarle County probate inventories, though blurred by time, cannot be dismissed as anomalous.

What forces in Albemarle County and other Virginia regions mitigated against the replacement of pewter? For a product, such as creamware, to be generally adopted in a region, it must be affordable, available, and desirable. As discussed above, Albemarle County was marked by a large number of "middling" farmers, as well as quite a few rich landowners compared to many more eastern regions of the state. Many householders had already gained land and slaves to produce capital and enter commercial agriculture. Isaac Weld (1799:206) observed that the county's common people were able to "procure the necessaries of life upon very easy terms." Pewter was certainly purchased by those common people, and the few shillings necessary to purchase a dozen of the less expensive creamware plates was not beyond the means of most of the population.

In addition, the product must be available. First, creamware was stocked in each of the sample stores after the early 1770s, despite their location. Second, while no specific estimates are available for the number of stores in late 18th century Albemarle County, her inhabitants most likely had access to ample retail facilities. Charles Farmer's study of country stores in the Virginia southside demonstrates a wide range of facilities for the purchase of goods. Although Farmer did not study variation within a general stock of goods, he found that these smaller stores sold items not unlike those at fall line towns, although prices were slightly higher and finding a particular item at any given time was more difficult. In addition, there was extensive shopping at higher order retail places, like the towns at the fall line. Business and agricultural products moved regularly between frontier and established regions, not only among the wealthy, but among the cast of wagoners, herdsmen, and tobacco rollers who made purchases for neighbors and friends (Farmer 1984). It is unlikely that creamware was not available to Albemarle County residents.

It seems, therefore, that consumer desire probably played the paramount role in the acquisition of ceramic tablewares in places like Albemarle County. The county elite were certainly mirroring the lifestyles of their tidewater peers even before the Revolution, when one of the wealthiest residents paid for dancing lessons for the children of relatives and neighbors (Moore 1976). At the end of the century, Isaac Weld found "several gentlemen of large landed property, who farm their own estates, as in the lower parts of Virginia.'' Yet, he also thought the ''common people'' of the county to be ''of a more frank and open disposition, more inclined to hospitality, and to live more contentedly on what they possessed than the people of the same class in any other part of the United States I passed through'' (Weld 1799:205–206). If the common people of Albemarle County ''lived more contentedly on what they possessed,'' does this suggest that they did not choose to purchase items that were unnecessary or beyond their means? Thus, even if those at the top like Thomas Walker or Thomas Jefferson lived and moved in a world not unlike that of established tidewater society, perhaps those of the middling ranks chose a different set of cultural values, tied to the relative simplicity and egalitarianism of a prosperous piedmont economy.

Pewter's Value and Use

The rejection of mere fashion or conspicuous consumption in Albemarle County as one explanation for the continued presence of pewter fits nicely, but begs one final question. What was the function of the pewter recorded there? The final answer must lie in an object's use and value: its cost in the marketplace, its long-term worth for resale or reuse, its function or functions, and its ''meaning,'' if any, to those who used it.

The cost of new pewter to an Albemarle County consumer can easily be established in Thomas Walker's store in the late 1760s. A dozen white salt glazed stoneware plates cost him a modest two-and-a-half shillings while the same number of pewter plates ranged from eight to fourteen shillings. Assuming a constant mark-up for Mr. Walker's profit, a customer choosing pewter would spend four to six times more than had he or she chosen white salt glaze. The new fashionable creamware was no less a bargain to that customer. Between 1770 and 1779 the cost of pewter plates was consistently three to four times the cost of creamware plates, and even a bit higher than porcelain ones in stores throughout Virginia and Maryland.

This initial start-up cost, however, was offset by pewter's durability and resale value. Suppose that hypothetical customer dropped a new ceramic plate a few weeks later. It could be repaired and placed on a shelf, but re-use was far less certain. In contrast, if the new pewter plate had been dropped, it would not have suffered more than a dent and could continue in use for years. If it had become a bit too battered, its owner could send it off to a pewterer to be recast, and for about half of his original cost could have a new plate in perfect condition (Greene 1965:1060). Perhaps he or she would sell it to a tradesman like James Haldane, who advertised that he gave ''the best prices for old . . . pewter'' or perhaps pass it on to an itinerant peddler (*Virginia Gazette,* February 6, 1772). One tradesman offered about 40 per cent of the retail cost of a new pound of pewter in the early 1770s, and a similar ratio was used for ''old pewter'' or ''pewter unfit for use'' in probate inventories throughout the century (Carter 1773: 26; York County Wills and Inventories 12:277, 23:414). In contrast, even intact ceramic items retained little value in probate inventories.

Thus pewter cost more initially but was a wise long-term investment. Was it perceived that way? According to James Deetz (1973: 28), pewter was a traditional symbol of wealth in 17th century America, its display serving as both ornament and social statement. Evidence from travellers' records, literary sources, and contemporary prints demonstrate some continuation of that tradition throughout the next century. For instance, upon entering a small log cabin in Connecticut in 1744, a wealthy traveller was horrified to find ''several superfluous things which showed an inclination to finery in these poor people,'' such as six pewter plates ''old and wore out but bright and clean.'' His suggestion that they sell the pewter—''too fine for such a cottage''—and substitute wooden plates which would be ''as good for use, and, when clean . . . almost as ornamental'' clearly articulates pewter's multiple role with utilitarian, decorative, and social functions (Bridenbaugh 1948:55). The description of the interior of a 14 by 18 foot cabin in 1800 still included brightly shining pewter, where make-shift shelves supported by pins driven into the logs displayed "in ample order a host of pewter plates, basins, dishes, and spoons, scoured and bright." More formal arrangement was on a "kind of sideboard or dresser with shelves called the pewter rack. Women prided themselves on keeping the whole [dinner set] brilliant as silver" (Montgomery 1973:16,14).

Even the famous tale of "The Legend of Sleepy Hollow" contains evidence of pewter's symbolic role. In this story, Washington Irving sets the scene of the home of a traditional wealthy Dutch family in New York. As the poor schoolmaster enters the hall "which formed the center of the mansion and the place of usual residence . . . rows of resplendent pewter, ranged on a long dresser, dazzled his eyes" (Irving 1978:781). Perhaps the immediate acknowledgment of wealth and material abundance dazzled Ichabod Crane as much as its gleaming metal. New fashions in refined earthenwares were less likely to impress in these traditional rural pockets of wealthy conservatism, where yeoman values were reinforced by religion and ethnicity. An 1816 description of Dutch and Quaker households in Virginia acknowledges the material culture of such conservatism where "the dresser[s] glistening with pewter-plates, still stand their ground, while the baseless fabrics of fashion fade away" (Paulding 1835:109). Thus, pewter for some may have represented both a solid economic investment and an accepted realm for display of one's wealth as late as the early 19th century.

Obviously some who could easily have afforded to purchase a dozen creamware or even porcelain plates chose to do so; yet others did not. Their foodways carried clear social meaning, and that message may have been remarkably conservative. Jack Goody points to the "nature and order of meals and courses, and the etiquette of eating" as an important factor for this conservatism in foodways (Goody 1977:151). Thus an early 19th century English poet lamented the disintegration of the traditional common table "Where master, son, and serving-man and clown/Without distinction daily sat them down," in households "where bright rows of pewter by the wall/Served all the pomp of kitchen or of hall." The author chose these images as the final evidence of the transformation of ancient agrarian relationships and scorned the modern farmer who ate alone with his family, aspiring "to ape the country squire" (Snell 1985: 67).

Contemporary prints also confirm the display of pewter on shelves or in cupboards. In some households, however, ceramics and pewter stood side-by-side. Thus, acquired ceramics were not necessarily in competition with pewter as status symbols but actually reinforced the metal's statement about wealth. For instance, a household scene illustrated in 1796 depicts both pewter and ceramic gleaming from the parlor corner cupboard (Figure 8). Irving's wealthy Von Tassel "knowingly left open" his corner cupboard to display "old silver and well-mended china" while pewter dazzled in his hall (Irving 1978:782).

Just as the display of pewter and ceramic were not exclusive, neither were their functions in daily usage. Open cabinets were for storage of items as well as showmanship. As only the upper groups seemed to have more than enough plates than were required for daily usage, these scenes of display in most households could only have been one part of pewter's role. When a family owned both pewter and ceramics, what was the function of each?

Personal choice may have dictated that pewter still be used at the household table despite the introduction of more refined earthenwares. John Hancock, for one, claimed that pewter was preferable for "the contents of the plates were not so apt to slide off" and the use of them "caused no clatter in contact with knives and forks" (Montgomery 1973:13). A village clergyman refused to give up his pewter because, he explained, "I can't sharpen my knife on the new stuff" (Sprackling 1958:7). If Von Tassel displayed his pewter in the great hall and his china in the parlor he may have preferred the traditional pewter.

An alternative to uses of display or at the family table may have been the passing of pewter tablewares down for kitchen usage. A 1770 print depicts both black and white servants dancing below a shelf of pewter in the kitchen (Figure 9). As early as 1757 pewter dishes, plates, and basins

FIGURE 8. "Diligence and Dissipation", London, 1796–1797; engraving by Gaugain and Hellyer after a painting by James Northcote, 1746–1831 (Photograph courtesy of the Colonial Williamsburg Foundation).

were included with "kitchen furniture" in 15 general categories of goods for stocking stores (Gill 1984:III, 7). In addition, the inventory data often distinguished between "old" and "new" pewter, and the older pewter is often listed in the constellation of kitchen, or food preparation, objects.

Yet, these kinds of impressions do not completely bear quantification from the probate data. If pewter replaced either food preparation or food serving ceramics, the ratio of items within these functional categories should change with the ownership of pewter. Overall some 60 per cent of the ceramics in the 170 Albemarle households fell in a loosely-defined food preparation/storage category while the other 40 per cent were tablewares. This ratio of ceramic table and kitchen wares was nearly the same in households with or without pewter. Pewter did not seem to take the place of either ceramic classification, or thus to be confined to one function.

Second, the pewter may have descended even farther down the household hierarchy and slaves, overseers, or servants could have used the cast-offs in their own homes. A 1797 Albemarle County probate inventory gives an enticing hint of slave usage, for on the second day of inventory taking only eleven slaves and "sundry pewter in basins and porrangers" were listed, despite an earlier extensive kitchen listing. Parker Potter found in

FIGURE 9. "High Life Below Stairs", England, 1770 (Photograph courtesy of the Colonial Williamsburg Foundation).

19th century Rockbridge County, Virginia, inventories that pewter is often listed in association with items from the "outside" realm, such as dairying items, farm equipment, and specialized tools (Potter 1983). This could also suggest slave use. Finally, excavation at slave structure 'S' at Thomas Jefferson's Monticello in Albemarle County revealed a large pewter basin, evidence suggesting at least some form of usage by the structure's occupants. It should be cautioned, however, that this phenomenon may not have been related to the introduction of newly-fashionable earthenwares. A precedent can be found as early as 1704 in the York County inventory of Joseph Ring, where a parcel of old pewter was found in the "Mattapany Quarter" assumedly for the use of overseer or slave (York County Deeds and Wills 12:285).

Thus the relationship between pewter and ceramic tableware items was complex. First, the assumption cannot be made that pewter had one "meaning" that was shared across time, space, and the social hierarchy. As Sidney Mintz (1985: 122) has vividly demonstrated in the case of sugar, differing social groups may transform or recast "meanings specific to the social and cultural position of the users." Second, alternative usages within the household may provide a partial explanation for a coexistence of pewter and ceramics in probate inventories. Pewter may have retained its function as a symbol of conservative stability and wealth long after its daily usage had passed. It may have been merely personal preference that dictated the continued usage of pewter in households that could afford to replace it. If ceramics were purchased, pewter may have become designated a less prestigious kitchen ware, continuing in standard service while ceramic plates and their supporting serving items graced the new mahogany dining table increasingly requisite for an elite lifestyle. Perhaps as these plates grew more derelict they were even passed down to slaves or servants for their own household. The puzzling anomaly in that case must lie in the curation of pewter despite its resale value as metal, and the seeming lack of desire within these households to regain part of their investment in cash or kind. Yet, whatever the use of the pewter recorded in Albemarle County inventories, other constraints balanced the pressures of marketing and social emulation to obtain new ceramic items.

The evidence presented here is not necessarily contradictory, but points to a period of transition within Virginia society in which many were unable—or in some cases, unwilling—to participate in a particular kind of behavior. Food and its presentation carried a strong message about one's place in the social hierarchy. Dining was undoubtedly ceremonial and gracious in the elite world of Thomas Jefferson (1790), who returned home to Albemarle County from Paris in 1790 with four cases of porcelain. But few on the farms and plantations there lived in the world of their famous neighbor. While some may have tried to imitate the gentry, food and food serving for others was still simple and hearty in the yeoman tradition. For the less fortunate, foodways were repetitious and mundane. Eating, not dining, was the norm, and that eating was often done from pewter plates.

Creamware plates were relatively inexpensive, but if the ubiquitous pewter plate was already owned, the purchase of ceramics was an "amenity." In urban or more established tidewater society, the upper and middling classes were clearly being wooed and won by the Staffordshire manipulation of fashion in the 18th century. There too the middling ranks were purchasing supporting artifacts of elite social behavior. Yet, less wealthy Virginians, or the more rural, frontier, or conservative of varying ranks, may not have been so easily convinced. Pewter remains an important "missing artifact" until the early 19th century.

ACKNOWLEDGMENTS

Research in merchants' records was funded by a 1986–87 grant from the National Endowment for the Humanities: "English Ceramics in America: Prices, Availability and Marketing"(# RO-21158-86), directed by George L. Miller. Research in Albemarle County probate records was partially funded by the Thomas Jefferson Memorial Foundation in 1983 when William M. Kelso incorporated the original probate study into the archaeology program at Monticello. James P. Whittenburg of the College of William and Mary guided my stumbling steps in 1983 and 1984 into the world of computer analysis with patience and enthusiasm, and carefully read the final product. J. Mark Wittkofski similarly made helpful comments on the original paper, and provided certain research materials on Albemarle County. Many on the staff of the Colonial Williamsburg Foundation have since helped refine and expand this research. My faithful partner George L. Miller read numerous drafts and made helpful suggestions for improvement. John Davis, Curator of Metals, was generous with his time and information, and arranged for all photographs. Harold Gill kindly provided me with his draft manuscript on the Virginia retail trade and Lorena Walsh shared probate data from her research. Marley R. Brown III helped inestimably through his critical insights of an earlier draft, and Greg Brown patiently proofed the final manuscript. Graphics were prepared by Virginia Caldwell Brown and Tamera Mams of the Department of Archaeological Research.

REFERENCES

ALBEMARLE COUNTY, VIRGINIA
1752–1809 Will and Inventory Books 2–4, Albemarle County Courthouse, Charlottesville, Virginia.

ALLASON, WILLIAM
1760 Letter to James Mitchell, August 19. Letter Book 1757–1770, Allason Papers, Virginia State Library, Richmond. Microfilm Holdings, Colonial Williamsburg Foundation.

AYRES, S. EDWARD
1966 Albemarle County, 1744–1770: An Economic, Political, and Social Analysis. *Magazine of Albemarle County History* 25:37–72.

BAYARD, FERDINAND
1950 *Travels of a Frenchman in Maryland and Virginia with a Description of Philadelphia and Baltimore in 1791.* Translated and edited by Ben C. McCary. Edward Brothers, Ann Arbor, MI.

BEAUDRY, MARY C., JANET LONG, HENRY M. MILLER, FRASER D. NEIMAN, AND GARRY WHEELER STONE
1983 A Vessel Typology for Early Chesapeake Ceramics: The Potomac Typological System. *Historical Archaeology* 17(1):18–43.

BERGSTROM, PETER VICTOR
1980 *Markets and Merchants: Economic Diversification in Colonial Virginia, 1700–1775*. Ph.D. Dissertation, Department of History, University of New Hampshire, University Microfilms, Ann Arbor.

BRIDENBAUGH, CARL (EDITOR)
1948 *Gentleman's Progress: The Itenerarium of Dr. Alexander Hamilton in 1744*. University of North Carolina Press, Chapel Hill.

BUSHMAN, RICHARD L.
1984 American High-Style and Vernacular Cultures. In Jack P. Greene and J.R. Pole, editors. *Colonial British America: Essays in the New History of the Early Modern Era,* pp. 345–383. Johns Hopkins University Press, Baltimore.

CARR, LOIS GREEN AND LORENA WALSH
1988 The Standard of Living in the Colonial Chesapeake. *William and Mary Quarterly* 3rd series 45 (1):124–134.
1985 Changing Life Styles and Consumer Behavior in the Colonial Chesapeake. Paper presented at the Conference on Anglo-American Social History, Williamsburg, Virginia.
1980 Inventories and the Analysis of Wealth and Consumption: Patterns in St. Mary's County, Maryland, 1658–1777. *Historical Methods,* 13(2):81–104.

CARTER, ROBERT
1773 Day Book. Volume XIII (1773–1776). Manuscript Division, Duke University Library. Typescript, Foundation Library, Colonial Williamsburg Foundation.

CLARK, PETER
1988 Clubs and Sociability in Britain and the American Colonies in the 18th Century. Paper presented at an Institute of Early American History and Culture Colloquium, Williamsburg, Virginia.

COOMBE, WILLIAM
1790 *Anderson's Historical and Chronological Deductions of the Origin of Commerce . . . A History of the Great Commercial Interests of the British Empire*. revised and continued to the year 1789. P. Byrne, Dublin.

CORFIELD, P.J.
1987 "Class by Name and Number in Eighteenth-Century Britain." *History,* 72(234):38–61.

DEETZ, JAMES F.
1973 Ceramics from Plymouth, 1635–1835: The Archaeological Evidence. In Ian M.G. Quimby, editor, *Ceramics in America,* Winterthur Conference Report 1972. Charlottesville, Virginia. pp. 15–40.

DOUGLAS, MARY AND BARON ISHERWOOD
1979 *The World of Goods: Toward an Anthropology of Consumption.* W. W. Norton and Company, New York.

EDDIS, WILLIAM
1969 *Letters from America,* edited by Aubrey C. Land. Belknap Press of Harvard University, Cambridge.

FARMER, CHARLES JAMES
1984 *Country Stores and Frontier Exchange Systems in Southside Virginia During the Eighteenth Century.* Ph.D. Dissertation, Department of Geography, University of Maryland.

FELTON, DAVID L. AND PETER D. SCHULZ
1983 *The Diaz Collection: Material Culture and Social Change in Mid-Nineteenth Century Monterey.* California Archaeological Reports, No. 23. California Department of Parks and Recreation, Sacramento.

GILL, HAROLD
1984 The Retail Business in Colonial Virginia. Draft ms. on file, Colonial Williamsburg Foundation.

GLASSE, MRS. [HANNAH]
1797 *The Art of Cookery, Made Plain and Easy.* Reprint edition, 1945. Randolph Carter Williams, Richmond.

GOODY, JACK
1977 *Cooking, Cuisine and Class: A Study in Comparative Sociology.* Cambridge University Press, New York.

GREENE, JACK P. (EDITOR)
1965 *The Diary of Colonial Landon Carter of Sabine Hall, 1752–1778.* The University Press of Virginia, Charlottesville.

HANTMAN, JEFFREY
1985 *The Archaeology of Albemarle County: Results of a Systematic Survey of Proposed Development Areas in Albemarle County, Virginia.* Laboratory of Archaeology, Department of Anthropology, University of Virginia. Submitted to the Virginia Division of Historic Landmarks, Richmond, Virginia.

HATCHER, JOHN, AND T. C. BARKER
1974 *A History of British Pewter.* Longman, London.

HENING, WILLIAM WALTER
1823 *The Statutes at Large: Being a Collection of all the Laws of Virginia, from the First Session in the Legislature to 1823.* Richmond, Virginia.

HERMAN, BERNARD L.
1984 Multiple Materials, Multiple Meanings: The Fortunes of Thomas Mendenhall. *Winterthur Portfolio* 19(1): 67–86.

IRVING, WASHINGTON
1978 The Legend of Sleepy Hollow. In *Anthology of American Literature,* edited by George McMichael. McMillan, New York, pp. 575–595. Originally published 1819.

ISAAC, RHYS
1982 *The Transformation of Virginia: 1740–1790.* University of North Carolina Press, Chapel Hill.

JEFFERSON, THOMAS
1790 Memorandum of the Objects Made and Furnished by me Grevin Master Boxmaker for Mr. de Jefferson minister of the United States of North America. July 17. Typescript on file, Thomas Jefferson Memorial Foundation, Charlottesville, Virginia.

JERDONE, FRANCIS
1743 Letter to Neill Buchanan, August 4. Jerdone Letter book, 1736–1744. E.G. Swem Library, College of William and Mary, Williamsburg, VA.

KULIKOFF, ALLAN
1986 *Tobacco and Slaves: The Development of Southern Cultures in the Chesapeake 1680–1800*. University of North Carolina Press, Chapel Hill.

LARABEE, LEONARD W. (EDITOR)
1969 *The Papers of Benjamin Franklin*, Vol. 13. Yale University Press, New Haven.

LA ROCHEFOUCAULD, FRANCOIS ALEXANDRE FREDERIC
1799 *Travels through the United States of North America, the Country of the Iroquois, and Upper Canada in the Years 1795, 1796, 1797*. Translated by Henry Norman. R. Phillips, London.

LEMAY, J.A. LEO (EDITOR)
1987 *Benjamin Franklin: Writings*. The Library of America, New York.

MCKENDRICK, NEIL, JOHN BREWER AND J.H. PLUMB
1982 *The Birth of a Consumer Society: The Commercialization of the Eighteenth Century*. University Press, Bloomington, Indiana.

MCKENDRICK, NEIL
1985 The Cultural Response to a Consumer Society: Coming to Terms with the Idea of Luxury in Eighteenth Century England. Paper presented at the Conference on Anglo-American Social History, Williamsburg, Virginia.

MCKUSKER, JOHN J. AND RUSSEL R. MENARD
1985 *The Economy of British North America, 1607–1789*. University of North Carolina Press, Chapel Hill.

MAIN, GLORIA
1982 *Tobacco Colony: Life in Early Maryland, 1650–1720*. Princeton University Press, Princeton, New Jersey.

MAIN, JACKSON TURNER
1954 The Distribution of Property in Post-Revolutionary Virginia. *Mississippi Valley Historical Review* 41: 241–258.

MAIR, JOHN
1905 "The Produce and Commerce of Virginia and Maryland." Extract from *Book-keeping Modernized* (3rd Edition, 1784) *William and Mary Quarterly*, 1st Series, XIV (2):87–93.

MARTIN, ANN SMART
1988 *To Supply the Real and Imaginary Necessities: The Retail Trade in Table and Teawares, Virginia and Maryland, c. 1750–1810*. Submitted to the National Endowment for the Humanities, Grant No. RO-21158-86.

MATTHEWS, ELIZABETH
1957 *The Life of Reverend Devereux Jarrett*. Master's thesis, Department of History, College of William and Mary.

MAURY, J.
1768 Letter to T. Walker, January 21. Dr. Thomas Walker Papers, Library of Congress. Microfilm Holdings, Colonial Williamsburg Foundation.

MILLER, GEORGE L.
1980 Classification and Economic Scaling of Nineteenth Century Ceramics. *Historical Archaeology* 14(1):1–40.

MINTZ, SIDNEY W.
1985 *Sweetness and Power: The Place of Sugar in Modern History*. Viking Penguin, New York.

MONTGOMERY, CHARLES
1973 *A History of American Pewter*. Praeger, New York.

MOORE, JOHN HAMMOND
1976 *Albemarle: Jefferson's County, 1727–1976*. University Press of Virginia, Charlottesville.

NEIMAN, FRASER D.
1978 Domestic Architecture at the Clift's Plantation: The Social Context of Early American Buildings. *Northern Neck of Virginia Historical Magazine*: 3096–2138.

NOEL HUME, IVOR
1969 *A Guide to Artifacts of Colonial America*. Alfred A. Knopf, New York.

NORFOLK GAZETTE AND PUBLICK LEDGER
1814 January 26. Norfolk, VA.

O'MARA, JAMES
1983 *An Historical Geography of Urban System Development: Tidewater Virginia in the Eighteenth Century*. York University Geographical Monographs 13. York University Press, York, Canada.

OTTO, JOHN SOLOMON
1975 *Status Differences and the Archaeological Record*. Ph.D. dissertation, Department of Anthropology, University of Florida. University Microfilms, Ann Arbor.

[PAULDING, JAMES]
1835 *Letters from the South by a Northern Man*. 2nd edition, Harper and Brothers, New York.

PAPENFUSE, EDWARD C.
1975 *In Pursuit of Profit: The Annapolis Merchants in the Era of the American Revolution: 1763–1805*. Johns Hopkins University Press, Baltimore.

POTTER, PARKER, JR.
1983 *Down the Rabbit Hole: An Application of the Structuralist Principal of Binary Opposition to a Historical Material Culture Problem.* Ms. on file, Historic Annapolis.

PREISSER, THOMAS M.
1977 *Eighteenth-Century Alexandria, Virginia, before the Revolution, 1749–1776.* Ph.D. Dissertation, Department of History, College of William and Mary.

PRICE, JACOB L.
1980 *Capital and Credit in British Overseas Trade: The View from the Chesapeake, 1700–1776.* Harvard University Press, Cambridge.
1979 *Joshua Johnson's Letterbook: Letters from a Merchant in London to his Partners in Maryland.* London Record Society, London.
1954 The Rise of Glasgow in the Chesapeake Tobacco Trade, 1707–1775. *William and Mary Quarterly,* 3rd series, XI: 179–199.

RISJORD, NORMAN K.
1978 *Chesapeake Politics, 1781–1800.* Columbia University Press, New York.

SCHUMPETER, ELIZABETH BOODY
1960 *English Export Trade Statistics.* Clarendon Press, Oxford.

SHEFFIELD, JOHN BAKER HOLROYD
1783 *Observations on the Commerce of the American States with Europe and the West Indies; including the Several Articles of Import and Export.* Reprint edition, Research Reprints, Inc. New York, 1970.

SMART, ANN MORGAN
1986 *The Urban/Rural Dichotomy of Status Consumption: Tidewater, Virginia 1815.* Master's thesis, Program in American Studies, College of William and Mary.

SMYTH, J.F.D.
1784 *A Tour in the United States of America.* G. Robinson, London.

SNELL, K.D.M.
1985 *Annals of the Labouring Poor: Social Change and Agrarian England, 1660–1900.* Cambridge University Press, Cambridge, England.

SPOEDE, ROBERT WILLIAM
1973 *William Allason: Merchant in an Emerging Nation.* Ph.D. Dissertation, Department of History, College of William and Mary.

SPRACKLING, HELEN
1958 *Customs on the Table Top: How New England Housewives Set Out Their Tables.* Old Sturbridge Village Booklet Series.

TEUTE, FREDERICKA J.
1976 *The Commercial Endeavors of a Virginia Merchant during the Confederation Period: The Rise and Fall of Richard Blow.* Master's thesis, Department of History, College of William and Mary.

UNITED STATES BUREAU OF THE CENSUS
1975 *Historical Statistics of the United States, Colonial Times to 1970, Bicentennial Edition, Part 1,* Series E 52–63:202. Government Printing Office, Washington, D.C.

VALLETE, ELIE
1774 *The Deputy Comissary's Guide Within the Province of Maryland Together with Plain and Sufficient Directions for Testators to Form and Executors to Perform their Wills and Testaments; for Administrators to Compleat their Administrations and for Every Person any Way Concerned in Deceased Person's Estates, to Proceed Therein with Safety to Themselves and Others.* printed by Ann Catherine Green and Son, Annapolis.

VIRGINIA GAZETTE
1772 February 6. Williamsburg: Purdie and Dixon, publishers.

WALSH, LORENA S.
1983 Urban Amenities and Rural Sufficiency: Living Standards and Consumer Behavior in the Colonial Chesapeake, 1643–1777. *Journal of Economic History* XLIII (1) 109–117.

WATTS, CHARLES WILDER
1947 Land Grants and Aristocracy in Albemarle County, 1727–1775. *Magazine of Albemarle County History* 8:6–26.

WELD, ISAAC
1799 *Travels Through the States of North America.* Reprint edition, 1968. Johnson Reprint Corporation, New York.

WILKINS, JOHN
c. 1773 Letter to John Norton. John Norton and Sons Papers, Colonial Williamsburg Foundation.

WOODS, EDGAR
1900 *Albemarle County in Virginia.* C.J. Carrier Company, Bridgewater, Virginia.

YORK COUNTY, VIRGINIA
1702–1706 Deeds, Orders, and Wills Book 12. Typescript. Foundation Library, Colonial Williamsburg Foundation, Williamsburg, Virginia.
1783–1811 Wills and Inventories Book 23. Typescript. Foundation Library, Colonial Williamsburg Foundation, Williamsburg, Virginia.

ANN SMART MARTIN
DEPARTMENT OF ARCHAEOLOGICAL RESEARCH
COLONIAL WILLIAMSBURG FOUNDATION
WILLIAMSBURG, VIRGINIA 23185

APPENDIX

For the purpose of this study, food-related items were all those ceramic, glass, pewter, brass, tin, copper, bell metal, iron, flint, horn, lead, silver, silver plate and wooden items used in the preparation, storage, and serving of foods. Table 1 lists the broad range of vessels and utensils found in Albemarle County probate inventories between 1770 and 1799. Excluded were agricultural implements or large-scale storage containers, as well as textiles. Descriptive statistics were generated by SAS on an IBM mainframe at the College of William and Mary.

The problem of price fluctuations and inflation was a serious one, especially with the depreciation of paper money in the Revolutionary war era and after. A crude weighting was performed using Warren and Pearson's wholesale price indices found in U.S. Bureau of the Census (1975:202). While the total effects of national price trends on Albemarle County is debatable, its participation in a market economy predicts a smoothing relationship. A price series from probate data was beyond the scope of this work.

Wealth groups were devised based on the statistical profile of the probate population. Those households below the median wealth level were designated the bottom group (50 per cent of the population with weighted estate valued between £0 and £284); those above the median and below the mean became the second wealth level (22 per cent, £284 to £887 estate values); between this line and one standard deviation lay an upper middle group (20 per cent, £888 to £2333); and those beyond this point were the wealthiest elite, Wealth Group 4 (9 per cent, £2333 +). My thanks to James Whittenburg of the College of William and Mary for his suggestion of this method.

A listing of sources of merchants' records follows.

Microfilm Holdings, Foundation Library, Colonial Williamsburg Foundation, Williamsburg, Virginia:

William Allason Papers, Virginia State Library.

Edward Dixon Papers. Library of Congress.

Eilbeck, Ross and Company Papers. Miscellaneous Collections, Duke University.

John Glassford and Company Papers, Library of Congress.

Frederick Hall Account Books. Southern Historical Collection, University of North Carolina at Chapel Hill.

Hooe, Stone, and Company Papers. Invoice Book. New York Public Library.

Neil Jamieson Account Books, Library of Congress.

James Lawson-John Semple Accounts, Scottish Record Office, Currie-Dal Misc. Bundle 20.

Logan, Dunmore and Company Inventory, Original: P.R.O./A.O. 13/30 Loyalist Claims 1782–1790, Reel 252.

John Norton and Sons Papers, London. 1769–1780.

Wallace, Davidson and Johnson Order Book, Annapolis. Maryland Hall of Records.

Dr. Thomas Walker Papers, Rives Papers, Library of Congress.

Willison, Stewart and Company Invoice. U.S. Circuit Court, Eastern District of Virginia Records—Record Books # 1 A–# 2 B. 1790–November 1794.

Swem Library, Manuscripts Department, College of William and Mary, Williamsburg, Virginia:

Henry Bedinger Invoice Book, 1785–1796.

Briggs and Blow Letter Book, Blow Family Papers.

Virginia State Library, Richmond, Virginia:

William Allason Papers, Loose papers.

Dramgoole Family Papers.

KATHERINE R. SINGLEY

Caring for Artifacts After Excavation—Some Advice for Archaeologists

ABSTRACT

As the concern for long-term curation of artifacts grows in the United States, more responsibility will fall on the archaeologist and the laboratory assistant to provide adequate care for artifacts during and after excavation. In this article various systems are presented for packing and storing the range of artifacts found on historic sites in North America. A list of suppliers of some materials mentioned in the text is included.

Introduction

As soon as an artifact is removed from its burial environment, it is subjected to certain physical and chemical changes. The equilibrium the artifact has achieved with its surroundings is upset. For instance, increased temperature of the air may promote chemical reactions. Abundance of oxygen in the new surroundings may stimulate corrosion on metals. Soluble salts from ground water may move through porous materials and, when exposed to a drier environment, crystallize on surfaces. Increased levels of light may destroy painted surfaces (Sanford 1975:55–56).

A conservator stabilizes an artifact to prevent its further deterioration. This should be done as soon as possible after excavation. Because some of the treatments can be quite exacting and complicated, archaeologists should employ trained conservators. Ideally, a conservator should be involved both in the planning of fieldwork and in the excavation (Grosso 1978). The presence of a conservator during all stages of excavation and subsequent analysis is a critical factor in the survival of artifacts. To a conservator, the excavation by archaeologists of artifacts without adequate measures for their preservation is irresponsible.

However, the conservation treatment itself is not enough: the preservation of any archaeological artifact may be regarded as a maintenance problem of curation. Artifacts undergo more changes during storage as temperature and moisture in the air change seasonally as well as daily. Greater factors in the survival of artifacts indeed may be proper storage and handling. The actual conservation treatment, then, constitutes an important but small part of the long-term preservation scheme. Even the most laborious of treatments can be undone by placing an artifact back into an improper storage environment.

In reality, the current lack of trained archaeological conservators and curators in the United States means that artifacts in collections may wait years for any kind of treatment. This situation will change in the future as awareness of endangered collections grows, co-operation between archaeologist and conservator increases, and support for conservation and curation is mandated (Bourque et al. 1980). However, because of the present situation, more responsibility must be taken by the excavators to safeguard their finds during and after archaeological projects. Even if a conservator cannot be provided, the curatorial process of labelling, packing, and storing must be regarded as equally important as the excavation. Before the excavation, adequate funds must be included in budgets prepared by the archaeologist for suitable packing materials of good quality. Moreover, time and care must be given by excavators in labelling and packing their finds.

This article provides some advice concerning handling of artifacts in the field and storing them in the transitional period between excavation and conservation. The measures are relatively simple and inexpensive. Some of the ideas are not new and are similar to those presented in two British publications by Dowman (1970) and Leigh (1972). Hopefully this article will reach a wider audience of American archaeologists and provide more useful suppliers for materials. Emphasis has been placed equally on what to do and not to do. Unfortunately, because of space, only basic advice could be given. The advice will help, but not guarantee, the survival of artifacts. It should not be regarded as a substitute for professional conservation and long-term curation. No attempt is made to discuss conservation treatments found elsewhere. For more information on the kinds of treatments available, one is referred instead to two general books (Plenderleith and Werner 1971; UNESCO 1968) as well as a small selection of publications cited below.

Some sources for materials and suppliers marked by an asterisk (*) are provided in the appendix. A more complete discussion of packing materials has been presented by Fall (1965). Archaeologists dealing with artifacts from marine sites should consult Lawson (1978).

Marking, Bagging, and Boxing—General Advice

Although every archaeologist has his own way of recording artifacts, certain methods in marking, bagging, and boxing can be suggested to minimize confusion.

If an artifact is given temporary identification in the field, it is advisable to use a dual marking system—a notation on the bag *as well as* a duplicate card or tag inside. Waterproof pencil, marker, or ink should be used. Waterproof plastic paper* may be useful in damp conditions. The plastic paper can also be cut into tags that are more resistant than paper to damage by insects and dampness in storage.

If an artifact is actually marked, the field or catalog number should be applied in India ink on two thin coats of a reversible resin (PVA-AYAF* in acetone*; Acryloid B72* in xylene* or toluene*) which seals the surface of the artifact. Clear nail polish is a readily available alternative. Caution should be exercised in using any of these resin solutions for marking artifacts. Always use in a well-ventilated area. Toluene is especially dangerous if used for long periods without proper precautions. Avoid contact with these solvents on the skin by wearing solvent resistant gloves* and avoid inhalation of vapors by using a cartridge respirator*. Do not use near open flame or store in extreme heat.

Once the number is applied, another coat of resin is applied for protection. It is unadvisable to mark directly on any unstable surface that is flaky or heavily encrusted with dirt or corrosion. In these cases tags (preferably plastic paper, as above) would be better. Pottery sherds should not be marked along the edges but on the inside surfaces as inconspicuously as possible.

While artifacts recovered from wet environments will require special packing, artifacts from dry sites should not be damp when bagged and marked. The artifacts should be dried slowly in the shade. Any moisture trapped in bags will encourage corrosion on metals and the growth of mold and mildew on artifacts. "Zip-lock" bags are especially dangerous for this reason. Paper bags may be used (except for lead and pewter), if they are of good quality. Double bagging is recommended for added strength.

Small, more fragile artifacts, like worked bone, glass, or buckles, are better stored in hinged clear plastic boxes* with labels (Figure 1). Acid-free tissue paper* and/or flexible

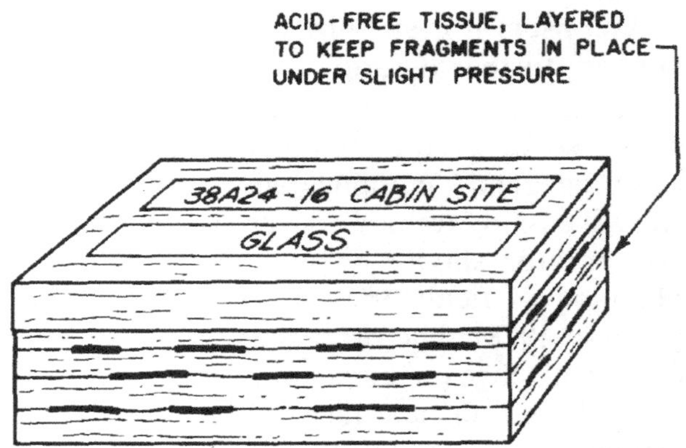

FIGURE 1. Fragile artifacts packed in plastic boxes with padding.

foam sheeting* should be used as padding around the find, although only the tissue paper should be in direct contact with the artifact. These packing materials not only will protect the surface but also will serve as buffers to lessen the effects of daily fluctuations in temperature and relative humidity. Cotton wool should be avoided as a packing material because it catches easily on rough edges. Newspaper, so strongly acidic, should not be used in direct contact with artifacts.

Additionally, a cheaper alternative to individual boxing is to staple small plastic polyethylene bags (2″ × 2″) containing finer fragments of glass or porcelain to index cards which can be boxed together. Galvanized staples are preferable to others which may rust in time. Pharmaceutical vials* also are useful for storing small fragments, but any empty space should be packed with acid-free tissue paper.*

Industrial polyethylene tote boxes* are more durable but more expensive than cardboard for transporting and storing artifacts. Some have internal dividers that are removable. If sturdy cartons like liquor boxes are used to store artifacts, heavier artifacts like brick, tile, and ceramics should be placed on the bottom. It may be necessary to reinforce the bottom with rigid foam sheeting.* The weight should be evenly distributed. Packing material like newspaper or polystyrene p-nuts in stapled plastic bags may be used to fill in holes to minimize shifting and reduce physical damage. Air-entrapped polyethylene sheeting, like "Bubble-Pack," may also be useful. The exterior of the box should be marked clearly to give contents and any special instructions (Figure 2). Finally, boxes do have limits in load, and should be transportable by one person of normal strength.

Thought and care should be given as well to shelving and storing of the cartons. The curatorial area should be accessible, well-ventilated, and free of dust and vermin. A general stable environment, with ideal levels of relative humidity at 45–55% and temperature at 65–75°F, is preferable to an environment with severe daily and seasonal fluctuations. Constancy of relative humidity is probably more

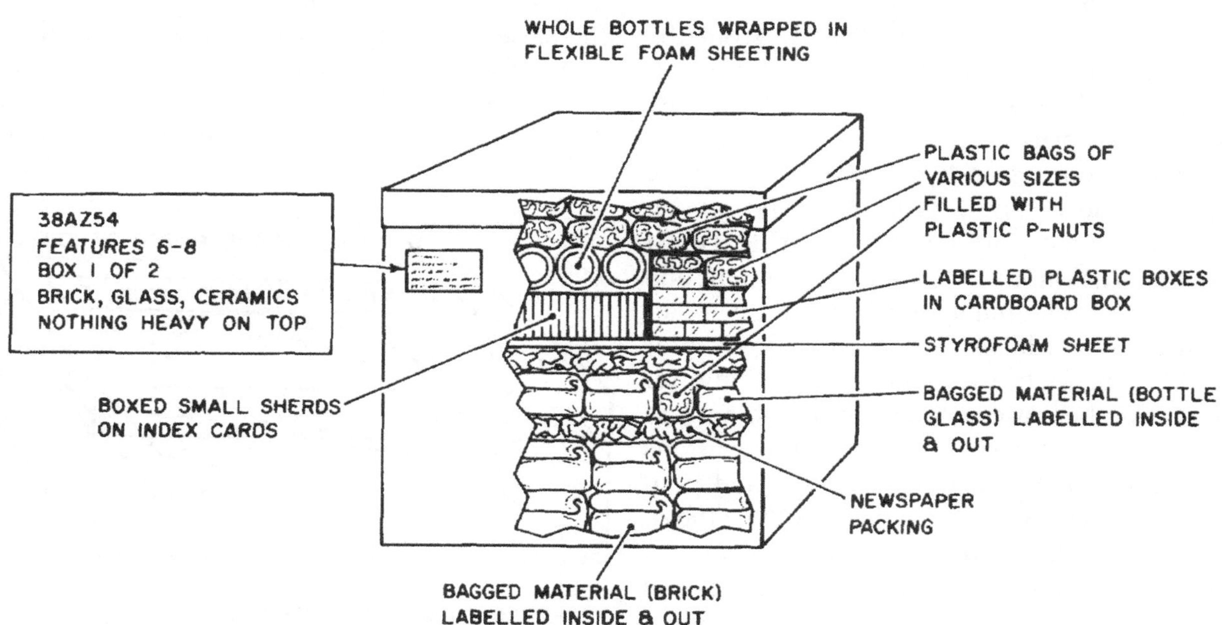

FIGURE 2. Sample label and packing system.

critical than constancy of temperature. Some artifacts, like metals and unstable glass, require special storage (see below).

Shelving units for a collection should be selected with a regard for strength rather than economy. Some cheaper metal utility shelving units may collapse under the weight of boxed artifacts. Enough boxes and shelving units, then, should be available to avoid overloading. Any necessary heavy boxes should be marked as such and placed on lower shelves. Stacking of heavier cartons of tile, brick, or iron on top of boxes of glass or bone should be avoided. An arbitrary placement of boxes just to retain sequence may be disastrous for more delicate artifacts. Partially or totally reconstructed pots should either be boxed or covered with plastic bags to prevent dust accumulation. Finally, some containers, i.e., those holding metals or waterlogged organic materials, may require placement where the archaeologist or laboratory assistant can get to them for frequent inspection.

Metals

Most metal artifacts recovered from historical sites may be removed directly from the ground. Metal artifacts should not be washed; if superficial cleaning is attempted, it only should be to brush off loose adhering dirt. No removal of corrosion by chisel, pick, or wire brush should be tried. Not only may impressions of organic material (wood, textiles) exist in the corrosion layer, but also the extent and condition of remaining metal may not be readily apparent. Ideally, a trained conservator should treat metals as soon as possible after excavation because much information may be lost with secondary corrosion. For various discussions of corrosion processes and conservation treatments, see Stambolov (1969), Hamilton (1976), and Brown et al. (1977).

Metal artifacts recovered from terrestrial sites should be thoroughly dry before bagging, especially if plastic bags are used for packing; otherwise, moisture will be trapped and further corrosion stimulated. For this reason plastic bags should be used for storing metals only in conjunction with indicating silica gel.* Indicating silica gel is an absorptive silica which changes color from blue to pink as moisture is removed from the surroundings. Pink indicates the silica gel's exhaustion, but the desiccant may be renewed by heating it in a domestic oven at no higher than 350°F until the deep blue color returns. The silica gel must not come in contact with the artifact's surface. Most important: artifacts stored with silica gel must be inspected monthly and the desiccant rejuvenated as necessary. A more complete discussion of the nature and applications of silica gel is found in Stolow (1977).

Fine or delicate metal artifacts may be packed individually in plastic boxes* as mentioned above. However, a small perforated plastic bag of silica gel* should be used as a desiccant (Figure 3).

Small metal finds like buttons or coins can be bagged in small plastic bags and stapled to cards filed in a plastic food container (i.e., Tupperware) with a perforated packet of silica gel* (Figure 4a). This system permits easy inspection of the artifacts. Plastic containers for shoes and clothing also may be useful.

A larger storage container for metals (Figure 4b) recently has been devised by the York Archaeological Trust in England (Spriggs

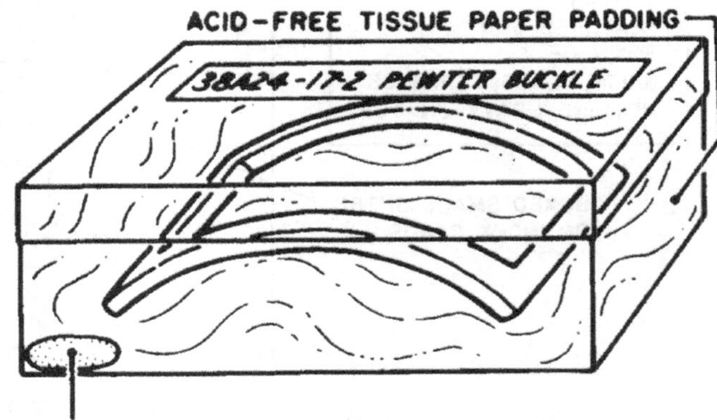

FIGURE 3. Metal artifact packed individually with padding and desiccant.

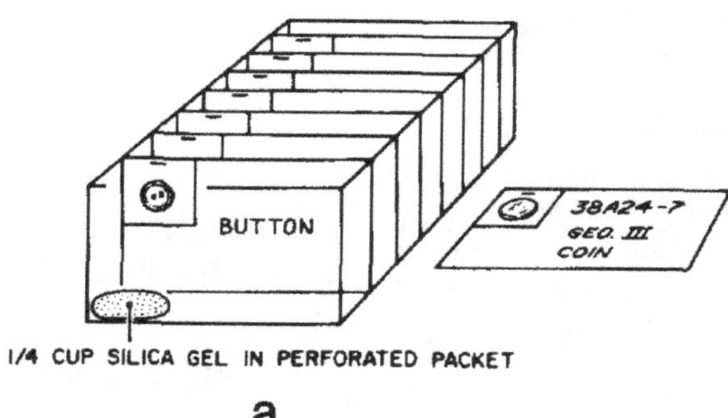

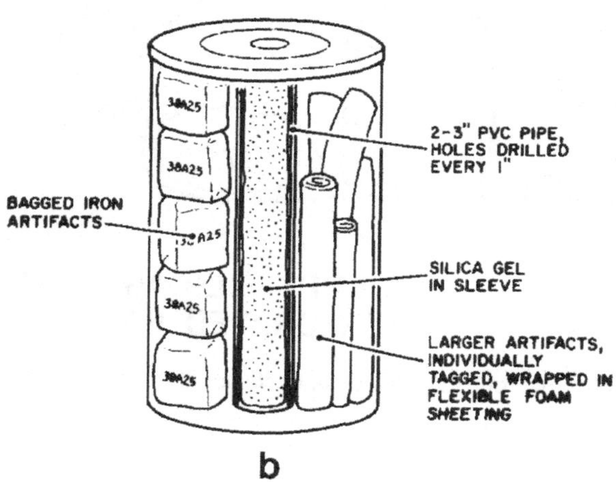

FIGURE 4. Metal artifacts packed as a group in closed containers with desiccant. a) Small finds on cards in a sandwich container. b) Larger artifacts in a bucket.

1979) using a 5 gallon polyethylene utility bucket, often available cheaply from franchise food concerns, such as Hardees or McDonalds. The cover should be tight fitting. Indicating silica gel* is placed in a muslin sleeve that slides down a drilled PVC pipe (Poly Vinyl Chloride), the kind used in plumbing. The sleeve system permits easy removal of the silica gel for inspection and regeneration without disturbing the bagged artifacts.

If covered plastic containers are unobtainable, metal artifacts (except lead and pewter) may be stored in cardboard boxes as recommended by Leigh (1972) provided that the box is placed inside a heavy gauge plastic bag (8 mil minimum) with a perforated bag of silica gel* (Figure 5).

It is very important that all metals before *and* after conservation be stored in areas that are as dry as possible, ideally not more than 30% Rh. Domestic dehumidifying units will help lower the overall relative humidity in a storage area. However, because the lower level is so difficult to achieve in most storage areas, a system of individual containers with silica gel* may be more advisable, despite the need for maintenance.

Metals recovered from waterlogged sites should be kept wet (Hamilton 1976; Lawson 1978).

Finally, archaeologists should be aware of four special considerations for metals:

1. Outbreaks of active corrosion on *iron* take the form of shiny, wet areas, often pustules of ferrous chloride ("weeping iron"). Weeping iron indicates very unstable iron which needs the immediate attention of a conservator as well as a sealed dry storage environment.
2. Active corrosion on *copper and brass* takes the form of an electric green, soft powder (basic cupric chloride—"bronze disease"). Again, the artifact is unstable and a dry environment and conservation treatment are needed.
3. *Lead and pewter* should not be stored in paper bags and cardboard boxes because the organic acids emitted from paper will attack the lead. Similarly, wooden shelving (oak, fiberboard, plywood) should be avoided. Lead and pewter exhibiting a whitish powder need immediate conservation treatment. Plastic boxes* padded with acid-free tissue* are recommended.
4. *Silver* artifacts in storage should be kept away from any sulfur containing materials because the hydrogen sulfide emitted from them will tarnish the silver. Included in this group are rubber materials like rubber bands, mats, and molding strips as well as some latex paints and treated textiles (Oddy 1975a).

Ceramics

Occasionally pottery (especially coarse Indian) is so weak and friable that consolidation is necessary before the fragments can be lifted from the ground. In general, consolidation is the exception to the rule and should be avoided unless totally necessary. Consolidation of any material should be regarded as a last resort; often resin heavily applied in the field is very

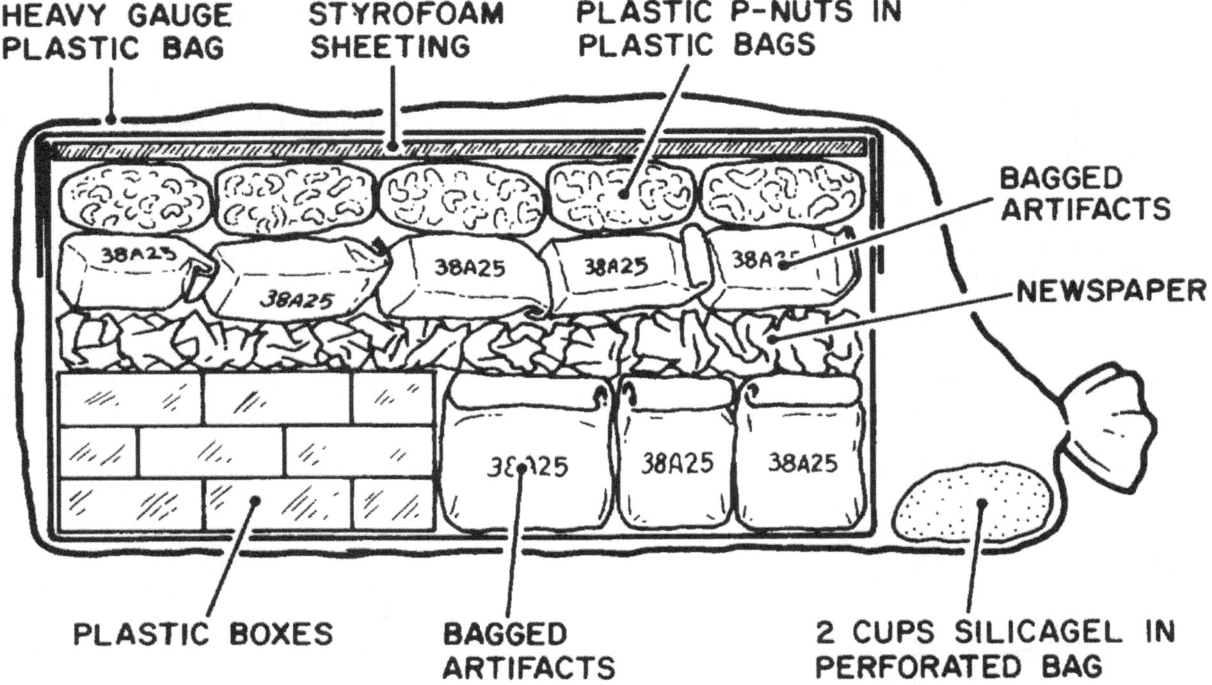

FIGURE 5. Metal artifacts packed as a group in a cardboard box with desiccant.

difficult to remove later. If the situation seems complicated, the advice of a trained conservator should be sought first. More complete discussions of consolidants and lifting techniques, including block lifting and encasement with plaster, are provided in Dowman (1970).

When simple consolidation is necessary, soil conditions will determine the type of consolidant used. If conditions are damp, a waterbased emulsion of polyvinyl acetate (PVA)* or acrylic (Rhoplex 234)* should be used. Both of these may be removed later with ethyl alcohol.* If the soil is dry, a 10% solvent-based solution of Acryloid B72* in xylene* or toluene* or PVA-AYAF resin* in acetone* may be applied.

While emulsions come prepared and may be thinned with water to aid penetration, solutions are made in a weight per volume ratio expressed as grams per liter. For example, a 10% solution is 10 grams of resin crystals dissolved in 100 mls of solvent; a 15% solution is 15 grams in 100 mls. Wrapping the resin beads in cheesecloth tied with string and then suspending the bundle in a jar of solvent will aid dissolution of the beads.

Again, care should be exercised in handling solvents like acetone,* xylene,* and especially toluene* in preparing, using, and removing consolidants. Cartridge respirators* and protective solvent-resistant gloves* should be worn. The solvents should be kept from heat, flame, and sunlight and always used in a well-ventilated space. Additionally, for larger applications and prolonged use, it may be wiser to use an emulsion.

The selected consolidant may be applied by brush, spray, or pipette. Dripping on the consolidant is advised if the surface is friable or painted; however, the solubility of the paint should be tested first. Applying the solvent alone first will encourage penetration of the consolidant. Successive coats of a thinner consolidant usually are more effective than one heavier coat, but care must be taken that the consolidant does not dry to leave a skin between coats. The consolidant should be applied until the ceramic appears saturated. Most importantly, do not attempt to lift the fragments until the consolidant is totally dry, usually in an hour depending on temperature, sunlight, wind, etc. After removal fragments should be supported on boards or packed in a padded box for transport.

It should be noted that consolidation will eliminate the possibility of any future analysis of the ceramic, so a small fragment should be kept separate for this purpose. The type of consolidant used in the field should be recorded as well.

While consolidated pottery will require special cleaning with the respective solvent, the bulk of historic (and prehistoric) ceramics may be washed easily in plain water provided that some care is taken. Wash water should be changed frequently, because accumulated grit can act as an abrasive. If soap is needed, a few drops of a non-ionic wetting agent like Tergitol-NPX* is preferable to household detergents which may have additives. Surfaces with burnishing or deteriorated glaze should be not scrubbed vigorously but cleaned carefully and gently using a soft paintbrush. On porcelain care should be exercised to notice overpainting and lifting glaze. These pieces, as well as any poorly fired pottery or terra cotta which may disintegrate totally in the water should *not* be washed, but cleaned by dry methods (scalpel, dry brush, pin-vice). Consolidation with a 10% resin solution* could follow if necessary.

Joining sherds with tape before packing is a temptation which must be avoided; otherwise, damage will result from long-term contact of the tape to the ceramic surface. Bagging together possibly joining sherds is preferable.

Complete reconstruction is best done by a trained conservator; methods have been examined by Mibach (1975). However, if sherds must be glued for photography and study, then an easily reversible adhesive like Duco cement, which can be dissolved in acetone, should be employed. One should use as little glue as possible and record the brand. Cyanoacrylate ("Crazy Glue") and other instant adhesives, rubber cement, epoxy, and even Elmer's Glue should be avoided. A sandbox will be useful for supporting the sherds. Masking tape or Scotch Magic tape may be used to temporarily hold sherds during drying if their surfaces are not friable or painted. Even with sherds in good condition, care should be taken not to lift the surface as the tape is removed. Acetone* will soften the tape.

Most ceramics can be processed and packed easily. In general, ceramics are relatively inert and require no special storage requirements. They may be stored under normal conditions, i.e., 45–55% Rh, 65–75°F.

However, one complication which may arise is that of infestation of pottery with soluble salts absorbed from ground water which can crystalize in drier surroundings and disrupt the surface. Salts also may be present because of the artifact's original use (i.e., meat curing). If a white efflorescence of salt appears on the surface or if the surface begins to flake, it may be advisable to soak the pottery for about a week in daily changes of tap water to remove as many salts as possible. A small sherd should be tested first, and the advice of a conservator should be sought before attempting to desalt ceramics with severe flaking or surface disruption. Total removal of soluble salts requires deionized or distilled water and is best done in a conservation laboratory (Jedrzejewska 1971). Nevertheless, for processing ceramics in good condition from saline environments, a small inexpensive deionizing cartridge* that hooks directly into a tap and needs no special plumbing may be a wise investment.

Stone and Brick

Most stone may be washed like ceramics and will need very little subsequent attention. In saline environments some porous stones may be subject to salt infestation and should be examined for flaking and efflorescence before packing. Chemical cleaning, stain removal, etc. can be complicated for stone (Thomson 1971) and should be carried out by a conservator.

Well-fired brick and glazed brick in good condition may also be washed as well as soaked to remove salts if they are suspected. Unfired mud bricks and adobe, however, should *not* be washed or soaked. The advice of a conservator should be sought instead.

Care should be taken in the storage and packing of stone and brick to minimize damage to other artifacts. Like ceramics, stone and brick may be stored under normal conditions.

Glass

Most historical glass (bottle, window glass) may be washed in tap water with a drop or two of Tergitol-NPX* for a wetting agent. Large amounts of glass may be stored in plastic or paper bags; "zip-lock" bags should not be used because of the danger of trapping moisture. If glass is packed with heavier artifacts in the same box, care must be taken to cushion and isolate the glass against shifting.

Very fine pieces, like wineglass stems, should be cleaned more carefully by dry methods or by "Q-tips" using a minimum amount of water, or half water/half ethyl alcohol,* to loosen the dirt. The unusual or fine fragments can be stored individually on cards (as above) or packed in layers in plastic boxes* padded with acid-free tissue paper* (Figure 1).

Painted or enamelled glass should be cleaned only by a conservator. Moreover, glasses that are highly deteriorated, flaky, powdery, or exhibiting beading or onionskins are unstable and also should *not* be washed. Instead, these fragments should be packed carefully on layers of acid-free tissue.* The advice of a conservator should be sought immediately.

Storage boxes containing glass should be kept at a moderate level of relative humidity, ideally 40–55%, and normal temperature. Even if these levels are unobtainable, the environment should be as stable as possible. Extremes of relative humidity (above 70% and below 25%) can be particularly harmful for glass. Unstable glasses as described above will need a more closely monitored environment using silica gel especially conditioned to the exact level required (Brill 1978). For this reason professional advice will be needed.

Pieces of glass may be joined for photography and study with Duco cement provided that the join is not critical or load-bearing, because the hold will not be as strong on glass as it is on more porous ceramics. Again, taping glass together before packing should be avoided.

If glass is found in a damp environment, a small fragment should be allowed to dry. If there are no changes like clouding, cracking, or a rainbow effect, the rest of the glass can be dried slowly. Otherwise, the glass should be stored damp, laid flat on layers of damp acid-free tissue paper* in a covered sandwich container with waterproof labels.* The advice of a conservator should be sought immediately.

Bone

Bone from dry or somewhat damp soils should be dried slowly to prevent distortion. Drying bone in direct sunlight should be avoided. Because of the likelihood of bone's weakened condition in both acidic and basic soils, it may be necessary to consolidate it before lifting. Again, consolidation may be carried out *only* if the bone cannot carry its own weight. After the bone is cleaned by brush and dental picks, consolidation can be carried out as described in the section on ceramics, although a thinner solution of either resin* or emulsion* (5–10%) is advisable. Following consolidation and drying, the bone may be removed directly or in block sections. If future analysis may be required, some samples that are not consolidated should be kept separate.

Only bone in good condition should be washed using a minimum of scrubbing and exposure to water. More friable or delicate pieces, skulls and diagnostic fragments, or artifacts of worked bone should be cleaned dry by scalpel or pick, perhaps using a 50–50 mixture of ethyl alcohol* and water applied in swabs to loosen the dirt. The bone can be consolidated with a 5–10% solution of resin* or emulsion* as cleaning proceeds. Bone fragments may be glued with a viscous PVA emulsion.*

Sections of bone should be packed carefully in cardboard or plastic boxes using acid-free tissue* or flexible foam sheeting* as padding. No bone should be packed in a plastic bag unless totally dry because mildew and mold will grow.

If bones are found in totally waterlogged conditions, they should not be allowed to dry, but should be stored wet with a fungicide (see sections on leather and wood).

The care and classification of bone are covered more thoroughly in Coy (1978).

Leather

Leather is best preserved when little attack by microorganisms has occurred; acid waterlogged conditions with their anaerobic environments are most conducive to preservation. Leather has been found in privies, wells, swamps, and rivers. Leather from somewhat damp terrestrial sites should be treated as waterlogged.

Damp or waterlogged leather should be handled carefully because it probably will be weaker than it appears. It should be kept wet continuously. If allowed to dry, wet leather will harden and curl irreversibly. Therefore, waterlogged leather should be submerged in water in a closed container (i.e., Tupperware sandwich container). Smaller pieces may be stored with some added water in "zip-lock" bags, but these too should be stored in a secondary covered container with more water (Figure 6). A fungicide will be needed, and for this purpose a quick application of Lysol spray (non-foaming kind) on the leather before storing will help but may need to be repeated. Storage containers and bags should have a dual label system using waterproof plastic paper* or plastic tags inside and out. Dymo tapes also have been used for labelling, but they may deteriorate with time. Teflon tapes may be more durable. Storage systems are discussed further in the following section on wood. It is unadvisable to use neat's-foot oil, cedarwood, or linseed oil for storing wet leather or for dressing dry leather. Treatments for wet leather have been presented by Mühlethaler (1973) and Morris and Seifert (1978).

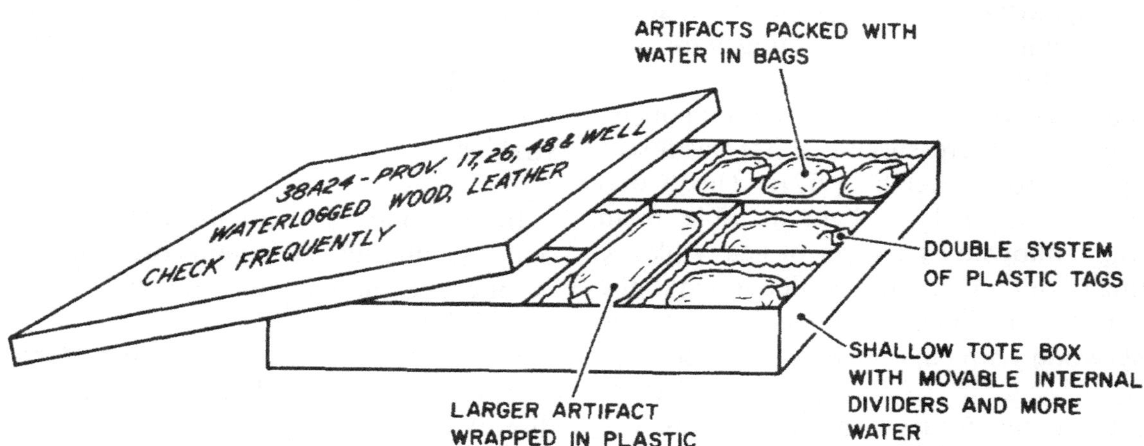

FIGURE 6. Small waterlogged artifacts packed in plastic bags in a covered plastic tote box.

Dry or dessicated leather should be handled carefully and packed on layers of acid-free tissue.*

Wood

As with leather, wood is usually best preserved in anaerobic waterlogged environments. Wet wood also will suffer irreversible damage if allowed to dry, even if for a few minutes. Exposed wood must be covered with a wet blanket or hosed repeatedly during in situ drawing and photographing. Because of the problems and costs associated with handling, storing, and preserving waterlogged wood (Mühlethaler 1973; Oddy 1975b; Grosso 1976), the advice of a conservator should be sought immediately if waterlogged wood is found on an excavation.

Small, fragile pieces of waterlogged wood may be packed in individual "zip-lock" bags* with a little water and then placed in a covered plastic container with more water. Covered industrial tote boxes with internal dividers* also may be useful for organizing and storing small pieces of wet wood and leather from various proveniences (Figure 6). Larger pieces should be wrapped in three layers of polyethylene bags or sheeting* that are sealed; however, this system is not advisable for prolonged storage. A dual system of waterproof labels* is advised. Dymo or Teflon labels or plastic tags attached to the wood with stainless steel staples or nylon fishing wire also may be useful.

If the waterlogged wood cannot support its own weight, a board should be used as a secondary support (Leigh 1972). The wood should be wrapped in damp flexible foam sheeting* followed by a layer of heavy plastic sheeting (8 mil minimum) and tied down to the support. Care must be taken not to cut into the cheesy wood with rope or masking tape (Figure 7).

All these temporary storage systems will require a generous application of non-foaming Lysol spray to the wood before wrapping. Lysol (a dilute solution of orthophenyl phenol in alcohol) is recommended for field use because of its availability and ease of application. However, for prolonged storage of wet wood (and leather) a suitable fungicide should be used in solution form. If no fungicide is used, then the water in the storage containers should be changed at least three times a week. Factors to be considered in the selection of a particular fungicide are cost, effectiveness, toxicity, pH value, compatability with the wood, and compatability with any future conservation treatment. A conservator should be able to help make the best selection. Archaeologists should also realize that exposure of the wood to a carbon containing fungicide or preservative will change Carbon 14 values. Samples of wet wood for Carbon 14 or dendrochronology will require special handling (Keene 1977).

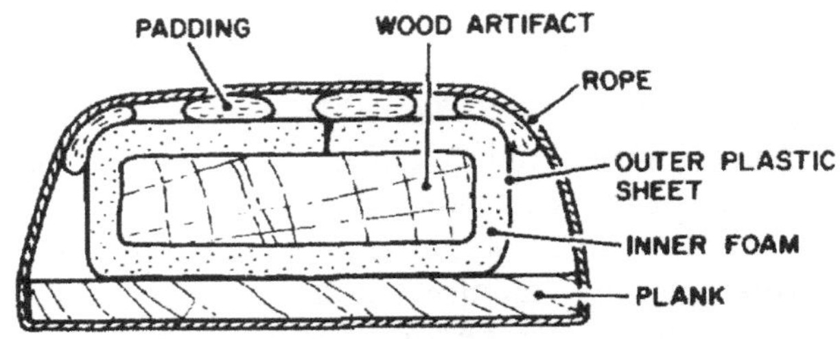

FIGURE 7. Support system for waterlogged wood.

For prolonged storage of larger pieces of waterlogged wood, submersion in a covered tank containing water and fungicide is preferable to plastic bags and sheeting. The wet wood should be checked frequently.

Textiles

In dry conditions, textiles usually are found only as mineralized remains on metals, which is one reason cleaning metals in the field should be avoided.

If a textile is waterlogged, it will be very fragile. No attempt should be made to lift it directly. Rather, the textile should be removed with its surrounding dirt as a block and wrapped damp in heavy gauge plastic or three layers of thinner plastic bags or sheeting and then placed in a covered plastic container or tote box.* Plastic paper* and tags are advisable for labelling. However, unlike wet wood, bone, and leather, *no* fungicide should be used in storing wet textiles. The advice of a conservator should be sought immediately.

Conclusion

Numerous ways of packing and storing artifacts have been presented in this article in order to make archaeologists more familiar with some of the problems of long-term curation. The care of artifacts begins with excavation. Even if a conservator cannot be provided, an archaeologist has a responsibility to insure that artifacts are handled properly and packed adequately. Developing a storage scheme will require time and thought. Artifacts may have to be separated and stored by material, not provenience. Some artifacts may require periodic checking. Cataloging and shelving systems should be devised to accommodate these separations. Finally, a good packing system will require money. A few hundred dollars' worth of appropriate supplies should be regarded as equally important as tools and equipment for excavation. With these efforts, the material remains from an excavation will have a better chance for survival.

ACKNOWLEDGMENTS

I would like to thank the following people for their help in the preparation of this article: William Marquardt and Stanley South, Institute of Archeology and Anthropology, University of South Carolina, for their encouragement; artist Darby Erd, also of the Institute, for his drawings; and members of the Conservation Department, Walters Art Gallery, Baltimore, for their comments and suggestions.

REFERENCES

Bourque, Bruce J., Stephen W. Brooke, Ronald Kley, and Kenneth Morris
1980 Conservation in Archaeology: Moving Toward Closer Cooperation. *American Antiquity* 45(4): 794–99.

Brill, Robert H.
1978 The Use of Equilibrated Silica Gel for the Protection of Glass with Incipient Crizzling. *Journal of Glass Studies* 9:100–18.

Brown, B. Floyd, Harry C. Burnett, W. Thomas Chase, Martha Goodway, Jerome Kruger, and Marcel Pourbaix, editors
1977 *Corrosion and Metal Artifacts—A Dialogue Between Conservators and Archaeologists and Corrosion Scientists.* U.S. Department of Commerce, National Bureau of Standards Special Publication 479, Washington, D.C.

Coy, Jennie
1978 *First Aid for Animal Bones.* Rescue and Department of Archaeology, University of Southampton, Southampton.

Dowman, Elizabeth A.
1970 *Conservation in Field Archaeology.* Methuen and Co., London.

Fall, Frieda K.
1965 New Industrial Packing Materials: Their Possible Uses for Museums. *Museum News* Technical Supplement 10.

Grosso, Gerald H., editor
1976 *Pacific Northwest Wet Site Wood Conservation Conference.* 2 Vols. Papers presented at Neah Bay, Washington, September 19–22, 1976.

Grosso, Gerald H.
1978 After Excavation, then What? *Society for California Archaeology: Occasional Papers in Method and Theory in California Archaeology* 2:53–58.

Hamilton, Don L.
1976 *Conservation of Metal Artifacts from Underwater Sites: A Study in Methods.* Texas Antiquities Committee Publication 1, published jointly with the Texas Memorial Museum, Austin, Texas.

Jedrzejewska, Hanna
1971 Removal of Soluble Salts from Stone. In *Conservation of Stone, the Proceedings of the 1970 New York Conference on Conservation of Stone and Wooden Objects*, edited by Garry Thomson, Vol. 1, pp. 19–33. The International Institute for Conservation of Historic and Artistic Works, London.

Keene, Suzanne
1977 An Approach to the Sampling and Storage of Waterlogged Timbers from Excavation. *The Conservator* 1:8–11. The United Kingdom Group of the International Institute for Conservation of Historic and Artistic Works, London.

LAWSON, ERIC
1978 In Between: The Care of Artifacts from the Seabed to the Conservation Laboratory and Some Reasons Why it is Necessary. In *Beneath the Waters of Time: The Proceedings of the Ninth Conference on Underwater Archaeology*, edited by J. Barto Arnold III, pp. 69–91. Texas Antiquities Committee Publication 6, Austin, Texas.

LEIGH, DAVID
1972 *First Aid for Finds*. Rescue and Department of Archaeology, University of Southampton, Southampton.

MIBACH, LISA
1975 The Restoration of Coarse Archaeological Ceramics. In *Conservation in Archaeology and the Applied Arts*, edited by Norman Brommelle and Perry Smith, pp. 55–61. International Institute for Conservation of Historic and Artistic Works, London.

MORRIS, KENNETH AND BETTY L. SEIFERT
1978 Conservation of Leather and Textiles from *The Defence*. *Journal of the American Institute for Conservation* 18(1):33–43.

MÜHLETHALER, BRUNO
1973 *Conservation of Waterlogged Wood and Wet Leather*. Editions Eyrolles, Paris.

ODDY, W. A.
1975a The Corrosion of Metals on Display. In *Conservation in Archaeology and the Applied Arts*, edited by Norman Brommelle and Perry Smith, pp. 235–37. International Institute for Conservation of Historic and Artistic Works, London.

ODDY, W. A., EDITOR
1975b *Problems in the Conservation of Waterlogged Wood*. Maritime Monographs and Reports 16, The National Maritime Museum, Greenwich, England.

PLENDERLEITH, H. J. AND A. E. A. WERNER
1971 *The Conservation of Antiquities and Works of Art*. Oxford University Press, London.

SANFORD, ELIZABETH
1975 Conservation of Artifacts: A Question of Survival. *Historical Archaeology* 9:55–64.

SPRIGGS, JIM
1979 Workshop Notes-The Y. A. T. Bin. *Conservation News* 9:3. United Kingdom Group of the International Institute for Conservation of Historic and Artistic Works, London.

STAMBOLOV, T.
1969 *The Corrosion and Conservation of Metallic Antiquities and Works of Art*. Central Research Laboratory for Objects of Art and Science, Amsterdam.

STOLOW, NATHAN
1977 The Microclimate: A Localized Solution. *Museum News* 56(2):52–63.

THOMSON, GARRY, EDITOR
1971 *Conservation of Stone, the Proceedings of the 1970 New York Conference on Conservation of Stone and Wooden Objects*, Vol. I. The International Institute for Conservation of Historic and Artistic Works, London.

UNESCO
1968 *The Conservation of Cultural Property, Museum and Monument* series XI. UNESCO, Paris.

KATHERINE R. SINGLEY
INSTITUTE OF ARCHEOLOGY AND ANTHROPOLOGY
UNIVERSITY OF SOUTH CAROLINA
COLUMBIA, SOUTH CAROLINA 29208

Appendix

Supplies and Suppliers

The following is a partial list of suppliers of materials mentioned in the text. It is not intended as an endorsement of the products or of the distributors.

The following are available from local distributors: cardboard boxes; plastic (polyethylene) bags and sheeting; "zip-lock" bags; flexible polystyrene or polyethylene foam sheeting; polystyrene p-nuts; air-entrapped polyethylene sheeting; industrial tote boxes.

Consult the Yellow Pages of local phone book under "Packing Materials," "Bags," and "Boxes." Some distributors may fabricate bags and boxes to specifications; others may require a minimum order.

Selection and prices may vary. Various sizes of small plastic bags can be 2–4 mils thick, but a thickness of at least 8 mils will be needed for storing metals or wrapping wet wood. Boxes should be of several sizes and modular to fit within each other.

Industrial tote boxes in various sizes, some with lids and internal dividers, are also available from:

Regal Plastic Company
4405 E. 11th (CLOON)
Kansas City, Missouri 64127

Hinged clear plastic boxes are available in various sizes from:

Ward's
Company Headquarters
P.O. Box 1712
Rochester, N.Y. 14603

Flexible polyethylene foam sheeting in various thicknesses (i.e., 1/16", 1/8", 3/16") is also available from:

Sentinel Foam Products, Inc.
Hyannis, Massachusetts 02601

Acid-free tissue paper in sheets or rolls is available from:

University Products
P.O. Box 101
Holyoke, Massachusetts 01040

Talas
104 Fifth Avenue
New York, New York 10011

Plastic paper (Nalgene Poly Paper); specimen vials; acetone (laboratory grade); xylene (laboratory grade); toluene (laboratory grade); silica gel (indicating, 6–16 mesh); ethyl alcohol (laboratory grade); cartridge respirators; protective, solvent resistant gloves; Tergitol-NPX (non-ionic wetting agent); disposable demineralizing cartridge (Barnstead "Hose-Nipple" High Capacity) are available from:

Fisher Scientific Company
Corporate Headquarters
711 Forbes Avenue
Pittsburg, Pennsylvania 15219
(regional offices throughout the U.S.)

Arthur A. Thomas
Vine Street at Third
Philadelphia, Pennsylvania 19105

Sargent-Welch
35 Stern Avenue
Springfield, New Jersey 07081
(regional offices throughout the U.S.)

Some state or university purchasing offices may get special discounts from these or other scientific supply companies.

Acryloid B-72 (ethyl methacrylate copolymer); PVA-AYAF (polyvinyl acetate resin); CM Bond M-3 (polyvinyl acetate emulsion); Rhoplex AC-234 (acrylic emulsion) are all available from:

Conservation Materials, Ltd.
340 Freeport Blvd.
Box 2884
Sparks, Nevada 89431

Polyvinyl acetate and acrylic emulsions will come prepared and can be thinned with water to a desired consistency. They may be removed later with alcohol. Both Acryloid B-72 and PVA-AYAF resins come as beads and are prepared as solutions in toluene and acetone. As mentioned in the text, safety precautions must be used in handling solvents and resin solutions.

Part II: Interpreting Dates and Meaning From Artifacts

PATTERN RECOGNITION IN HISTORICAL ARCHAEOLOGY

STANLEY SOUTH

The process of pattern recognition using data from historic sites is illustrated with data from the British colonial system. The Brunswick Pattern of Refuse Disposal *monitors eighteenth century refuse disposal behavior patterns. The* Carolina Pattern *monitors artifact relationships from domestic occupation. The* Frontier Pattern *is seen on frontier sites as well as the area inside domestic ruins, and is characterized by a high architecture to kitchen artifact relationship. The formula concept of pattern recognition demonstrated by the Mean Ceramic Date Formula is a tool based on the recognition of highly regular patterns of variation in the popularity of ceramics through time. Such pattern recognition is foundational for historic site data to contribute to the explanation of culture processes. Historical archaeology has an as yet unrealized potential for contributing to method-refinement and theory building in archaeology generally. This is the exciting promise historical archaeology holds for the future.*

TRADITIONALLY, HISTORICAL ARCHAEOLOGY in America has been oriented to site-specific goals focused on filling in historical documentation, locating architectural features, recovering and describing artifacts associated with architecture, and correlating archaeological with historical data. Most of this involvement can be termed "heritage studies" from sponsorship by agencies concerned with research founded on a priori beliefs about the past. Under this traditional format historical archaeology has come to have a particularistic image.

In spite of the fact that data from historic sites lend themselves admirably to the study of high energy cultural systems, few archaeologists have concerned themselves with a search for pattern on an intra- and intersite level to explore site function, chronology, structure, as well as status, trade routes, ethnicity, settlement patterns, frontier phenomena, and environmental variables. Once replicated patterns are demonstrated, the accompanying variability in the archaeological record can be understood with reference to the basic regularity. This strategy can be carried out as an integral part of a research program whose sponsor may well be concerned primarily with heritage goals, provided the archaeologist maintains as the primary responsibility an allegiance to the data base with which he is testing his ideas about the past.

To use such an approach the archaeologist must make use of quantitative analysis so that comparison can be made between sets of data in addition to those based on presence and absence alone. This quantification strategy can also be applied to historical documentation and ethnographic data sets to abstract generalized systemic pattern rather than the biased perspective afforded by a more particularistic orientation.

Some historians have long emphasized the broader, more generalized perspective, and the failure of historical archaeologists to do likewise accounts for the general lack of communication between archaeological particularists and the historical generalists. Historical archaeologists looking beyond their particular site can begin to delineate regularity and variability reflective of cultural systems in the form of patterned relationships from sites with similar temporal and cultural associations. Historical documentation is most effectively used to derive some degree of independent control of function, status, ethnic background, time, etc., against which archaeological patterns can be projected for exploring the relationship between past behavioral processes and the archaeological record. In order to identify behavior and process reflected in the archaeological record the archaeologist must concern himself with pattern recognition using all data sets at his disposal.

With the delineation of archaeological pattern that says to the archaeologist "this was a tavern," "this was a domestic dwelling," "this was a slave quarters," "this was a planter's mansion," the heavy dependence now placed on historical documentation can be replaced with a reliance on, and a confidence in, the archaeological record. The archaeologist who depends on documentation exclusively to interpret the ruin being excavated must always live in fear that a new document will turn up to refute the interpretation, since that interpretation was anchored in a particular document to begin with. Once functional and other behavioral processes have been delineated in the form of archaeological pattern the archaeologist will be in a position to take issue with particularistic historical documentation not in keeping with the general archaeological pattern. For example, once the pattern is known for the by-products associated with eighteenth century tavern activity in the British colonial system, the documentation of the site as that of a tavern will carry less weight than that the archaeological record demonstrates this fact. With such control via the archaeological record the archaeologist can come to rely more on the primary archaeological record and less on the secondary historically documented sources.

As the variables are isolated the archaeologist may express the pattern as reflecting a law predictive of past human behavior. Postulates can be tested as new sites are examined and by this means the pattern can be verified from which hypotheses directed at the cultural system can be formulated and tested. In some cases empirical data may be contrary to expectations and in such cases both the historical and archaeological, and other data bases must again be examined for isolating other variables. This process of data manipulation, this free exploration of the regularity and variation in the archaeological record is a major part of pattern recognition aimed at understanding the dynamics of past cultural systems.

The process of pattern recognition using data from historic sites will be illustrated here using artifact distribution frequencies and quantitative relationships between artifact types, classes and groups. Several patterns have been delineated by use of data from the British colonial system. Four of these will be summarized here (from South 1977a): the *Brunswick Pattern* of refuse disposal, the *Carolina Pattern* of artifact relationships, the high architecture group ratio I have termed the *Frontier Pattern*, and the Mean Ceramic Date Formula.

The *Brunswick Pattern* of refuse disposal results from the practice on British colonial sites of discarding refuse at the entranceways to houses, shops and forts. It is a refuse density dispersion phenomenon identified by simply measuring the relative density of secondary refuse around a structure. The *Carolina Pattern* of artifact relationships is a statement of the relative frequency of the artifact groups recovered in the secondary refuse around a structure, a high percentage of Kitchen Group artifacts in relation to Architecture Group artifacts being the characteristic pattern.

The *Frontier* or architecture pattern has a high Architecture to Kitchen Group artifact ratio. This pattern has been seen on eighteenth century frontier military and trading post sites, but also characterizes the artifact group relationship seen inside ruins of domestic function not located on the frontier. Nondomestic structures also reveal this high Architecture to Kitchen Artifact ratio.

The Mean Ceramic Date Formula is a tool based on the recognition of highly regular patterns of variation in the popularity of ceramics through time. This tool monitors site chronology via ceramics. The *Brunswick Pattern* monitors refuse disposal behavior via dispersion of all artifact classes and groups, while the *Carolina* and *Frontier* patterns monitor function via the frequency relationship between artifact groups. The *Kitchen Artifact Pattern* monitors specific function through variability in patterns based on artifact class relationships within the kitchen artifact group, but this pattern is not dealt with in this paper (South 1977a).

THE FORMULA CONCEPT OF PATTERN RECOGNITION

Artifact patterning reflecting the occupation period during which the archaeological sample accumulated is being examined by means of the formula concept of pattern recognition. This concept is focused on determining a mean manufacture date of artifacts for use in deriving an interpreted median occupation date represented by the artifact sample. Artifacts such as ceramics, wine bottles and other types and classes of objects for which the manufacture period is known can be used with the formula concept.

An assumption on which the formula concept is based is that artifact fragments can be used to determine an archaeologically relevant comparison of surviving material remains of culture. A second assumption is that artifacts surviving in the archaeological record reflect the use of the artifacts in time as a unimodal curve having a beginning, a rise in use to a peak, and a decrease to extinction. For the purpose of illustration of the formula concept we will use British ceramic types, a frequently recovered class of artifacts on American historic sites.

The mean manufacture date for the group of British ceramic types from an eighteenth-century historic site taking into consideration the frequency of occurrence of fragments of the types, can be determined by a mean ceramic date-frequency formula as follows:

The mean ceramic date, Y, is expressed:

$$Y = \frac{\sum_{i=1}^{n} X_i \cdot f_i}{\sum_{i=1}^{n} f_i} \qquad -1.1$$

Where X_i = the median date for the manufacture of each ceramic type
f_i = the frequency of each ceramic type (fragments)
n = the number of ceramic types in the sample

The median manufacture date for each ceramic type in the sample is determined from the documents (Noël Hume 1970, and personal communication). This information has been compiled into a list of 78 ceramic types. In order to use the formula the archaeologist places the sherd count for each type in a column beside the median date and these are multiplied, producing a third column, which is a product of the median date times the frequency of occurrence. The sum of the frequency column is divided into the sum of the product column, producing the mean ceramic date for the sample. Although this frequency-adjusted manufacture date might be assumed to have nothing to do with the occupation date for an historic site, it has been found that there is a remarkable degree of similarity between the mean ceramic date derived from the use of the formula and the historically known median occupation date of the eighteenth century historic sites on which it has been used.

The application of the formula concept to ceramics is illustrated with data from the Hepburn-Reonalds ruin (S7) in the town of Brunswick, North Carolina. This ruin was a stone-lined cellar located on lot 71 in Brunswick, and was excavated in 1959. The records reveal that the structure was probably standing by 1734, and was burned in 1776, with a median historic date of 1755. The collection of ceramic fragments from the entire ruin was used as the sample.

A total of 13 ceramic types for which the median manufacture dates were known was recovered from the ruin, for a total of 1,960 ceramic fragments. When the number of fragments for each type was multiplied by the assigned median manufacture date for each type and these products totalled, the sum was 3,446,567, which, when divided by the total number of sherds, 1,960, produced a mean ceramic date of 1758.4, a date only 3.4 years from the median historic date of 1755 for the ruin.

Since its first introduction in 1972 (South 1972a) the Mean Ceramic Date Formula has proven highly predictive of the median occupation dates for sites, demonstrating the great redundancy of the pattern on which it was based. For example, 16 sites from the Carolinas, Virginia, Tennessee, Michigan, and Newfoundland were found, on the average, to overestimate the median historic occupation date by only 1.025 years. These sites had an R^2 value of .980 for the relationship between the known median occupation dates and the mean ceramic dates derived from the formula (South 1977a:236). The formula, therefore, appears to be a valid tool for helping the archaeologist to infer the occupation period represented by archaeological samples from British colonial sites.

In using the formula concept it has been found that eighteenth century British American sites of varied functions, from port town ruins, to townhouse mansions, to frontier forts and Indian villages have similar groups of ceramic types present at similar periods of time. This has been interpreted in terms of the horizon concept outlined by Gordon R. Willey and Philip Phillips (1958). The time required for the spread of the cultural material representing the horizon is a factor to be considered. Therefore, an approximate contemporaneity is involved for a group of ceramic types leaving the source of manufacture and being distributed throughout the British empire.

In demonstrating the regularity of the pattern, and expressing this as an empirical generalization in terms of the horizon concept, we still have not *explained* the phenomenon in terms of the processes of culture. This can be done by stating hypotheses relating the horizon concept to processes at work in the British colonial cultural system, postulating the mechanism whereby these are related, and presenting arguments of relevance within a research design directed at the collection of new data.

Hypotheses for explaining the horizon phenomenon described by the Mean Ceramic Date Formula could be focused on a specified set of variables expected to provide explanatory power. These range from broad phenomenon such as the distribution system of colonial empires to refuse disposal practices in domestic households. Historical documentation and archaeological inference permit us to control the following regular variables which, in turn, should provide some degree of explanation for the success of the formula concept: the distribution of goods from the mother country to the colony and the subsequent dispersal mechanisms in the colony; the procurement, preparation, serving and consumption of food; the cleaning, display, and storage of ceramics; and the modes of discard of broken ceramics and other refuse.

If these variables are archaeologically monitored we can hypothesize that a highly regular patterned relationship would exist between ceramic types from domestic refuse deposits of various occupation periods. Disruption of the regularity would occur with variation in any of the major causal variables just mentioned having an effect on the ceramic relationships in the archaeological record, such as non-domestic occupation, change in the distributive system, etc.

If the above variables are highly regular, and we know the manufacture period for the various ceramic types involved, then it should come as no surprise that a formula designed to monitor the regularity between ceramic types from domestic refuse deposits within a cultural system is found to be predictable as a dating tool. Hopefully future investigations directed at testing this and other explanatory hypotheses will elucidate the specific cultural processes at work that led to this useful regularity.

THE BRUNSWICK PATTERN OF REFUSE DISPOSAL

For over a decade the pattern of refuse disposal at the ruins of the town of Brunswick, North Carolina has been used as a guide for predicting the location of refuse deposits reflecting eighteenth century behavior on British colonial sites. Excavations at Brunswick Town State Historic Site were carried out from 1958 to 1968, through the North Carolina Department of Archives and History. This archaeology revealed that the occupants of these structures, from about 1725 to about 1776, discarded their refuse adjacent to their homes, primarily at the back door, but also adjacent to the front doorway. Nearby depressions were also used, as well as the public street. So firmly established was this pattern of refuse disposal that entrance areas to structures could be identified by the increased quantity of midden at the doorways, even if no architectural data had been present. This practice of discarding secondary refuse adjacent to the dwellings is the basis for what I call the *Brunswick Pattern of Refuse Disposal* (South 1977a), expressed as a generalization as follows: On British American sites of the eighteenth century a concentrated refuse deposit will be found at the points of entrance and exit in dwellings, shops, and military fortifications.

The *Brunswick Pattern of Refuse Disposal* is seen specifically in the distribution of ceramic fragments around the Public House-Tailor Shop ruin (Fig. 1). The concentration of ceramic fragments in two areas to the rear of the structure reveals the location of a doorway as well as a major refuse disposal area at the rear corner of the building. These midden deposits resulted from occupants throwing refuse outside a rear door, and behind the buildings from the direction of the front yard. The contrast between the slight amount of refuse around the front entrance and the concentration at the rear is a characteristic of the *Brunswick Pattern*.

Most secondary refuse artifacts will reveal this same *Brunswick Pattern* whereas any primary refuse classes will vary from this dispersion. The importance of frequency variability in the distribution of different classes of artifacts is seen when pins and beads are examined (Fig. 2). The high concentration of these inside the structure as "loss refuse," with few in the secondary refuse behind the ruin reflects the fact that these artifacts were not discarded, but were lost accidentally inside five of the six rooms, having fallen through the cracks in the floorboards. The virtual absence of these artifacts in the sixth room reveals that a different function was involved here, probably that of an office or merchandizing

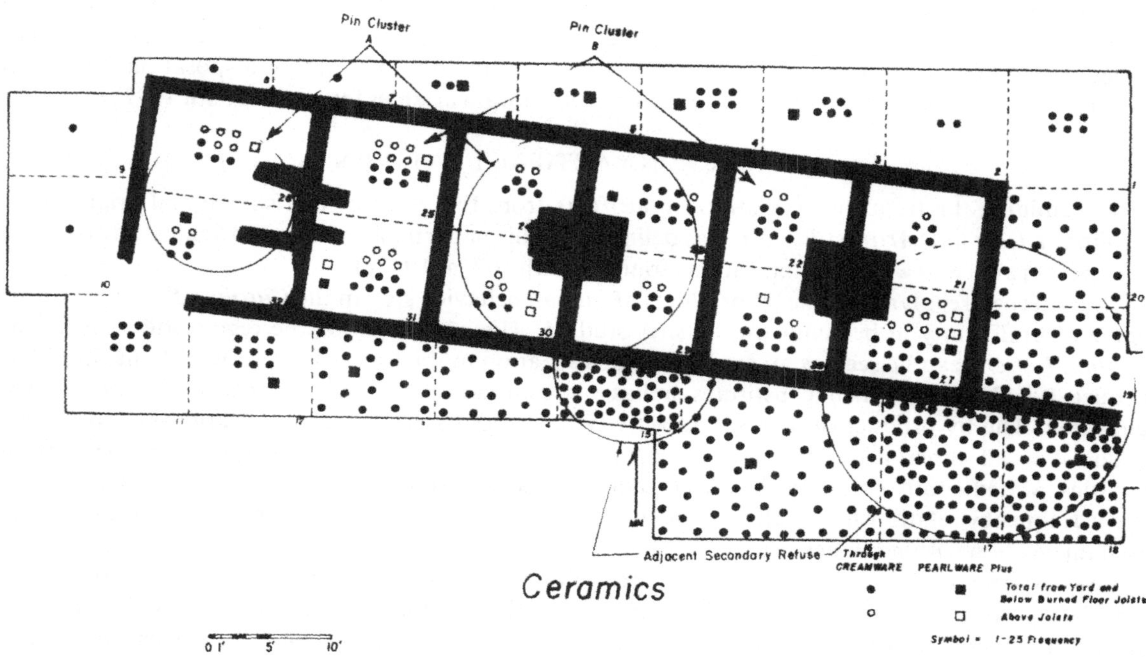

Fig. 1. Plan of the Public House-Tailor Shop (S25), at Brunswick Town, North Carolina. Ca. 1732-1776. Dispersion of ceramics.

room. These pins and beads, plus a similar concentration of other tailoring objects inside the rooms, suggests this ruin functioned as a tailor shop. This, plus documentation that the owner of this lot once operated a public house, plus the architectural plan revealing a number of small rooms in a row, resulted in a public house-tailor shop interpretation for this structure.

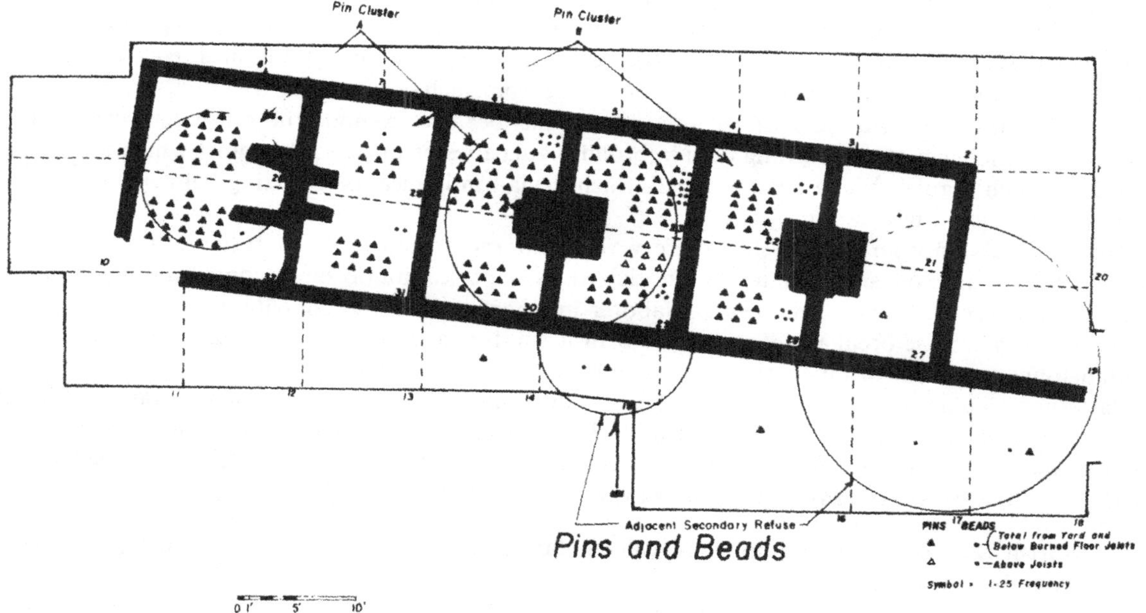

Fig. 2. Plan of the Public House-Tailor Shop (S25), at Brunswick Town, North Carolina. Ca. 1732-1776. Dispersion of pins and beads.

The *Brunswick Pattern* is mainly applicable, it is thought (in the absence of comparative data from other cultural systems), to sites of British American, or British colonial origin. There is some evidence to suggest that German American settlements will reveal far different refuse disposal patterns than that of the *Brunswick Pattern* due to the different behavioral variables involved (South 1972b).

THE CAROLINA ARTIFACT PATTERN

By examining the frequency variations in artifacts from five ruins of British colonial origin in the Carolinas a *Carolina Artifact Pattern* was delineated. This pattern has been tested against sites outside the Carolina area and a similar pattern was found (South 1977a, 1977b).

The patterned regularity in the by-products of human behavior seen in the *Carolina Pattern* reflect a degree of uniformity in behavior on the sites studied. The expression of the regularities seen in the *Carolina Pattern* can be seen as an empirical generalization in the form of "A Law of Behavioral By-product Regularity," which constitutes a basic assumption on which the *Carolina Pattern* was delineated: The by-product of a specified activity has a consistent frequency relationship to the by-products of all other activities in direct proportion to the organized integration of the various activities. Stated another way, the broken ceramics discarded from a domestic kitchen will have a consistent frequency relationship to all other associated artifact classes in direct proportion to their organized integration within kitchen activity.

The question remains as to what types of sites will fall into the predicted range of the *Carolina Pattern*. The pattern was derived from sites both domestic and military in nature, and they have in common the fact that they are in the mainstream of a colonial cultural system. That system was British colonial in origin, even though two ruins contained materials dating to 1830. The application of the pattern to data outside the Carolinas suggests that the phenomena we are dealing with is certainly not limited to the Carolina area from which the pattern was derived. This data suggest applicability extends at least as late as about 1860 (South 1977a, 1977b).

Patterns contained within data from historic sites can be compared with what is known about such sites historically. Therefore, the archaeologist working with documented as well as archaeological data sets has an advantage in that some of the information sought for variable control is available as a given. A group of known domestic house ruins from varying areas and known cultures can be selected, such as those from British American communities, German American communities, French American communities, and Spanish American communities, for abstracting patterns from each group for comparative analysis. Frontier fort sites, manufacturing sites, high and low status sites, etc., can also be used to determine the covariation of patterns resulting from such occupation.

In delineating the *Carolina Pattern*, the concern has been to examine the ratios between artifact groups with the view of establishing certain broad regularities or pulsations against which any deviation from such regularity can be contrasted. Such deviation is seen as reflecting behavior somewhat different from expected margins.

The basic assumption here is that there was a patterned casting off of behavioral by-products around an occupation site that might be viewed as a per-capita-per-year contribution to the archaeological record. Since a middle-class laborer in Charleston would contribute his per-capita-per-year procurement-use-breakage-discard record in a similar ratio to his counterpart in Savannah or Philadelphia, some uniformity in the record would certainly be expected.

Patterned regularity in the archaeological record does indeed exist, and steps must be taken to define it before much progress can be made toward elevating historical archaeology from a study of the unique and particular to a study of lawful regularities of culture. The postulates involved in the delineation of the *Carolina Pattern* might be expressed as follows:

1. British colonial behavior should reveal regularities in patterning in the archaeological record from British colonial sites.
2. Specialized behavioral activities should reveal contrasting patterns on such sites.
3. These patterns will be recognized through quantification of the fragmented by-products from such behavior comprising the archaeological record.

The sites used in the *Carolina Pattern* are the Public House-Tailor Shop ruin (S7) at Brunswick, North Carolina, occupied about 1732 to 1776; Nath Moore's Front ruin (S10), at Brunswick, occupied about 1728 to 1776; the American occupation at Fort Moultrie, South Carolina, from 1775 to about 1794; the British occupation at Fort Moultrie from 1780 to 1782; and a Cambridge cellar midden deposit at Ninety Six, South Carolina, representing an occupation about 1783 to about 1800. All of these sites were excavated under the direction of the author through the North Carolina Department of Archives and History, and the Institute of Archeology and Anthropology, University of South Carolina.

The artifacts from these ruins were classified by type, class, and group, with the eight groups being used for delineating the *Carolina Pattern*. The percentage range and mean for all five sites were determined, and this constitutes the *Carolina Pattern* (Table 1).

Table 1. The Carolina Artifact Pattern.

Artifact Group	Mean	% Range
Kitchen	63.1	51.8–69.2
Architecture	25.5	19.7–31.4
Furniture	.2	.1– .6
Arms	.5	.1– 1.2
Clothing	3.0	.6– 5.4
Personal	.2	.1– .5
Tobacco Pipes	5.8	1.8–13.9
Activities	1.7	.9– 2.7
Total	100.0	

Other British colonial sites within and outside the Carolina area have been found to fall within the predictive ranges of the *Carolina Pattern*. It is obvious that in order to compare new data with the *Carolina Pattern* the archaeologist must recover and quantify all artifacts in the collection in order to have a comparable data set.

An explanation of *why* the *Carolina Pattern* exists on British colonial sites is to be found in the examination of hypotheses directed at cultural processes in the British colonial system. These hypotheses would focus on questions such as the logistics of the British distributive system, the production system, discouragement or encouragement of colonial manufacture and self sufficiency by the British power structure, British expansionist and empire-building policies, status-enforcing rituals, and role-regulating mechanisms. The archaeological patterning resulting from such processes would be expected to vary between British American, German American, French American, and Spanish American occupations, reflecting variability in these cultural systems. Patterning would also vary with the functional role of the site in the social system.

THE FRONTIER PATTERN

The same procedure used to delineate the *Carolina Pattern* was used to define a *Frontier Pattern* using sites of the eighteenth century British colonial frontier. This pattern contrasts with the *Carolina Pattern* in the reversal of the frequencies for Kitchen and Architecture Group artifacts (South 1977a). This pattern was delineated using data from Spalding's Lower Store, Florida, a British trading post site; Fort Ligonier, Pennsylvania, a British anti-Indian fort site; and Fort Prince George, South Carolina, a British anti-French and Cherokee Indian trading post site (South 1977a). All three sites date from the period of the French and Indian War.

By deriving the mean for each artifact group for these three sites the *Frontier Artifact Pattern* mean and range can be determined (Table 2).

The most apparent contrast between the *Carolina Pattern* and the *Frontier Pattern* is the inverse ratio between the Architecture and Kitchen Groups. When we question the cause of this reversal, an increase in by-products associated with architecture in frontier situations can be suggested. This might result from a shorter occupation period per architectural unit on the frontier than in the settlements

Table 2. The Frontier Artifact Pattern.

Artifact Group	Mean	% Range
Kitchen	27.6	22.7-34.5
Architecture	52.0	43.0-57.5
Furniture	.2	.1- .3
Arms	5.4	1.4- 8.4
Clothing	1.7	.3- 3.8
Personal	.2	.1- .4
Tobacco Pipes	9.1	1.9-14.0
Activities	3.7	.7- 6.4
Total	100.0	

not on the frontier, thus increasing the Architecture Group artifacts in relation to secondary midden deposits of Kitchen Group artifacts. This might also be the result of sampling error in that from the forts very little secondary refuse from the moat ditches (where refuse is most often thrown) was recovered, whereas more architectural objects were recovered from inside the fort where the major excavation was concentrated. The *Frontier Pattern* could perhaps best be termed an *Architectural Artifact Pattern* to reflect the variable distinguishing it from the *Carolina Pattern* since a similar high architectural ratio is often found *inside* the area of a ruined structure compared with the *Carolina Pattern* usually seen to prevail in the yard *around* the structure.

The delineation of patterns for comparing archaeological data from historic sites toward understanding more about the archaeological record and the processes that produced it is a necessary step that must be taken if historic site data are to contribute to explanation of culture processes. The role of historical documentation in controlling some variables while archaeological pattern is defined and compared is the major role of the historical record in the future of historical archaeology. By controlling for variability relating to national origin, distributive systems, status and function through documents providing the basis for classification of historic sites, and then delineating the patterns from such sites through archaeology, we will eventually develop the ability to interpret cultural processes from historic site patterns without dependence on historical control. When we achieve this level of archaeological sophistication we can apply this knowledge to sites for which there is no historical control: prehistoric sites, for instance. This potential for contributing to method-refinement and theory building in archaeology generally is the exicting premise historical archaeology holds for the future.

Noël Hume, Ivor
1970 *A guide to artifacts of colonial America.* Knopf, New York.
South, Stanley
1972a Evolution and horizon as revealed in ceramic analysis in historical archaeology. *The Conference on Historic Site Archaeology Papers 1971* 6:71-116. Institute of Archeology and Anthropology, University of South Carolina, Columbia.
1972b Discovery in Wachovia. Manuscript on file with the Institute of Archeology and Anthropology, University of South Carolina, Columbia.
1977a *Method and theory in historical archeology.* Academic Press, New York.
1977b (Editor) *Research strategies in historical archeology.* Academic Press, New York.
Willey, Gordon R., and Philip Phillips
1958 *Method and theory in American archaeology.* University of Chicago Press, Chicago.

14. Ceramic Analysis Tools for the Interpretation of Eighteenth Century British American Sites

Stanley South

[This table is an excerpt from South, S., 1971. Evolution and Horizon as Revealed in Ceramic Analysis in Historical Archaeology. Conference on Historic Site Archaeology Papers 6, 71-106. It contains the types and dates used by South in the previous chapter, I:13, to create mean ceramic dates.]

A. The Ceramic Types Used to Construct the Analysis Tools

Porcelain

Type Number	Date Range	Median Date	Ceramic Type Name and Page Reference [to Noel Hume 1969]
5.	c. 1800-1830	1815	Canton Porcelain (262).
7.	c. 1790-1825	1808	Overglaze Enamelled China Trade Porcelain (258 and 261).
26.	c. 1660-1800	1730	Overglaze Enamelled Chinese Export Porcelain (261).
31.	c. 1745-1795	1770	English Porcelain (137).
39.	c. 1660-1800	1730	Underglaze Blue Chinese Porcelain (257).
41.	c. 1750-1765	1758	"Littler's Blue" (119-23) (On White Salt-Glazed Stoneware, Porcelain, and Creamware).
69.	c. 1574-1644	1609	Chinese Porcelain, Underglaze Blue, Late Ming (257 and 264).

Stoneware, Brown

Type Number	Date Range	Median Date	Ceramic Type Name and Page Reference [to Noel Hume 1969]
1.	c. 1820-1900+	1860	Brown Stoneware Bottles for Ink, Beer, Etc. (78-79).
46.	c. 1700-1810	1755	Nottingham Stoneware (Lustered) (114).
52.	c. 1700-1775	1738	Burslem "Crouch" Pale Brown Stoneware Mugs.
53.	c. 1690-1775	1733	Brown Salt-Glazed Mugs (Fulham) (111-13).
54.	c. 1690-1775	1733	British Brown Stoneware (Excluding 1, 52, 53) (112-14).
66.	c. 1620-1700	1660	Deteriorated Bellarmine Face Bottles (One Dated Example to The 1760's) (56-57).
74.	c. 1550-1625	1588	Bellarmine, Brown Salt-Glazed Stoneware, Well Molded Human Face
75.	c. 1540-1600	1570	Rhenish Brown-Glazed Sprigged, Mould-Decorated, Cologne Type Stoneware (277-79).

Stoneware, Blue, Grey

Type Number	Date Range	Median Date	Ceramic Type Name and Page Reference [to Noel Hume 1969]
44.	C. 1700-1775	1738	Westerwald, Stamped Blue Floral Devices, Geometric Designs (284-85).
58.	c. 1650-1725	1668	Sprig Molding, Combed Lines, Blue and Manganese Decorated Rhenish Stoneware (280-281).
59.	c. 1690-1710	1700	Embellished Hohr Gray Rhenish Stoneware (284).
77.	c. 1700-1775	1738	Westerwald Chamber Pots (148, 281).

Stoneware, White

Type Number	Date Range	Median Date	Ceramic Type Name and Page Reference [to Noel Hume 1969]
16.	c. 1740-1765	1753	Moulded White Salt-Glazed Stoneware (115).
24.	c. 1765-1795	1780	Debased "Scratch Blue" White Salt-Glazed Stoneware (118).
30.	c. 1755-1765	1760	Transfer Printed White-Saltglazed Stoneware (128).
34.	c. 1744-1775	1760	"Scratch-Blue" White Salt-Glazed Stoneware (117).
40.	C. 1720-1805	1763	White Salt-Glazed Stoneware (Excluding Plates and Moulded) (115-17).
41.	c. 1750-1765	1758	"Littler's Blue" (119-23) (On White Salt-Glazed Stoneware, Porcelain, and Creamware).
43.	c. 1740-1775	1758	White Salt-Glazed Stoneware Plates (115-17).
48.	c. 1715-1775	1745	Slip-Dipped White Salt-Glazed Stoneware (114-15).
55.	c. 1720-1730	1725	"Scratch Brown of Trailed" Whiter Salt-Glazed Stoneware (117).

Stoneware, Other

Type Number	Date Range	Median Date	Ceramic Type Name and Page Reference [to Noel Hume 1969]
3.	c. 1813-1900	1857	Ironstone and Granite China (131).
27.	c. 1750-1820	1785	"Black Basaltes" Stoneware (121-22).
28.	c. 1763-1775	1769	Engine-Turned Unglazed Red Stoneware (121).
37.	c. 1690-1775	1733	Refined Red Stoneware, Unglazed, Sprigged (120-21).
50.	c. 1732-1750	1741	Ralph Shaw, Brown, Slipped Stoneware (118-19).

Earthenware, Slipware

Type Number	Date Range	Median Date	Ceramic Type Name and Page Reference [to Noel Hume 1969]
56.	c. 1670-1795	1733	Lead Glazed Slipware (Combed Yellow) (107, 134-36).
63.	c. 1650-1710	1680	North Devon Sgraffito Slipware (104-05).
67.	c. 1612-1700	1656	Wrotham Slipware (103-04).
70.	c. 1610-1660	1635	Red Marbelized Slipware (North Italian) (77).
50.	c. 1580-1625	1603	Wanfried Slipware (139).

Earthenware, Refined

Type Number	Date Range	Median Date	Ceramic Type Name and Page Reference [to Noel Hume 1969]
2.	c. 1820-1900+	1860	Whiteware (130-31).
6.	c. 1795-1890	1843	Mocha (131).
29.	c. 1740-1780	1760	"Jackfield" Ware (123).
33.	c. 1759- 1775	1767	Green Glazed Cream-Bodied Ware (124-25).
36.	c. 1740-1770	1755	"Clouded" Wares, Tortoiseshell, Mottled Glazed Cream-Colored Ware (123).
42.	c. 1740-1775	1758	Refined Agate Ware (132).
51.	c. 1725-1750	1738	"Ashbury" Ware, White Sprigged and Trailed (123).
78	c. 1790-1840	1815	Luster Decorated Wares.

Earthenware, Coarse

Type Number	Date Range	Median Date	Ceramic Type Name and Page Reference [to Noel Hume 1969]
35.	c. 1750-1810	1780	Coarse Agate Ware (Excluding Doorknobs) (132).
38.	c. 1745-1780	1763	Iberian Storage Jars (143).
47.	c. 1720-1775	1748	Buckley Ware (132-33, 135)
61.	c. 1650-1775	1713	North Devon Gravel Tempered Ware (133).

Earthenware, Tin-Enameled

Type Number	Date Range	Median Date	Ceramic Type Name and Page Reference [to Noel Hume 1969]
21.	c. 1775-1800	1788	Debased Roven Faience (141-42) (c. 1755 on French Sites).
32.	c. 1730-1830	1780	Pedestal-Footed Type Delft Ointment Pot (204-05).
45.	c. 1700-1800	1750	Everted Rim, Plain Delft Ointment pot (204-05).
49.	c. 1600-1802	(1650) (1750)	(17th Century) (18th Century) Decorated Delftware (105-11). [See the discussion of Mean Ceramic Dating in the introduction, Chenoweth I:1]
57.	c. 1750-1800	1775	Plain Delft (108-11).
60.	c. 1710-1740	1725	Mimosa Pattern Delft (108-11).
62.	c. 1620-1720	1670	English Delftware (Blue Dash Chargers) (108-09).
64.	c. 1630-1700	1665	Cylindrical Delft Ointment Pots (109, 203-10).
65.	c. 1640-1800	1720	Plain White Delftware (109).
71.	c. 1620-1775	1698	Delft Apothecary Jars (Monochrome).
72.	c. 1580-1640	1610	Delft Apothecart Jars and Pots (Polychrome) (203).
76.	c. 1660-1800	1730	Delft Chamber Pots (146-47).

Earthenware, Creamware

Type Number	Date Range	Median Date	Ceramic Type Name and Page Reference [to Noel Hume 1969]
8.	c. 1790-1820	1805	"Finger-Painted" Wares (Polychrome) Slip on Creamware or Pearlware (132).
14.	c. 1780-1815	1798	"Annular Wares" Creamware (131).
15.	c. 1775-1820	1798	Lighter Yellow Creamware (126-28).
18.	c. 1765-1810	1788	Overglaze Enameled Hand Painted Creamware.

Earthenware, Creamware

Type Number	Date Range	Median Date	Ceramic Type Name and Page Reference [to Noel Hume 1969]
8.	c. 1790-1820	1805	"Finger-Painted" Wares (Polychrome) Slip on Creamware or Pearlware (132).
14.	c. 1780-1815	1798	"Annular Wares" Creamware (131).
15.	c. 1775-1820	1798	Lighter Yellow Creamware (126-28).
18.	c. 1765-1810	1788	Overglaze Enameled Hand Painted Creamware.
22.	c. 1762-1820	1791	Creamware (125-26).
23.	c. 1765-1815	1790	Transfer Printed Creamware (126-28).
25.	c. 1762-1780	1771	Deeper Yellow Creamware (126-28).
41.	c. 1750-1765	1758	"Littler's Blue" (119-23) (On White Salt-Glazed Stoneware, Porcelain, and Creamware).

Earthenware, Pearlware

Type Number	Date Range	Median Date	Ceramic Type Name and Page Reference [to Noel Hume 1969]
4.	c. 1820-1840	1830	Underglaze Polychrome Pearlware, Directly Stenciled Floral Patterns, Bright Blue, Orange, Green, Pinkish Red (129).
6.	c. 1795-1890	1843	Mocha (131).
8.	c. 1790-1820	1805	"Finger-Painted" Wares (Polychrome Slip on Creamware of Pearlware) (132).
9.	c. 1800-1820	1810	Embossed Feathers, Fish Scales, Etc. on Pearlware (131).
10.	c. 1795-1840	1818	"Willow" Transfer-Pattern on Pearlware (130).
11.	c. 1795-1840	1818	Transfer-Printed Pearlware (128-130).
12.	c. 1795-1815	1805	Underglaze Polychrome Pearlware (129).
13.	c. 1790-1820	1805	"Annular Wares" Pearlware (131).
17.	c. 1780-1820	1800	Underglaze Blue Hand Painted Pearlware (128-29).
19.	c. 1780-1830	1805	Blue and Green Edged Pearlware (131).
20.	c. 1780-1830	1805	Undecorated Pearlware.

B. An Application of the Mean Ceramic Dating Formula

The Mean Ceramic Dating Formula Using Presence-Absence and Frequency

The mean manufacture date for a group of colonial English ceramic types from an historic site taking into consideration the frequency of occurrence of fragments of the types, can be determined by a mean ceramic date-frequency formula as follows:

Where the mean ceramic date, Y, is expressed:

$$Y = \frac{\sum_{i=1}^{n} Xi \bullet fi}{\sum_{i=1}^{n} fi}$$

Where X_i = the median date for the manufacture of each ceramic type
f_i = the frequency of each ceramic type
n = the number of ceramic types in the sample

Brunswick Town, North Carolina, Ruin 57

Ceramic Type	Type Median (X_i)	Sherd Count (f_i)	Product (X_i * f_i)
22	1791	483	43953
33	1767	25	1675
26	1730	62	1860
34	1760	32	1920
36	1755	55	3025
37	1733	40	1320
43	1758	327	18966
49	(1750)	583	29150
44	1738	40	1520
47	1748	28	1344
39	1730	241	7230
53,54	1733	52	1716
56	1733	286	9438
29	1760	9	540
		2263	**123657 ÷ 2263 (+1700) = 1754.6**

Historic Dates 1734-1776
Historic Median Date 1755
Mean Ceramic Date 1754.6
Pipestem Date 1756

WILLIAM TURNBAUGH
SARAH PEABODY TURNBAUGH

Alternative Applications of the Mean Ceramic Date Concept for Interpreting Human Behavior

ABSTRACT

By illuminating inconsistencies between material culture chronology and historically documented occupation periods, seemingly "erroneous" dates derived from uses of South's mean ceramic date formula can be fully as valuable as is the technique's more traditional application for dating. Our paper formally recognizes and extends the use of the mean ceramic date approach as a tool for furthering the interpretation and explanation of human behavior in three categories: intrasite/intrafeature, intersite/interfeature, intrasite/interfeature. In-depth treatment of the latter category considers the excavation of two structures pertaining to Fort Independence in Boston. Three hypotheses are tested and serve to illustrate the use and limitations of the concept as a tool for cultural explanation. This quantitative approach to ceramic analysis is combined with qualitative considerations of artifacts, features, and stratigraphy to reach a consistent explanation of past lifeways at the 1803–33 fort.

Since its presentation in 1972, South's mean ceramic date formula (South 1972, 1977: 201–74) has revolutionized historical archaeologists' considerations of ceramic artifacts and analyses of English-American assemblages, features and sites. Initially, the technique was applied to ceramic assemblages from individual sites in order to provide a mean date of occupation which might also "be used with the historical data, or with *terminus post quem* dates, . . . (or) with mean pipestem dates, as well as other artifact data to arrive at an interpretation of the site occupation period (South 1977: 217)."

Occasionally, however, the use of the formula has yielded a mean ceramic date which has seemed to be inconsistent with the historically documented median occupation date for a particular site. A number of researchers have discarded the method as unworkable in such cases. Yet, productive reexamination of their data, by archaeologists who persist in accepting the validity of the formula's tenets, often has resulted precisely when such "unworkable" dates have been obtained. In some of these instances, the discrepancy between dates has triggered imaginative uses of the mean ceramic date concept as a tool to search for other, less obvious explanations of human behavior.

The literature, to date, has neither formally recognized nor systematized the innovative manipulation of the formula as a tool for archaeological explanation. Consequently, this study describes three major types of analysis where such uses of the approach may be particularly relevant. These are intrasite/intrafeature analyses, intersite/interfeature considerations, and intrasite/interfeature treatments. Within these categories, the appropriateness of certain inventive applications of the mean ceramic date formula will vary, of course, depending upon the types of questions with which an archaeologist is concerned, upon the specific nature of the data base, and upon the number of sites, features, and stratigraphic levels involved in the consideration.

Since research pertaining to the first two categories of analysis has been aired and is beginning to emerge in published form, it will be summarized only briefly below. The intrasite/interfeature classification, however, seems to have the most exciting potential for recognizing, interpreting, and explaining specific patterns of human behavior. Subsequently, it will be explored in greater depth.

Intrasite/Intrafeature

Intrasite/intrafeature analyses have been peformed occasionally with data from sites which provided accurate mean ceramic dates that conformed excellently to results of independent dating methods including documentation. S. Turnbaugh (1977: 201–08), for example, obtained a mean ceramic date of 1731.66, a median occupation date of 1732.50, "may result from a basic 17th vs. 18th century difference in ceramic distribution and use patterns," or, second, it "may also reflect differences between behavior in a small pioneer settlement, whose settlers brought old possessions with them and had relatively little opportunity to replenish them, and in an active port town, where there were many more opportunities for ostentatious display, as well as more frequent contact with sources of supply (Salwen and Bridges 1977: 169)."

Sarah Turnbaugh has tested the quantitative bracketing method, using the ceramic assemblage from the Salem Village Parsonage site, and has found that the delimitation of site occupation falls between approximately 1685–1782, which fits well with the documented occupation of 1681–1784.

Intrasite/Interfeature

As mentioned previously, intrasite/interfeature analysis which makes use of the mean ceramic date approach may have the greatest potential for explanation of specific cultural processes and human behavior. Due to the emphasis upon a single site, it is possible to take advantage of the combined benefits of spatial and temporal control, plus the greater complexity of interpretation afforded by systemic integration of more than one feature or assemblage within the archaeological site. In this way, description and explanation may be produced which can be more thorough and detailed than that of intrasite/intrafeature analyses. Furthermore, the use of the mean ceramic date formula in this manner can add synergistically both to the methodological control and to the quality of interpretation when data from a number of sites are later integrated in the search for explanation of more general culture process.

Consideration of the post-Colonial occupation of Fort Independence can indicate the usefulness of intrasite/interfeature analyses which apply the mean ceramic date approach to further the explanation of past lifeways.

Fort Independence is a former military post now owned by the Commonwealth of Massachusetts and administered through its Metropolitan District Commission (MDC). The present structure, a large granite pentagon built ca. 1850, is situated on the northern half of Castle Island (now connected to City Point, Dorchester, and South Boston by a broad causeway) in Pleasure Bay. Castle Island is one of the innermost Boston Harbor islands. Since 1972, Fort Independence and vicinity have been undergoing restoration and development under MDC auspices. The Fort Independence Archaeological Project, 1973–74, was directed by W. Turnbaugh, then a research associate at Harvard University. Since that time, further archaeological work for the MDC has been undertaken by the Brown University Public Archaeology Laboratory.

This discussion is concerned exclusively with two buildings which were excavated in 1973–74 and which apparently pertain to the post-Revolutionary utilization of the site. Consequently, the post-Colonial history of the fort (Turnbaugh 1974: 1–5) is relevant to the subsequent treatment and will be summarized briefly.

Castle Island has been fortified since 1634, making it one of the oldest continually occupied military sites in the nation. Following its colorful role in the Revolution, in 1785 the post was used as the first state prison. During 1794 it was regarrisoned when the threat of undeclared war with France loomed. In 1798. Massachusetts' primary defensework was ceded to the United States, and the following year, President John Adams inspected Castle Island and called for the construction of a new fortification to be known as "Independence" (Figure 1).

Between 1801 and 1803, a French military engineer, Jean Foncin, designer of the contemporary Fort McHenry at Baltimore, leveled the site and constructed Fort Independence, a large pentagonal structure with fairly low earth-embanked walls and steep glacis. Once built, the 1803 fortification was occupied until the garrison was withdrawn in 1833. The first Fort Independence apparently had lapsed

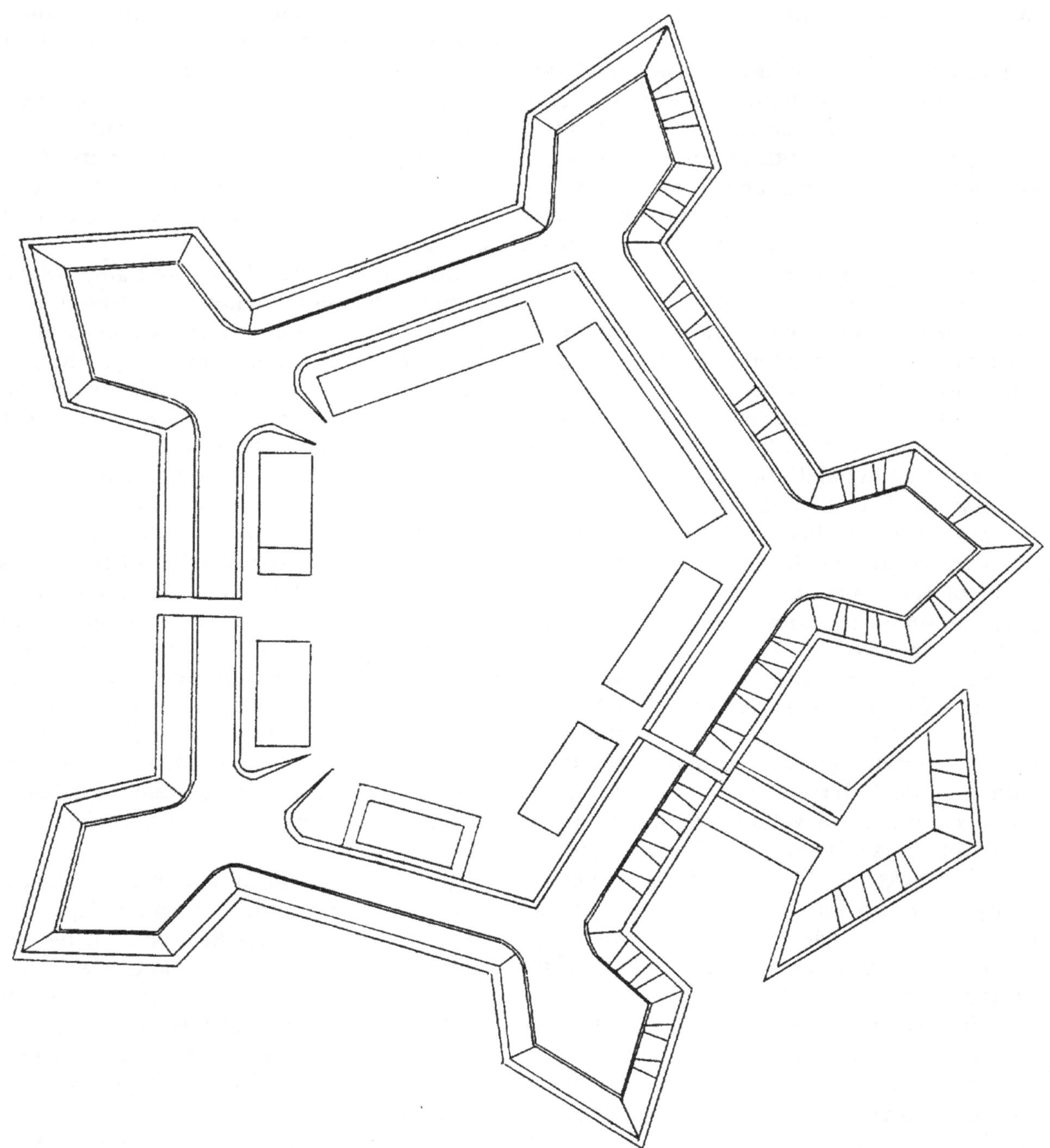

FIGURE 1. Fort Independence, Boston, adapted from prospectus of Jean Foncin, dated November 26, 1802, in the U.S. National Archives.

into poor repair for some time; during the ensuing 18 years, the current structure was begun and completed. This fort continued to be manned intermittently until well within the present century.

The two structural foundations with which this inquiry is concerned are located within the walls of the standing fort, yet pertain to the 1803 Fort Independence. They possibly served as half-cellars under barracks buildings. These two features will be referred to as Structure A and Structure C.

Structure A represents the basal foundation around a cellar hole which had a north-south length of 22 feet and an east-west width of 18 feet. Its south-east outside corner is situated at a point 38 feet north and 51 feet six inches west of the established datum at the northwest interior corner of the present fort's entryway. Observation of patterned grass development in 1973 prompted the digging of a small test trench near the midpoint of the western wall of Structure A, which intersected the mortared stone foundation. Subsequent work demonstrated that the remaining foundation walls and associated interior fill averaged little more than two feet in height/thickness. On the basis of historical and archaeological evidence, there is reason to believe that several feet of the parade ground, including the upper portions of the foundations, were cut away in preparation for the construction of the present fort, begun about 1833.

Excavation by natural stratigraphic units revealed four levels: Level 1 was sodded topsoil; Level 2 was a mixture of fine shale and plaster containing some artifacts that dated from the late 19th to early 20th century; Level 3a was a matrix of yellow clay incorporating small amounts of comminuted building debris; Level 3b held larger building debris, including many stones obviously derived from the upper portions of the adjacent foundation walls, and Level 4 was the original basement floor of the building, consisting of a mantle of shale resting directly upon the native boulder clay into which the cellar hole had been dug.

The lowest two strata (Levels 3b and 4) yielded a majority of the artifacts. Many of these objects had worked into the shale of Level 4 and many more were encountered just above this stratum, in Level 3b. Smaller quantities of similar material occurred throughout the upper unit of Level 3. Since Levels 3 and 4 have every appearance of containing comparable and contemporary early 19th century items that pertained directly to the structure in which they were found, it seems legitimate to consider the artifacts from both levels as a single unit in the following discussion. Levels 1 and 2 are general site strata which probably pertain to two episodes of grading the entire parade ground close to the middle and near the end of the 19th century, so they do not enter into this discussion of the mean ceramic date concept.

Structure C was discovered and excavated in much the same manner as Structure A. In 1974, 24 five foot square excavation units were opened to expose the 18 by 26 foot foundation, whose southeast outside corner was 37 feet north and seven feet west of the established datum point (Figure 2).

As with Structure A, the remaining foundation averaged little more than two feet in height. In this instance, however, somewhat more wall rubble remained in association with the structure, either as part of the interior fill or as loose *in situ* debris on top of the wall's intact portions. The Structure C stratigraphy is comparable to that of Structure A, although in this case Level 3 was more homogenous. As with Structure A, Levels 3 and 4 will be combined in the following treatment while Levels 1 and 2, which do not pertain specifically to the structure, will not be discussed further (Figure 3).

In analyzing the assemblages from Structure A and Structure C at Fort Independence, some alternative applications of the mean ceramic date concept can be useful in testing three hypotheses which relate to the culture history of the post. These three propositions were presented and tested qualitatively by Turnbaugh (1974: 12–35). The premises are as follows:

> *Hypothesis 1:* Both Structure A and Structure C were contemporary and pertain to the 1803 Fort Independence of Jean Foncin.
>
> *Hypothesis 2:* Structure A was occupied somewhat longer than was Structure C.
>
> *Hypothesis 3.* Structure A was occupied by officers, Structure C by enlisted men.

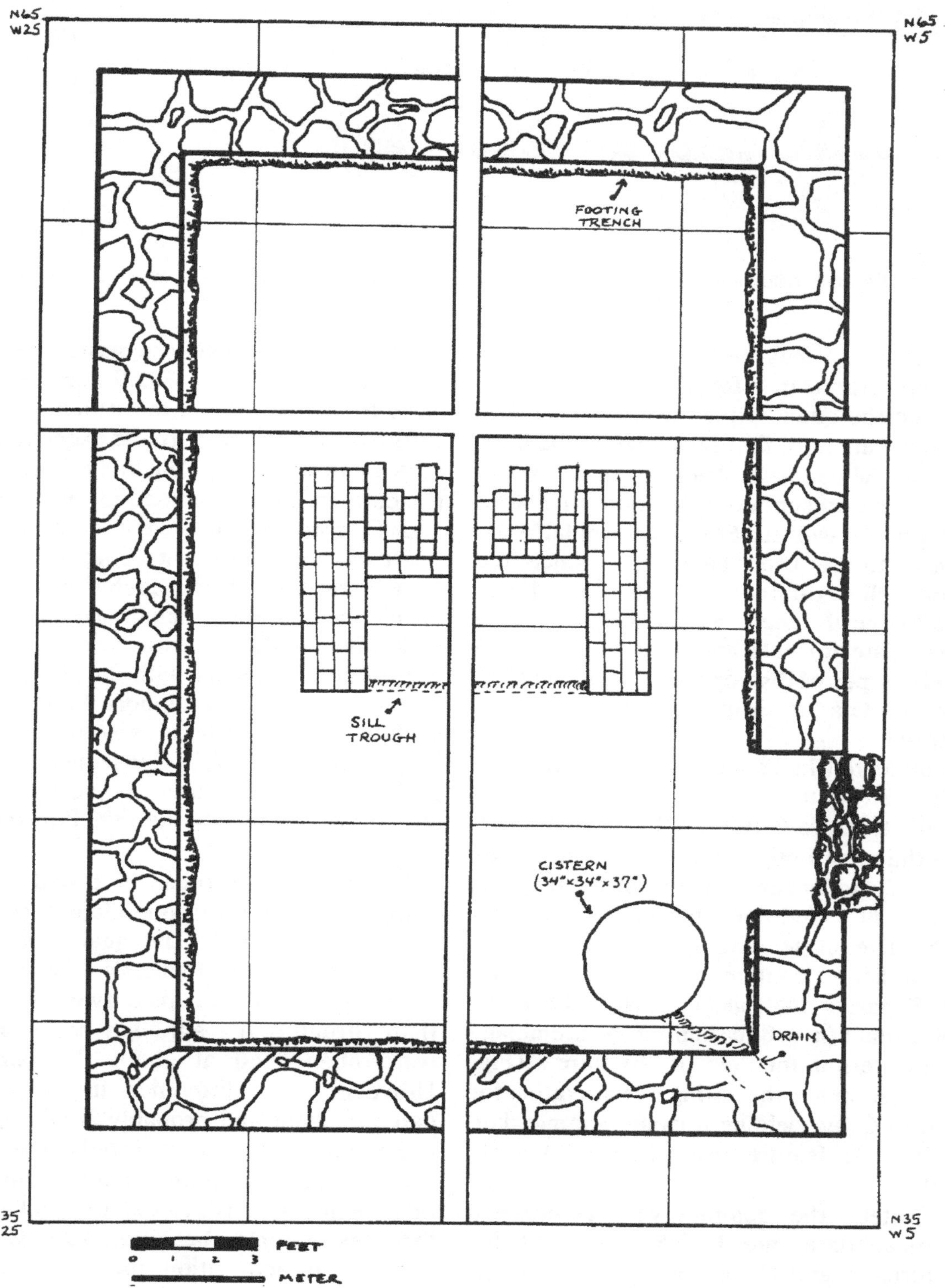

FIGURE 2. Plan view of Structure C during 1973–74 excavations at Fort Independence. Structure A plan and profiles are similar.

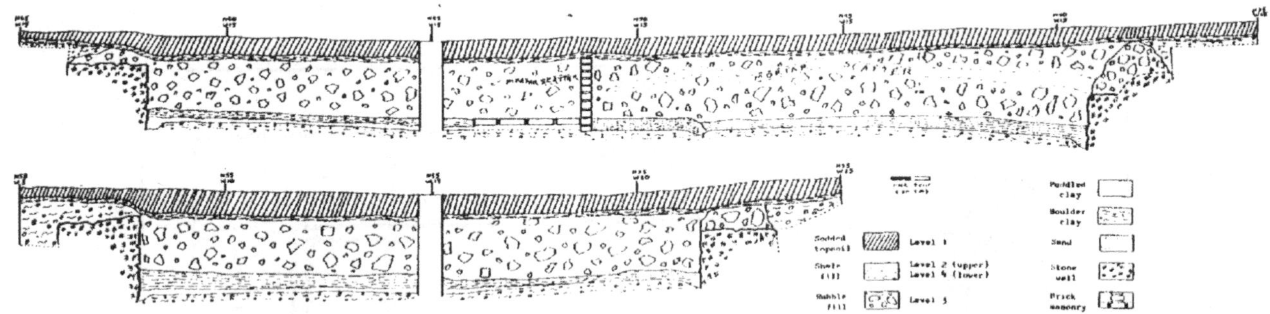

FIGURE 3. Profiles through Structure C, Fort Independence (upper, north-south; lower, east-west).

Hypothesis 1 may be tested by using both the mean ceramic date formula of South (1972, 1977) and the quantitative mean ceramic date bracketing method, first presented in the literature by Salwen and Bridges (1977). While useful in the present consideration, this latter approach, as well as South's formula, must continue to be used cautiously, since the method relies on the same theoretical and methodological tenets as the original mean ceramic date formula and may be subject to the same types of discrepancies with regard to historical data as South's formula has encountered.

As indicated in Table 1, the mean ceramic date for Structure A (Levels 3/4) is 1805.96, and for Structure C (Levels 3/4) it is 1807.82. Using the quantitative bracketing method, the period of site occupation for Structure A is 1782.2–1829.5 and for Structure C, 1785.0–1829.8. The close correspondence of these values indicates contemporaneity of the structures. Separate analysis (Turnbaugh 1974: 29–30) of a small (n = 8) ceramic sub-assemblage from a cistern in the floor of Structure C (Figures 2,4) supports the dating interpretation for Structure C by yielding a mean ceramic date of 1807 and feature use range of 1796.3–1830.0.

As noted, the quantitatively determined final mean dates are 1829.5 and 1829.8 for Structures A and C, respectively. These figures are consistent with the historically documented withdrawal of troops from the 1803 Fort Independence by 1833. On the other hand, the quantitatively suggested initial mean dates of 1782.2 and 1785.0 seem somewhat early for association of the structures with the 1803 fort. However, with the exceptions of the gray stoneware and "Jackfield" ware, all of the ceramic types included in the Structure A and C computations were at their median point of manufacture at about 1800 or later. Considerations of the architecture and the artifactual contents, including datable buttons and coins, of the two structures indicate they are totally consistent with an early 19th century date and firmly support the probable association of the structures with the 1803 fort (cf. Turnbaugh 1974). Consequently, the hypothesis that Structures A and C were contemporary and date to the 1803 Fort Independence is confirmed.

Hypothesis 2 also can be tested in part by using the mean ceramic date formula and bracketing method. The quantitative values presented in Table 1 suggest that Structure A may have been occupied two years earlier than Structure C, although both apparently were abandoned at about the same time. However, this difference in the beginning dates is slight and probably is not significant since numerous unrecognized variables may be operating here. Standard quantitative methods are not sensitive to specific qualitative differences in human behavior, such as differential rates of acquisition, use, and breakage of ceramics. As a further strictly idiosyncratic example, debris from three meals and fires encountered on the shale floor of Structure C at

TABLE 1
APPLICATION OF THE MEAN CERAMIC DATE FORMULA AND THE BRACKETING METHOD TO FORT INDEPENDENCE STRUCTURE A AND STRUCTURE C ASSEMBLAGES

Structure A, Levels 3 and 4 (N = 337)

Ceramic Type	Mfg. Date Range	X_i	(X_i-1805)	F_i	$(X_i-1805)(F_i)$	Initial Mfg. Date(A)	F_i	$(A)(F_i)$	Final Mfg. Date(B)	F_i	$(B)(F_i)$
3	1813–1900	1857	52	2	104	1700	1	1,700	1775	1	1,775
6	1795–1890	1843	38	1	38	1740	5	8,700	1780	5	8,900
10	1795–1840	1818	13	2	26	1775	20	35,500	1815	6	10,890
11	1795–1840	1818	13	65	845	1780	239	425,420	1820	65	118,300
13	1790–1820	1805	0	2	0	1790	2	3,580	1830	190	347,700
14	1780–1815	1798	− 7	6	− 42	1795	68	122,060	1840	67	123,280
15	1775–1820	1798	− 7	20	−140	1813	2	3,626	1890	1	1,890
17	1780–1820	1800	− 5	43	−215		337	600,586	1900	2	3,800
19	1780–1830	1805	0	36	0					337	616,535
20	1780–1830	1805	0	154	0						
29	1740–1780	1760	−45	5	−225						
44	1700–1775	1738	−67	1	− 67						
				337	+324						

Mean Ceramic Date: 324/337 + 1805 = 1805.96

Initial Mean Date: 600,586/337 = 1782.2

Final Mean Date: 616,535/337 = 1829.5

Structure C, Levels 3 and 4 (N = 98)

Ceramic Type	Mfg. Date Range	X_i	(X_i-1805)	F_i	$(X_i-1805)(F_i)$	Initial Mfg. Date(A)	F_i	$(A)(F_i)$	Final Mfg. Date(B)	F_i	$(B)(F_i)$
6	1795–1890	1843	38	1	38	1700	2	3,400	1775	2	3,550
11	1795–1840	1818	13	35	455	1765	1	1,765	1810	1	1,810
13	1790–1820	1805	0	14	0	1775	5	8,875	1820	25	45,500
15	1775–1820	1798	− 7	5	− 35	1780	40	71,200	1830	34	62,220
17	1780–1820	1800	− 5	6	− 30	1790	14	25,060	1840	35	64,400
18	1765–1810	1788	−17	1	− 17	1795	36	64,630	1890	1	1,890
19	1780–1830	1805	0	6	0		98	174,930		98	179,370
20	1780–1830	1805	0	28	0						
44	1700–1775	1738	−67	2	−134						
				98	+277						

Mean Ceramic Date: 277/98 + 1805 = 1807.82

Initial Mean Date: 174,930/98 = 1785.0

Final Mean Date: 179,370/98 = 1829.8

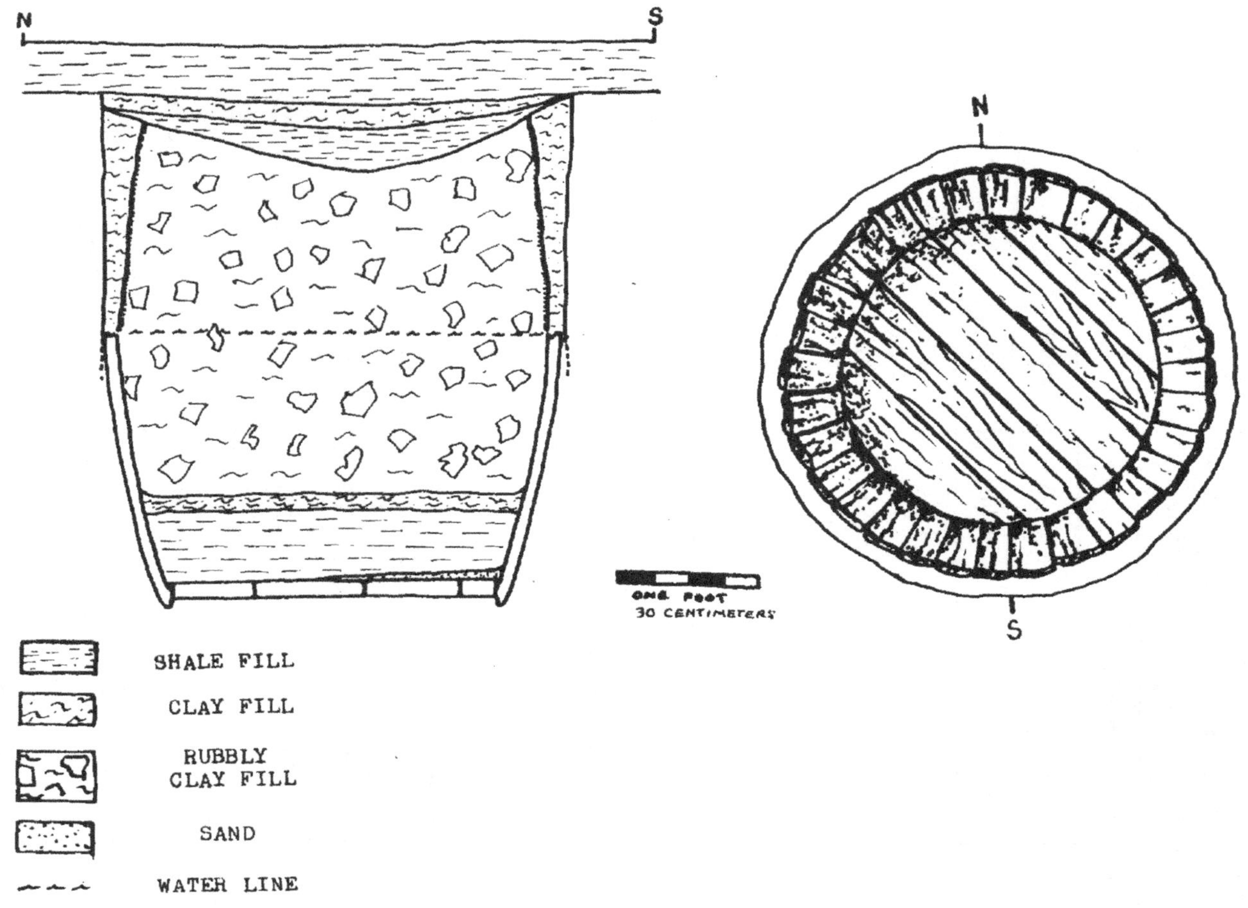

FIGURE 4. Profile and top view of cistern feature in the floor of Structure C.

Fort Independence can be interpreted only qualitatively, i.e. they probably were the leavings from the work crew who demolished the building after having used the cellar hole as a convenient windbreak (cf. Turnbaugh 1974: 16). Thus, incorporatng analyses of additional non-ceramic artifact categories and their qualitative interpretation is perhaps the more useful approach in such instances.

Objects other than ceramics yield a rough dating estimate (cf. Noël Hume 1969, 1970; Cotter 1968; Nelson 1963; Harrington 1954; Binford 1962; Olsen 1963; Campbell 1965; Dunnigan 1975). In Structure A these include kaolin clay pipe fragments. The bowls are of late 18th and 19th century styles and the pipestem bore diameters corroborate the bowls' stylistic evidence. Nail typology suggests that an early 19th century placement is likely, for both handmade and machine examples occurred in quantity, with a ratio of about one to two. Improvements in nail technology made about 1820 are reflected in a number of specimens from Structure A.

Military buttons, a coin and coin impressions on lead sheathing offer the most direct internal dating evidence. Three brass military buttons were found in Structure A. One was marked with a foliate "LA" (denoting Light Artillery), a design of 1813–1815 (Campbell 1965; Dunnigan 1975). The second was a brass officer's button displaying an eagle and a shield, worn between 1815 and 1821. The final example was an early version of an artillery corps button in use after 1821, depicting an eagle bearing a shield marked "A"; the reverse side of this specimen carried the maker's stamp, "RR."

The only coin found in the excavation's lower levels was an 1823 Netherlands (Belgian) cent; it was in good condition, showing little wear. In addition, five coin impressions had been hammered into two sheets of lead sheathing for an unknown reason. Unfortunately, the impressions of these coins (three half-dimes and two large cents) were of the reverse undated sides except for one example where the date was distorted beyond recognition. Coins of these types were in common use throughout the early 19th century.

Although no one artifact category specifically indicates the terminal date of Structure A, a general qualitative impression gleaned from examining its assemblage, stratigraphy, and architecture is that this building may have been demolished ca. 1830–33, which is consistent with the bracketing method's final mean date of 1829.5. Artifacts seem to suggest that the razing of Structure A occurred sometime later than Structure C. While this conclusion is not definitive, it could be the case if, for example, these quarters were reserved as the command center during the first phase of the new fort's construction, begun ca. 1830–33.

In Structure C, as with Structure A, the non-ceramic artifacts associated with the lower levels offer some general information on dating, and suggest a *terminus post quem* date. Again, the pipe fragments are of very late 18th or very early 19th century types. Furthermore, as in Structure A, machine made nails outnumbered handmade nails by approximately two to one.

Thirty-one military buttons were excavated from the lower levels of Structure C. Many of the brass military button patterns common between 1802 and 1821 are represented in this sample. The largest number from Structure C depict an eagle perched atop a cannon, surrounded by a stack of cannonballs, a drum and unfurled flags; these are the First Regiment of Artillery buttons made by Armitage between 1802 and 1810. Others pertain to units of the First Regiment of the Light Artillery. A single button of the Second Regiment of Artillery may be one which was supplied by the Quartermaster General without regard to unit designation, something which was done when production failed to meet demands during the War of 1812 and when excess supplies were available in later years (Campbell 1965). Button manufacturers represented by marked examples include, in addition to George Armitage of Philadelphia, Leavenworth and Hayden of Waterbury and Scoville, also of Waterbury.

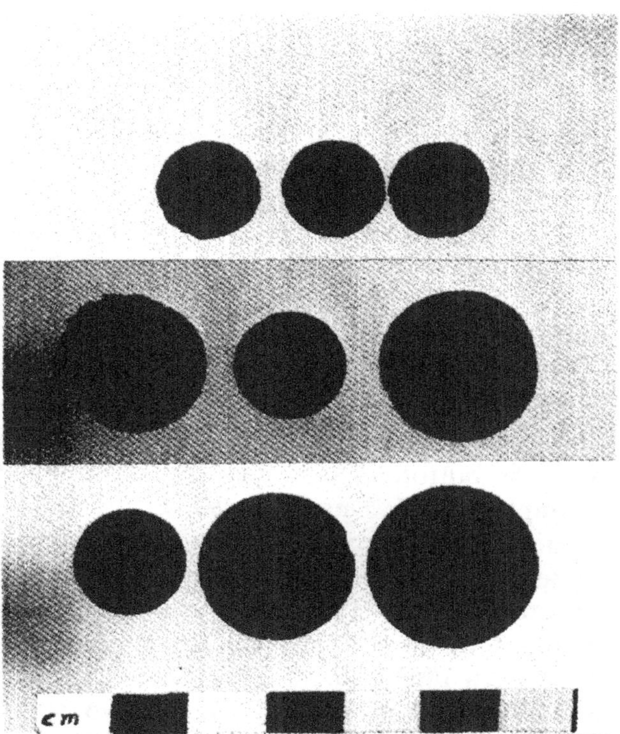

FIGURE 5. Decorated and military buttons from Fort Independence.

Plain brass buttons also occur, as do gilded and tinned examples. One unusual gilded button had been engraved with "LA" above a flying eagle which grasps a bolt of lightning and an olive wreath. Several general issue buttons of pewter, marked with a bold "US," were excavated from Structure C; these probably were worn on work uniforms. Another button, designed with an eagle bearing a shield, was the pewter counterpart of a brass button recovered from Structure A; the pewter issue was for enlisted men, while the brass button of the same design was reserved for officers (Campbell 1965; Dunnigan 1975).

All of the military buttons appear to date to the first quarter of the 19th century; few could be later. The Light Artillery specimens are particularly useful for dating purposes since they first appeared in 1810, were revised in 1813 and again in 1815. The unit was abolished by Congress in 1821. Buttons firmly associated with Level 4, the floor of the structure, included several Light Artillery specimens of the 1815 design, a First Regiment of Artillery button of 1802–1810, and the Second Regiment of Artillery button of 1813–15. Buttons from Level 3 likewise have a general termination date of 1821, the year when extensive military button design changes were made (Campbell 1965; Dunnigan 1975).

Finally, three coins excavated from Levels 3 and 4 provide corroborative evidence for the structure's early 19th century existence, although they do not suggest when it was abandoned. An 1803 U.S. cent in little worn condition appeared in Level 3, while two silver Spanish one *real* pieces of 1774 and 1782 came from the floor level. Spanish coins remained standard currency until about 1800 after which time the U.S. mint was producing a steady supply of coins of various denominations.

Thus, on the evidence of these non-ceramic artifacts, particularly the military buttons, it could be concluded that Structure C was not in use much later than 1821. This date seems somewhat earlier than that of ca. 1833 for Structure A's assemblage which, for example, included an artillery button post-dating 1821. While Hypothesis 2 might be confirmed on the basis of such evidence, an alternative explanation, dependent upon the acceptance of Hypothesis 3, seems more consistent and probable to us: officers had greater access than did their enlisted men to the latest products in such categories as button and ceramics.

If the latter proposition is accepted, then the two structures conceivably could have been occupied for the same duration. This alternative suggestion can be shown to be the favored explanation since it is more consistent with the cultural processes considered to confirm Hypothesis 1 and Hypothesis 3. It is sustained further by the Structure C cistern data (see above). Internal stratigraphic evidence demonstrates that the feature had been filled sometime prior to the abandonment and filling of Structure C itself. Thus, supported by the results of the application of the mean ceramic date formula and bracketing method to the cistern's ceramic assemblage, Structure C, like Structure A, probably has an actual *terminus post quem* date of ca. 1830–1833.

Hypothesis 3 will be tested both with a less formal application of South's mean ceramic date concept and with qualitative interpretation of other non-ceramic artifacts.

As presented in Table 2, Levels 3 and 4 of Structure A contained 12 ceramic types, which were considered in the application of the mean ceramic date formula (see Table 1), while Structure C's levels 3 and 4 contained only nine types. Furthermore, each of the Structure A types usually is represented by a considerably larger number of vessels and sherds (N = 337) than are the Structure C types (N = 98). Differential breakage, varied housekeeping habits, and dissimilar numbers of occupants are among the possible variables which might skew the frequencies of ceramic items represented in the respective assemblages. Yet, in consideratons of late 18th century Rhode Island and Massachusetts inventories, Teller (1968), Stone (1970), Brown (1973), and Turnbaugh (1977) have found that larger numbers of finer wares were listed in inventories of wealthier households than in those of more modest socioeconomic levels. In a military situation such as at Fort Independence, where the regimen of life often obscures actual socioeconomic differentation, this distinction may occur, instead, along lines of rank.

Consideration of the proportion (rather than frequency) of ceramic types supports the assumption that officers inhabited Structure A and enlisted men Structure C. Although the same uncontrolled variables which may skew the frequency might also be operating here and are not simply explained away by using this approach, the consideration of the grosser categories of proportion may more readily reflect patterned human behavior.

Table 2 divides the ceramic types repre-

TABLE 2
CERAMIC TYPES AND PROPORTIONS REPRESENTED IN FORT INDEPENDENCE STRUCTURE A AND STRUCTURE C ASSEMBLAGES

Structure A, Levels 3 and 4 (N = 337)				Structure C, Levels 3 and 4 (N = 98)			
Ceramic Type	Mfg. Date Range	X_i	Description	Ceramic Type	Mfg. Date Range	X_i	Description
3	1813–1900	1857	plain ironstone	6	1795–1890	1843	mocha
6	1795–1890	1843	mocha	11	1795–1840	1818	transfer-printed pearlware
10	1795–1840	1818	"willow" transfer pearlware	13	1790–1820	1805	annular pearlware
11	1795–1840	1818	transfer-printed pearlware	15	1775–1820	1798	light creamware
13	1790–1820	1805	annular pearlware	17	1780–1820	1800	underglaze blue painted pearlware
14	1780–1815	1798	annular creamware	18	1765–1810	1788	overglaze painted creamware
15	1775–1820	1798	light creamware	19	1780–1830	1805	blue and green edged pearlware
17	1780–1820	1800	underglaze blue painted pearlware	20	1780–1830	1805	undecorated pearlware
19	1780–1830	1805	blue and green edged pearlware	44	1700–1775	1738	gray stoneware
20	1780–1830	1805	undecorated pearlware				
29	1740–1780	1760	"Jackfield" ware				
44	1700–1775	1738	gray stoneware				
pre-1805.96 wares = 8, or 67% of types				pre-1807.82 wares = 7 or 78% of types			
post-1805.96 wares = 4, or 33% of types				post-1807.82 wares = 2 or 22% of types			

sented in the Structure A and Structure C assemblages into "early" and "late" units of probable acquisition according to whether their mean date of manufacture precedes or post-dates the probable mean date of occupation. For Structure A, eight types or 67% of the assemblage probably were acquired prior to the assumed mean date of occupation (1805.96) and four types or 33% probably were acquired after 1806. By the same token, only two types or 22% of the Structure C assemblage probably were acquired after the assumed mean date of occupation (1807.82). These figures suggest that the occupants of Structure A managed to acquire a significantly larger number of newer ceramic types than did the inhabitants of Structure C. In the absence of exclusively feminine artifacts or possible socioeconomic distinctions in a civilian sense, the existence of a difference in military rank may explain this variation between the Structure A and Structure C ceramic assemblages.

Furthermore, of the 13 ceramic types included in Table 2, the Structure A assemblage contains all except 18th century overglaze painted creamware. The Structure C assemblage, on the other hand, includes no "willow" transfer pearlware, annular creamware, "Jackfield" ware, or ironstone. Several of these wares were especially decorative, while ironstone, in particular, was a ceramic type which first appeared in the second decade of the 19th century. These trends also tend to support the hypothesis that officers inhabited one barracks and enlisted men the other, especially if the assumption that officers had greater access to new wares is accepted.

Consideration of non-ceramic artifacts also tends to support this premise. Overall distinctions between the assemblages lead to the suggestion that Structure A may indeed have been the residence of some of the fort's officers. Yet, positive documentary proof is lacking, and Foncin's 1802 plans are of little help since his prospectus for the specific location of structures appears to have been modified and was not confirmed archaeologically.

The major point of inference is in the quality of artifacts associated with Structure A. A number of these items differ from what one might expect to find among the personal possessions of enlisted men serving their term of duty at the fort. A small piece of serpentine is in the form of a Classic column, and probably functioned as a decorative element on a clock. Two sections of a sterling silver spoon handle marked "Churchill" and another handle of silver plate with a scallop design were also found. A piece of mother-of-pearl inlay, a large clasp knife with a handsome checkered bone handle, a domino face, a scrimshaw finial, and a key to a trunk were retrieved form Structure A.

In addition, 19 bone, shell, gilded brass, and ornamental buttons (vs. three military buttons) were excavated from Levels 3 and 4 of Structure A. Three sleeve or waistcoat buttons of English manufacture displaying a radial pattern, and a gilded button with a fly or honeybee in low relief on its field and marked "R.J. & Co. Superfine" were the most unusual examples found. Such buttons might have been worn by high ranking officers (or perhaps their

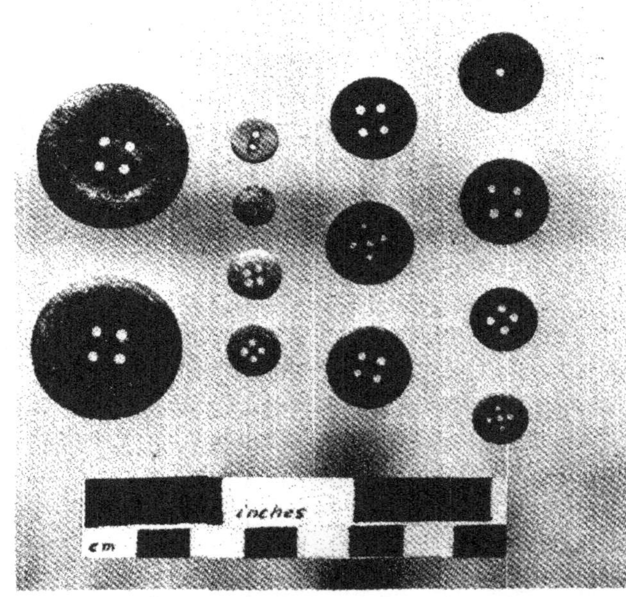

FIGURE 6. Plain buttons from Fort Independence structures.

wives), who were not required to be in standard uniform at all times.

Military buttons were many times more plentiful in Structure C (N = 31) than in Structure A (N = 3). It is possible that the number of buttons relates directly to the number of men housed in the respective quarters, and if this premise is accepted, then Structure C seems to have housed the greater number of men in uniform. The fact that pewter buttons were found only in Structure C and included the enlisted man's counterpart of an officer's brass button type excavated in Structure A supports this interpretation.

Similarly, Structure A ceramics included the greater frequency of wares displaying decorative motifs (including Canton, "Gaudy Dutch," and one "Cauliflower" ware sherd not heretofore considered since they are not included in the mean ceramic date calculations). Plates, teacups, sugar bowls, and pitchers were represented. On the other hand, the smaller Structure C assemblage included only a few forms and they were associated directly with eating (i.e., plates).Three chamberpots or their fragments came from Structure A, while the lack of even one sherd of such a vessel from Structure C suggests that its occupants were required to use an outside convenience. Here again, the distinction may be due to differences in rank. Finally, two brass doorknobs, a brass keyhole plate, and a brass hinge from Structure A had no equivalent counterparts in Structure C.

On the basis of faunal evidence, the quality of food consumed in both structures did not differ. Bones of cow, suckling pig, sheep/goat, chicken, and soft-shelled clams and oysters were represented in each structure in approximately equal proportions.

After using the mean ceramic date concept to define behavioral trends in the ceramic assemblages, the authors have proceeded to examine other artifactual sub-assemblages from Levels 3 and 4 of Structures A and C. Based on the indications that Structure A was occupied by officers and Structure C by enlisted men, Hypothesis 3 is confirmed. In light of the acceptance of Hypothesis 3, the slight temporal differences between assemblages which figures in the discussion of Hypothesis 2 seem to be explained most convincingly by distinctions in human behavior rather than by differences in length of occupation of each structure. Consequently, Hypothesis 1 and Hypothesis 3 are confirmed and Hypothesis 2, though plausible, is rejected in favor of an alternative which addresses human behavior and is more compatible with the variables of culture process delineated in this analysis. Thus, South's mean ceramic date concept seems to be a useful tool for interpreting processes of past human activity on the intrasite/interfeature level.

Summary

In each category of analysis, then—intrasite/intrafeature, intersite/interfeature and intrasite/interfeature—the mean ceramic date approach can help to elicit valuable information and patterns which otherwise may be hidden in less precise considerations. Yet, the overall value of the approach is not realized fully unless it is used to complement qualitative and quantitative analyses of their artifactual and architectural categories, historical documentation, and stratigraphy in order to provide a synergistic, consistent explanation of culture process. In this way, the ability of the mean ceramic date approach to point up inconsistencies between material culture and historically documented site occupation periods can be fully as valuable to the archaeologist as is its more traditional application as a dating tool.

REFERENCES

BINFORD, LEWIS R.

1962 A New Method of Calculating Dates from Kaolin Pipe Stem Samples. *Southeastern Archaeological Conference, Newsletter* 9(1): 19–21.

BROWN, MARLEY R., III

1973 Ceramics from Plymouth, 1621–1800: The Documentary Record. In, *Ceramics in America*, edited by I. M. G. Quimby, pp. 41–74. University Press of Virginia, Charlottesville.

CAMPBELL, J. DUNCAN
1965 Military Buttons, Long-Lost Heralds of Fort Mackinac's Past. *Mackinac History Leaflet*, No. 7.

COTTER, JOHN L.
1968 *Handbook for Historical Archaeology*, Part 1. Wyncote, Pennsylvania.

DEETZ, JAMES J. F.
1977a *In Small Things Forgotten*. Anchor Press, New York.
1977b Parting Ways: A Rural New England Black Community. Paper presented at the 1977 Annual Meeting of the Northeastern Anthropological Association, Providence.

DUNNIGAN, BRIAN L.
1975 Military Buttons and Insignia from Mackinac. *Mackinac History Leaflet*. 2(3).

HARRINGTON, JEAN C.
1954 Dating Stem Fragments of Seventeenth Century Clay Tobacco Pipes. *Archaeological Society of Virginia Quarterly Bulletin* 9(1): 10–14.

NELSON, LEE H.
1963 Nail Chronology as an Aid to Dating Old Buildings. *American Association for State and Local History Technical Leaflet*, No. 15.

NOËL HUME, IVOR
1969 *Historical Archaeology*. Alfred A. Knopf, New York.
1970 *A Guide to the Artifacts of Colonial America*. Alfred A. Knopf, New York.

OLSEN, STANLEY J.
1963 Dating Early Plain Buttons by Their Form. *American Antiquity* 28(4): 551–54.

SALWEN, BERT, AND SARAH T. BRIDGES
1977 Cultural Differences and the Interpretation of Archaeological Evidence: Problems with Dates. *Researches and Transactions of the New York State Archaeological Association* 17(1): 165–73.

SOUTH, STANLEY A.
1972 Evolution and Horizon as Revealed in Ceramic Analysis in Historical Archaeology. *Conference on Historic Site Archaeology Papers* 6(2): 71–116.
1977 *Method and Theory in Historical Archaeology*. Academic Press, New York.

STONE, GARY W.
1970 Ceramics in Suffolk County, Mass., Inventories, 1680–1775. *Conference on Historic Site Archaeology Papers* 3: 73–90.

TELLER, BARBARA G.
1968 Ceramics in Providence, 1750–1800: An Inventory Survey. *Antiques* 94(4): 570–77.

TURNBAUGH, SARAH PEABODY
1977 Ideo-Cultural Variation and Change in the Massachusetts Bay Colony. *Conference on Historic Site Archaeology Papers* 11: 169–235.

TURNBAUGH, WILLIAM
1974 Archaeological Investigations at Fort Independence on Castle Island in Boston Harbor, 1973–74. Report to the Commonwealth of Massachusetts, Metropolitan District Commission.

TURNBAUGH, WILLIAM, AND SARAH PEABODY TURNBAUGH
1977 Recovery of Ceramics from a Revolutionary Warship. Paper presented at the 1977 Annual Meeting of the Northeastern Anthropological Association, Providence. Typescript.

TURNBAUGH, WILLIAM, SARAH PEABODY TURNBAUGH, AND ALBERT P. DAVIS, JR.
1979 Ceramics from the HMS Orpheus. *Archaeology*. 32(3).

WILLIAM TURNBAUGH
SARAH PEABODY TURNBAUGH
DEPARTMENT OF SOCIOLOGY/ANTHROPOLOGY
UNIVERSITY OF RHODE ISLAND
KINGSTON, RHODE ISLAND 02881

A NEW METHOD OF CALCULATING DATES FROM KAOLIN PIPE STEM SAMPLES

by

Lewis R. Binford

In 1954 Harrington published an article on the study of metrical changes in kaolin pipe stem hole diameters through time. He found that there was a general and regular reduction in the hole diameters as you go from 1620 to 1800. In attempting to use this correlation to date Indian occupations in the Virginia-North Carolina area in 1954-55, I found that Harrington's method of data presentation was rather clumsy when attempting to compare archaeological samples of pipe stems to the control data or basic data on which the correlation was originally determined. Harrington had presented the observed correlation as a series of percentages for the occurrence of various hole diameters by forty year time periods. Very seldom is an archaeological sample likely to correspond to the forty year time periods set up by Harrington, so that when comparing observed percentages with the basic chart it was very difficult to arrive at an accurate age estimate. While attempting to eliminate this cumbersome difficulty it became quite obvious that Harrington's observed correlation of a metrical attribute with time was ideal for regression analysis. I computed from Harrington's percentages a straight line regression and arrived at a formula which would allow me to substitute values from any archaeological sample into the formula and determine an absolute date which would be the mean date for the period of sample accumulation. This I was able to do by using Harrington's original percentages and converting them to mean hole diameters for the given time period. This allowed me to calculate a straight line regression formula using years and mean hole diameters. The resulting formula is: $Y = 1931.85 - 38.26X$, Y being the date you are attempting to determine, 1931.85 being the theoretical date, if we project this correlation, at which the stem hole diameters would reach zero, and 38.26 being the slope of the line, that is, the interval of years between a mean of any one of the various metrical categories 5, 6, 7, 8, or 9/64 of an inch. If you had a sample with a mean of 5/64ths, and another with a mean of 6/64ths, there is an interval of 38.26 years between them according to Harrington's correlation. X in the formula is the mean pipe stem diameter for the sample you are attempting to date, and this is determined simply by measuring the hole diameters of the pipe stems in the sample and computing the arithmetic mean for the sample. The formula then gives you the mean date of the pipe stem sample, and is the mean date for the period of accumulation.

The first set of data on which I used this particular formula was the historic Nottoway and Meherrin Indian sites in the Virginia area. I had very good data as to the period of occupancy for at least four documented sites, and in all cases (this was the first application of the formula as such) I was amazed. I couldn't believe the results could be so close to the known dates. On one particular site, a Warrasqueoc occupation of 1675-1702, the mean pipe stem date determined by this formula was 1683, and with the other sites I found equally good results. In conversing with Carol Erwin, who is writing up the historic material from the Macon Trading Post, I learned that she had found, in using the formula, that the mean pipe stem dates fall between the known estimated periods of occupation for the site. H. Geiger Omwake, who is one of our better authorities on pipe makers' marks, originally analyzed five fairly well dated historic sites, using Harrington's method in an attempt to demonstrate that the correlation was in fact valid. I have reapplied my formula to his data and was able to make more refined temporal estimates for the sites which were actually closer to the known dates. The other cases of application of the formula are Fort Michilimackinac and Brunswick Town. For the former site we have excellent documentation on the date of abandonment although its date of establishment is in dispute, being somewhere between 1700 and 1720. In addition to the documented span of the site, we have documented dates for the period of use of various structures, one of which was a soldiers' barracks built in 1769 and torn down in 1781. From the fireplace and a small closet that was adjacent to the fireplace of this structure a large sample of kaolin pipe stems were recovered yielding a mean pipe stem date of 1776, right in the middle of the known period of occupancy. These cases of application have convinced me and others that Harrington's correlation and this method is valid and quite useful for dating historic sites.

There are certain limitations to the method. When I applied the formula in the analysis of a sample from Mackinac Island, occupied from 1780 until the present, I found that the correlation fell to pieces. Known samples of pipe stems derived from hearths dated 1805 yielded pipe stem dates of 1732. In other cases of the application of the technique to late materials the results were equally disturbing. In the way of explanation it is quite obvious that with the influx of pipes manufactured in Montreal and at other seats of American pipe making there is a corresponding reoccurrence of certain "early" styles, in addition to the appearance of a new style of elements. This break in the traditional direction of stylistic change is responsible, I feel quite sure, for the breakdown in the correlation after roughly 1780.

I will mention certain sampling problems which also will affect the validity of any mean date determined by this technique. First, it must be kept in mind that you must have an adequate sample, that is, a large enough sample to be representative of the population being dated. The next major caution was brought forcibly to my attention by the material from Fort Michilimackinac. Early in the analysis of the Fort material it was obvious that throughout the span of the fort there had been an increasing logistics efficiency as well as an increase in population. The factors taken together resulted in there being many more pipes in use during the late period as contrasted with the early period. Thus, the increased rates of accumulation for the late period tend to skew the total sample from the site in favor of a later date. This brings us to the point that the accuracy of the date depends upon the possession of a random sample of a population which was stable with regard to rates of deposition through the period of sample accumulation. If either one of these conditions are not met, then you can expect less accuracy in dating.

I might briefly mention that by calculating the standard deviations of the means of samples, you have a rough estimate of the length of time over which the sample was accumulating.

In summary the regression formula presented here allows you to estimate from the variation observed in the hole diameters of kaolin pipes, a mean date for the period of sample accumulation and by using standard deviations estimate the length of time involved in accumulating the sample. The accuracy of the date depends upon (1) derivation of the sample from a population deposited prior to 1780, (2) randomness of the sample, (3) representativeness of the sample, and (4) a constant rate of accumulation throughout the period of sample building. I might mention that these limitations apply whether using Harrington's percentage technique or my regression formula.

GEORGE L. MILLER

A Revised Set of CC Index Values for Classification and Economic Scaling of English Ceramics from 1787 to 1880

ABSTRACT

This paper presents an updated and expanded set of CC index values for plates, teas, and bowls for the period 1787 to 1880. It is meant to replace the index values in the article "Classification and Economic Scaling of 19th-Century Ceramics" (Miller 1980). In addition to expanding the range of years covered, it adds values for dishes and for Irish size teas, as well as correcting a misconception about the stability of the price of CC ware during the first half of the 19th century. A better understanding of the discount rates has made it necessary to recalculate the index values for the post-1844 period. This paper also presents extensive chronological and descriptive information on the common types of ceramics that were imported from the 1780s to the 1880s.

Introduction

During the second half of the 18th century, a revolution took place in the English ceramic industry in Staffordshire. Developing technology, transportation, introduction of new raw materials, glazes, and marketing culminated in the Staffordshire industry becoming one of the dominant suppliers of ceramics to a world market (Miller et al. 1989). One of the major products of that revolution was creamware, which was introduced in the early 1760s and went on to become the dominant ceramic ware used during the rest of the century.

By the late 1790s, however, the demand for creamware was declining, and it had become the cheapest refined ware available. From that time on, creamware was referred to as "CC ware" in potters' and merchants' records. CC ware remained the cheapest type available from the late 1780s through the 19th century. While it consistently remained the cheapest ceramic, its appearance changed over that period. By the 1830s, CC ware was considerably lighter in color and would be classed as a whiteware by most archaeologists.

Because CC ware remained the cheapest type available for over a century, it makes an excellent bench mark to gauge the cost of other wares in terms of its price. A set of index values based on the cost of CC ware was published in *Historical Archaeology* in 1980 (Miller 1980). Over the last decade, those index values have been widely used to examine and compare expenditure patterns represented in archaeological assemblages. The CC index values presented here are the results of research made possible by a recent fellowship and two grants and are intended to supersede those prices provided in the earlier 1980 article.

CC Index Values: An Update

One of the basic assumptions of the 1980 article was that the cost of CC ware was relatively stable from 1796 to around 1860. That assumption was based on the prices of 16 dozen CC vessels from the Staffordshire Potters' price fixing lists of 1796, 1814, 1833, and 1846 (1796, 1846 reprinted in Mountford 1975:11–14; 1814 reprinted in Miller 1984; Staffordshire Potters 1833), and from the 1855 price list of the Fife Pottery (Miller 1980:23). Because the prices of these vessels in the above lists remained somewhat stable, it was assumed that CC index values from various years could be used to compare expenditure patterns from different time periods.

Research funded by the National Endowment for the Humanities (NEH) located Staffordshire potters' price fixing agreements from 22 different years between 1770 and 1885, and individual potters' price lists for an additional eight years during that period (Miller 1988:Appendix D). In addition to these price fixing lists, 167 potters' invoices with discount information for the period 1809 to 1875 have been located (Miller 1988: Appendix B).

This new information provides a clearer picture of the price structure for English ceramics and the relationship between the *list* prices in the price fixing lists and the *net* prices being charged by the

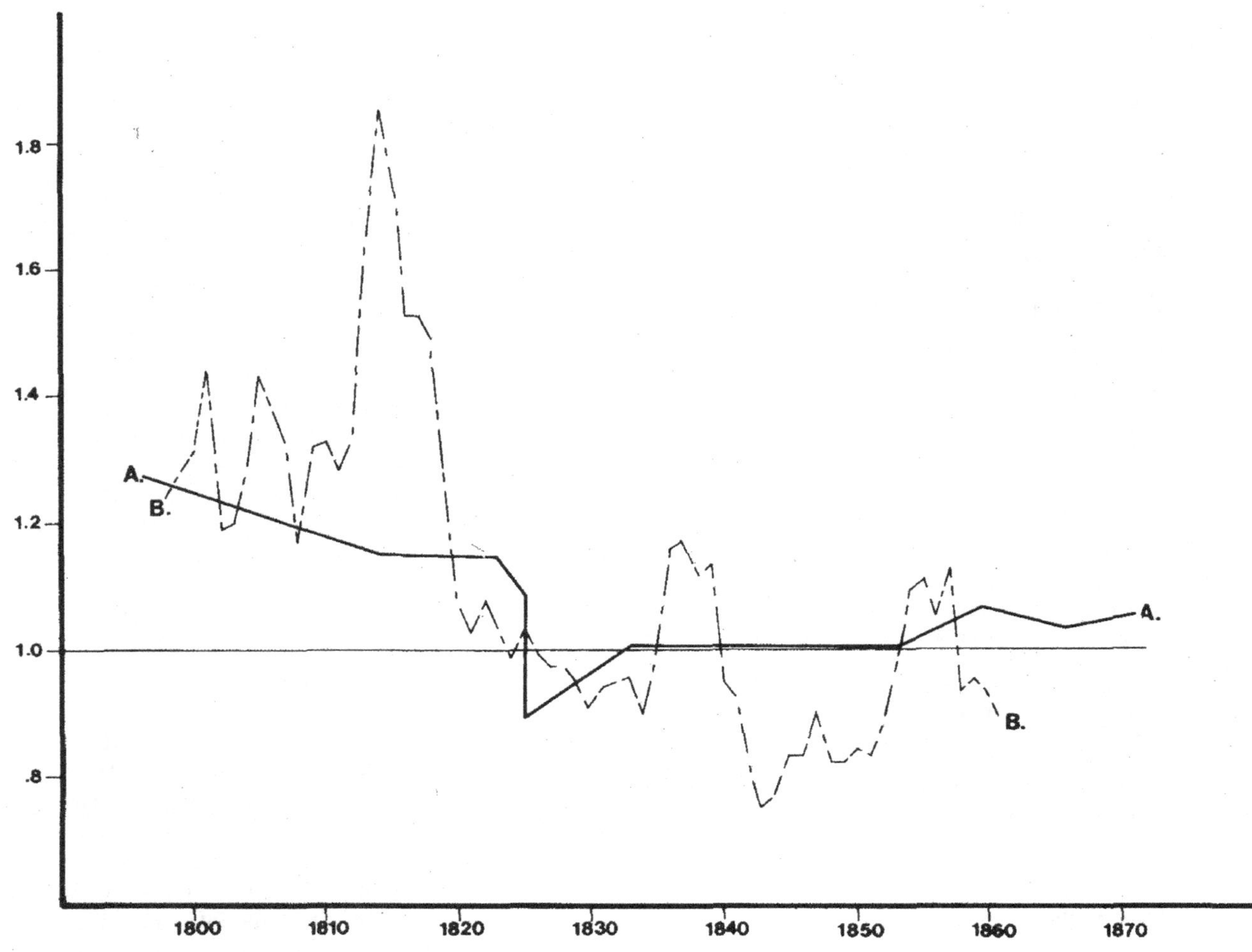

FIGURE 1. Comparison of Ceramic *List* Prices with the New York All Commodities Index of Wholesale Prices, both indexed to the period 1824 to 1842. A. = *list* prices for 48 dozen vessels, one-third creamware, shell edge, and printed wares for 1796, 1814, 1816, 1817, 1818, 1823, 1825, 1833, 1846, 1853, 1859, 1866, and 1871. B. = New York All Commodities Index of Wholesale Prices (Cole 1969: 135–136; Miller et al. 1989).

Staffordshire potters. Using these data, the list prices of 48 dozen vessels (one-third CC, edged, and printed wares) were extracted from 14 potters' price fixing lists and catalogues from 1796 to 1871 (Miller 1988:Appendix A). These *list* prices were then indexed to the period 1824 to 1842 and plotted against the New York All Commodities Index of Wholesale Prices (Cole 1969:135–136). Figure 1 illustrates the results of that price comparison. The graph suggests that prices of the common Staffordshire wares were relatively stable from 1796 to 1871.

That stability, however, is an illusion. Using the discount information from 122 potters' invoices from 25 different years, the Staffordshire average *net* prices per year were calculated for the period 1809 to 1848 (Miller 1988:Appendix C). These prices were also indexed to the period 1824 to 1842 and plotted against the New York All Commodities Index. Figure 2 presents that data. From this graph it can be seen that English ceramic prices dropped significantly from 1809 to 1848.

Clearly the prices of all wares, including CC, were dropping. CC ware remained the cheapest

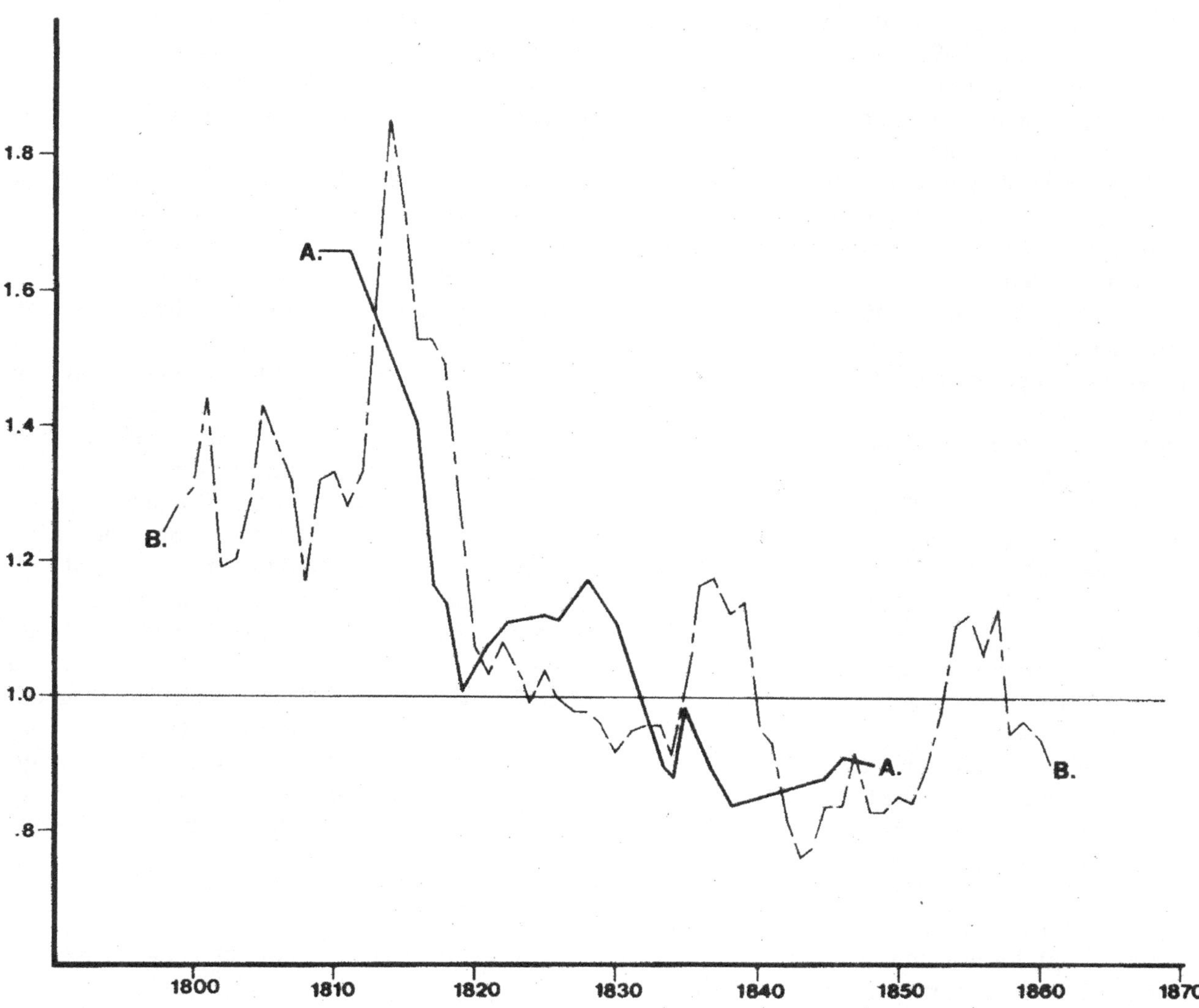

FIGURE 2. Comparison of Ceramic *Net* (wholesale) Prices with the New York All Commodities Index of Wholesale Prices, both indexed to the period 1824 to 1842. A. = *list* prices for 48 dozen vessels, one-third creamware, shell edge, and printed wares for 25 different years between 1809 and 1848. B. = New York All Commodities Index of Wholesale Prices (Cole 1969: 135–136; Miller et al. 1989).

refined earthenware throughout the entire period; however, it was dropping in price just like the other wares. This means that CC index values from one period should not be compared to those from another period without taking into consideration the declining prices and changing tariff rates. From the discount information gathered so far, indices within the following four periods appear to be comparable:

1780–1814 Period of the traditional discount, which was 5 percent for breakage plus 5 percent for cash payment, for a total discount of 10 percent. There was a 5 percent tariff on imported earthenware from 1789 until 1816.

1816–1830 The discount from the invoices for this period averages 28.8 percent. In addition, the tariff on earthenware had been raised to 20 percent in 1816.

1832–1842 The discount from the invoices for this period averages 39.5 percent. The tariff on earthenware continued at 20 percent until 1842.

1844–1859 The discount rate is more volatile during this period; however, the average rate of discount is 39.8 percent which is close to the previous period. The tariff rate went up to 30 percent in 1842 and remained at that rate until the Civil War.

For the periods after 1860, the quality of the information is not sufficient to set up periods or provide average discount rates. During the Civil War, the tariff rates went up and the exchange rate on the dollar dropped because of the large volume of greenback currency issued to finance the War. Assemblages from the Civil War period probably should not be compared to other time periods, and those from after the War probably should not be compared to earlier periods without taking into consideration differences in tariff and discount rates. A summary of the rates of discount and United States tariff rates on ceramics is covered more fully in appendices given in Miller (1988).

Around 1844, a change took place in the way that wares were discounted. Prior to that time, a single rate of discount was applied to all the wares on an invoice. After 1844, printed wares began to be discounted at a different rate than the other wares. As a result, the index values provided in Miller (1980) for printed wares from the post-1844 period had to be corrected. Table 1 provides a comparison of the old and new values for printed wares for 1846.

The index values for edged, painted, and dipt—or dipped—wares remained the same as those published in 1980.

The set of 1980 index values was created from a variety of sources, including potters' price fixing lists, invoices, jobbers' bills, and account books. Until now, there has not been a sufficient amount of data to build a set of index values based solely on potters' price records. Funding provided by NEH remedied this problem (Miller 1988). All of the index values presented here are based on prices from English potters' documents, such as their price fixing lists, catalogues, and invoices.

This paper presents four times as many CC index values as were available in 1980. The earlier article had values for 24 different years, while the current index values cover 38 years and also extend over a longer time period. In addition, index values are provided for new decorative types and vessel forms. Along with the above data is an expanded description of the basic decorative types and information on their periods of popularity. Further information on the technology of decoration can be found in Majewski and O'Brien (1987).

TABLE 1
CORRECTED INDEX VALUES

	1980	Corrected
Plates		
10 inch	2.63	2.11
8 inch	2.57	2.42
7 inch	2.50	2.37
Teas		
unhandled	2.45	2.27
handled	3.00	2.77
Bowls	2.80	2.58

The Use of CC Index Values

Using CC index values is quite simple. Once the minimal vessel count has been completed, the plates, cups, and bowls are grouped by their decorative type. Then the user selects a year from the indexes in the appendices that follow. In dealing with sites that have been occupied for a long period of time, one should attempt to break down the site assemblages into meaningful time units such as periods of occupation for different families or generations of a family. Generating average CC index values for lumped assemblages representing over 20 years of occupation seems to be a meaningless exercise.

Once one has established the assemblage or assemblages to be compared, the index value for each vessel type is multiplied times the number of vessels of that type. The results for each vessel type are summed and divided by the total number of vessels, which yields the average CC index value for the assemblage. This analysis is done for plates, cups, and bowls which provides three sets of index values for each archaeological assemblage under consideration. For a more detailed explanation of how the index values were derived and are used in the study of expenditure patterns see Miller (1980:11–12).

The most common expenditure pattern that has emerged from the study of archaeological assemblages has been for the highest average index value to be from the teas and the lowest to be from the bowls. The resulting index values can be compared with ceramic index values from other sites. A recent article lists ceramic index values for 44 archaeological assemblages (Adams and Boling 1989).

In the current study, the term "white granite" has replaced "white ironstone." This term was adopted for two reasons. First, it is the most common name used for white ironstone in the potters' documents. Second, "white granite" avoids the confusion between the highly decorated stone chinas, such as Mason's 1813 "Patent Ironstone," with the plain white and molded wares from the second half of the 19th century.

Descriptions of Common Decorative Types

The following descriptions of the types of decoration used on English ceramics are to be used in conjunction with the appendices of CC index values. They cover the most common types of ceramic tea, table, and toilet wares found on North American sites occupied from the 1790s to the 1880s and provide some new chronological information. Guidance to an extensive literature on English ceramics can be found in Miller and Martin (1989).

CC Ware

CC is the potters' term for cream colored or creamware. When the term CC was used by itself, it referred to undecorated creamware. Almost all underglaze decorated, refined earthenwares from the 1780s on were either pearlware or whiteware. Those wares, however, were consistently referenced in potters' and merchants' records by their type of decoration rather than by ware type.

Early creamware has a deep yellow tint. In 1775, the Staffordshire potters gained the right to use kaolin clays from Cornwall (Miller 1987:88), resulting in a lighter colored creamware which became common after that date. By 1830, an even lighter colored CC ware had evolved. The resulting product is what most archaeologists call whiteware. Some have attempted to attribute this change to the development of a leadless glaze around 1820; however, lead glazes continued to be the dominant type throughout the 19th century (Binns 1907:83).

Before the War of 1812, CC ware was common in most forms of tea, table, kitchen, and toilet wares (Miller et al. 1989:17). CC ware remains in the potters' price fixing lists and continues to show up in invoices of wares imported to America into at least the 1890s. However, from the 1830s on, it was more commonly found in utilitarian forms such as bowls, mugs, and chamber pots, which were less involved in status display.

Because CC ware is the base for measuring the cost of the other types, its index value is always one. Therefore, it is not listed in the tables of index values. Index values are given for CC teas, however, because the addition of handles or fluting can create CC teas with an index value greater than one.

Shell Edge Decorated Wares

"Edged" is the most common potters' term for what was called "shell edge" in Wedgwood's 1775 pattern book and in Leeds' pattern book of 1783 (Mankowitz 1966:59; Towner 1965:57–61). The 1783 Staffordshire potters' price fixing list, reprinted in Mountford (1975:9), enumerates a full range of tableware vessels available in shell edge that are listed as "edged in blue," indicating that shell edge was an item of considerable production by that date. Overglaze painted, shell-edged creamware was first produced in the 1770s (Mankowitz 1966:59). Underglaze painted shell edge was most commonly available on pearl or white wares with blue or green edges. By around 1840, green shell edge had become rare, while blue shell edge remained a commonly available type listed in potters' and merchants' invoices into the 1860s. After that date, shell edge is not commonly found in archaeological assemblages, although production continued into the 1890s and possibly later (Miller 1989).

Edged wares are generally limited to flat wares, sauce boats, tureens, and butter boats, which as a general class are known as tablewares. From the index values presented in this study, it can be seen that edged wares were the cheapest decorated tableware available for most of the 19th century.

Sponge Decorated Wares

Spatter and sponge decorated wares are two closely related types under this classification. Spattered wares have the color powdered on, whereas sponged wares have their color applied with a sponge. Powdered decoration, which has been labeled "spatter" by collectors, has a long tradition, dating back to the delft wares from the 17th century (Shlasko 1989:39). Spattered decoration occurs on "China glaze," i.e., early pearlware from the late 1770s (Ferguson 1975:6). Most of the pre-1830s wares with this type of decoration are spattered (or powdered), and they often are found with simple painted birds which collectors have called peafowl (Godden 1966:160). These painted wares continued into the mid-19th century with the broader sponged decoration.

Sponged wares without painting are not common before the introduction into the Staffordshire potteries of cut sponges with simple patterns in the late 1840s (Turner 1923:149). Most of the early examples are tea wares. After the introduction of the cut sponge, this type of decoration became more common on table, tea, and toilet wares. CC price index values for sponged wares are only available for the period from 1848 to 1871. In the 1855 Fife pottery list, sponged wares were the same price as edged wares. For their period, sponged wares are usually the cheapest vessels available with decoration (Finlayson 1972:118).

Dipped Wares

Dipped—or dipt—wares cover various types of decoration that were produced by the application of a colored clay slip. Potters' terms for these types include: variegated, mocha, moco, common cable, chainband, banded, blue banded, French gray, brick, and checkered (Mountford 1975:20; Miller 1987:91). Collectors have added to this list terms such as annular, finger-painted, finger-trailed, tree, wave, worm, and cat's eye. The most common terms used in the potters' price lists, invoices, and account books are dipt, dipped, colored, mocha, and banded.

Dipped wares were slip decorated on the green ware before it was bisque fired. Most underglaze decoration was applied to bisque fired wares. Colors of dipped wares are generally muted earth tones such as tan, rust, brown, olive drab, ocher yellow, and gray. An exception is blue-banded ware which became the most common type of dipped ware after the 1840s.

These wares occupied a grouping by themselves that was commonly referred to as "Mugs and Jugs Ware." Dipped decoration was generally limited to bowls, mugs, jugs (the English term for pitchers), chamber pots, mustard pots, castors, or shakers. Dipped teas and teapots exist, but they are rare. Dipped wares were the cheapest holloware available with decoration. These wares were not finger-painted.

The term mocha should only be used to describe those dipped wares with the dendritic pattern (Evans 1970[1846]:31). Mocha was most popular from the period 1795 to 1835 on American sites; however, mocha mugs continued to be produced in England for tavern use until the 1930s. Mocha was also developed on yellowware and was common throughout the second half of the 19th century. Index values for yellowware have not yet been worked out.

With the exception of simple banded types,

dipped wares are not common after the 1840s. Blue-banded wares continued to be produced well into the 20th century.

Underglaze and Enamelled Lined Wares

Underglaze-lined and enamelled-upon-glaze-lined wares are types listed on Staffordshire potters' price fixing lists from 1814 to 1833. They have a simple line painted around the rim and the inner edge of the marley that can be either on or under the glaze. The Wedgwood catalog for 1774 lists green double lines, brown double lines, and blue lines as decorative types (Mankowitz 1966: 57; Finer and Savage 1965:116–118). These early versions of lined types would have been enamelled on the glaze.

Underglaze-lined and enamelled-upon-glaze wares are different from the other decorative types in that they often occur on creamware with brown lines. Most other types of underglaze decoration were on pearl or white wares. Lined wares were almost always limited to tableware and are rare in teaware. Creamware and pearlware plates with one or two lines around the rim and marley are common on British military sites that have been excavated by Parks Canada from the period of the War of 1812.

Band-and-Line Wares

Band-and-line wares became common during the last quarter of the 19th century and are usually associated with hotel wares. The band-and-line type is underglaze painted with the two lines usually right next to each other at the vessel's rim. Green was the most common color. Green band-and-line hotel wares remained a common institutional ware into the late 1950s when they began to be replaced by paper plates. One still occasionally finds these wares being used in small non-chain restaurants such as "Hank's Place" in Chadds Ford, Pennsylvania, as recently as December 1989. Band-and-line wares were available in tea and table wares.

Painted and Enamelled Wares

Enamelled means painted on top of the glaze. It is not necessary to refer to such wares as enamel painted wares. This type of decoration is most commonly associated with creamware and porcelain. However, it is also found on white salt-glazed stoneware, pearlware, whiteware, and the stone chinas. Because enamel painting was done after the pottery had been produced, the enameler did not have to be associated with the pottery that produced the ware and often worked independently (Prime 1929:128; Gottesman 1965:127).

Because enamel painting is fired at a lower temperature, a wider range of colors is available than is the case for underglaze colors which had to withstand the high temperature of the glazing oven. In addition to a greater color range, enamel painting produces a sharper image because the colors were not melted into the glaze. Underglaze painting has a slight blurring of the line due to the acidity of the glaze. The main disadvantage of enamelled decoration is that it was subject to being worn away by use. Enamelled wares were more expensive than underglaze painted wares because overglaze painting was added after the pottery was produced and required an additional firing.

By the late 1760s, a series of enamelled border patterns was being developed by Wedgwood (Mankowitz 1966:59–66). These patterns were copied and augmented by other potters. Many of those designs were later used as underglaze painted patterns. Enamelling was the most common type of decoration on creamware and did not begin to be superseded by underglaze painting until late in the 1780s (Miller 1987:90).

The term painted refers to underglaze decoration. Production of underglaze painted cream and pearl wares became more common after 1772, when the technology for the refining of cobalt for blue paints was introduced into Staffordshire (Shaw 1968[1829]:211). Staffordshire did not have much of a tradition of painting or enamelling prior to the development of creamware. The rapid rise of the popularity of creamware slowed the growth of the porcelain industry and destroyed the delft ware industry in England during the last quarter of the 18th century. Blue painters from both of these industries began to migrate to Staffordshire looking for employment in the late 1760s (Finer and Savage 1965:90).

Unlike the enamelers, the blue painters had to work within the factory structure because the painting was done prior to glazing. Widespread use of blue painting existed by 1775 when the potters developed "China Glaze" ware, which was a direct copy of Chinese porcelain in an earthenware. It contained kaolin clays from Cornwall and had a blue tinted glaze in imitation of Chinese porcelain. In addition to these elements, the wares were painted in a Chinese style to take the place of Chinese porcelain which was being eliminated from the English market by a tariff that by 1799 had reached over 100 percent (Haggar 1972:185). This ware was named "pearl white" by Josiah Wedgwood in 1779, and today it is generally known as pearlware (Miller 1987).

Blue painted wares in a Chinese style were the dominant painted ware from ca.1775 to around the War of 1812. The demand for wares painted in a Chinese style was somewhat stemmed by the introduction of underglaze transfer printing, introduced in Staffordshire around 1784. According to Shaw (1968[1829]:215), the "Blue Painters experienced such a diminution of employment and remuneration, that they employed every artifice to prevent" the development of underglaze printing. The blue painters working for Josiah Wedgwood were able to extract a promise from him not to produce blue printed ware (Shaw 1968[1829]: 123).

Around 1795, various other high temperature colors began to be introduced for underglaze painting (Noël Hume 1982:129). The new colors were brown, mustard yellow, and olive green. These colors remained common through the 1820s and are most commonly painted in floral motifs on tea wares.

In the 1820s, blue painted tea wares with floral motifs became popular, and on many sites they are more common than polychrome painted tea wares. Around the 1830s, a new color grouping came into use which included red, black, and some lighter shades of blue and green. These may be related to the introduction of chrome colors. It is at this time that painting again became more common on plates as well as teas. From the 1840s on, it is common to have painted wares in which part of the motif has been done with a cut sponge.

A series of style changes occurred in the floral painting, such as sprig painted wares, which became common after the late 1840s. Large painted floral polychrome motifs come back into popularity during the 1870s, and these often are found on table and tea ware. Flow-painted wares in blue and purple also appear from the 1840s through the 1870s and possibly later.

Gaudy Dutch and peasant painted ware are two 20th-century collectors' terms that have been applied to painted wares, but have no historical timedepth (Anne Wolfe 1989, pers. comm.; Laidacker 1938:82). There is no evidence of these terms having been used by the potters or merchants selling these wares. It would be better to refer to these wares simply as painted.

"Willow Ware"

Willow is a pattern rather than a ware. The term "willow ware" had close to universal usage in the potters' records. By 1814, willow had been set aside as the cheapest available transfer printed pattern in the potters' price fixing lists. It appears to remain in that position throughout the 19th century. Willow ware was made by many potters in England and other countries. Its production was, for the most part, limited to tableware until the second half of the 19th century, when tea wares begin to appear in the willow pattern.

Willow, according to many accounts, was the earliest underglaze printed pattern developed in Staffordshire. It is a composite of two or more Chinese porcelain patterns. A good history of the pattern can be found in Copeland's book on Spode's Willow Pattern. The pattern became standardized around 1790 and has been in production ever since (Copeland 1980:33–44). Shaw (1968[1829]:216) refers to an "Old Willow" with a "dagger boarder," which is probably the first underglaze transfer printed pattern developed in Staffordshire.

Brosley is another pattern that was copied from Chinese porcelain. Like willow, it was a generic pattern that was made by many potters. Brosley was almost always limited to tea wares (Shaw 1968[1829]:212–216).

Printed Wares

"Printed" is the most commonly used term in the potters' and merchant's records to refer to transfer printed wares. The first patent application for transfer printing was made in 1751 (Williams-Wood 1981:53). Large-scale printing of ceramics, however, did not begin until after Saddler and Green's patent for the process was taken out in 1756 in Liverpool (Williams-Wood 1981:103). All of this early printing was on top of the glaze.

Printing under the glaze was first used around 1760 on English porcelain, which was over 20 years before its first use on Staffordshire earthenware (Watney 1964: 52–53). Underglaze blue printing was introduced around 1783 into Staffordshire (Shaw 1968[1829]:214). Like the blue painted wares, the early blue printed earthenwares were also done in Chinese patterns which remained popular until around the War of 1812.

Early blue printed wares were line engraved and have cruder and heavier designs with minimal shading. Early in the 19th century, the engravers began to use stipples—small dots in the engraving—as a shading device which gave greater perspective to the prints. The earliest dated piece with stipple engraving is from 1807 (Coysh and Henrywood 1982:9). Around 1810, prints of English and foreign landscapes began to become more common on Staffordshire wares, as did American scenes following the War of 1812. These patterns began to be replaced by romantic views by the 1830s (Samford 1985).

Color is another area that can be helpful chronologically. Around 1818 there was an American craze for very dark blue printed wares (Stachiw 1988). The Staffordshire potters accommodated it by producing a series of dark blue prints, many of which were negative patterns—that is, the subjects of the views were left white while the background was filled with blue. Dark blue patterns were popular through the 1820s, which was also a period of popularity for blue painted floral patterns. Brown printed pearlwares were being imported into the American market as early as 1809 (Smith 1809).

Simeon Shaw's 1829 account stated that "very recently several . . . Manufacturers . . ." had introduced red, green, and brown transfer printed patterns (Shaw 1968[1829]:234–235). Potters' invoices from 1829 into the 1840s list quantities of red, green, brown, and purple printed wares. The printed wares from this period, however, are on white wares with minimal traces of blue in the glaze.

The last major change in printed wares came with the introduction of flowing colors in the 1840s. The earliest known advertisement for this ware in North America occurs in the *Montreal Gazette* for April 10, 1844, where it is described as "the new . . . FLOWING STONEWARE" (Collard 1967:118).

Transfer printed wares declined in popularity in the 1850s and were replaced by white granite ware (Miller 1990). The demand for printed wares picked up again in the early 1870s (Warburton 1931:155–156). Many patterns in a Japanese style were introduced in that period, and these were commonly printed in brown on an ivory tinted body. Kamm illustrates six different Japanese style patterns registered between 1877 and 1882 (Kamm 1970:75,76,87,91–93).

Stone Chinas

One of the most confusing terms used to describe the 19th-century ceramics is ironstone. The term ironstone comes from "Mason's Patent Ironstone China," patented in 1813 (Godden 1980:102). Several potters produced early stone chinas including: William Turner's Stone China, patented 1800 (Hillier 1965:22); John Davenport's Stone China, produced ca.1805–1820 (Godden 1980:221); Josiah Spode's Stone China, introduced ca.1814 (Godden 1980:248–249); and Hicks & Meigh, ca.1804–1822, also an early producer of stone china (Godden 1980:227).

These stone chinas were vitrified or semi-vitrified heavy, dense wares. Most of those produced prior to the 1830s were heavily decorated, commonly combining painting or enamelling with printing. Stone chinas were mostly copies of Chinese porcelains. Decoration for the early period was usually in a Chinese style, and the glaze was almost always tinted blue with cobalt as were the china glazed and pearl wares of that period.

There is strong evidence that the stone chinas were produced by potters such as Spode, Davenport, and Turner (Copeland 1980:97) to take the place of Chinese porcelain which the British East India Company stopped importing in 1791 (Godden 1980:22–25). In 1799, a customs duty of over 100 percent was placed on the importation of Chinese porcelain in England (Godden 1980:29). Miles Mason was a London Chinaman, a merchant who dealt in Chinese porcelain imported by the British East India Company. When the source of that porcelain was closed off, Mason purchased a pottery in Staffordshire and began trying to make porcelain (Godden 1980:17–32). That attempt was not as successful as a subsequent product, Mason's "Patent Ironstone China."

White Granite Wares

"White granite" and ironstone are the most common names applied to a group of hard white wares which were often vitrified or semi-vitrified. These wares evolved out of Mason's Ironstone and the stone chinas, discussed above, and are still evolving today. White granite has been selected as the term for their classification because it avoids the confusion of these plain white wares with the highly decorated stone chinas or early ironstone.

Invoices for earthenware shipped to Philadelphia show that white granite was being imported in the United States by the 1840s. Terms used in these documents include "White Glaze" (Ridgway 1844, 1846) and "White Granite" (Heath 1848). After the 1850s, the term white granite, or "W.G.," becomes very common in invoices for wares sent to America. From the invoices and price lists examined for this study, it is clear that white granite became the dominant type in use from the 1850s until the end of the 19th century.

Gold-Banded Earthenware

Gold gilding on porcelain was perfected at Meissen ca.1723 (Hunt 1979:118). The early process involved grinding the gold by hand in mediums like honey, then applying the gilding on top of the glaze. In addition, the gold had to be burnished after firing. Because gilding was expensive, its use was mostly associated with porcelain and finely enamelled earthenware. The process was to change in the 19th century with the development of "liquid bright gold" in Germany in 1836 (Hunt 1979:124). In this process, the gold was dissolved by acids and mixed with chemicals which produced a gold that could be fired with enamel colors and would come out of the muffle kiln bright and shiny without having to be burnished (Hunt 1979: 124).

Wenger Company, a pottery supply company, introduced liquid gold gilding into the Staffordshire potteries by 1870 (Wenger 1893). After that date, bright gilding began to be more commonly found on cheap earthenwares such as the gold-banded plates listed in Appendix A. Use of cheap gilding increased on common wares by the late 19th century and continues today.

Basalt Ware

Basalt is Wedgwood's name for what other potters called "Egyptian Black." It is a dense, fine-grained stoneware that has been dyed black with cobalt and manganese (Savage and Newman 1976: 44–45). These wares were usually unglazed; however, there is a glazed variety which was referred to as "Shining Black" (Shaw 1968[1829]:209).

Basalts are most commonly found in teapots, creamers, sugars, and bowls for tea slops. They were also used for decorative wares such as vases and busts, but these rarely show up in archaeological collections. The CC index values for basalt wares presented in this paper are from bowls associated with teawares in the Staffordshire potters' price fixing lists.

Black-dyed stonewares were produced as early as the 1690s by the Elers brothers in Staffordshire (Shaw 1968[1829]:118). Wedgwood perfected his version of Egyptian Black in 1768, which he renamed Basalt (Savage and Newman 1976:44). The other potters continued to call it Egyptian Black, which is the name used in the Staffordshire price fixing lists of 1795, 1796, 1814, and 1846 (in Mountford 1975:9–14; Miller 1984:42–43).

English Porcelains

Beginning in the 1740s, various soft paste porcelains were developed in England. These were attempts to discover the secret of how to produce Chinese porcelain, which was a hard paste made with kaolin and petuntse. Different soft paste formulas were developed. Then, in 1768, William Cookworthy produced the first English true hard paste porcelain using kaolin and petuntse from Cornwall (Watney 1964:116–119). However, the growth of the English porcelain industry was checked by the success of Josiah Wedgwood's creamware.

Most of the porcelain types developed in the 18th century were replaced by bone china which was introduced by Josiah Spode around 1794 (Savage and Newman 1976:51). Bone china became the dominant type produced in England by the early 19th century and holds that position today. Even the Worcester porcelain factory, which had a very successful soapstone porcelain, made the switch to bone china in the 1830s (Sandon 1978:189). Bone china had a couple of advantages over hard paste porcelain, including a lower firing temperature which means it can be decorated with a wider color range. In addition, it is a very translucent white porcelain. One of its disadvantages for consumers is that it will stain if the glaze is crazed.

English porcelains are relatively rare in invoices of wares sent to America and in American archaeological assemblages prior to the second half of the 19th century. Therefore, this section of CC index values is very limited, and the descriptions from the invoices are minimal. The porcelains indexed here are most likely bone china which was the dominant type for the period.

Discussion

The following appendices provide an expanded and updated set of index values for platters, plates, twifflers, muffins, London size teas, Irish size teas, and bowls. They are meant to replace the previously published index values (Miller 1980). The tables are organized chronologically by vessel form. The forms and their size ranges are described at the beginning of each appendix.

Appendix A: Flatware

The late 18th- and 19th-century Staffordshire potters' price fixing lists consistently use the following terms to describe the most common types of flatware:

Dish	10–20-inch platters (commonly oval or oblong-hexagonal in shape)
Table plate	10-inch plates
Supper plate	9-inch plates
Twifflers	8-inch plates
Muffins	3–7-inch plates

All of the above vessels are generally larger than their stated sizes. One of the ways in which the potters got around the price fixing agreements was to provide their customers with slightly larger sized vessels for the cost of smaller ones. For example, a potter might sell 9.75-inch plates as "Suppers" which, by the price list for 1796 (in Mountford 1975:11), should only have been 9 inches in diameter.

CC INDEX VALUES FOR SHELL EDGE WARES

		Dishes		Plates	Twifflers		Muffins	
	14	12	10	10–9	8	7	6	5
1787	1.5	2.0	2.0	1.67	2.0	2.11		
1793				1.35				
1796	1.67	1.5	1.5	1.33	1.28	1.33	1.41	
1802	1.6	1.58	1.67	1.38	1.23	1.4		
1804	1.5	1.25	1.25	1.33	1.5	1.51	1.49	
1814	1.64	1.57	1.2	1.33	1.28	1.33	1.41	1.24
1816	1.64	1.57	1.2	1.43	1.32	1.28	1.33	1.41
1821	1.64	1.57	1.2	1.33	1.28	1.33	1.49	1.24
1823	1.64	1.43	1.2	1.33	1.28	1.4	1.41	1.49
1825	1.64	1.57	1.2	1.33	1.28	1.33	1.41	1.5
1833	1.64	1.57	1.64	1.33	1.43	1.33	1.4	1.5
1836				1.33	1.25	1.38	1.45	1.25
1838	1.64	1.57	1.2	1.33	1.29	1.33	1.4	1.25
1846	1.64	1.57	1.2	1.14	1.13	1.14	1.17	1.2
1848		1.57	1.2	1.33	1.28	1.33	1.41	
1853	1.64	1.57	1.2	1.12	1.11	1.13	1.16	1.2
1859	1.13	1.05	1.09	1.09	1.05	1.06	1.07	1.09
1866	1.13	1.1	1.08	1.12	1.11	1.13	1.15	1.2
1869	1.13	1.1	1.08	1.14	1.11	1.13	1.15	1.2
1870	1.1	1.08	1.13	1.07	1.08	1.1	1.09	1.12
1871	1.13	1.1	1.08	1.08	1.11	1.12	1.25	1.3
1874				1.09	1.10	1.11	1.14	1.18
1880				1.09	1.1	1.12	1.14	1.18

UNDERGLAZE LINED WARES

		Dishes		Plates	Twifflers		Muffins	
	14	12	10	10–9	8	7	6	5
1814	2.18	2.0	1.6	1.67	1.71	1.68	1.81	2.0
1816	2.18	2.0	1.6	1.43	1.5	1.43	1.5	1.6
1823	2.18	2.0	1.6	1.67	1.71	1.8	1.81	1.99
1825	1.82	1.71	1.4	1.5	1.5	1.5	1.61	1.75
1833	2.18	2.0	1.6	1.67	1.71	1.67	1.8	2.0

BAND-AND-LINE WARES

		Dishes		Plates	Twifflers		Muffins	
	14	12	10	10–9	8	7	6	5
1873	1.27	1.43	1.2	1.2	1.29	1.22	1.32	1.2
1886	1.22	1.33	1.13	1.13	1.17	1.2	1.25	1.18

ENAMELLED-UPON-GLAZE LINED WARES

		Dishes		Plates	Twifflers		Muffins	
	14	12	10	10–9	8	7	6	5
1814	2.73	2.68	2.4	2.33	2.35	2.5	2.41	1.99
1816	2.6	2.67	2.86	2.22	2.0	1.83	1.69	1.5

PAINTED WARES

		Dishes		Plates	Twifflers		Muffins	
	14	12	10	10–9	8	7	6	5
1787				1.5	1.67			
1822							2.1	2.25
1838				2.17	2.36	2.25	2.1	2.25
1853	2.73	3.0	2.4	1.68	1.67	1.63	1.62	1.8
1854							1.56	1.5
1859	1.88	2.0	2.18	1.64	1.58	1.53	1.5	1.64
1866	1.88	2.1	2.0	1.75	1.67	1.62	1.62	1.8
1869	1.88	2.1	2.0	1.71	1.67	1.62	1.62	1.8
1871	1.88	2.1	2.0	1.57	1.5	1.45	1.5	1.64

ENAMELLED WARES

		Dishes		Plates	Twifflers		Muffins	
	14	12	10	10–9	8	7	6	5
1804	3.0	3.0	3.0	3.67	4.0	3.61	2.99	
1814	5.45	6.0	4.8	4.67	5.13	5.0	4.82	5.22
1833	3.27	3.57	3.0	2.33	2.57	2.5	2.7	2.62

SPONGED WARES

		Dishes		Plates	Twifflers		Muffins	
	14	12	10	10–9	8	7	6	5
1855	1.22	1.33	1.25	1.2	1.25	1.2	1.25	1.33
1871					1.5	1.45		1.5

CHILDREN'S ABC AND MOTTO PLATES—PAINTED

		Dishes		Plates	Twifflers		Muffins	
	14	12	10	10–9	8	7	6	5
1845						1.71	1.67	1.8
1868							1.16	1.3
1874								1.74

CHILDREN'S ABC AND MOTTO PLATES—PRINTED AND COLORED

		Dishes		Plates	Twifflers		Muffins	
	14	12	10	10–9	8	7	6	5
1871							6.94	8.12

WILLOW WARE

		Dishes		Plates	Twifflers		Muffins	
	14	12	10	10–9	8	7	6	5
1793				4.0	5.0			
1814	3.82	4.29	3.6	2.67	3.0	3.0	3.01	2.99
1823	3.82	4.29	3.6	2.67	3.0	3.0	3.01	2.99
1825	3.82	4.29	3.6	3.00	3.21	3.25	3.49	3.37
1836				2.5	2.44	2.77	2.73	
1854	1.4	1.38	1.5	1.62	1.5	1.5	1.33	1.38
1855	1.44	1.5	1.5	1.6	1.5	1.8	1.5	1.67
1870	1.25	1.32	1.38	1.52	1.33	1.4	1.22	1.25

PRINTED WARES

	Dishes			Plates	Twifflers		Muffins	
	14	12	10	10–9	8	7	8	5
1796	6.0	5.25	7.5	4.33	3.93	4.0	4.22	
1814	5.45	6.0	4.8	3.33	3.42	3.5	3.61	3.73
1816	5.45	5.14	4.8	2.86	3.0	3.0	3.0	3.01
1823	5.45	6.0	4.8	3.33	3.41	3.5	3.61	3.73
1825	4.91	5.14	4.0	3.00	3.21	3.25	3.49	3.37
1833	3.82	4.29	3.6	2.67	3.0	3.0	3.0	3.0
1836				3.0	2.81	3.0	3.0	
1838	3.82	4.29	3.6	2.67	3.0	3.0	3.0	3.0
1844				2.11	2.44			
1845	3.82	4.29	3.6	2.67	3.0	3.0	3.0	3.0
1846	3.52	3.96	3.32	2.11	2.42	2.37	2.31	2.22
1848	3.47	3.9	3.27	2.42	2.72	2.73	2.74	2.72
1854	2.2	2.46	2.3	1.86	1.75	1.8	1.67	1.62
1855	2.22	2.67	2.25	1.6	1.5	1.8	1.5	1.67

DARK BLUE PRINTED WARES

	Dishes			Plates	Twifflers		Muffins	
	14	12	10	10–9	8	7	8	5
1846	3.82	4.29	3.6	2.29	2.63	2.57	2.5	2.4

FLOW PRINTED WARES

	Dishes			Plates	Twifflers		Muffins	
	14	12	10	10–9	8	7	6	5
1846	4.41	4.95	4.15	2.64	3.03	2.97	2.88	2.77
1848	4.14	4.64	3.9		3.25	3.25		3.25
1855	3.11	3.33	2.75	2.4	2.5	2.4	2.25	2.5

DECORATED STONE CHINA WARES

	Dishes			Plates	Twifflers		Muffins	
	14	12	10	10–9	8	7	6	5
1833		"JAPAN PATTERN"		3.33	3.43	3.5		

WHITE GRANITE WARES

	Dishes			Plates	Twifflers		Muffins	
	14	12	10	10–9	8	7	6	5
1846	3.23	3.63	3.05	1.93	2.22	2.18	2.12	2.03
1858	3.27	3.63	3.09		2.0	1.93	1.98	
1868						1.93	2.06	2.06
1871	2.25	2.57	2.57		2.07	2.0	2.09	2.20
1874	1.93	2.2	2.21		1.66	1.59	1.73	1.81
1880	1.84	2.11	2.11		1.57	1.53	1.67	1.73

GOLD-BANDED EARTHENWARE

	Dishes			Plates	Twifflers		Muffins	
	14	12	10	10–9	8	7	6	5
1871		3.57	3.57		2.98	2.9	3.06	3.24

ENGLISH PORCELAINS

			Dishes		Plates	Twifflers		Muffins	
		14	12	10	10–9	8	7	6	5
1836	White							7.14	
1838	Enamelled							7.0	
1871	White						4.0	3.92	3.4
1871	Gold-Banded								5.06
1871	Sprig								5.54

Appendix B: Teas, London Size

Teas, the potters' terms for cups and saucers, are more complex than tablewares because of available options, different shapes, and the size system. Two sizes were commonly referred to in the price fixing lists and potters' invoices. "London" size was the most common and the smaller of the two. "Irish," the larger size, was sometimes referred to as "Breakfast" size. The great majority of the cups recovered from American sites are of the London size. In addition to London and Irish size teas, there were also bowls and saucers which are a size larger than Irish size. These are rarely reported in archaeological assemblages, perhaps because they have not been recognized. Evidence of this combination would be confirmed by a matching bowl and saucer.

The term London size is further complicated by the fact that the most common cup shape for the period from 1810 to 1840 has been labeled "London Shape," which is the name that the Spode factory gave to this shape. London shape cups look like an inverted truncated cone with a steeply angled shoulder just above a high standing foot ring. Other potters appear to have called this shape "Grecian," which is what an illustration of this shape is labeled in the Wedgwood catalogue of 1880 (des Fontaines 1971:28). London or Grecian shape occurs in all sizes of cups as well as bowls.

Some of the options that were available with teas included handles, color-lined rims, fluted shapes, and scalloped rims. These options all involved an additional cost which, on the potters' price fixing lists, commonly added a shilling per dozen to the teas. This resulted in a greater range of prices for teas for most of the period under consideration. For example, taking all of the combinations of these options in the 1796 price fixing list, there were 18 options which are listed below:

TEAS

	Unhandled			Handled		
		Fluted			Fluted	
	Simple	or edged	& edged	Simple	or edged	& edged
CC	1.0	1.8	2.6	1.8	2.6	3.4
Painted	1.8	2.6	3.4	2.6	3.4	4.2
Printed	3.4	4.2	5.0	4.2	5.0	5.8

One can see that a set of handled, fluted or edged CC teas would cost as much as a simple printed set of teas. However, edged, fluted, and handled teas are not very common in American archaeological assemblages.

The following descriptions apply to the forms indexed in the appendices.

Handled The great majority of cups were unhandled until the second half of the 19th century. A New York merchant writing to his Liverpool agents in 1816 stated that "Handled cups & saucers will Never never sell in our Market there can not be a worse article" (Ogden 1816). The above range of index values provides a possible clue as to why handled cups may have remained unpopular. For the price of CC teas with handles, one could have painted teas without handles. A set of fluted painted teas with handles could have cost more than a set of simple printed teas. In other words, the consumer may have chosen to have a more highly decorated set of teas without handles rather than a simpler handled set for the same amount of money.

Brown Edged Brown Edged or "Topped" teas have an enamelled or painted brown line on the top of the rim of the cups and saucers, in imitation of the brown iron rim line on Chinese porcelain. Edged teas are listed in the Staffordshire potters' price fixing lists for 1795, 1796, 1808, and 1825 (1795, 1796 in Mountford 1975:9–11; Staffordshire Potters 1808, 1825). Occasionally the rim was lined with blue. Lined teas seem to have been most popular from the 1790s to around the War of 1812.

Fluted These teas have molded fluting, usually spiraled, up the outside surface of the cups and on the inside surface of the saucers. Fluted teas are listed in the Staffordshire potters' price fixing lists for 1796, 1808, 1814, 1846, 1853, and 1859 (1796, 1846 in Mountford 1975; 1814 in Miller 1984; Staffordshire Potters 1808, 1853, 1859). They seem to be most popular from the 1790s to the 1820s.

Scalloped Scalloped teas appear to be a good time marker, as they appeared for a short period from the mid-1820s through the 1830s (Staffordshire Potters 1825). These teas have a slight rim scallop.

Extra Thick These teas were hotel wares meant for use in institutions such as hotels, restaurants, hospitals, and schools.

Pressed Most teas were wheel thrown until the Jolly came into use in the potteries after 1863 (Lamb 1977:6). The Jolly was an automatic throwing device that used a plaster mold to shape the cups with the aid of a template mounted on the wheel to form the inside profile of the cup. Teas could be pressed, a slower process than throwing. In 1859, pressed teas were the same price as fluted teas (Staffordshire Potters 1859:2). These are listed as "pressed shapes" and appear to refer to eight-, 10-, and 12-sided teas which make their appearance in the 1850s.

CC TEAS—LONDON SIZE

	Unhandled			Handled		
	Simple	Fluted or Edged	Fluted & Edged	Simple	Fluted or Edged	Fluted & Edged
1796	1.0	1.8	2.6	1.8	2.6	3.4
		Fluted			Fluted	
1804	1.0			1.28		
1814	1.0	1.67		1.67	2.33	
18.16	1.0	1.5		1.5	2.0	
1823	1.0	1.67		1.67	2.33	
		Scalloped			Scalloped	
1825	1.0		1.17	1.67		1.83
1833	1.0			1.57		
1836	1.0			1.67		
1838	1.0			1.67		
1845	1.0			1.67		
1846	1.0			1.55		

CC TEAS—LONDON SIZE (continued)

	Unhandled			Handled		
	Simple	Fluted or Edged	Fluted & Edged	Simple	Fluted or Edged	Fluted & Edged
1848	1.0			1.67		
1853	1.0			1.55		
		Fluted or Pressed	Extra Thick		Fluted or Pressed	Extra Thick
1859	1.0	1.63	2.0	1.5	2.13	2.5
1866	1.0		2.0	1.5		2.5
1871	1.0		1.92	1.38		2.31

PAINTED TEAS—LONDON SIZE

	Unhandled			Handled		
	Simple	Fluted or Edged	Fluted & Edged	Simple	Fluted or Edged	Fluted & Edged
1787	2.5					
1796	1.8	2.6	3.4	2.6	3.4	4.2
		Fluted			Fluted	
1802	1.6					
1804	1.71			2.14		
1814	1.5	2.17		2.17	2.83	
1816	1.25	1.75		1.75	2.25	
1823	1.5	2.17		2.17	2.83	
			Scalloped			Scalloped
1825	1.5		1.67	2.17		2.33
1833	1.43			2.0		
1836	1.5					
1838	1.5					
1845	1.5					
1846	1.23			1.77		
1848	1.5					
1853	1.23			1.77		
		Fluted or Pressed	Extra Thick		Fluted or Pressed	Extra Thick
1859	1.13	2.0	2.13	1.63	2.5	2.63
1866	1.17		2.17	1.67		2.67
1868	1.16					
1869	1.17					
1871	1.15		2.08	1.54		2.46

ENAMELLED TEAS—LONDON SIZE

	Unhandled		Handled	
	Simple	Fluted or Edged	Simple	Fluted or Edged
1814	3.0	3.67	3.67	4.33
1823	3.0	3.67	3.67	4.33
1833	2.0		2.57	

DIPT TEAS—LONDON SIZE

	Unhandled		Handled	
	Simple	Scalloped	Simple	Scalloped
1825	1.5	1.67	2.17	2.33

SPONGED TEAS—LONDON SIZE

	Unhandled	Handled
	Simple	Simple
1848	1.5	2.17
1858	1.5	2.17
1871	1.16	

BAND-AND-LINE TEAS—LONDON SIZE

	Unhandled	Handled
	Simple	Simple
1873	1.22	1.45
1886		1.18

PRINTED TEAS—LONDON SIZE

	Unhandled			Handled		
	Simple	Fluted or Edged	Fluted & Edged	Simple	Fluted or Edged	Fluted & Edged
1795	4.09	5.18	6.27	5.18	6.27	7.36
1796	3.4	4.2	5.0	4.2	5.0	5.8
		Fluted			Fluted	
1799	5.36	5.95				
1804	3.42	4.29	5.14			
1814	3.0	3.67		3.67	4.33	
1816	2.25	2.75		2.75	3.25	
1823	3.0	3.67		3.67	4.33	
			Scalloped			Scalloped
1825	3.0		3.17	3.67		3.83
1833	2.57			3.14		
1836	3.0					
1838	3.0					
1845	3.0			4.0		
1846	2.27	2.52		2.77	3.02	
1848	2.89					

DARK BLUE PRINTED TEAS—LONDON SIZE

	Unhandled		Handled	
	Simple	Fluted	Simple	Fluted
1834	3.0			
1846	2.45	3.15	2.73	3.27

FLOW PRINTED TEAS—LONDON SIZE

	Unhandled		Handled	
	Simple	Fluted	Simple	Fluted
1846	2.83	3.15	3.46	3.78
1848		3.25		

WHITE GRANITE TEAS—LONDON SIZE

	Unhandled		Handled	
	Simple	Fluted	Simple	Fluted
1846	2.08	2.31	2.54	2.77
1868	2.15			
1871	2.04		2.45	
1874	1.71		2.05	
1875	2.0		2.75	
1880	1.69		1.95	

ENGLISH PORCELAIN TEAS—LONDON SIZE

	Unhandled	Handled	
1823		14.5	Gilded
1835	4.44		Decorated
1836	3.70	4.20	Decorated
1871	2.20	3.01	White

Appendix C: Teas, Irish Size

Irish size teas have been discussed above. Their index values are given here.

CC TEAS—IRISH SIZE

	Unhandled			Handled		
	Simple	Fluted or Edged	Fluted & Edged	Simple	Fluted or Edged	Fluted & Edged
1796	1.0	1.67	2.6	1.67	2.33	3.4
		Fluted			Fluted	
1814	1.0	1.5		1.5	2.0	
1816	1.0	1.4		1.4	1.8	
1823	1.0	1.5		1.5	2.0	
			Scalloped		Scalloped	
1825	1.0		1.13	1.5		1.65
1833	1.0			1.5		
1846	1.0			1.43		
1853	1.0			1.43		
		Fluted or Pressed	Extra Thick		Fluted or Pressed	Extra Thick
1859	1.0	1.42	1.67	1.33	1.75	2.0
1866	1.0		1.73	1.36		2.09
1871	1.0		1.73	1.36		2.09

PAINTED TEAS—IRISH SIZE

	Unhandled			Handled		
	Simple	Fluted or Edged	Fluted & Edged	Simple	Fluted or Edged	Fluted & Edged
1787	2.4					
1796	1.83	2.5	3.17	2.5	3.17	3.83
		Fluted			Fluted	
1814	1.38	1.88		1.88	2.38	
1816	1.2	1.6		1.6	2.0	
1823	1.38	1.88		1.88	2.38	
			Scalloped			Scalloped
1825	1.38		1.5	1.88	2.0	
1833	1.5			2.0		
1846	1.18			1.61		
1853	1.29			1.71		
		Fluted or Pressed	Extra Thick		Fluted or Pressed	Extra Thick
1859	1.17	1.67	1.83	1.5	2.0	2.17
1866	1.27		2.0	1.64		2.36
1869	1.27					
1871	1.27		2.0	1.64		2.36

ENAMELLED TEAS—IRISH SIZE

	Unhandled		Handled	
	Simple	Fluted	Simple	Fluted
1814	3.0	3.67	3.67	4.33
1823	3.0	3.67	3.67	4.33
1833	2.25		2.75	

BAND-AND-LINE TEAS—IRISH SIZE

	Unhandled	Handled
1886		1.07

PRINTED TEAS—IRISH SIZE

	Unhandled			Handled		
	Simple	Fluted or Edged	Fluted & Edged	Simple	Fluted or Edged	Fluted & Edged
1795	4.07	4.93	5.79	4.93	5.79	6.64
1796	3.5	4.17	4.83	4.17	4.83	5.5
		Fluted			Fluted	
1814	2.75	3.25		3.25	3.75	
1816	2.2	2.6		2.6	3.0	
1823	2.75	3.25		3.25	3.75	
			Scalloped			Scalloped
1825	2.75		2.88	3.25		3.38
1833	2.75			3.25		
1846	2.18	2.37		2.57	2.77	

DARK BLUE PRINTED TEAS—IRISH SIZE

	Unhandled	Handled
1846	2.36	2.79

FLOW PRINTED TEAS—IRISH SIZE

	Unhandled		Handled	
	Simple	Fluted	Simple	Fluted
1846	2.72	2.97	3.21	3.46

WHITE GRANITE TEAS—IRISH SIZE

	Unhandled		Handled	
	Simple	Fluted	Simple	Fluted
1846	1.99	2.18	2.36	2.54

Appendix D: Bowls

Bowls' sizes were ranked by the potters' dozen. The potters' dozen began as a unit of pay for throwers and other workers. After a vessel was thrown, it was placed on a 6-ft. drying board. A board full of wares of a single size counted as a dozen. Thus, a dozen bowls could range from four one-gallon punch bowls to 30 half pint bowls (Copeland 1983). The former would be called 4s while the latter would be called 30s. Bowls were available in the following sizes: 3s, 4s, 6s, 12s, 18s, 24s, 30s, 36s, 42s, and 48s. The potters attempted to stabilize the capacities assigned to these various sizes, but they got larger as various potters attempted to get around the price fixing lists by selling bigger bowls under smaller potters' dozen sizes. A 1796 potters' agreement (in Mountford 1975:11) set the following sizes:

BOWLS AND WASH BASINS

Size	Maximum volume
3s	6 pints
4s	4 pints
6s	3 pints
12s	1 1/2 pints
24s	3/4 pints
30s	1/2 pints

Sometimes the size number was impressed in the bottom of hollowares. The following summary, for example, gives prices per dozen bowls from the 1814 Staffordshire potters' price fixing list, reprinted in Miller (1984:42–43), and the cost per individual bowl:

COST, IN PENCE, FOR BOWLS

		Individual bowl prices			
	Price per potters' dozen	6s	12s	24s	30s
CC	30d	5.0@	2.5@	1.25@	1.0@
Dipt	36d	6.0	3.0	1.5	1.2
Painted	48d	8.0	4.0	2.0	1.6
Printed	84d	14.0	7.0	3.5	2.8

Thus, a potters' dozen of bowls purchased in 1814 could range from 6 to 30 bowls depending on the size ordered. The price per potters' dozen would be the same with adjustments made for the size by varying the quantity of bowls included, rather than by changing the price for each size category.

CC INDEX VALUES FOR BOWLS

	Dipt	Painted	Sponged	Enamelled	Flow Painted	Printed	Dark Blue	Flow Printed	White Granite	Basalt	"White China" Porcelain
1787		3.75 (sortable)									
1795						4.32 (Sortable)					
1799	1.6	2.0									
1802		2.33									
1804		2.0				3.14					
1814	1.2	1.6				2.8				6.0	
1821	1.2	1.6				2.8					
1822	1.2	1.6		2.8		2.8					
1823	1.2	1.6				2.8				6.0	
1825	1.2	1.6				2.6					
1832	1.2	1.6									
1833	1.2	1.6		2.4		2.8					
1836	1.2	1.8				3.0					
1838	1.2					2.8					
1842	1.22					3.0					
1846	1.2	1.6				2.58	2.8	3.25	2.37	6.0	
1848	1.2					2.91		3.03			
1853		1.64									
1854	1.14					2.0		2.29			
1855			1.11			2.0		2.4			
1858									2.49		
1859	1.08	1.38									
1866	1.17	1.5									
1868									2.29		
1869	1.17	1.17									
1870	1.13	1.38		3.5	1.5	2.0		2.25	2.25		
1871	1.16	1.5							2.42		2.54
1873	1.11	1.33			1.67						
1874									2.46		
1877	1.08	1.33									
1880									2.34		
1886	1.08										

ACKNOWLEDGMENTS

The generation of this expanded set of index values was made possible by funding from a fellowship and two grants. I would like to thank the Winterthur Museum for awarding me a NEH/Winterthur Fellowship in 1979. I would also like to thank Pat and Barbara Garrow of Garrow and Associates for a grant in 1985 to work on the 1814 Staffordshire potters' price list. In 1986, Ann Smart Martin, Nancy Dickinson, and I received a two-year grant from the National Endowment for the Humanities for our project "English Ceramics in America, 1760–1860: Marketing, Prices, and Availability" (NEH Grant RO-21158-86). Working as a team, we were able to cover a very broad range of documents from many areas. I also thank my boss, Marley Brown, for his support during this project. I would like to thank Colonial Williamsburg for providing the matching funds for this project.

I would like to thank the following institutions for generous access to their archives and records: in

England, Josiah Wedgwood and Sons; Keele University Library; the Stoke-on-Trent City Museum and Art Gallery; the Spode Company Archives; the Minton Company; the Horace Barks Reference Library in Hanley; and the Stafford County Record Office; on this side of the Atlantic, Winterthur Museum; New York Historical Society; Massachusetts Historical Society; Maryland Historical Society; Virginia State Archives; Smithsonian Institution; Colonial Williamsburg Foundation Library; National Archives, Washington, D.C.; Canadian National Archives, Ottawa; Hagley Museum, Wilmington; Pennsylvania Historical Society; Kress Library of Business and Economics of Harvard University; and University of Delaware Library.

My research in England was greatly facilitated by Robert Copeland and Helen Dent. Others in England to whom I owe special thanks include: Martin Phillips, Pat Halfpenny, Gaye Blake Roberts, Una and John des Fontaines, Eileen and Rodney Hampson, David Barker, David Furniss, Christine Fyfe, Margaret Morris, John Smith, Arnold Mountford, and Terry Lockett. On this side of the Atlantic, I thank Susan Myers, Reggie Blaszczyk, Lynne Sussman, Elizabeth Collard, Arlene Palmer Schwind, Mary Beaudry, Georgeanna Greer, Barbara Teller, Rob Hunter, Silas Hurry, Henry Miller, Kate Hutchins, Neville Thompson, Rich McKinstry, Beatrice Taylor, Karen Stuart, Bill Adams, Steve Pendery, Myron Stachiw, Ellen Shlasko, Sarah Peabody Turnbaugh, Suzanne Spencer-Wood, and John L. Seidel.

Many people were more than generous with help in the form of suggestions, sending copies of price lists, invoices, and other records. Because this research has been going on for over a decade, it is difficult to remember everyone who provided help and information. I apologize to anyone I may have left off the list of acknowledgments.

REFERENCES

Adams, William H., and Sarah Jane Boling
1989 Status and Ceramics for Planters and Slaves on Three Georgia Coastal Plantations. *Historical Archaeology* 23(1):69–96.

Binns, Charles F.
1907 *The Manual of Practical Potting.* Scott, Greenwood and Son, London.

Cole, Arthur H.
1969 *Wholesale Commodity Prices in the United States, 1700–1861.* Johnson Reprint Corporation, New York.

Collard, Elizabeth
1967 *Nineteenth-Century Pottery and Porcelain in Canada.* McGill University Press, Montreal.

Copeland, Robert
1980 *Spode's Willow Pattern and Other Designs after the Chinese.* Rizzoli International Publications, Inc., New York.
1983 Pottery Trade Sizes. Ms., on file with the author.

Coysh, A. W., and R. K. Henrywood
1982 *The Dictionary of Blue and White Printed Pottery, 1780–1880.* Antique Collectors' Club, Woodbridge, England.

Evans, William
1970 Art and History of the Potting Business, Compiled from the Most Practical Sources, for the Especial Use of Working Potters. Reprint of 1846 edition. *Journal of Ceramic History* 3:21–43.

Ferguson, Leland G.
1975 Analysis of Ceramic Materials from Fort Watson, December 1780–April 1781. *Conference on Historic Site Archaeology Papers, 1973* 8:2–28.

Finer, Ann, and George Savage (editors)
1965 *The Selected Letters of Josiah Wedgwood.* Cory, Adams and Mackay Ltd., London.

Finlayson, R. W.
1972 *Portneuf Pottery.* Longman Canada Limited, Don Mills, Ontario.

des Fontaines, John K.
1971 *The Wedgwood 1880 Illustrated Catalogue of Shapes.* The Wedgwood Society, London.

Godden, Geoffrey A.
1966 *An Illustrated Encyclopedia of British Pottery and Porcelain.* Crown Publishers, New York.
1980 *Godden's Guide to Mason's China and the Ironstone Wares.* The Antique Collectors' Club Ltd., Woodbridge, England.

Gottesman, Rita S. (compiler)
1965 *The Arts and Crafts in New York, 1800–1804: Advertisements and News Items from New York City Newspapers.* New York Historical Society, New York.

Haggar, Reginald
1972 Miles Mason. *English Ceramic Circle* 2:183–199.

Heath, Joseph
1848 Invoice for Earthenware Sold by Joseph Heath, Manufacturer of Earthenware, Tunstall, to P. A. Rovendt of Philadelphia, 12/9/1848. Customs House Collection, University of Delaware Library, Newark.

Hillier, Bevis
1965 *Master Potters of the Industrial Revolution: The Turners of Lane End.* Cory, Adams and Mackay Ltd., London.

Hunt, L. B.
1979 Gold in the Pottery Industry. *Gold Bulletin* 13(3): 116–127.

KAMM, MINNIE WATSON
1970 *Old China*. Kamm Publications, Grosse Pointe, Michigan.

LAIDACKER, SAM (EDITOR)
1938 *The Standard Catalogue of Anglo-American China from 1810 to 1850*. Sam Laidacker, Scranton, Pennsylvania.

LAMB, ANDREW
1977 The Press and Labour's Response to Pottery-making Machinery in the North Staffordshire Pottery Industry. *Journal of Ceramic History* 9:1–8.

MAJEWSKI, TERESITA, AND MICHAEL J. O'BRIEN
1987 The Use and Misuse of Nineteenth-Century English and American Ceramics in Archaeological Analysis. *Advances in Archaeological Method and Theory* 11: 97–209. Academic Press, New York.

MANKOWITZ, WOLF
1966 *Wedgwood*. Spring Books, London.

MILLER, GEORGE L.
1980 Classification and Economic Scaling of 19th-Century Ceramics. *Historical Archaeology* 14:1–40.
1984 George M. Coates, Pottery Merchant of Philadelphia, 1817–1831. *Winterthur Portfolio* 19:42–43.
1987 Origins of Josiah Wedgwood's Pearlware. *Northeast Historical Archaeology* 16:80–92.
1988 Prices and Index Values for English Ceramics from 1787 to 1860. Ms., on file with the author.
1989 *A Chronology of English Shell Edged Pearl and White Wares*. George L. Miller, Williamsburg, Virginia.
1990 The 'Market Basket' of Ceramics Available in Country Stores from 1790 to 1860. Paper Presented at the Annual Meeting of the Society for Historical Archaeology Conference on Historical and Underwater Archaeology, Tucson, Arizona.

MILLER, GEORGE L., AND ANN SMART MARTIN
1989 English Ceramics in America. In *Decorative Arts and Household Furnishings Used in America, 1650–1920: An Annotated Bibliography*, edited by Kenneth L. Ames and Gerald W. R. Ward, pp. 201–219. University Press of Virginia, Charlottesville.

MILLER, GEORGE L., ANN SMART MARTIN, AND NANCY S. DICKINSON
1989 Changing Consumption Patterns: English Ceramics and the American Market from 1770 to 1840. In *Everyday Life in the Early Republic 1789–1828*, edited by Catherine E. Hutchins. Twenty-ninth Winterthur Conference, Wilmington, Delaware, in press.

MOUNTFORD, ARNOLD R.
1975 Documents Relating to English Ceramics of the 18th and 19th Centuries. *Journal of Ceramic History* 8: 3–41.

NOËL HUME, IVOR
1982 *A Guide to the Artifacts of Colonial America*. Alfred A. Knopf, New York.

OGDEN, JONATHAN
1816 Letter to Bolton and Ogden in Liverpool, 9/12/1816. Letterbook of Jonathan Ogden. Ferguson, Day and Successor Company papers, New York Historical Society, New York.

PRIME, ALFRED COXE (COMPILER)
1929 *The Arts and Crafts in Philadelphia, Maryland, and South Carolina, 1721–1785*. The Walpole Society, Philadelphia.

RIDGWAY, JOHN
1844 Invoice for Earthenware Sold by John Ridgway & Company, Manufacturer of Earthenware, Cauldon Place, to J. Y. Rushton of Philadelphia, 12/28/1844. Collection of Business Americana, National Museum of American History, Smithsonian Institution, Washington, D.C.
1846 Invoice for Earthenware Sold by John Ridgway & Company, Manufacturer of Earthenware, Cauldon Place, to Adam Southern of Philadelphia, 10/31/1846. Collection of Business Americana, National Museum of American History, Smithsonian Institution, Washington, D.C.

SAMFORD, PATRICIA M.
1985 Response to a Market: English Transfer Printed Wares in North America. Paper Presented at the 18th Annual Meeting of the Society for Historical Archaeology, Boston.

SANDON, HENRY
1978 *Flight and Barr Worcester Porcelain: 1783–1840*. Antique Collectors' Club, Woodbridge, England.

SAVAGE, GEORGE, AND HAROLD NEWMAN
1976 *An Illustrated Dictionary of Ceramics*. Van Nostrand Reinhold Company, New York.

SHAW, SIMEON
1968 *History of the Staffordshire Potteries and the Rise and Progress of the Manufacture of Pottery and Porcelain*. Reprint of 1829 edition. Beatrice C. Weinstock, Great Neck, New York.

SHLASKO, ELLEN
1989 Delftware Chronology: A New Approach to Dating English Tin-Glazed Ceramics. Unpublished M.A. thesis, Department of Anthropology, College of William and Mary, Williamsburg, Virginia.

SMITH, MATTHEW
1809 Letter to Jonathan Wyld of Liverpool from the Baltimore Earthenware Dealer Matthew Smith, 12/20/1809. *Matthew Smith Letterbook, 1803–1812* 1: M3621-1. Maryland Historical Society, Baltimore.

STACHIW, MYRON O.
1988 Research notes on the Letter and Order Books of Horace Collamore, a Boston Earthenware Dealer, 1814–1818. Ms., on file with the author.

STAFFORDSHIRE POTTERS
1808 A List of Prices, Settled, and Finally Agreed to by the Manufacturers, as the Lowest Prices, of the Following Articles, Below which None of Them Are to Sell after 1st of March, 1808. *Enoch Wood Scrapbook* 1. Stoke-on-Trent City Museum and Art Gallery, Hanley, Staffordshire.
1825 Staffordshire Potteries, Price Current of Earthenware, July 1, 1825. Ferguson, Day and Successor Company papers. New York Historical Society, New York.
1833 Staffordshire Potteries. General Meeting of Manufacturers, Held at the Swan Inn, Hanley, October 21, 1833; Mr. Ralph Stevenson in the Chair. Ferguson, Day and Successor Company papers. New York Historical Society, New York.
1846a At a Meeting of Manufacturers Engaged in the American Trade, Held Pursuant to Notice, At the Trentham Inn, on Monday, January 26th, 1846. John Ridgway, Esq., in the Chair. Foxwell Collection of Broadsides and Circulares, Item 24954. Kress Library of Business and Economics, Baker Library, Harvard University, Cambridge, Massachusetts.
1853 Prices Current of Earthenware, 1853. Wedgwood Archives, Keele University Library, Keele Staffordshire.
1859 Prices Current of Earthenware, 1859. Wedgwood Archives, Keele University Library, Keele, Staffordshire.

TOWNER, DONALD
1965 *The Leeds Pottery*. Taplinger Publishing Co., New York.

TURNER, WILLIAM
1923 *William Adams, An Old English Potter*. Chapman and Hall Ltd., London.

WARBURTON, W. H.
1931 *The History of Trade Union Organization in the North Staffordshire Potteries*. George Allen & Unwin, Ltd., London.

WATNEY, BERNARD
1964 *English Blue and White Porcelain of the 18th Century*. Thomas Yoseloff, New York.

WENGER, A.
1893 *Liquid Gold of the Highest Standard, for Earthenware, China, and Glass; Introduced by Me to the English Potters, Since 1870*. A. Wenger, Hanley, Staffordshire. One-page circular, on file with the author.

WILLIAMS-WOOD, CYRIL
1981 *English Transfer-Printed Pottery and Porcelain: A History of Over-Glaze Printing*. Faber and Faber, London.

GEORGE L. MILLER
DEPARTMENT OF ARCHAEOLOGICAL RESEARCH
COLONIAL WILLIAMSBURG FOUNDATION
WILLIAMSBURG, VIRGINIA 23187

DIANA DI ZEREGA WALL

Sacred Dinners and Secular Teas: Constructing Domesticity in Mid-19th-Century New York

ABSTRACT

In this study, the ceramics from two mid-19th-century middle-class homes in New York's Greenwich Village are analyzed to begin to explore consumer patterns among the women of this group. The analysis suggests that during this period, "domesticity" was defined differently by women at the poorer and richer ends of the middle-class spectrum.

Introduction

When Julia Harkness Lay, a bookkeeper's wife who lived on New York's Allen Street, noted in her diary in November 1852 that she had just "bought some new crockery," she described neither the crockery nor the social and cultural factors that she took into account when she made her selection as a consumer (Lay 1851–1878). In this study, archaeological materials are used to explore some of the issues which she and other women of New York's middle class may have considered in making such consumer decisions in the mid-19th century. The ceramics from two sites in Greenwich Village in New York City—from wealthier and poorer middle-class homes—are analyzed to provide the data for the study.

During the last decade or so, a literature on consumerism and mass-produced goods has begun to appear in several disciplines (e.g., Douglas and Isherwood 1979; Csiksentmihalyi and Rochberg-Halton 1981; McKendrick et al. 1982; Bourdieu 1984; Appadurai 1986; Campbell 1987; D. Miller 1987; McCracken 1988). Some of these studies offer subtle and sophisticated approaches to the study of consumer behavior and make several important points which are used as the underlying assumptions in the present study. Foremost, goods are regarded as texts that are open to multiple readings (cf. D. Miller 1987:176). Consumers actively decode these texts and thereby help to "produce" them in the act of their appropriation (cf. Bourdieu 1984:100). In selecting and appropriating goods, consumers use them to transform the world into an intelligible universe (e.g., Douglas and Isherwood 1979:102). Goods do not merely *reflect* various aspects of culture; rather, they *constitute* the very fabric of culture itself.

In *Distinction,* Pierre Bourdieu (1984) shows that tastes in goods and other phenomena helped to create and maintain the power structure among socioeconomic classes in France in the mid-20th century. When entertaining, for example, French working-class women tended to set their tables with earthenware plates and ordinary glasses, while executive and professional families tended to use china plates and crystal glasses (Bourdieu 1984:198). Bourdieu suggests that the rationale behind these differences does not reside simply in the cost of these commodities. Rather, for the working-class family, necessity prevailed outside the home, but domestic life inside the home was the realm of freedom. Working-class people stressed the substance of the food over the form of the service and restricted invitations to a meal to family or those who could be treated as family—people they felt "at home with." For Bourdieu's bourgeois family, in contrast, the order, restraint, and propriety of the outside world could not be abandoned in domestic life. The form of the meal was stressed over its substance, and professional or business acquaintances were often entertained at home (Bourdieu 1984:175–200).

In this paper, two ceramic assemblages from households in Greenwich Village are used to explore the appropriation of goods from a similar perspective. Unlike Bourdieu's households, however, the households here would all be defined as members of the middle class. The question is whether women at the wealthier and poorer ends of the middle-class spectrum were using goods to construct similar or different domestic worlds in New York in the mid-19th century. While it is obviously "reaching" to examine a subject as complex as this one with data from only two sites, this study shows the potential of using data generated by historical archaeology for addressing questions of this nature.

Archaeological Context

The domestic materials analyzed for this study come from backyard features at two sites in Greenwich Village. One assemblage came from the uppermost domestic deposit in a privy (Feature 9) in the backyard of 50 Washington Square South at the Sullivan Street Site (Salwen and Yamin 1990). The assemblage has a *terminus post quem* of 1854 (Rebecca Yamin 1989, pers. comm.), indicating the materials were deposited during or after that year.

The other assemblage came from a cistern in the backyard of 25 Barrow Street (Bodie and Wall [1991]). Here, a coin with a date of 1863 provides a *terminus post quem*. The feature also contained several drug bottles embossed with the name and address of a druggist who moved from his Bleecker Street address in 1870 (Geismar 1989), suggesting that the materials were probably not deposited too long after this year.

Both the nature of the soil matrices and the consistency of the dates of the materials from each level within each deposit suggest that the materials were dumped into each of the features in single episodes.

Cultural Context

As Stuart Blumin (1989) has recently shown, the 19th century was the period which saw the emergence of the urban middle class as known today. Although the middle class was defined ambiguously in the early part of the century, it was described in the 1860s in an article in *The New York Times [NYT]* as including "professional men, clergymen, artists, college professors, shopkeepers, and upper mechanics" who presumably owned their own businesses (*NYT* in Blumin 1989: 247). This broad definition suggests that for men in the mid-19th century (as now), a broad spectrum of cultural experience was subsumed under the rubric of "middle class." This may have been true of their wives as well.

In the mid-19th century, the mistresses of middle-class households were in charge of domestic life. Their role had been increasingly sanctified in the early part of the century and, by mid-century, was defined around the two interrelated ideals of domestic duty and refined gentility (Blumin 1989). Women not only used material goods to exert their influence in shaping the domestic environment, but also were active in procuring these goods (Blumin 1989:187–188). Contemporary diaries show that New York women shopped for household goods at least as early as the turn of the century. Elizabeth Bleecker, for example, noted in her diary the multitude of shopping expeditions she undertook to buy the furnishings and dishes she needed to set up house after her marriage in 1800 (Bleecker 1799–1806). Julia Harkness Lay, the bookkeeper's wife referred to at the beginning of this study, also recorded many purchases of household goods, including dishes, in the diary which she kept at mid-century (Lay 1851–1878). Although New York's middle-class husbands shopped for the family's food at the city's large public markets in the early part of the century, by mid-century their wives had taken on this role, shopping in the smaller neighborhood retail shops that proliferated in this period (Dudden 1983: 137).

The ceramics from the Greenwich Village sites were used by families at opposite ends of the middle-class spectrum. The houses at 50 Washington Square South and 25 Barrow Street were both built in the 1820s, during the period when the Village of Greenwich was being developed into one of the city's first suburbs; it was soon to be swallowed by the lower city. Both sites lie to the east of the area of the 18th-century Hudson River village, and were part of farm or estate lands until their development in the early 19th century. The sites lie in separate neighborhoods to the east and west of the present Sixth Avenue (Figure 1).

These neighborhoods are similar in that they were both among the city's first residential areas, marking the end of the "walking city" with its pattern of integrated homes and workplaces (Wall

FIGURE 1. Map of southern Manhattan, showing the 25 Barrow Street and 50 Washington Square South sites in Greenwich Village. (Courtesy of the City of New York, Department of City Planning.)

1987). Throughout much of the 19th century, Greenwich Village as a whole remained a relatively exclusive enclave for the wealthy and middle class—in the 1860s, fewer than a quarter of the buildings there were tenements. With the exception of those working as domestic servants, working-class German and Irish immigrants (the most numerous immigrant groups in the city) were for the most part excluded from these neighborhoods until later in the century (Ernst 1949:45, 235).

In other ways, however, these two adjacent neighborhoods were quite different from each other. Fifty Washington Square South was located to the east of Sixth Avenue and, as its address implies, on the south side of Washington Square, a parade ground and park which had been developed as the focus of an enclave of wealthy homes in the late 1820s. The southern side of the square was somewhat less expensive than the northern side because of its proximity to a poorer neighborhood which was developing immediately to its south. Twenty-five Barrow Street, to the west of Sixth Avenue, was located in a middle-class residential neighborhood composed of artisans, shopkeepers, and clerks.

The house at 25 Barrow Street (Figure 2) was originally built by a mason in 1826 as a 2½-story Federal-style house. The property had a small gangway leading from its backyard to the street (Perris 1854), which was probably used as a passageway for horses. Tax assessment records indicate that in the early 1870s, the house was altered, and the top-most half-story was converted into a full third floor (City of New York [CNY] 1873). During the second half of the century, the house was home to two and sometimes three separate families.

FIGURE 2. 25 Barrow Street, New York City. The sloping roof and dormer windows of this late Federal-style house were removed when the full third story was added in the 1870s.

The date range for the assemblage from 25 Barrow Street suggests that the domestic goods were used in one or more of the middle-class households whose members lived in the house in the 1860s or early 1870s. Like most of their neighbors, all of the families that have been documented as living in the house during this period were either native-born or were Protestant English-speaking immigrants from England or Scotland (U.S. Bureau of the Census [USBC] 1860, 1870, 1880; Bodie 1989).

Throughout this period, the house was owned by an absentee landlord. The tenancy pattern suggests that there may have been a primary, long-term tenant, living perhaps on the ground and basement floors, and one or two other, transient families, who perhaps lived on the upper floors. Samuel Hirst, an English-born baker, his wife, Emeline (who was also born in England), and their six native-born children moved into the house in 1858. Although Samuel died in 1860 or 1861, his family stayed on in the house for more than a decade. They presumably supported themselves through the earnings of Emeline (who became a nurse and later ran a boardinghouse) and the older children, who were in their 20s when they moved in. Other tenants in the house were there only briefly. David Sinclair, a Scottish locksmith, his wife, Selina (who was born in New York), and their two children lived there for only a few years, from 1858 until 1862. Sinclair had his shop in the neighborhood, on Bleecker Street. The Sinclairs were probably succeeded in the house by other families or boarders taken in by the widowed Emeline Hirst. However, their presence in the house has not been documented.

The Hirst family was followed in 1870 by that of Edward M. Seaman, a native-born expressman (or delivery man) who also ran a feed store. He lived there until 1883 with his New York-born wife, Mary, and their three children, who ranged in age from 14 to 28 in 1870. Seaman had his store nearby, on West Fourth Street. Their two documented co-tenants both lived in the house only briefly. David Andrews, a Scottish shipping clerk, his American-born wife, Catherine, and young son apparently lived there for only about a year, in 1870. Theodore Thorp, a painter, his wife, Ann, and their grown son, Theodore, who was also a painter, lived there from 1870 through 1874. All of the Thorps were born in New York. Thorp had his shop downtown, first on Centre Street and later on Fulton Street (USBC 1860, 1870, 1880; Trow 1858–1874).

These families were members of the city's middle class. Most of the household heads had their own small businesses (as inferred from their listing their business addresses in the city directories, implying they were business proprietors) or described themselves as "clerks," the quintessential middle-class occupation in the late 19th century. However, the families apparently belonged near the bottom of the middle class. They rented, rather than owned, their homes, which were apartments, not houses. The value of the house itself was assessed at only $2600 in 1860 (CNY 1841–1873). None of the families enjoyed the services of live-in domestic help, unlike many middle-class New Yorkers at mid-century. The personal estates of David Sinclair, the locksmith, and Samuel Hirst, the baker, were assessed at only $600 and $300, respectively (USBC 1860).

The presence of a toy teacup and saucer and three china dolls in the artifact assemblage (Figures 3, 4) suggest that the domestic materials excavated from the cistern may well have belonged at least in part to the Hirst or Seaman families.

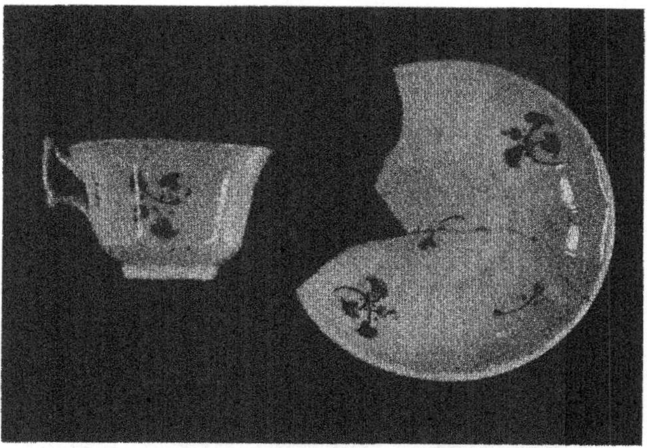

FIGURE 3. Miniature cup and saucer, painted and molded whiteware, from 25 Barrow Street. The saucer's diameter is 4¼ in.

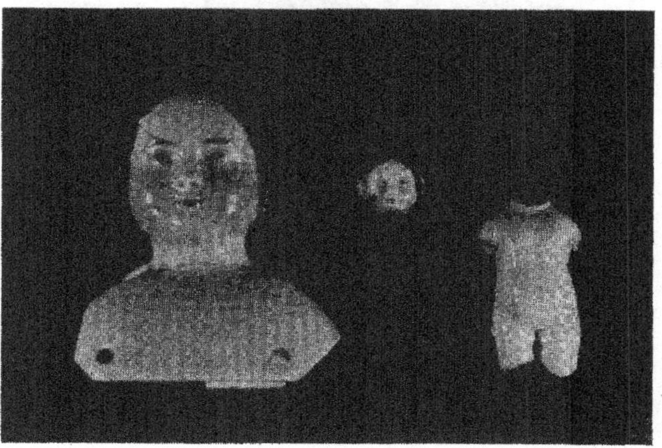

FIGURE 4. Parts of three dolls from the 25 Barrow Street site. The doll torso is 2½ in. high.

These are the only families with young daughters documented as living on the property during the period in question: Emma and Catherine Hirst, who were approximately six and 11 years old, respectively, in 1860 at the beginning of the period in question, and Ada Seaman, who was 14 when her family moved on to the property in 1870—as calculated from the USBC (1860, 1870). All of the other families either had young boys, grown children, or were childless. In subsequent sections of the text the people associated with the Barrow

FIGURE 5. The Old Merchant's House, a house-museum on Fourth Street a few blocks east of Washington Square, is similar in style to the late Federal-period house at 50 Washington Square South, which was torn down at the turn of the century.

Street assemblage are referred to as a "household" for clarity of style. It should be remembered, however, that it is unclear which particular family (or families) used the objects in question. The identity of the particular household that used the objects is not relevant, however, because all of the households documented as living on the lot during the period when the materials were disposed of fit neatly into the socioeconomic group examined here: the poorer members of the middle class.

The house at 50 Washington Square South (Figure 5) was built in 1826 on a parcel of land which had been owned previously by John Ireland and Alfred Pell. Both men were local landowners who had been active in petitioning the city for the creation of the square which subsequently enhanced the value of their property. The house changed hands several times in the late 1820s and 1830s, as its owners speculated on the northward growth of the city (Salwen and Yamin 1990).

In 1841, Benjamin R. Robson, a physician, purchased the property and moved into the house with his wife, Eliza, and her brother James Bool. The Robsons' grown daughter, Mary Sage, lived next door with her husband, Francis, a South Street flour merchant, and their children. The Robsons continued to live on the property until Benjamin's death almost four decades later (Longworth 1842; Doggett 1843, 1844, 1845–1849, 1851; Rode 1852–1854; Trow 1853, 1855–1874). Throughout this period, the family had a series of live-in Irish female domestics (a pair at a time) and, at least in 1850, an African-American coachman, Samuel Stevens (USBC 1850, 1860, 1870). Before they moved to Washington Square, the Robsons had lived downtown on East Broadway, where Benjamin had conducted his practice out of the family home (e.g., Longworth 1835). After they moved, the doctor continued to run his practice from his old downtown office (e.g., Longworth 1842) and presumably kept the coachman and carriage for his commute. He probably kept his horse and carriage in his stable, which was located at the back of the property, fronting on Third Street.

The Robsons were clearly among the wealthier families in the middle class. They lived in the relatively exclusive enclave of Washington Square in a 3½-story brick single-family home that they owned themselves and that was assessed for $10,000 in 1855 (CNY 1841–1873). They consistently had live-in domestic help and even kept a carriage and a coachman for at least part of the period that they lived there (USBC 1850, 1860, 1870). On his death, Benjamin Robson left an estate worth $300,000 (*NYT* 1878).

The persistence of the Robson family in this house throughout the entire period when the domestic materials may have been deposited in the backyard privy allows one to infer that the domestic materials, in fact, came from their home.

TABLE 1
THE TABLEWARES FROM THE TWO GREENWICH VILLAGE SITES

Decorative Type	Site Distribution: 50 Washington Square South n[b]	%	25 Barrow Street n	%	Relative Value[a]: Table Plates 1846	Table Plates 1850s	Twifflers 1846	Twifflers 1850s
Plain/cc	4	12.1	5	38.5	1	1	1	1
Edged	5	15.2	1	7.7	1.14	1.12	1.13	1.11
Sponged	—		—		—	1.2	—	1.25
Willow	—		1	7.7	—	1.6	—	1.5
White granite	19	57.6	6	46.2	1.93	—	2.22	2.0
Printed	5	15.2	—		2.11	1.6	2.42	1.5
Dark blue printed	—		—		2.29	—	2.63	—
Flown	—		—		2.64	2.4	3.03	2.5
Total	33	100	13	100				

[a]After Miller (1988); 1853 is the year quoted for the relative value of the edged plates, 1858 is quoted for the white granite ones, and 1855 is used for all other plates.

[b]The frequencies are derived from the minimum number of table plates and twifflers of each decorative type in each assemblage.

Note. A chi-square test of association corrected for continuity (Siegel 1956: 107–110) comparing the distributions of the white granite versus all of the other wares combined yielded a value of .14, with a significance level of $p<.05$ and *df* 1. This indicates that there is no significant difference between the distributions of these two samples. These data follow:

	Molded granite/ ironstone	Other
25 Barrow Street	6	7
50 Washington Sq. So.	19	14

The Ceramics

This study examines the ceramics in the assemblages from these two sites to see whether these poorer and richer middle-class women were using their choices in household furnishings to construct domestic worlds that were similar to or different from each other's. To do this, the vessels used in two different domestic arenas are examined: tea, where non-family members were entertained, and family meals, where participation was usually limited to family members.

The ceramics from the households are divided into three groups: tablewares, teawares, and other vessels. The vessels in the tableware and teaware categories are compared for this study. Vessels in the tableware category consist of larger plates like table plates and twifflers (or medium-sized plates), while cups and saucers make up those in the teaware category. Serving dishes like platters, sauceboats, teapots, and creamers are not included, because they could have been made of silver or silver plate, and therefore might not have been discarded to form part of the archaeological record. Vessels of other forms were not analyzed further for this study. Small plates or muffins present a problem as they could have been used both in family meals and for serving desserts at tea parties. Therefore they are not included in the main part of the analysis, but are discussed separately below.

The tableware assemblages from both households are similar to each other (Table 1). Approximately half of the tablewares from each of the households are white granite ironstone with pan-

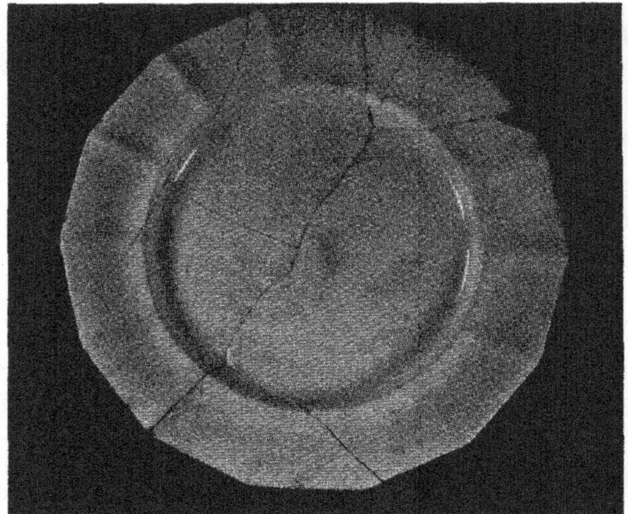

FIGURE 6. White ironstone plate in the Gothic pattern, from the 50 Washington Square South site. The plate's diameter is 10¼ in.

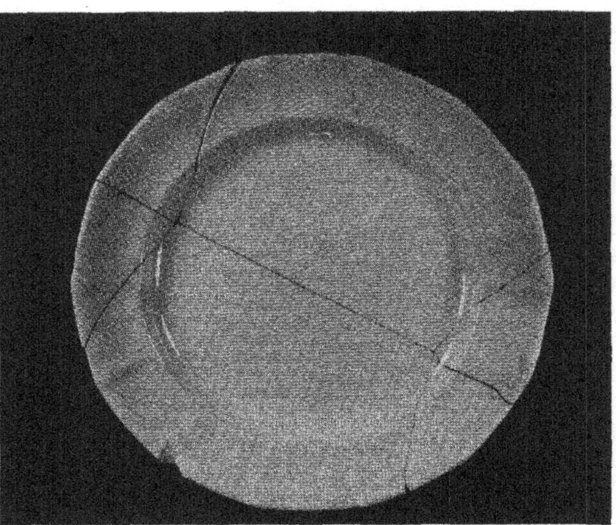

FIGURE 7. White ironstone plate in the Gothic pattern, from the 25 Barrow Street site. The plate's diameter is 8⅜ in.

elled rims, a pattern referred to as Gothic in the ceramics literature (Figures 6, 7; Wetherbee 1985: 176). In the Robson household, shell-edged plates and light- and medium-blue transfer-printed plates are the next most common patterns in the assemblage. The printed patterns are not from a single set of dishes, however, but rather are odd, unmatched plates. There are also some plain, undecorated (or cream-colored) plates in the Robson assemblage. For the Barrow Street assemblage, the total sample size is much smaller, and the next most common pattern here is plain, undecorated white. Finally, there is a single plate of edged ware and one in the willow pattern.

The two households show strikingly different preferences in teaware cups and saucers, however (Table 2). Three-quarters of the Robsons' tea vessels are porcelain. Half of these vessels have molded panels and are similar in style to the ironstone tablewares (Figure 8), while the others are pedestalled and decorated with gilt floral bands (Figure 9). Painted whiteware, white granite ironstone, and transfer-printed cups and saucers together make up the remaining quarter of the assemblage.

Almost two-thirds of the teawares in the Barrow Street assemblage, in contrast, are made out of white granite ironstone, and most are panelled to match the vessels in the tableware assemblage (Figure 10). The single porcelain saucer recovered also matches the panelled granite tablewares. The two remaining tea vessels in the assemblage are made of plain, undecorated (or cream-colored) ware.

There is only one vessel for serving tea in either assemblage—a soft-paste porcelain teapot with both molded panels and gilt trim in the Barrow Street collection. The absence of serving vessels in the Robsons' assemblage suggests that they may have used ones made of silver or silver plate. These vessels would naturally not turn up in the archaeological record. They became more accessible to members of the middle class with the discovery of the rich Comstock Lode in Nevada and the development of the electroplating process just before the Civil War (Rainwater 1987).

Both of the assemblages included small plates, or muffins. As mentioned above, these plates could have been used in family meals and/or for serving desserts or sandwiches at tea parties. The

TABLE 2
THE TEAWARES FROM THE TWO GREENWICH VILLAGE SITES

	Site Distribution				Relative Value[a]	
	50 Washington Square South		25 Barrow Street		Handled, Simple Cups	
Decorative Types	n[b]	%	n	%	1846	1850s
Plain/cc	—		2	25	1.55	1.5
Painted	6	13.6	—		1.77	1.77
Sponged	—		—		2.17	2.17
White granite	3	6.8	5	62.5	2.54	—
Printed	2	4.5	—		2.77	—
Dark blue printed	—		—		2.73	—
Flown	—		—		3.46	—
European porcelain						
Molded only	17	38.6	1	12.5		
Gilded	16	36.4	—		4.2	
Total	44	100	8	100		

[a]After Miller (1988); 1853 is the year quoted for the relative value of the plain and painted cups and 1852 is quoted for the sponged cups.

[b]The frequencies are derived from the minimum number of cups and saucers of each decorative type in each assemblage.

Note. A chi-square test of association corrected for continuity (Siegel 1956: 107–110) comparing the distributions of the molded granite cups and saucers and those of all the other wares combined yielded a value of 12.12, with $p>.05$ significance level and df 1. This indicates that there is in fact a significant difference in the distributions of these two samples. The data used in the X^2 calculation follow:

	Molded granite/ ironstone	Other
25 Barrow Street	5	3
50 Washington Sq. So.	3	41

seven muffins from the Robson assemblage and the single muffin from Barrow Street, however, were all made out of porcelain and had plain, flat rims: several of them were also embellished with gilt overglaze decoration. Both the fabric and the decoration of these muffins suggest that they were used for tea parties rather than for family meals.

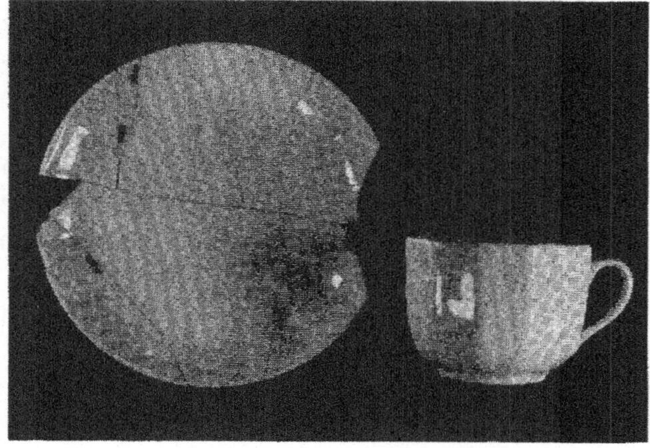

FIGURE 8. Porcelain cup and saucer decorated with molded panels, from the 50 Washington Square South site. The saucer's diameter is 6¼ in.

Discussion

One way to begin to compare the meaning of domesticity in these households is to examine the similarities and differences in the styles of the ceramic vessels that were used in these two homes.

FIGURE 9. Gilded and pedestalled porcelain cup and saucer from the 50 Washington Square South site. The saucer's diameter is 5½ in.

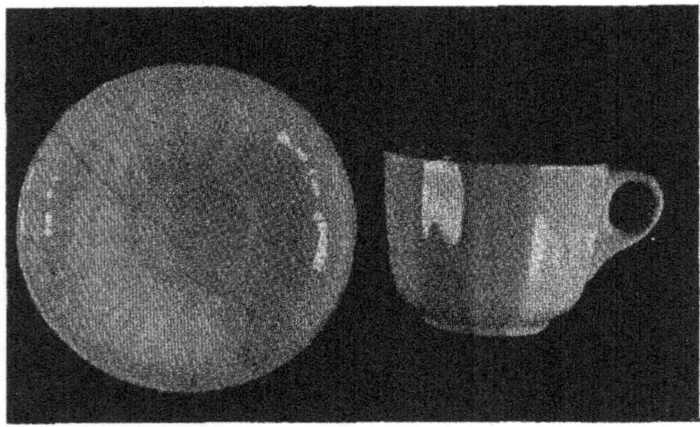

FIGURE 10. Panelled ironstone cup and porcelain saucer from the 25 Barrow Street site. The saucer's diameter is 5⅞ in.

Archaeologists can look on similarities in the styles of objects from similar contexts of use within a single cultural system as inferential evidence that both the objects and the arenas in which they were used had similar meanings. Archaeologists can also look on differences in the styles of objects used in similar contexts as implying that the meaning of both the objects and the arenas in which they were used were quite different.

The similarities and differences in the styles of the ceramic assemblages used in these two households are provocative. They suggest that during this period, women in wealthier and poorer middle-class households were constructing domestic worlds which in some ways were similar to and in other ways were quite different from each other's.

Both of these mid-century families in this suburb used similarly panelled ironstone tablewares for their family meals. The similarity of the ceramics suggests that the meals where the ceramics were used had the same social meaning for the relatively wealthy Robsons as for the poorer Barrow Street family (Figures 6, 7). These dishes were made at Britain's Staffordshire potteries. These women were rejecting for the most part both the cheaper edged, plain, and sponged dishes as well as the more expensive printed and flown plates that Americans were also importing from these potteries at this time (Table 1; G. Miller 1990). Ironstone dishes were made specifically for the North American market and were not sold at all in Britain where they were made (Sussman 1985: 7), presumably because there was no demand for them there. These panelled-ironstone dishes apparently had a cultural meaning for North American consumers that was not shared by their British contemporaries.

These tablewares were used for serving breakfast, lunch, and dinner, meals which were intended to be the focus of family life and which were seen as "constant and familiar" family reunions (Calvert Vaux in Clark 1986:42). They were not seen as appropriate for entertaining guests—dinner parties became common among the American middle classes only later, in the 1880s (Clark 1986:42, 1987:154–156, 162). It is particularly interesting that Eliza Robson, who certainly could have afforded tablewares in more expensive printed and flown patterns, instead consistently chose the ironstone vessels which were middle range in cost for her family's meals (Table 1).

The actual meaning that dishes in this style held for those who acquired and used them can only be surmised. It is suggestive, however, that the style is referred to as Gothic in the ceramics literature. When Gothic revival architecture became popular in New York in the 1840s, it was used predominately in church design (Landau 1982). As Susan Williams (1985:67) has pointed out, Gothic furniture was also considered appropriate for dining rooms at this time. The presence of both furniture and vessels in the Gothic style could only have enhanced the sacred aspect of women's domestic role within the ritual of family meals. Like Bourdieu's working-class women, middle-class women in New York also used vessels to distinguish domestic life in the home from commercial life in the marketplace. The New York women, however, apparently defined their domestic role by the cult of domesticity (Cott 1977) and equated private family meals (with both dishes and furnishings displayed in the Gothic style) with the sanctity and community of Gothic churches and contrasted them to the more competitive arena of the capitalist marketplace.

The styles of the teawares in these homes, however, tell a different story. Both families had sets of panelled teawares that were similar to their panelled ironstone plates (Table 2). Most of the tea vessels belonging to the Barrow Street family were made of ironstone, like their plates. Most of the Robsons', however, were made of porcelain. The Robsons (unlike the Barrow Street family) also had a second set of teaware. This set, too, was made of porcelain, but was formed in a pedestalled shape and had gilt-painted decoration—it did not match their dinnerwares at all (Figure 9). This suggests that these families participated in two different kinds of teas. One, where panelled teawares were used, was partaken of by members of both households. The other, where the fancier pedestalled, gilt-painted vessels were used, was indulged in only by the wealthier Robsons.

Teawares were used in two different settings: women served tea (or coffee) at breakfast, which took place at the dining table, and also as the keystone of afternoon tea. Afternoon tea parties were held in the parlor. The parlor was the most luxuriously furnished room in a middle-class home and was the arena where the middle-class members aspired to make their claims to refined gentility (Blumin 1989:184). Tea was particularly important for middle-class women because they otherwise were often isolated from each other in their private homes (Williams 1987:9–11). Unlike family meals at the dining table, where the community of family members was stressed, afternoon tea in the parlor with non-family guests was an occasion where the display of family social status could be important.

The sets of panelled teawares that matched the tablewares were probably used for serving tea with meals in both households. These teawares, like the similar tablewares, may well have embodied the sacred aspects of family and community life of the dining table. The Robsons may also have used their panelled porcelain teacups for intimate, less formal tea parties in the upstairs parlor.

Eliza Robson probably used her fancy gilt-decorated and pedestalled teaware at the more elaborate and formal afternoon tea parties she gave for her friends. Like the china and crystal that Bourdieu's bourgeois families used for dinner parties, these fancier tea vessels suggest that this home was not simply a haven from the competitive world of the capitalistic marketplace—Eliza Robson may well have used her dishes in a series of competitive displays designed to impress her friends and acquaintances with the refined gentility of her family.

The fact that the Barrow Street family did not have such fancy wares, however, does not necessarily simply mean that these women could not afford the fancier cups or that they did not have their friends in for tea. It could also mean that when they entertained their friends at afternoon tea, the meal had a different meaning. Instead of trying to impress and compete with their friends for family status, as Eliza Robson may have done, the Barrow Street tenants (like Bourdieu's working class) perhaps only invited those equated with family and community into their homes for any meal at all. The panelled cups and saucers (whether in porcelain or ironstone) may have served to elicit the almost sacred values of community and mutual help—values which could be very useful for those at the lower end of the middle-class spectrum—among the women who were gathering together for tea.

When Julia Harkness Lay noted in her diary in 1852 that she had gone shopping for crockery, she did not mention what she bought or how she made her choice. But the analysis of the archaeological materials from the middle-class homes of contemporary New Yorkers allows one to begin to explore how the cultural experiences of the women who constructed and maintained domestic life inside these 19th-century homes may have varied. They suggest that as a bookkeeper's wife who kept house in mid-century New York, Julia Lay may well have bought most of her teaware and tableware in the panelled Gothic pattern, and researchers can begin to understand why she made that choice.

DEDICATION AND ACKNOWLEDGMENTS

Both the 25 Barrow Street and 50 Washington Square South sites were excavated under the direction of Bert Salwen. This study is dedicated to his memory. I am very grateful to Arlene and Harry Nance, who generously made the archaeologists welcome at their home at 25 Barrow Street. I also thank Rebecca Yamin for sharing information about the analysis of the materials from 50 Washington Square South at the Sullivan Street site with me and Paul Pearson for his help with the photographs. This paper was infinitely improved by the comments of Anne-Marie Cantwell, Nan A. Rothschild, Donna Seifert, and three anonymous reviewers. Any remaining errors of fact or interpretation are, unfortunately, my own.

REFERENCES

APPADURAI, ARJUN (EDITOR)
1986 *The Social Life of Things: Commodities in Cultural Perspective*. Cambridge University Press, Cambridge.

BLEECKER, ELIZABETH
1799–1806 Diary kept in New York City. Rare Books and Manuscripts Division, New York Public Library, New York.

BLUMIN, STUART M.
1989 *The Emergence of the Middle Class: Social Experience in the American City, 1760–1900*. Cambridge University Press, Cambridge.

BODIE, DEBRA C.
1989 Twenty-five Barrow Street. Ms. on file with the author.

BODIE, DEBRA C., AND DIANA DIZEREGA WALL
[1991] Final Report, Excavation of a Cistern at the Nance House, 25 Barrow Street, Greenwich Village Historic District, New York. Ms. on file with the authors.

BOURDIEU, PIERRE
1984 *Distinction: A Social Critique of the Judgement of Taste*, translated by Richard Nice. Harvard University Press, Cambridge.

CAMPBELL, COLIN
1987 *The Romantic Ethic and the Spirit of Modern Consumerism*. Basil Blackwell, Oxford.

CITY OF NEW YORK (CNY)
1841–1873 Tax Assessment Records. Municipal Archives, Department of Records and Information Services, New York.

CLARK, CLIFFORD E.
1986 *The American Family Home, 1800–1960*. University of North Carolina Press, Chapel Hill.
1987 The Vision of the Dining Room: Plan Book Dreams and Middle-Class Realities. In *Dining in America, 1850–1900*, edited by Kathryn Grover, pp. 142–172. University of Massachusetts Press, Amherst, and The Margaret Woodbury Strong Museum, Rochester, New York.

COTT, NANCY F.
1977 *The Bonds of Womanhood: "Woman's Sphere" in New England, 1780–1835*. Yale University Press, New Haven.

CSIKSENTMIHALYI, MIHALYI, AND EUGENE ROCHBERG-HALTON
1981 *The Meaning of Things*. Cambridge University Press, Cambridge.

DOGGETT, JOHN, JR.
1843 *The New-York City and Co-Partnership Directory for 1843 and 1844*. John Doggett, Jr., New York.
1844 *The New-York City Directory*. John Doggett, Jr., New York.
1845–1849 *Doggett's New York City Directory*. John Doggett, Jr., New York.
1851 *Doggett's New York City Street Directory for 1851*. John Doggett, New York.

DOUGLAS, MARY, AND BARON ISHERWOOD
1979 *The World of Goods*. W.W. Norton, New York.

DUDDEN, FAYE E.
1983 *Serving Women: Household Service in Nineteenth-Century America*. Wesleyan University Press, Middletown, Connecticut.

ERNST, ROBERT
1949 *Immigrant Life in New York City, 1825–1863*. Kings Crown Press, Columbia University, New York.

GEISMAR, JOAN
1989 History and Archaeology of the Greenwich Mews Site, Greenwich Village, New York. Prepared by Greenwich Mews Associates. Submitted to the New York City Landmarks Preservation Commission.

LANDAU, SARAH BRADFORD
1982 Greek and Gothic Side by Side: Architecture Around the Square. In *Around the Square, 1830–1890: Essays on Life, Letters, and Architecture,* edited by Mindy Cantor, pp. 12–29. New York University Press, New York.

LAY, JULIA HARKNESS
1851–1878 Diary. Rare Books and Manuscripts Division, New York Public Library, New York.

LONGWORTH, THOMAS
1835 *Longworth's American Almanac, New-York Register, and City Directory.* Thomas Longworth, New York.
1842 *Longworth's American Almanac, New-York Register, and City Directory.* Thomas Longworth, New York.

MCCRACKEN, GRANT
1988 *Culture and Consumption: New Approaches to the Symbolic Character of Consumer Goods and Activities.* Indiana University Press, Bloomington.

MCKENDRICK, NEIL, JOHN BREWER, AND J.H. PLUMB
1982 *The Birth of a Consumer Society: The Commercialization of Eighteenth-Century England.* Indiana University Press, Bloomington.

MILLER, DANIEL
1987 *Material Culture and Mass Consumption.* Basil Blackwell, Oxford.

MILLER, GEORGE
1988 Prices and Index Values for English Ceramics from 1787 to 1880. Ms. on file with the author, Colonial Williamsburg.
1990 The "Market Basket" of Ceramics Available from 1780 to 1860. Paper presented at the Annual Meeting of the Society for Historical Archaeology Conference on Historical and Underwater Archaeology, Tucson, Arizona.

THE NEW YORK TIMES (NYT)
1878 Contesting the Copy of a Will. *The New York Times,* 30 January:8.

PERRIS, WILLIAM
1854 *Maps of the City of New York.* William Perris, New York.

RAINWATER, DOROTHY
1987 Victorian Dining Silver. In *Dining in America, 1850–1900,* edited by Kathryn Grover, pp. 173–204. University of Massachusetts Press, Amherst, and The Margaret Woodbury Strong Museum, Rochester, New York.

RODE, CHARLES R.
1852–1854 *The New York City Directory.* Charles R. Rode, New York.

SALWEN, BERT, AND REBECCA YAMIN
1990 The Archaeological History of Six Nineteenth Century Lots: Sullivan Street, Greenwich Village, New York City. Prepared by New York University Law School. Submitted to the New York City Landmarks Preservation Commission.

SIEGEL, SIDNEY
1956 *Non-Parametric Statistics for the Behavioral Sciences.* McGraw-Hill, New York.

SUSSMAN, LYNNE
1985 *The Wheat Pattern: An Illustrated Survey.* National Historic Parks and Sites Branch, Parks Canada, Ottawa.

TROW, JOHN F.
1853 *Trow's New York City Directory.* John F. Trow, New York.
1855–1874 *Trow's New York City Directory.* John F. Trow, New York.

UNITED STATES BUREAU OF THE CENSUS (USBC)
1850 *Population Schedule, Seventh Census of the United States.* Research Division, New York Public Library, New York.
1860 *Population Schedule, Eighth Census of the United States.* Research Division, New York Public Library, New York.
1870 *Population Schedule, Ninth Census of the United States.* Research Division, New York Public Library, New York.
1880 *Population Schedule, Tenth Census of the United States.* Research Division, New York Public Library, New York.

WALL, DIANA DIZEREGA
1987 At Home in New York: The Redefinition of Gender Among the Middle-Class and Elite, 1783–1840. Unpublished Ph.D. dissertation, Department of Anthropology, New York University, New York.

WETHERBEE, JEAN
1985 *A Second Look at White Ironstone.* Wallace-Homestead, Lombard, Illinois.

WILLIAMS, SUSAN
1985 *Savory Suppers and Fashionable Feasts: Dining in Victorian America.* Pantheon Books, New York.
1987 Introduction. In *Dining in America, 1850–1900,* edited by Kathryn Grover, pp. 3–23. University of Massachusetts Press, Amherst, and The Margaret Woodbury Strong Museum, Rochester, New York.

DIANA DIZEREGA WALL
SOUTH STREET SEAPORT MUSEUM
207 FRONT STREET
NEW YORK, NEW YORK 10038

Laurie A. Wilkie

Culture Bought: Evidence of Creolization in the Consumer Goods of an Enslaved Bahamian Family

ABSTRACT

Archaeologists working in the Caribbean have identified evidence of African continuities in the craft and architectural traditions of enslaved peoples. Less attention has been paid to the role of the abundant, European-produced goods that are also found in the homes of enslaved families. The material culture from one enslaved Bahamian family is explored here, looking at how European-produced goods were selected by enslaved Africans and imbued with meanings in the creation of a Creole culture. The family discussed lived on Clifton plantation, on the island of New Providence, and consisted of an African-born couple and their two island-born children. The enslaved population, due to the paternalistic attitudes of the plantation owner, enjoyed an unusual degree of access to island markets. Using analyses of ceramics and pipes recovered from the household, it is argued that African-based aesthetics directed the selection and composition of the artifacts recovered from the dwelling.

Introduction

Since the inception of African-American archaeology, researchers have attempted to identify artifacts from the New World that are African in style, manufacture, or origin (Handler and Lange 1978; Armstrong 1983, 1990; Handler 1996, 1997; Gaucher 1997; Haviser 1997). Much of this research has focused upon studies of hand-made ceramics, such as Colono Ware in the southern United States, or Yabba wares in Jamaica (Armstrong 1990; Ferguson 1992) or unique or distinctive artifact types (Handler and Lange 1978; Brown and Cooper 1990; Pearce 1993; Emerson 1994; Wilkie 1995; Samford 1996). Enslaved Africans and African Americans also expressed cultural values, such as religious beliefs and aesthetic preferences, through the reinterpretation of European-produced consumer goods.

The degree to which African cultural practices survived the Middle Passage and the brutality of slavery has long interested anthropologists and historians (Herskovits 1962; Mintz and Price 1976; Thompson 1983). Since European-American planters were likely to discourage the expression of African culture, and were themselves cultural outsiders who may not have recognized African traditions, the documentary record has limited potential for identifying evidence of continuities. For this reason, archaeology provides the most promising avenue for studying the African cultural contribution during the period of enslavement.

Archaeologists in the Caribbean have been successful in identifying objects that were either African in origin or African in their style of manufacture. For instance, in excavating the slave cemetery of Newton Plantation in Barbados, Jerome Handler and Frederick Lange (1978) recovered the skeleton of an individual who wore 2 copper bracelets on his left arm, 2 metal rings, 1 copper ring and a necklace of 7 cowry shells, 21 drilled dog canines, 14 glass beads, 5 drilled fish vertebrae, and 1 large agate bead. Handler and Lange argued that these were likely to be materials of extremely high status that had been brought from Africa. Handler (1996) has recently argued that one of the individuals buried at Newton Plantation was a witch or other negatively viewed person, based upon their burial position. Working in Jamaica, at Drax Hall plantation, Douglas Armstrong (1990) identified, in the material form of Yabba wares, a ceramic manufacturing tradition that grew from West African pottery traditions.

In addition to finding materials that reflect a West African heritage, archaeologists have also identified behaviors that reflect West African traditions. For instance, Grace Turner (1993:116) has noted that human teeth have been recovered near the rooflines of houses in the Bahamas. Drawing upon oral traditions, Turner ties this to the contemporary Bahamian practice of throwing lost teeth over the shoulder and onto the roof to bring good luck. Herskovits (1962:195) also noted this tradition in other parts of the New World, and attributed the origin of the practice to Dahomey. Working in Jamaica, Matthew Reeves (1996) discovered two bottles near the doorway of an enslaved person's house, which he has interpreted as Obeah bottles, intended to harm the occupants of the house. The use of bottles as containers for conjure is well-documented in the Caribbean as well as throughout the American South (Thompson 1983; Franklin 1995; Samford 1996; Wilkie 1997). Again, this magical practice appears to have a West African basis. Lydia Pulsipher (1993), working in Montserrat, has found continuities in the formation and use of house-yard compounds on that island with house gardens in West Africa. While these studies have been important in establishing the successful adaptation of African technologies and traditions in the Caribbean they ultimately ignore the vast majority of materials recovered from these sites–materials that are of European manufacture.

Enslaved people did not merely adopt the material culture of their enslavers in European ways. Instead, African-Americans selectively appropriated those goods that best reflected their cultural sensibilities and that enabled them to construct New World creolized identities through new material culture. To varying degrees at different times and places, the conditions of enslavement limited access that any enslaved person had to goods other than through the planter. The degree to which cultural expressions could be made through European-manufactured goods also varied through time and space.

For this work, creolization is seen as a process that is represented by retentions in cultural values that become expressed in new ways due to cultural contact and relocation (Wilkie 1997:93). This definition contrasts with that of syncretism, the fusion of two existing traditions into a new, third cultural reality. Creolization and syncretism are both cultural processes through which individuals create cultural change. Herein, the process of creolization is conceptualized similar to the manner of Charles Joyner (1984) and Leland Ferguson (1992). The underlying cultural values that enslaved Africans brought with them to the New World shaped their perceptions and attitudes regarding their new surroundings. These underlying values were in essence the grammar that guided the way individuals explained, categorized, and navigated the alien terrain of New World enslavement. While some of the patterns and activities that became part of the Diaspora experience may have been new, they were still undertaken in a way that was informed by the enslaved person's underlying African sensibility. In such a view of creolization, artifacts can be likened to words in a language. While new words may be incorporated into a language quickly, the underlying grammar is slower to change and directs the ways in which new words are organized within the language.

There are shortcomings to such a definition of creolization. African-American cultures did not develop in a vacuum. Racism, oppression, new environments, new economies, and new personal and family histories all shaped the ways that African Americans created themselves and their cultures in the New World. Joyner and Ferguson's grammar model of creolization should not be extended to account for cultural change or continuities in long-established immigrant communities, for to do so would minimize the increasing importance of the experiences that shaped daily life after arrival in the New World. The model is useful for exploring the ways that the first generation of enslaved Africans encountered and experienced life as slaves, and how they attempted to raise their children in a way that was faithful to their beliefs, while also recognizing the different social and physical landscapes native to their children. In a very real way, creolization, as conceptualized here, represents the intergenerational negotiation of group identity. In this study, the focus is not concerned with long-term macro-scale culture, but rather with short-term, micro-scale change, i.e., within a single family and within a single generation. An archaeological study of a single enslaved household at Clifton plantation in the Bahamas will be presented.

Clifton Plantation: Evidence of African Consumer Choices

Clifton plantation, located on the western end of New Providence Island, Bahamas, was occupied by William Wylly and an enslaved population of Africans and African-Bahamians from ca. 1813 to 1821, after which Wylly moved from the Bahamas to St. Vincent (Wilkie and Farnsworth 1997). The archaeological remains include 15 standing limestone structures, including 8 structures associated with the enslaved population. Despite the excellent state of preservation of the buildings, the site does not, based on archaeological testing, appear to have been extensively re-inhabited since the period of Bahamian enslavement. Several of the buildings do not appear to have been used after Wylly left for St. Vincent.

Clifton plantation offers a unique opportunity to study the material culture of an enslaved population who were able to participate as both buyers and sellers in the markets of Nassau. This market access was due to the paternalistic philosophy of planter William Wylly, Attorney General of the Bahamas from 1799 to 1821 (Wilkie and Farnsworth 1996, 1997). Wylly strove to reform the conditions of enslavement in the Bahamas and held up his own Clifton plantation as an example of a model plantation. Wylly's goal was to make his enslaved population self-sufficient and God-fearing. He provided each enslaved family with a plot of land on which they could grow their own provisions and raise hogs and fowl (Colonial Office Records [CO] 1812).

In exchange for the right to work in their gardens on Saturdays, enslaved families on Clifton agreed to a decreased corn ration. Such an arrangement lessened Wylly's overhead costs. In addition, the enslaved families were allowed to sell any surplus from their gardens at the market in Nassau. To encourage this practice, Wylly even loaned (Wylly's term for the arrangement) the families his boat so that heavy items could be more easily moved to market (CO 1818a). To create additional work for his enslaved population, Wylly also provided enslaved men with the opportunity to earn cash wages by building plantation field and compound walls. Not only did the enslaved people of Clifton have the opportunity to participate in the Nassau market as sellers, the combination of earnings from their garden produce sales and wages from wall-building provided them with ample means to participate as consumers.

The material culture of the enslaved families at Clifton is very different from that seen at other Bahamian plantations, and markedly different from the material culture of William Wylly. The differences between the planter and enslaved people's assemblages, it will be argued, are the result of distinct African-influenced consumer behavior. In particular, comparisons between the planter and enslaved populations of Clifton demonstrate that enslaved people favored polychrome decorated ceramics, while Wylly and his family preferred monochromes, particularly blue monochromes. The enslaved people of Clifton consistently favored hand-painted and annular wares, while Wylly's household preferred shell-edged and blue transfer-prints (Wilkie and Farnsworth 1997; Farnsworth 1999). The analysis presented here will focus upon materials recovered from a cabin at Clifton identified as the driver's house.

The Driver's House at Clifton: Locus G

During the summer of 1996, archaeological testing was conducted at Clifton plantation by the author and Paul Farnsworth of Louisiana State University. During the course of the field season, 15 standing structures were tested archaeologically. Among the buildings tested were those of the Clifton slave quarters. The quarters consisted of one slave kitchen, a driver's cabin, and six additional cabins. While the short duration of the field season limited the amount of archaeological testing that could be completed, it was possible to excavate 22 1 x 1m square units in and around the driver's cabin, which was designated Locus G (Figure 1). Surface survey revealed that the largest concentrations of materials were located to the north and west of the cabin, therefore excavations were concentrated in these areas.

The structure has been designated the driver's cabin based upon multiple lines of evidence. First, the structure is the southernmost one in the line of cabins, making it closest to the planter's residence and the plantation chapel. Wylly's personal papers indicate that he subscribed to a strongly hierarchical arrangement within the plantation. The driver was the enslaved person afforded greatest access to the planter, and the person assigned by the planter to oversee the religious training of the enslaved population. Spatially, the arrangement of Clifton is atypical for Bahamian plantations, in that it utilizes a linear row of cabins more reminiscent of the Georgian plantations of Wylly's birthplace and young adulthood. In southern plantations, it is not unusual for the driver's cabin to be placed at the head of the row (Vlach 1993:139). The cabin is also located in front of the slave kitchen, where weekly provisions for the enslaved families were stored and distributed. Historical documents indicate that the driver at Clifton had considerable prestige and responsibility within the plantation. Among his various duties, the driver was required to supervise the allocation and distribution of weekly rations (CO 1818a).

While these spatial attributes of the cabin strongly suggest that the cabin was likely that of the driver and his family, additional historical evidence also points to this conclusion. Ledger records kept in 1817 by Wylly's overseer, James Rutherford, reveals the driver was a man named Jack and that he was married to a plantation cook named Sue Eve (CO 1818b). While described as a plantation cook, Sue Eve was not the woman listed as working in Wylly's kitchen, meaning that she must have worked in the only other kitchen on the plantation, the enslaved peoples' kitchen. The family that lived in Locus G would have had the greatest access to and control over this kitchen. Slave registers, required by the British government on a triennial basis, provide the only consistent accounting of enslaved people in the Bahamas. Initial register lists were compiled by the planter or his agent. Some planters organized the register by the age and sex of the individuals. More often, people were listed by family groups. After the first register, the original lists were updated as necessary, with individuals added or deleted from the list (Saunders 1985). The first Bahamian register was compiled for the year 1821. Jack and Sue Eve are the first couple listed in the 1821 slave register of William Wylly. While this placement in the list may reflect their status within the slave community (from Wylly's perspective), it may also denote a spatial relationship. If the slave inventory were made, house by house, going down the row, from south to north (walking away from the planter's house), then Locus G would be the first house encountered, supporting the argument that this structure was the driver's cabin. The register contains seven families who lived on Clifton plantation, corresponding to the number of cabins in the quarters.

In the 1821 register, Jack is described as a 53-year-old African-born male, and Sue Eve is a 46-year-old African-born woman. Also living with them were their two island-born children, a son, Cato, aged 16, and a daughter, Maria, aged 10 (Register of Slaves 1821). The family does not appear in Wylly's 1822 Register of Slaves entry (Register of Slaves 1822). By 1822, Wylly had left the Bahamas and was living in St. Vincent. It seems likely that the driver and his family accompanied Wylly to St. Vincent. More documentary research is necessary, however, to confirm this interpretation. None of the family members are mentioned specifically in Wylly's (1827) will. There is no evidence in the Bahamas to suggest that Wylly sold this family or that they died, ran away, or were manumitted. The house at Locus G does not appear to have been occupied after the Wylly period. As a consequence, it appears that the materials recovered from around this cabin are associated with the activities of the Jack and Sue Eve's household.

Unlike many of the other structures in the quarters, the standing architecture at Locus G is poorly preserved, with no intact walls, only crumbled foundation walls. Archaeological testing suggests that the structure was only occupied during William Wylly's ownership of the plantation, from approximately 1813 to 1827. The archaeological remains associated with the cabin provide a unique opportunity to study creolization within a single family over a short span of time. Artifacts recovered in association with this structure include creamwares, pearlwares, free-blown and dip-molded bottles, buttons, clay pipes, and faunal remains (Wilkie and Farnsworth 1997). While it is unusual to be able to tie a specific enslaved family to a particular house, what is even more significant about this household is that was composed of two African-born individuals and their children. Through the archaeological exploration of Locus G at Clifton plantation, it is possible to investigate the negotiation of creole identities through consumer choices of an African family.

Africans in the Bahamas

The island of New Providence was home to a large, thriving, African community during the Loyalist Period (1793-1835). After the formal abolition of the African slave trade in 1807 (Higman 1984), Britain seized large numbers of Africans bound for Cuba as contraband. Many of these individuals were conscripted into the British West Indies Regiments, while others were "apprenticed" to planters on different islands (CO 1811; Craton and Saunders 1992). Free African settlements grew in the "Over the Hill" section of Nassau and on the western end of the island. Some of these settlements retained distinctive African ethnic identities. For instance, Baintown residents maintain that they are descendants of the Yoruba peoples (from modern Nigeria), while their neighbors, in Contabutta, are Congos (from modern Congo) (Eneas 1976:7-8). Eneas (1976:36), in a synthesis of oral histories from Baintown, reported that throughout the late 19th and early 20th centuries, the two groups maintained distinct communities and had minimal social interaction.

A relatively large African population appears to have lived and worked at Clifton. In 1821, at the time of the first Bahamas Slave Register, Wylly was listed as owning 67 slaves who were spread across three plantations. Fifteen of these individuals were registered as having been born in Africa, representing slightly more than 20% of the total enslaved population. Based upon an 1818 record of families allotted provisioning grounds (CO 1818b), at least 44 of the enslaved individuals lived at Clifton, of whom at least 10 were African-born.

Although the geographic origins of the Clifton slaves are not known, given the strong sense of Yoruba and Congo identities that survived elsewhere on New Providence Island, it seems appropriate to focus particularly upon potential continuities in Yoruba and Bakongo (Congo) cultural ideals and practices. According to Higman (1984:127, Table 5.10), as many as 31% of the African slaves brought to the British Caribbean between 1790 and 1807 were from central Africa. A majority of these people were Bakongo. Slave registers from the Bahamas, as well as newspaper advertisements for runaways, mention individuals with names such as "Congo Jim," or individuals of Congo background (Register of Slaves 1825; Saunders 1985:82). The documentary record suggests that enslaved and free Congo peoples lived in the Bahamas. Less clear is how much of the Yoruba population was free versus enslaved. Yoruba influences continue in modern-day New Providence, most strikingly perhaps in the traditions of Junkanoo, where representations of the *orisha* are incorporated into celebratory parades (Bethel 1991). An annual street carnival, taking place on Boxing Day (26 December) and New Year's Day each year, Junkanoo consists of masked reveling to the rhythms of cow bells and drums. While scholars disagree on the origin of the Christmastime celebrations found throughout the Caribbean, Bethel (1991) has argued, at least for the Bahamas, that the festival has a distinctly Yoruba influence.

Saunders (1991:22-23) describes the Congo, Ibo, Mandigo, and Yoruba as the most represented African ethnic groups brought to the Bahamas as slaves. A survey of names found on slave registers also indicates the presence of Akan peoples (Wilkie 1993). Saunders (1991:22-23) further states "most of these [African] tribes had maintained the separate identity down to 1960 in the form of the Congo Lodges I and II and the Yoruba Lodge." The lodges were similar to the social aid organizations associated with African-American churches in the southern United States, in that they provided members' families with access to health care and a decent burial (Saunders 1996:26).

In analyzing the material culture of the Clifton plantation households, designs, styles, and decorations found on the ceramics selected by the seven slave households were closely compared with the material culture of Yoruba and Bakongo peoples (Wilkie [1999]), and contrasted with the ceramics recovered from Wylly's household. A number of distinctive attributes of the driver's house assemblage suggest Bakongo aesthetic and religious traditions. Most striking was evidence drawn from ceramics and tobacco pipes.

Ceramics

Ceramics were identified according to ware, decoration, pattern, decorative colors, vessel form, vessel size, and alterations. In addition to these attributes, the minimum number of vessels was determined through reconstructable elements. First, it was necessary to determine whether the assemblages recovered from the slave quarters reflect the consumer decision-making of the enslaved population versus actions of the planter, such as provisioning or gifting of ceramics. To this end, the diversity and distribution of ceramic types from the planter assemblages and slave cabins were compared. This analysis was completed by the project co-director (Farnsworth 1999). In his analysis, Farnsworth compared

TABLE 1
DISTRIBUTION OF DRIVER'S CABIN CERAMICS BY VESSEL FORM

Vessel Form	MNV	%
Flatwares	12	18.5%
Hollowwares	19	29.2%
Soup plates	1	1.5%
Tea wares/Coffee wares	20	30.8%
Food Preparation/Service	8	12.3%
Storage	4	6.2%
Health/Hygiene	0	0
Other	1	1.5%

diversity of ceramic types (based upon ware, decoration, and color) recovered from the planter house and slave cabin assemblages. He found that 154 distinct ceramic types were recovered from Clifton. Only one type was found at the plantation house, kitchen, and slave cabins: undecorated creamware. In comparing the assemblages from the slave cabins, Farnsworth found that undecorated creamware is still the only type common to each household. Farnsworth hypothesizes that Wylly distributed undecorated creamware to his enslaved people. This said, undecorated creamware only accounts for 9% of the driver's assemblage.

Farnsworth then compared the ceramic types recovered from the cabins. He found that 31 types were unique to the quarters, representing 28% of the ceramic assemblages recovered there. Each cabin with more than 10 vessels had at least 2 types unique to that cabin. The diversity of the assemblages within the quarters suggested to Farnsworth that the majority of ceramics used by the enslaved people were not supplied by the planter, but rather were purchased by individual families. Given the results of Farnsworth's analysis, it is appropriate to consider the cultural factors that influenced selection criteria in one of these households.

During analysis of the ceramics from the driver's house, a minimum of 65 vessels were identified. All of these vessels are of English manufacture and represent types common to the time period. When analyzed according to form (Table 1) (Otto 1984), the vast majority of vessels are tea wares and hollowwares. Teacups and saucers were recovered from the site in nearly even numbers, with eight saucers and seven teacups represented. Such a pattern superficially suggests that the items were being used together. When these vessels are analyzed by decoration, however, it is clear that the saucers and teacups overlap little in decoration type, let alone pattern (Table 2). Six of the eight saucers recovered from the house are hand-painted, whereas the teacups include hand-painted, annular, transfer-printed and over-glazed porcelain decorative examples. While both cups and saucers were obviously used within the household, it is not clear that they were used (or even obtained) as matched pairs in any way. It is likely that these vessels were being used in ways different from the ways they would have been used in English households.

Leland Ferguson (1992) has discussed the importance of condiments within West African cuisine, stating that these are often served in small individual bowls, similar in size and shape to teacups. Starches and meats may be served communally from larger bowls or platters (Ferguson 1992). Condiments, particularly homemade pepper sauces that have the consis-

TABLE 2
DISTRIBUTION OF DECORATIVE TYPES BY VESSEL FORM

	Undecorated	Shell-edged	Dipped	Sponged	Hand-painted	Printed	Porcelain
Bowls	2	0	9	1	6	1	0
Plates	2	5	0	0	1	4	0
Saucers	1	0	0	0	6	1	0
Teacups	1	0	1	0	0	2	2
Tea service	0	0	0	0	0	0	0
Mugs	2	0	2	0	1	0	0
Service vessels	1	1	1	0	2	1	0
Health and Hygiene	0	0	0	0	0	0	0

Note. Refined white earthenwares and porcelain only

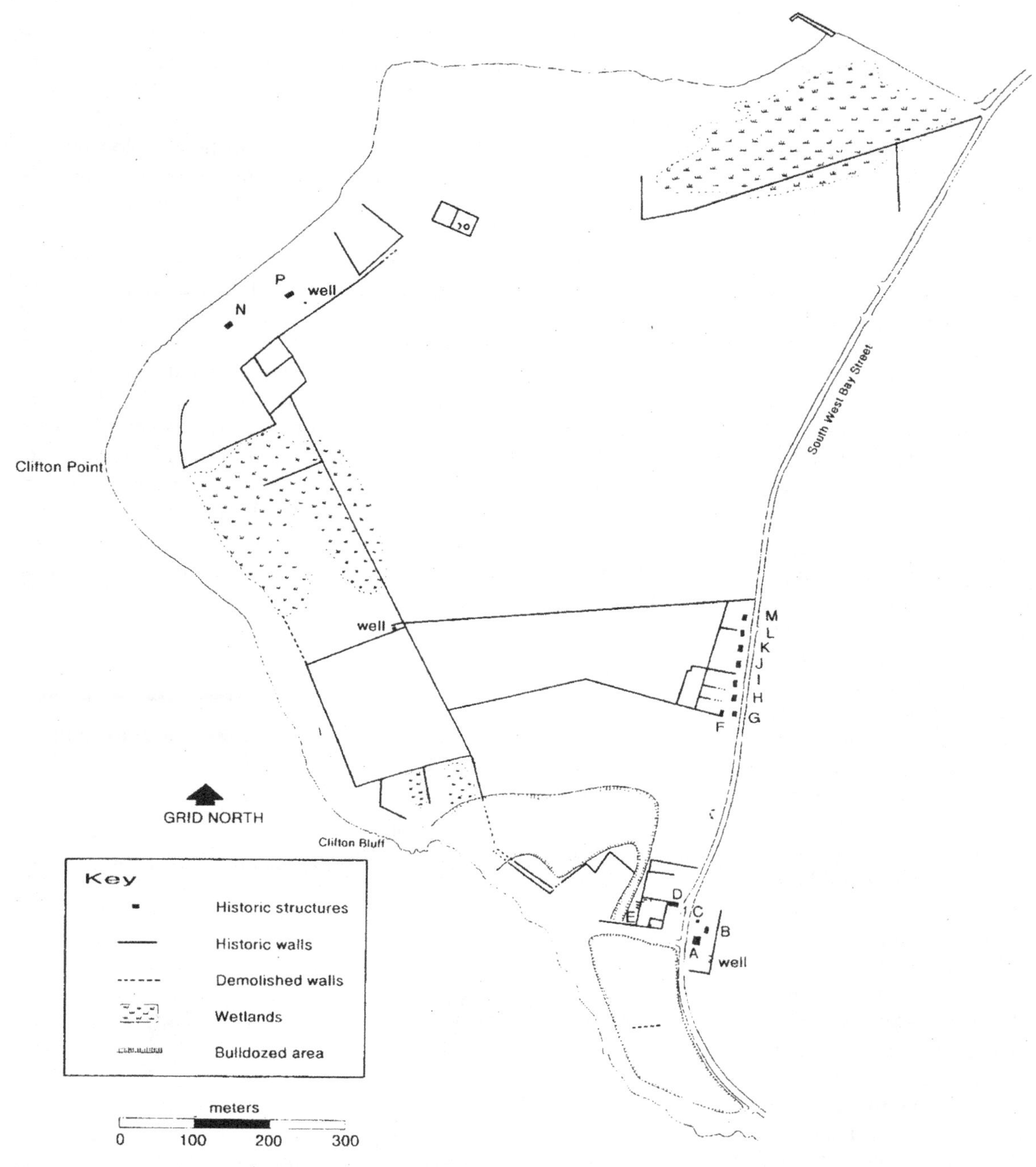

FIGURE 1. Map of Clifton Plantation.

tency of tomato paste, are an important element of Bahamian cuisine. The teacups recovered from the site could have been used to serve such condiments, in addition to any other role they served.

Bowls selected at the site tend to be high-sided and deep (Figure 2) rather than shallow. Of the five bowls that could be identified as to height, base diameter, and rim diameter dimensions, four were deep bowls with 8 cm base diameters and 18 cm rim diameters. Based upon sherd curvature, as many as 14 of the 17 bowls recovered from the site could have been of this morphology. These bowls imitate in form Colono Ware vessels reported from South Carolina, and Yabba wares from Jamaica (Armstrong 1983; Ferguson 1992).

Food preparation items recovered from the house include two stoneware cooking crocks. Bahamians today often serve liquid-based one-pot meals, such as souses (a hot and sour soup) and stews. Leftovers have new ingredients added to them, and the dish evolves over time. The mixture that results at the bottom is referred to locally as "pot-cake." Faunal remains from the house and associated slave kitchen indicate that a variety of locally procured fish and queen conch (*Strombus gigas*) were among the most important meat sources. Today, these animals are commonly prepared as stews, souses, teas (thin broths), and chowders. Such meals are most easily consumed from bowls. People today can be seen consuming chowders and teas by drinking them from cups, perhaps also providing another potential interpretation of the large numbers of tea wares found archaeologically.

An analysis of the households' ceramics by decorative type suggests specific styles were selected over others. The analysis has been completed using the four broad decorative categories defined by Miller (1980, 1991). It was decided not to use Miller's (1980, 1991) available year by year price indices, since it is not clear that these numbers would accurately reflect the relative value of these wares to one another within the Bahamian market. Farnsworth (1996) has a fuller discussion of the ceramic trade in the Bahamas. Of the 53 decorated refined white earthenware ceramics from the household, 17% were plain, 33.9% were minimally decorated, 32.1% were hand-painted, and 17% were transfer-printed. While plain ceramics were the least expensive wares available (Miller 1980, 1991), archaeological evidence clearly demonstrates that the family preferred more expensive ceramics. Within the group of the minimally decorated ceramics, 11 of the 18 vessels in this class were annular or mocha decorated. This distribution contrasts with ceramic use among European planter populations in the Bahamas and southeastern United States, whose assemblages often contain high proportions of flatwares, and particularly shell-edged wares (Baker 1980; Otto 1984; Farnsworth 1996, 1999). At Clifton, four out of the five minimally decorated ceramics recovered from Wylly's residence were fragments from shell-edged flatware. At Wylly's kitchen, a building that possibly doubled in function as housing for servants, shell-edged wares were also slightly greater in frequency than dipped wares, consisting of 13 to 12 vessels, respectively. A comparison of the styles of dipped wares recovered between the planter's kitchen and the driver's cabin deserves note. Nine of the 11 dipped ware vessels recovered from the driver's cabin were decorated with annular band designs. The remaining vessels included one mocha ware and one inlaid slip-decorated vessel (Sussman 1997:33). In contrast, the dipped wares from the planter's kitchen consist of six annular vessels; one cat's eye vessel; three cable-decorated vessels, and one marbled vessel (Sussman 1997). The selection of annular wares over other dipped

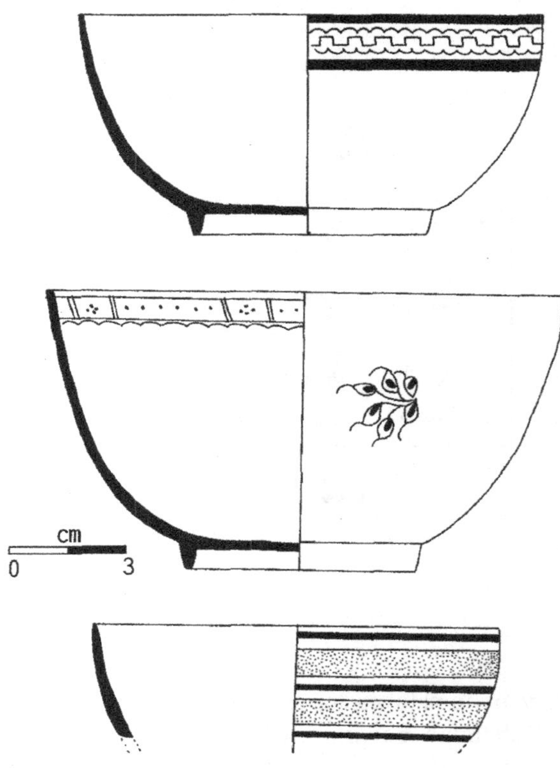

FIGURE 2. Examples of bowls recovered from Locus G.

wares may reflect an African cultural preference. Two early 20th-century photographs of chiefs' graves in Zaire demonstrate that annular and mocha vessels were used to decorate the surface of the graves (Thompson 1981:183-187; Figures 165 and 170). Although the photographs date to the early 20th century, the bottles and ceramics covering the surface of the graves suggest an earlier, possibly mid-19th-century, depositional date.' The photographs suggest that similar preferences shaped the selection of European-manufactured goods by these groups.

The composition of the ceramic assemblage's color pallet also suggests an African aesthetic, rather than European preferences. Hand-painted and dipped wares (mocha, banded, cat's eye, etc.) were analyzed to see if certain colors were represented to a greater degree than others in the assemblages. The analysis was limited to these decorative types since they were available in a wide range of colors through the Nassau market (Farnsworth 1996). In contrast, transfer-prints during this time were limited almost exclusively to blue, and it is unclear whether edged wares in colors other than blue or green were available. The planter assemblages from Clifton clearly indicate that Wylly's family selected predominately blue-decorated vessels for their household. Of the minimally decorated and hand-painted vessels from that residence 60% included the color blue, and 50% of these decorative types from Wylly's kitchen had this color (Wilkie 1997). Jack and Sue Eve's table demonstrated a different range of color choices. In analyzing the hand-painted and dipped wares from the site, although a range of different-colored decorations were available, the driver's family preferred brown and orange over all other colors. Brown was found on 63% of the vessels, while 44.4% of the vessels had orange decoration. Only 29.6 % of the vessels contained the color blue. In contrast, 20% of the vessels from the planter's residence, and 40% of those from the planter's kitchen included brown decoration. A total of 40% of the vessels from the planter's residence, and 5% from his kitchen had orange decoration. A comparison of specific designs recovered from the two house sites failed to identify any patterns that were common to the driver and planter families. In other words, there is no evidence that the planter was provisioning the driver with "hand-me-down" ceramics.

The analysis of the color composition of the assemblage can be viewed in another way. Based upon the reconstruction of minimum vessel counts, to some degree it has been possible to identify the range of color mixing visible on particular vessels. As previously mentioned, minimum vessel counts were derived using decorative patterns, colors, ware, vessel form, vessel size, and reconstructability. Since complete vessels were not reconstructable, the colors attributed to each vessel represent the minimum of colors found on any particular vessel. Of the 29 dipped and hand-painted vessels identified from the driver's cabin, 11 were decorated with one color, 13 with at least two colors, and 5 with at least three colors. The majority of vessels, therefore, were decorated with polychromes.

In contrast, the planter's house had five hand-painted and dipped vessels, of which only one had at least two colors. The planter's kitchen follows a similar pattern. From this structure, 11 vessels were decorated with one color; 3 with at least two colors; 2 with at least three colors; and 3 with at least four colors. The kitchen assemblage also suggests a predominance of less colorful vessels, yet at the same time contains vessels that have more colors on them than any from the driver's house. As mentioned previously, the planter's kitchen assemblage contains styles of dipped wares not found at the driver's cabin. The vessels containing at least four colors were all examples of cat's eye, worm and finger-swirled dipped wares.

Differences in the color pallets between the planter and driver assemblages are also visible in the incidence and pairing of colors. At Wylly's house, orange and green are the only paired colors. Brown and blue occur only as monochromes. In the planter kitchen assemblage, the color blue is most likely to occur on a monochrome (Table 3) and the colors that occur together on the same vessel with the greatest frequency are brown and blue. These colors occur together on 3 of the 19 dipped and hand-painted vessels. In the driver's assemblage a very different color assortment is visible (Table 4). Brown, the most prevalent color in the assemblage, is found as a monochrome as well

TABLE 3
COLOR-MIXING ON DIPPED AND HAND-PAINTED VESSELS:
PLANTER'S KITCHEN

Incidence of Color	Blue	Brown	Yellow	Orange	Green	Black	Gray-Brown
Alone	5	2	0	1	3	0	0
With 1 other color	0	3	1	0	0	0	0
With 2 other colors	1	2	1	0	2	0	0
With 3 other colors	3	2	2	0	0	2	1

Note. Number of Vessels = 19

as paired with one or two other colors. Orange, however, is found only paired with other colors. Brown and orange appear paired together on 8 of the 12 vessels that contain orange. Blue and brown, despite the relative abundance of each color, are paired on only one vessel. These differences suggest that alternate values and taste preferences may have shaped the construction of the two assemblages.

As noted above, the ceramic assemblage from the driver's house demonstrates a preference for annular or mocha wares over shell-edged flatwares, as well as a preference for expensive hand-painted and annular-decorated ceramics over other categories of ceramics. A brief consideration of Bakongo art traditions may provide some insight into these patterns. Important Bakongo crafts traditions include the production of ceramics, wood-carving, and cloth production. Personal and ethnic aesthetics were also commonly expressed through body art such as scarification, tattooing, hair braiding, or the wearing of ornamental art such as beads and piercings. As artistic elements, geometric lines, chevrons, bands, and lines of dots are commonly used to adorn crafts and bodies (Thompson 1981, 1983).

Bakongo pottery is decorated with incised and applied decorations, and little use of paint (Thompson 1981). Decorative elements are often organized in concentric bands that horizontally decorate a vessel. Within these bands, chevrons, dots, zigzags, and crosses are often used. A number of different bands of decorations can found along the horizontal axis of the pot and the elements are visually separated from one another by solid incised lines or raised clay bands (Figure 3*a*). Chevrons and bands and dots are also commonly found on the refined white earthenwares English potters marketed as dipped, which includes annular, mocha, cat's eye, engine-turned wares, etc. (Figure 2)(Miller 1980, 1991; Sussman 1997). English hand-painted wares also frequently include these elements. While dipped wares derive their decorations from their glaze, many vessels include incised decorations. In addition, dipped wares often consist of several different bands of decoration

TABLE 4
COLOR-MIXING ON DIPPED AND HAND-PAINTED VESSELS:
DRIVER'S CABIN

Incidence of Color	Blue	Brown	Yellow	Orange	Green	Gray
Alone	3	4	0	0	2	0
With 1 other Color	3	6	3	7	2	0
With 2 other colors	1	4	1	5	2	1

Note. Number of vessels = 29

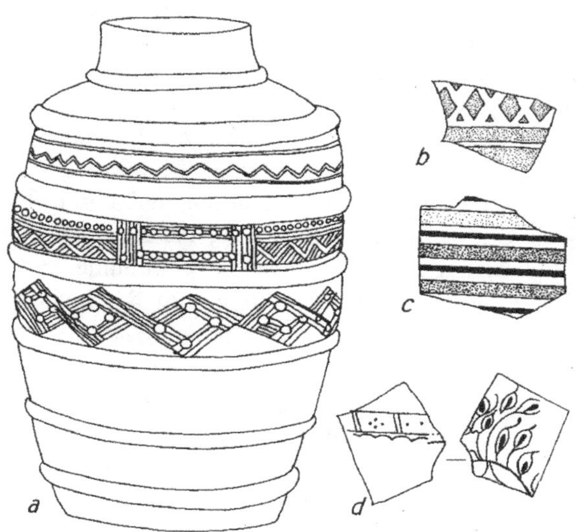

FIGURE 3. Comparison of design elements from Bakongo pottery with vessels found at Locus G, Clifton Plantation: *a*, Bakongo funerary pot (after Thompson 1981:82, Figure 47); *b*, engine-lathed design; *c*, banded bowl; *d*, hand-painted bowl, note how the dots mimic those on a. The series of four dots represent the four moments of the sun in Bakongo cosmology.

that are delineated from one another through the use of dark or different colored annular rings (Figure 3*c*). Hand-painted wares also often contain polychrome banded borders, while transfer-printed vessels do not. At the driver's cabin, at least 3 of the 11 annular decorated vessels were decorated with engine-turned chevrons, while an additional vessel was engine-lathed with cross-hatching similar to that found on some Bakongo pots (Figure 3*b*).

While the vessel forms and decoration method used in the production of the English hollowwares are very different, the design elements and the organization of the designs conform to Bakongo decorative elements for pots. While the dipped ceramics are certainly not the equivalents of the African pots, to an African consumer faced with an array of English hollowwares to choose from, the dipped wares were likely the most appropriate selection.

In addition to the organization of the ceramics decorative elements, the color pallet associated with the assemblage from Locus G may also reflect cultural preferences. The browns, oranges, yellows, and greens found on both banded and hand-painted ceramics are commonly found in West African cloth (Thompson 1983), perhaps suggesting another motivation for the selection of these ceramics. While painted ceramics were not typically used by Bakongo people, when faced with industrially manufactured ceramics that were decorated, they possibly selected familiar colors that were commonly used in different African artistic media that appealed to their aesthetic sensibilities.

The specific designs on hand-painted English ceramics that may have held additional cultural meanings to African and African-Bahamian people also need to be considered. While many of the hand-painted patterns were geometric designs and floral patterns, portions of birds were represented on at least three vessels. In each instance, the birds portrayed are peacocks, or at least their feathers (Figure 3*d*). Birds are commonly found in West African sculpture, and are often associated with deities, witchcraft, and wisdom (Thompson 1983). Among the Bakongo, birds represent souls in flight or spirits because their wings fan the air, like spirits or witches (MacGaffey 1986:131). Thompson (1983:76, plate 48) illustrates a fan from Cuba that was made for the Yoruba *orisha Yemayá* and was adorned with peacock feathers, which he states denotes witchcraft. In other contexts, African-styled pipes decorated with animal and bird imagery have been recovered archaeologically from slave quarters throughout the Chesapeake region (Emerson 1988, 1994). While these pipes were manufactured by African or African-American craftsmen, the potential importance of such imagery should not be discounted when found on English-made pottery in the households of enslaved Africans.

Additional Bakongo imagery may be conveyed in the ceramics from Locus G. Examples of Colono-Ware pottery found in South Carolina are incised with X's and quartered circles. The elements were located on the exterior and interior bases of bowls. Leland Ferguson (1992) has convincingly argued that these symbols may represent New World versions of the Bakongo cosmogram, like those identified by Robert Ferris Thompson (1981, 1983) in Haiti. In its original form, the Bakongo cosmogram is a quartered circle, with smaller circles on the end of each axis representing the four movements of the sun.

The cosmogram represents the circle of life and death and the progression of the seasons.

When placed on the base of a bowl, whether it in the interior or exterior, the cosmogram signifies a bowl used to create *nkisi*, or sacred medicine. *Nkisi* can take many forms, including statuettes, bowls and their contents, and bundles of magical ingredients tied in cloth (MacGaffey 1991). Magical bundles of herbs and cloth can commonly be seen hanging from or immediately outside Bahamian houses, and are believed to serve as protective medicine for the house's occupants. This practice may be Bakongo in origin.

The ceramic assemblage from the driver's house (Locus G) may provide archaeological evidence of *Nkisi* (Wilkie 1997). One of the hand-painted ceramic sherds recovered from the driver's cabin (Figure 4*c*) bears a design remarkably similar to the Bakongo cosmogram (Figure 4*a*). When part of a complete vessel, this design would have been located on the interior base of the bowl, similar to the South Carolina Colono-Ware designs (Figure 4*b*). On the broken sherd, the design is nearly centered, and perhaps was curated after the bowl broke.

Although this industrially manufactured design bears a remarkable resemblance to the South Carolina examples of Bakongo cosmograms, several important differences should be noted. First, the South Carolina examples are predominately recovered from water contexts, on nearly intact vessels, not from midden contexts. It cannot be assumed, based upon the house yard context, that the sherd was intentionally discarded. Objects of some value, such as coins, beads, and gilt buttons have been recovered from the house yards. The thick, dusty soil of the swept yards provides poor visibility for locating dropped artifacts. At the same time, the recovery of this symbol, a symbol of great sacred importance in South Carolina, from among household debris in the Bahamas, could alternately suggest that the symbol's meaning was different to the Bahamian user. As stated previously, the driver was responsible for the Christian training of the enslaved population. How sincerely the driver may have embraced Christianity cannot be known. At least one of the enslaved families on Clifton abandoned the Methodist beliefs that Wylly encouraged when they joined a local black Baptist church (Craton and Saunders 1992:302). The midden context from which this sherd was recovered may suggest a secularization of the cosmogram symbol's meaning to the family. Instead of retaining the full sacred meaning, the cosmogram may have been seen as a familiar and comforting decorative device. Likewise, the significance of the design may have been to communicate a sense of ethnic identity both within the house-

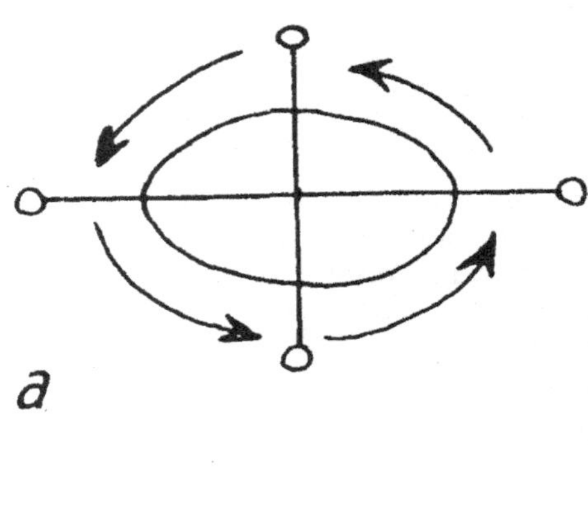

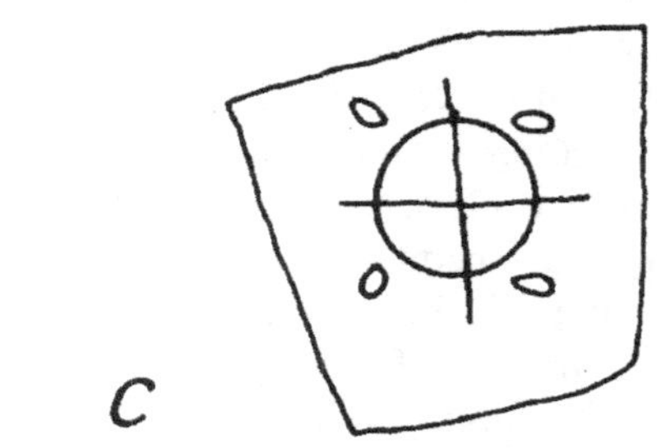

FIGURE 4. Various representations of the Bakongo cosmogram: *a*, as found in Africa (after Thompson 1981); *b*, as found on Colono wares in South Carolina (after Ferguson 1992); *c*, as found at Clifton Plantation.

hold and within the community. The enslaved population of Clifton was undoubtedly ethnically mixed. Ethnographies from the late-19th and early-20th centuries demonstrate that strong ethnic identities provoked tensions between different descendant communities (Eneas 1976). The cosmogram-decorated bowl may have been a means of communicating a sense of ethnic solidarity within the enslaved community.

Tobacco Pipes

At Clifton plantation, tobacco was used by planter and enslaved person alike. The greatest frequencies of pipe fragments were found at the planter residence and kitchen (Wilkie and Farnsworth 1997). While fewer pipes were recovered from the slave quarters, a greater diversity of pipe types was recovered from the cabins than the planter complex. Twenty-four pipe fragments, representing a minimum of five pipes, were recovered from the driver's cabin. At least four distinct designs were represented on the five vessels. Wylly is known to have distributed tobacco to his enslaved population at Christmas (Saunders 1985:231), but the decoration differences suggest contrasting consumer preferences. Like the ceramics, the diversity of pipes styles recovered from the quarters likely reflects the consumer choices of the enslaved population.

African-styled and decorated pipes manufactured in the New World have been recovered from the Chesapeake region of the United States. The pipes were incised with significant motifs, including a Nigerian *kwardata* motif, that symbolized the transition to adulthood among the Ga'anda. Other designs consist of a cattle motif found throughout West and Central Africa, and a lozenge with surrounding circlets, which has also been found on Ashanti vessels from Ghana (Emerson 1988:148-152). While Emerson (1988) has not interpreted the potential meanings of pipes bearing ritual symbols, their presence suggests that tobacco pipes in other American settings have been manufactured and used to express ethnic affiliation and ritual practice. It is important to consider how the imagery on Bahamian pipes may have been viewed by African consumers.

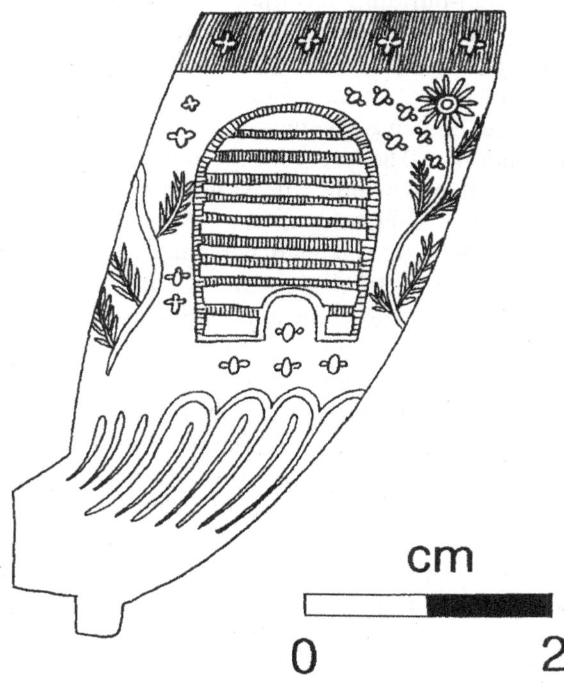

FIGURE 5. Tobacco pipe recovered from Locus G bearing beehive design.

One pipe recovered from Locus G was embossed with a prominent bee hive surrounded by flying bees, and was additionally decorated with flowering vines (Figure 5). The manufacturer of these pipes has not yet been identified, although they were undoubtedly manufactured in Europe or the United Kingdom. The distinctiveness of this pipe design led to a consideration of whether these motifs could have had any additional meanings to a Bakongo slave. Further exploration of Bakongo imagery revealed that ant and termite hills were powerful physical and metaphysical objects within Bakongo cosmology. MacGaffey (1986:74) cites termite hills as locations inhabited by the dead. Termite hills are important parts of the spiritual landscape, and people passing by them may be expected to make small offerings to them (MacGaffey 1986:80). "Termites are like the dead in that they fly, like souls and spirits, but live 'underground' in a gravelike mound" (MacGaffey 1986:263). Like birds, flying insects often symbolize divination or spiritual revelation within Bakongo belief systems (MacGaffey 1986:133).

Mound-building termites are not limited to West Africa; termites that build large, dome-shaped mounds, sometimes standing up to 4 to 5 ft. [1 to 1.5 m], are commonly found throughout the Bahamas, including the site of Clifton plantation. The presence of these mounds in the Bahamas would allow the opportunity to construct a continuity in the spiritual landscape to an enslaved Bakongo person. The tobacco pipe potentially represents a very powerful iconographic image to a Bakongo user. What was a beehive surrounded by bees to someone of European descent, to a viewer of Bakongo descent could be a termite hill surrounded by flying insects. Like the Bakongo cosmogram, which emphasizes the relationship between life and death, and the interrelationship of each in the life cycle, the tobacco pipe could portray the same juxtaposition between the living and the dead. The dead in the termite hill exist among the living, symbolized by the flying insects, with one stage of existence always balancing the other. This artifact potentially represents the appropriation of a common European design element for a sacred Bakongo one. Again, it is necessary to recognize that while the imagery of the pipes suggests symbolic continuity in Bakongo beliefs, the meaning of this imagery may have been transformed from that of its African origin.

Conclusion

Efforts to identify the ethnicity of African groups in the New World have traditionally attempted to use items manufactured through craft production or architectural types. It should be apparent, hoever, that through the application of a grammar-based creolization model, a clearer recognition of how mass-produced materials could be used and perceived in uniquely African ways can be reached. Archaeologists must closely examine material assemblages to attempt to recognize the multiple meanings or symbolic attributions artifacts may have held to multiple users, in this case, enslaved Africans. Such consideration is essential when considering how much of enslaved assemblages are composed of mass-produced European goods. Enslaved people, in the ways that they incorporated mass-produced goods into daily interactions and routines, not only created a means for constructing African-based identities in the New World, but were also provided a means of masking distinct African identities. If modern archaeologists who explicitly search for evidence of African continuities in material culture have failed to recognize the importance of mass-produced goods, it is likely that 18th- and 19th-century planters were victims of the same oversight.

A close inspection of materials recovered from the driver's house at Clifton plantation suggests that household assemblages, even when comprised exclusively of European-manufactured goods, still had the potential to convey African aesthetic sensibilities. When acquiring ceramics, color, decoration, and vessel form, were all dictated by distinct cultural values. Through comparison of ceramic styles and iconographic imagery found on mass-produced goods, it is even possible to suggest a Bakongo ethnicity for Jake and Sue Eve. Dipped wares recovered from the house are decorated much like Bakongo ceramics, using bands of decoration and incising. Several artifacts recovered from the driver's house could be interpreted as having Bakongo meanings. A very close likeness of a Bakongo cosmogram was recovered on a ceramic sherd from the house. When it was a complete vessel, the location of the symbol would have paralleled the same placement of this symbol on a handmade pot. Vessels bearing the likeness of birds, also powerful spiritual symbols, were recovered. Finally, the embossed design of the beehive on the clay tobacco pipe evokes iconography surrounding termite hills that were considered to be sacred objects. The ceramic sherd bearing a likeness of the Bakongo cosmogram and a ceramic vessel depicting birds, with their Bakongo symbolic implications, found in association with a tobacco pipe bearing another potentially significant Bakongo iconographic image, seems more than coincidental. Jack and Sue Eve may be recorded in the documentary record of the Bahamas as "African," but the archaeological record more explicitly seems to suggest that they were Bakongo.

The point here is not to contribute an example of cultural historical particularism to the archaeological literature. Rather, there are several underlying intentions. First, this essay should be viewed as an illustration of how ethnographic ties can be used in attempting to understand the multiple meanings that objects, particularly industrially produced goods, may have held to different consumers. Although it is possible to identify through the documentary record the possible cultural origins of enslaved populations, with a few notable exceptions (Ferguson 1992; Haviser 1997), archaeologists have been hesitant to explore the possibility that distinct ethnic identities survived the Middle Passage, opting instead to adopt a "pan-African" model to explain continuities.

The first generation of African individuals brought to the New World often hoped to return to their homes (Mullin 1992). As parents, these individuals had every reason to instill a sense of ethnic identity and heritage in their children. Craft and industrially manufactured goods offered opportunities to express cultural values. The grammar-based model of creolization provides a means of understanding how African-born enslaved people sought to organize and explain the new sensations, experiences, materials, and ideas that they faced in the New World. They confronted their new lives as transplanted Africans. While these African-born individuals underwent the process of creolization, their children, however, were already creoles. The world so foreign to their parents was, for better or worse, the homeland of these first African-Americans. During childhood, this generation would have encountered the values and practices of their parents' homeland as filtered through their New World experiences. As this first generation of creoles reached adulthood, some would marry other creoles, some would marry African-born mates. Like their parents before them, they would negotiate African and New World identities with their children, and possibly extended family, within their homes and communities. As the African slave trade grew to a close, fewer and fewer members of the community would have had first-hand memories of Africa.

African cultures could not be simply duplicated or replicated in the New World. Interactions with members of different ethnic heritage (be that heritage African, European, or Native American), intermarriage, and adaptations to new environments all influenced the ways individuals came to conceptualize their new lives. Any constructions of New World African identity were embedded within the context of the racism and oppression of enslavement. Enslaved people negotiated a sense of self that navigated around these obstacles. Ultimately, these are the forces that shaped the process of creolization.

ACKNOWLEDGMENTS

The 1996 archaeological research at Clifton Plantation was supported by grants from the University of California Committee on Research and the University of California Berkeley Stahl Endowment for Archaeology. Additional financial and logistical support was provided by the Bahamian Departments of Archives, Lands and Surveys, Ministries of Tourism and Education, the Bahamas National Defense Force, and the Bahamas National Trust. The field season was a success due to the efforts of numerous staff and students from UC Berkeley and Louisiana State University. I thank Paul Farnsworth for his tireless support. I would particularly like to thank Shannon Dawdy, Mark Groover, Paul Mullins and an anonymous reviewer for their thoughtful comments and suggestions. Their insights have greatly enriched my interpretations, though, of course, I take responsibility for any remaining flaws. Finally, thank you to Alexandra, who personally supervised much of the writing of this paper.

REFERENCES

ARMSTRONG, DOUGLAS V.

1983 *The Old Village at Drax Hall Plantation: An Archaeological Examination of an Afro-Jamaican Settlement.* Ph.D. dissertation in Anthropology, University of California, Los Angeles. University Microfilms International, Ann Arbor, MI.

1990 *The Old Village and the Great House.* University of Illinois Press, Urbana.

BAKER, VERNON

1980 Archaeological Visibility of Afro-American Culture: An Example from Black Lucy's Garden, Andover, Massachusetts. In *Archaeological Perspectives on Ethnicity in America: Afro-American and Asian-American Culture History*, Robert Schuyler, editor, pp. 29-37. Baywood Publishing Co., Farmingdale, NY.

BETHEL, E. CLEMENT

1991 *Junkanoo: Festival of the Bahamas.* Macmillan Caribbean, London, England.

BROWN, KENNETH L., AND DOREEN C. COPPER

1990 Structural Continuity in an African-American Slave and Tenant Community. *Historical Archaeology,* 24(4):7-19.

COLONIAL OFFICE RECORDS (CO)

1811 African List on Service of the Customs, Port of Nassau, CO 23/63:292-307. Original Correspondence, Colonial Office Records, Public Records Office, Kew, Richmond, Surrey, England.

[1812] Wylly's Rules of Clifton Plantation. CO 23/67:147. Original Correspondence, Colonial Office Records, Public Records Office, Kew, Richmond, Surrey, England.

1818a Letters from Wylly defending management of Clifton Plantation, enclosed in letter from Munnings to Bathurst, 31 August 1818, CO 23/67:147-153. Original Correspondence, Colonial Office Records, Public Record Office, Kew, Richmond, Surrey, England.

1818b Account of Provisioning Grounds at Clifton Plantation, enclosed in letter from Munnings to Bathurst, 5 September 1818, CO 23/67:164-165. Original Correspondence, Colonial Office Records, Public Record Office, Kew, Richmond, Surrey, England.

Craton, Michael, and Gail Saunders

1992 *Islanders in the Stream: A History of the Bahamian People*. University of Georgia Press, Athens.

Emerson, Matthew C.

1988 *Decorated Clay Pipes from the Chesapeake*. Ph.D. dissertation, Department of Anthropology, University of California, Berkeley. University Microfilms International, Ann Arbor, MI.

1994 Decorated Clay Tobacco Pipes from the Chesapeake: An African Connection. In *Historical Archaeology of the Chesapeake*, Paul A. Shackel and Barbara J. Little, editors, pp. 35-39. Smithsonian Institution Press, Washington, DC.

Eneas, Cleveland W.

1976 *Bain Town*. Cleveland and Muriel Eneas, Nassau, Bahamas.

Farnsworth, Paul

1996 The Influence of Trade on Bahamian Slave Culture. *Historical Archaeology*, 30(4):1-23.

1999 Isolation and the Development of Bahamian Culture. *Proceedings of the 17th Caribbean Archaeological Congress*.

Ferguson, Leland

1992 *Uncommon Ground: Archaeology and Early African America, 1650-1800*. Smithsonian Institute Press, Washington, DC.

Franklin, Maria

1995 Rethinking the Carter's Grove Slave Quarter Reconstruction: A Proposal. *Kroeber Anthropological Society Papers*, 79:147-164.

Gaucher, Conduce

1997 African-Caribbean Technology: Forging Cultural Survivals. Paper presented at the 17th International Congress for Caribbean Archaeology, Nassau, Bahamas.

Handler, Jerome S.

1996 A Prone Burial from a Plantation Slave Cemetery in Barbados, West Indies: Possible Evidence for an African-Type Witch or Other Negatively Viewed Person. *Historical Archaeology*, 30(3):76-86.

1997 An African-Type Healer/Diviner and His Grave Goods: A Burial from a Plantation Slave Cemetery in Barbados, West Indies. *International Journal of Historical Archaeology*, 1(2):91-130.

Handler, Jerome S., and Frederick W. Lange

1978 *Plantation Slavery in Barbados: An Archaeological and Historical Investigation*. Harvard University Press, Cambridge, MA.

Haviser, Jay B.

1997 Social Repercussions of Slavery as Evident in African-Curaçaoan "Kunuku Houses." Paper presented at the 17th International Congress for Caribbean Archaeology, Nassau, Bahamas.

Herskovits, Melville

1962 *Myth of the Negro Past*, reprint of 1941 edition. Beacon Press, Boston, MA.

Higman, Barry W.

1984 *Slave Populations of the British Caribbean, 1807-1834*. Johns Hopkins University Press, Baltimore, MD.

Joyner, Charles

1984 *Down by the Riverside: A South Carolina Slave Community*. University of Illinois Press, Urbana.

MacGaffey, Wyatt

1986 *Religion and Society in Central Africa*. University of Chicago Press, Chicago, IL.

1991 *The Art and Healing of the Bakongo*. Folkens museum-etnografiska, Stockholm, Sweden.

Miller, George L.

1980 Classification and Economic Scaling of 19th-Century Ceramics. *Historical Archaeology*, 14:1-40.

1991 A Revised Set of CC Index Values for Classification and Economic Scaling of English Ceramics from 1787 to 1880. *Historical Archaeology*, 25(1):1-25.

Mintz, Sidney W., and Richard Price

1976 *The Birth of African-American Culture*, 1992 edition. Beacon Press Edition, New York, NY.

Mullin, Michael

1992 *Africa in America: Slave Acculturation and Resistance in the American South and the British Caribbean 1736-1831*. University of Illinois Press, Urbana.

Otto, John Solomon

1984 *Cannon's Point Plantation, 1794-1860*. Academic Press, Orlando, FL.

Pearce, Laurie

1993 To Whom do They Belong?: Cowrie Shells in Historical Archaeology. *African-American Archaeology*, 9:1-3.

Pulsipher, Lydia M.

1993 Changing Roles in the Life Cycles of Women in Traditional West Indian Houseyards. In *Women and Change in the Caribbean*, J. H. Momsen, editor, pp. 50-64. Indiana University Press, Bloomington.

REEVES, MATTHEW
1996 "To Vex a Teif": An African-Jamaican Ritual Feature. Poster and text, presented at the Society for American Archaeology Conference, New Orleans, LA.

REGISTER OF SLAVES
1821 Return of William Wylly. Department of Archives, Nassau, Bahamas.
1822 Return of William Wylly. Department of Archives, Nassau, Bahamas.
1825 Register of 1825. Department of Archives, Nassau, Bahamas.

SAMFORD, PATRICIA
1996 The Archaeology of African-American Slavery and Material Culture. *The William and Mary Quarterly*, 3rd series, 53(1):87-114.

SAUNDERS, GAIL
1985 *Slavery in the Bahamas 1648-1838.* Gail Saunders, Nassau, Bahamas.
1996 *Social Life in the Bahamas 1880s-1920s.* Rosebud, Nassau, Bahamas.

SAUNDERS, HARTLEY C.
1991 *The Other Bahamas.* Bodab Publishers, Nassau, Bahamas.

SUSSMAN, LYNNE
1997 Mocha, Banded, Cat's Eye, and Other Factory-Made Slipware. *Studies in Northeast Historical Archaeology,* No 1. Council for Northeast Historical Archaeology, Boston, MA.

THOMPSON, ROBERT F.
1981 *Four Moments of the Sun.* National Art Gallery, Washington, DC.
1983 *Flash of the Spirit.* Vintage Books, New York, NY.

TURNER, GRACE
1993 An Archaeological Record of Plantation Life in the Bahamas. In *Amerindians, Africans, Americans: Three Papers in Caribbean History.* G. Lafleaur, S. Branson and G. Turner, editors, pp. 107-125. Department of History, University of West Indies, Mona, Jamaica.

VLACH, JOHN MICHAEL
1993 *Back of the Big House: The Architecture of Plantation Slavery.* University of North Carolina Press, Chapel Hill.

WILKIE, LAURIE A.
1993 Continuities in African Naming Practices among the Slaves of Wade's Green Plantation, North Caicos. *Journal of the Bahamas Historical Society,* 15(1):32-37.
1995 Magic and Empowerment on the Plantation: An Archaeological Consideration of African-American World View. *Southeastern Archaeology,* 14(2):136-148.
1997 Secret and Sacred: Contextualizing the Artifacts of African-American Magic and Religion. *Historical Archaeology,* 31(4):81-106.
1999 Evidence of African Continuities in the Material Culture of Clifton Plantation, Bahamas. *Proceedings of the 17th International Caribbean Congress.*

WILKIE, LAURIE A., AND PAUL FARNSWORTH
1996 Preliminary Results of the 1996 Excavations at Clifton Plantation. *Journal of the Bahamas Historical Society,* 18:50.
1997 Daily Life on a Loyalist Plantation: Results of the 1996 Excavations at Clifton Plantation. *Journal of the Bahamas Historical Society,* 19:2-18.

WYLLY, WILLIAM
1827 Last Will and Testament. Supreme Court Wills, W-Y, 18 March 1827, Department of Archives, Nassau, Bahamas.

LAURIE A. WILKIE
DEPARTMENT OF ANTHROPOLOGY
UNIVERSITY OF CALIFORNIA
BERKELEY, CA 94720

"What'll Thou Have": Quakers and the Characterization of Tavern Sites in Colonial Philadelphia

John M. Chenoweth

In 1766, Ebenezer Robinson, an active Quaker and middle-class tradesman, was one of the first to develop the land just north of Independence Hall, then at the edge of urban Philadelphia. Recent work on Independence Mall sponsored jointly by the National Park Service and the National Constitution Center has uncovered several features on this property, but analysis and historical documentation has suggested that a low-class tavern occupied the spot while Robinson owned it. This paper examines artifacts from a privy associated with this period of the site and compares the finds with several other sites to characterize this tavern, explore the different roles taverns played in colonial communities, and clarify the relationship of the tavern with its Quaker landlord. The study is further contextualized with a discussion of Quakerism and attitudes towards alcohol in the colonial period.

En 1766, un membre actif de la communauté Quaker et marchand de la classe moyenne nommé Ebenezer Robinson fut l'un des premiers à développer la terre au nord de l'édifice Independance Hall qui se trouvait à cette époque en bordure du centre urbain de Philadelphie. Des travaux récents, organisés par le National Park Service et le National Constitution Center, ont été menés sur la place Independence Mall. Ces travaux ont révélé plusieurs éléments architecturaux sur cette propriété. Les analyses et la documentation historique suggèrent que l'emplacement ait appartenu à Robinson et qu'une taverne populaire s'y trouvait. Cet article examine les artefacts des latrines associés à cette période d'occupation du site et offre une comparaison entre les découvertes faites sur ce site et celles d'autres sites dans le but de caractériser cette taverne, d'explorer les différents rôles joués par les tavernes dans les communautés coloniales et de clarifier la relation entre la taverne et le propriétaire Quaker. L'étude est de plus mise en contexte à l'aide d'une discussion sur les Quakers et les attitudes sur l'alcool à l'époque coloniale.

Introduction

Modern views of colonial taverns are colored by reconstructions such as those in Philadelphia and Colonial Williamsburg, which are expensive and elegant dining places for upper-class tourists. Members of the Religious Society of Friends—better known as Quakers—are often perceived as being somber and—literally—sober, plainly dressed and mild mannered, disapproving of alcohol and other entertainments. Given this, the discovery of a low-class colonial alehouse on Quaker-owned land might come as a bit of a surprise. In fact, Quaker morals (past and present) cannot be so easily summed up, and taverns served many vital and sometimes conflicting roles in colonial society. This discovery not only offers the opportunity to study the small, ephemeral taverns that represented the vast majority of colonial drinking establishments, but also invites us to problematize popular conceptions of Quakerism.

Background

In 1766, Ebenezer Robinson purchased an empty lot of ground at the corner of Fifth Street and Cherry Alley, then at the edge of urban Philadelphia (FIG. 1), from the Cresson brothers, land developers and fellow Quakers. Robinson was one of the first to buy and to build in the area, just three blocks north of Independence Hall. He erected a one-story house, insured it in May of 1768, and rented it to various tenants until he and his family moved there in 1781.

In 1999, this site was chosen for the construction of the National Constitution Center. Figure 2 shows the National Constitution Center in 2005; Robinson's plot of land would have been partly under and partly just in front of the furthest right-hand corner of the building as pictured. Archaeological investigations took place in advance of the construction. Sponsored jointly by the National Park Service (NPS) and the National Constitution Center, this work was conducted by the CRM firm

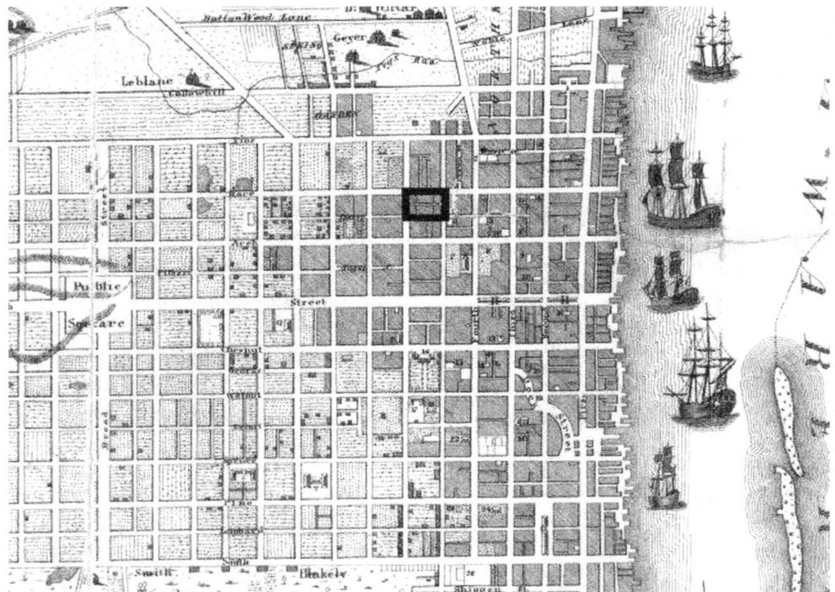

Figure 1. Map of Philadelphia in 1775 with 5th and Cherry block highlighted. Robinson owned part of the southeast (bottom right) corner of this block (Varte 1875, Library of Congress, Map Collection).

Figure 2. The National Constitution Center in 2005. Robinson's land is under and in front of the right-hand corner of the building (photo by the author).

Kise, Straw and Kolodner (KSK) and recovered over one million artifacts in hundreds of features. The NPS and KSK kindly allowed me access to these materials, and this paper presents the findings from one feature on this site—Feature 209—coupled with archival and historical research. The analysis suggests that this feature is associated with a low-class tavern, present on Robinson's land while he owned it, but before he himself moved there. I compare this site to others in order to characterize this tavern, explore the different roles taverns played in colonial communities, and clarify the relationship this tavern may have had with its Quaker landlord.

Ebenezer Robinson and his Community

Ebenezer Robinson was an active member of the Philadelphia Quaker congregation or "Monthly Meeting" from his arrival in the city in 1745, bearing a letter of recommendation from the Burlington Meeting which stated that he "behaved himself orderly whilst amongst us Was [*sic.*] pretty diligent in attending our Religious Meetings" (Certificates and Removals of the Philadelphia Monthly meeting, 4th day of 3rd month, 1745). He remained in Philadelphia for much of the next 65 years, living for brief periods in Morristown, Burlington, and Bristol, dying in the latter town in 1810 probably about the impressive age of 85. He married twice and had at least four children, two of whom—daughters Sarah and Mary—survived to adulthood. From 1748 until his death, he was a landowner and a successful landlord. Although his occupation is listed as "mason" and "bricklayer" in the early years, and "brushmaker" later in life, he owned at least five houses simultaneously, and several others in both Philadelphia and Bristol over the course of his long life. This was in an era when only about 20 percent of Philadelphians owned the house

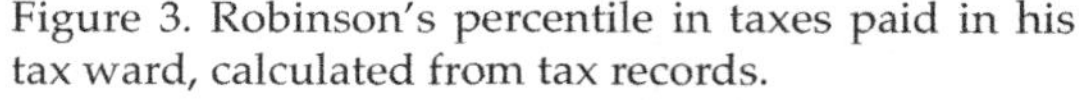

Figure 3. Robinson's percentile in taxes paid in his tax ward, calculated from tax records.

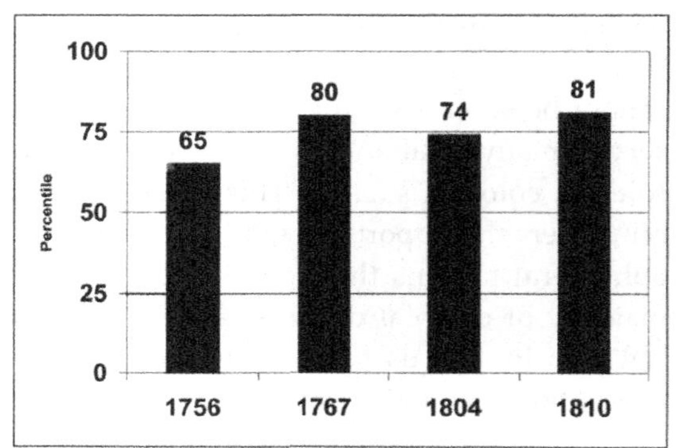

they themselves lived in, let alone others (Toogood 2004).

Tax records reveal him to be in the upper percentiles in his tax ward in terms of tax paid for much of his life (FIG. 3), and late in life he stopped calling himself a "brushmaker" and is listed as a "gentleman," indicating that he had attained a level of stability and success. At his death in 1810, his will reveals a picture of a man who is at least upper-middle class: besides his considerable real estate holdings, his probate inventory and the accounts of his executors list household goods, debts owed to him, and cash in the bank worth $1,819.72 1/2.

Ebenezer Robinson's success was more than financial, however, and his standing within the Quaker community was evident. Each time he moved to a new area and began attending a new Meeting for Worship, a certificate of removal—always favorable—went with him and was formally entered into the receiving Meeting's records. Lacking a hierarchical power structure by design, Quaker Meetings made many decisions and performed many actions in committees of their trusted and respected members. It is considered a duty to serve on a committee, but it also represents a level of confidence and trust on the part of the community (Philadelphia Yearly Meeting [PYM] 1997: 177–8), and so committee involvement can be used to assess a Quaker's social standing (Brown 1987: 251).

In years following, the minutes of the Monthly Meeting show that Robinson was asked to help "preserve order and quiet among our Youth during the term of Worship," to visit and "treat with" other members in "melancholy and disorder'd" states, and to help those "laboring in distress and want in this time of close tryal and deep suffering [the Revolutionary War]." He traveled as far as Burlington, New Jersey, to give recommendations on behalf of other Quakers and was even asked to see to the whitewashing and repair of the meetinghouse itself. Perhaps his greatest honor was to be elected six times as one of the four representatives to the Quarterly Meeting. In all, Robinson was given an assignment from the Meeting a total of 50 times in the 17-year period between 1781 and 1798. Clearly he was, and continued to be, an important and trusted member of the community throughout the period.

The Excavation and Finds

Feature 209 is a round, 4 ft (1.2 m) diameter, brick-lined shaft feature, approximately 5 1/2 ft (1.67 m) of which remained when the area was excavated in June 2001. The firm of Kise, Straw and Kolodner conducted the work under contract to the National Park Service. KSK also cleaned and cataloged the artifacts, and pieced some vessels back together before this analysis began. The feature was excavated in four natural levels, defined in the forthcoming report as Strata I through IV, and artifacts from this feature were assigned a "Field Specimen" or "FS" number which either corresponded to one of these strata, represented an area of interface between two strata, or—in two cases—represented an arbitrary bisect of a single stratum to facilitate collection and storage (FIG. 4). Most of the artifacts were recovered from a dense, 4 in (10 cm) layer at the bottom of the excavation. Feature 209 yielded 7,350 artifacts, mostly bottle and window glass and ceramic sherds along with

Figure 4. Schematic cross section of Feature 209, with strata and FS labeled (by the author after Kise, Straw and Kolodner forthcoming, and Douglas Mooney, personal communication 2005).

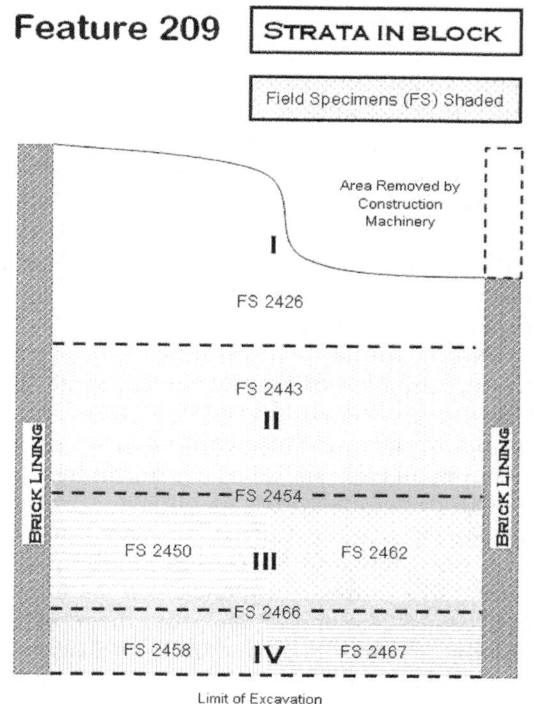

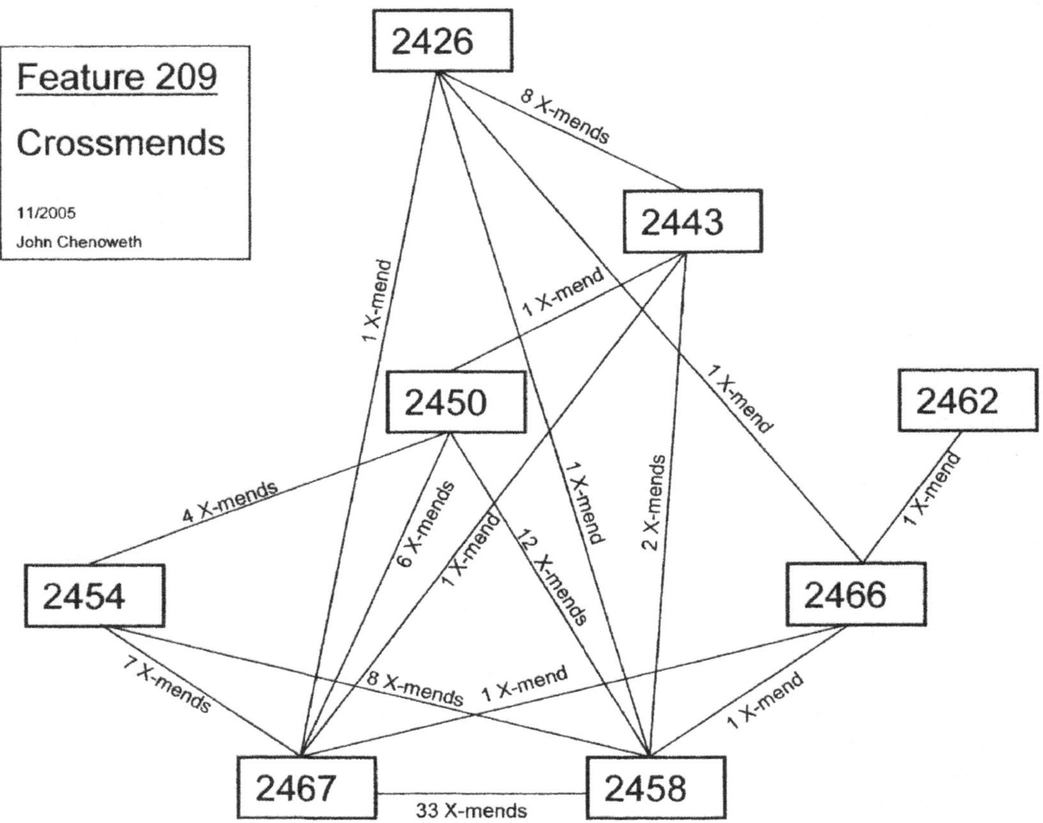

Figure 5. Diagram of crossmends between Feature 209 contexts.

dense areas of brick and gravelly construction debris overlaying and intermixing with the artifacts. The deposits of the feature seem to date from a short time frame. The *terminus post quem* for the feature is 1762 in all levels, and the mean ceramic dates have been calculated by KSK as ranging between 1743 and 1771 (all data in this paragraph from Kise, Straw and Kolodner forthcoming, and Douglas Mooney personal communication 2005).

Notable in the analysis of this feature was the high number of crossmends that could be made between contexts ("FS" numbers), including one vessel reassembled out of pieces found in all eight divisions of the feature (FIG. 5). Out of the 138 vessels identifiable by form, 50 (36%) were reconstructed from sherds found in more than one FS (although the most impressive number of mends—the 33 found between FS 2458 and FS 2467—are the result of an arbitrary division of a stratum as described above). Several items were whole or almost completely reconstructable, suggesting that they were deposited whole and not broken beforehand. This coupled with the high number of crossmends makes it possible that the entire deposit represents a single cleanout event.

In general, the artifactual assemblage is characterized by a high proportion of simple red-bodied earthenwares, which comprise 67% of the entire ceramic collection of almost 2,500 sherds (FIG. 6). Most have a simple lead glaze, often only on the inside, and this sloppily applied. Many items, such as the porringers and mugs, are highly uniform in size and appearance (FIG. 7), suggesting that they were made at the same time and purchased from the same source. Several pieces, mostly rough platters or pie-plates, have simple yellow and brown slip-glaze, all only on the inside. At first glance, this modest assemblage is in keeping with a pious Quaker intent on living a simple, plain life. However, neither the assemblage nor Quaker morals are so easily explained.

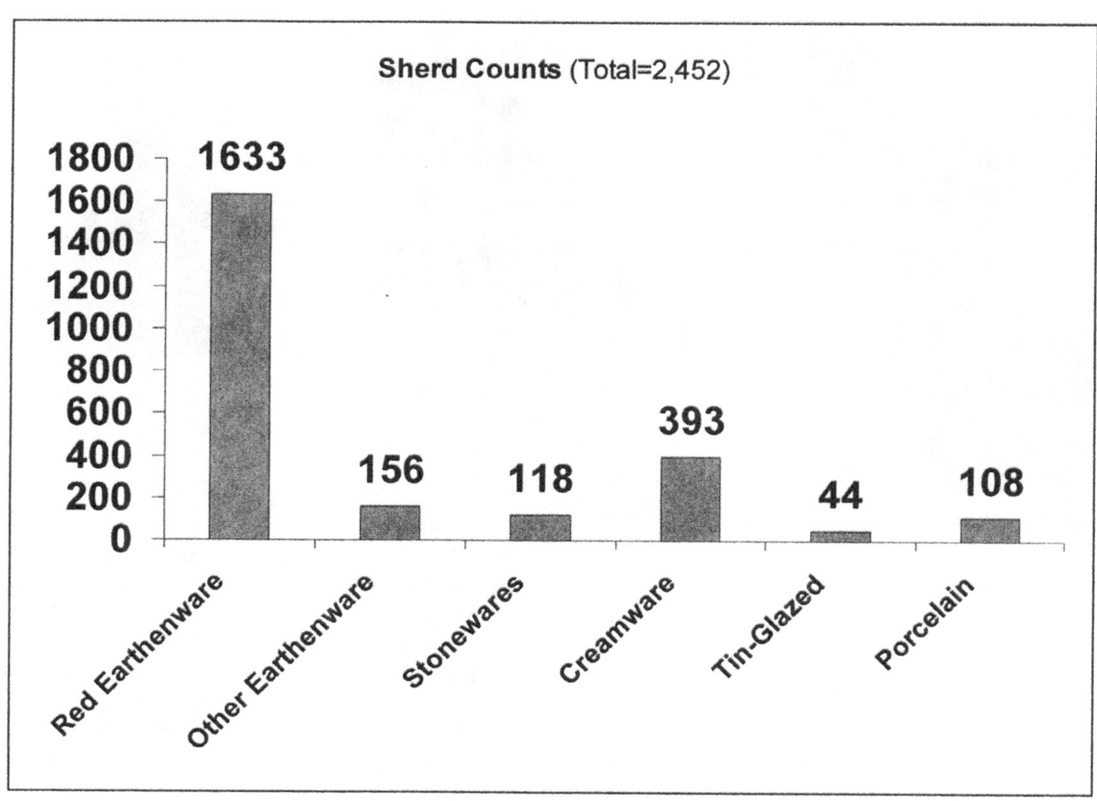

Figure 6. Sherd counts by type for Feature 209 (Kise, Straw and Kolodner forthcoming).

Perhaps the most significant aspect of the assemblage is revealed by an analysis of the vessels by form. Prominent in the assemblage were the numbers of mugs, porringers, teawares and serving platters (TAB. 1). From the ceramic and bottle glass fragments recovered, 138 separate vessels could be identified. The largest single group was that of glass bottles (including wine/liquor and case bottles), which numbered 44, almost a third (32%) of the entire number of vessels identifiable by form.

As the analysis continued, it became clear that the assemblage was not representative of an ordinary home, even that of a person of extremely modest means or one intent on living a "plain" life. The presence of many cheap redware porringers and very few plates suggested a simple stew or porridge instead of formal dining, and the high number of bottles and rough redware mugs looked distinctly more like a tavern of modest means. This interpretation is supported by Bragdon's (1981) description of a six-part "tavern signature," although this "signature" is considered more below. This represents an interesting case where archaeological evidence actually determined the course of documentary research, and a search of the lists of tavern licenses issued during this time yielded the name of one of Robinson's known tenants: Melchior Neff was issued a "license to retail Liquors by small Measure" in July of 1780, while he was living at the Fifth and Cherry property.

The city's licensing laws (discussed in greater detail below) make it highly unlikely that Neff could have operated a tavern on the site without Robinson's knowledge and consent. At some point between July of 1780 and the following spring the historical record suggests that the tavern closed down, and Neff was explicitly denied when he tried to renew his license in 1781. The quick deposition of Feature 209 suggests that it is a cleanout as noted above, and its contents imply connection to the tavern on the site. This makes it possible that the cleanout may have been the result of Robinson's returning to live on the site in the

Figure 7. Reconstructed porringers (photo by the author).

Table 1. Minimum vessel counts by form in Feature 209.

Form	*N*	*%*
Drinking		
Mugs	10	7.2
Teacups	10	7.2
Saucers	10	7.2
Tumblers	7	5.1
Wine Glasses	1	0.7
Eating		
Porringers	11	8.0
Platters (Redware)	10	7.2
Bowls	4	2.9
Plates (Creamware)	3	2.2
Storage/Serving		
Storage Pots	14	10.1
Creamers	1	0.7
Round Bottles	36	26.1
Case Bottles	8	5.8
Decanters	1	0.7
Health/Hygiene		
Chamber Pots	6	4.3
Galley Pots	2	1.4
Medicine Bottles	2	1.4
Ointment Jars	1	0.7
Lids	1	0.7
Total vessels	138	

spring of 1781, and disposing of the last of the tavern equipment Neff left behind.

Like other colonial cities, Philadelphia hosted many—perhaps hundreds (Cotter et al. 1992: 162; Thompson 1999: 27)—of ephemeral, local, low-class taverns. These taverns are largely unrecorded because their clientele is largely unrecorded by history and because they do not survive long enough to be noted in and of themselves, unlike more famous, purpose-built establishments such as Philadelphia's "City Tavern," frequented by the founding fathers. Most of these ephemeral taverns would have been little more than private homes known to possess liquor licenses where a drink might be had, and this conflation with private homes, along with their short duration, means that tavern-related deposits for such sites are likely to become mixed with preceding and following occupation deposits. But here, the tightly packed nature of the deposit in Feature 209 suggests that the privy had been cleaned regularly during its use, and its short deposition period makes it possible that it contains artifacts almost exclusively from the tavern period of the Fifth and Cherry building, an extraordinarily narrow window. Therefore, this feature offers an opportunity to explore both the character of such taverns and how the existence of this one reflects on its landlord and Quaker culture during this time.

Quakers and Taverns

The suggestion that a pious, active Quaker was the landlord to a tavern certainly raises questions. Quakers were well known to disfavor strong drink, a position they adopted long before the rise of the "temperance" movement in the first half of the 19th century. For instance, Anthony Benezet, a prominent Friend, is primarily known to history as an anti-slavery activist, but his famous "Potent Enemies of America Laid Open" (1774) referred to two equally (in his estimation) dangerous evils: slavery and "Distilled Spirituous Liquors."

As early as 1706, "advices" were issued to members of Quaker meetings that "none accustom themselves to...sipping or tippling of Drams and strong Drink" (PYM 1797: 86). These increased in Ebenezer's day, and an advice issued both in 1777 and 1781 discouraged any Friends from using spirits, distilling them for sale, encouraging distillation, or even selling grain to one who intended to use it for distillation into liquor (PYM 1797: 86–87). This trend continued in the last years of the century, to the point that Quakers insisting on distilling liquor were explicitly threatened with the church's highest punishment, disownment (removal from the Meeting), until such time as they repented (PYM 1797: 89).

All of these sentiments were felt strongly by the community in which Ebenezer Robinson lived. Just two months after Melchior Neff was approved for his license, the minutes of the Philadelphia Quarterly Meeting, a body that Robinson was elected to join as a representative six times (although not at this particular Meeting), included the following statement about Friends' business and alcohol:

> The accounts also in general import, that Friends are nearly clear of keeping Houses of public entertainment—Distilling spirituous liquors from grain—Selling their Grain for that purpose, or purchasing spirits so made.—The few instances excepted are said to be under care (Minutes of the Philadelphia Quarterly Meeting, 7th day of 8th Month, 1780).

Considering this, would Ebenezer Robinson not have been in violation of his community's standards? If owning a tavern, frequenting a tavern, and participating even tangentially in the manufacture of spirits are all disallowed, being a tavern landlord would appear to break the spirit of the law, even if it was not itself prohibited. Nonetheless, Ebenezer continued to receive assignments and to be trusted with responsibilities for his Meeting. No comments appear in the minutes of the meeting suggesting that Ebenezer's was a case "under care" for any transgression.

Quaker Attitudes toward Liquor Reexamined

For Quakers, as for others in colonial America, taverns and liquor were a much more complex issue than the last paragraph implied. Fundamentally, Quakerism is rooted in an individual relationship with the divine, and as such entails a strong element of individual conscience. Although Meeting organizations did exert considerable control over many aspects of their members' lives, Quaker beliefs are based in individual experience, and therefore rules of being a "good Quaker" cannot be seen as entirely prescriptive. For Friends, religious decisions—matters of conscience included—were not to be handed down from a hierarchical structure but were reserved for the small worship group and, ultimately, the individual (PYM 1997: i, 175). It may be that individual members of the Meeting, especially respected and trusted members like Ebenezer Robinson, would have been allowed a certain latitude, for instance to engage with the alcohol trade at arm's length. In certain cases, this would certainly have enabled Ebenezer to rent to a tavern without fear of reprisal from his community or his own conscience. The question is: what cases?

In and of themselves, early Friends had no particular animosity toward taverns or alcohol. The principle founder of the movement, George Fox, was himself known to stay at "alehouses" when traveling (Fox 1952: 306), and it was not uncommon for Friends to be innkeepers in the early days (Cadbury 1952: 744). In Ebenezer Robinson's time, the Philadelphia Yearly Meeting even admits the necessity of occasionally visiting taverns on business (PYM 1797: 125). Thus Quakers' problems with taverns may be seen as more complicated than a simple distrust of liquor itself. Quaker priorities lay with family and community life, and spiritual and temporal security, which allowed them to practice their faith. It is only certain secondhand effects of involvement in the liquor trade and consumption of liquor that threaten these, namely damage done to Quakers' reputations and prospects for their financial security.

First, public perceptions of Quakers were directly tied to their safety and their continued ability to act within their consciences because the renewal of laws of religious toleration was contingent on Friends being seen as "behaving as responsible subjects" (Frost 2003: 25). Raucous taverns were disapproved of even by the non-Quaker public which might easily blame "outsider" Quakers involved, but a respectable establishment posed no threat of public disapproval to anyone. Second, although Quakers are publicly imagined as rejecting of the world's wealth, several historical (Walvin 1997) and archaeological (Brown 1987; Cotter et al. 1992) studies have shown that Quakers had no fear of financial success. On the contrary, the pursuit of some degree of wealth was required by Quaker morals, for it was only with a certain level of financial security that one could provide adequately for one's family. "Excessive" spending was the problem, but this was very much a relative term—spending more than one was able while still providing for the family (Frost 2003: 27). In the same vein, even though alcohol was demonized as a waste of money, many Quakers saw drink in moderation by those who had plenty as perfectly acceptable.

Quaker Restrictions on Tavern Licensing

With all of these conditional problems with taverns and drink, Quakers sought not their elimination, but their regulation. In truth, they could not have eliminated taverns if they tried, for taverns have been widely acknowledged to be a fundamental part of life in the colonial world, frequented by all elements of society and serving a vital role for workmen, merchants, and travelers. Though originally tempted to forbid them from his colony altogether, Pennsylvania's Quaker proprietor William Penn soon realized their necessity as places of commerce, and for other functions (Thompson 1999: 21).

Beginning with Penn's 1701 "Charter of Privileges," taverns were carefully regulated, and only those owners judged to be of "appropriate" moral character were allowed to operate them. Since taverns were needed for accommodation and food for travelers, all taverns were required to provide these functions and so fill that need in the community. While a crooked tavern working against these rules would bring vice, waste, sin, and the wrath of the community, it was hoped that a well-run, respectable tavern would counter all these forces. In this view, there would certainly have been opportunities for Quakers to protect their public image, avoid waste, and protect—even help to provide for—their families, and yet take part in the tavern trade on some level.

If Quakers had no inherent problems with taverns, then what was the situation of Melchior Neff? In July of 1781, only one year after being granted a tavern license, Neff was explicitly turned down for a renewal and the tavern seems to have closed. If Quaker rejection of taverns hinged on their irresponsible use, then their acceptance of them hinged on their being used well, moderately, by those who could afford it, and on their filling a vital community need. So, what sort of tavern was the house of Melchior Neff?

Characterizations of Taverns from Archaeological Remains

Archaeological considerations of taverns have used several statistical measures to shed light on the character of public houses in colonial America. Bragdon (1981) built on South's (1977) artifact pattern ideas and attempted to define an archaeological "tavern signature." Her comparison of taverns with domestic sites produced six characteristics one would expect to see in the archaeological assemblage of a tavern: 1) a large number of vessels; 2) a large percentage of drinking vessels; 3) a large percentage of those ceramic types most often used for making drinking vessels; 4) large numbers of wine glasses; 5) specialized glassware; and 6) large numbers of pipe stems.

Rockman and Rothschild (1984) built on Bragdon's work, recognizing that different taverns fill different functions within their communities and that they will therefore produce different archaeological deposits. In particular, they reasoned that rural taverns would primarily be places of accommodation for travelers, while urban taverns would be frequented by those who lived close by, and so would be more specialized and social in function. Since tobacco was an integral part of social activity throughout the colonial period, they hypothesized that the number of pipe stem fragments

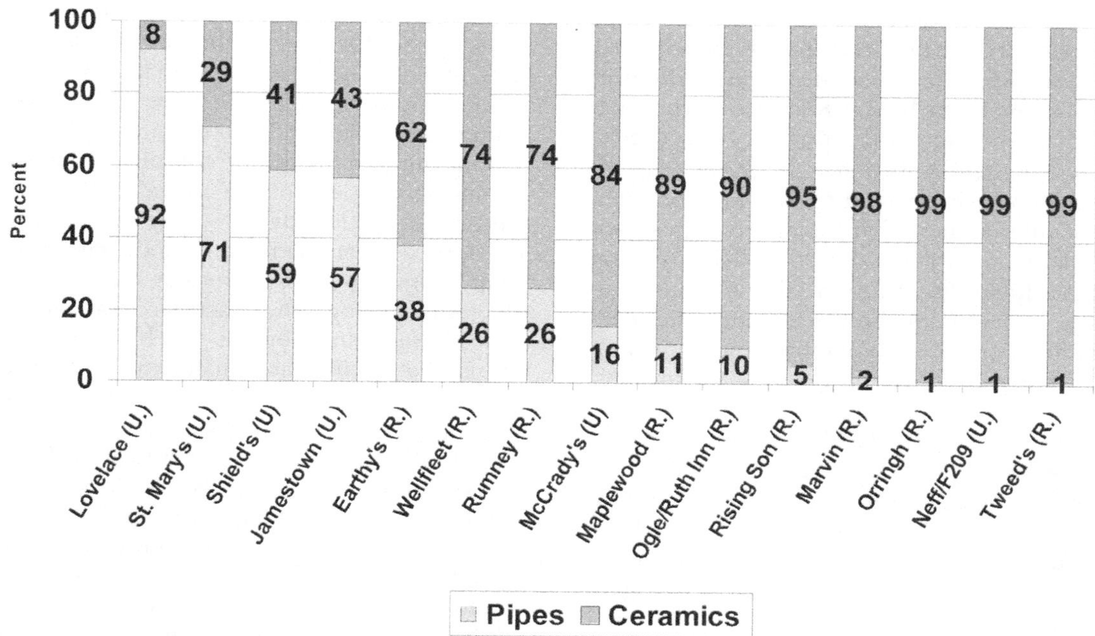

Figure 8. Ceramic sherds compared to pipe fragments (in percentage) for 15 taverns, marked "U" for urban and "R" for rural, as identified by each separate source's author (sources: Lovelace, Jamestown, Earthy's, and Wellfleet: Rockman and Rothschild 1984; St. Mary's ["Inn" occupation only]: King 1988; Shield's ["Early-" and "Transitional" layers only]: Brown et al. 1990; .McCrady's ["Tavern" occupation only]: Zierdan et al. 1982; Orringh: Hayes 1965; Marvin: Espenshade 1998; Maplewood: Rees et al. 1993; Ogle/John Ruth: Coleman et al. 1990; Rumney: Kerns-Nocerito 2004; Rising Son ["18th Century" occupation only]: Thompson 1987; Tweed's: Burrow et al. 2003).

would vary proportionally to the amount of social activity which occurred. On the other hand, ceramics, used in personal care and hygiene as well as cooking and eating—all aspects that had to occur at a traveler's inn but not as much or at all in a city tavern where people met only to socialize—would vary proportionally with the accommodation function of a tavern. Taken together, the two would vary inversely, and this variance should directly correlate to the distance from a city center with more pipe stems relative to ceramics being found in the more urban environments. Their analysis of four sites known to be taverns produced the anticipated inverse relationship, and the authors cautiously concluded that the analysis could separate specialized (usually urban) from generalized (usually rural) taverns.

Several other authors have repeated the Rockman and Rothschild analysis, and the results of some of these, along with additional sites, have been compiled into Figure 8 and Table 2. Clearly, Rockman and Rothschild's method generally holds true, and separates most urban and rural taverns. However, it is notable that there is a great deal of variation.

Table 2. Pipe and ceramic data from comparative taverns (for sources see FIG 8.).

Tavern (Date Range)	*Pipes*	*Ceramics*	*% Pipes*
Lovelace (1677–1706)	4220	388	91.5
St. Mary's (1668–1690s)	1117	462	70.7
Shield's (1708–1751)	7764	5439	58.8
Jamestown (late 17th cen.)	543	411	56.9
Earthy's (late 17th cen.)	2863	4769	37.5
Wellfleet (1690–1740)	9090	26336	25.6
Rumney (1700–1780)	854	2382	23.3
McCrady's (1770's–1801)	144	739	12.9
Maplewood (1743–1754)	367	3014	10.8
Ogle/John Ruth (1730–1780)	1049	9137	10.3
Rising Son (18th cen.)	46	857	5.0
Marvin (1750–1850)	17	705	2.3
Orringh (1790–1830)	7	461	1.5
Neff/F209 (1780's)	33	2452	1.3
Tweed's (1802–1831)	37	4589	0.8

Sites range from 92 percent to 16 percent pipes for most urban taverns, and 38 percent to 1 percent pipes for rural sites. The position of Neff's tavern in Figure 8 is also surprising. This assemblage is dominated by ceramics over pipe fragments, indicating a rural tavern focused on accommodation and food preparation, but we know that this tavern is just two blocks from Independence Hall in thriving Philadelphia. Furthermore, the vessel assemblage as discussed above does not indicate an emphasis on food preparation and consumption, having few cooking and storage items, and little variety among the serving ones.

Other authors (Coleman et al. 1990, Coleman et al. 1993) have placed more emphasis on this variability, and their analysis combined with the historical discussion above and the wider sample shown here than previously published (the 15 sites shown in Figure 8) suggests that although Rockman and Rothschild's method is a valuable tool, since the variation between sites is so great, an analysis would benefit from a way of parsing out *which* functions a specialized tavern specialized in, and to what extent.

Tavern Function Analysis

As the preceding discussion suggests, while all colonial communities used taverns as a central part of life, different taverns served different functions for their communities. Therefore a method of analysis that is able to judge the relative importance of the primary functions taverns served would be beneficial to understanding the role each tavern played. In our present case of Ebenezer Robinson and Melchior Neff, it might also suggest an explanation for the tavern's short life span, and shed light on the character of small, ephemeral taverns of which Neff's is an example.

To this end, I propose to compare drinking, eating, and "living" (the latter including the hosting of travelers) as three of the principal functions taverns are known to have served. Taking cues from the previous literature, each of these activities may be associated with a category of artifact among ceramic and glass vessels identifiable by form, and the relative proportions of each can then be compared across sites. On one level this is an artifact pattern analysis, like South's or Bragdon's. However, this does not attempt to be predictive, and there is no effort to establish a "tavern pattern." Indeed, the argument is that such a pattern cannot exist in a simple way. The connection of past action and present archaeological remains is usually more complex than we assume—this is one of the central critiques of processualism (Hodder 1986). For this study, an effort has been made to make the necessary "leap" from artifacts to actions as small as possible and, through the discussions above, to place these connections as much as possible within the cultural and historical context of their time. Does the lack of expected wine glasses (discussed below) call the pattern or site identification into question or offer a window into social perceptions of alcohol use? In this study of Philadelphia in the 18th century, I suggest it is more the latter, and so, while this analysis certainly may have application to other sites, it will not yield an equation into which any site may be plugged without consideration of cultural context.

Eating

Eating-related items include platters, plates, porringers, bowls, pans, colanders, and any other form most likely used for the preparation, storage, consumption, or presentation of food. Many previous analyses have separated "storage" verses "serving" items, but each points to the same event: a meal. All taverns in Philadelphia were required to provide food for travelers and workers, and it is part of Rockman and Rothschild's assumption that the extent to which a tavern filled this role would be indicated in the proportion of ceramics. However, this study attempts to delineate between ceramic vessels used for food and those used for drink, and also incorporates glasswares into these categories.

Living

This group covers most of the forms identified that do not fit either of the other categories, and includes chamber pots and other hygiene related forms, as well as inkwells, flowerpots, and similar items. The idea behind this seemingly haphazard category is that these forms are associated with activities that are not transient and therefore would be expected in quantity only at sites where at least some people lived as well as ate and drank, such as an inn or boarding house, or a private home. It should be noted, of course, that some level of these items is to be expected from most taverns since most "publicans" lived at their taverns. Precisely because these artifacts have no inherent connection to taverns, they speak to the generalized character of (some) taverns which the authors of Philadelphia's licensing laws hoped to promote, as they hoped that such places would be more for the hosting of travelers than the drinking of rum.

Drinking

Although this final category is the most obvious, it is also the most telling. Drinking alcohol was almost universal in the 18th century, but the questions being examined here are ones of quantity, the exclusion of other activities, and social meanings. The drinking component was the one lawmakers hoped to keep in check, balanced by taverns' other roles. This category of artifacts would be associated, as Bragdon points out, with large numbers of drinking vessels. However, her suggestion that there would necessarily be a large number of wine glasses in particular at any tavern site is problematic. In Philadelphia, the sale of wine required a special license—one which cost more and Neff did not have—and many taverns sold no wine at all. The separation of higher-class wine consumption from lower-class beer and spirits in the law points to the attitude of those who wrote these laws towards different drinks and those who consumed them. Legal scrutiny might well have been more intense for the latter, and the poor were seen as less able to control their own drinking habits.

"Drinking" would also include any other items most likely related to beverages, such as bottles and jugs for their storage, decanters for presentation, and large, deep bowls for mixing and serving punches. Ideally, teawares would be excluded from this category on the grounds that they represent a different kind of drinking which lawmakers were not opposed to, and a different kind of social practice. The use of tea at tavern sites would be interesting to study in its own right. Although one rarely thinks of imported porcelain teawares in the smoky rooms of colonial taverns, they are found at virtually all tavern sites. However, at the present time separating teawares out is not practical as too few published reports include enough detail to separate the different kinds of drinking vessels. For the time being, teawares have been included in this category, except for saucers. Since saucers and teacups were intended for use as a set, counting each separately might skew this measure even further, so saucers have been excluded entirely. Lids of all sorts also have been excluded from all of these counts on the same grounds.

Results and Analysis

Few reports on taverns have included analysis of vessels by form. For this project, I was able to gather this information for five taverns for comparative purposes. The results, in percentage of vessels identifiable by form in each of the categories defined above, are presented in Table 3 and Figure 9. Numbers for Feature 209 and all comparative taverns were calculated the same way, and including all identifiable vessels regardless of material.

The most notable result is the wide range of figures in the "drinking" category. They

Table 3. Proportional categorization of tavern assemblages. The numbers in parenthesis give the actual vessel count for each category, excluding saucers and lids (see Figure 9 for sources).

Site Name	*Date*	*% Drinking (N)*	*% Eating (N)*	*% "Living" (N)*
Neff's/ F209	1780s	58 (74)	33 (42)	9 (11)
Wellfleet Tavern*	1690–1740	50 (143)	50 (140)	(N/A)*
Shield's Tavern	1708–1800	48 (252)	40 (206)	12 (61)
Maplewood Ordinary	1743–1754	37 (30)	61 (50)	2 (2)
Ogle/John Ruth Inn	1730–1780	24 (106)	72 (317)	4 (20)
Tweed's Tavern	1790s–1831	22 (39)	76 (137)	2 (4)

*See note in caption for Figure 9.

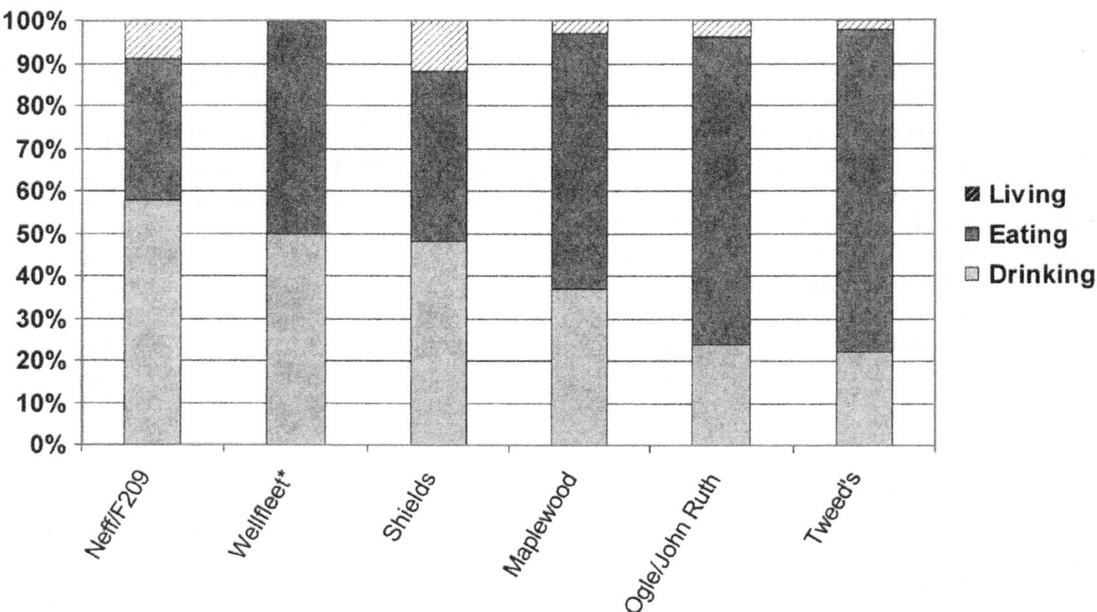

Figure 9. Proportion of vessels at six tavern sites associated with the living, eating, and drinking categories defined in the text (sources: Ogle/John Ruth: Coleman et al. 1990; Tweed's: Burrow et al. 2003; Shields Tavern ["Early-" and "Transitional" layers only]: Brown et al. 2001; Wellfleet: Bragdon 1981 [*Note: Bragdon gives vessel count only for food- and drink-related items, and it is unclear if this excludes other forms or if there were no other forms]; Maplewood: Rees et al. 1993).

range from 58 percent of vessels being drink-related to a mere 22 percent for Tweed's Tavern. Although one would assume drink to be the primary function of colonial taverns from a 21st-century perspective, it seems that other functions are dominant, except in the case of Neff's tavern. This only serves to highlight the diversity of their roles in colonial communities.

Melchior Neff's Tavern as Revealed through Feature 209

The archaeology suggests that Melchior Neff's tavern was not likely to have functioned predominantly as an inn or boarding house, although Neff himself is likely to have lived there as suggested by tax records and a moderate level of "living" items. Nor was it a place where one went and stayed for a great deal of time, chatting and debating with friends, indicated by the low proportion of pipe-stems. Food, as indicated by the proportion of food-related items to drink- and living-related items and lack of variety in the former, was not a major focus of activity (compared to other taverns). The high number of drinking forms—primarily bottles (44) and tankards (10) as well as glass tumblers (7, all heavy bottomed and undecorated forms)—suggests that drink was the primary function of Neff's tavern. This appears to be unusual among colonial taverns, as most other assemblages are dominated by food-related items.

Epilogue: The Rise and Fall of Melchior Neff

Research conducted on Neff produced none of the solid, middle-class records so abundant for his landlord, Robinson. No will was ever registered for him in Pennsylvania, he shows up on none of the Pennsylvania census records which begin in 1790, and his name was not found in the records of any area church or Meeting. In the mid 1770s he had apparently owned some land in Westmoreland County, in rural Pennsylvania, but by 1780 this land is not taxed as his. He appears in two advertisements in the *Pennsylvania Gazette* in

1778, hoping to reclaim a lost horse, and is referred to as a tavern keeper living on Market Street near Front Street. However, no record of his receiving a license to keep a tavern was found for those years, so it is likely that he worked in another keeper's tavern. It may well have been that Neff lost his land in Westmoreland and came to the city to get back on his feet. It appears that he had previous connections to tavern-keeping, and his move to Robinson's land may have been an effort to strike out on his own when he received permission to operate a tavern there in July of 1780.

But something went wrong, and Neff was rejected when he attempted to renew his tavern license in July of 1781. Historian Timothy Thompson (1999: 37) writes that "if a person broke the licensing law…he or she could expect to be barred from the trade, but unless or until a publican broke the law, he had a reasonable chance of keeping house for as long as he desired." The archaeology suggests that the patrons of Neff's tavern came for the rum, not accommodation or food or even to socialize. The tavern was not being used moderately if all its patrons did was drink, and the archaeology suggests a poor tavern which would likely have been frequented by those who were similarly poor and—according to Quaker morals—could ill afford to waste their money on alcohol. While there are many other potential causes for Neff's rejection, the archaeology suggests that Neff's tavern may not have been seen as serving the community, as defined by the contemporary tavern regulations. Whether this led to objections by Robinson himself or other members of the Quaker or non-Quaker community we will probably never know, but if anyone showed that Neff was neglecting his duties to offer other services and keep his patrons from drinking to excess this could easily have resulted in the cancellation of his license.

His particular position as the tenant of a Quaker made Neff more susceptible to critique, since Robinson would have been more sensitive than the average landlord to the effect such a tavern would have had on both his, and by extension his community's, public image. Furthermore, Robinson may well have considered the dangers of waste and disorder associated with such a tavern—without the benefits to the community it was required to serve—to be reason enough to turn Neff out of his building. The disposal of a nearly complete bar set, some items still in perfectly usable condition, might suggest that this cleanout was more than spring tidying-up or readying for a new tenant. Perhaps the cleanout event even represents more of an eviction, a forcible discard of the material remains of the offending establishment.

The only other mentions of Neff in the available records are in the notebook of William McMullin and George Smith, Esq., agents charged with the accounting for and sale of lands and possessions forfeited over debt in Philadelphia. These are two brief, cryptic notations about Neff's having fled from debts in the 1780s (Montgomery 1906, Vol. 12, 804, 806).

Conclusion

Research has shown the presence of a tavern on land owned by an active member of the Quaker community, and this paper has suggested some more complicated views on Quakers and alcohol that help to contextualize this tavern. Specifically, it has been suggested that despite popular perceptions of colonial Quakers as teetotalers, their concerns were not always incompatible with taverns, and Robinson would most likely have been allowed latitude to rent to a tavern in some cases. The conditions under which this could have occurred are reflected in tavern license regulations of the time—written by Quakers—which allowed for taverns in the city primarily in order to fulfill certain economic roles. They functioned as places where food and accommodation could be purchased, where people could meet for business and personal discussion, and last *and* least, where alcohol could be consumed. I have suggested a method of analyzing tavern assemblages that allows us to examine the extent to which each of these activities may have occurred at a particular site. A comparative analysis of six sites has suggested that for the most part (although to varying degrees) taverns abided by these mores and emphasized food and accommodation. The exception was the house of Melchior

Neff. Archaeologically, Feature 209 represents a unique opportunity to study small, ephemeral taverns in a closely-dated context with a significant historical record. The historical and archaeological analyses together contextualize and clarify the relationship of Quakers and taverns in colonial Philadelphia, and offer some possible explanations to the particular case of Ebenezer Robinson and Melchior Neff.

Acknowledgements

I would like to thank the National Constitution Center and National Park Service, whose joint project made these artifacts available for study. In particular, I appreciate the assistance of Jed Levin and his staff at Independence National Historic Park. Thanks also to Douglas Mooney, Robert L. Schuyler, Robert Preucel, Laurie Wilkie, and two anonymous reviewers whose comments on previous drafts of this paper were invaluable. Of course, any errors that remain are my own.

References

Benezet, Anthony
1774 *The Potent Enemies of America Laid Open*. Joseph Crukshank, Philadelphia.

Bragdon, Kathleen Joan
1981 Occupational Differences Reflected in Material Culture. *Northeast Historical Archaeology* 10: 27–39.

Brown, Marley III
1987 Among Weighty Friends: The Archaeology and Social History of the Jacob Mott Family, Portsmith, Rhode Island. Ph.D. dissertation, Brown University, Providence.

Brown, Gregory, Thomas F. Higgins III, David F. Muraca, S. Kathleen Pepper, and Roni K. Polk
1990 *Archaeological Investigations of the Shields Tavern Site, Williamsburg, Virginia*. The Colonial Williamsburg Foundation, Williamsburg.

Burrow, Ian, William Liebknecht, Damon Tvaryanas, Douglas Scott, Nadine Sergejeff, and Rebecca White
2003 John Tweed's Log Tavern: The Archaeology, History, and Achitecture of the Gutherie-Giacomelli House. Delaware Department of Transportation Archaeological Series No 167. Delaware Department of Transportation, Dover.

Cadbury, Henry J.
1952 George Fox's Later Years. In *The Journal of George Fox*, ed. by John L. Nickalls. Cambridge University Press.

Coleman, Ellis C., Wade Catts, Angela Hoseth, and Jay F. Custer
1990 Final Archaeological Investigations of the John Ruth Inn Site. Delaware Department of Transportation Archaeological Series No 77. Delaware Department of Transportation, Dover.

Coleman, Ellis C., Wade Catts and Angela Hoseth
1993 Entertained at Ye Tavern Close By: Historical Archaeological Inquiry at Thomas Ogle's Tavern, Ogletown. *Bulletin—Archaeological Society of Delaware* 30 (New Series): 5–16.

Cotter, John L., Daniel G. Roberts, and Michael Parrington
1992 *The Buried Past: An Archaeological History of Philadelphia*. University of Pennsylvania Press, Philadelphia.

Espenshade, Christopher T.
1998 *Not a Good House: Archaeological Evaluation of the Marvin Tavern Site*. TRC Environmental Corporation, Atlanta.

Feister, Lois M.
1975 Analysis of the Ceramics Found at the Vereberg Tavern Site, Albany County, New York. *Man In The Northeast* 10: 2–16.

Fox, George
1952 [1691] *The Journal of George Fox*. John L. Nickalls, ed. Cambridge University Press, Cambridge.

Frost, J. William
2003 From Plainness to Simplicity: Changing Quaker Ideals for Material Culture. In *Quaker Aesthetics: Reflections on a Quaker Ethic in American Design and Consumption*, ed. by Emma Jones Lapsansky and Anne A. Verplanck, 16–40. University of Pennsylvania Press, Philadelphia.

Hayes, Charles F. III
1965 *Orringh Stone Tavern and Three Seneca Sites of the Late Historic Period*. Research Records of the Rochester Museum of Arts and Sciences No 12. Rochester Museum Association, Rochester.

Hodder, Ian
1986 *Reading the Past*. Cambridge University

Press, Cambridge.

Kerns-Nocerito, Mechelle
2004 The History of London Town, Maryland: 18th Century Chesapeake Tobacco Port. M.A. thesis, University of St. Andrews, Scotland.

King, Julia A.
1988 A Comparative Midden Analysis of a Household and Inn in St. Mary's City, Maryland. *Historical Archaeology* 22: 17–39.

Kise, Straw, and Kolodner
Forthcoming. The Forgotten Founding Father: The Archaeology of the James Oronoco Dexter Site, Independence National Historical Park, Philadelphia, Pennsylvania. Report prepared for the National Constitution Center and the National Park Service, Philadelphia.

Montgomery, Thomas Lynch, ed.
1906 *Pennsylvania Archives, Sixth Series*. Harrisburg Publishing Company.

Philadelphia Mayor's Court
n.d. *Docket*. Historical Society of Pennsylvania microforms XR 519.
n.d. *Docket*. Philadelphia City Archives.

Philadelphia Monthly Meeting
n.d. *A Record of Certificates of Removal for the Philadelphia Monthly Meeting 1681–1758*. Historical Society of Pennsylvania, Ph 1F:5.
n.d. *Minutes of the Philadelphia Monthly Meeting*. Friends Historical Library, Swarthmore, PA, microforms MR-Ph383.

Philadelphia Monthly Meeting, Northern District
n.d. *Abstracts of Minutes, Northern District Monthly Meeting, Philadelphia, Marriages 1772–1907, Births, Deaths and Burials 1772–1882*. Historical Society of Pennsylvania, Ph 1F.
n.d. *Minutes of the Philadelphia Monthly Meeting, Northern District*. Friends Historical Library, Swarthmore, PA, microforms MR-Ph 411.
n.d. *Certificates of Removal Sent by the Philadelphia Monthly Meeting, Northern District*. Friends Historical Library, Swarthmore, PA, microforms MR-Ph 416.

Philadelphia Quarterly Meeting
n.d. *Minutes of the Philadelphia Quarterly Meeting*. Friends Historical Library, Swarthmore, PA, microforms MR Ph-445.

Philadelphia Yearly Meeting
n.d. *Minutes of the Philadelphia Yearly Meeting*. Friends Historical Library, Swarthmore, PA, microforms MR Ph-445.
1797 *Rules of Discipline and Christian Advices of the Yearly Meeting of Friends for Pennsylvania and New Jersey*. Samuel Sansom, Jr., Philadelphia.
1997 *Faith and Practice*. Philadelphia Yearly Meeting.

Rees, Mark A, Tad Britt, and Jeffrey L. Holland
1993 Maplewood Ordinary: Data recovery on an 18th Century Tavern in Amelia County, Virginia. Garrow and Associates (TRC Environmental), Smyrna, GA.

Rockman, Diana DiZ. and Nan A. Rothschild
1984 City Tavern, Country Tavern: An Analysis of Four Colonial Sites. *Historical Archaeology* 18 (2): 112–121.

South, Stanley
1977 *Method and Theory in Historical Archaeology*. Academic Press, New York.

Thompson, Peter
1999 *Rum Punch and Revolution*. University of Pennsylvania Press, Philadelphia.

Thompson, Timothy A.
1987 Final Archaeological Excavations at the "Rising Son Tavern" Route 7—Limestone Road. Delaware Department of Transportation Archaeology Series 51. Delaware Department of Transportation, Dover.

Toogood, Anna Coxe
2004 Historic Resource Study Independence Mall The 18th Century Development Block Three Arch to Race, Fifth to Sixth Streets. Cultural Resources Management Division of Independence National Historic Park, Philadelphia. Electronic Resource, http://www.cr.nps.gov/history/online_books/inde/hrs/hrs.htm, accessed July 18, 2005.

Varte, P. C.
1875 *Map of Philadelphia in 1775*. J. Toudy & Co, Philadelphia. Library of Congress, Geography and Maps Division, Electronic Resource, http://hdl.loc.gov/loc.gmd/g3824p.ct000737, accessed February 2, 2006.

Walvin, James
1997 *The Quakers: Money and Morals*. John Murray Publishers, London.

Zierdan, Martha, Elizabeth Reitz, Michael Trinkley, and Elizabeth Paysinger
1982 *Archaeological Investigations at McCrady's*

Longroom. The Charleston Museum Archaeological Contributions Number 3. The Charleston Museum, Charleston.

John M. Chenoweth received his MA in Anthropology from the University of Pennsylvania in 2006, and is currently a PhD student at the University of California, Berkeley. His focus is on the historical archaeology of colonialism, the British Empire, and the study of social, racial and religious identity.

John M. Chenoweth
Archaeological Research Facility
University of California, Berkeley
Berkeley, CA 94720
chenoweth@berkeley.edu

WILLIAM HAMPTON ADAMS
SARAH JANE BOLING

Status and Ceramics for Planters and Slaves on Three Georgia Coastal Plantations

ABSTRACT

Previous work on Georgia plantations has provided useful data about life on the large plantations on barrier islands. More recent work on small to mid-sized plantations reveals that slaves' acquisition of ceramics may reflect more of their own decisions on what was purchased and what was used. Coarser ware frequencies indicate food preparation and storage in the slave quarters. Porcelain was often found in greater numbers in the slave quarters than in the plantation bighouse kitchen. Like earlier research, slaves at Kings Bay were found to have relatively more small bowls, but surprisingly they had relatively more plates as well. Comparison of slaves and planters using CC Index revealed that for several vessel forms the slaves had more expensive ceramics than their masters. This suggests that the slaves themselves viewed ceramics as status indicators and purchased them accordingly.

Introduction

The plantation is basically an agricultural factory using capital to manage labor to grow a product for the world market. Inherent in plantations is the creation of separate social and economic classes. While the degree of separation varied greatly through time and space, the presence of this dichotomy was inherent in the system. This article examines status as revealed by material culture on three plantations on the Georgia coast, and compares those plantations to ones elsewhere on that coast. The discussion centers upon the following research questions for different status groups (slave vs. planter; tenant vs. planter; small planter vs. middle planter; slaves of small planter vs. slaves of middle planter). The following analyses were run on these status groups for comparative purposes:

- Do these status groups differ in the ceramic wares used?
- Do these status groups differ in the ceramic vessel forms used?
- Do these status groups differ in the value of the ceramic tableware used?

These data were obtained from three nearly adjacent plantations on the mainland portion of the Georgia coast, in the southern-most county, Camden County. The plantations examined here were: Kings Bay Plantation (9CAM172; 1791-ca. 1850); Cherry Point Plantation (9CAM182, 1801–1806; 9CAM183, 1791–1823), and Harmony Hall Plantation (9CAM194; 1793-ca. 1832) (Figure 1).

While this article primarily focuses upon economic status, as revealed by goods produced for the mass market, economic status was related to social status in the antebellum South. The two are different, but interrelated. Furthermore, this is an etic analysis, from the perspective of a American society as a whole, and with an emphasis on manufactured items. This is not an emic analysis of social status within slave society where status was defined in ways which were not likely to leave traces in the archaeological record. Status among slaves was based upon occupations, as well as the ability to control the supernatural and fool their masters. Much slave material culture was made by them of perishable materials, so if one is to investigate relative status it is through the mass-produced materials bought by them or furnished to them.

Status in the Antebellum South

In the antebellum South, one's parents' statuses determined whether one was ascribed the status of being free or slave. While clearly linked to race, it was much more arbitrary than commonly believed for some planters were black or Native American (Adkins 1980; Olmsted 1856:636; Woodson 1968: 3–4). Status for slaves in the antebellum South was largely a legal condition, rather than one of race or skin color. However, their occupation and

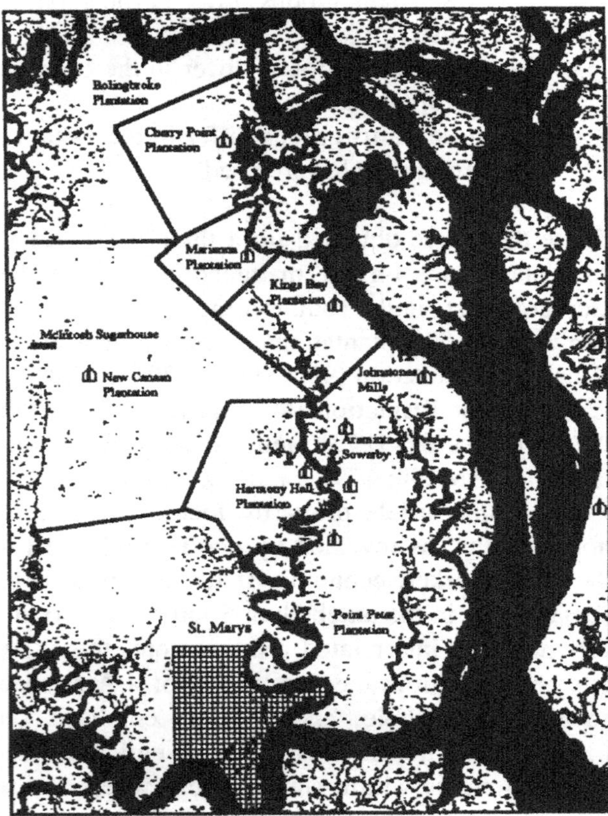

FIGURE 1. Plantations at Kings Bay, Georgia.

the status of their owners played an even greater role in their daily lives.

Slaves of planters with a higher status regarded their own status as being higher than that of slaves owned by poorer planters. "They seemed to think that the greatness of their masters was transferable to themselves. It was considered bad enough to be a slave; but to be a poor man's slave was deemed a disgrace indeed" (Rawick 1972:3). Many slaves considered their economic status to be superior to that of poor whites; as David Hundley (1860:256) has remarked these were the "Poor White Trash, a name said to have originated with the slaves, who look upon themselves as much better off than all 'pó white folks' whatever." The slaves' social status on each plantation also depended upon their occupation. Field slaves had a lower social status than house slaves as viewed by the planter and their fellow slaves alike (Frazier 1930:209; Hundley 1860:351–52; Kelso 1984:26; Orser 1987:126–28), because their acculturation was influenced through interacting with the planter's family and guests.

Slaves on task system plantations had a potentially different economic status than the slaves on gang system plantations because they provided more of their own subsistence needs and participated within the region's market economy selling their own produce and handcrafts; plantations with task systems permitted slaves to garden and raise chickens, eggs, and pigs, as well as making baskets, canoes, and other handcrafts for sale (Adams 1987:11–13; Adams et al. 1987:228–34; Morgan 1982, 1983). Such slaves were very much akin to peasants working on their landlord's manor or hacienda. Because of this participation, most of the material culture slaves possessed on a task system plantation were made by them or purchased using their own funds. Of course, on any plantation the slaves made much of what they possessed. One may hypothesize that the task labor plantation slaves could have had a higher amount of material goods through their own individual initiative.

Achieved status is that position in society obtained by an individual through his or her own achievements in life, like elected positions, and sometimes wealth and power or the lack of such. Status is relational; an individual's status is determined by reference to someone else's status. Each person has many different statuses, depending upon the circumstances of the moment and the people present (see Orser 1987:124–26 for discussion of this). One can be a father in one's own household, and a son in one's parents' household, wealthier than a beggar, and poorer than a merchant. The planters' relative economic status can be measured by the number of slaves owned, or acreage controlled. The planters' relative social status can be inferred by levels of interaction with their fellow planters and townspeople, as well as from the material culture indicating such interaction.

Three main classification schemes have been developed for the relative status of free whites in the South (Figure 2). David R. Hundley's (1860)

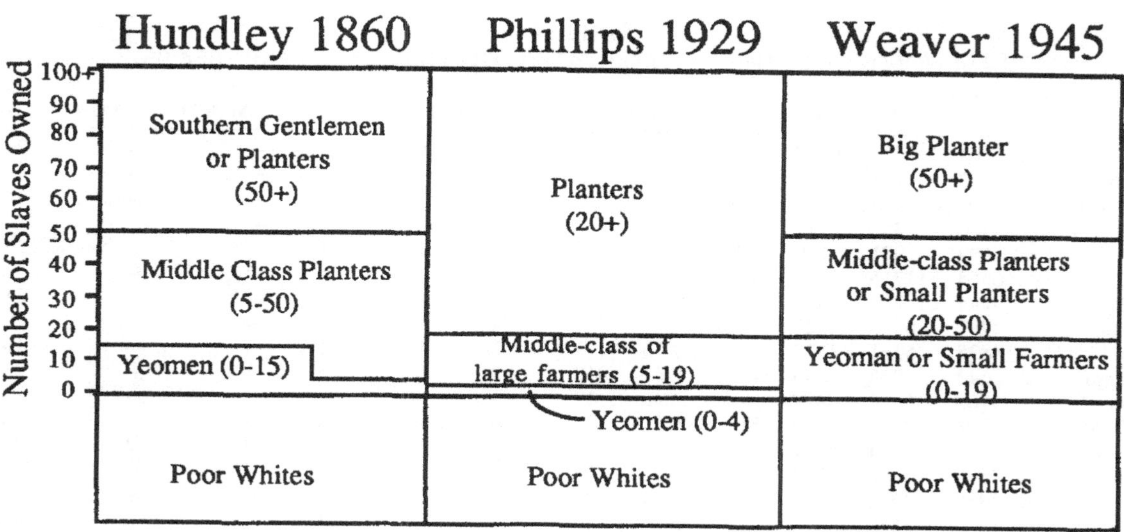

FIGURE 2. Comparison of social status of free whites on the basis of number of slaves owned.

classification centered upon slave ownership, with three classes of slave owners and a fourth class, Poor Whites, who owned no slaves. Ulrich B. Phillips (1929:339) thought a minimum of 20 slaves was needed to define a plantation, whereas owners of 5–19 slaves formed "a middle-class of large farmers and comfortable townsmen." Phillips admired Hundley's work and differs from it only by not distinguishing between middle class and upper class planters. Herbert Weaver (1945) objected to the above classifications because those were based solely upon slave ownership and did not take into consideration landownership. The problem in classifying slaveowners as planters, without considering their land as well, is that the two were not necessarily the same. "Quite frequently men without land owned large numbers of slaves whom they hired out to plantation owners; others were found to own extensive tracts of improved land but no slaves. The former were obviously not planters and the latter were probably middle-class farmers" (Weaver 1945:37).

Does Weaver's classification add anything to what Hundley or Phillips had done, or does it merely complicate it by adding a second variable? Weaver still based the definition of each class on the number of slaves owned. His Big Planter is the same, in terms of slaves, as Hundley's Southern Gentleman or Planter. He uses Phillips' dividing line of owning 20 slaves to distinguish planter from yeoman farmers. While he did not label these groups as upper, middle, and lower class, the distinction is implicit in his designating one group as middle-class planters. How does one classify a person with 150 slaves and only 100 acres who rented out his slaves or put them to work in a mill, or one with 5000 acres but only 10 slaves, using Weaver's classification? The economic control which can be brought to bear, not ownership, provides the relative economic status or worth. For example, at Waverly Plantation in Mississippi, George H. Young, owned 916 hectares (324 improved hectares) and 117 slaves in 1850, 1368 hectares (594 tillable) and 137 slaves in 1860, or ratios of 10.0 and 11.6 acres per slave (Adkins 1980:85–87). Young would be classified as a big planter on the basis of acreage and slave ownership, but he also rented other plantations and controlled twice as much land. Land control is as important as landownership as a socio-economic variable. Furthermore, to use acreage owned as the only criterion is misleading. How much of that land is forest or swamp? How much is in pasture or fields? While a census provides information on

TABLE 1
SLAVEHOLDERS IN THE UNITED STATES, 1850 (FROM DEBOW 1854:95)

	1	2–4	5–9	10–19	20–49	50–99	100–199	200–299	300–499	500–999	1000+	Total
Alabama	5204	7737	6572	5067	3524	957	216	16	2	—	—	29,295
Arkansas	1383	1951	1365	788	382	109	19	2	—	—	—	5,999
Columbia, D. of	760	539	136	39	2	1	—	—	—	—	—	1,477
Delaware	320	352	117	20	—	—	—	—	—	—	—	809
Florida	699	991	759	588	349	104	29	—	1	—	—	3,520
Georgia	6554	11716	7701	6490	5056	764	147	22	4	2	—	38,456
Kentucky	9244	13284	9579	5022	1198	53	5	—	—	—	—	38,385
Louisiana	4797	6072	4327	2652	1774	728	274	36	6	4	—	20,670
Maryland	4825	5331	3327	1822	655	72	7	—	1	—	—	16,040
Mississippi	3640	6228	5143	4015	2964	910	189	18	8	1	—	23,116
Missouri	5762	6878	4370	1810	345	19	—	1	—	—	—	19,185
North Carolina	1204	9668	8129	5898	2828	485	76	12	3	—	—	28,303
South Carolina	3492	6164	6311	4955	3200	990	382	69	29	2	2	25,596
Tennessee	7616	10582	8314	4852	2202	276	19	2	1	—	—	33,864
Texas	1935	2640	1585	1121	374	82	9	1	—	—	—	7,747
Virginia	11385	15550	13030	9456	4880	646	107	8	1	—	—	55,063
U.S. TOTAL	68,820	105,683	80,765	54,595	29,733	6,196	1,479	187	56	9	2	347,525
U.S%	19.80	30.41	23.24	15.71	8.56	1.78	0.42	0.05	0.02	<0.01	<0.01	100.0
Georgia %	17.04	30.47	20.03	16.87	13.15	1.99	0.38	0.06	0.01	<0.01	0.00	100.0

improved acreage, often this information is not available for a particular archaeological site.

While the above classifications can be used for mid-19th century plantations, using them for earlier plantations is riskier because the slave population was increasing during the 18th and early 19th centuries. And, of course, it is entirely useless after Emancipation, even though plantations continued to the present day. What is not clear from the literature is whether this increase meant more people could be slaveholders with time or if the increase was relative. Would a slaveholder with 30 slaves in 1780 be the equivalent of a slaveholder of 50 slaves in 1860? Furthermore, applying this classification to an individual plantation has problems, for a plantation may change classes through time with growth or from difficulties. Like most discussions of plantations, these classifications are ahistorical. Does a big planter who sells or emancipates his slaves lose status as a big planter?

Federal census-takers collected information on slaveholding within specific categories of slaveowners (Table 1; Figure 3). Whether these were emic categories or bureaucratic ones, they surely would have affected classification systems of later historians. The 1850 U.S. Census of Population summarized by DeBow (1854:95) revealed that Georgia slaveholders were in very similar proportions to the U.S. average, with 47.51% owning one to four slaves, 36.90% owning 5–19 slaves, 13.15% owning 20–49 slaves, and only 2.44% owning more than 50 slaves (Table 1; Figure 3). Thus, 84.41% of the *slaveholders* in Georgia in 1850 would be classified as small planters, 13.15% middle planters, and 2.44% large planters. Using these large planters to characterize plantation life is as valid as using millionaires to portray American life.

Figures for the county north of Kings Bay, Glynn County, during the 1820–1860 period also reveal that large and middle planters comprised only a small portion of the total population and of the slaveholders. Small planters comprised roughly 60–80% of the slaveholders, while slaveholders themselves were less than 15% of the white population (Otto 1979). The latter figure is somewhat misleading, however, for it does not show slave-

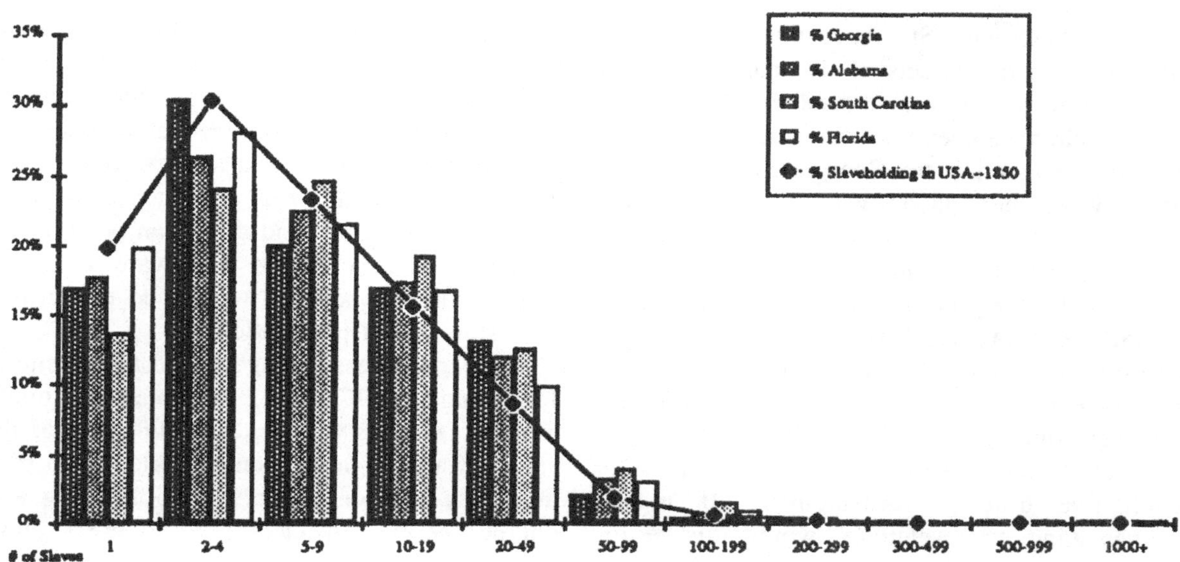

FIGURE 3. Slaveownership in the South, 1850.

holding by household, which would be a much higher percentage. In 1860, only a small number of free Southerners were involved directly with slavery, for most were small farmers or city dwellers who could not afford the expense of providing for slaves (Stampp 1956:29–30). For every plantation, there were many more small farms with no slaves at all.

Using the numbers of slaves owned as the determining factor in assigning status presents other problems. Knowing the total number of slaves on a plantation is not as useful as knowing the demography of that population. A plantation with about 50 slaves in a normal distribution of ages and sexes provides fewer full hands than one with about 30 young male slaves; in terms of economic output of the labor, the latter plantation would provide much more production for the short term. Yet to use the above classifications of Hundley and Weaver, one would be a big planter, while the latter plantation would be of a middle class planter. Furthermore, the labor system used determines the slave population to a great extent. For example, if two adjacent plantations having identical acreage cultivated and identical crops planted, were to use the different labor systems, gang labor and task labor, the number of slaves required would differ. The plantation with task labor would have relatively more slaves, since each one would produce less than they would in a gang system; the planter can afford to have more slaves because he is providing proportionately less in weekly rations and the slaves are using their free time in gardening, raising meat, and hunting (Adams 1987:11–13; Morgan 1982, 1983; Reitz, Gibbs, and Rathbun 1985:165–166, 183–184). So if one uses the numbers of slaves owned by a planter as a status criterion, one should adjust for the labor system used.

More meaningful classifications need to be developed using other criteria. Clearly, a planter with more than 50 slaves was wealthy, even if his capital was invested only in slaves. Such individuals were upper class, economically (and probably socially as well). But based upon the investigation of one plantation with about 28 slaves—the Kings Bay Plantation—the Thomas King family would also have to regarded as upper class during the 1791–1819 period. The planter, Thomas King, served as an officer in the local militia, owned a town house as well as a plantation bighouse, and entertained at parties friends who were coming from Savannah and St. Augustine. He poured drinks from matched sets of decanters into gold inlaid goblets and decorated tumblers. His prominence would have been known outside the county, probably for much of the Georgia coast, since his parties were mentioned even in the Savannah paper.

By contrast, John King and son James King, who owned Cherry Point Plantation (1791–1823), had only eight slaves and, while locally prominent, were on a different economic and social level as Thomas King (not a relative). John and James King were small planters, while Thomas King was a middle planter, if we use slave ownership as the quantitative unit of measurement. If indeed Thomas King was wealthier, would this be revealed in the ceramic assemblages from these two planter's kitchens? Using the CC Index (Miller 1980) to compare these assemblages should (and does) reveal significant differences, as will be examined later here.

Status and Ware

Much of what we know about the planters' more mundane lives comes from archaeology and from studying probate inventories. Few descriptions of kitchens can be gleaned from historical sources, although what few do exist would offend most modern ideas of cleanliness. Fanny Kemble described her kitchen at Cannon's Point in 1838 as "a mere wooden outhouse, with no floor but bare earth" (Kemble 1863:26). Each kitchen at Kings Bay was dirt floored also and contained hundreds of broken ceramic vessels inside them and in the middens just outside.

Small plantations may have provided food storage and preparation in the planter's kitchens, whereas this was less feasible when one was feeding 28 slaves as Thomas King was faced with doing at the Kings Bay Plantation. Since coarse wares, tablewares, and food bone were all found at the small plantations' slave quarters we know some food preparation was done at the quarters.

Utilitarian vessels for storage and processing foods were made from coarse stoneware, coarse redware, and yelloware. The higher frequency of coarser wares at the slave sites was evidence that food storage and processing was undertaken at the slave quarters. Refined stonewares included Westerwald from Germany and white saltglazed tableware from England. But few such vessels were found at Kings Bay, and those can be considered heirlooms. Coarser wares (yelloware, coarse redware, coarse stoneware) were used primarily for food storage and preparation.

The ceramic assemblage at the tenant site (the John King Site, 9CAM182, occupied by Woodford Mabry, 1801–1806), yielded only 7.3% of these coarser wares by vessel count (Tables 2 and 3); this may be a function of the short occupation which did not permit sufficient time to break enough vessels, or it may reflect less storage and food preparation at that site. Small planters at Harmony Hall Plantation and at Cherry Point Plantation had 8.4% coarser wares in their kitchen middens, compared to 6.4% at the middle planter's kitchen and yard at Kings Bay Plantation. Lumping planters together, the average for coarse wares was 7.6%, compared to the slave average of 15.7% (Table 3; Figure 4). The slave and planter site areas on small plantations were nearly identical in the amount of coarse wares, with 8.5% for slaves and 8.4% for planters. On the middle-sized plantation, the slaves' assemblage contained 22.8% coarse wares, compared with 6.4% of the planter's assemblage. Taken as a whole, the importance of coarse wares was essentially the same on all sites, except the Kings Bay Plantation slave quarters. This may reflect a different provisioning system on the middle-sized plantation, with the slaves there being responsible for their own food storage and preparation.

Porcelain was not a commonly recovered ware from the Kings Bay sites, as would be expected due to its cost. No porcelain was found at the John King Site (the tenant house), while the other sites had less than 7% of their ceramic assemblage in porcelain. Harmony Hall kitchen (9CAM194A) had the highest frequency of porcelain, 6.2%, while the slave quarters there (9CAM194B) had the next highest at 4.2%, followed by the Kings Bay Plantation slave quarters (9CAM172B),

TABLE 2
VESSELS BY WARE FOR SITES AT KINGS BAY

Site	John King Sawyer 182		James King Planter 183a		James King Planter 183c		Harmony Hall Planter 194a		Kings Bay Planter 172a		James King Slave 183 d		Harmony Hall Slave 194b		Kings Bay Slave 172b	
	N	%	N	%	N	%	N	%	N	%	N	%	N	%	N	%
Yelloware	0	0.0	4	3.7	3	1.3	3	1.6	5	1.4	1	2.9	0	0.0	13	8.5
Redware, coarse	0	0.0	3	2.8	6	2.6	4	2.1	6	1.7	2	5.9	2	1.7	12	7.8
Stoneware, coarse	3	7.3	1	0.9	14	6.0	6	3.1	11	3.0	3	8.8	5	4.2	10	6.5
Other earthenwares	0	0.0	0	0.0	0	0.0	1	0.5	1	0.3	0	0.0	0	0.0	0	0.0
Redware, refined	0	0.0	4	3.7	3	1.3	3	1.6	4	1.1	0	0.0	1	0.8	3	2.0
Stoneware, refined	0	0.0	3	2.8	3	1.3	2	1.0	1	0.3	1	2.9	0	0.0	0	0.0
Porcelain	0	0.0	2	1.8	2	0.9	12	6.2	9	2.5	0	0.0	5	4.2	6	3.9
Delft/Majolica	0	0.0	0	0.0	0	0.0	0	0.0	2	0.6	0	0.0	2	1.7	1	0.7
Creamware	18	43.9	26	23.9	33	14.0	37	19.3	62	17.1	6	17.6	7	5.9	31	20.3
Pearlware	20	48.8	66	60.6	171	72.8	124	64.6	259	71.6	21	61.8	97	81.5	77	50.3
Whiteware	0	0.0	0	0.0	0	0.0	0	0.0	2	0.6	0	0.0	0	0.0	0	0.0
Total	41	100.0	109	100.2	235	100.2	192	100.0	362	100.2	34	99.9	119	100.0	153	100.0

TABLE 3
VESSELS BY WARE AND STATUS AT KINGS BAY

	Sawyer		Small Planter		Middle Planter		Slave of Small Planter		Slave of Middle Planter		Kings Bay Planters		Kings Bay Slaves	
	N	%	N	%	N	%	N	%	N	%	N	%	N	%
Yelloware	0	0.0	10	1.9	5	1.4	1	0.7	13	8.5	15	1.7	14	4.6
Redware, coarse	0	0.0	13	2.4	6	1.7	4	2.6	12	7.8	19	2.1	16	5.2
Stoneware, coarse	3	7.3	21	3.9	11	3.0	8	5.2	10	6.5	32	3.6	18	5.9
Other earthenwares	0	0.0	1	0.2	1	0.3	0	0.0	0	0.0	2	0.2	0	0.0
Redware, refined	0	0.0	10	1.9	4	1.1	1	0.7	3	2.0	14	1.6	4	1.3
Stoneware, refined	0	0.0	8	1.5	1	0.3	1	0.7	0	0.0	9	1.0	1	0.3
Porcelain	0	0.0	16	3.0	9	2.5	5	3.3	6	3.9	25	2.8	11	3.6
Delft/Majolica	0	0.0	0	0.0	2	0.6	2	1.3	1	0.7	2	0.2	3	1.0
Creamware	18	43.9	96	17.9	62	17.1	13	8.5	31	20.3	158	17.6	44	14.4
Pearlware	20	48.8	361	67.4	259	71.6	118	77.1	77	50.3	620	69.0	195	63.7
Whiteware	0	0.0	0	0.0	2	0.6	0	0.0	0	0.0	2	0.2	0	0.0
Total	41	100.0	536	100.1	362	100.2	153	100.1	153	100.0	898	100.0	306	100.0

which at 3.9% was higher than the planter's kitchen at 2.5%. For porcelain, the planters do not differ significantly in their ceramic assemblages (3.0% vs. 2.5% for small vs. middle; Table 3). Slaves on the two small plantations had 3.3% of their ceramics as porcelain, compared to 3.9% for slaves on the middle plantation. The slaves' porcelain average was 3.6%, compared to the planter average of 2.8%. Due to porcelain's being more expensive, we would not expect it to be found frequently on slave sites, much less in higher quantities than at their masters'. Otto found at Cannon's Point, that porcelain was 1.1% on the slave site, 2.8% at the overseer's, and 1.4% at the planter's kitchen (Otto 1984:90). Perhaps the mistress of that bighouse simply wiped out or rinsed the tea service and that this resulted in less breakage of it there. Porcelains were most often found in tea service.

Pearlware gradually supplanted creamware as the vessel of choice for the table, so much so that by the early 1800s creamware was the cheapest tableware available (Miller 1980). The Kings Bay sites can be seriated (ordered) on the basis of the relative frequency of creamware and pearlware, with later sites having more pearlware. For example, the 1801–1806 John King Site had 48.8% pearlware, while the longer occupied and later sites like Harmony Hall had 64.6%. While the range of creamware:pearlware ratios is considerable between some of these sites, it is not part of this analysis. The ratio is thought to be mostly influenced by time, and we are considering distinct marks of status. On the basis of ware types, we found little meaningful difference between small and middle planter assemblages, or between their slaves' assemblages. Slave sites tended to have a few more coarse ware vessels than did the planters (or fewer refined wares for the table).

Status and Vessel Form

Vessel form has been suggested as indicating status on plantations (Otto 1977, 1984). If vessels were used for the purpose each was made, then the more vessel forms in a site, the greater the complexity of the meals partaken there. Researchers have observed that slave sites yielded a disproportionate amount of bowls and have inferred this has resulted from the cooking methods employed by the slave, particularly using *pot-au-feu*. The interpretation for Cannon's Point Plantation was that slaves ate from bowls, while at the planter's house people ate from plates, reflecting different methods of cooking there, stewing and roasting (Otto 1977:98, 1984:167). Others also found that slaves used bowls more (Booth 1971:33).

At Kings Bay, small bowls at the planters' kitchens ranged from 7.9% to 22.4% of the ce-

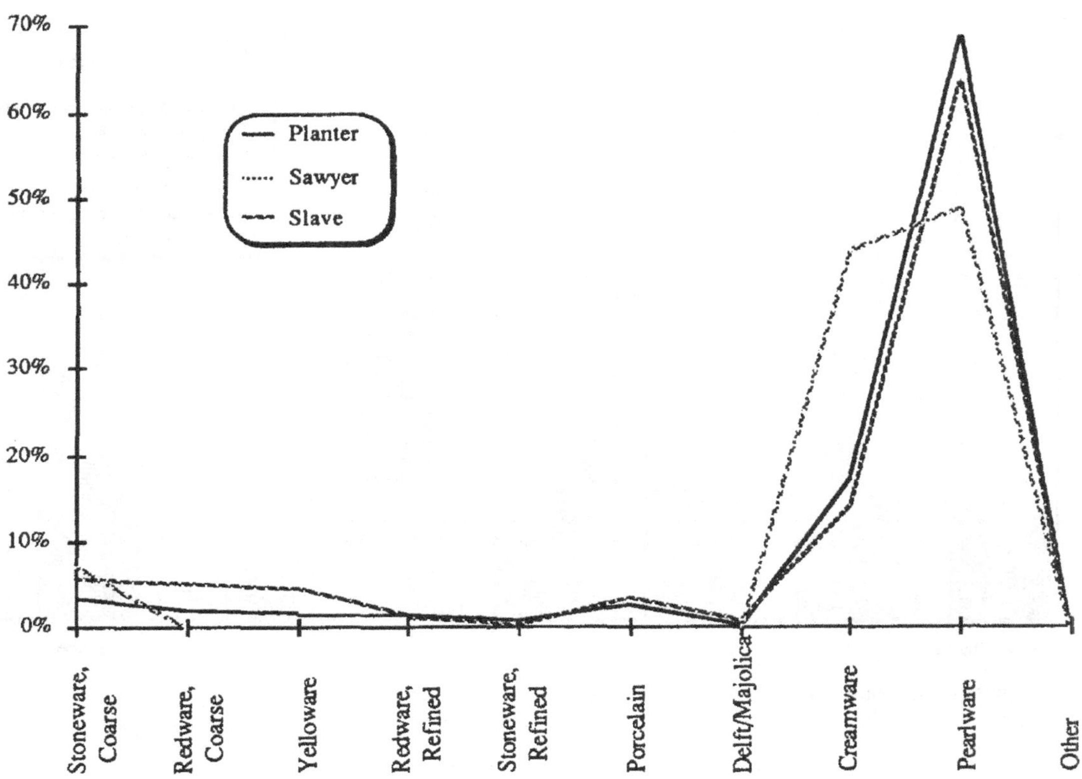

FIGURE 4. Vessels by ware for planters, sawyer, and slaves at Kings Bay.

ramic assemblage, while at the slave quarters there the small bowls ranged from 15.4% to 32.2%, consistently more than for the planters' kitchen (Table 4; Figures 5–8). If small bowls and large bowls are combined, the planters' kitchens totals ranged from 15.8% to 28.5%, while those at the slave quarters ranged from 24.1% to 35.8%. When we compare bowl frequency for planter and slave on the same plantation, the slave always has relatively more small bowls and fewer large bowls than the planter, but the range for slaves on one plantation overlaps that for planters on other plantations. Plates ranged from 23.2% to 37.6% at the planters' kitchens and from 24.8% to 40.4% at the slave quarters. Plates were more frequent at the Harmony Hall Plantation Slave Cabin and the Kings Bay Plantation Slave Quarters, compared to their planters. But for the Cherry Point Plantation, the slaves' plate frequency is less than that of the planter.

Oral histories of ex-slaves collected in the 1930s indicated wooden implements and tableware were common in many areas of the South (Cade 1935: 300–301). Conversely, planters likely used pewter plates as well as ceramic ones (even though few pewter vessels were found in the Kings Bay sites). These are biases for which there can be no control. While it is true slave sites at Kings Bay did have relatively more small bowls (20.5% vs. 13.2%), they also had relatively more plates (31.2% vs. 30.7%) than the planters (Tables 4–6). The reason for this is that slaves had relatively few vessels other than plates and bowls, while the planter's assemblage contained a fuller complement of tableware vessels like cups, platters, teapots, and miscellaneous vessels. With the sites at Kings Bay we can now see that the variation between slave sites is much the same as the variation between planter sites, and that some slaves had higher frequencies of plates than the planters did.

Research suggests the tea ceremony in British-

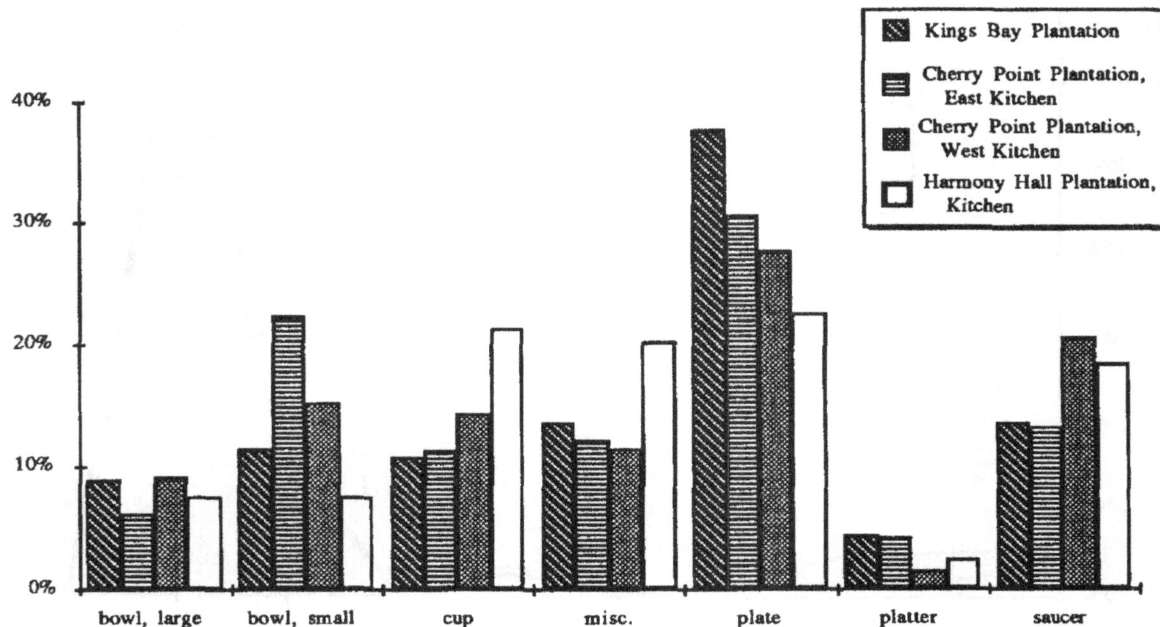

FIGURE 5. Vessel forms for the planters at Kings Bay.

American society had important status implications on a plantation, even though elsewhere after the Revolution its importance as a status indicator becomes less distinct (Roth 1961). On a plantation, however, the tea ceremony (not just tea drinking) should have been restricted to the planters and their guests; it would seem unlikely that slaves partook of it and hence the presence of tea service, especially porcelain, might have valid usage in defining status of site occupants. However, some archaeologists believe household servants may have become acculturated to the tea ceremony and acquired tea service for their personal use (K. Lewis 1985:58; Otto 1977:106, 1984:166). But we do not know whether the presence of tea pots and tea cups at a slave site implies the tea ceremony, or other uses. Otto noted that while the slaves and the overseer had teawares, these were not matched sets like the planter used (Otto 1984:166). Some of the slave sites at Kings Bay had more porcelain vessels for tea service than did the planter's assemblage. At Kings Bay, porcelain was not a common ware, only 1.8%, 0.9%, 6.2%, 2.5% at the four planter's kitchens, and 0.0%, 4.2%, and 3.9% at the slave quarters (Table 2). This porcelain was almost always teaware, but matching vessels were found only at planter kitchens. At Kings Bay Plantation, the slave quarters had more porcelain than the planter's kitchen, not at all what would be expected on the basis of cost, for porcelain was more expensive than earthenwares (Miller 1980).

Comparing the Kings Bay vessels to other plantations on the Georgia coast is difficult because the level of analysis between reports differs considerably. Sue Mullins Moore in a study of status on the coastal plantation (Moore 1985:153) lumped all vessels into either holloware or flatware without defining either category or noting whether the data included pitchers, chamberpots, and other vessels associated with an assortment of activities in the bedroom, kitchen, dairy, and elsewhere. John S. Otto (1984) lumped cups, mugs, and other vessels into teaware, but did not explicitly define the category for Cannon's Point. Singleton (1980) did not distinguish between cups and bowls in her analysis of the material from Butler Island. Given the lack of any detailed analysis by previous

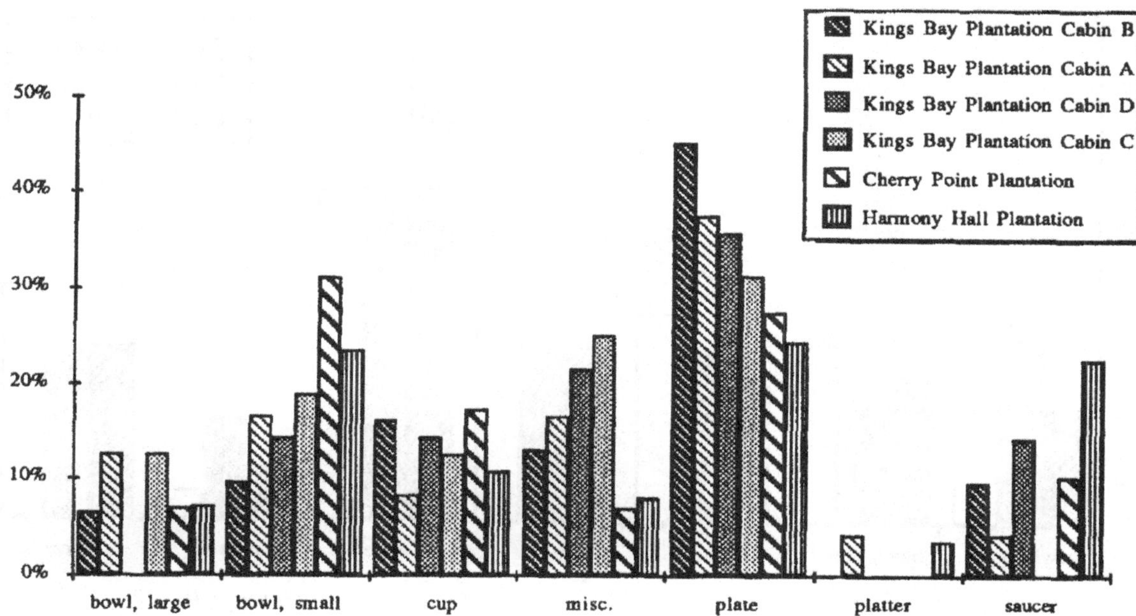

FIGURE 6. Vessel forms for the slaves at Kings Bay.

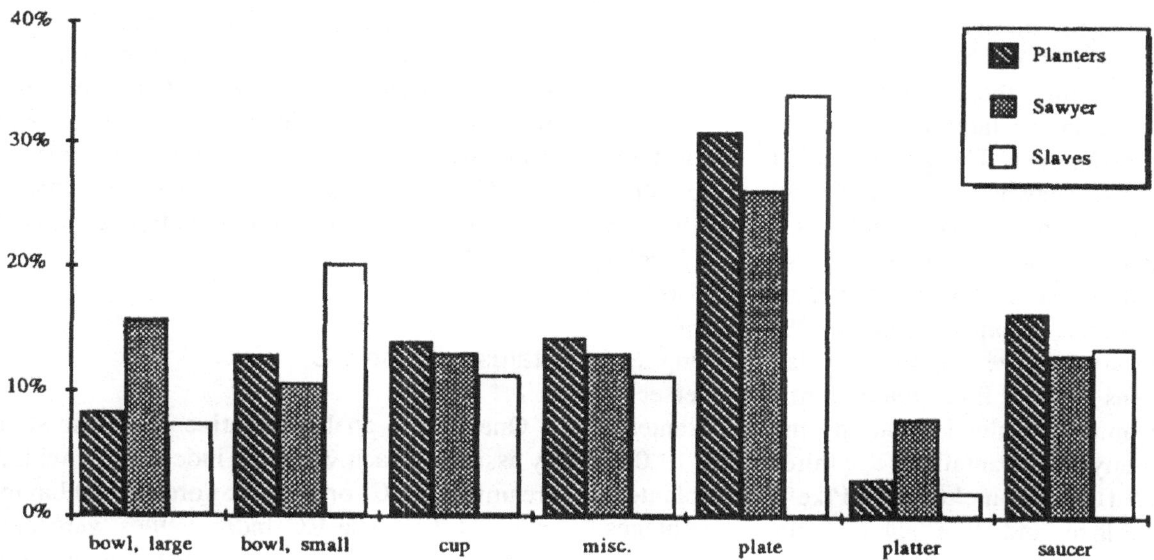

FIGURE 7. Vessel forms, comparing the planters, sawyer, and slaves at Kings Bay.

researchers, we can only compare using the simplistic dichotomy of flatware versus holloware.

For the following discussion, cups, teapots, miscellaneous vessels, and bowls will be subsumed into holloware, while saucers, plates, and platters will be lumped together as flatware. As one can easily see, functional groupings like vessels for serving food or liquids, for eating, for

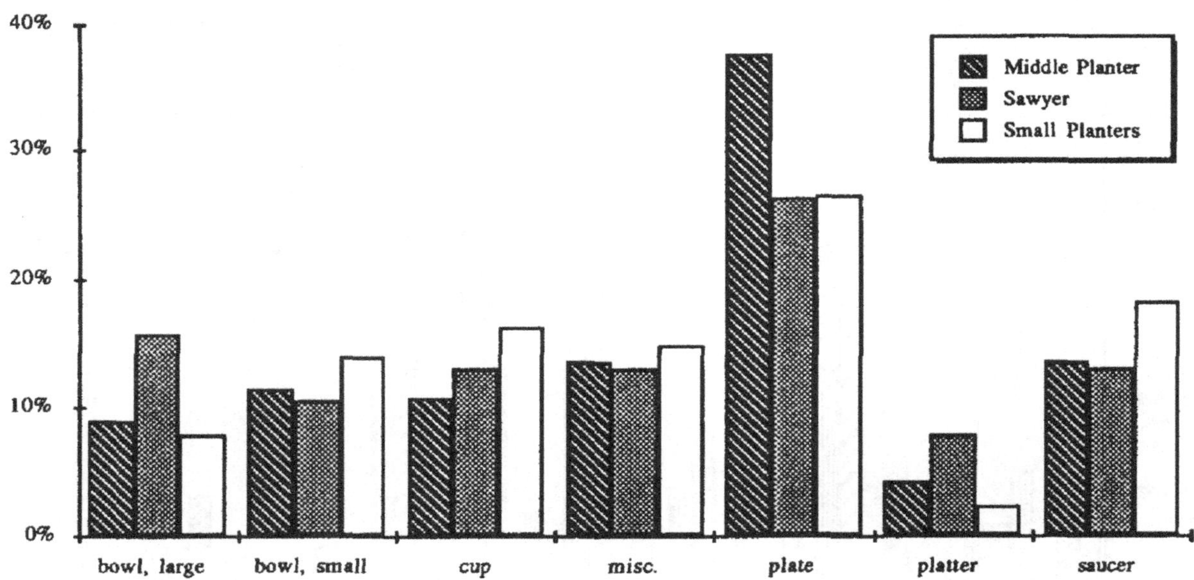

FIGURE 8. Vessel forms, comparing the middle planter, sawyer, and small planters at Kings Bay.

drinking, for storage, cross-cut these two arbitrary shapes of flat and hollow.

By ranking these sites on the frequency of flatwares in the tableware asemblage we derived three groupings. The group with the highest frequency of flatwares—roughly 55%—are planters' kitchens from the large planter at Cannon's Point Plantation, and the middle planters at Sinclair Plantation and at Kings Bay Plantation (Table 4). The second group, 45.1%–51.4% flatware, includes two slave cabins, the James King Site kitchens (Cherry Point Plantation), the overseer at the Cannon's Point Plantation, and the planter at Harmony Hall Plantation. The third group, 19.0%–39.3% flatware, includes the Pike's Bluff planter's assemblage and five slave cabin assemblages. Thus, we may conclude that this analysis, as simple as it is, does provide useful information regarding relative status.

Slaves had higher quantities of holloware, mostly bowls, while planters had more flatware. This generality simply confirms what Otto (1975) found at Cannon's Point more than a decade ago, but with a greater range of data we now see the situation is much more complicated. Indeed, some slave sites were found to have a higher flatware frequency than some planter sites had. Thus, while there is a strong linear correlation between vessel form and status, with lower status sites having more hollowares, too many sites show exceptions to this trend for it to be any more than suggestive. In addition to this kind of analysis we must therefore turn to other methods to determine relative status.

Status and the CC Index

One way to analyze relative economic status is by assigning each vessel an index value, with plain creamware (CC, or cream colored ware) having an index of 1.0. The CC Index values were derived from potters' price fixing lists assembled by George Miller (1980); thus, vessels with a higher index were more expensive than ones with lower indices. Because the initial settlement of the Kings Bay sites began about 1791, the authors chose to use the 1796 price list whenever possible, or the next closest one when certain categories were not available. The price list chosen should be the one nearest to the date when the ceramics are assumed to have been purchased.

TABLE 4
PERCENTAGE OF CERTAIN VESSEL FORMS IN THE CERAMIC TABLEWARE ASSEMBLAGE FOR KINGS BAY SITES COMPARED TO OTHER PLANTATIONS ON THE GEORGIA COAST

Site	Area	Cup	Teapot	Misc.	Plate	Saucer	Platter	Large Bowl	Small Bowl
Kings Bay Plantation	Kitchen	10.5	1.0	12.7	37.6	13.1	4.2	9.2	11.6
James King Plantation	Kitchen, East	11.2	1.0	11.2	30.6	13.2	4.1	6.1	22.4
James King Plantation	Kitchen, West	14.5	3.4	7.2	28.0	20.7	1.4	9.2	15.5
Harmony Hall Plantation	Kitchen	22.6	4.2	12.1	23.2	19.5	2.4	7.9	7.9
John King	House	13.2	—	13.2	26.3	13.2	7.9	15.8	10.5
Kings Bay Plantation	Slave Cabins	10.6	0.9	16.4	40.4	6.7	1.0	8.7	15.4
Harmony Hall Plantation	Slave Cabin	11.0	1.8	4.6	24.8	22.9	3.7	7.3	23.8
James King Plantation	Slave Cabin	17.9	—	7.1	28.6	10.7	—	3.6	32.2

Site	Area	FLATWARE	TEAWARE	MISC.	BOWLS
Cannon's Point Plantation[1]	Planter's Kitchen	55.3	34.0	5.7	4.9
Cannon's Point Plantation[1]	Overseer	46.7	35.0	2.5	15.8
Cannon's Point Plantation[1]	Slave Cabin	36.4	24.3	5.6	32.7

Site	Area	FLATWARE	HOLLOWARE
Sinclair[3]	Planter	55.9	44.1
Cannon's Point Plantation[1]	Planter's Kitchen	55.3	44.7
Kings Bay Plantation	Planter's Yard and Kitchen	54.9	45.1
Harmony Hall Plantation	Slave Cabin	51.4	48.6
James King Plantation	Planter's West Kitchen	50.1	49.9
Kings Bay Plantation	Slave Cabins	48.1	51.9
James King Plantation	Planter's East Kitchen	47.9	52.1
John King	House	47.4	52.6
Cannon's Point Plantation[1]	Overseer	46.7	53.3
Harmony Hall Plantation	Planter's Kitchen	45.1	54.9
James King Plantation	Slave Cabin	39.3	60.7
Cannon's Point Plantation[1]	Slave Cabin	36.4	63.6
Pikes Bluff[3]	Planter	35.2	64.8
Sinclair[3]	Slave Cabin	28.6	71.4
Butler Island[2]	Slave Cabin	26.1	73.9
Jones[3]	Slave Cabin	19.0	81.0

[1]calculated from Otto 1984:180 and Table 3.14; Teaware was not defined by Otto, but presumably included teapots, cups, creamers, and saucers; Flatware was defined (Otto 1984:69) as plate, platter, soup plate. The figures here differ from those calculated by Moore (1985:153) for the Cannon's Point assemblages apparently because Moore used Otto's 1975 dissertation.
[2]from Singleton 1980: Table 8; cups and bowls were not distinguished
[3]from Moore 1985:153

The inhabitants of these sites bought their dishes between 1770 and 1834 (median date ranges from 1795 to 1820); it is impossible to tell what year, or at what price, any given vessel was purchased. Likewise, one cannot take into account birthday presents, inheritance, shipping delays, or estate sales. The authors used the price list from the earliest year a decorative type was mentioned in the lists, as long as it was between 1796 and 1834, to evaluate the whole range of decorative types. Porcelain and sponged wares appeared on the price lists so late that the former was left out of the calculations and the latter treated as dipped. All edgeware and transferprinted vessel prices were taken from the 1796 price lists, even when some patterns had not been manufactured until a later date, to avoid confusing the issue. Each tally of indices is made up of scores for different years. Analysis used 1.33 as CC Index for edged large serving bowls.

Ceramics were divided into gross types based on form as shown above: plates, platters, cups, saucers, small and large (≥6") bowls, teapots, chamberwares and other ceramic forms (Table 7). Over-

TABLE 5
TABLEWARE VESSEL FORMS FOR THE PLANTATIONS AT KINGS BAY.

	CHERRY POINT PLANTATION				HARMONY HALL PLANTATION		KINGS BAY PLANTATION	
vessel	WOODFORD MABRY 182	PLANTER KITCHEN 183a	PLANTER KITCHEN 183c	SLAVE CABIN 183d	PLANTER KITCHEN 194a	SLAVE CABIN 194b	PLANTER KITCHEN 172a	SLAVE CABIN 172b
bowl, large	6	6	19	1	13	8	28	9
bowl, small	4	22	32	9	13	26	36	17
cup	5	11	30	5	37	13	35	13
plate	10	30	58	8	40	26	111	45
platter	3	4	3	0	4	5	12	1
saucer	5	13	43	2	32	25	44	9
miscellaneous	5	12	24	3	26	8	40	20
Tableware Totals	38	98	209	28	165	111	306	114

TABLE 6
PLATE INDEX FOR TABLEWARE VESSEL FORMS FOR THE PLANTATIONS AT KINGS BAY.

	CHERRY POINT PLANTATION				HARMONY HALL PLANTATION		KINGS BAY PLANTATION	
vessel	WOODFORD MABRY 182	PLANTER KITCHEN 183a	PLANTER KITCHEN 183c	SLAVE CABIN 183d	PLANTER KITCHEN 194a	SLAVE CABIN 194b	PLANTER KITCHEN 172a	SLAVE CABIN 172b
bowl, large	.60	.20	.33	.12	.32	.31	.25	.20
bowl, small	.40	.73	.55	1.12	.32	1.00	.32	.38
cup	.50	.37	.52	.62	.92	.50	.32	.29
plate	1.00	1.00	1.00	1.00	1.00	1.00	1.00	1.00
platter	.30	.13	.05	.00	.10	.19	.11	.02
saucer	.50	.43	.74	.25	.80	.96	.40	.20
miscellaneous	.50	.40	.41	.38	.65	.31	.36	.44

glaze polychrome and plain blue painted pearlware received the same value, although overglaze painted wares may not have been in the potters' lists. Willow cups and saucers were classified with other blue transferprinted wares, porcelain was omitted, and blue or green scalloped edging on any vessel not plate or platter was classified as painted.

The results are quite surprising and indicate that while this method is useful, its application on slave sites must be done with caution. First, each plantation kitchen will be compared with its slave site. At the James King Site, the slaves had more expensive cups, the saucers and plates were of similar cost, but small and large bowls were considerably less expensive than the planter's assemblage (Figure 9). At Harmony Hall Plantation, the CC Index shows that the slaves' small bowls were considerably less expensive, while the plates and platters were more expensive, and the cups and saucers considerably more expensive, than those of the planter there. Large bowls were about the same cost, for the ceramics *discarded at their site*. For the Kings Bay Plantation, the slaves also had somewhat less expensive small bowls, but at least one cabin had more expensive bowls than did the planter; otherwise the slaves had less expensive ceramics.

Comparison between slave sites at Kings Bay reveals that cups and saucers form one subset of the ceramic assemblage as do large and small bowls, because when the assemblage is ordered on the basis of cup CC Index values, the bowl values are inversely proportional. In other words, slave sites with expensive cups and saucers have inex-

TABLE 7
CC INDEX FOR VARIOUS SITES ARRANGED BY INDEX YEAR AND MEAN

SITE	AREA	LOCATION	DATE	INDEX	STATUS	N	CUPS	PLATES	BOWLS	MEAN	SOURCE
Diaz	Privy	Monterey, CA	ca. 1842-ca. 1858	1846	merchant	74	3.59	1.92	1.68	2.69	c
Walker Tavern	—	Detroit, MI	ca. 1834-ca. 1850	1846	tavern	35	2.31	2.44	2.32	2.37	b
Moses Tabbs	Context #1	St. Marys, MD	1800–1840	1846	tenant farmer	16	1.44	1.46	1.29	1.42	b
Green Mansion	—	Windsor, VT	1814–1870	1833	merchant	94	3.04	1.83	1.59	2.29	d
Black Lucy's Garden	—	Andover, MA	1815–1845	1833	freed slave	58	1.68	1.61	1.24	1.53	c
Cannon's Point	Kitchen	St. Simons, GA	1820s–1850s	1824	big planter	166	2.50	2.79	1.22	2.61	d
Franklin Glass	House	Portage Co., OH	1824–1832	1824	glass worker	94	2.15	1.86	1.54	1.90	b
Franklin Glass	Factory	Portage Co., OH	1824–1832	1824	laborers	62	2.11	1.47	1.37	1.67	b
Skunk Hollow	B	NJ	—	1824	black laborer	64	1.53	1.51	1.18	1.43	e
Moses Tabbs	Context #2	St. Marys, MD	1840–1860	1824	tenant farmer	41	1.50	1.43	1.20	1.44	b
Jonathan Hale Cabin	—	Summit Co., OH	1810–ca. 1830	1824	farmer	45	1.45	1.23	1.36	1.34	b
Kings Bay Plantation	Kitchen	Camden Co., GA	1791–ca. 1840	1814	middle planter	274	1.94	1.87	1.60	1.81	f
Harmony Hall	Slave Cabin	Camden Co., GA	ca 1793–ca. 1832	1814	slave	98	2.10	1.88	1.36	1.72	f
Cannon's Point	Slave Cabin	St. Simons, GA	1820s–1850s	1814	slave	80	1.71	2.07	1.27	1.68	c
Kings Bay	Planter average	Camden Co., GA	1791–1850	1814	planter	672	1.78	1.67	1.63	1.68	a
Kings Bay	Slave Average	Camden Co., GA	1791–1832	1814	slaves	208	1.95	1.62	1.61	1.66	f
Kings Bay Plantation	Slave Cabin C	Camden Co., GA	1791–ca. 1815	1814	slave	11	2.25	1.13	1.45	1.64	f
James King	West Kitchen	Camden Co., GA	ca. 1806–ca. 1823	1814	small planter	184	1.72	1.55	1.71	1.62	f
Harmony Hall	Kitchen	Camden Co., GA	ca. 1793–ca. 1832	1814	small planter	129	1.69	1.53	1.56	1.60	f
James King	Slave Cabin	Camden Co., GA	1791–ca. 1823	1814	slave	26	2.30	1.53	1.36	1.59	f
Kings Bay Plantation	Slave Cabin Avg.	Camden Co., GA	1791–ca. 1815	1814	slave	93	1.71	1.37	1.84	1.55	f
James King	East Kitchen	Camden Co., GA	1791–ca. 1806	1814	small planter	83	1.72	1.42	1.62	1.53	f
Kings Bay Plantation	Slave Cabin A	Camden Co., GA	1791–ca. 1815	1814	slave	34	1.33	1.44	1.57	1.47	f
Kings Bay Plantation	Slave Cabin B	Camden Co., GA	1791–ca. 1815	1814	slave	24	2.00	1.44	1.28	1.47	f
John Hamlin	House	Warren Co., NJ	1810–1856	1814	wealthy farmer	18	1.50	1.31	1.86	1.45	f
175 Water St.	Fea. 43	New York, NY	1795–1820	1814	merchants	58	1.80	1.19	1.29	1.33	a
175 Water St.	Fea. 49	New York, NY	1795–1820	1814	merchants	44	1.46	1.00	1.28	1.26	f

John Richardson	Privy/Cistern	Wilmington, DE	1810–ca. 1816?	1802	wealthy	21	3.40	1.93	2.53	2.31	a
Kings Bay Plantation	Kitchen	Camden Co., GA	1791–ca. 1840	1796	middle planter	274	2.22	2.08	1.81	2.03	f
Harmony Hall	Kitchen	Camden Co., GA	ca 1793–ca. 1832	1796	slave	—	2.30	2.11	1.60	1.95	f
Kings Bay	Planter average	Camden Co., GA	1791–1850	1796	planter	672	2.06	1.84	1.90	1.89	a
Kings Bay	Slave average	Camden Co., GA	1791–1832	1796	slaves	208	2.23	1.77	1.93	1.88	f
James King	West Kitchen	Camden Co., GA	ca. 1806–ca. 1823	1796	small planter	184	2.02	1.69	2.03	1.84	f
Harmony Hall	Kitchen	Camden Co., GA	ca 1793–ca. 1832	1796	small planter	129	1.94	1.68	1.77	1.77	f
James King	East Kitchen	Camden Co., GA	1791–ca. 1806	1796	small planter	83	2.02	1.52	2.00	1.74	f
James King	Slave Cabin	Camden Co., GA	1791–ca. 1823	1796	slave	26	2.60	1.61	1.43	1.74	f
Kings Bay Plantation	Slave Cabin C	Camden Co., GA	1791–ca. 1815	1796	slave	11	2.60	1.13	2.00	1.71	f
Thomas Hamlin	—	Warren Co., NJ	ca. 1790–1810	1796	farmer	74	1.67	1.19	2.14	1.68	a
Telco	Test Cut AX	New York, NY	ca. 1810	—	elite	33	1.65	2.02	1.39	1.68	a
Kings Bay Plantation	Slave Cabin A	Camden Co., GA	1791–ca. 1815	1796	slave	37	1.53	1.51	2.02	1.68	f
Kings Bay Plantation	Slave Cabin Avg.	Camden Co., GA	1791–ca. 1815	1796	slave	93	2.00	1.46	1.89	1.66	f
John King	House	Camden Co., GA	ca. 1801–ca. 1806	1796	sawyer	32	2.10	1.37	1.85	1.64	f
Kings Bay Plantation	Slave Cabin B	Camden Co., GA	1791–ca. 1815	1796	slave	24	2.33	1.54	1.57	1.64	f
Kings Bay Plantation	Slave Cabin D	Camden Co., GA	1791–ca. 1815	1796	slave	11	1.80	1.37	1.76	1.52	f
Barclays	Fea. 48	New York, NY	ca. 1800	1796	several occupants	60	1.53	1.48	1.25	1.39	a

Sources: a Morin et al. 1986:6.43–45; Morin and Klein n.d.
b Miller 1980
c Felton and Schulz 1983:76–81
d Spencer-Wood and Heberling 1984
e Geismar 1982
f Adams and Boling 1987

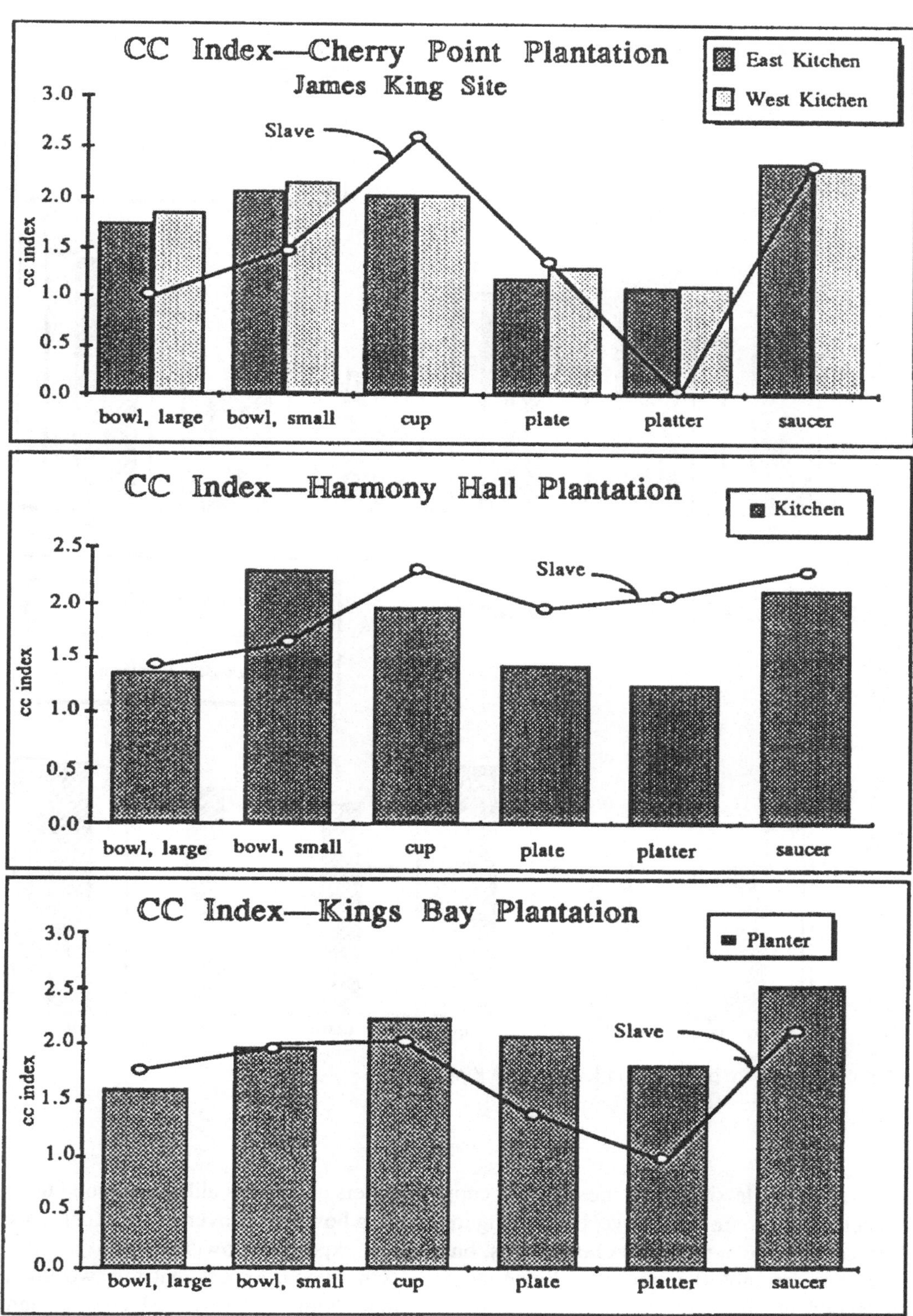

FIGURE 9. CC index for the planters and slaves on different plantations at Kings Bay.

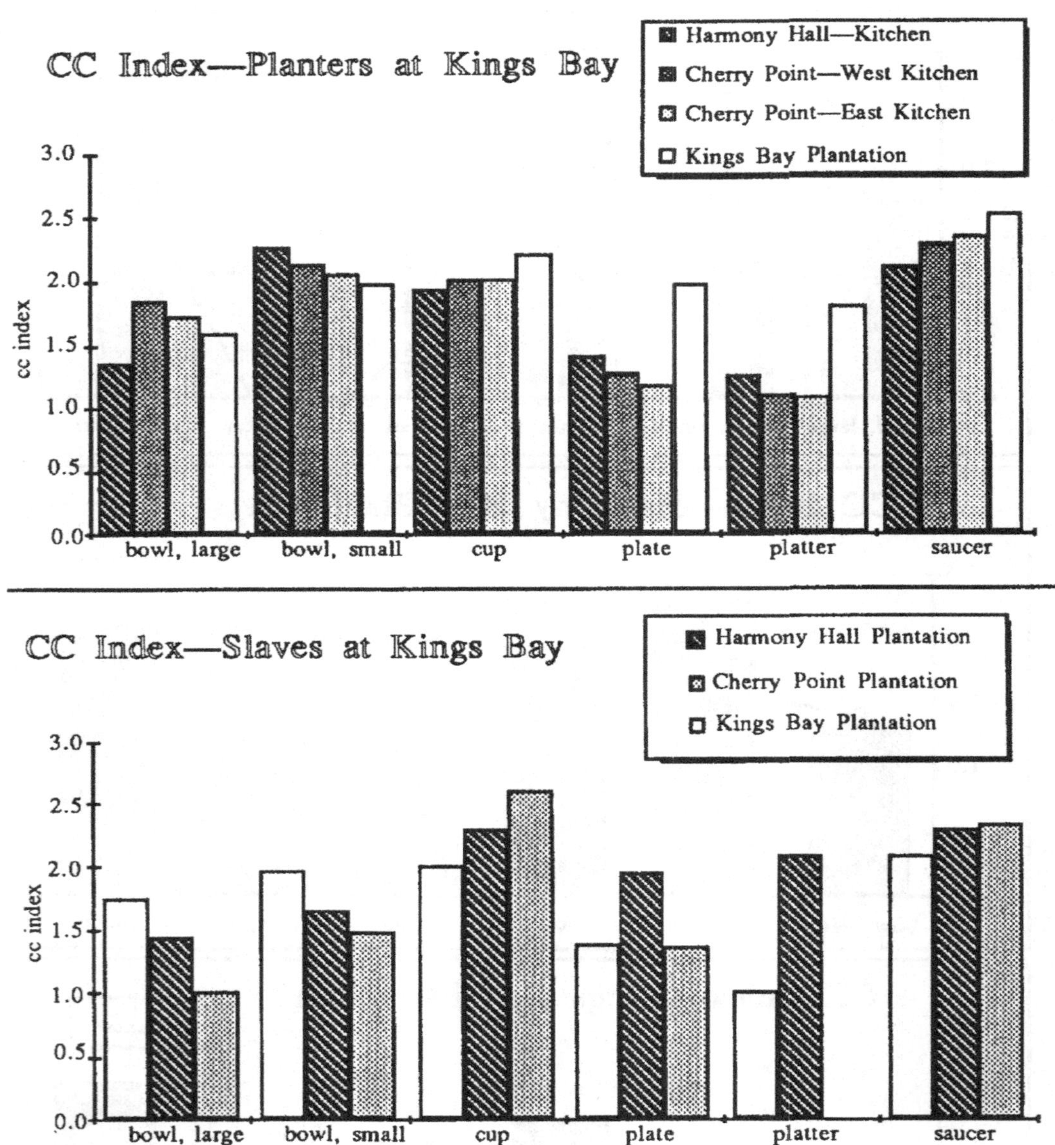

FIGURE 10. CC index for planters and for slaves at Kings Bay.

pensive bowls, while sites with inexpensive cups and saucers have more expensive bowls (Figure 10). The same is true in the planter households, but the differences are not as impressive. Since these are not dependent values, except in terms of capital expended on a given amount of ceramic vessels, this observation has some meaning. Why would planters and slaves alike have good tea service and cheap bowls or conversely cheaper tea service and more expensive bowls?

One would expect that the two kitchens at the James King Site (the east one is slightly earlier than the other) would have similar CC Index values, since they represent the same household.

Indeed, the two assemblages have very similar CC Indices, with the later kitchen having a slightly higher (1.84 vs. 1.74) value. If other evidence were available to support it, one would suggest a slightly higher economic status for James King, than for his parents (who built the first kitchen). Unfortunately, such supportive data do not exist for this site.

If the two kitchens at the James King Site are combined with the planter assemblage from the Harmony Hall Plantation to represent the small planter at Kings Bay, one can compare that with the CC Index for a middle planter, Thomas King at Kings Bay Plantation, a free white sawyer at the John King Site (Woodford Mabry), and their slaves. One would assume that order (based upon posited wealth) would be revealed in the ceramic assemblages of each. For the whites, this was true, but this was not the case if the slaves were included (Figure 11). The one middle planter had more expensive plates and saucers, the small planter had the most expensive small bowls and large bowls, and the slaves had the most expensive cups and platters. In every ceramic vessel form except bowls, the slave had more expensive vessels than the small planter and the sawyer. The middle planter generally had better ceramics than his neighboring small planters, bowls being the only exception. But this was tempered somewhat by the slaves having some even better ceramic vessels.

Grouping the planters together, to compare with the sawyer and slaves, yields essentially the same observations. Planter and renter had nearly the same price large bowls and cups, but in every other vessel the sawyer renter, Woodford Mabry at the John King Site, had much less expensive items (Figure 11). But the slaves had more expensive small bowls, cups, and platters. With the exception of large bowls, the slaves had more expensive ceramics than the white renter. (The identification of Woodford Mabry as white is based upon the paucity of free blacks in the county in 1800 and the fact that he rented the land from John King. He does not show up in the 1800 or 1810 censuses.)

The Thomas King ceramics do stand out for all but cups, large bowls, and small bowls. Thomas and Mary King's plates and platters were nearly half again as expensive as those of the other planters, but their cups and saucers were only somewhat more expensive. If glassware could be considered on a similar scale the entire dinner table of Thomas and Mary King would stand high over those of the smaller landowners, who had nothing near the splendor represented by gold-painted goblets, other fine stemware, and decanters. Likewise if porcelain tablewares could be calculated in the Thomas King and Harmony Hall tea equipages, well supplied with porcelain, would rise in apparent status. If miscellaneous tableware (teapots, vases, soup tureens) could be measured the small planters would cluster more closely, and Thomas King would again come out far above them.

Since this discussion treats ceramics as indicators of household finances, platters and serving dishes, which are nonessential, even luxury items, must be taken into account somehow. For convenience in this analysis, platters were given the index value of a 10″ plate of the same decorative category. However, a platter's price varied as much with size as it did with decoration. The price lists used have little chance of providing a ranking between archaeological assemblages, in which two or three broken rim fragments were classified as "platter," because the size of a platter must be known before its price can be attached, and determining if an oval platter was 10″ or 11″ from a small sherd is impossible. Also, the price difference between the two is comparatively large (Miller 1980:23–25). However, it hardly seems reasonable to exclude platters from this analysis, since they were such valuable items. A large creamware platter was more of of a luxury item than a transferprinted dinner plate—half again as expensive, and not as generally useful.

Therefore, a system of ranking sites by the value of serving dishes in the assemblage was necessary. In this case the results fit well with the other ceramic price patterns. Estimations, based on the dimensions of the few measurable platters, and how rim and base fragments of the others compared to them, were made of the size of each platter found on a site. Serving dishes of types listed on the Staffordshire Potters' price list for 1796, used by Miller, were counted from each site.

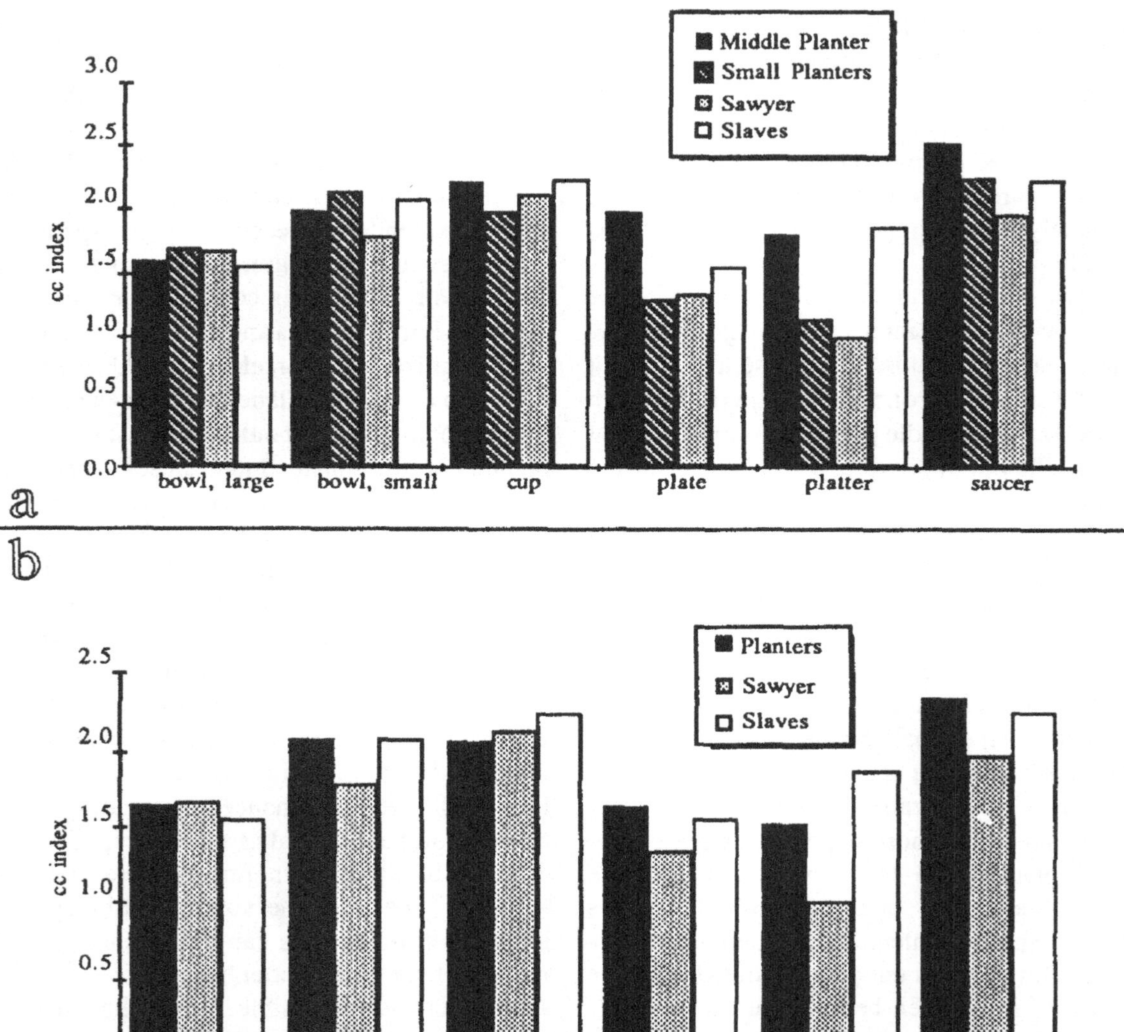

FIGURE 11. CC index by economic status at Kings Bay.

The price in English pence per dozen for each vessel was determined, and various weighting systems were tested to find one which made sense for Kings Bay.

The system which proved most useful for ranking sites by average value of platters also was least meaningful, in that it did not correct for the sample size (which in most cases was one to three vessels). That index gave a 12″ creamware platter, which seemed to be a good generic vessel, a value of 1.00 (in real terms, 48 pence/dozen). When all platters from all sites were run through this equation, the results were: Harmony Hall Slave, 3.75; Kings Bay Plantation Kitchen, 2.40; James King West Kitchen, 1.75; Harmony Hall Kitchen, 1.44; James King East Kitchen, 1.00; Woodford Mabry, 0.75, Kings Bay Plantation Slave, 0.62 (dividing the total 2.50 by the four cabins), and James King Slave 0.00, for there were no platters there.

This order, with one exception, is in keeping

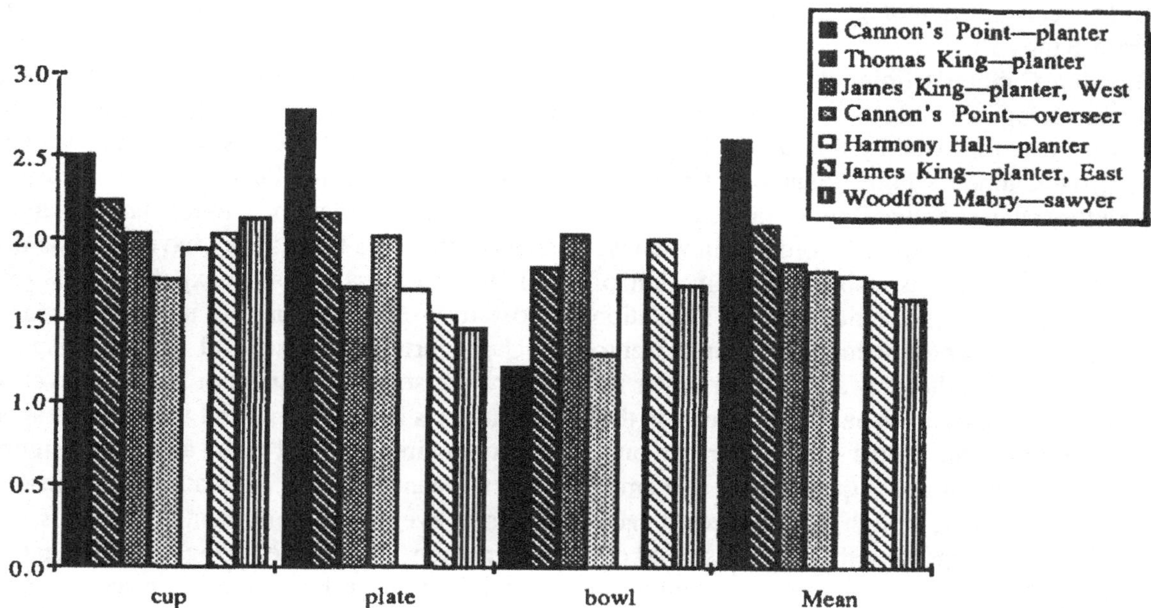

FIGURE 12. CC index for planters, overseer, and sawyer on the Georgia coast.

with the expected economic ranking of the occupants. The middle planter is first, the small planters next and close together, the sawyer close below them and the slaves, last; the Harmony Hall slave site does not fit into any appropriate pattern. One other approach which proved equally interesting was to add up the raw prices of all the platters and serving dishes for which prices were available, and rank the sites by this sum. In this case, the costliness of the Kings Bay Plantation ceramics was even more marked, and the anomalous Harmony Hall slave site became much more nearly equal to the small planter sites. It seemed to be the most vivid measure of conspicuous consumption possible.

The Harmony Hall Plantation slave quarters cannot, in fact, be compared well to any other site examined here in terms of average ceramic value, and another approach will be necessary to describe it. Its expensive platters distorted comparison of slaves and planters, in which a 40% lead in cost of platters appears in the slave column. Only one platter was recovered among the five other slave cabins excavated around the bay, and it was of the most inexpensive variety. Plates, which are important in tableware in Kings Bay area slave quarters, come out the same in both social classes. Leaving aside platters as an unmanageable form to sample, one can see some of the cruder trends already mentioned reestablished as general. Specifically, cups and saucers are higher in average price among the slaves, large bowls are very close, and small bowls inexpensive, at a price between dipped and painted. The next detail to consider is, of course, how many of the different-priced wares each domestic site possessed.

Comparison of the Kings Bay sites with those at Cannon's Point Plantation reveals that the large planter there had far more expensive ceramics (Figure 12). One explanation for the high index values there may be that a later price list should have been used to calculate it—the 1814 and 1824 price lists were used, instead of the 1833 list (Spencer-Wood and Heberling 1984). While the Cannon's Point Plantation dates from 1791 to 1860 (and later), re-examination of the ceramics from those sites revealed no creamware and no other ceramics with dates definitely earlier than about

1830. The entire assemblage is much later than that from Kings Bay.

Following Cannon's Point Plantation in value, the Thomas King assemblage from Kings Bay Plantation was next, followed by the James King West Kitchen, the Cannon's Point Plantation Overseer, and the other sites at Kings Bay. Clearly, using the mean CC Index, the sites can be ordered in what we would surmise is a reasonable approximation of wealth, except that the Cannon's Point Plantation overseer should, it would seem, have been closer to the values for Woodford Mabry, the sawyer on Cherry Point Plantation. What this suggests is that the relative economic status of an overseer on a large plantation is roughly equal to that of a small planter. That overseer, though, had the lowest value of cups, perhaps suggesting that his household did not have a public position to maintain through entertaining guests on the premises.

Comparison of the Kings Bay sites with others outside the Southeast provides a way of ranking these sites (Figures 13, 14; Table 7). Selection of these sites was based upon the available published data (Felton and Schulz 1983:76–81; Geismar 1982; Morin et al. 1986:43–45; Morin and Klein n.d.; Miller 1980; Spencer-Wood and Heberling 1984). These were divided into three groups, those with a mean over 2.0, with a mean of between 1.5 and 2.0, and those with a mean below 1.5. Each of the individuals in the high grouping is known to have been a wealthy individual, upper class would not be an unreasonable label for these people (Table 5). The individuals with a mean less than 1.5 could be labelled lower class, for they are small farmers, tenant farmers, and tenement dwellers. The middle group, 1.5–2.0 is not necessarily what would be called middle class, and should not be labelled such. It is most interesting that each of the slave sites analyzed falls into this group, along with the small planters, factory worker, plantation overseer, and so forth.

A number of sites have been identified as having been occupied by blacks exclusively, for example, Black Lucy's Garden (Baker 1980) and Skunk Hollow (Geismar 1982). Comparing those sites to Cannon's Point and to the Kings Bay site averages revealed that in every vessel category, the slaves had more expensive ceramics than the free blacks (Figure 15a). However, when the sites at Kings Bay are compared individually with the free black sites, the free black was found to have more expensive plates than half of the Kings Bay slave sites (Figure 15b). The general implication of this, bearing further investigation with a much larger sample of sites, is that free blacks may have had less disposable income, less access to expensive cast-offs, or chose to use their income in a different manner.

Using crude measures of income-disposal to determine status is a difficult process. Even when the subjects are still alive and willing to respond to questionnaires on what their, and their neighbor's, dishes mean to them, evaluating the household's status is even more complicated. For this reason, information about the Kings Bay inhabitants' dishes, beyond relative market price, is included here. Clear differences existed among the decorative quality of dishes on the various sites. By this we mean that a coherent taste, or devotion to ornament, of the family which had purchased the dishes emerged from the ceramic assemblages. The Harmony Hall planter household had a wide selection of fruit decorated early polychrome vessels, plenty of which represented partial sets. The household also owned a small selection of restrained blue transferprinted teawares and a miscellaneous collection of lathe decorated dipped bowls, plain creamware, and edged plates. The two James King kitchens were furnished with a heterogeneity of small-patterned printed, early polychrome painted, blue painted, overglaze painted, saltglazed, and creamwares. The Kings Bay Plantation kitchen had several sets of elaborate, large-pattern printed dishes, in tea and table sets, more variety in edged plates and dipped bowls than any other site, and a minimal assortment of unmatched painted dishes. Woodford Mabry set plain tablewares. The slaves had plain ceramics, like their masters did also, along with a few expensive decorated ones.

Conclusions

While the plantation bighouse has been studied in numerous circumstances as part of architectural

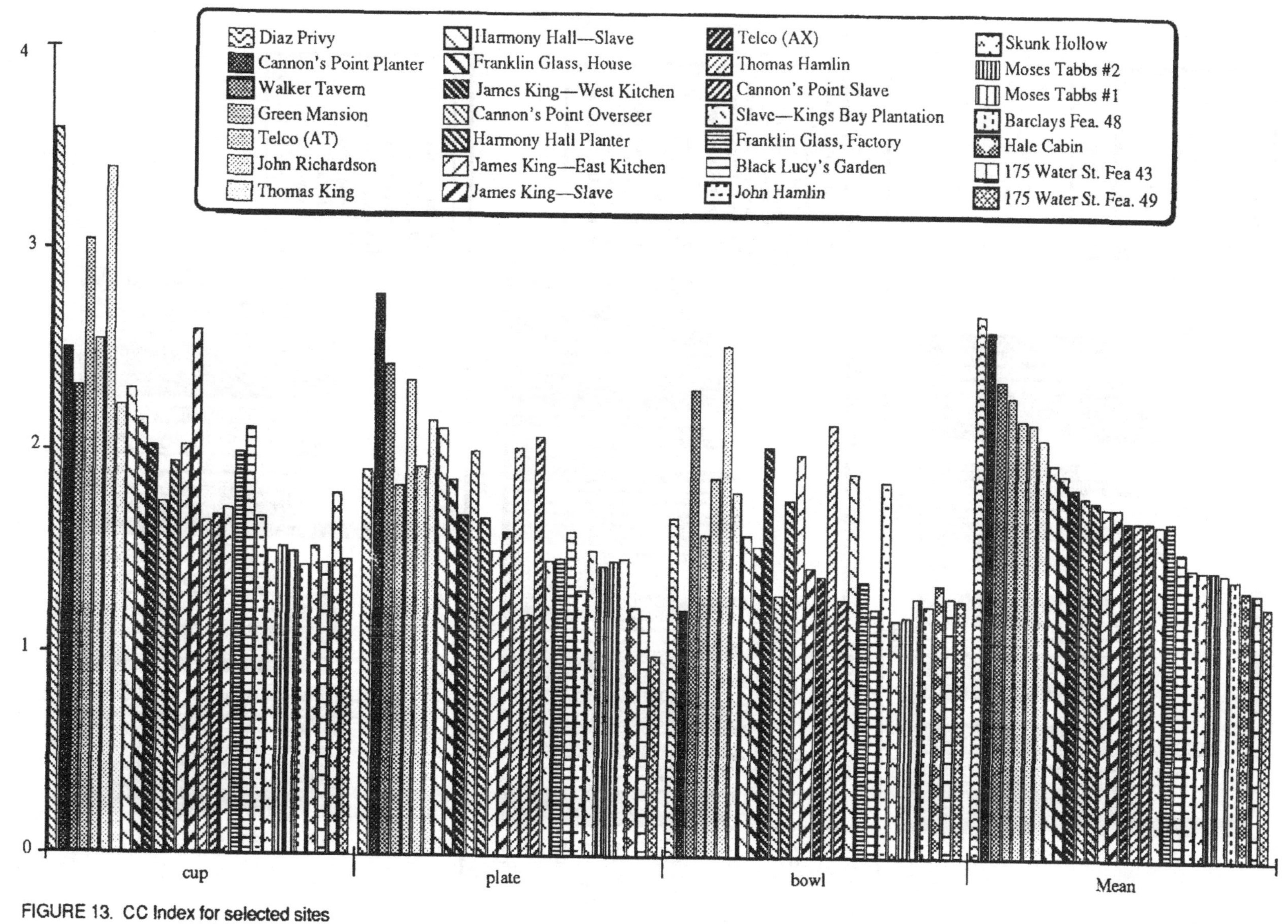

FIGURE 13. CC Index for selected sites

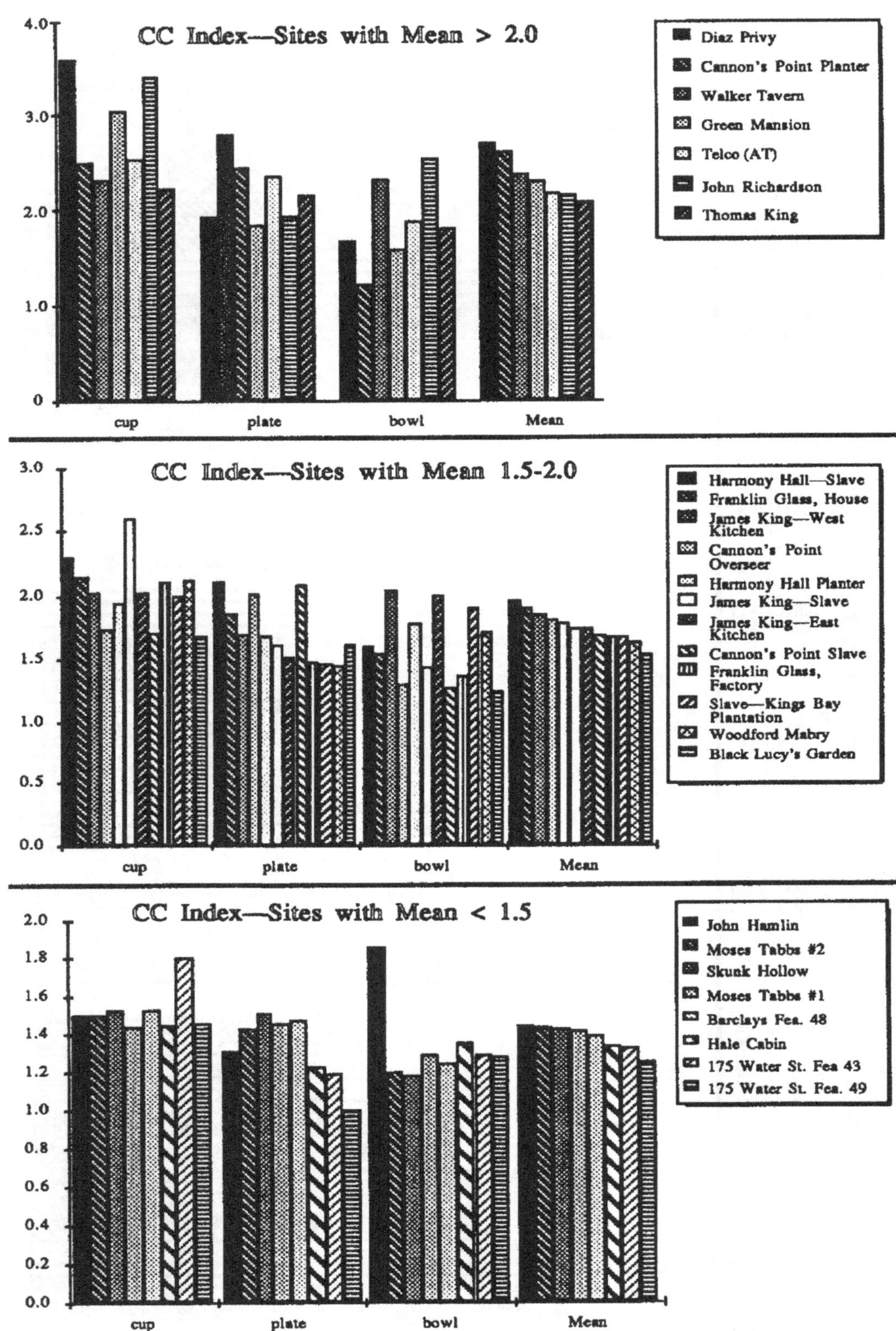

FIGURE 14. CC Index, comparing sites by mean range.

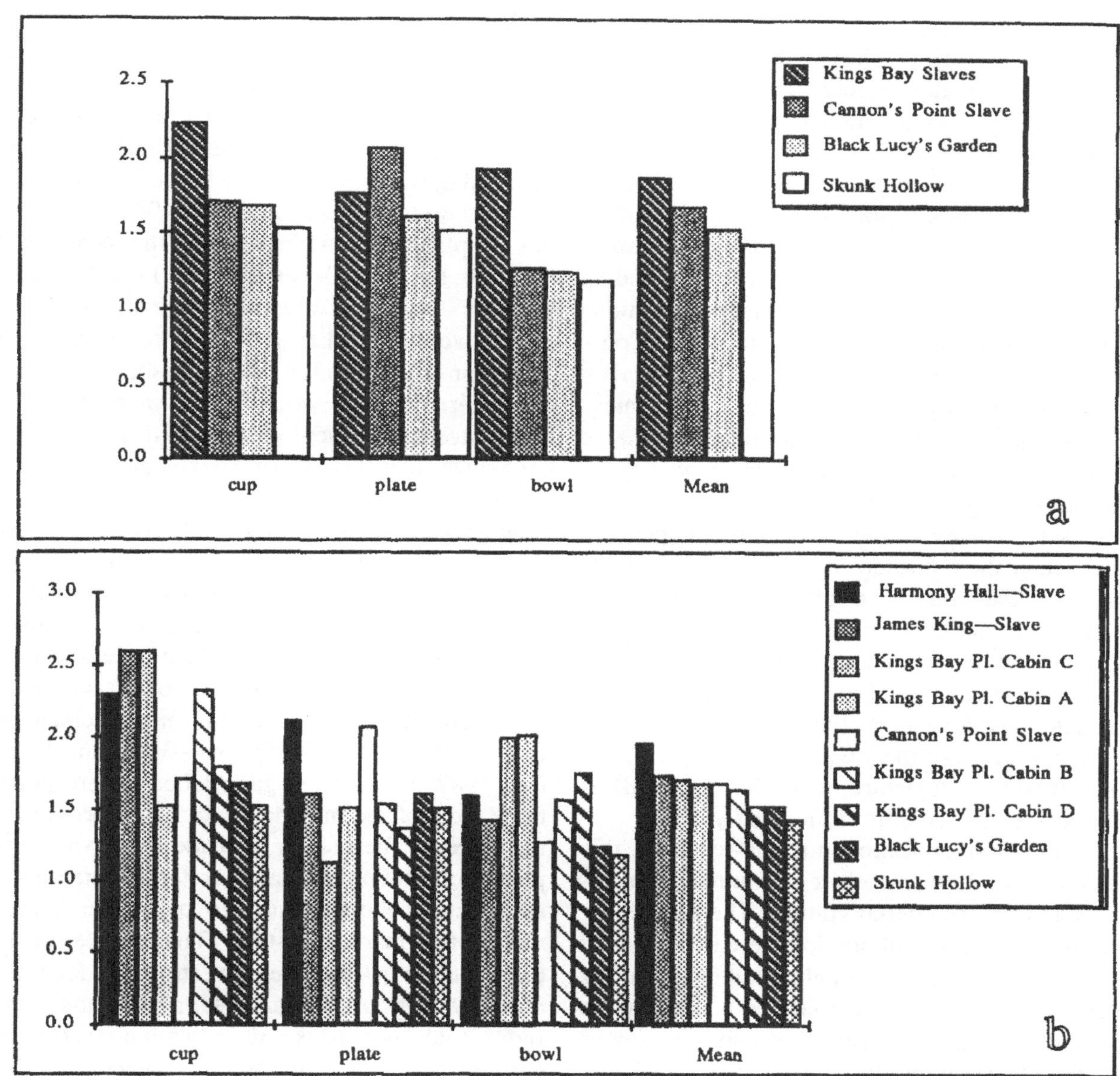

FIGURE 15. CC Index for sites with black occupants.

reconstruction, less work has been done on the material culture of the planter class. Otto found that the planter's wife at Cannon's Point set her table primarily with transferprinted plates, in sharp contrast to the banded bowls of the slave cabins (1984:151). Charles Orser (n.d.) in a re-analysis of the published data on Cannon's Point artifacts, found that ceramics were among the least sensitive indicators of status. William Kelso argued that it is in other material culture that we should be looking for status indicators. "As for other artifact patterns, matched sets of ceramics, monogrammed wine bottles, book clasps, jewelry, and coats of arms are indisputably all items that indicate wealth and high status far more strongly than whatever one can tentatively conjecture from masses of numbers of mugs or cups or bowls that happened to have been broken and thrown away" (Kelso

1984:205–206). The work at the various plantations at Kings Bay suggested that the wealthier planter had a greater variety of vessel forms for ceramics and glassware, rather than simply more expensive ones.

Status can be inferred from the artifacts, when we have sufficient sample size and a regional data base for comparison. Comparison by ceramic wares, for instance, revealed that slaves tended to have more coarse wares, that planters had more refined wares, or both possibilities together. Comparison by vessel form showed that while slaves did have many bowls, they also had many plates.

Using the CC Index was useful, because it showed that when one examines a larger variety of sites and distinguishes their ceramic assemblages by vessels, slaves might have more expensive vessels than their masters had for certain forms, and the slaves on these plantations had more expensive ceramics than many of the Northern white farmers and businessmen had on their table. Ceramics provide a good indicator of status, when approached as done here, but other indicators are also important, like the frequency of French gunflints, durable architecture, and reliance on different food species (Adams et al. 1987).

One important question not answered by this analysis was where the slaves acquired their ceramics and other material culture. The underlying assumption of nearly all previous research was that of a paternalistic system of the planter providing the ceramics and other material goods used by the slave. Whether these consisted of hand-me-downs from the planter's family or items purchased specifically for the slaves is an important distinction, but another alternative must be considered. The plantations at Kings Bay used the task system, which meant the slaves had the opportunity to earn outside income. The slaves may have purchased their own ceramics with money they themselves earned. Few, if any, of the ceramics from the slave quarters of the three plantations were hand-me-downs, for the matches between the planter and slave assemblages were in the commonest types of dishes and those assemblages showed no evidence of any substantial time lag. This means the ceramics were purchased and were used immediately: perhaps the planter bought the ceramics solely for the slaves' usage, or the slaves bought them. Quite possibly the planter bought expensive transferprinted dishes for his slaves, even when plain creamware or pearlware would have sufficed. The slave assemblages ranged from 7.81% to 19.33% transferprinted wares, compared to 10.94% to 24.31% for the planter assemblages, with the means being 13.17% for slaves' vessels and 17.61% for the planters' vessels. Conversely, is it likely that the slaves would spend their income on more expensive items? Perhaps not, if one wishes to continue the paternalistic viewpoint of so many historians and historical archaeologists. But if one wishes to recognize that the slaves developed their own culture and some participated freely within the Southern market economy, archaeologists should reassess the evidence collected previously.

In the future, it is hoped that researchers will not eliminate slave data just because it does not fit their preconceived notion of slave access to material culture. Yet current studies of market access only tend to perpetuate this misunderstanding (e.g., Orser 1987:127; Spencer-Wood and Heberling 1987:70, 80). On gang labor system plantations most of the material culture was provided to the slave by the planter or made by slaves on the plantation, but on task labor system plantations the slave had the opportunity to participate directly within the market system. The degree of this participation has not been investigated adequately, but if the work of Morgan (1982, 1983) and the CC Index analysis here is any indication, that market participation was considerable. Indeed, on such plantations slaves may be better understood within the context of being peasants or serfs, regarding their economic status. Their legal status was still as chattel slave, of course, but their economic freedoms were much greater than most people realize.

ACKNOWLEDGMENTS

Archaeological research was conducted at Kings Bay with a contract (N00025-79C-0013) between the U.S. Navy and the University of Florida; the senior author served as Principal Investigator. We would like to thank Stephen Alexandrowicz, Susan Alexandrowicz, George L. Miller, and Timothy B. Riordan for their assistance in the ceramic analysis. This article was adapted from Chapters 12 and 13 of the site report (Boling and Adams 1987; Adams and Boling 1987). We would like to thank the anonymous reviewers of *Historical Archaeology* for their comments and suggestions.

REFERENCES

ADAMS, WILLIAM HAMPTON
1987 Plantation Archaeology: An Overview. *In* Historical Archaeology of Plantations at Kings Bay, Camden County, Georgia, edited by W.H. Adams, pp. 9–22. *Reports of Investigations* 5. Department of Anthropology, University of Florida, Gainesville.

ADAMS, WILLIAM HAMPTON, WILLIAM R. ADAMS, CAROLYN ROCK, AND JANIS KEARNEY-WILLIAMS
1987 Foodways on the Plantations at Kings Bay: Hunting, Fishing, and Raising Food. *In* Historical Archaeology of Plantations at Kings Bay, Camden County, Georgia, edited by W.H. Adams, pp. 225–76. *Reports of Investigations* 5. Department of Anthropology, University of Florida, Gainesville.

ADAMS, WILLIAM HAMPTON AND SARAH JANE BOLING
1987 Material Culture and Status on the Plantations at Kings Bay. *In* Historical Archaeology of Plantations at Kings Bay, Camden County, Georgia, edited by W. H. Adams, pp. 293–310. *Reports of Investigations* 5. Department of Anthropology, University of Florida, Gainesville.

ADKINS, HOWARD G.
1980 The Antebellum Waverly Community. *Waverly Plantation: Ethnoarchaeology of a Tenant Farming Community,* edited by W.H. Adams, pp. 75–100. National Technical Information Service, Washington, D.C.

BAKER, VERNON G.
1980 Archaeological Visibility of Afro-American Culture: An Example from Black Lucy's Garden, Andover, Massachusetts. *Archaeological Perspectives on Ethnicity in America,* edited by Robert L. Schuyler, pp. 29–37. Baywood, Farmingdale, New York.

BOLING, SARAH JANE, AND WILLIAM HAMPTON ADAMS
1987 Foodways on the Plantations at Kings Bay: Putting Food on the Table. *In* Historical Archaeology of Plantations at Kings Bay, Camden County, Georgia, edited by W.H. Adams, pp. 277–92. *Reports of Investigations* 5. Department of Anthropology, University of Florida, Gainesville.

BOOTH, SALLY S.
1971 *Hung, Strung, and Potted: A History of Eating in Colonial America.* Potter, New York.

CADE, J. B.
1935 Out of the Mouths of Ex-Slaves. *Journal of Negro History* 20:294–337.

DEBOW, J.D.B.
1854 *Statistical View of the United States.* Beverley Tucker, Washington, D.C.

FELTON, DAVID L. AND PETER D. SCHULZ
1983 The Diaz Collection: Material Culture and Social Change in Mid-Nineteenth-Century Monterey. *California Archeological Reports 23.* Cultural Resource Management Unit, Resource Protection Division, California Department of Parks and Recreation.

FRAZIER, E. FRANKLIN
1930 The Negro Slave Family. *Journal of Negro History* 15(1):198–259.

GEISMAR, JOAN H.
1982 *The Archaeology of Social Disintegration in Skunk Hollow, A Nineteenth Century Rural Black Community.* Academic Press, New York.

HUNDLEY, DAVID ROBINSON
1860 *Social Relations in Our Southern States.* Henry B. Price, New York. [reprinted 1973, Arno Press]

KELSO, WILLIAM M.
1984 *Kingsmill Plantations, 1619–1800: Archaeology of Country Life in Colonial Virginia.* Academic Press, New York.

KEMBLE, FRANCIS ANNE
1863 *Journal of a Residence on a Georgian Plantation in 1838–1839.* Longman, Green, Longman, Roberts, & Green, London.

LEWIS, KENNETH E.
1985 Plantation Layout and Function in the South Carolina Lowcountry. *The Archaeology of Slavery and Plantation Life,* edited by Theresa Singleton, pp. 35–65. Academic Press, New York.

MILLER, GEORGE L.
1980 Classification and Economic Scaling of 19th Century Ceramics. *Historical Archaeology* 14:1–41.

MOORE, SUE MULLINS
1985 Social and Economic Status on the Coastal Plantation: An Archaeological Perspective. *The Archaeology of Slavery and Plantation Life,* edited by Theresa Singleton, pp. 141–60. Academic Press, New York.

MORGAN, PHILIP D.
1982 Work and Culture: The Task System and the World of Low Country Blacks, 1700 to 1880. *William and Mary Quarterly* 39(Series 3):563–99.
1983 The Ownership of Property by Slaves in the Mid-19th Century Low Country. *Journal of Southern History* 49(3):399–434.

MORIN, EDWARD M., TERRY H. KLEIN, AMY FRIEDLANDER, MALLORY GORDON, AND META JANOWITZ
1986 *Hamlin Site (28WA532) Archaeological Data Recovery I-78, (103) Section Four Pohatcong Township, Borough of Alpha, Warren County, New Jersey.* Report prepared by Louis Berger & Associates, East Orange, New Jersey, for the Federal Highway Administration and the New Jersey Department of Transportation.

MORIN, EDWARD M., AND TERRY H. KLEIN
n.d. The Hamlin Site, 1780 to 1856: A Study of Rural Consumer Behavior. *Pennsylvania Archaeologist.* In press.

OLMSTED, FREDERICK LAW
1856 *Journey in the Seaboard Slave States: With Remarks on Their Economy.* Dix and Edwards, New York.

ORSER, CHARLES E., JR.
n.d. Archaeology and Antebellum Plantation Society in the American South. Ms.
1987 Plantation Status and Consumer Choice: A Materialist Framework for Historical Archaeology. *Consumer Choice in Historical Archaeology,* edited by S. Spencer-Wood, pp. 121–37. Plenum, New York.

OTTO, JOHN SOLOMON
1975 *Status Differences and the Archaeological Record: A Comparison of Planter, Overseer, and Slave Sites from Cannon's Point Plantation (1794–1861), St. Simons Island, Georgia.* PhD dissertation, Department of Anthropology, University of Florida. University Microfilms, Ann Arbor.
1977 Artifacts and Status Differences—A Comparison of Ceramics from Planter, Overseer, and Slave Sites on an Antebellum Plantation. *Research Strategies in Historical Archaeology,* edited by Stanley South, pp. 91–118. Academic, New York.
1979 Slavery in a Coastal Community—Glynn County (1790–1861). *Georgia Historical Quarterly* 64(2): 461–68.
1984 *Cannon's Point Plantation, 1794–1860: Living Conditions and Status Patterns in the Old South.* Academic Press, New York.

PHILLIPS, ULRICH BONNELL
1929 *Life and Labor in the Old South.* Little, Brown, Boston.

RAWICK, GEORGE P.
1972 The American Slave: A Composite Autobiography. (Vol. 1. From Sundown to Sunup: The Making of the Black Community.) *Contributions in Afro-American and African Studies* 11. Greenwood Press, Westport, Connecticut.

REITZ, ELIZABETH J., TYSON GIBBS, AND TED A. RATHBUN
1985 Archaeological Evidence for Subsistence on Coastal Plantations. *The Archaeology of Slavery and Plantation Life,* edited by Theresa Singleton, pp. 163–91. Academic Press, New York.

ROTH, RODRIS
1961 Tea Drinking in Eighteenth Century America: Its Etiquette and Equipage. *United States National Museum Bulletin 225.* Washington, D.C.

SINGLETON, THERESA A.
1980 The Archaeology of Afro-American Slavery in Coastal Georgia: A Regional Perspective of Slave Household and Community Patterns. Unpublished Ph.D. dissertation, Department of Anthropology, University of Florida, Gainesville.

SPENCER-WOOD, SUZANNE M. AND SCOTT D. HEBERLING
1984 Ceramics and Socio-Economic Status of the Green Family, Windsor, Vermont. *Northeast Historical Archaeology* 13:33–52.
1987 Consumer Choices in White Ceramics: A Comparison of Eleven Early Nineteenth-Century Sites. *Consumer Choice in Historical Archaeology,* edited by S. Spencer-Wood, pp. 55–84. Plenum, New York.

STAMPP, KENNETH
1956 *The Peculiar Institution.* Vintage, New York.

WEAVER, HERBERT
1945 *Mississippi Farmers, 1850–1860.* Peter Smith, Gloucester, Massachusetts.

WOODSON, CARTER G. (EDITOR)
1968 *Free Negro Owners of Slaves in the United States in 1830, Together with Absentee Ownership of Slaves in the United States in 1830* (reprint of 1924 ed.). Negroe Universities Press, New York.

WILLIAM HAMPTON ADAMS
DEPARTMENT OF ANTHROPOLOGY
OREGON STATE UNIVERSITY
CORVALLIS, OREGON 97331

SARAH JANE BOLING
LIBRARY AND INFORMATION SCIENCE
SIMMONS COLLEGE
BOSTON, MASSACHUSETTS 02115

DEATH'S HEADS, CHERUBS, AND WILLOW TREES: EXPERIMENTAL ARCHAEOLOGY IN COLONIAL CEMETERIES[1]

EDWIN DETHLEFSEN AND JAMES DEETZ

ABSTRACT

Seventeenth- and eighteenth-century gravestones in Massachusetts are decorated with a traditional set of designs which have distinctive spatial and temporal limits. By treating them as archaeological phenomena, one can demonstrate and test methods of inferring diffusion, design evolution, and relationships between a folk-art tradition and the culture which produced it. Early popularity of death's-head designs reflects Puritan attitudes toward death, while the later cherub, willow tree, and urn motifs indicate the breakdown of these values. Although cherubs appear earliest among an innovating urban class in Cambridge, they remain a relatively minor type in this central area but are rapidly adopted in outlying districts further removed from the center of influence. Imperfect reproduction of certain designs gives rise to distinctive local styles of other areas. The distribution of these local styles in time and space provides further insights regarding religious change in the Colonial period, including a clear indication of how this change proceeded in different geographical areas at different times. Future analysis of this material promises to be quite productive in the areas of experimental archaeology, kinship analysis, demographic studies, style change, and religious change in Colonial America.

And know, reader, that though the stones in this wilderness are already grown so witty as to speak, they never yet that I could hear of, grew so wicked as to lye.

Cotton Mather, 1693

THE PROBLEM of deriving meaningful inferences from an artifactual assemblage concerning the culture which created it is an ever-present one with which the prehistorian must be concerned. A number of specific methods have been devised to aid in coping with this problem, and much of the cultural reconstruction which has been done to date is indicative of the success of such methodology. However, in most instances interpretive methods, such as seriation, typology, and various space-time unit concepts, are devised, tested, and subsequently employed in situations which are not rigorously controlled. The purpose of this paper is to direct attention to a corpus of artifactual material in which a wide variety of archaeological methods may be tested, refined, and perhaps improved under highly controlled circumstances. Colonial gravestones are uniquely and admirably suited to such a study. Produced by a literate people whose history is known, these markers show design variations in time and space which can be projected against known historical data, thereby detailing the dynamics of change in material objects as a function of changes in the society which produced them. Gravestones are peculiarly suited to such an investigation for a number of specific reasons:

(1) Although produced in a civilized milieu, Colonial gravestones were not carved by full-time specialists. Stonecarvers might have been ropemakers, leatherworkers, smiths or printers who pursued stonecutting as a secondary specialty. Gravestones are therefore true folk products as is much of the artifactual material with which the prehistorian is routinely involved.

(2) New England stonecutters produced stones for the population immediately surrounding the towns in which they lived. There is no evidence of itinerant stonecutters, and few stones were erected at a great distance from the town in which they were carved. In spite of this local pattern and the absence of a professional stonecarving group, all carvers participated in a decorative tradition which extended unbroken over an area vastly larger than that served by any one individual. While local variations can be seen between any two areas at the same point in time, these are minor when compared with the adherence to a larger design tradition, shown by stones over all of eastern Massachusetts, and probably even farther.

(3) Gravestones, by their very function, carry their own elegant chronological control. All are dated, and in those instances when one can determine the time interval between the death of the individual whose resting place is marked by a stone and its purchase and erection, this period is relatively brief, usually within a year.

(4) It is possible to project design patterns against genealogy, since the stones bear kinship data. Thus one can investigate the effect, if any, of familial affiliation on designs employed. Adequate information also exists regarding the carvers of the stones. Many of them are known by name, their products have been identified, and it is possible to investigate the nature of kin-based micro-traditions of design among the carvers.

(5) Since age at death is also stated in most cases, life tables can be constructed and, through them, certain demographic information can be derived.

(6) Since a large number of the stones bear epitaphs, it is possible to arrive at some statement concerning values regarding death, which can be shown to change in harmony with designs. This literary dimension provides a small measure of psychological control.

(7) The distinctive symbols employed as decorative elements are in part a function of religion, and therefore changes in this aspect of culture can be investigated as they relate to other areas of change.

[1] This is an expanded version of a paper presented at the 29th Annual Meeting of the Society for American Archaeology, Chapel Hill, North Carolina, May 9, 1964.

It can be seen that gravestones are probably unique in permitting the anthropologist to investigate interrelated changes in style, religion, population, personal and societal values, and social organization under absolute chronological control with a full historical record against which to project results for accuracy. As such, they form a valuable laboratory in which to test many of the inferential methods employed by the archaeologist who works with material culture.

The present study, which is still in its early stages, began with a tabulation of design types in a number of cemeteries in eastern Massachusetts. The area presently under investigation is approximately 100 mi. long and 50 mi. wide, centering on Boston, with the long axis running north and south along the Atlantic coast (Fig. 1). These limits are purely arbitrary and in the near future will be expanded to include all of New England and ultimately the entire eastern seaboard area which formed the sphere of 17th- and 18th-century English Colonial development. The temporal limits extend from about 1680 to the early years of the 19th century. Preservation of gravestones erected before 1680 is generally not so reliable as that of later stones; by 1830, stonecarving had become a full-time specialty, bringing into effect a different set of forces to act upon stylistic selection and change. Between these two dates, nearly all stones in the area are made from native slate. The widely held notion that most of the raw material from which the stones were cut was imported from the British Isles is incorrect. Harriet Forbes (1927: 5–7) makes an excellent case for the extensive utilization of native stone by citing the absence of slate from the shipping bills of merchant ships of the period and by correctly pointing out that the low prices usually paid for these stones precludes their having been imported in either worked or unworked form. In addition to the commonly used slate, sandstones and schists were employed for gravestones in some cases, these materials being particularly popular in the area south of Boston, where good-quality slate was lacking in any quantity.

Three basic designs are universally present in the Colonial cemeteries of eastern Massachusetts. A number of other design types have a more local distribution, but local styles do not eclipse the universal motifs. The normal location of the primary design is at the top of the headstone. Although decorated footstones are present in many cases, their designs were not included in this study, since they do not seem to provide the regularity of patterning as universally as headstone designs do, nor are they present in adequate numbers for statistical treatment. Beneath the design is the inscription, usually giving the name, age, and date of death of the individual, and the epitaph, if any. In addition to the main top design, the sides of most stones are embellished with various floral, geometric, and anthropomorphic motifs.

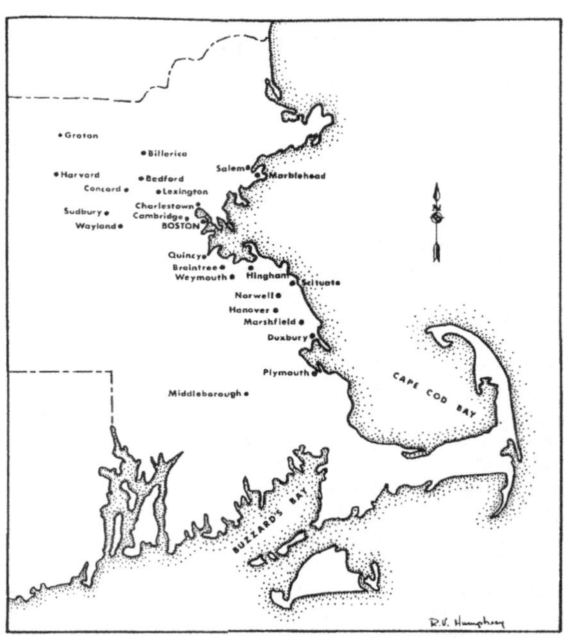

FIG. 1. Eastern Massachusetts, showing cemetery locations.

The three universally occurring design types are as follows:

(1) *Death's Heads* (Fig. 2 *a*). Usually some type of winged skull, this design is early in New England and is found on the oldest stones as the most common motif. At times it is combined with other elements such as bones, hourglasses, coffins, and palls. This design undergoes a gradual simplification through time.

(2) *Cherubs* (Fig. 2 *b*). A human face with wings, this style is characteristic of stones carved after the middle 18th century. Like the death's-head motif, the cherub motif undergoes considerable modification through time, chiefly marked by a trend toward simplification.

(3) *Urns and Willow Trees* (Fig. 2 *c*). The urn and willow motif appears at the close of the 18th century and becomes universal in a very short time. It is the latest design of the three, and its appearance signals the end of the slate-gravestone tradition in New England. Associated with this design is a marked alteration in the shape of the stone. Earlier stones have arched shoulders flank-

FIG. 2. Universal motifs. *a*, death's head; *b*, cherub; *c*, urn and willow.

ing the curved major-design area, while the urn-and-willow design is preponderantly associated with a square-shouldered stone.

The method employed in this study consisted of making photographic collections of all stones in a number of key cemeteries and supplementing these with selections from a number of other locations. Epitaphs were also collected so that a study of the relationship between epitaph and design, if any, could be made. Each complete cemetery sample was then quantified by determining the relative popularity of all designs through the time represented by the cemetery, broken down by decade, and presented in graphic form showing the percentage of each design type used in each ten-year period. This procedure enables one to determine by rapid inspection the time of initial appearance, maximum popularity, and final disappearance of each design involved. After these graphs were prepared, the data were viewed synchronically in an effort to determine the direction of movement of certain designs or attributes thereof, and then both aspects of design distributions were projected against known historical data. Cemeteries at Sudbury, Concord, Lexington, Cambridge, and Plymouth were treated in this manner, although over 40 cemeteries were visited and inspected to ascertain that the pattern in the five intensively treated cemeteries was a valid and universal one. The results of this initial effort are extremely promising in a number of ways.

When the three types are plotted against time, it appears that gravestone designs produce classic examples of the well-known "battleship-shaped" curve which is the mainstay of seriation methods (Fig. 3). Each cemetery so far examined in depth shows the gradual replacement of skulls by cherubs and the subsequent eclipse of the cherub motif by the urn-and-willow design. While the general pattern of replacement is repeated in each of the cemeteries treated, as well as in each of those visited, there are significant differences in the time and rate of change. While cherubs replace death's heads over the entire area, they do so later in Cambridge and progressively earlier as one moves out from the Boston area, although their time of initial appearance is earlier in the Boston area and correspondingly later in areas farther removed. This change is more marked in the southern direction toward Plymouth.

Another significant difference is in the number of local styles in the cemeteries in question. Although Cambridge has none, many cemeteries in the surrounding area have at least one design type of only local occurrence. Most of these local styles occur with highest frequency during the 20-year period between 1740 and 1760. Gravestone designs in the 5000-square-mile area in question cluster rather naturally by type into three time periods between 1680 and 1820. These are as follows: Period I, 1680–1740;

TABLE 1. SEQUENCE OF UNIVERSAL STYLES IN COLONIAL CEMETERIES

Universal Styles	*Period*
Death's heads	I, II
Cherubs	II, III
Urns and willows	III

Period II, 1740–1760; and Period III, 1760–1820. These are seriated in Table 1.

Of the six local styles described in Table 2, four are found in the area south of Boston, two occur primarily to the west, and none as yet has been isolated in the area north of Boston in the direction of Salem or Cape Ann. With one exception, these designs are derived in some way from one of the universal motifs. The portraits, which are nearly universal, occurring in most cemeteries outside the Boston area and the region immediately to the north and east, seem to be analogous in many ways to the cherub motif. In fact, many of the cherubs probably have some aspect of portraiture. In the Cambridge and Charlestown cemeteries, cherubs marking male burials differ from those marking females in a single aspect, the style of hair, with male cherubs exhibiting a downward curl and female hair styles done in an upsweep (Fig. 5). This distinction is probably an idiosyncrasy of one family of carvers, the Lamsons of Charlestown, since the distinction cannot be shown to carry over to cherub motifs executed by other carvers. The essential functional identity between cherubs and portraits is further indicated by their similar distribution in time, both reaching their highest frequencies in the third quarter of the 18th century or somewhat later. The Medusas and birdlike death's heads of the Plymouth-Scituate area are derived from the death's head design. In both cases, there seems to have been a change in the features of the lower face, with the typical death's head nose enlarging to form a smiling mouth, with a subsequent reduction or complete loss of the teeth. The curious heart-mouthed death's heads, on the other hand, appear to derive from some other source, as yet unclear.

Among these local styles, the so-called Roman motif is unique in its remarkable conservatism. Although in use for a period of approximately 30 years, little change can be seen between its earliest and latest form. Slight variations in the number of turns in the flanking spirals and the occasional addition of a second, smaller, six-pointed element within the larger ones at the sides are the only changes which take place. This design was probably the product of a single carver, Jonathan Worcester (Forbes 1927: 77–8), but other carvers whose work is known in detail show considerable variation and change in their work over a comparable period of time, as can be seen in the reduction of complexity in the cherub motif employed by Nathaniel and Caleb Lamson between 1740 and 1760 (Fig. 5). Worcester's work is also unique in that he retains upper-case lettering for inscriptions, a practice which was abandoned for more conventional lower case by all other carvers in the first two decades of the 18th century. It is tempting to view the intense conservatism of Worcester's

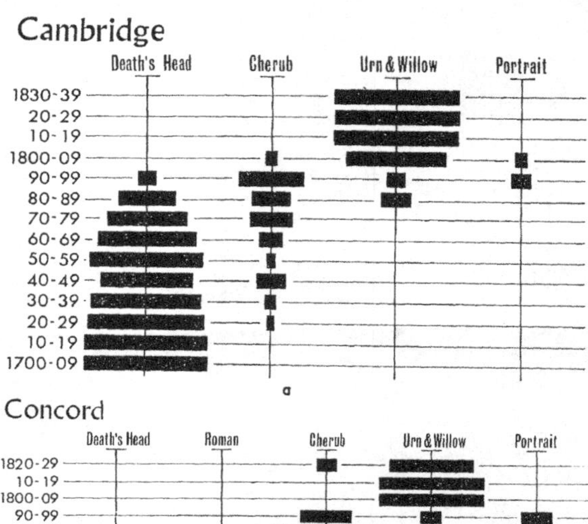

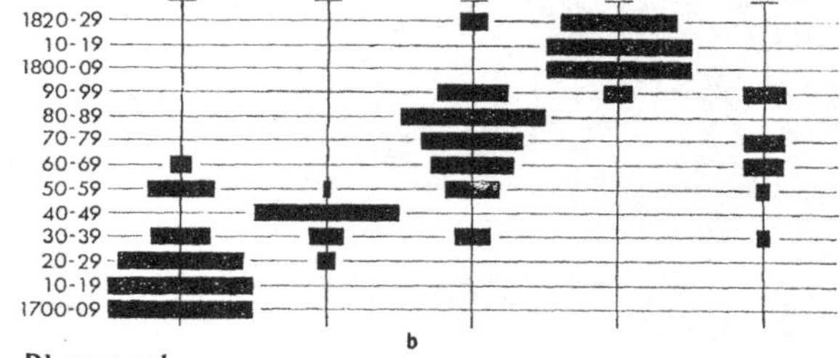

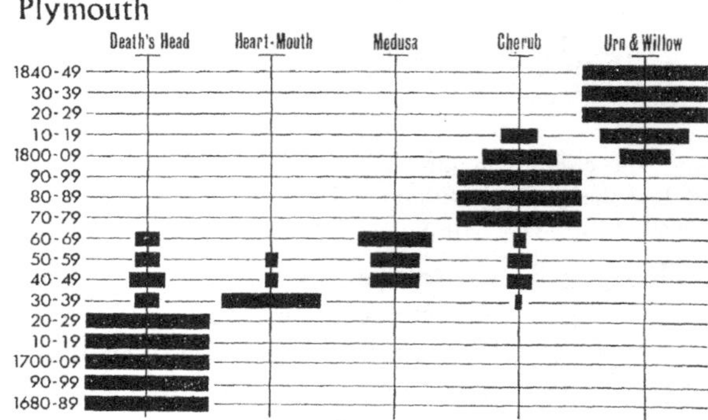

FIG. 3. Graphs showing stylistic sequences in three cemeteries.

TABLE 2. LOCAL STYLES IN COLONIAL CEMETERIES (FIG. 4)

Style	*Carver*	*Dates and Period*	*Known Distribution*
"Roman"	Worcester	1730–1760 (II)	West of Boston (Concord, Lexington, Wayland, Sudbury, Billerica, Bedford, Harvard).
Large, red sandstone portraits	Unknown	1770–1800 (III)	South of Boston, Old Plymouth Colony (Hanover, Hingham, Quincy, Braintree, Weymouth, Norwell, Plymouth).
Black slate, portraits or bulldoglike death's heads	Park	1756–1785 (III)	West of Boston (Lexington, Concord, Billerica, Bedford, Wayland, Sudbury).
Green schist Medusas	Unknown	1745–1770 (II)	South of Boston to Cape Cod (Middleboro, Marshfield, Plymouth, Buzzards Bay, Duxbury).
Birdlike death's head	Vinal?	1740–1770 (II)	A local style of limited distribution, centered on Scituate, home of Vinal. (Scituate, Norwell, Braintree, Marshfield).
Death's head with heart-shaped mouth	Unknown	1730–1745 (I, II)	Middleboro, Marshfield, Plymouth, Scituate.

curious design as resulting from its unique qualities. The design in toto could have been taken as a minimal significant unit, rather than its constituent attributes, while cherubs and death's heads could more easily have been perceived as made up of rather discrete, semi-independently variable elements such as wings, skulls, faces, and different hair styles.

This pattern of design change and replacement, rigidly placed in time and space by the peculiar nature of the material which demonstrates it, reflects a wealth of information concerning the times during which it was produced. The interpretive aspects of this study, only recently begun in detail, already show considerable promise of providing a model of interrelated change in many aspects of culture, based primarily on its material remains. For example, the replacement of one universal motif by another through time over the entire area is certainly a function of changes in religious values combined with significant shifts in views regarding death. Considered synchronically, it can be seen that these changes did not proceed uniformly but were proceeding at different rates and probably for different reasons. It is a safe assumption that Cambridge and Boston were apparently the 18th-century cultural focus in eastern Massachusetts. Harvard was a divinity school at the time, and religious attitudes and beliefs must have been intensified and initially changed in this central area. Since the death's-head motif was the modal design which accompanied early Puritanism in the colony, the shift from death's heads to cherubs may be viewed as indicative of a departure from a prior form of Puritan religion. Such an assumption is strongly supported by the epitaphs normally found on stones of the late 17th and early 18th centuries, which are in close harmony with the major tenets of New England Puritanism. Mortality is stressed, little or no mention being made of an afterlife or resurrection of the dead, as shown by the following example:

Remember me as you pass by
As you are now so once was I
As I am now you soon must be
Prepare for death and follow me.

Other epitaphs mention moldering dust, worms, and decay. When cherubs become modal after midcentury, epitaphs take on a lighter, more hopeful note, although the earlier type does not disappear, occurring even on urn-and-willow stones. Frequent mention of ascent to God, or afterlife in general, is common on cherub stones:

Farewell my wife and children dear,
I leave you for a while
For God has called and I must go
And leave you all behind.

It is important to note that while the death's head can be viewed as a graphic representation of one's mortal remains, cherubs are indicative

FIG. 4. Four local styles. *a*, Roman; *b*, black slate death's head; *c*, Medusa; *d*, birdlike death's head.

of the immortal component of the deceased. However, both designs are personal representations, while the later urn-and-willow motif is a depersonalized memorial.

In addition to this religious dimension of design change, there may be a significant social dimension. A survey of the literature dealing with English gravestones of the 17th and 18th centuries shows that a change from death's heads to cherubs occurred in the British Isles approximately 70 years before it occurred in New England (Chin 1963; Christison 1902; Graham 1957–58; Yentsch 1963). Cherubs were therefore modal in England in the opening decades of the 18th century, and they appear in small numbers in Cambridge and Charlestown as early as the second decade of that century. The association of these early cherub stones in Cambridge is largely with members of the cosmopolitan minority of the populace. High church officials, a governor's daughter, Harvard College presidents and their wives, and even a Londoner have graves marked by stones bearing elaborate cherub designs. While the cherub motif remains a minor component in

FIG. 5. Cherub designs carved by the Lamson family of Charlesdown, Massachusetts, showing reduction in design complexity from 1720 to 1760. *a–c*, from stones marking male burials; *d*, from stone marking female burial.

Cambridge gravestone design, the association with members of a higher, more worldly urban class suggests that they are the source of innovation in this case. The remainder of the population still employs stones with the typical death's heads, and cherubs never become a truly popular design in the central Cambridge-Boston area (Fig. 3*a*). The upward slope of the horizon marking the initial appearance of cherubs in the cemeteries progressively farther from the center probably indicates that this influence diffused outward. However, from the point in time when cherubs become popular, the slope is in the other direction, downward as one moves out from Boston. This can be most economically interpreted as indicating the progressive reduction in intensity of the Puritan ethic in places farther removed from the center of its formulation and transmission. It appears that change is primarily initiated by a small segment of the population and then spreads to the majority, with the rate of spread being inversely proportional to the strength with which religious belief is regulated by a central authority. This interpretation is tentative, subject to the accumulation of additional data.

The distribution pattern of local styles supports these general interpretations. The preponderance of local stylistic diversity in the area which until 1692 was Plymouth Colony, with a somewhat different religion, is expectable according to the general conclusions drawn from the pattern of change seen through time in all cemeteries studied. The only local styles which exist outside of the Old Colony are the two which occur in the Concord-Lexington-Harvard sphere, and these are somewhat different from those to the south. The Roman style was the work of one man, and it continued only during his productive years; William Park's massive black-slate stones, while distinctively local, are usually decorated with one of the universal motifs. In marked contrast, the area south of Boston abounds with designs which are truly peculiar, and the pattern of highly individualistic designs, derived from the universal motifs but quite different from them in detail, is distinctive of this area.

The period from 1740 to 1760 stands out as a time of initial departure from death's heads and of considerable experimentation in new designs. West of Boston it is the peculiar Roman style; to the south, birdlike skulls, Medusas, and the first cherubs occur in quantity. This sudden variability is not seen in Boston, in Cambridge, or in the area immediately to the north. In all other cemeteries, however, it is the time during which the maximum number of designs occurs. After 1760, cherubs preponderate; prior to 1740, death's heads are virtually universal. This two-decade span was noted at an early stage of this study, and only much later did we discover that it coincided with the time of the "Great Awakening." This movement within New England Puritanism, sparked by Jonathan Edwards, began in 1740 in the Connecticut Valley in Central Massachusetts, and spread rapidly east, reaching but not entering Boston. It was characterized by a newly placed stress on the joys of life after death and resurrection of the dead, rather than the earlier stern emphasis on judgment and mortality. While the cemeteries surrounding Boston on the west and south do not share in the precise motifs introduced during this period, the cherub is one design universally shared, and its subsequent rise to popularity, eclipsing other local styles, in all probability relates in some way to the influence of the Great Awakening.

The end of the Great Awakening is also the time of the final demise of Puritanism. The year 1760 marks the beginning of yet another change in religious views, leading to the rise of Unitarianism and Methodism in the early years of the 19th century. This change is reflected in the cemeteries by the final shift in design types from cherub to urn-and-willow. The urn-and-willow motif becomes the hallmark of Victorian gravemarkers. In direct contrast to the earlier highly personalized designs, urns and willows reflect a trend toward the depersonalization of death and memorial. By the beginning of the 19th century this design becomes absolutely universal, and even today draped urns are a favorite element in gravestone style. The depth to which chroniclers of American funeral custom trace the historic roots of modern practices probably cannot pass this point of time. Much of modern "grief therapy" (Mitford 1963) may be traceable to this initial step in depersonalization, but certainly funeral customs in the period preceding 1800 belong to another age and another set of values.

The data and tentative conclusions presented above are but a very small part of a program already planned and in process in this study of Colonial gravestone design. This paper is primarily a preliminary statement of aims and methods, with a number of tentative conclusions included to direct attention to the value of the study in its entirety. That this project is of importance to general anthropological theory has already been suggested above. A brief enumeration of future plans will make this more obvious. The following objectives are among those to be reached in the next three to five years:

(1) A complete photographic sample of all cemeteries in the study area, plus a large number of comparative cemeteries in the area from Maine to Georgia and west to the Appalachians will be accumulated. Eastern Massachusetts alone is expected to provide 20,000 stones from hundreds of locations. These are now being photographed; the size of the photographic sample at this writing is approximately 3000 stones from 20 cemeteries.

(2) For each stone an IBM card will be punched according to a design vocabulary now being prepared. In addition, the cards will bear punches for person, age, kinship term, date of death to the day, cemetery, cause of death if given, and stone material.

(3) Using the coded cards, a study of design change in terms of discrete stylistic elements as well as multiattribute configurations will be pursued.

(4) Using the data regarding date of death, sex, and location, a demographic study of colonial New England will be carried out. It is reasonable to expect that the paths of epidemics, differences in mean age of death in time and space, and other significant information regarding Colonial populations can thus be derived. One such pattern has already emerged with great clarity; there is a marked tendency for young people to die during the summer months, while elderly people have a higher death rate during the winter. Gravestones are a much more detailed source of such information than many town records, which often provide only yearly summaries of fatalities. A projection of cemetery data against town death-lists in Plymouth indicates that most of the population is represented in that cemetery at least until 1800.

(5) All stones bear kinship terms, such as mother, son, and daughter. Preliminary analysis suggests that changes in terminology and shifts in emphasis between consanguinial and affinial kinship terms as they occur spatially and temporally can be determined and explained. As an example of this type of investigation, inscriptions indicate a heavy paternal bias in the period preceding 1800. Stones marking the graves of males are inscribed with name only, with no kinship affiliation indicated. Women and unmarried children, on the other hand, are almost always identified in terms of their husbands or fathers, with "wife of," "child of," "son of," and "daughter of" as the kinship terms utilized in the inscription. Between 1800 and 1840, this strong paternal emphasis is seen to break down, and a brief period of sexual equality is reflected by the general use of Mr. and Mrs. or the deceased's name only. From 1840 until the beginning of the present century, some slight maternal bias is present, as shown by the placement of the wife's name first on stones marking the remains of couples or by larger letters being used for wives' names. The modern pattern contrasts with all previous ones, with most individuals being referred to as mother or father of individuals still alive, indicating a filial bias in the perception of deceased kin. It may well be that gravestones are one of the richest sources of information regarding changes in the cognitive aspect of kin terminology through time in American culture.

(6) Genealogies will be constructed, and the correlation between design types and families will be further investigated. Preliminary study suggests that familial affiliation has little or no effect on selection of design.

(7) By consulting the probate records, it is possible to determine the average price of stones of each design type in different places at different times. These records are also informative concerning the social status, occupation, and net worth at death of the estate of the individual whose resting place is marked by a stone. Thus the economic dimension of style change can be detailed.

(8) Using the discrete design elements which occur on the stones, rate of stylistic change within each major type will be measured to determine if a difference in rate of change exists between waxing and waning styles.

(9) Seriation methods will be tested by arranging single-decade samples from different cemeteries in chronological order and investigating the effect of direction and rate of diffusion on the sequential ordering of sites at different locations. Analysis completed to date suggests that if a series of sites is sampled along a line which is parallel to the direction of diffusion, successively more recent sites in the direction of diffusion will produce a curve for the rate of change which is more gradual than the true rate, while a sequence ordered in a line running against the direction of diffusion will produce an apparently greater rate of change. This phenomenon is analogous to the Doppler effect in physics, where frequencies of sound and light appear to rise or fall depending on whether the observer is traveling toward or away from the source of energy.

(10) Investigation of the degree of social and commercial intercourse between towns, as shown by an index stating the percentage of shared surnames and relatives, will be pursued, and between-town design sharing will be studied in these terms.

(11) An attempt will be made to reconstruct extinct political boundaries. Preliminary analysis suggests that the Massachusetts Bay–Plymouth Colony line is reflected in a disruption of an otherwise smooth continuum of design variation along a line connecting Boston and Plymouth. All of the local styles in the Plymouth Colony area are restricted to that region, and the red-sandstone portraits and birdlike skulls reach their northern limit along a line approximating this boundary. A similar phenomenon may occur at the Rhode Island–Plymouth Colony line and at the junction of any two of the original colonies.

(12) The totality of New England mortuary art will be traced back to its Old World antecedents.

This project holds great potential for several aspects of general anthropology, going far beyond the area of archaeological method. Practically every factor which might have an effect on the changes observed in one area of material culture can be controlled and investigated in considerable depth. This control is not restricted to the cultural realm of human existence; with the demographic dimension added, an important biological integration is provided. That the archaeologist must at all times keep before him a sense of the articulation between his excavated material and the rich and colorful culture which produced it is a frequently repeated injunction which is all too often not adequately heeded. Colonial gravestones provide the anthropologist with a highly complex pattern of material change, in which the dominant theme is the highly integrated nature of the various aspects of culture change.

While most of the intrinsic value of this study arises from the rigorously positive historical control which allows observation in considerable detail of the causes of various changes in gravestone decorative style, it has further value in providing detailed information concerning social changes and historical events which did *not* have an effect on gravestone design. The most striking example of this latter negative type of control is the fact that the American Revolution, a most moving and disruptive event in New England Colonial culture, has not as yet been detected in the gravestone data. With the exception of certain epitaphs which commemorate an individual killed in action or which cite his military prowess, no discernible change in design is registered in the period between 1750 and 1800 which could in any way be attributed directly to the effects of the Revolution. Such a lack of indication in an otherwise rather sensitive tradition should be noted and heeded as a plea for due caution in interpretation, particularly the postulation of the lack of cultural elements based on negative evidence.

The success with which the initial phases of this study have been completed points strongly to a successful final conclusion. Since ethnographic data are frequently lacking in the kind of information which is of maximum value to the prehistorian, controlled studies of this type may provide a valuable alternative solution to the problem of joining man's material products with his culture in a meaningful sense. Archaeology must be viewed as a technique employed by the ethnologist for the purpose of adding a time dimension to his analysis of culture. As such, the prehistorian must be an ethnologist first and an archaeologist second, since he cannot possibly perform meaningful and sophisticated reconstructions of past cultures unless he is aware of the nature of the articulation between culture and its products. A study like the present one is therefore a problem in general anthropology, as well as a valuable exercise in experimental archaeology. Future work in this area should help to delineate the nature of the links between archaeological and ethnological data and thus serve both subdisciplines well.

Acknowledgments. We wish to express appreciation for constructive comments and suggestions made by Richard Comstock, Edward Hunt, William Mayer-Oakes, John New, and Gordon Willey.

Chin, Roberta

1963 English Tombstones: An Attempt to Trace Their Relationship to Social Attitudes and to the Tombstone Trends of Colonial New England. Unpublished manuscript, Peabody Museum, Cambridge.

Christison, D.

1902 The Carvings and Inscriptions of the Kirkyard Monuments of the Scottish Lowlands, Particularly in Perth, Fife, Angus, Mearns and Lothian. *Proceedings of the Society of Antiquaries of Scotland*, Series 3, Vol. 12, pp. 280–457.

Forbes, H.

1927 *Gravestones of Early New England, 1653–1800.* Houghton Mifflin, Boston.

Graham, A.

1957–58 Headstones in Post Reformation Scotland. *Proceedings of the Society of Antiquaries of Scotland*, Vol. 91, pp. 1–9.

Mitford, Jessica

1963 *The American Way of Death.* Simon and Schuster, New York.

Yentsch, Anne E.

1963 Design Elements in Scottish Gravestones. Unpublished manuscript, Peabody Museum, Cambridge.

Harvard University
Cambridge, Massachusetts

University of California
Santa Barbara, California

March, 1965

Made in the USA
Las Vegas, NV
25 April 2024

89145338R00195